Fodor's 98

Ireland

The complete guide, thoroughly up-to-date

Packed with details that will make your trip

The must-see sights, off and on the beaten path

What to see, what to skip

Mix-and-match vacation itineraries

City strolls, countryside adventures

Smart lodging and dining options

Essential local do's and taboos

Transportation tips, distances and directions

Key contacts, savvy travel tips

When to go, what to pack

Clear, accurate, easy-to-use maps

Books to read, videos to watch, background essays

Fodor's Travel Publications, Inc.
New York • Toronto • London • Sydney • Auckland
www.fodors.com/

Fodor's Ireland '98

EDITOR: Matthew Lore

Editorial Contributors: Jonathan Abrahams, Robert Andrews, David Brown, Georgina Campbell, Kevin Courtney, Dermot Gilleece, Jennifer Grimes, Ian Hill, Alannah Hopkin, Vincent Jamison, Sarah McQuaid, Hugh Oram, Andrew Sanger, Heidi Sarna, Helayne Schiff, M. T. Schwartzman (Gold Guide editor), Dinah A. Spritzer, Sylvia Thompson, Colm Tóibín

Editorial Production: Laura M. Kidder

Maps: David Lindroth, *cartographer*; Steven Amsterdam, *map editor*

Design: Fabrizio La Rocca, *creative director*; Guido Caroti, *associate art director*; Jolie Novak, *photo editor*

Production/Manufacturing: Mike Costa

Cover Photograph: Wendy Carlson

Copyright

Special Sales

Fodor's Travel Publications are available at special discounts for bulk purchases for sales promotions or premiums. Special editions, including personalized covers, excerpts of existing guides, and corporate imprints, can be created in large quantities for special needs. For more information, contact your local bookseller or write to Special Markets, Fodor's Travel Publications, 201 East 50th Street, New York, NY 10022. Inquiries from Canada should be directed to your local Canadian bookseller or sent to Random House of Canada, Ltd., Marketing Dept., 1265 Aerowood Drive, Mississauga, Ontario L4W 1B9. Inquiries from the United Kingdom should be sent to Fodor's Travel Publications, 20 Vauxhall Bridge Road, London SW1V 2SA, England.

PRINTED IN THE UNITED STATES OF AMERICA

10 9 8 7 6 5 4 3 2 1

CONTENTS

Maps

ON THE ROAD WITH FODOR'S

WE'RE ALWAYS THRILLED to get letters from readers, especially one like this:

It took us an hour to decide what book to buy and we now know we picked the best one. Your book was wonderful, easy to follow, very accurate, and good on pointing out eating places, informal as well as formal. When we saw other people using your book, we would look at each other and smile.

Our editors and writers are deeply committed to making every Fodor's guide "the best one"—not only accurate but always charming, brimming with sound recommendations and solid ideas, right on the mark in describing restaurants and hotels, and full of fascinating facts that make you view what you've traveled to see in a rich new light.

About Our Writers

Our success in achieving our goals—and in helping to make your trip the best of all possible vacations—is a credit to the hard work of our extraordinary writers and editors. 1998 marks the debut of a raft of new contributors to our guide, among them six Dublin-based journalists and one from Belfast.

Kevin Courtney came on board this year to cover the rapidly changing state of pubs and nightlife in Dublin. A rock journalist with the *Irish Times,* he has reviewed practically every Irish artist on the scene, including U2, The Cranberries, Sinéad O'Connor, Hothouse Flowers, and Van Morrison. He also covers emerging new Irish talent, so remember you heard it here first: Ash and The Divine Comedy are his top picks for the best new groups to come out of Ireland in the past couple of years.

Also debuting this year, as the updater of our golf chapter, is Dublin native and resident **Dermot Gilleece,** the golf correspondent for the *Irish Times* and author of several books on golf, including a biography of Harry Bradshaw. In the course of his work he reports on all of the game's leading events, including the U.S. Masters, U.S. Open, British Open, and the U.S.P.G.A. Championships.

American-born writer **Jennifer Grimes** has made Dublin her home since 1994, where she has written for the New York–based *Irish Echo* newspaper. She has generously agreed to tell all about her weekend stomping grounds in the far reaches of Counties Mayo, Sligo, and Donegal, where she's brought us up-to-date on the best guest houses and villages, a wealth of sporting activities, and increasingly fine food.

Belfast-based **Ian Hill** also joins us this year, to give us a fresh look at Belfast and the rest of our chapter on Northern Ireland. He has written extensively for the *Irish Times,* the *Sunday Tribune,* and the *Guardian,* and he has also written, contributed to, and edited, many books on Ireland, including *The Fish of Ireland, Northern Ireland, The North,* and *Irish Counties.* Having worked on both sides of the Irish border, Ian offers an impartial, well-informed commentary.

A full-time freelance writer who lives near the sea in County Cork, **Alannah Hopkin,** our valued veteran contributor, has worked on the guide since 1985. This year she covered the Midlands, Southeast, Southwest, and much of the West of Ireland. Alannah has published an acclaimed book on the cult of St. Patrick, a book-length guide to County Cork, two novels, and several short stories. She writes on the arts for the London *Sunday Times* and contributes regularly to the *Cork Examiner.*

Our Dublin restaurant coverage is the handiwork of **Vincent Jamison,** new to *Fodor's Ireland* this year. He is the food and wine critic for *The Sunday Business Post,* Ireland's leading business publication, a college lecturer in journalism, and co-author of the books *Writing for the Media* and *The Media Primer.* Vincent brings his broad travel experience and wide-ranging interest in exotic cuisines and wines from the New World and the Old to his reviews.

Dublin-based journalist **Sarah McQuaid,** who also joins us for the first time in 1998, writes for *Hot Press* and *Irish Music* magazines and for the *Evening Herald.* She is the author of *The Irish DADGAD Guitar Book: Playing and Backing Traditional Irish Music on Open-Tuned Guitar* (1995) and has recently released *When Two Lovers Meet,* an album of traditional tunes and songs. Her essay on the West's traditional music scene (☞ Chapter 7) should help lead you right to the best traditional music Ireland has to offer.

Sylvia Thompson, another new contributor for 1998, edits the *Irish Times'* "Pursuits" page and writes a summer column in the *Times* on festivals and seasonal events. She won the Association of Irish Festival Events annual trophy for best media coverage of festivals in 1996. We're thrilled to have her join us this year: She updated our Gold Guide, our festivals coverage (natch!), and Dublin and Dublin Environs. She lives in County Wicklow with her husband, an illustrator, and their baby daughter.

Editor **Matthew Lore** fell hard for all things Irish at the first annual San Francisco Celtic Music Festival in March 1993, when he first heard County Clare musician Sharon Shannon electrify the crowd as she peeled through a few jigs on her button accordion. With Shannon's music still ringing in his ears 3½ years later, he jumped at the chance to edit the 1998 *Fodor's Ireland* guide. Alas, Shannon wasn't performing in County Clare when he swung through in November 1996, on the first of two trips he made to Ireland in the course of his year working on the guide. Between that trip and a follow-up trip in April 1997, he covered 1,500 miles in both the Republic and Northern Ireland, visiting Dublin, Belfast, Galway City (twice), Sligo Town (twice), Donegal Town, Kinsale, and dozens of villages, pubs, restaurants, historic houses, parks, and other sights.

For their help in putting together this guide, the editor wishes especially to thank Ruth Moran, Orla Carey, and Joe Lynam with Bord Fáilte (the Irish Tourist Board); Maebeth Fenton of the Northern Ireland Tourist Board; Damien Brennan with Northwest Tourism in Sligo Town; and Dave Watson. Thanks also to Anna Mazzarotto Coleman at the Clarence Hotel, Dublin; Martin Cooley at the Davenport Hotel, Dublin; Myrtle, Ivan, Darina, and Tim Allen at Ballymaloe House, Shanagarry; Stephen Quinn at Adare Manor; Michael Cunningham at the Great Southern Hotel, Galway City; Charles Cooper

at Markree Castle, Coolloney; Kay O'Flynn at Rathsallagh House, Dunlavin; Jas Mooney at Madison's Hotel in Belfast; Mary Breslin, Patrick McLarnon, and Maebeth Fenton (again!) at Ardtara Country House in Upperlands; Robin, Bob, and Mark Wheeler at Rathmullan House (*especially* for retrieving a very important lost book)—all for their courteous hospitality. Finally, thanks to Dan Dooley Rent-a-Car and Aer Lingus for their generous support, without which the editor's trips might not have been possible.

New This Year

1998 has been a big year for *Fodor's Ireland,* as we've done a major overhaul on the guide. To do justice to the enormous changes taking place throughout Ireland, we've rewritten and expanded our coverage of many sections—most notably Dublin, Galway City, Belfast, and Sligo Town. We've also substantially revised our coverage of dozens of smaller towns and cultural and natural sites. From Glenveagh National Park in the wilds of County Donegal to Emo Court and Gardens in County Laois, we now provide you with more detailed, up-to-date historical and contextual information than ever before. We've also added two "Close-Up" essays—one on James Joyce in Chapter 2 and the other on traditional music in the West in Chapter 7. In our Dublin chapter, we've added a map to help you find the best of the capital's 1,000 pubs.

And this year, Fodor's joins Rand McNally, the world's largest commercial mapmaker, to bring you a detailed color map of Ireland. Just detach it along the perforation and drop it in your tote bag.

We're also proud to announce that the American Society of Travel Agents has endorsed Fodor's as its guidebook of choice. ASTA is the world's largest and most influential travel trade association, operating in more than 170 countries, with 27,000 members pledged to adhere to a strict code of ethics reflecting the Society's motto, "Integrity in Travel." ASTA shares Fodor's devotion to providing smart, honest travel information and advice to travelers, and we've long recommended that our readers consult ASTA member agents for the experience and professionalism they bring to the table.

On the Web, check out Fodor's site (www.fodors.com/) for information on major destinations around the world and travel-savvy interactive features. The Web site also lists the 85-plus radio stations nationwide that carry the *Fodor's Travel Show,* a live call-in program that airs every weekend. Tune in to hear guests discuss their wonderful adventures—or call in for answers to your most pressing travel questions.

How to Use This Book

Organization

Up front is the **Gold Guide,** an easy-to-use section divided alphabetically by topic. Under each listing you'll find tips and information that will help you accomplish what you need to in Ireland. You'll also find addresses and telephone numbers of organizations and companies that offer destination-related services and detailed information and publications.

The first chapter in the guide, **Destination: Ireland,** helps get you in the mood for your trip. New and Noteworthy cues you in on trends and happenings, What's Where gets you oriented, Pleasures and Pastimes describes the activities and sights that really make Ireland unique, Fodor's Choice showcases our top picks, and Festivals and Seasonal Events alerts you to special events you'll want to seek out.

Chapters in *Ireland '98* are arranged by geographical region. Dublin—our one city chapter—leads off the guide, beginning with an Exploring section subdivided by neighborhood; each subsection recommends a walking tour and lists sights in alphabetical order. Each regional chapter is divided by geographical area; within each area, towns are covered in logical geographical order, and attractive stretches of road and minor points of interest between them are indicated by the designation En Route. Throughout, Off the Beaten Path sights appear after the places from which they are most easily accessible. And within town sections, all restaurants and lodgings are grouped together. Chapter 10 covers the 28 finest of Ireland's 330 golf courses; references to many others appear throughout the guide.

An additional note about the organization of *Ireland '98:* Occasionally the exigencies of organizing the guide require us to separate one town from its geographic neighbor, covering the two in separate chapters. This situation happens on the fringes of a tour, where one county meets another. Because Irish counties are so significant in Irish culture and to the Irish themselves, we try, as much as possible, to contain our coverage of a county to a single chapter. That sometimes means that one place we may be covering in the guide is within shouting distance of another, across a county line. We have made a point to cross-reference our coverage wherever this situation appears.

To help you decide what to visit in the time you have, all chapters begin with recommended itineraries; you can mix and match those from several chapters to create a complete vacation. The A-to-Z section that ends all chapters covers getting there and getting around. It also provides helpful contacts and resources.

At the end of the book you'll find **Portraits,** including a map showing the county of origin of Irish family names, and an essay by leading Irish writer Colm Tóibín, followed by suggestions for any pretrip research you want to do, from recommended reading and audiotapes to movies on tape with Ireland as a backdrop.

Icons and Symbols

★	Our special recommendations
✕	Restaurant
🏠	Lodging establishment
✕🏠	Lodging establishment whose restaurant warrants a special trip
🐤	Good for kids (rubber duckie)
☞	Sends you to another section of the guide for more information
✉	Address
☎	Telephone number
FAX	Fax number
☉	Opening and closing times
💷	Admission prices (those we give apply to adults; substantially reduced fees are almost always available for children, students, and senior citizens)

Numbers in white and black circles (e.g., ② or ❷) that appear on the maps, in the margins, and within the tours correspond to one another.

Dining and Lodging

The restaurants and lodgings we list are the cream of the crop in each price range. Price categories are as follows:

For restaurants:

CATEGORY	(A) COST: THE REPUBLIC*	(B) COST: NORTHERN IRELAND*
$$$$	over £25	over UK£25
$$$	£20–£25	UK£15–£UK25
$$	under £20	UK£10–£UK15
$	under £15	under UK£15

All prices are per person for a first course, a main course, and dessert, including sales tax, excluding wine or tip.

For hotels:

CATEGORY	(A) COST: DUBLIN	(B) COST: ELSEWHERE IN THE REPUBLIC
$$$$	over £180	over £140
$$$	£140–£180	£100–£140
$$	£100–£140	£80–£100
$	under £100	under £80

All prices are for two people in a double room, including 12.5% local sales tax (VAT) and a service charge (often applied in larger hotels).

Note: Separate lodging price charts appear in Chapter 8 for the Northwest, where the majority of lodging still tends to be less expensive than elsewhere in the Republic, and in Chapter 9, for Northern Ireland.

Hotel Facilities

We always list the facilities that are available—but we don't specify whether they cost extra: When pricing accommodations, always ask what's included.

Restaurant Reservations and Dress Codes

Reservations are always a good idea; we note only when they're essential or when they are not accepted. Book as far ahead as you can, and reconfirm when you get to town. Unless otherwise noted, the restaurants listed are open daily for lunch and dinner. We mention dress only when men are required to wear a jacket or a jacket and tie. Look for an overview of local habits in the Gold Guide

Credit Cards

The following abbreviations are used: **AE,** American Express; **DC,** Diners Club; **MC,** MasterCard; and **V,** Visa.

Don't Forget to Write

You can use this book in the confidence that all prices and opening times are based on information supplied to us at press time; Fodor's cannot accept responsibility for any errors. Time inevitably brings changes, so always confirm information when it matters—especially if you're making a detour to visit a specific place. In addition, when making reservations be sure to mention if you have a disability or are traveling with children, if you prefer a private bath or a certain type of bed, or if you have specific dietary needs or other concerns.

Were the restaurants we recommended as described? Did our hotel picks exceed your expectations? Did you find a museum we recommended a waste of time? If you have complaints, we'll look into them and revise our entries when the facts warrant it. If you've discovered a special place that we haven't included, we'll pass the information along to our correspondents and have them check it out. So send us your feedback, positive *and* negative: E-mail us at editors@fodors.com (specifying the name of the book on the subject line) or write the Ireland editor at Fodor's, 201 East 50th Street, New York, New York 10022. Have a wonderful trip!

Karen Cure

Karen Cure
Editorial Director

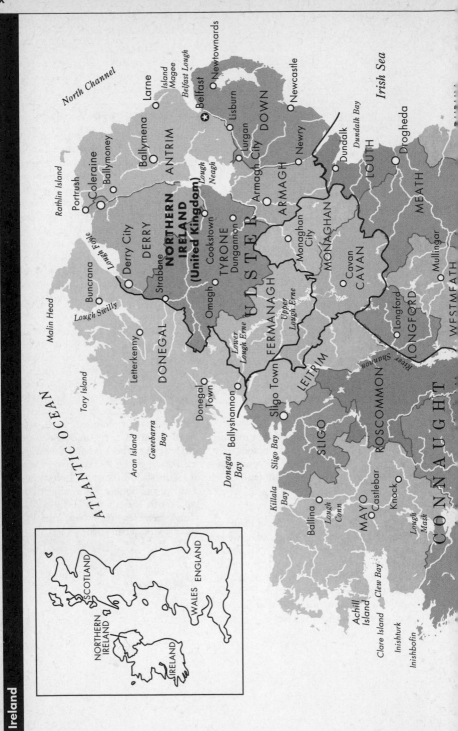

Ireland

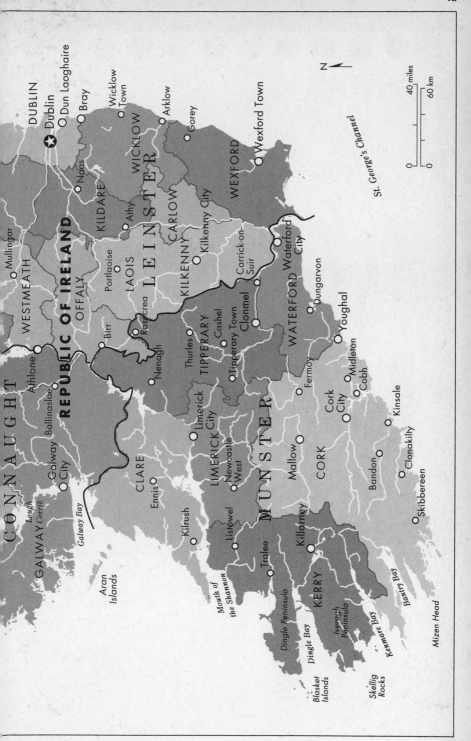

World Time Zones

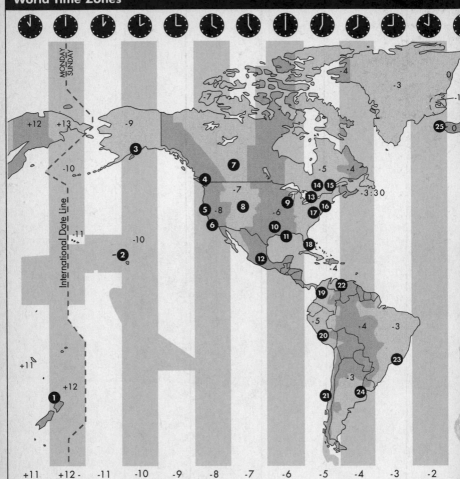

Numbers below vertical bands relate each zone to Greenwich Mean Time (0 hrs.).
Local times frequently differ from these general indications,
as indicated by light-face numbers on map.

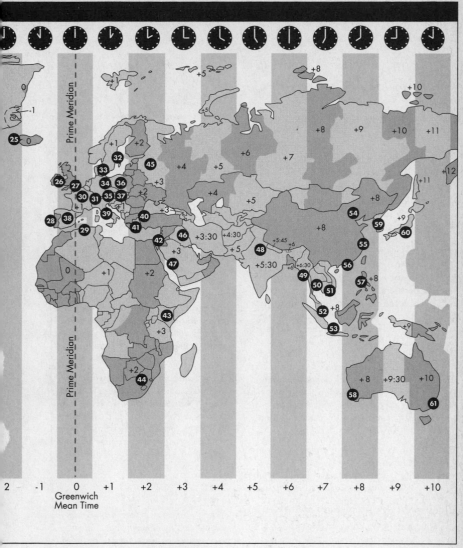

Greenwich
Mean Time

SMART TRAVEL TIPS

THE GOLD GUIDE / SMART TRAVEL TIPS

SMART TRAVEL TIPS A TO Z

Basic Information on Traveling in Ireland, Savvy Tips to Make Your Trip a Breeze, and Companies and Organizations to Contact

A

AIR TRAVEL

MAJOR AIRLINE OR LOW-COST CARRIER?

Most people choose a flight based on price. Yet there are other issues to consider. Major airlines offer the greatest number of departures; smaller airlines—including regional, low-cost and no-frill airlines—usually have a more limited number of flights daily. Major airlines have frequent-flyer partners, which allow you to credit mileage earned on one airline to your account with another. Low-cost airlines offer a definite price advantage and fewer restrictions, such as advance-purchase requirements. Safety-wise, low-cost carriers as a group have a good history, but **check the safety record before booking** any low-cost carrier; call the Federal Aviation Administration's Consumer Hotline (☞ Airline Complaints, *below*).

Aer Lingus is the major air carrier to Ireland, with regularly scheduled flights to Shannon and Dublin from JFK, Newark, Boston's Logan, and Chicago's O'Hare. Delta jointly operates with Aer Lingus's JFK flights and also has a daily departure from Atlanta that flies first to Dublin and on to Shannon. Aeroflot flies twice weekly from Miami, three times weekly from Washington, DC (Dulles), and once a week from Chicago.

➤ MAJOR AIRLINES: **Aer Lingus** (☎ 212/557–1110 or 800/223–6537). **Aeroflot** (☎ 888/340–6400). **Delta** (☎ 800/241–4141).

FLYING TIME

Flying time to Ireland is 6½ hours from New York and 7½ hours from Chicago.

GET THE LOWEST FARE

The least-expensive airfares to Ireland are priced for round-trip travel. Major airlines usually require that you **book far in advance and stay at least seven days** and no more than 30 to get the lowest fares. Ask about "ultrasaver" fares, which are the cheapest; they must be booked 90 days in advance and are nonrefundable. A little more expensive are "supersaver" fares, which require only a 30-day advance purchase. Remember that penalties for refunds or scheduling changes are stiffer for international tickets, usually about $150. International flights are also sensitive to the season: **plan to fly in the off season** for the cheapest fares. If your destination or home city has more than one gateway, **compare prices to and from different airports.** Also price flights scheduled for off-peak hours, which may be significantly less expensive.

To save money on flights from the United Kingdom and back, **look into an APEX or Super-PEX ticket.** APEX tickets must be booked in advance and have certain restrictions. Super-PEX tickets can be purchased at the airport on the day of departure—subject to availability.

DON'T STOP UNLESS YOU MUST

When you book, **look for nonstop flights** and **remember that "direct" flights stop at least once.** International flights on a country's flag carrier are almost always nonstop; U.S. airlines often fly direct. Try to **avoid connecting flights,** which require a change of plane. Two airlines may jointly operate a connecting flight, so ask if your airline operates every segment—you may find that your preferred carrier flies you only part of the way.

USE AN AGENT

Travel agents, especially those who specialize in finding the lowest fares (☞ Discounts & Deals, *below*), can be especially helpful when booking a plane ticket. When you're quoted a price, **ask your agent if the price is likely to get any lower.** Good agents know the seasonal fluctuations of airfares and can usually anticipate a sale or fare war. However, waiting can be risky: The fare could go *up* as seats become scarce, and you may wait so long that your preferred flight sells out. A wait-and-see strategy works best if your plans are flexible, but if you must arrive and depart on certain dates, don't delay.

CHECK WITH CONSOLIDATORS

Consolidators buy tickets for scheduled flights at reduced rates from the airlines then sell them at prices that beat the best fare available directly from the airlines, usually without advance restrictions. Sometimes you can even get your money back if you need to return the ticket. Carefully read the fine print detailing penalties for changes and cancellations, and **confirm your consolidator reservation with the airline.**

➤ CONSOLIDATORS: **United States Air Consolidators Association** (✉ 925 L St., Suite 220, Sacramento, CA 95814, ☎ 916/441–4166, FAX 916/441–3520).

AVOID GETTING BUMPED

Airlines routinely overbook planes, knowing that not everyone with a ticket will show up, but sometimes everyone does. When that happens, airlines ask for volunteers to give up their seats. In return these volunteers usually get a certificate for a free flight and are rebooked on the next flight out. If there are not enough volunteers the airline must choose who will be denied boarding. The first to get bumped are passengers who checked in late and those flying on discounted tickets, **so get to the gate and check in as early as possible,** especially during peak periods.

Always **bring a photo ID to the airport.** You may be asked to show it before you are allowed to check in.

ENJOY THE FLIGHT

For more legroom, **request an emergency-aisle seat**; don't however, sit in the row in front of the emergency aisle or in front of a bulkhead, where seats may not recline.

If you don't like airline food, **ask for special meals when booking.** These can be vegetarian, low-cholesterol, or kosher, for example.

To avoid jet lag try to maintain a normal routine while traveling. At night **get some sleep.** By day **eat light meals, drink water (not alcohol), and move about the cabin** to stretch your legs.

Some carriers have prohibited smoking throughout their systems; others allow smoking only on certain routes or even certain departures from that route, so **contact your carrier regarding its smoking policy.**

COMPLAIN IF NECESSARY

If your baggage goes astray or your flight goes awry, complain right away. Most carriers require that you file a claim immediately.

➤ AIRLINE COMPLAINTS: U.S. Department of Transportation **Aviation Consumer Protection Division** (✉ C-75, Room 4107, Washington, DC 20590, ☎ 202/366–2220). **Federal Aviation Administration (FAA) Consumer Hotline** (☎ 800/322–7873).

WITHIN IRELAND

Although air travel does not play a big role in internal travel, a recent increase has led to the development of provincial airports, some with regular flights from the United Kingdom. See the relevant regional chapters for details on airports at Kerry, Sligo Town, Galway, Knock, Waterford, and Derry City (for Donegal). Several flights daily are scheduled between Shannon, Dublin, and Cork, with a flying time of 30–40 minutes between each city. There is also a regular service to all three of the Aran Islands from Connemara Airport. Operated by Aer Arann, the flights take six minutes, weather permitting.

AIRPORTS

The major gateways to the Republic of Ireland are Shannon Airport on the west coast, 25½ km/16 mi west of Limerick City, and Dublin Airport, 10 km/6 mi north of the city center. Two airports serve Belfast: Belfast International Airport at Aldergrove, 24 km/15 mi from the city, handles all international traffic; Belfast City Airport, 6½ km/4 mi from the city, handles local and United Kingdom flights only. In addition, the City of Derry Airport receives flights from Manchester, Birmingham, and Glasgow in the United Kingdom (Loganair).

THE GOLD GUIDE / SMART TRAVEL TIPS

➤ AIRPORT INFORMATION: **Shannon Airport** (☎ 061/471444). **Dublin Airport** (☎ 01/844–4900). **Belfast International Airport at Aldergove** (☎ 01849/422888). **Belfast City Airport** (☎ 01232/457745).

B

BUS TRAVEL

FROM THE U.K.

Numerous bus services run between Britain and the Irish Republic, but **be ready for long hours on the road and possible delays.** All buses to the Republic use either the Holyhead–Dublin or Fishguard/Pembroke–Rosslare ferry routes. National Express, a consortium of bus companies, has Supabus (as its buses are known) services from all major British cities to more than 90 Irish destinations. Slattery's, an Irish company, has services from London, Manchester, Liverpool, Oxford, Birmingham, Leeds, and North Wales to over 100 Irish destinations.

Buses to Belfast run from London and from Birmingham, making the Stranraer–Larne crossing. Contact National Express (☞ below).

➤ BUS LINES: **National Express** (☎ 0171/724–0741). **Slattery's** (☎ 0171/482–1604).

WITHIN THE IRISH REPUBLIC

Buses are a cheap, flexible way to explore the countryside. Expressway bus services, with the most modern buses, cover the country's major routes. Outside the peak season, services are limited, and some routes (e.g., Killarney–Dingle) disappear altogether. There is often only one service a day on the express routes—and one a week to some of the more remote villages!

Long-distance bus services are operated by Bus Éireann, which also provides local services in Cork, Galway, Limerick, and Waterford. To ensure that your proposed bus journey is feasible, **buy a copy of Bus Éireann's timetable**—80p from any bus terminal.

Many of the destination indicators on bus routes are in Irish, so **make sure you get on the right bus.** Asking someone to translate is often the best way to avoid a mishap.

➤ BUS LINES: **Bus Éireann** (☎ 01/836–6111).

WITHIN NORTHERN IRELAND

In Northern Ireland, all buses are operated by the state-owned Ulsterbus. Service is generally good, with particularly useful links to those towns not served by train. Ulsterbus also offers tours. (For details *see* Northern Ireland A to Z *in* Chapter 9.)

➤ BUS LINES: **Ulsterbus** (☎ 01232/333000).

DISCOUNT PASSES

There is a Freedom of Northern Ireland ticket that costs U.K.£28 for seven days' unlimited travel. A one-day ticket costs U.K.£9. Several passes offer discounts on both the bus and rail system in the Irish Republic, including the **Irish Explorer Rail & Bus Pass,** the **Go as You Please Rambler Card,** and the **Emerald Isle Card** (☞ Discount Passes *in* Train Travel, *below*).

BUSINESS HOURS

IN THE IRISH REPUBLIC

Most shops are open 9–5:30 or 6, Monday–Saturday. Once a week—normally Wednesday, Thursday, or Saturday—they shut at 1 for the afternoon. These times do *not* apply to Dublin, and they can vary from region to region, so it's best to check locally. Larger shopping malls usually stay open late once a week—generally until 9 on Thursday or Friday.

Banks are open 10–4, Monday–Friday. In small towns they may close from 12:30–1:30. They remain open until 5 one afternoon per week; again, the day of week varies. Post offices are open weekdays 9–5 and Saturdays 9–1; some of the smaller country offices close for lunch.

Pubs are open Monday–Saturday 10:30 AM–11:30 PM May–September, closing at 11 the rest of the year. The famous Holy Hour, which required city pubs to close from 2:30 to 3:30, was abolished in 1988, and afternoon opening is now at the discretion of the owner or manager; few bother to close. On Sunday, pubs are open 12:30–2 and 4–11. All pubs close on Christmas Day and Good Friday, but hotel bars are open for guests.

IN NORTHERN IRELAND

Shops in Belfast are open 9–5:30, Monday–Friday, with a late closing on Thursday, usually at 9. Elsewhere, shops close for the afternoon once a week, usually Wednesday or Thursday; check locally. In addition, most smaller shops close for an hour or so at lunch.

Bank hours are weekdays 9:30–4:30. Post offices are open weekdays 9–5:30, Saturday 9–1. Some close for an hour at lunch.

Pubs in Northern Ireland are open 11:30 AM–11 PM Monday–Saturday and 12:30 PM–2:30 PM and 7 PM–10 PM on Sunday. Sunday opening is at the owner's or manager's discretion.

C

CAMERAS, CAMCORDERS, & COMPUTERS

Always **keep your film, tape, or computer disks out of the sun.** Carry an extra supply of batteries, and **be prepared to turn on your camera, camcorder, or laptop** to prove to security personnel that the device is real. Always **ask for hand inspection of film,** which becomes clouded after successive exposure to airport x-ray machines, and **keep videotapes and computer disks away from metal detectors.**

➤ PHOTO HELP: **Kodak Information Center** (☎ 800/242–2424). *Kodak Guide to Shooting Great Travel Pictures,* available in bookstores or from **Fodor's Travel Publications** (☎ 800/533–6478; $16.50 plus $4 shipping).

CUSTOMS

Before departing, **register your foreign-made camera or laptop with U.S. Customs** (☞ Customs & Duties, *below*). If your equipment is U.S.-made, call the consulate of the country you'll be visiting to find out whether the device should be registered with local customs upon arrival.

CAR RENTAL

If you are renting a car in the Irish Republic and intend to visit Northern Ireland (or vice versa), make this clear when you get your car, and check that the rental insurance applies when you cross the border.

REPUBLIC OF IRELAND

Rates in Dublin for an economy car with a manual transmission, and unlimited mileage begin at $21 a day/$147 a week (Jan.–Apr. and Nov.–Dec. 15); $24 a day/$168 a week (May–June and Sept.–Oct.); and $38 a day/$266 a week (July–Aug. and Dec. 16–31). This does not include the Republic's 12½% tax on car rentals.

NORTHERN IRELAND

Rates in Belfast begin at $23 a day/$161 a week (Jan.–June, Sept.–Dec. 15) and $35 a day/$245 a week (July–Aug and Dec. 16–31). This does not include the 17½% tax on car rentals in the North.

➤ MAJOR AGENCIES: **Alamo** (☎ 800/522–9696 in the U.S.; 0800/272–2000 in the U.K.; 1800/343536 in Ireland). **Avis** (☎ 800/331–1084 in the U.S.; 800/879–2847 in Canada; ☎ 01/605–7500 in Ireland). **Budget** (☎ 800/527–0700 in the U.S.; 0800/181181 in the U.K.; 01/837–9611 in Ireland). **Dollar** (☎ 800/800–4000 in the U.S.; 0990/565656 in the U.K.; 01/842–3166 in Ireland [it is known as Eurodollar in the U.K. and Ireland]). **Hertz** (☎ 800/654–3001 in the U.S.; 800/263–0600 in Canada; 0345/555888 in the U.K.; ☎ 01/676–7476 in Ireland). **National Car Rental** (☎ 800/227–3876 in the U.S.; 0345/222525 in the U.K., where it is known as Europcar InterRent; 01/668–1777 in Dublin, where it is known as Murray's Rent-a-Car).

➤ LOCAL COMPANIES: **Argus** (☎ 01/490–4444 in Dublin). **Dan Dooley** (☎ 800/331–9301 in the U.S.; 081/994–2512 or 0800/282–189 in the U.K., 01/677–2723 in Dublin). **ECL Chauffeur Drive** (☎ 01/704–4062) offers chauffeur-driven Mercedes sedans, minivans, and coaches for a journey or daily rate.

CUT COSTS

To get the best deal, **book through a travel agent who is willing to shop around.**

Also **ask your travel agent about a company's customer-service record.** How has it responded to late plane arrivals and vehicle mishaps? Are there often lines at the rental counter, and, if you're traveling during a holiday period, does a confirmed reservation guarantee you a car?

Be sure to **look into wholesalers,** companies that do not own fleets but rent in bulk from those that do and often offer better rates than traditional car-rental operations. Prices are best during off-peak periods. Rentals booked through wholesalers must be paid for before you leave the United States.

➤ RENTAL WHOLESALERS: **Auto Europe** (☎ 207/842–2000 or 800/223–5555, FAX 800–235–6321). **Europe by Car** (☎ 212/581–3040 or 800/223–1516, FAX 212/246–1458). **DER Travel Services** (✉ 9501 W. Devon Ave., Rosemont, IL 60018, ☎ 800/782–2424, FAX 800/282–7474 for information or 800/860–9944 for brochures). The **Kemwel Group** (☎ 914/835–5555 or 800/678–0678, FAX 914/835–5126).

NEED INSURANCE?

When driving a rented car you are generally responsible for any damage to or loss of the vehicle. Before you rent, **see what coverage you already have** under the terms of your personal auto-insurance policy and credit cards.

Collision policies that car-rental companies sell for European rentals typically do not cover stolen vehicles. Before you buy additional coverage for theft, find out if your credit card or personal auto insurance will cover the loss.

BEWARE SURCHARGES

Before you pick up a car in one city and leave it in another, **ask about drop-off charges or one-way service fees,** which can be substantial. Note, too, that some rental agencies charge extra if you return the car before the time specified on your contract. To avoid a hefty refueling fee, **fill the tank just before you turn in the car,** but be aware that gas stations near the rental outlet may overcharge.

MEET THE REQUIREMENTS

In Ireland your own driver's license is acceptable. An International Driver's Permit is a good idea; it's available from the American or Canadian automobile association, or, in the United Kingdom, from the Automobile Association or Royal Automobile Club.

CHILDREN IN IRELAND

The Irish love children and will go to great lengths to make them welcome. Many hotels offer baby-sitting services, and most will supply a cot if given advance notice. Hotel and pub restaurants often have a children's menu and can supply a high chair if necessary. Unlike Great Britain, Irish licensing laws allow children under 14 into pubs—although they may not consume alcohol on the premises until they are 18, and they are expected to leave by about 7 PM. This is a boon if you are touring by car because pubs are perfect for lunch or tea stops.

While most attractions and bus and rail journeys offer a rate of half-price or less for children, **look for "family tickets,"** which may be cheaper and usually cover two adults and up to four children. The Irish Tourist Board (ITB) publishes "A Tour of Favorite Kids' Places," that covers a week's worth of sights around the country.

Involve your youngsters as you outline your trip. When packing, include things to keep them busy en route. On sightseeing days try to schedule activities of special interest to your children. If you are renting a car don't forget to **arrange for a car seat** when you reserve. Most hotels in Ireland allow children under a certain age to stay in their parents' room at no extra charge, but others charge them as extra adults; be sure to **ask about the cutoff age for children's discounts.**

FLYING

As a rule, infants under two not occupying a seat fly at greatly reduced fares and occasionally for free. If your children are two or older **ask about children's airfares.**

In general the adult baggage allowance applies to children paying half or more of the adult fare. When booking, **ask about carry-on allowances for those traveling with infants.** In general, for babies charged 10% of the adult fare you are allowed one carry-on bag and a collapsible stroller, which may have to be checked; you may be limited to less if the flight is full.

According to the FAA it's a good idea to use safety seats aloft for children weighing less than 40 pounds. Airlines, however, can set their own policies: U.S. carriers allow FAA-approved models but usually require that you buy a ticket, even if your child would otherwise ride free, since the seats must be strapped into regular seats. Airline rules vary regarding their use, so it's important to **check your airline's policy about using safety seats during takeoff and landing.** Safety seats cannot obstruct any of the other passengers in the row, so get an appropriate seat assignment as early as possible.

When making your reservation, **request children's meals or a free-standing bassinet** if you need them; the latter are available only to those seated at the bulkhead, where there's enough legroom. Remember, however, that bulkhead seats may not have their own overhead bins, and there's no storage space in front of you—a major inconvenience.

GROUP TRAVEL

If you're planning to take your kids on a tour, look for companies that specialize in family travel.

➤ FAMILY-FRIENDLY TOUR OPERATORS: **Grandtravel** (✉ 6900 Wisconsin Ave., Suite 706, Chevy Chase, MD 20815, ☎ 301/986–0790 or 800/247–7651) for people traveling with grandchildren ages 7–17. **Families Welcome!** (✉ 92 N. Main St., Ashland, OR 97520, ☎ 541/482–6121 or 800/326–0724, FAX 541/482–0660).

CONSUMER PROTECTION

Whenever possible, **pay with a major credit card** so you can cancel payment if there's a problem, provided that you can provide documentation. This is a good practice whether you're buying travel arrangements before your trip or shopping at your destination.

If you're doing business with a particular company for the first time, **contact your local Better Business Bureau and the attorney general's offices** in your state and the company's home state, as well. Have any complaints been filed?

Finally, if you're buying a package or tour, always **consider travel insurance** that includes default coverage (☞ Insurance, *below*).

➤ LOCAL BBBs: **Council of Better Business Bureau** (✉ 4200 Wilson Blvd., Suite 800, Arlington, VA 22203, ☎ 703/276–0100, FAX 703/525–8277).

CUSTOMS & DUTIES

When shopping, **keep receipts** for all your purchases. Upon reentering the country, **be ready to show customs officials what you've bought.** If you feel a duty is incorrect, appeal the assessment. If you object to the way your clearance was handled, get the inspector's badge number. In either case, first ask to see a supervisor, then write to the port director at the address listed on your receipt. Send a copy of the receipt and other appropriate documentation. If you still don't get satisfaction you can take your case to customs headquarters in Washington.

ENTERING IRELAND

Two categories of duty-free allowance exist for travelers entering both the Republic of Ireland and Northern Ireland: one for goods obtained outside the European Union (EU), on a ship or aircraft, or in a duty-free store within the EU; and the other for goods bought in the EU with duty and tax paid.

Of the first category, you may import duty-free: (1) 200 cigarettes or 100 cigarillos or 50 cigars or 250 grams of smoking tobacco; (2) 2 liters of wine, and either 1 liter of alcoholic drink over 22% volume or 2 liters of alcoholic drink under 22% volume (sparkling or fortified wine included); (3) 50 grams of perfume and ¼ liter of toilet water; and (4) other goods to a value of £142 per person (£73 per person for travelers under 15 years of age).

Of the second category, you may import duty-free a considerable amount of liquor and tobacco—800 cigarettes, 400 cigarillos, 200 cigars, 1 kilogram of pipe tobacco, 10 liters of spirits, 45 liters of wine, 25 liters of port/sherry and 55 liters of beer. You'll need a truck!

Goods that cannot be freely imported to the Irish Republic include firearms, ammunition, explosives, illegal drugs, indecent or obscene books and pictures, oral smokeless tobacco products, meat and meat products, poultry and poultry products, plants and plant products (including shrubs, vegetables, fruit, bulbs, and seeds), domestic cats and dogs from outside the United Kingdom, and live animals from outside Northern Ireland.

No animals or pets of any kind may be brought into Northern Ireland without a six-month quarantine. Other items that may not be imported include fresh meats, plants and vegetables, controlled drugs, and firearms and ammunition.

ENTERING THE U.S.

You may bring home $400 worth of foreign goods duty-free if you've been out of the country for at least 48 hours and haven't already used the $400 allowance or any part of it in the past 30 days.

Travelers 21 and older may bring back 1 liter of alcohol duty-free. In addition, regardless of your age, you are allowed 200 cigarettes and 100 non-Cuban cigars. (At press time, a federal rule restricting tobacco access to persons 18 years and older did not apply to importation.) Antiques, which the U.S. Customs Service defines as objects more than 100 years old, enter duty-free, as do original works of art done entirely by hand, including paintings, drawings, and sculptures.

You may also send packages home duty-free: up to $200 worth of goods for personal use, with a limit of one parcel per addressee per day (and no alcohol or tobacco products or perfume worth more than $5); label the package PERSONAL USE, and attach a list of its contents and their retail value. Do not label the package UNSOLICITED GIFT, or your duty-free exemption will drop to $100. Mailed items do not affect your duty-free allowance on your return.

➤ INFORMATION: **U.S. Customs Service** (Inquiries, ✉ Box 7407, Washington, DC 20044, ☎ 202/927–6724; complaints, Office of Regulations and Rulings, 1301 Constitution Ave. NW, Washington, DC 20229; registration of equipment, ✉ Resource Management, 1301 Constitution Ave. NW, Washington DC, 20229, ☎ 202/927–0540).

ENTERING CANADA

If you've been out of Canada for at least seven days you may bring in C$500 worth of goods duty-free. If you've been away for fewer than seven days but more than 48 hours, the duty-free allowance drops to C$200; if your trip lasts 24–48 hours, the allowance is C$50. You may not pool allowances with family members. Goods claimed under the C$500 exemption may follow you by mail; those claimed under the lesser exemptions must accompany you.

Alcohol and tobacco products may be included in the seven-day and 48-hour exemptions but not in the 24-hour exemption. If you meet the age requirements of the province or territory through which you reenter Canada you may bring in, duty-free, 1.14 liters (40 imperial ounces) of wine or liquor *or* 24 12-ounce cans or bottles of beer or ale. If you are 16 or older you may bring in, duty-free, 200 cigarettes and 50 cigars; these items must accompany you.

You may send an unlimited number of gifts worth up to C$60 each duty-free to Canada. Label the package UNSOLICITED GIFT—VALUE UNDER $60. Alcohol and tobacco are excluded.

➤ INFORMATION: **Revenue Canada** (✉ 2265 St. Laurent Blvd. S, Ottawa, Ontario K1G 4K3, ☎ 613/993–0534, 800/461–9999 in Canada).

ENTERING THE U.K.

If your journey was wholly within EU countries you needn't pass through customs when you return to the United Kingdom. If you plan to bring back large quantities of alcohol or tobacco, check on EU limits beforehand.

➤ INFORMATION: **HM Customs and Excise** (✉ Dorset House, Stamford St., London SE1 9NG, ☎ 0171/202–4227).

DINING

For information about restaurants beyond those reviewed in our guide, look for *Dining in Ireland* (free in the U.S.; £2.50 otherwise), an illustrated guide in which establishments are organized by region with accompanying price brackets. It's available from Bord Fáilte offices. *Where to Eat*

(U.K.£2.50), published by the Northern Ireland Tourist Board (NITB), contains lists many Northern Irish restaurants in the middle to lower price ranges.

DISABILITIES & ACCESSIBILITY

ACCESS IN IRELAND

Ireland has only recently begun to provide facilities such as ramps and accessible toilets for people with disabilities. Public transportation also lags behind. However, visitors with disabilities will often find that the helpfulness of the Irish often makes up for the lack of amenities.

TIPS & HINTS

When discussing accessibility with an operator or reservationist, **ask hard questions.** Are there any stairs, inside *or* out? Are there grab bars next to the toilet *and* in the shower/tub? How wide is the doorway to the room? To the bathroom? For the most extensive facilities meeting the latest legal specifications, **opt for newer accommodations,** which are more likely to have been designed with access in mind. Older buildings or ships may offer more limited facilities. Be sure to **discuss your needs before booking.**

➤ COMPLAINTS: **Disability Rights Section** (✉ U.S. Department of Justice, Box 66738, Washington, DC 20035–6738, ☎ 202/514–0301 or 800/514–0301, FAX 202/307–1198, TTY 202/514–0383 or 800/514–0383) for general complaints. **Aviation Consumer Protection Division** (☞ Air Travel, *above*) for airline-related problems. **Civil Rights Office** (✉ U.S. Department of Transportation, Departmental Office of Civil Rights, S-30, 400 7th St. SW, Room 10215, Washington, DC, 20590, ☎ 202/366–4648) for problems with surface transportation.

TRAVEL AGENCIES & TOUR OPERATORS

The Americans with Disabilities Act requires that travel firms serve the needs of all travelers. That said, you should note that some agencies and operators specialize in making travel arrangements for individuals and groups with disabilities.

➤ TRAVELERS WITH MOBILITY PROBLEMS: **Access Adventures** (✉ 206 Chestnut Ridge Rd., Rochester, NY 14624, ☎ 716/889–9096), run by a former physical-rehabilitation counselor. **Accessible Journeys** (✉ 35 W. Sellers Ave., Ridley Park, PA 19078, ☎ 610/521–0339 or 800/846–4537, FAX 610/521–6959), for escorted tours exclusively for travelers with mobility impairments. **CareVacations** (✉ 5019 49th Ave., Suite 102, Leduc, Alberta, T9E 6T5, ☎ 403/986–6404, 800/648–1116 in Canada) has group tours and is especially helpful with cruise vacations. **Hinsdale Travel Service** (✉ 201 E. Ogden Ave., Suite 100, Hinsdale, IL 60521, ☎ 630/325–1335), a travel agency that benefits from the advice of wheelchair traveler Janice Perkins. **Wheelchair Journeys** (✉ 16979 Redmond Way, Redmond, WA 98052, ☎ 206/885–2210 or 800/313–4751), for general travel arrangements.

DISCOUNTS & DEALS

Be a smart shopper and **compare all your options before making a choice.** A plane ticket bought with a promotional coupon may not be cheaper than the least expensive fare from a discount ticket agency. For high-price travel purchases, such as packages or tours, keep in mind that what you get is just as important as what you save. Just because something is cheap doesn't mean it's a bargain.

LOOK IN YOUR WALLET

When you use your credit card to make travel purchases you may get free travel-accident insurance, collision-damage insurance, and medical or legal assistance, depending on the card and the bank that issued it. American Express, MasterCard, and Visa provide one or more of these services, so **get a copy of your credit card's travel-benefits policy.** If you are a member of the American Automobile Association (AAA) or an oil-company-sponsored road-assistance plan, always **ask hotel or car-rental reservationists about auto-club discounts.** Some clubs offer additional discounts on tours, cruises, or admission to attractions. And don't forget that auto-club membership entitles you to free maps and trip-planning services.

DIAL FOR DOLLARS

To save money, **look into "1-800" discount reservations services,** which use their buying power to get a better price on hotels, airline tickets, even car rentals. When booking a room, always **call the hotel's local toll-free number** (if one is available) rather than the central reservations number—you'll often get a better price. Always ask about special packages or corporate rates.

When shopping for the best deal on hotels and car rentals **look for guaranteed exchange rates,** which protect you against a falling dollar. With your rate locked in you won't pay more even if the price goes up in the local currency.

➤ AIRLINE TICKETS: ☎ 800/FLY–4–LESS.

➤ HOTEL ROOMS: **Hotels Plus** (☎ 800/235–0909).

SAVE ON COMBOS

Packages and guided tours can both save you money, but don't confuse the two. When you buy a package your travel remains independent, just as though you had planned and booked the trip yourself. Fly/drive packages, which combine airfare and car rental, are often a good deal. If you **buy a rail/drive pass** you'll save on train tickets and car rentals. All Eurail and Europass holders get a discount on Eurostar fares through the Channel Tunnel.

JOIN A CLUB?

Many companies sell discounts in the form of travel clubs and coupon books, but these cost money. You must use participating advertisers to get a deal, and only after you recoup the initial membership cost or book price do you begin to save. If you plan to use the club or coupons frequently you may save considerably. Before signing up, find out what discounts you get for free.

➤ DISCOUNT CLUBS: **Entertainment Travel Editions** (✉ 2125 Butterfield Rd., Troy, MI 48084, ☎ 800/445–4137; $23–$48, depending on destination). **Great American Traveler** (✉ Box 27965, Salt Lake City, UT 84127, ☎ 800/548–2812; $49.95 per year). **Moment's Notice Discount Travel Club** (✉ 7301 New Utrecht Ave., Brooklyn, NY 11204, ☎ 718/234–6295; $25 per year, single or family). **Privilege Card International** (✉ 237 E. Front St., Youngstown,

OH 44503, ☎ 330/746–5211 or 800/236–9732; $74.95 per year). **Sears's Mature Outlook** (✉ Box 9390, Des Moines, IA 50306, ☎ 800/336–6330; $14.95 per year). **Travelers Advantage** (✉ CUC Travel Service, 3033 S. Parker Rd., Suite 1000, Aurora, CO 80014, ☎ 800/548–1116 or 800/648–4037; $49 per year, single or family). **Worldwide Discount Travel Club** (✉ 1674 Meridian Ave., Miami Beach, FL 33139, ☎ 305/534–2082; $50 per year family, $40 single).

DRIVING

REPUBLIC OF IRELAND

A car journey on Ireland's many back roads and byways is the ideal way to explore the country's predominantly rural attractions. Roads are generally good, although four-lane, two-way roads are the exception rather than the rule. Most National Primary Routes (designated by the letter *N*) have two lanes with generous shoulders on which to pass. Brand-new divided highways, or motorways—designated by blue signs and the letter *M*—take the place of some *N* roads. They are the fastest way to get from one point to another, but use caution: They sometimes end as abruptly as they begin. In general, traffic is light, especially off the national routes. Still it's wise to **slow down on the smaller, often twisty roads** and **watch out for cattle and sheep;** they may be just around the next bend. Speed limits are generally 96 kph (60 mph) on the open road and 48 kph (30 mph) or 64 kph (40 mph) in urban areas.

Road signs are generally in both Irish (Gaelic) and English; in the northwest and Connemara, most are in Irish only, so **make sure you have a good road map.** On the new green signposts distances are in kilometers; on the old white signposts their given in miles. Because of the coexistence of both old and new signs, the route number is not always referred to on the signpost, particularly on National Secondary Roads (*N*-numbered routes) and Regional roads (*R*-numbered routes). On such roads, knowing the name of the next town on your itinerary is more important than knowing the route number: Neither the small local signposts nor the local people refer to roads by official numbers. At unmarked intersections, a good rule of thumb is to **keep going straight if there's no sign directing you to do otherwise.**

The Irish, like the British, **drive on the left-hand side of the road.** Safety belts must be worn by the driver and front passenger, and children under 12 must travel in the back. It is compulsory for motorcyclists and their passengers to wear helmets.

Traffic signs are the same as in the rest of Europe, and roadway markings are standard. Note especially that a continuous white line down the center of the road prohibits passing. Barred markings on the road and flashing yellow beacons indicate a crossing, where pedestrians have right of way. At a junction of two roads of equal importance, the driver to the right has right of way.

Despite the relatively light traffic, parking in towns can be a problem. Signs with the letter *P* indicate that parking is permitted; a stroke through the *P* warns you to stay away or you'll be liable for a fine of £15 to £40. In Dublin and Cork, parking lots are your best bet, but check the rate first in Dublin; they can vary wildly.

Drunk-driving laws are strict. Ireland has a Breathalyzer test, which the police can administer anytime. If you refuse to take it, the odds are you'll be prosecuted anyway. As ever, the best advice is **don't drink if you plan to drive.**

NORTHERN IRELAND

The road network in Northern Ireland is excellent and, outside Belfast, uncrowded. Road signs and traffic regulations conform to the British system. Speed limits are 48 kph (30 mph) in towns, 96 kph (60 mph) on country roads, and 112 kph (70 mph) on two-lane roads and motorways.

There are plenty of parking lots in the towns (usually free except in Belfast), and you should use them. In Belfast, you cannot park your car in some parts of the city center, more because of congestion than security problems.

BORDER CROSSINGS

Army checkpoints are a thing of the past between the North and the

South, though there are some border checkpoints to check the cattle (in an effort to contain BSE-contaminated livestock).

FROM THE U.K.

All ferries on *both* principal routes to the Irish Republic—Holyhead–Dublin and Fishguard/Pembroke–Rosslare—take cars. Fishguard and Pembroke are relatively easy to reach by road. The car trip to Holyhead, on the other hand, is sometimes difficult: Delays on the A55 North Wales coastal road are not unusual.

Car ferries to Belfast leave from the Scottish port of Stranraer and the English city of Liverpool; those to Larne leave from Stranraer and Cairnryan.

For reservations and information, *see* Ferry Travel, *below.*

➤ AUTO CLUBS: In the U.S., **American Automobile Association** (AAA; ☎ 800/564–6222). In the U.K., **Automobile Association** (AA; ☎ 0990/ 500–600), **Royal Automobile Club** (RAC; membership ☎ 0990/722–722; insurance 0345/121–345).

E

ELECTRICITY

To use your U.S.-purchased electric-powered equipment, **bring a converter and adapter.** The electrical current in Ireland is 220 volts, 50 cycles alternating current (AC); wall outlets take plugs with three prongs.

If your appliances are dual-voltage, you'll need only an adapter. Don't use 110-volt outlets, marked FOR SHAVERS ONLY, for high-wattage appliances such as blow-dryers. Some laptops operate equally well on 110 and 220 volts and so require only an adapter; check with your laptop's manufacturer before leaving home to be sure you're equipped with the proper adapter.

F

FERRY TRAVEL

FROM THE U.K.

There are two principal ferry routes to the Irish Republic: to Dublin from Holyhead on the Isle of Anglesea, and to Rosslare from Fishguard or Pembroke in Wales. Two companies sail the Dublin route: Irish Ferries from Dublin port and Stena Sealink, whose ferries go both to Dublin port and Dun Laoghaire, 4 km/2½ mi south of the city center. Prices and departure times vary according to season, so call either company to confirm. In summer, reservations are strongly recommended. Dozens of taxis wait to take you into town from both ports, or you can take DART or a bus to the city center.

Irish Ferries operates the Pembroke–Rosslare route; Stena Sealink operates the Fishguard–Rosslare route. To connect with the Fishguard sailings, take one of the many direct trains from London (Paddington). A connecting train at Rosslare will get you to Waterford by about 8:30 PM, to Cork by about midnight. For the Pembroke sailings, you have to change at Swansea. Sailing time for both routes is 4½ hours.

Swansea Cork Ferries operate a service between Swansea and Cork from mid March to early January. The crossing takes 12 hours, but easy access by road to both ports make this longer sea route a good choice for motorists heading for the Southwest.

The cost of your trip can vary substantially, so **spend time with a travel agent and compare prices carefully;** flying is sometimes cheaper, and fares to Dublin are cheapest. **Book well in advance at peak periods.** Students and others under 26 should take advantage of the cheap fares offered by Eurotrain.

Car ferries run to Northern Ireland from the Scottish port of Stranraer. Trains leave London (Euston) for Stranraer Harbour several times a day. Sealink Ferries crosses the water to the port of Larne, where you pick up a train to Belfast. The whole trip is around 13 hours. Much faster and more convenient is the SeaCat, a huge, car-ferry catamaran that crosses from Stranraer right into Belfast in just 1½ hours. There is also a 9-hour crossing from Liverpool to Belfast, operated by Belfast Ferries. Trains leave London (Euston) for Liverpool throughout the day.

➤ FERRY CONTACTS: **Irish Ferries** (✉ Merrion Row, ☎ 01/661–0511).

Stena Sealink (✉ Ferryport, Dun Laoghaire, ☎ 01/204–7777 or 204–7700).

WITHIN THE IRISH REPUBLIC

If you're traveling from County Kerry to County Clare and the West of Ireland, you can take the ferry from Tarbert (in County Kerry), leaving every hour on the half hour. Going the other way, ferries leave from Killimer (in County Clare) every hour on the hour. The 30-minute journey across the Shannon Estuary costs £7 per car, £2 for foot passengers.

A 10-minute car ferry crosses the River Suir between Ballyhack in County Wexford and Passage East in County Waterford. It saves you a boring drive through New Ross on the N25 and also introduces you to two pretty fishing villages, Ballyhack and Arthurstown. The ferry operates continuously during daylight hours and costs £3.50 per car, 80p for foot passengers.

The Cork Harbour crossing is a scenic route that allows those traveling from west Cork or Kinsale to Cobh and the east coast to bypass the city center. The five-minute car ferry runs from Glenbrook (near Ringaskiddy) in the west to Carrigaloe (near Cobh) in the east and operates continuously from 7:15 AM to 12:45 AM daily. It costs £3 per car, 60p for foot passengers.

You can reach many, but not all, of Ireland's offshore islands by ferry. There are regular services to the Aran Islands from Galway City, Rossaveal in County Galway, and Doolin in County Clare. Ferries also sail to Inishbofin off the Galway coast and Arranmore off the Donegal coast, and to Bere, Sherkin, and Cape Clear islands off the coast of County Cork. The islands are all small enough to explore on foot, so the ferries are for foot passengers and bicycles only. Other islands—the Blaskets and the Skelligs in Kerry, Rathlin, and Tory off the Donegal coast—can be reached by private arrangements with local boatmen (*see* the relevant regional chapters). Full details on ferries to the islands are available in a publication from the ITB (☞ Visitor Information, *below*).

FISHING

The salmon season is normally from January 1 to September 30, but dates vary from one district to another. The best period for sea trout is from June to late September. Permits are necessary on privately owned waters or club waters: the latter will cost £5–£15 a day for salmon, £2–£10 for trout. There is no closed season for coarse angling. Besides the permit for the use of a certain stretch of water, those who wish to fish for salmon and sea trout by rod and line must also have a state license. No license is required for brown trout, rainbow trout, or coarse fish, including pike. Sea angling is available on rocks and piers around the coast.

Licenses for salmon and sea-trout fishing by rod and line in the Irish Republic (£25 annually, or £10 for 21 days) are available in some tackle shops or from the **Central Fisheries Board** (⊠ Balngowan House, Mobhi Boreen, Glasnevin, Dublin 9, ☎ 01/837–9206).

To game fish in Northern Ireland, you need a rod license. The **Foyle Fisheries Commission** (⊠ FFC, 8 Victoria Rd., Londonderry BT47 2AB, ☎ 01504/42100) distributes licenses for game fishing in the Foyle area, and the **Fisheries Conservancy Board** (⊠ FCB, 1 Mahon Rd., Portadown, Craigavon, Co. Armagh BT62 3EE, ☎ 01762/334666) handles all other regions. A license costs approximately U.K.£10 for eight days. You must also obtain a permit from the owner of the waters in which you plan to fish. Most of the waters are owned by the **Department of Agriculture** (⊠ Fisheries Division, Stormont, Belfast BT4 3PW, ☎ 01232/523431), which charges about U.K.£15 for an eight-day permit, U.K.£3.50 for a daily one. If you plan to fish outside the jurisdiction of the Department of Agriculture, you must obtain a permit from one of the local clubs. For more information, and for Department of Agriculture permits and FFC and FCB rod licenses, contact the NITB (☞ Visitor Information, *below*).

G

GAY & LESBIAN TRAVEL

In 1993 the Republic of Ireland began to replace virulently homophobic laws (inherited from British rule and enforced up to the 1970s) with some of the most gay-progressive statutes in the EU. Homosexual acts have been decriminalized and hate crimes and discrimination in the workplace and public accommodation are now illegal. Leading these efforts was Ireland's progressive president, Mary Robinson, the first woman to hold this office. (She was named United Nations High Commissioner for Human Rights in June 1997.)

This enlightened legal environment, however, doesn't readily translate into the same public lesbian and gay presence you find in U.S. and European cities. Outside the Republic's major cities—Dublin, Cork, and Galway—signs of gay life can be difficult to find, and even in these cities you're likely to find them only in small pockets—a pub here, a café there. If you do encounter any difficulties as a gay traveler, it's likely to be with lodging establishments. Proprietors at even some of most upscale places may resist letting a room with one bed to same-sex couples; at other establishments, no one may so much as raise an eyebrow. Test the waters in advance: Be explicit about what you want when you make your reservation.

➤ IRISH CONTACTS: *Gay Community News* (GCN; ☎ 01/671–9076 or 01/671–0939), Ireland's free monthly lesbian and gay newspaper, is widely available in Dublin and in gay-friendly venues in larger cities such as Cork, Galway, Limerick, Derry, and Belfast.

CORK

Ireland's second largest city has the country's only lesbian and gay community center and a decade-old gay bar. The Cork International Film Festival (☞ Festivals and Seasonal Events *in* Chapter 1), held in October, incorporates the Irish Lesbian and Gay Film Festival.

➤ CORK CONTACTS: **Lesbian and Gay Line** (☎ 021/271087) operates Wednesday 7 PM–9 PM and Saturday 3 PM–5 PM; it functions as a lesbian hot line Thursday 8 PM–10 PM. **Loafers** (⊠ 26 Douglas St., ☎ 021/311612) is Cork's main gay bar. **The Other Place** (⊠ 8 S. Main St., ☎ 021/278745), the lesbian and gay community center, houses a bookstore and café and hosts Friday and Saturday night dances.

DUBLIN

By far, Dublin has more accessible lesbian and gay life than any other city in Ireland. Consult *Gay Community News* and *In Dublin* for current information about what's going on in the community.

➤ DUBLIN CONTACTS: **Gay Switchboard Dublin** (☎ 01/872–1055) operates Sunday–Friday 8 PM–10 PM and Saturday 3:30 PM–6 PM. **The George** (⊠ 89 S. Great George's St., ☎ 01/478–2983). **Out on the Liffey** (⊠ 27 Ormond Quay, ☎ 01/872–2480).

GALWAY

A young populace, a progressive university, and a few outstanding theater companies help make Ireland's bohemian left-coast city one of the country's most gay-friendly places. Neither Le Graal nor Neaćhtain's are specifically gay, but they are among the gay-friendlier places in town.

➤ GALWAY CONTACTS: **Galway Gay Helpline** (☎ 091/566134) operates Tuesday 8 PM–10 PM. **Galway Lesbian Helpline** (☎ 091/564611) operates Wednesday 8 PM–10 PM and Saturday noon–2 PM. **Le Graal** (⊠ 38 Lower Dominick St., ☎ 091/567614). **Neaćhtain's** (⊠ 17 Cross St., ☎ 091/561720).

➤ GAY- AND LESBIAN-FRIENDLY TRAVEL AGENCIES: **Advance Damron** (⊠ 1 Greenway Plaza, Suite 800, Houston, TX 77046, ☎ 713/850–1140 or 800/695–0880, FAX 713/888–1010). **Club Travel** (⊠ 8739 Santa Monica Blvd., West Hollywood, CA 90069, ☎ 310/358–2200 or 800/429–8747, FAX 310/358–2222). **Islanders/Kennedy Travel** (⊠ 183 W. 10th St., New York, NY 10014, ☎ 212/242–3222 or 800/988–1181, FAX 212/929–8530). **Now Voyager** (⊠ 4406 18th St., San Francisco, CA 94114, ☎ 415/626–1169 or 800/255–6951, FAX 415/626–8626). **Yellowbrick Road** (⊠ 1500 W. Balmoral Ave., Chicago, IL 60640, ☎ 773/561–1800 or 800/642–2488, FAX 773/561–4497). **Skylink Women's Travel** (⊠ 3577 Moorland Ave., Santa Rosa, CA 95407, ☎ 707/585–8355 or 800/225–5759, FAX 707/584–5637), serving lesbian travelers.

H

HEALTH

MEDICAL PLANS

No one plans to get sick while traveling, but it happens, so **consider signing up with a medical-assistance company.** Members get doctor referrals, emergency evacuation or repatriation, 24-hour telephone hot lines for medical consultation, cash for emergencies, and other personal and legal assistance. Coverage varies by plan, so **review the benefits carefully.**

➤ MEDICAL-ASSISTANCE COMPANIES: **International SOS Assistance** (⊠ Box 11568, Philadelphia, PA 19116, ☎ 215/244–1500 or 800/523–8930; ⊠ 1255 University St., Suite 420, Montréal, Québec H3B 3B6, ☎ 514/874–7674 or 800/363–0263; ⊠ 7 Old Lodge Pl., St. Margarets, Twickenham TW1 1RQ, England, ☎ 0181/744–0033). **MEDEX Assistance Corporation** (⊠ Box 5375, Timonium, MD 21094-5375, ☎ 410/453–6300 or 800/537–2029). **Traveler's Emergency Network** (⊠ 3100 Tower Blvd., Suite 1000B, Durham, NC 27707, ☎ 919/490–6055 or 800/275–4836, FAX 919/493–8262). **TravMed** (⊠ Box 5375, Timonium, MD 21094, ☎ 410/453–6380 or 800/732–5309). **Worldwide Assistance Services** (⊠ 1133 15th St. NW, Suite 400, Washington, DC 20005, ☎ 202/331–1609 or 800/821–2828, FAX 202/828–5896).

HOLIDAYS

Irish national holidays are as follows: January 1 (New Year's); March 17 (St. Patrick's Day); April 10 (Good Friday); April 13 (Easter Monday); May 1 (May Day); May 18 (Whit Monday); August 3 (August Holiday); October 26 (October Holiday); and December 25–26 (Christmas and St. Stephen's Day). If you plan to visit at Easter, remember that theaters and cinemas are closed for the last three days of the preceding week.

I

INSURANCE

Travel insurance is the best way to **protect yourself against financial loss.**

The most useful policies are trip-cancellation-and-interruption, default, medical, and comprehensive insurance.

Without insurance you will lose all or most of your money if you cancel your trip, regardless of the reason. It's essential that you **buy trip-cancellation-and-interruption insurance,** particularly if your airline ticket, cruise, or package tour is nonrefundable and cannot be changed. When considering how much coverage you need, look for a policy that will cover the cost of your trip plus the nondiscounted price of a one-way airline ticket, should you need to return home early. Also **consider default or bankruptcy insurance,** which protects you against a supplier's failure to deliver.

Medicare generally does not cover health-care costs outside the United States, nor do many privately issued policies. If your own policy does not cover you outside the United States, **consider buying supplemental medical coverage.** Remember that travel health insurance is different from a medical-assistance plan (☞ Health, *above*).

Citizens of the United Kingdom can buy an annual travel-insurance policy valid for most vacations during the year in which it's purchased. If you are pregnant or have a preexisting medical condition, make sure you're covered.

If you have purchased an expensive vacation, particularly one that involves travel abroad, comprehensive insurance is a must. **Look for comprehensive policies that include trip-delay insurance,** which will protect you in the event that weather problems cause you to miss your flight, tour, or cruise. A few insurers sell waivers for preexisting medical conditions. Companies that offer both features include Access America, Carefree Travel, Travel Insured International, and Travel Guard (☞ *below*).

Always **buy travel insurance directly from the insurance company**; if you buy it from a travel agency or tour operator that goes out of business you probably will not be covered for the agency or operator's default, a major risk. Before you make any purchase, **review your existing health and home-owner's policies** to find out whether they cover expenses incurred while traveling.

➤ TRAVEL INSURERS: In the U.S., **Access America** (✉ 6600 W. Broad St., Richmond, VA 23230, ☎ 804/285–3300 or 800/284–8300), **Carefree Travel Insurance** (✉ Box 9366, 100 Garden City Plaza, Garden City, NY 11530, ☎ 516/294–0220 or 800/323–3149), **Near Travel Services** (✉ Box 1339, Calumet City, IL 60409, ☎ 708/868–6700 or 800/654–6700), **Travel Guard International** (✉ 1145 Clark St., Stevens Point, WI 54481, ☎ 715/345–0505 or 800/826–1300), **Travel Insured International** (✉ Box 280568, East Hartford, CT 06128–0568, ☎ 860/528–7663 or 800/243–3174), **Travelex Insurance Services** (✉ 11717 Burt St., Suite 202, Omaha, NE 68154-1500, ☎ 402/445–8637 or 800/228–9792, FAX 800/867–9531), **Wallach & Company** (✉ 107 W. Federal St., Box 480, Middleburg, VA 20118, ☎ 540/687–3166 or 800/237–6615). In Canada, **Mutual of Omaha** (✉ Travel Division, 500 University Ave., Toronto, Ontario M5G 1V8, ☎ 416/598–4083, 800/268–8825 in Canada). In the U.K., **Association of British Insurers** (✉ 51 Gresham St., London EC2V 7HQ, ☎ 0171/600–3333).

L
LANGUAGE

Irish (also known as Gaelic)—a Celtic language related to Scottish Gaelic, Breton, and Welsh—is the official national language. Though English is technically the second language of the country, it is, in fact, the everyday tongue of the majority of the population. Nowadays all Irish speakers are fluent in English.

Irish-speaking communities are found mainly in sparsely populated rural areas along the western seaboard, on some but not all offshore islands, and in pockets in West Cork and County Waterford. Irish-speaking areas are known as Gaeltacht. While most road signs in Ireland are given in both English and Irish, within Gaeltacht areas the signs are often in Irish only. A good touring map will give both Irish and English names to places within the Gaeltacht. You really need only know two Irish words: *Fir* (men) and *mná* (women)—useful vocabulary for a trip to a public toilet.

LODGING

Accommodations in Ireland range from deluxe renovated castles and stately homes to thatched cottages and farmhouses. Room standards are rising all the time, especially in the middle and lower price ranges. Pressure on hotel space reaches a peak from June to September, but it's always a good idea to **reserve in advance.** Many Irish hotels can be booked directly from the United States. Ask your travel agent.

The ITB has an official grading system and publishes a list of "approved accommodations," which includes hotels, guest houses, bed-and-breakfasts, farmhouses, hostels, and camping parks. For each accommodation, the list gives a maximum charge that no hotel may exceed without special authorization. Prices must be displayed in every room, so if the hotel oversteps its limit, do not hesitate to complain to the hotel manager and/or the ITB.

Ideally, visitors should **sample a range of accommodations.** The very expensive country-house hotels and renovated castles offer a unique combination of luxury and history. Less impressive, but equally charming, are the provincial inns and country hotels with simple but adequate facilities. Many visitors, seeking to meet a wide cross section of Irish people, prefer a different B&B every night. Others enjoy the simplicity of self-catering for a week or two in a thatched cottage. ITB-approved guest houses and B&Bs display a green shamrock outside and are usually considered more reputable than those without.

Hotels and other accommodations in Northern Ireland are similar to those in the Republic of Ireland. The NITB publishes a complete list—called *Where to Stay* (U.K. £3.99)—of hotels, guest houses, farmhouses, bed-and-breakfasts, self-catering accommodations, youth hostels, and camping and trailer parks; prices and full information are included. There is more of a choice in the middle and lower price ranges than at the top.

➤ PUBLICATIONS: The ITB and NITB distribute five accommodation guides produced under separate auspices; all are free if obtained in the U.S.: *Be Our Guest* (£2) covers hotels and guest houses; *Bed & Breakfast Ireland* (£3) covers thousands of B&Bs; *Ireland's Blue Book* (free) includes 37 prestigious country houses and restaurants; *Friendly Homes of Ireland*, (£1) covers family homes and small hotels; *Self Catering Guide* (£4) covers family homes and holiday cottages on short term lettings.

➤ RESERVATIONS: **Dublin Tourism** (✉ Suffolk St, Dublin 2, ☎ 01/605–7777, ⊠ 01/605–7787; ☎ 01/602–4129, ⊠ 01/475–8046 for non–credit card accommodation inquiries) operates a credit card central reservations service for hotels and other accommodations, including guest houses and B&Bs throughout Ireland. There's a booking fee of £3 plus a charge of 10% of the cost of the accommodations.

APARTMENT & VILLA RENTALS

If you want a home base that's roomy enough for a family and comes with cooking facilities, **consider a furnished rental.** These can save you money, however some rentals are luxury properties, economical only when your party is large. Home-exchange directories list rentals (often second homes owned by prospective house swappers), and some services search for a house or apartment for you (even a castle if that's your fancy) and handle the paperwork. Some send an illustrated catalog; others send photographs only of specific properties, sometimes at a charge. Up-front registration fees may apply.

➤ RENTAL AGENTS: **At Home Abroad** (✉ 405 E. 56th St., Suite 6H, New York, NY 10022, ☎ 212/421–9165, ⊠ 212/752–1591). **Drawbridge to Europe** (✉ 5456 Adams Rd., Talent, OR 97540, ☎ 541/512–8927 or 888/268–1148, ⊠ 541/512–0978). **Elegant Ireland** (✉ 15 Harcourt St., Dublin 2, Ireland, ☎ 01/475–1632, ⊠ 01/475–1012). **Europa-Let/Tropical Inn-Let** (✉ 92 N. Main St., Ashland, OR 97520, ☎ 541/482–5806 or 800/462–4486, ⊠ 541/482–0660). **Hometours International** (✉ Box 11503, Knoxville, TN 37939, ☎ 423/690–8484 or 800/367–4668). **Property Rentals International** (✉

1008 Mansfield Crossing Rd., Richmond, VA 23236, ☎ 804/378–6054 or 800/220–3332, FAX 804/379–2073). **Rental Directories International** (✉ 2044 Rittenhouse Sq., Philadelphia, PA 19103, ☎ 215/985–4001, FAX 215/985–0323). **Rent-a-Home International** (✉ 7200 34th Ave. NW, Seattle, WA 98117, ☎ 206/789–9377 or 800/488–7368, FAX 206/789–9379). **Villas and Apartments Abroad** (✉ 420 Madison Ave., Suite 1003, New York, NY 10017, ☎ 212/759–1025 or 800/433–3020, FAX 212/755–8316). **Hideaways International** (✉ 767 Islington St., Portsmouth, NH 03801, ☎ 603/430–4433 or 800/843–4433, FAX 603/430–4444) is a travel club whose members arrange rentals among themselves; yearly membership is $99.

B&BS

B&Bs are classified by the ITB as either town homes, country homes, or farmhouses. Town and country B&Bs are listed in the ITB's "Quality Approved Irish Homes Accommodation Guide." Many now have at least one bedroom with a bathroom, but don't expect this as a matter of course. B&Bs often charge an extra 50p–£1 for a bath or shower. If this is taken in the family bathroom, you should ask first whether you can use the facility. Many travelers do not bother booking a B&B in advance. They are so plentiful in rural areas that it's often more fun to leave the decision open, allowing yourself a choice of final destinations for the night.

CAMPING

This is the cheapest way of seeing the country, and facilities for campers and caravaners are improving steadily. An abundance of coastal campsites compensates for the shortage of inland ones. All are listed in *Caravan and Camping Ireland* available from the ITB. Rates start at about £4 per tent, £6 per caravan overnight.

COTTAGES

In more than 100 locations there are clusters of holiday cottages for rent. Although often built in the traditional style, they have central heating and all the other modern conveniences. A three-bedroom cottage equipped for six adults is around £250 per week in

mid-season. It is essential to reserve in advance. The ITB's publication *Self-Catering* lists individual properties and clusters of traditional cottages available by the week. For information on booking, contact the ITB.

FARM VACATIONS

Many Irish farms offer holidays with part board or full board on a weekly basis. These are listed in the ITB's illustrated publication *Farmhouse Accommodation*. You will notice at once from the booklet that very few are picturesque: They are more likely to be modern bungalows or undistinguished, two-story houses than creeper-clad, Georgian mansions—though exceptions do exist. Room and part board—breakfast and an evening meal—costs from £170 per week.

GUEST HOUSES

To qualify as a guest house, an establishment must have at least five bedrooms, but in major cities they often have many more. Some guest houses are above a bar or restaurant; others are part of a family home. As a rule, they're cheaper (some include an optional evening meal) and offer fewer amenities than hotels. But often that's where the differences end. Most have high standards of cleanliness and hospitality. Some even have a bathroom, a TV, and a direct-dial phone in each room.

HOME EXCHANGES

If you would like to exchange your home for someone else's, **join a home-exchange organization,** which will send you its updated listings of available exchanges for a year and will include your own listing in at least one of them. Making the arrangements is up to you.

➤ EXCHANGE CLUBS: **HomeLink International** (✉ Box 650, Key West, FL 33041, ☎ 305/294–7766 or 800/638–3841, FAX 305/294–1148) charges $83 per year.

M
MAIL

RATES

Airmail rates to the United States and Canada from the Irish Republic are 52p for letters, 38p for postcards.

Mail to all European countries goes by air automatically, so airmail stickers or envelopes are not required. Rates are 32p for letters, 28p for postcards.

Rates from Northern Ireland are 43p for letters and 37p for postcards (not over 10 grams). To the rest of the United Kingdom and the Irish Republic, rates are 26p for first-class letters and 20p for second class. These rates may well increase before or during 1998.

RECEIVING MAIL

Mail can be held for collection at any post office free of charge for up to three months. It should be addressed to the recipient "c/o Poste Restante." In Dublin, use the **General Post Office** (✉ O'Connell St., Dublin 1, ☎ 01/7057000).

MEDIA

PRINT

In Ireland, there are three national daily broadsheet newspapers, *The Irish Times* and *The Irish Independent*—both Dublin based—and *The Examiner* (formerly the *Cork Examiner*), which is published in Cork. *The Irish Times* is the most authoritative and esteemed of the three, *The Irish Independent* is the most popular, and the *Examiner* is widely read in the southern counties. The *British Daily Star* also has an Irish edition.

The Evening Herald is the only nationwide evening newspaper. The *Evening Echo* is published by the Examiner group and sold in the Cork region. There are four Irish Sunday newspapers: the very popular and opinion-focused *Sunday Independent*, the more intellectual *Sunday Tribune*, the business-oriented *Sunday Business Post*, and the popular tabloid, *Sunday World*. Regional weekly newspapers are published in almost every county. The British broadsheet and tabloid dailies and Sunday newspapers are widely available throughout Ireland.

BROADCAST

Radio Telefis Eireann (RTE) is Ireland's national television and radio network. There are two television channels—RTE 1, which concentrates on news and documentaries, and Network 2, which carries more feature films and light entertainment shows. TnaG (Telifis na Gaelige) is an Irish-language channel (with English subtitles). The British television channels (BBC 1, BBC 2, UTV, Channel 4) and many satellite channels—including SkyNews, SkyMovies, SkySports, MTV, and TV5 Europe are also widely available.

There are two 24-hour national radio stations in Ireland—Radio 1 (mainly talk shows) and the popular music-dominated station, 2FM. FM3 is a classical music station which is broadcast in the early mornings and evenings on the same wavelength as the daytime Irish-language radio station, Raidio Na Gaeltachta. There are more than 25 local commercial radio stations whose broadcasting standards vary from county to county.

MONEY

The unit of currency in the Irish Republic is the pound or punt, pronounced *poont*. It is divided into 100 pence (abbreviated 100p). In this guide, the £ sign refers to the Irish pound; the British pound is referred to as the pound sterling and is written U.K.£.

Irish notes come in denominations of £100, £50, £20, £10, and £5. Coins are available as £1, 50p, 20p, 10p, 5p, 2p, and 1p. £1 coins are not exchangeable outside the Republic of Ireland. Dollars and British pounds are accepted only in large hotels and shops geared to tourists. Elsewhere you will be expected to use Irish currency.

At press time (July 1997), the punt stood at around US$1.50, Canadian $2.10, and U.K.£.93; however, these rates will inevitably change both before and during 1998; keep a sharp eye on the exchange rate.

The unit of currency in Northern Ireland is the pound sterling, divided into 100 pence. Notes come in denominations of U.K.£50, U.K.£20, U.K.£10, and U.K.£5, and coins of U.K.£1, 50p, 20p, 10p, 5p, and 1p. At press time (summer 1997), the pound sterling stood at around US$1.65, Canadian $2.26, and punts £1.08.

ATMS

Before leaving home, **make sure that your credit cards have been pro-**

grammed for ATM use in Ireland.
Note that Discover is accepted mostly
in the United States. Local bank cards
often do not work overseas or may
access only your checking account;
**ask your bank about a MasterCard/
Cirrus or Visa debit card,** which works
like a bank card but can be used at
any ATM displaying a MasterCard/
Cirrus or Visa logo. These cards, too,
may tap only your checking account;
check with your bank about their
policy.

Finally, ATMs in Ireland do not
typically have letters on their key-
pads, so be sure you know the numer-
ical translation of your code, if you
use letters.

➤ ATM LOCATIONS: **Cirrus** (☎ 800/
424–7787). A list of **Plus** locations is
available at your local bank.

COSTS

A modest hotel in Dublin costs about
£100 a night for two; this figure can
be reduced to under £70 by staying
in a registered guest house or inn,
and reduced to less than £35 by
staying in a suburban B&B. Lunch,
consisting of a good one-dish plate
of bar food at a pub, costs around
£6; a sandwich at the same pub,
about £1.80. In Dublin's better
restaurants, dinner will run around
£20 per person, excluding drinks
and tip. Theater and entertainment
in most places are inexpensive—
about £14 for a good seat, and
double that for a big-name, pop-
music concert. For the price of a few
drinks and (in Dublin and Killarney)
a small entrance fee of about £1.50,
you can spend a memorable evening
at a *seisún* (pronounced *say-shoon*)
in a music pub. Entrance to most
public galleries is free, but stately
homes and similar attractions normally charge about £2.50 per person. Just about everything is more
expensive in Dublin, so add at least
10% to these sample prices: cup of
coffee, 65p; pint of beer, £2; soda,
95p; and 1-mi taxi ride, £3.

Hotels and meals in Northern Ireland
are less expensive than in the United
Kingdom and the Republic of Ireland.
Also, the lower level of taxation
makes dutiable goods such as gasoline, alcoholic drinks, and tobacco
cheaper.

CURRENCY EXCHANGE

For the most favorable rates, **change
money at banks.** Although fees
charged for ATM transactions may
be higher abroad than at home,
Cirrus and Plus exchange rates are
excellent, because they are based on
wholesale rates offered only by major
banks. You won't do as well at
exchange booths in airports or rail
and bus stations, in hotels, in restaurants, or in stores, although you may
find their hours more convenient. To
avoid lines at airport exchange
booths, **get a small amount of local
currency before you leave home.**

➤ EXCHANGE SERVICES: **International
Currency Express** (☎ 888/842–0880
on the East Coast or 888/278–6628
on the West Coast for telephone
orders). **Thomas Cook Currency
Services** (☎ 800/287–7362 for telephone orders and retail locations).

TRAVELER'S CHECKS

Whether or not to buy traveler's
checks depends on where you are
headed. **Take cash if your trip includes
rural areas** and small towns, traveler's checks to cities. If your checks
are lost or stolen, they can usually be
replaced within 24 hours. To ensure a
speedy refund, buy your checks
yourself (don't ask someone else to
make the purchase). When making a
claim for stolen or lost checks, the
person who bought the checks should
make the call.

P
PACKING FOR IRELAND

In Ireland you can experience all
four seasons in one day, so pack
accordingly. Even in July and
August, the hottest months of the
year, a heavy sweater and a good
waterproof coat or umbrella are
essential. You should **bring at least
two pairs of walking shoes:** It can
and does rain at any time of the
year, and shoes can get soaked in
minutes.

The Irish are generally informal about
clothes. In the more expensive hotels
and restaurants most people dress
formally for dinner, and a jacket and
tie may be required in bars after 7 PM,
but very few places operate a strict
dress policy. Younger travelers should
note that old or tattered blue jeans

are forbidden in certain bars and dance clubs.

Bring an extra pair of eyeglasses or contact lenses in your carry-on luggage, and if you have a health problem, **pack enough medication** to last the entire trip or have your doctor write you a prescription using the drug's generic name, because brand names vary from country to country. It's important that you **don't put prescription drugs or valuables in luggage to be checked**: it might go astray. To avoid problems with customs officials, carry medications in the original packaging. Also, don't forget the addresses of offices that handle refunds of lost traveler's checks.

LUGGAGE

In general, you are entitled to check two bags on flights within the United States and on international flights leaving the United States. A third piece may be brought on board, but it must fit easily under the seat in front of you or in the overhead compartment.

If you are flying between two foreign destinations, note that baggage allowances may be determined not by piece but by weight—generally 88 pounds (40 kilograms) in first class, 66 pounds (30 kilograms) in business class, and 44 pounds (20 kilograms) in economy. If your flight between two cities abroad *connects* with your transatlantic or transpacific flight, the piece method still applies.

Airline liability for baggage is limited to $1,250 per person on flights within the United States. On international flights it amounts to $9.07 per pound or $20 per kilogram for checked baggage (roughly $640 per 70-pound bag) and $400 per passenger for unchecked baggage. Insurance for losses exceeding these amounts can be bought from the airline at check-in for about $10 per $1,000 of coverage; note that this coverage excludes a rather extensive list of items, which is shown on your airline ticket.

Before departure, **itemize your bags' contents** and their worth, and label the bags with your name, address, and phone number. (If you use your home address, cover it so that potential thieves can't see it readily.) Inside each bag, **pack a copy of your itinerary.** At check-in, **make sure that each bag is correctly tagged** with the destination airport's three-letter code. If your bags arrive damaged or fail to arrive at all, file a written report with the airline before leaving the airport.

PASSPORTS & VISAS

Once your travel plans are confirmed, **check the expiration date of your passport.** It's also a good idea to **make photocopies of the data page;** leave one copy with someone at home and keep another with you, separated from your passport. If you lose your passport, promptly call the nearest embassy or consulate and the local police; having a copy of the data page can speed replacement.

U.S. CITIZENS

All U.S. citizens, even infants, need only a valid passport to enter Ireland for stays of up to 90 days.

➤ INFORMATION: **Office of Passport Services** (☎ 202/647–0518).

CANADIANS

You need only a valid passport to enter Ireland for stays of up to 90 days.

➤ INFORMATION: **Passport Office** (☎ 819/994–3500 or 800/567–6868).

U.K. CITIZENS

Citizens of the United Kingdom do not need a passport to enter Ireland.

S

SAFETY

The theft of car radios, mobile phones, cameras, video recorders and any other item of value from cars is common in Dublin and other major cities and towns. Never leave any valuable items on car seats or in the foot space between the back and front seats or in the glove compartments. In fact, never leave anything whatsoever in sight in your car—even if you're leaving it for only a short time. You should also think twice about leaving valuables in your car while visiting tourist attractions anywhere in the country.

SENIOR-CITIZEN TRAVEL

To qualify for age-related discounts, **mention your senior-citizen status up front** when booking hotel reservations (not when checking out) and before you're seated in restaurants (not when paying the bill). Note that discounts may be limited to certain menus, days, or hours. When renting a car, **ask about promotional car-rental discounts,** which can be cheaper than senior-citizen rates.

➤ EDUCATIONAL TRAVEL PROGRAMS: **Elderhostel** (✉ 75 Federal St., 3rd floor, Boston, MA 02110, ☎ 617/426–8056). **Interhostel** (✉ University of New Hampshire, 6 Garrison Ave., Durham, NH 03824, ☎ 603/862–1147 or 800/733–9753, FAX 603/862–1113).

STUDENTS

To save money, **look into deals available through student-oriented travel agencies.** To qualify you'll need a bona fide student ID card. Members of international student groups are also eligible.

➤ STUDENT IDs AND SERVICES: **Council on International Educational Exchange** (✉ CIEE, 205 E. 42nd St., 14th floor, New York, NY 10017, ☎ 212/822–2600 or 888/268–6245, FAX 212/822–2699), for mail orders only, in the United States. **Travel Cuts** (✉ 187 College St., Toronto, Ontario M5T 1P7, ☎ 416/979–2406 or 800/667–2887) in Canada.

➤ HOSTELING: **Hostelling International—American Youth Hostels** (✉ 733 15th St. NW, Suite 840, Washington, DC 20005, ☎ 202/783–6161, FAX 202/783–6171). **Hostelling International—Canada** (✉ 400-205 Catherine St., Ottawa, Ontario K2P 1C3, ☎ 613/237–7884, FAX 613/237–7868). **Youth Hostel Association of England and Wales** (✉ Trevelyan House, 8 St. Stephen's Hill, St. Albans, Hertfordshire AL1 2DY, ☎ 01727/855215 or 01727/845047, FAX 01727/844126). Membership in the U.S., $25; in Canada, C$26.75; in the U.K., £9.30).

Independent Holiday Hostel Ireland (✉ 57 Lower Gardiner St, Dublin 1, ☎ 01/8364700) is a group of independent hostels with no membership requirements.

➤ STUDENT TOURS: **Contiki Holidays** (✉ 300 Plaza Alicante, Suite 900, Garden Grove, CA 92840, ☎ 714/740–0808 or 800/266–8454, FAX 714/740–2034). **AESU Travel** (✉ 2 Hamill Rd., Suite 248, Baltimore, MD 21210-1807, ☎ 410/323–4416 or 800/638–7640, FAX 410/323–4498).

T

TAXES

VALUE-ADDED TAX

When leaving the Irish Republic, U.S. and Canadian visitors **get a refund** of the value-added tax (VAT), which currently accounts for a hefty 21% of the purchase price of many goods and 12.5% of those that fall outside the luxury category. Apart from clothing, most items of interest to visitors, right down to ordinary toilet soap, are rated at 21%. Most crafts outlets and department stores operate a system called Cashback, which enables U.S. and Canadian visitors to collect VAT rebates in the currency of their choice at Dublin or Shannon Airport on departure. Otherwise, refunds can be claimed from individual stores after returning home. Forms for the refunds must be picked up at the time of purchase, and the form must be stamped by customs before leaving Ireland (including Northern Ireland). Most major stores deduct VAT at the time of sale if goods are to be shipped overseas; however, there is a shipping charge. VAT is not refundable on accommodation, car rental, meals or any other form of personal services received on holiday.

When leaving Northern Ireland, U.S. and Canadian visitors can also get a refund of the 17.5% VAT by the over-the-counter and the direct-export methods. Most larger stores provide these services upon request and will handle the paperwork. For the over-the-counter method, you must spend more than £75 in one store. Ask the store for Form VAT 407 (you must have identification—passports are best), to be given to customs when you leave the country. The refund will be forwarded to you in about eight weeks (minus a small service charge) either in the form of a sterling check or as a credit to your charge card. The direct-export method, where the goods are shipped directly to your home, is more cumbersome. VAT Form 704/1/93 must be certified by customs, police, or a notary public when you get home and then sent

THE GOLD GUIDE / SMART TRAVEL TIPS

back to the store, which will refund your money.

TELEPHONES

The country code for Ireland is 353; for Northern Ireland (the U.K.), 44. When dialing an Irish number from abroad, drop the initial 0 from the local area code.

Public pay phones are in all towns and villages. They can be found in street booths and in bars and shops, some of which display a sign saying YOU CAN PHONE FROM HERE. There are currently at least three different models of pay phones in operation; read the instructions or ask for assistance. A local call costs 20p for three minutes; long-distance calls within Ireland are around 80p for three minutes. A cheaper option is to **use a "callcard,"** sold in all post offices and at most newsagents. These come in denominations of 10, 20, and 50 units, and range in price from £2. for 10 to £16 for 100. Card phones are now more popular than coin phones.

Northern Ireland is part of the United Kingdom telephone system. A local call costs 10p.

If you are dialing Northern Ireland from the Republic, place 08 before the local code (e.g., Belfast is 08/01232, Derry is 08/01504 and Armagh is 08/01861). International dialing codes can be found in all telephone directories. The international prefix from Ireland is 00. For calls to Great Britain, dial 0044 before the exchange code, and drop the initial zero of the local code.

CALLING HOME

Before you go, **find out the local access codes** for your destinations. AT&T, MCI, and Sprint long-distance services make calling home relatively convenient, but you may find the local access number blocked in many hotel rooms. First ask the hotel operator to connect you. If the hotel operator balks, ask for an international operator, or dial the international operator yourself. One way to improve your odds of getting connected to your long-distance carrier is to travel with more than one company's calling card (a hotel may block Sprint, for example, but not MCI). If all else fails, call your phone company collect in the United States or call from a pay phone in the hotel lobby.

➤ ACCESS CODES: **AT&T USADirect** (☎ 1800/550000 from the Republic of Ireland, ☎ 0800/0130011 from Northern Ireland). **MCI Call USA** (☎ 1800/5551001 from the Republic of Ireland, ☎ 0800/890222 from Northern Ireland using BT or 0500/890222 using Mercury). **Sprint Express** (☎ 1800/552001 from the Republic of Ireland), ☎ 0800/890877 from Northern Ireland using BT or 0500/890877 using Mercury.

➤ FOR MORE INFORMATION: **AT&T USADirect** (☎ 800/874–4000). **MCI Call USA** (☎ 800/444–4444). **Sprint Express** (☎ 800/793–1153).

OPERATORS & INFORMATION

If the operator has to connect your call, it will cost at least one-third more than direct dial. **Do not make calls from your hotel room** unless it's absolutely necessary. Practically all hotels add 200% to 300% to the cost of a call.

➤ REPUBLIC OF IRELAND: Call 1190 for directory inquiries within the Republic and Northern Ireland, call 1197 for U.K. numbers, and call 1198 for international numbers. Call 114 for operator assistance with international calls and 10 for operator assistance for calls within Ireland and the U.K.

➤ NORTHERN IRELAND AND THE U.K.: Call 192 for directory inquiries within Northern Ireland and the U.K., 153 for international directory inquiries, which includes the Republic, 155 for the international operator, 100 for operator assistance for calls within the U.K. and Northern Ireland.

TIPPING

In some hotels and restaurants a service charge of around 10%—rising to 15% in a few plush spots—is added to the bill. If in doubt, ask whether service is included. In places where it is included, tipping is not necessary unless you have received particularly good service. But if there is no service charge, add a minimum of 10% to the total.

Tip taxi drivers about 10% of the fare displayed by the meter. Hackney cabs, who make the trip for a prearranged sum, do not expect tips. There are few porters and plenty of baggage trolleys at airports, so tipping is usually not an issue; if you use a porter, 50p is the minimum. Tip hotel porters about 50p per large suitcase. Hairdressers normally expect about £1. You don't tip in pubs, but for waiter service in a bar, a hotel lounge, or a Dublin lounge bar, leave about 20p.

TOUR OPERATORS

Buying a prepackaged tour or independent vacation can make your trip to Ireland less expensive and more hassle-free. Because everything is prearranged you'll spend less time planning.

Operators that handle several hundred thousand travelers per year can use their purchasing power to give you a good price. Their high volume may also indicate financial stability. But some small companies provide more personalized service; because they tend to specialize, they may also be more knowledgeable about a given area.

A GOOD DEAL?

The more your package or tour includes, the better you can predict the ultimate cost of your vacation. Make sure you know exactly what is covered, and **beware of hidden costs.** Are taxes, tips, and service charges included? Transfers and baggage handling? Entertainment and excursions? These can add up.

If the package or tour you are considering is priced lower than in your wildest dreams, **be skeptical.** Also, **make sure your travel agent knows the accommodations** and other services. Ask about the hotel's location, room size, beds, and whether it has a pool, room service, or programs for children, if you care about these. Has your agent been there in person or sent others you can contact?

BUYER BEWARE

Each year consumers are stranded or lose their money when tour operators--even very large ones with excellent reputations—go out of business. So **check out the operator.** Find out how long the company has been in business, and ask several agents about its reputation. **Don't book unless the firm has a consumer-protection program.**

Members of the National Tour Association and United States Tour Operators Association are required to set aside funds to cover your payments and travel arrangements in case the company defaults. Nonmembers may carry insurance instead. Look for the details, and for the name of an underwriter with a solid reputation, in the operator's brochure. Note: When it comes to tour operators, **don't trust escrow accounts.** Although the Department of Transportation watches over charter-flight operators, no regulatory body prevents tour operators from raiding the till. You may want to protect yourself by buying travel insurance that includes a tour-operator default provision. For more information, *see* Consumer Protection, *above.*

It's also a good idea to choose a company that participates in the American Society of Travel Agents' Tour Operator Program (TOP). This gives you a forum if there are any disputes between you and your tour operator; ASTA will act as mediator.

➤ TOUR-OPERATOR RECOMMENDATIONS: **National Tour Association** (✉ NTA, 546 E. Main St., Lexington, KY 40508, ☎ 606/226–4444 or 800/755–8687). **United States Tour Operators Association** (✉ USTOA, 342 Madison Ave., Suite 1522, New York, NY 10173, ☎ 212/599–6599, 𝖥𝖠𝖷 212/599–6744). **American Society of Travel Agents** (☞ Travel Agencies, *below*).

USING AN AGENT

Travel agents are excellent resources. In fact, large operators accept bookings made only through travel agents. But it's a good idea to **collect brochures from several agencies,** because some agents' suggestions may be influenced by relationships with tour and package firms that reward them for volume sales. If you have a special interest, **find an agent with expertise in that area;** ASTA (☞ Travel Agencies, *below*) has a database of specialists worldwide. Do some homework on your own, too: Local tourism boards can provide information about lesser-known and small-niche operators, some of which may sell only direct.

SINGLE TRAVELERS

Prices for packages and tours are usually quoted per person, based on two sharing a room. If traveling solo, you may be required to pay the full double-occupancy rate. Some operators eliminate this surcharge if you agree to be matched with a roommate of the same sex, even if one is not found by departure time.

GROUP TOURS

Among companies that sell tours to Ireland, the following are nationally known, have a proven reputation, and offer plenty of options. The classifications used below represent different price categories, and you'll probably encounter these terms when talking to a travel agent or tour operator. The key difference is usually in accommodations, which run from budget to better, and better-yet to best.

➤ SUPER-DELUXE: **Abercrombie & Kent** (⊠ 1520 Kensington Rd., Oak Brook, IL 60521-2141, ☎ 630/954–2944 or 800/323–7308, FAX 630/954–3324). **Travcoa** (⊠ Box 2630, 2350 S.E. Bristol St., Newport Beach, CA 92660, ☎ 714/476–2800 or 800/992–2003, FAX 714/476–2538).

➤ DELUXE: **Globus** (⊠ 5301 S. Federal Circle, Littleton, CO 80123-2980, ☎ 303/797–2800 or 800/221–0090, FAX 303/347–2080). **Maupintour** (⊠ 1515 St. Andrews Dr., Lawrence, KS 66047, ☎ 913/843–1211 or 800/255–4266, FAX 913/843–8351). **Tauck Tours** (⊠ Box 5027, 276 Post Rd. W, Westport, CT 06881-5027, ☎ 203/226–6911 or 800/468–2825, FAX 203/221–6828).

➤ FIRST-CLASS: **Aer Lingus** (☎ 212/557–1110 or 800/223–6537). **Brendan Tours** (⊠ 15137 Califa St., Van Nuys, CA 91411, ☎ 818/785–9696 or 800/421–8446, FAX 818/902–9876). **Brian Moore Tours** (⊠ 1208 VFW Pkwy., Ste. 202, Boston, MA 02132, ☎ 617/469–3300 or 800/982–2299). **British Airways Holidays** (☎ 800/247–9297). **Caravan Tours** (⊠ 401 N. Michigan Ave., Chicago, IL 60611, ☎ 312/321–9800 or 800/227–2826, FAX 312/321–9845). **Celtic International Tours** (⊠ 1860 Western Ave., Albany, NY 12203, ☎ 518/862–0042 or 800/833–4373). **CIE Tours** (⊠ Box 501, 100 Hanover Ave., Cedar Knolls, NJ 07927-0501, ☎ 201/292–3899 or 800/243–

8687). **Collette Tours** (⊠ 162 Middle St., Pawtucket, RI 02860, ☎ 401/728–3805 or 800/832–4656, FAX 401/728–1380). **Delta Dream Vacations** (☎ 800/872–7786). **Irish American International Tours** (⊠ Box 465, Springfield, PA 19064, ☎ 610/543–0785 or 800/633–0505, FAX 610/543–0786). **Trafalgar Tours** (⊠ 11 E. 26th St., New York, NY 10010, ☎ 212/689–8977 or 800/854–0103, FAX 800/457–6644). **United Vacations** (☎ 800/328–6877).

➤ BUDGET: **Cosmos** (☞ Globus, *above*). **Trafalgar** (☞ *above*).

PACKAGES

Like group tours, independent vacation packages are available from major tour operators and airlines. The companies listed below offer vacation packages in a broad price range.

➤ AIR/HOTEL/CAR: **Abercrombie & Kent** (☞ Group Tours, *above*). **Aer Lingus** (☞ Group Tours, *above*). **Brian Moore Tours** (☞ Group Tours, *above*). **British Airways Holidays** (☞ Group Tours, *above*). **Celtic International Tours** (☞ Groups Tours, *above*). **CIE Tours** (☞ Group Tours, *above*). **Delta Dream Vacations** (☞ Group Tours, *above*). **DER Tours** (⊠ 9501 W. Devon St., Rosemont, IL 60018, ☎ 800/782–2424, FAX 800/282–7474; FAX 800/860–9944, for brochures). **Irish American International Tours** (☞ Group Tours, *above*). **United Vacations** (☞ Group Tours, *above*).

➤ FLY/DRIVE: **American Airlines Fly AAway Vacations** (☎ 800/321–2121). **Delta Dream Vacations** (☞ Group Tours, *above*). **United Vacations** (☞ Group Tours, *above*).

THEME TRIPS

➤ BARGE/RIVER CRUISES: **Le Boat** (⊠ 10 S. Franklin Turnpike, Ste. 204B, Ramsey, NJ 07446, ☎ 201/236–2333 or 800/992–0291, FAX 201/236–1214).

➤ B&Bs: **Brendan Tours** (☞ Group Tours, *above*). **Value Holidays** (⊠ 10224 N. Port Washington Rd., Mequon, WI 53092, ☎ 414/241–6373 or 800/558–6850). **ITB** (☞ Visitor Information, *below*). **NITB** (☞ Visitor Information, *below*).

THE GOLD GUIDE / SMART TRAVEL TIPS

➤ BICYCLING: **Backroads** (✉ 801 Cedar St., Berkeley, CA 94710-1800, ☎ 510/527–1555 or 800/462–2848, FAX 510-527–1444). **Butterfield & Robinson** (✉ 70 Bond St., Toronto, Ontario, Canada M5B 1X3, ☎ 416/864–1354 or 800/678–1147, FAX 416/864–0541). **Classic Adventures** (✉ Box 153, Hamlin, NY 14464-0153, ☎ 716/964–8488 or 800/777–8090, FAX 716/964-7297). **Euro-Bike Tours** (✉ Box 990, De Kalb, IL 60115, ☎ 800/321–6060, FAX 815/758–8851). **Himalayan Travel** (✉ 110 Prospect St., Stamford, CT 06901, ☎ 203/359–3711 or 800/225–2380, FAX 203/359–3669).

➤ CULTURE: **Lynott Tours** (✉ 350 5th Ave., #2619, New York, NY 10118-2697, ☎ 212/760–0101 or 800/221–2474, FAX 212/695–8347).

➤ CUSTOMIZED PACKAGES: **Destinations Ireland & Great Britain** (✉ 13 Sterling Pl., Ste. 4-A, Brooklyn, NY 11217, ☎ 718/622–4717 or 800/832–1848, FAX 212/622–4874).

➤ FOOD AND WINE: **Annemarie Victory Organization** (✉ 136 E. 64th St., New York, NY 10021, ☎ 212/486–0353, FAX 212/751—3149).

➤ GOLF: **Abercrombie & Kent** (☞ Group Tours, *above*). **Aer Lingus** (☞ Group Tours, *above*). **Francine Atkins' Scotland/Ireland** (✉ 2 Ross Ct., Trophy Club, TX 76262, ☎ 817/491–1105 or 800/742–0355, FAX 817/491–2025). **Golf International** (✉ 275 Madison Ave., New York, NY 10016, ☎ 212/986–9176 or 800/833–1389, FAX 212/986–3720). **Golfpac** (✉ Box 162366, Altamonte Springs, FL 32716-2366, ☎ 407/260–2288 or 800/327–0878, FAX 407/260–8989). **ITC Golf Tours** (✉ 4134 Atlantic Ave., #205, Long Beach, CA 90807, ☎ 310/595–6905 or 800/257–4981). **Value Holidays** (☞ Bed-and-Breakfasts, *above*).

➤ HIKING/WALKING: **Abercrombie & Kent** (☞ Group Tours, *above*). **Backroads** (☞ Bicycling, *above*). **Butterfield & Robinson** (☞ Bicycling above). **Hiking Holidays** (✉ Box 711, Bristol, VT 05443-0711, ☎ 802/453–4816 or 800/537–3850, FAX 802/453–4806). **Himalayan Travel** (☞ Bicycling, *above*). **Mountain Travel-Sobek** (✉ 6420 Fairmount Ave., El Cerrito, CA 94530, ☎ 510/527–8100 or 800/227–2384, FAX 510/525–7710). **Wilderness Travel** (✉ 801 Allston Way, Berkeley, CA 94710, ☎ 510/548–0420 or 800/368–2794, FAX 510/548–0347).

➤ HORSEBACK RIDING: **Cross Country International Equestrian Vacations** (✉ Box 1170, Millbrook, NY 12545, ☎ 914/677–6000 or 800/828–8768, FAX 914/677–6077). **Equitour FITS Equestrian** (✉ Box 807, Dubois, WY 82513, ☎ 307/455–3363 or 800/545–0019, FAX 307/455–2354).

TRAIN TRAVEL

The Irish Republic's train services are generally reliable, reasonably priced, and comfortable. All the principal towns are easily reached from Dublin, though services between provincial cities are roundabout. To reach Cork City from Wexford, for example, you have to go via Limerick Junction. It is often quicker, though perhaps less comfortable, to take a bus. Most mainline trains have two classes: standard and superstandard. Round-trip tickets are usually cheapest.

In Northern Ireland, Northern Ireland Railways has three main rail routes, all operating out of Belfast's **Central Station** (☎ 01232/899400). These are north to Derry, via Ballymena and Coleraine; east to Bangor along the shores of Belfast Lough; and south to Dublin and the Irish Republic. Note that **EurailPasses are not valid in Northern Ireland.**

To save money, **look into rail passes,** but be aware that if you don't plan to cover many miles, you may come out ahead by buying individual tickets.

➤ INFORMATION: In the Irish Republic: **Irish Rail** (Iarnrod Éireann; ☎ 01/836–6222), the rail division of CIE. In Northern Ireland: **Northern Ireland Railways** (☎ 01232/899411).

DISCOUNT PASSES

Ireland (excluding Northern Ireland) is one of 17 countries in which you can **use EurailPasses,** which provide unlimited, first-class rail travel, in all of the participating countries, for the duration of the pass. If you plan to rack up the miles, get a standard pass. These are available for 15 days ($522), 21 days ($678), 1 month ($838), 2 months ($1,148), and 3 months ($1,468). If your plans call for combining a visit to Ireland with travel in Great Britain, **look into a BritRail Pass Plus Ireland,** which allows unlimited train travel in England, Scotland, Wales, Northern Ireland, and the Republic of Ireland. Prices start at $335 for 5 days of travel and $475 for 10 days of travel in a 1-month period—including round-trip Stena Sealink service between Ireland and Britain.

In addition to standard EurailPasses, **ask about special rail-pass plans.** Among these are the Eurail Youthpass (for those under age 26), the Eurail Saverpass (which gives a discount for two or more people traveling together), a Eurail Flexipass (which allows a certain number of travel days within a set period), the Euraildrive Pass and the Europass Drive (which combines travel by train and rental car).

The **Irish Explorer Rail & Bus Pass,** for use on Ireland's railroads, bus system, or both, covers all the state-run and federal railways and bus lines throughout the Republic of Ireland. It does not apply to the North or to transportation within the cities. An 8-day bus *or* rail ticket is $96. An 8-day ticket for use on buses *and* trains during a 15-day period is $136.

Also available is the **Go as You Please Rambler Card** that combines 8 days of travel on bus and rail with seven nights' accommodations in your choice of private homes or first-class hotels. The home-stay program is $345 per person, with extra nights available for $22 each. The pass with first-class hotel accommodations costs from $455 to $515 per person, depending upon time of travel. Additional nights are available for $43 per night.

The **Emerald Isle Card** offers unlimited bus and train travel anywhere in Ireland and Northern Ireland, valid within cities as well. A 15-day pass gives you 8 days of travel over a 15-day period; it costs $168, $84 for children. A pass for 15 days of travel over a 30-day period costs $288, $144 for children.

In Northern Ireland, **Rail Runabout** tickets, entitling you to 7 days' unlimited travel on scheduled rail services April–October, are available from main Northern Ireland Railway

stations. They cost UK£30 for adults, UK£15 for children under 16 and senior citizens. Interrail tickets are also valid in Northern Ireland; tickets for 8 days of unlimited travel cost UK£55 for adults, UK£27.50 for children under 16 and senior citizens; tickets for 15 days cost UK£80 for adults, UK£40 for children and senior citizens.

Whichever pass you choose, remember that you must **purchase your pass before you leave** for Europe.

Many travelers assume that rail passes guarantee them seats on the trains they wish to ride. Not so. **Book seats ahead even if you are using a rail pass**; reservations are required on some European trains, particularly high-speed trains, and are a good idea on trains that may be crowded—particularly in summer on popular routes. You will also need a reservation if you purchase sleeping accommodations.

Eurail and EuroPasses are available through travel agents and **Rail Europe** (⊠ 226-230 Westchester Ave., White Plains, NY 10604, ☎ 914/682–5172 or 800/438–7245; ⊠ 2087 Dundas E., Suite 105, Mississauga, Ontario L4X 1M2, ☎ 416/602–4195, **DER Tours** (⊠ Box 1606, Des Plaines, IL 60017, ☎ 800/782–2424, FAX 800/282–7474), or **CIT Tours Corp.** (⊠ 342 Madison Ave., Suite 207, New York, NY 10173, ☎ 212/697–2100 or 800/248–8687 or 800/248–7245 in western U.S.).

For information on the Irish Explorer Rail & Bus Pass or Emerald Isle tickets, or to book in advance, contact **CIE Tours International** (⊠ 108 Ridgedale Ave., Morristown, NJ 07960, ☎ 201/292–3438 or 800/243–8687).

BritRail Passes are available from most travel agents or from **BritRail Travel International** (⊠ 1500 Broadway, New York, NY 10036, ☎ 212/575–2667, FAX 212/575–2542).

TRAVEL AGENCIES

A good travel agent puts your needs first. Look for an agency that has been in business at least five years, emphasizes customer service, and has someone on staff who specializes in your destination. In addition, **make** sure the agency belongs to the American Society of Travel Agents (ASTA). If your travel agency is also acting as your tour operator, *see* Tour Operators, *above.*

➤ LOCAL AGENT REFERRALS: **American Society of Travel Agents (ASTA, ☎ 800/965–2782** for 24-hr hot line, FAX 703/684–8319). **Alliance of Canadian Travel Associations** (⊠ Suite 201, 1729 Bank St., Ottawa, Ontario K1V 7Z5, ☎ 613/521–0474, FAX 613/521–0805). **Association of British Travel Agents** (⊠ 55–57 Newman St., London W1P 4AH, ☎ 0171/637–2444, FAX 0171/637–0713).

TRAVEL GEAR

Travel catalogs specialize in useful items, such as compact alarm clocks and travel irons, that can **save space when packing.** They also offer dual-voltage appliances, currency converters, and foreign-language phrase books.

➤ MAIL-ORDER CATALOGS: **L. L. Bean Traveler** (☎ 800/221–4221, FAX 207/552–3080). **Magellan's** (☎ 800/962–4943, FAX 805/568–5406). **Orvis Travel** (☎ 800/541–3541, FAX 540/343–7053). **TravelSmith** (☎ 800/950–1600, FAX 800/950–1656).

U
U.S. GOVERNMENT

The U.S. government can be an excellent source of inexpensive travel information. When planning your trip, **find out what government materials are available.**

➤ ADVISORIES: **U.S. Department of State** (⊠ Overseas Citizens Services Office, Room 4811 N.S., Washington, DC 20520); enclose a self-addressed, stamped envelope. **Interactive hot line** (☎ 202/647–5225, FAX 202/647–3000). **Computer bulletin board** (☎ 301/946–4400).

➤ PAMPHLETS: **Consumer Information Center** (⊠ Consumer Information Catalogue, Pueblo, CO 81009, ☎ 719/948–3334) for a free catalog that includes travel titles.

V
VISITOR INFORMATION

For information on travel in the Irish Republic, contact the **Irish Tourist Board,** known as Bord Fáilte (pronounced "Board Falcha"). Information on travel in the North is available from the **Northern Ireland Tourist Board** (NITB) office.

➤ ITB: **U.S.** (⊠ 345 Park Ave., New York, NY 10154, ☎ 212/418–0800 or 800/223–6470, FAX 212/371–9052). **Canada** (⊠ 160 Bloor St. E, Suite 1150, Toronto, Ontario M4W 1B9, ☎ 416/929–2779, FAX 416/929–6783). **U.K.** (⊠ Ireland House, 150 New Bond St., London W1Y 0AQ, ☎ 0171/493–3201, FAX 0171/493–9065).

➤ NITB: **U.S.** (⊠ 551 5th Ave., Suite 701, New York, NY 10176, ☎ 212/922–0101 or 800/326–0036 , FAX 212/922–0099). **Canada** (⊠ 111 Avenue Rd., Suite 450, Toronto, Ontario M5R 3J8, ☎ 416/925–6368, FAX 416/961–2175). **U.K.** (⊠ 11 Berkeley St., London W1X 5AD, ☎ 0171/355–5040, written or telephone inquiries only, or the BTA's Ireland Desk, ⊠ 4–12 Lower Regent St., London BW1Y 4PQ, ☎ 0171/839–8416).

W
WHEN TO GO

Summer remains the most popular time to visit Ireland, and for good reason. The weather is pleasant, the days are long (daylight lasts until after 10 in late June and July), and the countryside is green and beautiful. But there will be crowds in popular holiday spots, and prices for accommodations are at their peak. As British and Irish school vacations overlap from late-June to mid-September, families, backpacking students, and other vacationers descend on popular coastal resorts in the South, West, and East. Unless you are determined to enjoy the short (July and August) swimming season, you would be well advised to **take your vacation in Ireland outside peak travel months.**

Fall and spring are good times to travel, although the weather can be unpredictable. Seasonal hotels, restaurants, and accommodations usually close from early- or mid-November until mid-March or Easter. During this off-season, prices are considerably lower than in summer, but your selection of hotels and restaurants is limited, and many minor attractions also close. St. Patrick's Week in March gives a focal point to a spring visit, but some American visitors may find the saint's-day celebrations a little less enthusiastic than the ones back home. Dublin, however, welcomes American visitors on March 17 with a parade and the Lord Mayor's Ball. If you're planning an Easter visit, don't forget that most theaters close from Thursday to Sunday of Holy Week (the week preceding Easter), and all bars and restaurants, except those serving hotel residents, close on Good Friday.

If you want to feel like the only tourist in town, **try a winter visit.** Many hotels arrange special Christmas packages with entertainment and outdoor activities. Horse races and hunting trips abound, although mid-November to mid-February is either too cold or too wet for all but the keenest golfers. There are cheerful open fires in almost all hotels and bars, and, with extra time on their hands, people tend to take an added interest in visitors.

CLIMATE

➤ FORECASTS: **Weather Channel Connection** (☎ 900/932–8437), 95¢ per minute from a Touch-Tone phone.

What follows are average daily maximum and minimum temperatures for some major cities in Ireland.

DUBLIN

Jan.	47F	8C	May	59F	15C	Sept.	63F	17C
	34	1		43	6		49	9
Feb.	47F	8C	June	65F	18C	Oct.	58F	14C
	36	2		49	9		43	6
Mar.	50F	10C	July	68F	20C	Nov.	50F	10C
	38	3		52	11		40	4
Apr.	56F	13C	Aug.	67F	20C	Dec.	47F	8C
	40	4		52	11		38	3

CORK

Jan.	49F	9C	May	61F	16C	Sept.	65F	18C
	36	2		45	7		50	10
Feb.	49F	9C	June	67F	19C	Oct.	58F	14C
	38	3		50	10		45	7
Mar.	52F	11C	July	68F	20C	Nov.	52F	11C
	40	4		54	12		40	4
Apr.	56F	13C	Aug.	68F	20C	Dec.	49F	9C
	41	5		54	12		38	3

BELFAST

Jan.	43F	6C	May	59F	15C	Sept.	61F	16C
	36	2		43	6		49	9
Feb.	45F	7C	June	65F	18C	Oct.	56F	13C
	36	2		49	9		45	7
Mar.	49F	9C	July	65F	18C	Nov.	49F	9C
	38	3		52	11		40	4
Apr.	54F	12C	Aug.	65F	18C	Dec.	45F	7C
	50	4		52	11		38	3

1 Destination: Ireland

ARCADIA UNBOUND

I F YOU FLY INTO IRELAND, your descent will probably be shrouded by gray clouds. As your plane breaks through the mists, you'll see the land for which the famed Emerald Isle was named: A lovely patchwork of rolling green fields speckled with farmhouses, cows, and sheep. Shimmering lakes, meandering rivers, narrow roads, and stone walls add to the impression that rolled out before you is a luxurious welcome carpet, one knit of the legendary "forty shades of green." (If you're lucky you may even see a rainbow—something you'll see again and again if you travel the countryside.) This age-old view of misty Ireland may be exactly what you imagined. Soon enough, however, you'll soon discover that Ireland has this and more—more than you could ever have dreamed.

The Celtic Tiger

Despite its turbulent history, Ireland has long been cast as a bucolic Arcadia (William Butler Yeats's early pastoral lyrics are partly to blame). Yet this is a myth that's rapidly nearing retirement age. The country is racing toward the future with profound economic, social, and cultural transformations. Consider these statistics: On the 150th anniversary of the apocalyptic Great Famine, Ireland's economy—recently christened the "Celtic Tiger" (a nod to the "Four Tigers of Asia," the term for the most rapidly growing economies of the last 20 years)—is now the fastest-growing in the industrialized world, up almost 25% in the last three years. Inflation is less than 2%. Ireland is the second-largest exporter of computer software in the world, after the United States. Unemployment is lower than in France or Spain. In two key industries—technology and tourism—there are growing labor shortages. Signs at Dublin and Shannon airports advise Irish-born technocrats returning from abroad for a visit that there are jobs awaiting them in the high-tech sector.

Socially, Ireland is changing no less substantially. Demographic and religious shifts have been strong in the last several years. Divorce became legal in 1997, and, astonishing in a country whose largest export has long been its children, the birthrate is declining. At the same time, more than 60% of Ireland's populace is under the age of 25, making it the youngest nation in Europe. While many young men and women are working in the high-tech jobs that fuel the booming economy, others are taking advantage of the government's enlightened tax code, which exempts the Irish from paying taxes on the proceeds of "products of creativity." (You won't, for example, pay sales tax on books.) Most telling of all, however, is that fact that Ireland's net emigration has reversed, a profound demographic shift that was unthinkable 5 or 10 years ago. The young who once left for London and New York are now staying, and more college graduates are returning than are leaving.

The foreign capital that has flowed into the country since it joined the Common Market (now the European Union) in 1973 has been crucial to this regeneration. But money alone doesn't guarantee culture, and Irish culture is thriving. You name it—food, music, movies, literature, poetry, theater, art, fashion—and something innovative is afoot among the Irish at home and abroad. Take just two examples in literature: In 1995, Seamus Heaney claimed Ireland's fourth Nobel Prize in Literature in less than 75 years, and two years later, *Angela's Ashes,* Frank McCourt's memoir of his early life in Limerick, found millions of readers and won every major American literary prize. Ireland resounds with stories of artistic accomplishment; a quest for expressiveness seems to have been renewed. No matter what your passion, Ireland has something to offer.

The Oft-Conquered Isle

Standing stones and court graves, mottes and dolmens, raths and cairns, holy wells and mass stones, round towers and Celtic crosses, churches and country houses: The artifacts of Ireland's long, turbulent history are everywhere, from the barren limestone Burren in County Clare to the

Neolithic tombs and defenses of New-grange in County Meath. Even an island off the main island—Inishmore, one of the Aran Islands far out in Galway Bay—claims its antiquity: Dun Aengus, which is 5,000 years older than the pyramids of Giza. Given how tempestuous the fortunes of this small island have been, you may be surprised by just how many of these sights remain.

Iron Age Celts from Central Europe settled in Ireland in the 4th century BC and left a legacy of an agrarian society based on a democratic kingship, a justice system known as the Brehon laws, and an artisan caste proficient in working gold and precious metals. (The National Museum in Dublin displays heaps of this Bronze Age gold jewelry.)

Christianity arrived in Ireland in 432 with St. Patrick (or, perhaps, as some scholars suggest, two and possibly more missionaries whose work became conflated into the Patrician story). By the 8th century, Ireland was in its Golden Age. In general, the country's proliferating religious orders received protection from God-fearing Irish kings. Monks labored for decades to produce the Book of Kells (now on display at Trinity College in Dublin). Having set up monasteries throughout Ireland, Irish monks set out for Europe, where they continued their expansion of monastic communities from England to northern Italy. According to a recent best-seller, Thomas Cahill's *How the Irish Saved Civilization,* the medieval Irish monks who copied and standardized the masterpieces of Virgil and Horace helped to prevent the loss of classical Latin, the written language of Rome, to the vernacular Romance tongues of Italy, Spain, and France.

About 800, Viking longboats scourged the island's coasts. The Norsemen established settlements in Wexford, Cork, and Dublin (and leaving the mark of bright-red hair behind on their Irish descendants). Brian Boru, last of the High Kings to sit at Tara, won the Battle of Clontarf, defeating a troop of Viking raiders off the coast near Dublin in 1014. But Boru's subsequent murder marked the end of an era. Without his leadership, the power of the Irish kings dissipated, and in 1155, English-born Pope Adrian IV boldly granted dominion over Ireland to his fellow Englishman King Henry II. Fourteen years later Norman Strongbow arrived in Ireland, opening the door to more than 800 years of strife between the English and the Irish.

By 1609, the last of the Irish chieftains had lost their land to the British and sailed for exile, making way for the Plantation period. During this era 200,000 Scottish Lowlanders were "planted" on native Irish lands. Oliver Cromwell, "the Avenger," arrived with his troops in 1649, intent on making Ireland a Protestant country. He conducted a ruthless campaign of persecution against the already bitter Irish Catholics—a campaign that included beheading thousands of men, women, and children. Worse was still to come: Cromwell's Act of Settlement (1652) called for the forced migration of all Catholics to west of the River Shannon. As Cromwell put it, the Irish were welcome to relocate either "to Hell or Connaught." (Connaught, Leinster, Munster, and Ulster constitute the four ancient provinces of Ireland; see our Ireland map for the borders of these provinces.) Whichever they chose, Catholics were driven from the Anglicized and increasingly commercialized east. Cromwell also established the "Penal Code," forbidding Irish Catholics to practice their religion or law, own land, vote, or hold office.

The Great Famine and Its Aftermath

Throughout the early 19th century, poverty was endemic and disease was a simple fact of life. Irish peasants worked for absentee British landlords and either paid exorbitant rents for land that had probably belonged to their parents or grandparents, or simply starved. The system was unjust, but somehow the bulk of Ireland survived the lean years prior to 1845. Within a year, however, potato blight ruined crops throughout the country. In a decade, the population was decimated, reduced from 8 to 6 million inhabitants. Starvation was largely to blame for the decline, but this period also marks the beginning of the large-scale emigration—to America, Canada, and Australia—that continued, albeit at a slower pace, until very recently. At last count, 70 million of Ireland's descendants are scattered abroad in the Irish diaspora—including 44 million in the United States.

The mid-19th-century also saw the rise of an Irish Nationalist movement. Various groups, including the Fenians and the Irish Republic Brotherhood, agitated for equal rights for Catholics, land reform, the revival of Ireland's Gaelic heritage, and the expulsion of the British from Ireland. The movement exploded—literally—on Easter Sunday 1916, when Nationalists proclaimed a republic. England's merciless vengeance on the patriots—it shot 15 of the uprising's leaders—galvanized the country to the bitter War of Independence, which ended in 1920 with the partitioning of Ireland into 26 counties in the South, constituting the Irish Free State, and 6 in the North, making up the British-ruled province of Northern Ireland. The defining event of modern Irish history, the severing of North from South eventually spawned nearly 30 years of Troubles in the North (though the roots of the Troubles date back 800 years) and cast a dark shadow over the country.

The Irish Ascendant

There is a place in an ancient Irish myth called Tír na nÓg ("the land of the ever-young"). Ancient though it may be, it's a surprisingly relevant image for Ireland today. The fact that the country is, for the first time in 150 years, holding onto many of its young, speaks volumes—it is the era of the ascendant Irish, of fabled Arcadia unbound from its tumultuous history. There's a growing body of evidence for this newfound Irish assuredness—both within Ireland's shores and among the Irish abroad.

Together both the North and South of Ireland welcome more visitors annually (5 million) than they have residents (4.9 million). Not surprisingly, Dublin, the booming capital of the Republic, is the best place to take the pulse of Ireland. Home to half of the Republic's citizens, it is the Celtic Tiger's beating heart, a far cry from Joyce's "our dear, dirty Dublin." Dozens of cranes hover over new office buildings and hotels, and Georgian terrace houses are being brought back to glorious life. Visitors—especially weekenders from the Continent—fill Dublin's buzzing cafés, pubs, restaurants, hotels, and pour out onto busy Grafton Street and the narrow cobblestone alleys of Temple Bar. Outside Dublin, the country's quickening pulse is also palpable. New golf courses, housing developments, and blue-signed, divided highways are signs of the changes afoot.

Less conspicuously, in villages throughout the country, heritage and genealogical centers have sprung up to accommodate the surge of interest among the Irish diaspora for information about their roots. This relationship between the past and the present, between those who left and those who stayed, is an elemental part of Ireland's identity. Today, throughout the Irish diaspora, there is a boundless yearning for all that Ireland embodies: indomitable strength against all odds, the romance of an ancient place, the longing for a lost world, the solace and transcendent possibility of art. It's likely that a trip to Ireland in the late 1990s will put you in touch with the sources—historical and concrete, ineffable and mysterious—of this longing. If you've been moved by seeing *Riverdance,* or *Lord of the Dance,* or reading *Angela's Ashes* or *How the Irish Saved Civilization,* or hearing Black 47, Sinéad O'Connor, Van Morrison, U2, or any of the hundreds of other prominent Irish musicians, you're likely to feel the spirit that touched you more palpably in Ireland itself, as you meet its people, and witness them imagining—and creating—the Irish spirit anew.

NEW AND NOTEWORTHY

Amid all the new cafés, restaurants, and hotels in **Dublin** (☞ Chapter 2 for specifics—there are simply too many new spots to mention here), a number of cultural attractions are in the news: The main reading room of the **National Library** has reopened after a yearlong renovation, and the **National Gallery of Ireland** has also been renovated and expanded. The **National Museum** has moved its decorative arts to the **Collins Barracks,** on the north side of the Liffey near Phoenix Park. We've added coverage of a number of other Dublin cultural institutions, including the **Irish Jewish Museum** and the **Gallery of Photography,** and significantly increased our coverage of **Temple Bar.**

Throughout the Republic, **new hotels** are opening in and near major hubs, including **Cork City** and **Galway City.** The **Adare Manor Golf Course** (☞ Chapter 10) is one of several new **courses** opened recently.

In the North, **Waterfront Hall,** opened in 1997, is the major new cultural venue in **Belfast,** which is also seeing its share of new restaurants, cafés, and hotels.

WHAT'S WHERE

You are never very far from anywhere in Ireland, but each of its 32 counties has its special character and history, and fierce loyalty from its sons and daughters. Below we give a preview of Ireland's cities and counties—organizing our discussion using the same groupings we use in this guide.

Dublin

Set in a broad river basin fringed by the majestic sweep of Dublin Bay, Dublin is the millennium-old capital. It has been, in sequence, a Celtic settlement by the ford of the River Liffey, a Norse encampment for raiding Viking and Danish pirates, and finally the citadel-seat of the British colonizers' power for centuries. And today it is a boomtown—the soul of the new Ireland in the throes of what is easily its most dramatic period of transformation since the Georgian era. It's also a colossally entertaining, engaging city—all the more astonishing considering its intimate size.

Dublin Environs

The counties that surround Dublin constitute the Pale, the area most strongly influenced by English rule from Norman times onward. Here (as in other parts of Ireland), the ancestral homes of the dwindling members of the Anglo-Irish ascendancy dot the landscape, and lords and baronets down on their luck have turned hoteliers and welcome guests to castle holidays with adaptable grace. The gorgeous Wicklow Mountains—to some tastes Ireland's finest—lie tantalizingly close to the capital on its southern edge. Wicklow's evocative monastic settlement at Glendalough, many later abbeys and churches, castles, and several of Ireland's grandest houses and gardens are dotted amid hidden,

scenic wooded valleys. Some of the country's most fascinating neolithic ruins—including the famous passage graves at Newgrange—lie to the north in the Boyne Valley, where layer upon layer of history penetrates down into earlier, unknowable ages.

The Midlands

These small, watery counties form the geographical heart of Ireland, yet are usually portrayed as places to get *through* on the way to somewhere more interesting. However, closer exploration of these unsung plains reveal historic towns, abbey ruins, grand houses, and a gamut of outdoor activities—including some of the finest fishing in Europe. County Tipperary's rolling green flatlands and Galtee mountains are known for champion greyhounds and the stud farms that have turned out winners for generations. The Midlands are home to fine cultural sites, including Strokestown House, Birr Castle Gardens, Emo Court and Gardens, and the magnificent monastic ruins of Clonmacnois, as well as a less stereotyped picture of Ireland: Visitors are welcomed with true hospitality, without experiencing any pressure to buy sweaters or shamrock table linen.

The Southeast

In sharp contrast to the scenic wildness often associated with Ireland, the landscape of the Southeast is mostly low-lying and docile. Rich pastureland watered by brimming rivers extends gently to a quiet coastline of estuarial mudflats of wading birds; low cliffs that fringe deep bays; and long, sandy beaches which, owing to the region's climate—sunnier and drier than elsewhere in Ireland—draw families in summer. The coast of County Wexford was the original beachhead of Ireland named by the Vikings after the consort of their one-eyed god Odin; it still bears the stamp of its fearless, seagoing settlers in its steep pathways and fine seafood. Wexford is a quick trip to Kilkenny, the finest medieval city in Ireland and one known for its artisans. Also nearby is Waterford City, where the crystal of the same name is produced, at the confluence of three great rivers—the Nore, the Barrow, and the Suir. Waterford City has one of the oldest forts in Ireland, Reginald's Tower, built in 1003 and named for the Viking warrior who founded the city. Ireland's most fertile farmland lies in Tipperary's Golden Vale. The Rock of Cashel, seat of the Kings of Munster for 700 years (where St. Patrick said his first mass in Ireland) is here, along with Cahir Castle, one of the few places that managed to resist Cromwell's hordes, now restored to its former impressiveness.

The Southwest

With their striking scenery, charming towns, mild climate, and deep-rooted history, the southwestern counties of Cork and Kerry are perennially popular with visitors. Long called "The Rebel County" (if you saw Neal Jordan's 1996 film *Michael Collins,* you know why), Cork is a Venice-like port city of canals and bridges, and a bustling mercantile center. It was once home to writers Sean O'Faolain and Frank O'Connor, and is today a city of sport. Its team is always in the championship finals of hurling, that fast and furious ancient game that makes soccer look like kick-the-can, and the city is one of the few places where they still play the traditional, 2,000-year-old game of bowls at which the Irish giant Cuchulain used to excel. If your taste runs to less athletic entertainment, head for the exquisitely quaint village and historically significant seaside village of Kinsale. Just to the north of Cork, summer travelers have been thrilling to Kerry's surfeit of natural beauty for centuries, as they've gazed down from the heights of Killarney, or the black rocks and green waves glistening at Slea Head on the Dingle Peninsula, or at the Blasket Islands, where St. Brendan the Navigator was said to have set sail in a wooden curragh to discover the Americas in the 7th century. Seabirds reel and wild donkeys graze among the fuschia hedges awash in crimson velvet flowers, and the fields explode with deep yellow gorse, may-blossom, and honeysuckle against a dark-blue sky. To the north of Kerry, County Limerick is famed as horse country.

The West

Within the three counties of Clare, Galway, and Mayo lies a colossal variety of landscapes and natural sights—from the barren limestone Burren to the majestic Cliffs of Moher to the looming Twelve Bens. The West's largest city, Galway is the fastest-growing place in Ireland—a buzzing, youthful university town and the favorite getaway city for many native Irish people. It's also the departure point for the Aran Islands, celebrated by playwright J. M. Synge in *Riders to the Sea* and Robert Flaherty in his classic documentary film *Man of Aran.* Just to the west of Galway City lies the wild and rugged coast and mountains of Connemara, loved by painters, who flock there in summer, by writers (from Yeats to Gogarty to Joyce), and by all seekers of silence and beauty. It, too, is a Gaeltacht (Irish-speaking area), celebrated for its simplicity of lifestyle and genuinely warm natives. Connemara is also known for its ponies, descendants of the Andalusian horses that swam to shore from the Spanish fleet and bred with the local Celtic stock (direct descendants of the original Ice Age horse of 20,000 BC). To the north, Mayo is quieter and less popular, although its peaceful scenery has always appealed to a discerning minority.

The Northwest

County Donegal, in the far northwest, is among the wildest, most ruggedly beautiful places in the world, with its long, rocky coastline, white beaches, turbulent surf, and forlorn, windswept mountains and plateaus, full of legendary lore of giants and witches, and fairies known as *pishogues.* Irish is widely spoken here, and the music is famous; traditional groups, such as Clannad and De Dannaan, named after the prehistoric followers of the goddess Dana, are local heroes. When Enya, daughter of local musicians, hit the top of the charts in Europe and the United States with her Irish–New Age instrumentals, the roof flew off Leo's pub in Gweedore, where spontaneous sessions for the music-loving community are regular happenings.

Northern Ireland

The ancient provinces of Munster, Leinster, and Connaught constitute the Irish Republic, plus three of the nine counties of Ulster; the other six remained part of Britain in 1921. ("One of Ireland's four green fields is still in strangers' hands," as a song goes.) Today Northern Ireland, thriving in its newfound era of peace, is definitely worth a trip: Here you have the beauty of the Antrim Coast from Carncastle to Bushmills; the Giant's Causeway, glorious as every other great geologic accident; the rich farmlands and lake lands of Fermanagh; and the austere beauty

of the Mourne Mountains. People are as friendly and helpful here as they are in the Republic, and, probably because of their history, perhaps even often a little sharper and wittier. Northern Ireland is also fascinating for any follower of history and politics, for you get an unforgettable glimpse of the winds of time changing, a scene not unlike the last days of the Raj, as Britain's first colony erodes to be her last.

PLEASURES AND PASTIMES

Beaches

Ireland has more than 3,200 km/2,000 mi of coastline, with an abundance of beaches—or strands, as they are called locally. Some are small rocky coves with shingle where you can enjoy utter privacy; others, like Tramore, County Waterford; Courtown, County Wexford; Salthill, near Galway; and Bundoran in County Donegal are long, sandy beaches fronting bustling resort towns. The Irish like their beaches kept simple, so you will not find much in the way of facilities outside the resort towns. At most, there might be a public toilet, or an isolated hotel or bar, but don't count on it. If bathing is unsafe there will probably be a notice to that effect, or a red flag. You should not assume that bathing is safe in the absence of any warnings: Ask locally to make sure. Few people swim outside the months of July and August, but beaches remain popular with walkers and runners throughout the year.

Dining

To the astonishment—and delight—of many visitors, Ireland is in the throes of a food revolution. Not far out of Dublin you begin to see some of the reasons all around you: livestock grazing in impossibly green fields, clear waters to spawn fish, and acres of produce thriving in the temperate climate. But it is Ireland's chefs who are the stars of the rapidly changing food scene. Many of them are young and have traveled widely and absorbed the best influences of Europe, North America, and the Pacific Rim, and they're producing a Pan-European, postmodern cuisine. This new Irish cuisine—sometimes referred to as *cuisine Irlandaise*—has moved beyond the heavy traditional roast beef and Yorkshire pudding styles of the old Anglo-Irish country houses. In their place an innovative, indigenous style is emerging, marrying simple treatments of traditional dishes—Clonakilty black pudding, Clare nettle soup, Galway oysters, Cong wild salmon—with more exotic, complicated dishes that feature unusual combinations of the best local, often organic ingredients.

Despite the new sophistication, there are many examples of the old Celtic cooking, particularly in bars serving lunches of Irish stew, boiled bacon and cabbage, or steamed mussels. The national drink, Guinness, is a pitch-black, malted stout, one of the great beers of the world. With raw oysters and Tabasco, it is a blissful marriage of opposites.

Regional cooking is a strength of Irish cuisine, and some of the best restaurants are tucked away in small fishing villages or remote locations. See Fodor's Choice, *below,* for our very top restaurant picks around the country, and keep an eye out throughout the guide for restaurants that merit a star. Hotel dining rooms vary in quality, but the best country-house hotels offer some of the finest dining in Europe (and most will take reservations for meals only).

Music

Ireland is the land of *ceol agus craic,* which, loosely translated, means "music and merriment." Wherever you go in Ireland, you'll hear a musical air to accompany the scenery, and every town buzzes with its own individual blend of styles and sounds. The traditional music scene, far from becoming fossilized as a permanent tourist fixture, has evolved with each generation, remaining lively and contemporary while still cherishing the craft and skill of its past exponents. Young traditional musicians are also unafraid to experiment with the music of other cultures, and it's not unusual to discover exciting mixtures of trad, folk, African rhythms, jazz improvisations, and even Appalachian mountain music. The deep-rooted musical tastes of the Irish are reflected in the live music scene in pubs, clubs, and theaters; a check of local event guides will turn up a wealth of live en-

tertainment from rock to folk to traditional, and it's often possible to go into a small local venue and find a world-class artist in performance, whose talents are unsung outside a small circle of knowledgeable friends and fans.

Outdoor Activities and Sports

BICYCLING➤ The combination of numerous side roads and very light traffic makes Ireland a terrific destination for cyclists. The less energetic can concentrate their itinerary on the relatively flat central area of the country; those who brave the mountains of the West and Southwest will be rewarded by magnificent scenery and a wonderfully varied coastline.

CRUISING➤ Fully equipped boats are rented by the week on the Shannon and the Grand Canal. It's a simple and relaxing holiday, allowing you to explore lesser-known, but beautiful, corners of Ireland. Boats can accommodate up to eight people and have toilets, showers, and well-equipped galleys. Prices start at about £190 per week.

FISHING➤ Ireland is well known as a game-angling resort: Wild Atlantic salmon, wild brown trout, and sea trout abound in the rivers, lakes, and estuaries; and offshore is the deep-sea challenge. Coarse fishing (for all fish that are not trout or salmon) is also available. *See* Fishing *in* the Gold Guide *and* Outdoor Activities and Sports *in* the A to Z sections of Chapters 4, 5, 6, 7, 8, and 9 for more detailed information.

GAELIC GAMES➤ Gaelic football and hurling are played in most parts of the Republic. Gaelic football is an extremely fast and rough form of football (closer to rugby than American football), which involves two teams of 15 who kick and run around a field with a round, soccerlike ball. The rules are complicated, but the skill and speed of the players make it exciting and impressive to watch, even if you don't quite understand what is going on. Hurling, considered by many to be the fastest field game in the world, also involves two teams of 15 who use a 3-foot wooden stick with a broad base to aggressively catch and hurl a leather-covered ball toward goalposts; a typical game produces several injuries. Gaelic games are organized by the Gaelic Athletic Association (GAA) and can be observed free of charge at local GAA

fields and sports centers around the Republic. Interprovincial games and All-Ireland finals are played in July and August at the GAA stadiums in Cork and Dublin. Croke Park in Dublin is usually where the annual All-Ireland finals are held. Tickets for these matches can be hard to obtain, but the events are televised.

GOLF➤ There are more than 330 golf courses in Ireland (including Northern Ireland), from world-famous championship links courses to scenic nine-holers. About 50 of these courses have opened in the last two years. Choose between the challenging links of the Atlantic coast, the more subtle layouts on the eastern seaboard, and the mature parklands of the inland courses. For the very best of Ireland's golf courses, *see* Chapter 10.

HIKING➤ Bord Fáilte (the Irish Tourist Board) provides free information sheets on long-distance paths, set up throughout the country over the last few years with the consent of local landowners. Routes are indicated by trail markers and signposts. Most are between 30 and 60 km/18 and 37 mi in length, with the exception of the **Wicklow Way,** the first to be opened and still one of the best, which is 137 km/85 mi long. Alternatively, you can plan your own walks with the help of a good touring map: Ireland is an excellent walking country, with its mild climate and virtually traffic-free byroads. In Northern Ireland, there is the challenge of the 790-km/491-mi **Ulster Way,** a footpath that travels through spectacular coastal scenery.

HORSE RACING➤ There is a horse race somewhere in Ireland almost every day of the year. The flat season runs from March to November; steeplechases are held throughout the year. Several courses—there are some 28 in all—are within easy reach of Dublin. Irish classics are run at the Curragh in County Kildare, and the **Irish Grand National** is at Fairyhouse in County Meath. Some of the best meetings are held in the summer at smaller courses: Killarney in mid-July, Galway in late July-early August, Tramore in mid-August, Tralee in late August, and Listowel at end of September.

The Pub

Just how important is
Pub, a Dublin-based com
more than 1,000 of its five s

to-pour" pubs—Victorian Dublin, Gaelic, Irish Brewery Pub, Irish Pub Shop, and Irish Country Cottage—to more than 35 countries around the world, at about $300,000 a pop. Back on their home turf, pubs are still among the pillars of Irish social life—places where you can chat, listen, learn, and gossip about everything from horse racing to music to philosophy. Pubs have diversified in the last few years, owing partly to increasingly strict drunk-driving laws. Many now serve food at lunchtime and could be mistaken for restaurants between the hours of 12:30 and 2; many but not quite all also serve tea and coffee during daylight hours. Especially in rural areas they can be an important source of local information. If you're stuck for a meal or a bed for the night, ask a friendly publican if he knows of anyone who can solve your problem. A word about music in pubs: If it's in the main bar of a pub, you'll seldom have to pay a cover charge. However, if you're really enjoying the *craic*, as it's called, it is good form to buy a pint for the performers. Dancing to a fully amplified band in a room adjacent to the bar costs anywhere from £1.50 to £8.

Shopping

Few visitors leave Ireland without purchasing a tweed hat or a hand-knit Aran sweater, a linen tablecloth or a piece of Waterford crystal. All these items are reasonably priced investments that can easily last a lifetime. Dublin is the country's political *and* shopping capital—especially if you're looking for antiques, books, and the most *au courant* European and Irish fashions. Cork City offers less choice but quite a few surprises, and Galway has its share of galleries, bookstores, and offbeat boutiques. Most crafts shops sell a mix of goods drawn from all over the country. If you're after something a little different, keep an eye open for signs indicating "craft workshops": There are at least 20 of them around the country, where independent craftspeople sell directly from their studios. Whatever you do, don't wait to buy all of your gifts at the airport duty-free shops; the selection simply doesn't match what you can find in stores throughout the country, whether in Dublin or a tiny two-street village like Ardara in County Donegal.

ANTIQUES➤ Top-quality antiques shops are concentrated around Dublin's Fran-

cis Street area, but it's ⸻ pick up modestly priced p⸻ and 19th-century silver, 1⸻ pewter, and antique period furn⸻ where in the country. Try Co⸻ Castlecomer, Kilkenny, Galway Cit⸻ Limerick.

CRYSTAL➤ Irish lead crystal is justifiably world famous. The best known of all, Waterford glass, is on sale all over Ireland in department stores and crafts shops. The demand is so great that substantial export orders can take weeks or even months to fill. Check out the lesser-known crystals—Cork, Dublin, Kinsale, Tipperary, Tyrone, and Galway crystal—and the less formal, uncut glass from Jerpoint and Stoneyford.

DRINKABLES➤ Irish whiskey has an altogether different taste from Scotch whisky, and a different spelling, too. Well-known brands include Powers, Paddy, Jameson, and Bushmills. There are also two excellent Irish liqueurs: Irish Mist, which contains whiskey and honey, and Bailey's Irish Cream, a concoction of whiskey and cream, sometimes drunk on ice as an aperitif.

FOOD➤ Smoked salmon can vary greatly in taste and quality. Make sure it's wild salmon, not farmed; and if the label tells you what sort of wood it was smoked over, opt for oak chips. A cheaper but also delicious alternative is smoked trout. Or go for whole farmhouse cheeses like St. Killian's—a Camembert-like pasteurized cheese. More exotic and more expensive are the handmade farmhouse cheeses, each from an individual herd of cows. Milleens, Durrus, and Gubbeen are all excellent, though strong when ripe. A milder alternative is the Gouda-like Coolea cheese, found in most duty-free shops.

JEWELRY➤ Dublin and Cork City are the best spots for antique jewelry, but don't despair if the prices there are beyond your resources. Beautiful modern reproductions of such Celtic treasures as the Tara brooch are on sale for a fraction of the antique price. Other good buys include Claddagh friendship rings (Galway City is a particularly good place to shop for these) and beautiful pieces made by modern silversmiths using polished Connemara marble.

KNITWEAR➤ Aran sweaters were developed by the women of the Aran Isles to *[partial text from torn corner:]* ...ill possible to ...ces of 18th- ...th-century ...ture else- ... City, ...and **9**

...nt that was ...atherproof. ...olk motifs ...s once en- ...one an- ...en today, ...ou want to buy ...your time and wait till ...ne that really strikes your fancy. ...fter all, it should last the rest of your life. Cheaper and less durable Arans are described as "hand-loomed," which is just another way of saying "machine-made," so be sure you are getting what you want. There is a wealth of other types of sweaters: classic, blue, fisherman's rib sweaters; homespun, hand-dyed hand-knits; picture sweaters, and sophisticated mohair garments.

LINEN➤ A pure linen blouse, like an Aran sweater, can last forever. Designs are classic, so they won't become dated. Linen handkerchiefs for men make useful gifts. Damask tablecloths and crocheted-linen place mats make ideal wedding gifts. Most Irish linen is made in Northern Ireland.

RUGS, SHAWLS, AND BLANKETS➤ Crafts shops sell fleece floor rugs made of goat or sheepskin. Handwoven shawls made from unspun, undyed wool are even more luxurious than mohair, though not as easy to find. Lightweight woolen blankets in traditional plaids are always popular gifts.

TABLEWARE➤ The Arklow pottery in County Wicklow is famous for its fine china, sold at all major department stores. Belleek, on the border with Northern Ireland, produces delicate Parian china, which is widely collected. Tableware by Ireland's many ceramic artists, with striking modern designs, can be a real bargain, especially if you order four or six place settings at once.

TWEEDS➤ The best selection of traditional tweeds is still found in the specialist tweed shops of Counties Galway and Donegal. Weavers can also be found at work in Kerry, Dublin, Wicklow, Cork, and elsewhere in Connemara. Tweeds vary a good deal in type, from rugged-looking garments to clothes with jewellike colors that have been popularized by Avoca Handweavers.

FODOR'S CHOICE

No two people will agree on what makes a perfect vacation, but it's fun and helpful to know what others think. We hope you'll have a chance to experience some of Fodor's Choices yourself while visiting Ireland. They are organized in the same order as our guidebook; for detailed information about each entry, refer to the appropriate chapters.

Historic Buildings and Monuments

★ **Bank of Ireland, College Green, Dublin.** Not many buildings have been both a house of parliament *and* a bank: This 18th-century landmark graciously shows off its history in the midst of its bustling present.

★ **Trinity College, Dublin.** Ireland's oldest university, opened as an Irish counterpart to Oxford and Cambridge in 1592, is an oasis of genteel charm in the middle of a bustling metropolis.

★ **Castletown House, Celbridge.** Ireland's largest Palladian-style house, begun in 1722, is one of the country's architectural glories.

★ **Newgrange, west of Drogheda.** Built in the 4th millennium BC, this is one of the most spectacular prehistoric tombs in Europe.

★ **Emo Court, Emo.** The domed rotunda of this James Gandon–designed house is fashioned after Rome's Pantheon and is one of the most impressive rooms in Ireland.

★ **Clonmacnoise Monastery, County Offaly.** This was once one of Ireland's most important monastic settlements and a center for learning famous throughout Europe.

★ **Kilkenny Castle, Kilkenny Town.** For more than 500 years the home to the dukes of Ormonde, the powerful Butler family, this house played an important role in the history of modern Ireland.

★ **The Rock of Cashel, Cashel.** Ireland's most dramatically situated ruins—including a cathedral, chapel, and round tower—are perched atop a hill from which there's a tremendous view.

★ **Bunratty Castle and Folk Park, Bunratty.** Near Limerick, this is one of Ireland's most visited sites, made all the more interesting by the re-created 19th-century Irish village that surrounds it.

★ **Charles Fort, Kinsale.** Once a bastion of British forces in Ireland, this star-shape fort might remind you of Fort Ticonderoga in New York.

★ **Dún Aengus, Inishmore, Aran Islands.** This fine prehistoric monument dating from 2000 BC sits on the edge of a 300-ft-high cliff overlooking a sheer drop.

★ **Kylemore Abbey, Connemara.** One of Ireland's most photogenic castles is now a school run by nuns—and might make you consider taking holy orders.

★ **Glenveagh Castle, County Donegal.** This 19th-century folly is a grand, luxurious house whose exotic, extensive gardens are a sheer delight.

★ **The Crown Liquor Saloon and the Grand Opera House, Belfast.** A tunnel is said to join these two great edifices of the city's Baroque Victorian splendor, allowing "stage-door Johnnies" to entertain, discreetly, the chorus girls of one in the private snugs of the other.

★ **Dunluce Castle.** Some of the most evocative ruins in Ireland tower over Antrim's northern coast.

★ **Castle Coole, near Enniskillen.** One of Ireland's finest examples of an Anglo-Irish manor home, with abundant Rococo plasterwork, 18th-century furnishings, and a fine porcelain collection.

Parks, Gardens, and Natural Sites

★ **Phoenix Park, Dublin.** On weekends, Europe's largest enclosed park accommodates family picnics, lovers' strolls, and sporting events, as well as a herd of elegant—but terribly shy—deer.

★ **Japanese Gardens, in Tully, near Kildare Town.** Laid out in meticulous fashion to represent the human journey from birth to death, these show what's possible when Japanese gardening traditions are imported into Europe.

★ **Birr Castle Demesne, Birr.** The 100 acres of gardens that surround an imposing Gothic castle are best viewed in spring, when a wonderful display of flowering cherries, magnolias, crab apples, and naturalized narcissi bathe the grounds in color.

★ **The Giant's Causeway.** Ireland's strangest and most impressive geological curiosity consists of huge masses of mostly hexagonal pillars of basalt clustered like honeycomb and stretching into the sea off northern Antrim.

Quintessential Ireland

★ **Deserted Georgian squares on a Sunday, Dublin.** There is hardly a more pleasant haven of tranquillity in the capital than its two most beautiful squares on a quiet Sunday, St. Stephen's Green and Merrion Square.

★ **Glendalough Valley, near Dublin.** Between forested mountains, this valley with two lakes is one of Ireland's most scenic and home to some of the most significant monastic ruins in the country.

★ **Ballyhack Village from Passage East, Waterford.** The view from Passage East of this attractive village and its imposing castle at the top of Waterford Harbor has inspired many a painter and photographer.

★ **The Blasket Islands from Slea Head, near Dingle.** The view of these rugged—and now uninhabited—islands from the top of the towering cliffs of Slea Head will stop most visitors in their tracks.

★ **Dusk over Killarney's Lower Lake as seen from Aghadoe Heights.** Queen Victoria was reputedly overwhelmed by the panoramic vista from this promontory, one of the most beautiful anywhere in Ireland.

★ **Salmon Weir Bridge, Galway.** From mid-April to early July, the view from the bridge of shoals of salmon working their way upstream to the spawning grounds of Lake Corrib is one of the most popular and memorable sights in Galway.

★ **Peat cutters in the bog country.** There is no sight more specific to Ireland than that of cutters driving their long shovels into the squelchy peat bogs of the lower country of the northwest, pausing to watch and wave as you drive past.

★ **Whitewashed single-story cottages with tied-on thatched roofs.** John Ford's *The Quiet Man* introduced the simple beauty of these very Irish dwellings to the world, an integral part of the rural panorama of northwest Ireland.

★ **Devenish Island viewed from Lough Erne's shore.** The 12th-century ruins of a former monastery and the exquisitely preserved round tower and high cross—the best examples of each in the country—are clearly visible on a good day from the western shore of Lough Erne.

★ **In the Mourne Mountains, gorse flowers warmed by the sun.** These poke up between the high drystone walls and perfume the air with their rich vanilla aroma.

★ **On Upper Lough Erne, great-crested grebe diving and rising again.** Watch for these among the yellow-flag irises before the bow wave of a hired cruiser.

★ **The Apple Blossom route.** Walk through Ulster's flowery vale in the month of May.

Restaurants

★ **Patrick Guilbaud, Dublin.** Ireland's highest-ranked restaurant was moving its flagship operation at press time (summer 1997) to the new Hotel Merrion opposite Leinster House; Guilbaud's chef and staff are French, and the cooking is highly professional. $$$$

★ **Peacock Alley, Dublin.** Chef-owner Conrad Gallagher trained in New York and cooks with great brio and style—and creates a buzz of expectation among devotees of his modern, elegant restaurant. $$$$

★ **Thornton's, Dublin.** Chef-owner Kevin Thornton takes a cool, precise approach to classic French cooking in his renovated period house on the north shore of the Grand Canal. $$$$

★ **Rathsallagh House, Dunlavin, County Wicklow.** The culinary talents of owner Kay O'Flynn have become legendary, as has the equally famous relaxed atmosphere. $$$$

★ **Tinakilly House, Rathnew.** The Irish country-house cuisine at this excellent restaurant uses fresh produce from the vegetable garden on the grounds—and it shows. $$$$

★ **Crookedwood House, near Mullingar.** This restaurant off the beaten track produces superb dishes you might only expect in a large city. $$$

★ **The Wineport, Athlone.** This pleasantly informal restaurant on the shores of Lough Ree has gained several prestigious awards for its imaginative cuisine. $$

★ **Chez Hans, Cashel.** The traditional French cuisine with a hint of nouvelle at this charming restaurant has been successfully adapted to take advantage of fresh Irish ingredients. $$$$

★ **Arbutus Lodge, Cork.** Gastronomic delights of French-Irish haute cuisine, including an eight-course "tasting" menu, await guests at this outstanding restaurant five minutes from the city center. $$–$$$

★ **Longueville House, Mallow.** William O'Callaghan trained with leading European chefs before returning to Ireland to cook in his family's 18th-century country-house hotel. It is one of the most elegant dining rooms in the country. $$$–$$$$

★ **Aherne's, Youghal.** This long-established family business is arguably Ireland's best seafood restaurant. $$$

★ **Oystercatcher, Kinsale.** Owner-chef Bill Patterson has built a fine reputation for imaginative food, especially seafood and game, at this rustic outpost. $$$$

★ **Dromoland Castle, Newmarket-on-Fergus.** One of the country's best-known hotels also has an excellent restaurant worth a detour—and within taxi reach of Shannon Airport. $$$$

★ **Moran's of the Weir, Clarinbridge.** The sea is at the front door of this traditional thatched-roof pub-restaurant, which serves fresh oysters from its own beds. $–$$

★ **Drimcong House, Moycullen, County Galway.** One of the elder statesmen of the new Irish cuisine, Gerry Galvin had no formal training as a chef, yet his country-house cooking can be sublime. $$$

★ **Cromleach Lodge, Castlebaldwin.** Moira Tighe's cooking is excellent and every table in the three dining rooms of this well-regarded country hotel has panoramic views of Lough Arrow. $$$

★ **Restaurant St. John's, Fahan.** The only fastidious element of the simple but elegant cuisine at this restaurant is in the choice of produce: "only the freshest, please," insists owner-chef Reg Ryan. $$–$$$

★ **Deane's, Belfast.** Michael Deane—at his best one of Ireland's finest chefs—trained in Thailand, and it shows in his innovative east-west dishes; at press time (summer 1997) he had just reopened in a new location. $$$$

★ **Roscoff, Belfast.** Paul and Jeanne Rankin, well-known TV cooks, serve stylish food in the long, elegant room of their Golden Mile restaurant. *$$$–$$$$*

★ **Shanks, Clandeboye, Bangor, County Down.** Robbie Miller and his wife Shirley run one of Northern Ireland's best restaurants, with excellent local scallops and wild venison from a 3,000-acre estate. *$$$–$$$$*

★ **Ardtara, Upperlands, County Derry.** Gifted young chef Patrick McLarnon turns out the finest country-house food in the North. *$$$*

★ **Portaferry Hotel, Portaferry.** Scallops, lobsters, oysters, and Dublin Bay prawns haven't far to go from sea to table via John Herlihy's straightforward kitchen. *$$$*

Bed-and-Breakfasts

★ **Kilronan House, Dublin.** The warm welcome and attention to personal detail make this a longtime favorite—particularly among classical music lovers who can indulge themselves at the National Concert Hall around the corner. *$*

★ **Old Rectory Country House, Wicklow Town.** The comforts at this Greek Revival–style inn prove that you can be treated like royalty without spending a king's ransom. *$$*

★ **Lennoxbrook, Kells.** This family-run inn has been welcoming travelers for more than 200 years—practice makes perfect. *$*

★ **Gurthalougha House, Terryglass.** Formality and stuffiness have no place at this simple, characterful, and cozy inn on the shores of Lough Derg. *$$*

★ **Diamond Hill Country House, Waterford City.** This creeper-covered, modern guest house has won several excellence awards for its decor and service. *$*

★ **Ballymakeigh House, Youghal.** The sort of creeper-clad Irish farmhouse visitors dream of finding, set amid lush dairy country. *$*

★ **Berryhill Farm, Inistioge, Thomastown.** This 18th-century farmhouse offers an exceptionally high standard of comfort. *$*

★ **Hanora's Cottage, Nire Valley.** This traditional Irish cottage is one of the country's leading B&Bs and has won many awards. *$*

★ **Kathleen's Country House, Killarney.** Everything is spotlessly clean at this imaginatively designed, two-story guest house. *$*

★ **Currarevagh House, Oughterard.** All the guest rooms at this B&B overlook either Lough Corrib or the pleasant gardens and the mountains. *$$$*

★ **Norman Villa, Galway City.** Style and comfort are combined in this cheerfully decorated, welcoming town house. *$*

★ **Delphi Lodge, Leenane.** A comfortable sporting lodge in the heart of what is arguably Mayo's most spectacular mountains-and-lakes scenery. *$$*

★ **Quay House, Clifden, County Galway.** The oldest building in Clifden, this 1820, Georgian, quayside house has been lovingly restored and stylishly decorated. *$–$$*

★ **Woodhill Guest House, Ardara.** High ceilings and marble fireplaces set the tone at this grand and spacious home where guest rooms have fine views of the mountains. *$*

★ **Ash-Rowan Guest House, Belfast.** Every room at this award-winning, Victorian B&B is appointed in its own individual style. *$$*

★ **Jamestown House, in Ballinamalla, near Enniskillen.** This dignified country house, dating from 1760, is tucked away in lush, tranquil countryside near Lower Lough Erne. *$$*

Hotels

★ **Shelbourne, Dublin.** The grande dame of Dublin hotels—an elegant meeting place for Dublin's high society—is centrally located on St. Stephen's Green. *$$$$*

★ **Hibernian, Dublin.** The personal touches like potpourri and chocolates contribute to this elegant hotel's warm, friendly atmosphere. *$$$*

★ **Ariel House, Dublin.** This redbrick Victorian guest house offers the best of Irish lodging— comfortable and elegant yet personable and economical. *$*

★ **Kildare Hotel and Country Club, Straffan, County Kildare.** The Arnold Palmer-designed, lush, wooded, golf course is just one of the many attractions at this onetime mansion reminiscent of a French chateau. *$$$$*

★ **Tinakilly House, Rathnew.** Everything is on a grand scale at this elegant country hotel, from the rooms with four-poster beds to the high-quality cuisine in the restaurant. *$$$$*

★ **Slieve Russell Hotel and Country Club, Ballyconnell.** This magnificent hotel just west of Cavan has a palatial, floodlit, neoclassical facade; the interior and the rooms are no less splendid. *$$$$*

★ **Mount Juliet, Thomastown, County Kilkenny.** This Georgian mansion within a walled estate of 1,400 acres has a championship golf course and extensive riding trails. *$$$$*

★ **Park Hotel, Kenmare.** Set on extensive grounds and formerly a bishop's palace, this establishment is now one of Ireland's premier country-house hotels. *$$$$*

★ **Sheen Falls Lodge, Kenmare.** Set amid 300 secluded acres of tropical gardens with an award-winning restaurant overlooking a waterfall, this is a perfect hideaway. *$$$$*

★ **Longueville House, Mallow.** A fine 18th-century house with a lovely Victorian conservatory overlooks the Blackwater River; it's home to one of Ireland's finest restaurants, and it has its own vineyard. *$$$*

★ **Dromoland Castle, Newmarket-on-Fergus.** This impressive, turreted Gothic-style luxury hotel is popular with affluent American and French visitors. *$$$$*

★ **Ballynahinch Castle, Recess.** This large house on the shores of a river has long been a favorite retreat of statesmen and movie stars, including Gerald Ford and Alec Guinness. *$$$*

★ **Rathmullan House, Rathmullan.** Behind the signature three-bay facade of this country house is one of Ireland's most relaxing, comfortable hotels; its perch on the shores of Donegal's Lough Swilly is icing on the cake. *$$$*

★ **St. Ernan's House, Donegal Town.** On its own wooded island on Donegal Bay, this 19th-century country house is an unbeatable getaway.*$$$$*

★ **Ardtara, Upperlands, County Derry.** A lovingly decorated, impeccably run linen baron's mansion has one of the North's finest dining rooms. *$$$*

FESTIVALS AND SEASONAL EVENTS

In both the Republic and Northern Ireland, festivals devoted to the arts, literature, sports, harvests, and animals fill up the calendar year-round. The Republic's Bord Fáilte and the Northern Ireland Tourist Board jointly produce an annual 80-page Calendar of Events (£1). (☞ Visitor Information *in* the Gold Guide). A horse race is run practically every day of the year in Ireland; the **Irish Horse Racing Authority**'s marketing and promotions department (☎ 01/289–2888) is a good source for information.

➤ JAN. 10: The first big horse race of the season is the **Ladbrook Handicap Hurdle** (✉ Turf Club, ☎ 01/289–3607) in Leopardstown, County Dublin.

➤ FEB. 28–MAR. 7: **Opera Northern Ireland** (☎ 01232/322338) performs Humperdinck's *Hansel and Gretel* during its spring 1998 season at Belfast's Grand Opera House.

➤ EARLY MAR.: For 10 days, the **Dublin Film Festival** (☎ 01/679–2937) presents an eclectic mix of the best independent and feature films from Ireland and around the world, plus lectures, seminars, and other events for cineasts. The 87th annual **Belfast Music Festival** (☎ 01232/668944) sponsors speech, drama, and music competitions for young people.

➤ MAR.: For three weeks on either side of St. Patrick's Day, the **Celtic Spring Festival** (☎ 01504/365151) brings theatrical and rock music performances, an Irish-language festival, and a parade to **Derry City**, County Londonderry.

➤ MID-MAR.: At the **Guinness Roaring 20's Festival** (☎ 064/41170) in **Killarney**, County Kerry, which leads up to St. Patrick's Day, revelers turn out in Great Gatsby outfits to enjoy afternoon teas, cocktail parties, and live music. Bands of every stripe and size march in step and blow their horns in the 28th annual **Limerick International Band Festival** (☎ 061/410777), which immediately precedes the city's St. Patrick's Day celebrations. The **Adare Jazz Festival** (☎ 061/396118) in County Limerick fills the town's pubs with great jazz. **St. Patrick's Day** celebrations throughout the country get under way three days before the climactic day itself, March 17. Ireland's major St. Patrick's event is the **Dublin Festival and parade** (☎ 01/671–3788), more elaborate every year, which includes guest bands from the United States; there's also a festival of traditional Irish music, the Dublin **Feis Ceoil**.

➤ APR.: Easter brings one of the biggest events of the racing calendar, the two-day **Irish Grand National** at Fairyhouse, County Meath (☎ 01/825–6167), about 19 km/12 mi north of Dublin. **Easter walking festivals** also get visitors and locals tootling around on foot at various venues throughout the country, including **Rathdrum**, County Wicklow (☎ 0404/46262), **Glencar**, County Kerry (☎ 066/60101), and **Kenmare**, County Kerry (☎ 064/41034). Contact **Walking World Ireland** (☎ 01/492–3030) for details on other walking festivals throughout the year.

➤ APR.28–30: The Punchestown Racecourse, just outside **Naas**, hosts the **Punchestown National Hunt Festival** (☎ 045/897704).

➤ EARLY MAY: Sixty-plus choirs reverberate through Cork City Hall and other venues throughout the city during the **Cork International Choral Festival** (☎ 021/308308). Sixty-plus traditional music sessions take place over the first weekend in May at **Kinvara**'s **Cuckoo Fleadh** (☎ 091/637145).

➤ MAY: Twenty-one days of concerts, competitions, and exhibitions take place during the **Belfast Civic Festival** (☎ 01232/270345); festivities kick off with the **Lord Mayor's Show,** a parade to be held in 1998 on May 2. Also during the festival, the **Belfast Marathon** (☎ 01232/270345) fills the streets on May 4 with 3,500 runners.

➤ MAY–JUNE: It's the height of flower season in **The Burren** in County

Clare, and the best time to take a **Burren Flora Tour.** (Contact Mary Angela Keane [☎ 065/74003] or Shane Connolly [☎ 065/77168] for a guided botanical walk.)

➤ MID-MAY: The **Bantry Mussel Fair** (☎ 027/50360) in **Bantry**, County Cork celebrates the peak of the harvest season for this delicacy *na mara* ("of the sea" in Irish). From mid-May to mid-June, the **County Wicklow Gardens Festival** (☎ 0404/66058) allows entry to lovely private gardens not ordinarily open to the public.

➤ LATE MAY: The **Galway Early Music Festival** (☎ 091/524411) in **Galway City** fills the city with the sounds of pre-Baroque Irish and European music. The **Fleadh Nua** ☎ 01/280–0295), the annual festival of traditional Irish music, song, and dance, takes place in **Ennis**, County Clare. Theater, literary readings, and plenty of music fill the calendar of the **Sligo Arts Festival** (☎ 071/69802), which continues into early June.

SUMMER

➤ EARLY JUNE: **Listowel Writers' Week** (☎ 068/21074), one of Ireland's leading literary festivals, brings writers, poets, and lovers of literature together in this County Kerry town. Cartoonists congregate in the Wicklow village of **Rathdrum** for the annual **Guinness International Cartoon Festival** (☎ 0404/46811). **Carlow** celebrates the arts

in its annual **Éigse Festival** (☎ 0503/40491). The **Weavers' Fair and Vintage Weekend** (☎ 075/41262) comes to **Ardara** in County Donegal June 5–7, although today the fair has as much to do with music, dance, and having fun as it does with selling homespun.

➤ JUNE: Pick up some decorating tips while you're swooning over Schubert lieder at the **AIB Music Festival in Great Irish Homes** (☎ 01/278–1528), which puts on classical-music concerts in some of Ireland's finest country houses.

➤ MID-JUNE: Ballycastle puts on its own lively, three-day music and dance folk festival, the **Fleadh Amhrán agus Rince** (☎ 012657/63703) Devoted Joyceans celebrate the fictional wanderings of *Ulysses*'s Leopold and Molly Bloom and Stephen Daedalus on June 16 (the day the novel was set, in 1904) in **Dublin** with **Bloomsday** (☎ 01/878–8547); readings, dramatizations, and pilgrimages take place around the city (☞ Close-Up: ReJoyce! in Chapter 2).

➤ LATE JUNE: The **Budweiser Irish Derby** (☎ 045/441205) at the **Curragh Racecourse**, County Kildare, is the biggest race event of the year.

➤ JUNE 28–JULY 5: The Borodin Quartet and other chamber groups perform at the third annual **West Cork Chamber Music Festival** (☎ 027/61105), held at Bantry House in **Bantry**, County Cork. Russian music is the theme of this year's programs.

➤ EARLY JULY: **Castlebar**, County Mayo, is the

venue for the **International Four-Day Walking Festival** (☎ 094/24102). The **Coalisland International Music Festival** (☎ 01868/748809) attracts traditional and folk bands from all over Europe to County Tyrone. **Murphy's Irish Open Golf Championship** (☎ 01/662–2433) is held at Druid's Glen, Newtownmountkennedy, County Wicklow (☞ Chapter 10).

➤ JULY–SEPT.: Over 25,000 rose bushes are on display in Belfast's riverside Dixon Park in the **City of Belfast International Rose Trials;** the highlight is **Rose Week** (☎ 01232/320202).

➤ MID-JULY: On July 12 Belfast commemorates the historic 1690 **Battle of the Boyne** (☎ 01232/322801). Bachelors from throughout the country strut their stuff in **Mullingar** for the **Guinness International Bachelor Festival** (☎ 044/44044). Galway is jam-packed for the two-week **Galway Arts Festival** (☎ 091/583800), the West's premier arts event, which includes theater, film, music of all kinds, art exhibits, and a not-to-be-missed kickoff parade. The **James Joyce Summer School** (☎ 01/706–8480) draws academics and aficionados from all over the world to University College **Dublin**. Also in **Dublin**, the streets and pubs of Temple Bar resound day and night to jazz and blues music for the seventh annual **Temple Bar Blues Festival** (☎ 01/677–2255). Kilmore Quay hosts a two-week-long **Seafood Festival** (☎ 053/29922) that runs through to the end of the month.

➤ JULY 26: On the last Sunday in July, thousands

of pilgrims, some in bare feet, climb the rocky slopes of **Croagh Patrick** (2,510 ft) in County Mayo to honor St. Patrick.

➤ LATE JULY–EARLY AUG.: The **Galway Races** (☎ 091/753870) start the day after Galway's Arts Festival ends for a week of revelry. **Boyle,** County Roscommon, hosts the **Boyle Arts Festival** (☎ 079/62066), one of the best performing and visual-arts festivals in the region. Would-be beauty queens come to **Dungloe,** County Donegal, from as far away as Australia and New Zealand to compete in the **Mary of Dungloe International Festival** (☎ 075/21254). The **Festivals of Classical Music** (☎ 028/36193) fill historic St. Barrahane's Church in **Castletownshend,** County Cork, with the sounds of chamber music.

➤ EARLY AUG.: You have even more festivals than usual to choose from at this time of year. The **Ballyshannon Folk and Traditional Music Festival** (☎ 072/51088) in County Donegal is one of the best of the season. Everyone's got the beat at the **Waterford Spraoi** (☎ 051/353088), an international rhythm festival. The **O'Carolan Harp and Traditional Music Festival** (☎ 078/47204) in Keadue, County Roscommon, is a great place to hear traditional music. The two-week **Yeats International Summer School** (☎ 071/42693) in Sligo Town celebrates its 40th anniversary in 1998.

➤ MID-AUG.: Kinvara, County Galway, hosts its long-standing sailing event, **Cruinniú na mBád**

("Festival of the Gathering of the Boats"; ☎ 091/595635), in which traditional brown-sailed Galway hookers laden with turf race across Galway Bay. The **Kerrygold Dublin Horse Show** (☎ 01/668–0866) attracts a fashionable set to watch the best in Irish bloodstock. Aeronautical enthusiasts should check out the **Abbeyshrule Fly-in Festival and Air Show** (☎ 044/57424) in County Longford. The three-day **Puck Fair** (☎ 066/62366) in **Killorglin,** County Kerry, one of the country's oldest and more mythical festivals, retains vestiges of old pre-Christian fertility rites, like the garlanding with flowers of a large billy goat to signify his being crowned king.

➤ LATE AUG.: Kilkenny hosts **Kilkenny Arts Week** (☎ 056/63663), a marvelous assemblage of classical music, art exhibits, and theater. The highlight of the traditional music calendar is the **Fleadh Ceoil na hEireann** (pronounced "flah kee'yo na erin," ☎ 01/280–0295); the venue, somewhere in the west of Ireland, won't be determined until early 1998. The world-famous **Rose of Tralee International Festival** (☎ 066/21322) selects a "Rose of Tralee" from an international lineup of young women of Irish descent, and packs this County Kerry town in the process. The competition coincides with the **Tralee Races.** On the third Thursday of the month, the **Connemara Pony Show** (☎ 095/21863) brings Ireland's finest yearlings and stallions to **Clifden,** County Galway.

➤ AUG. 24–25: If you're in the neighborhood of

Ballycastle, County Antrim, don't miss Ireland's oldest fair, **Oul' Lammas Fair** (☎ 012657/62024), held every year since 1606 on the last Monday and Tuesday in August. It's a modern version of the ancient Celtic harvest festival of Lughnasa (Irish for "August").

AUTUMN

➤ SEPT.: Single people of all ages from throughout Ireland and beyond flock to County Clare for the **Lisdoonvarna Matchmaking Festival** (☎ 072/51103) in the hopes of finding a spouse—or at least a date. The **Appalachian and Bluegrass Music Festival** (☎ 01662/243292) traces the roots of Appalachian music back to Ireland at the Ulster American Folk Park in **Omagh,** County Tyrone. The hugely popular **Hurling and Gaelic Football Finals** (☎ 01/836–3222) are played in Croke Park Stadium in Dublin.

➤ MID-SEPT.: The **Budweiser Clifden Blues Festival** (☎ 095/21349) brings an out-of-season crowd to this West County Galway seaside town.

➤ LATE SEPT.: Indulge in the "food of the gods" at the start of the oyster season at the **Galway International Oyster Festival** (☎ 091/527282); the season lasts through all the months with the letter *r*. Farmers compete in the **All Ireland Ploughing Championships** (☎ 0507/25125); 1998 dates are September 29 through October 1, and it will be held in **Ferns**, County Wexford. **Opera Northern Ireland** (☎ 01232/ 322338) kicks off its autumn season in the Grand Opera House in Belfast. Troupes from all over Europe compete at **Waterford's** Theatre Royal during the annual **International Festival of Light Opera** (☎ 051/ 54909), which continues into early October.

➤ OCT.: The **Dublin Theatre Festival** (☎ 01/ 677–8439) puts on 10 visiting international productions, 10 Irish plays (most of them new), a children's festival, and a fringe of 60-plus plays October 5–17. The beautiful coastal Cork town of **Kinsale** opens its best restaurants for the **International Gourmet Festival** (☎ 021/774026).

➤ MID-OCT.: One of Ireland's premier film events, the **Cork Film Festival** (☎ 021/271711) shows new feature-length films, documentaries, and short films—a specialty of the festival. Amateur and professional runners fill the streets of **Dublin** in the **Dublin City Marathon** (☎ 01/676–4647).

➤ OCT. 23–26: The **Cork Jazz Festival** (☎ 021/ 270463) draws jazz lovers from Ireland and beyond.

➤ LATE OCT.–EARLY NOV.: The **Wexford Opera Festival** (☎ 053/22144) brings in major international stars to stage and perform three rarely heard opera gems in a tiny Georgian theater.

➤ NOV.: The three-day **Millstreet Indoor International Horse Show** (☎ 029/70707) brings out-of-season equestrian enthusiasts to this County Cork town. The **Belfast Festival at Queen's University** (☎ 01232/667687) is the city's preeminent arts festival, with hundreds of musical, film, theater, and ballet performances.

➤ NOV.: The **Irish Rugby Football season** gets under way in **Dublin** with games between Ireland and nations *not* in the Five Nations group (Scotland, Wales, England, France, and Ireland). A limited number of tickets are available through the Irish Rugby Football Union (☎ 01/668–4601).

➤ MID-DEC.: The yearling, foal, and breeding stock sale at **Goff's Bloodstock Sales** (☎ 045/ 877211), **Kill**, County Kildare, gives visitors a peek at how the rich and famous buy and sell their prized horses.

➤ DEC. 26: On **St. Stephen's Day,** the traditional Wren Boys in blackface and fancy dress still wander the streets of some rural towns asking for money and singing (these days much of the money goes to charity); by far the most extravagant celebration of this ancient folktale takes place on Sandymount Green in **Dublin** from about 11 AM.

2 Dublin

You can practically hear the '90s roaring: Western Europe's most intimate capital is also its fastest-growing urban tourist destination—a boomtown of new construction and restoration. Ask Dubliners for their take on what's happening, and you may hear echoes of one of W. B. Yeats's most-quoted lines: "All changed, changed utterly," uttered with a hint of nostalgia. Nowhere are the changes more apparent than in Temple Bar— the cobblestoned arts and culture quarter. But the city's pleasures are uncontainable: historic Georgian buildings, 1,000-odd pubs, buzzing cafés and restaurants, museums of quiet glory, lovely green parks, and, best of all, the easy friendliness of the people.

Updated by
Sylvia
Thompson and
Kevin Courtney

THE ONLY ADEQUATE COMPARISON to the astonishing change that has swept through Dublin in the last decade and continues unabated today may be to the transformations underway in the major cities of Central Europe—particularly Berlin, Prague, and Budapest—in the wake of the revolutions of 1989. Geographically the westernmost of European countries, Ireland underwent no such profound historic, ideological upheaval as the revolutions that sent its relatives on the eastern fringe of Europe, for decades firmly locked behind the Iron Curtain, careening into the present. And yet, the scope of what is happening in Ireland's capital suggests that something almost as momentous has happened here—even if it's not possible to pinpoint the precise moment, as we can down to the day, that set in motion the rebirth of Central Europe. Even if the pace of change that has gripped Dublin in the 1990s has not been as politically profound as that underway at the other end of Europe, it has been no less furious.

How dramatic are the changes taking place? On a wintry November day in the fall of 1996, a visitor to Dublin counted 18 construction cranes from the sixth-story roof of his center-city hotel—18 massive cranes towering over the Dublin skyline, poised over shiny new hotels and old Georgian houses, each signifying commitments of large sums of money and a deep faith in the city's future. Is it an accident that in several scenes in the 1991 film *The Commitments* you can glimpse one of these cranes quietly whispering off in the distance—a portent of things to come? The cranes, of course, are just the most outsized signs of Dublin's vitality. For every crane there are hundreds of stories of transformation in this city, both big and tall and small and quiet.

But first, to Dublin's past. Its origins as a village date back some 1,500 years, when it was little more than a crossroads—albeit a critical one—of four of the main thoroughfares that traversed the country. It has two names dating back this far: Baile Atha Cliath, meaning City of the Hurdles, which was bestowed by Celtic traders in the 2nd century AD and which you can still see on buses and billboards throughout the city, and Dubhlinn or "dark pool," which is believed to have been where Dublin Castle now stands. Today, the area where the city's first inhabitants, members of the Gaelic order, built their dwellings is known as the Liberties; sections of the first town walls, dating back nearly 1,000 years, can still be seen off Thomas Street, west of Christ Church Cathedral.

In 837, Norsemen from Scandinavia carried out the first outside attack on Dublin, arriving in a fleet of 60 longboats. Four years later, the Vikings built their first port here and used it for raiding large tracts of the countryside. Despite the resistance of the Irish against Viking rule, the Norsemen made Dublin one of the principal centers of their empire, which stretched from Russia in the east to Ireland in the west and Iceland in the north. The power of the Scandinavians was finally broken by the Irish at the Battle of Clontarf in 1014, which took place north of Dublin. Native rule, however, was short-lived. The Anglo-Normans landed in County Wexford, in southeast Ireland, in 1169; a mere two years later, King Henry II of England finally subdued some of the Irish chieftains and granted Dublin its first charter.

Through the Middle Ages, the city developed as a trading center, though fraught with political difficulties. The last remaining relic of medieval trade in Ireland can be seen nearly opposite Christ Church Cathedral, in Tailor's Hall. In 1651, English soldier Oliver Cromwell occupied and ransacked Dublin, which at the time was still little more than a large village, with 15,000 inhabitants. Not until the 18th century did Dublin reach a period of glory, when a golden age of enlightened patronage by wealthy members of the nobility turned the city into one of Europe's most prepossessing cities. New streets and squares, such as Merrion and Fitzwilliam squares, were constructed with a classical dignity and elegance. Handel, the German-born English composer, wrote much of his great oratorio, the *Messiah*, in Dublin, where it was first performed in 1742. Many other crafts, such as bookbinding and silver making, flourished to cater to the needs of the often-titled and usually wealthy members of society. Ireland was granted a certain measure of political autonomy by the British, and in the new government buildings (now the Bank of Ireland) in College Green, opposite Trinity College, the independent parliament met for the first time in 1783. Throughout this period, until the early 19th century, social and economic power rested exclusively in Protestant hands.

The glory of this era was short-lived; in 1800, the Act of Union brought Ireland and Britain together in a common United Kingdom, and the seat of political power and patronage moved from Dublin to London. Dublin quickly lost its cultural and social sparkle, as many members of the nobility moved to London. The 19th century proved to be a time of political turmoil and agitation, although Daniel O'Connell, a lord mayor of Dublin, won early success with the introduction of Catholic emancipation in 1829. During the late 1840s, Dublin escaped the worst effects of the famine, caused by potato disease, that blighted much of southern and western Ireland. New industries, such as mineral-water manufacturing, were established, and with an emerging Victorian middle class introducing an element of genteel snobbery to the city, Dublin began its rapid outward expansion. Until the mid-19th century, Dublin extended little beyond St. Stephen's Green, but with the sudden demand for additional housing by the newly wealthy, many new suburbs were established, such as Ballsbridge, Rathgar, and Rathmines on the southside, and Clontarf and Drumcondra on the northside.

In the first decade of this century, Dublin entered a period of cultural ferment (☞ Literary Dublin *in* Pleasures and Pastimes, *below*)—an era that had its political apotheosis in the Easter Uprising of 1916, which lasted a week, damaging many buildings in and around O'Connell Street on the northside of the city center. In 1919, the war aimed at winning independence from Britain began in County Tipperary and lasted for three years. Dublin was comparatively unscathed during this period, but during the Civil War, which followed the setting up of the Irish Free State in December 1921, more harm came to a number of the city's historic buildings, including the Four Courts and the Custom House, which both burned down. The capital had to be rebuilt during the 1920s. After the Civil War was over, Dublin entered a new era of political and cultural conservatism, which continued until the late 1950s. In the 1960s, an era of economic optimism pervaded the city, but much of this enthusiasm waned again during the recessionary years of the 1970s.

If there was a major turning point in Dublin's fortunes in the last 25 years, it was in the 1980s, when Irish musicians stormed the American and British barricades of rock and roll. Bob Geldof and the Boomtown Rats ("I Don't Like Mondays") and Chris de Burgh were among the most prominent Irish musicians who found audiences well beyond Irish shores, but it was U2, which ascended to the farthest heights of rock-and-roll stardom, that forever changed the place of Irish musicians in international popular culture. Sinéad O'Connor and The Cranberries have since followed, and it's certain that more are on the way.

If the 1980s saw the ascent of Irish rock stars, the 1990s have truly been the boom years—a decade of broadly improved economic fortunes, major capital investment, declining unemployment, and reversing patterns of immigration—all set in motion to a great extent by Ireland's participation in the European Union, or EU. When Ireland approved the EU in 1992, it was one of the poorest European nations; it qualified for EU grants of all kinds. Money has, quite simply, *poured* into Ireland—nowhere more so than in Dublin. The International Financial Services Centre, gleaming behind the two-centuries-old Custom House, is just one of the most overt signs of the success the city has had in attracting leading multinational corporations into the city, particularly in telecommunications, software, and service industries. But Dublin's swift transformation is probably a result not only of macroeconomic changes but of more grassroots changes, as well: To discover just how generous and widespread the EU grant-giving has been here, ask random Dubliners whether they know any individual who has received a grant, and see what they say.

Today roughly half of the Irish Republic's population of 3.6 million people live in Dublin and its suburbs. It is a young city—astonishingly so. Students from all over Ireland attend Trinity College and the city's dozen other universities. On weekends, their counterparts from Paris, from London, and from Rome fly in, swelling the city's youthful contingent, filling its pubs and clubs to overflowing. After graduating from university, more and more of these young Irish men and women are sticking around rather than emigrating to New York or London, filling the raft of new jobs and contributing to the hubbub that's evident everywhere in the city. The city is also increasingly as heterogeneous as it is young, for as multinational corporations have set up shop in Dublin, a large number of Middle Easterners and many American, Dutch, German, and Japanese immigrants have settled here. Today, more and more Americans of Irish descent are obtaining citizenship and returning to the capital of the country their ancestors left 150 years ago during the Great Famine.

James Joyce immortalized Dublin in his short stories and his modernist masterpiece, *Ulysses,* filling his works with the people he knew, with their own words and the cadence of their Dublin patois. He was also one of Dublin's—and Ireland's—most famous exiles. In 1902, at the age of 20, he left Dublin and thereafter returned only for brief visits. (Samuel Beckett, his assistant and friend, followed him into exile.) Walking around the buzzing boomtown of late-'90s Dublin today, you have to ask yourself, would Joyce have forsaken "our dear, dirty Dublin," as he so famously called his hometown, were he alive today? What would he have made of this genteel city, a place that seems astonished at its newfound fortunes?

Pleasures and Pastimes

Literary Dublin

Dublin packs more literary punch than practically anywhere else on the planet—largely because of the ferment that took hold at the fin de siècle, when two main literary movements emerged. In 1893, Douglas Hyde, later the first president of Ireland, founded the Gaelic League (Conradh na Gaelige), whose goal was to preserve the Irish language. At the same time, W. B. Yeats played a pivotal role in the Irish literary renaissance. With the foundation of the ☞ **Abbey Theatre** in 1904 and the growing prominence of such playwrights as Sean O'Casey and J. M. Synge, Irish literature thrived. The ☞ **Dublin Writers Museum** gives a terrific introduction to this story and to the more than two dozen

major writers Ireland subsequently produced (at least the dead ones
living legends have to wait to be included). To go farther back in literary history, head for ☞ **Trinity College**, where you can see a few pages
of the 9th-century Book of Kells. Oscar Wilde fans should pay homage
at 1 Merrion Square. Our ☞ **"ReJoyce!"** close-up guides you through
some key sites connected with Joyce and *Ulysses*. And if you want to
stock up on anecdotes about the relationship between the pint and the
pen, take the "Dublin Literary Pub Crawl" (☞ Guided Tours *in* Dublin
A to Z, *below*).

Musical Dublin

Music fills Dublin's streets (especially ☞ **Grafton Street**) and its pubs,
where *talk* of music is as popular as the tunes themselves. Dubliners
are obsessed with music of every kind and will happily discuss anything from Elvis's earliest recordings (remember Jimmy's father in *The
Commitments*?) to U2's latest incarnation. The city has been the stomping ground of so many big-league rock and pop musicians that Dublin
Tourism has created a "Rock n Stroll" Trail (☞ Guided Tours *in*
Dublin A to Z, *below*) that covers 16 sites, most of them in the city
center and ☞ **Temple Bar**. It includes spots like ☞ **Bewley's**, where
Bob Geldof and the other members of the Boomtown Rats hung out,
and the Bad Ass Café, where Sinéad O'Connor once worked. You're
forgiven if you think some connections between the trail sites and the
musicians seem hokey, but you're not if you don't seek out Dublin's
lively, present-day music scene. A number of small pubs and larger halls
host live music, but the best places are mid-size venues such as ☞
Olympia Theatre and the ☞ **Temple Bar Music Centre**, where you can
hear well-established local acts *and* leading international artists (including
world-renowned Irish musicians), playing everything from traditional
and folk-rock to jazz-funk and—for the truly adventurous—"Dubcore,"
a term coined to describe the city's many noisy alternative bands.

A Thousand Pubs

Irish pubs are being exported at an unprecedented rate all around the
world (☞ The Pub *in* Pleasures and Pastimes *in* Chapter 1), but in Dublin,
it's a different story altogether. Modern, European-style café-bars are
fast replacing the capital's traditional drinking spots. The city center
is now dotted with high-concept designer pubs with bright, arty facades
and a pervasive scent of affluence. To be sure, in the City of 1,000 Pubs,
you're still certain of finding a good, old-fashioned watering hole.
And if you do find yourself in a new spot, surrounded by the trappings
of European chic, you'll soon discover that Dubliners still enjoy good
craic—quintessentially Irish friendly chat and lively conversation—wherever they congregate.

Taking in the Views

Although you may not be conscious of it while you're in the city center, Dublin boasts a beautiful setting: looped around the edge of Dublin
Bay and on a plain at the edge of the gorgeous, green Dublin and Wicklow Mountains, which rise softly just to the south. From the ☞ **Four
Courts** building, the sight of the city, the bay, and the mountains will
take your breath away. For another vantage, head for the ☞ **South Wall**,
which stretches far out into Dublin Bay and isn't far from the city center. There are also fantastic views from choice spots in the suburbs of
south and north County Dublin.

EXPLORING DUBLIN

From north to south, Dublin stretches 16 km/10 mi. From its center,
immediately adjacent to the port area and the River Liffey, the city spreads

westward for an additional 10 km/6 mi; in total, it covers 28,000 acres. But its heart is far more compact than these numbers indicate. Like Paris, like London, like Florence, like so many of the world's most beloved cities—a river runs right through the city. The River Liffey divides the capital into the "northside" and the "southside," as everyone calls the two principal center city areas. Virtually all of the major sights in and around the city center are within well less than an hour's walk of one another.

Our coverage is organized into five tours of the city center and the areas immediately surrounding it, and two excursions into County Dublin—the first to the southern suburbs, the latter to the northern. Our first tour—The Georgian Heart of Dublin—covers many of the southside's major sites: Trinity College, St. Stephen's Green, Merrion Square, and Grafton Street. We suggest you do this tour first, as it will quickly orient you to a good portion of the southside. Our second tour—Temple Bar—takes you through the recently revived Temple Bar neighborhood that's the hottest, hippest zone in the capital. Our third tour—Dublin Castle, Christ Church Cathedral, and Dublin West—picks up literally across the street from Temple Bar and gets you to the Guinness Brewery, the city's most popular attraction. A word about these three tours: Although we've split the southside into three, you'll soon realize that the distance between the areas in all of these tours is not very great. Our fourth walk—Northside Dublin—moves to the northside of the city center and covers all of the major cultural sites there. Phoenix Park and environs, at the western fringe of the northside city center, is the main focus of our fifth Dublin walk.

If you're visiting Dublin for more than two or three days, you will probably want to explore farther afield. There's plenty to see and do a short distance from the center city—in the suburbs of both north and south County Dublin—but since you need either a car or public transportation to reach these destinations, we cover them in our Side Trips section (☞ below). Still, if you are adventuresome and want to explore outside the city center, it's not difficult to reach these areas, even if your time in Dublin is limited.

Because of its compact size and traffic congestion—brought on in the last few years by an astronomical increase in the number of new vehicles, *pedestrian* traffic—especially on the city center's busiest streets during commute hours—is astonishing. Watch where you stop to consult your map or you're liable to be swept away by the ceaseless flow of the bustling crowds.

Numbers in the text correspond to numbers in the margin and on the Dublin City Center, Dublin West, County Dublin—Southside, and County Dublin—Northside maps.

Great Itineraries

In a week, you should be able to cover virtually all of our Dublin exploring suggestions, including the Side Trips. But in three or even two days, you can at least see many of the city-center sites and come away with a familiarity of the city greater than that you could establish in a similar length of time in any of Europe's other capital cities.

IF YOU HAVE 3 DAYS

On the first day visit **Trinity College**—exploring the campus and spending an hour at the **Book of Kells** exhibit. Move on to the surrounding south city-center area, taking in **St. Stephen's Green, Grafton Street,** and the main museums, such as the **National Museum** and the **National Gallery of Ireland**—most of which are located opposite **Merrion Square.** After an early dinner, take in a play at one of Dublin's half-dozen theaters. Dedicate your second day to the north and west of the city center. In the morning, cross the Liffey via O'Connell Bridge and walk up **O'Connell Street,** stopping to visit the **General Post Office,** on your way to the **Dublin Writers Museum** and the **Hugh Lane Municipal Gallery of Modern Art.** Be sure to join the thousands of Dubliners strolling down Henry, Moore, and Mary streets, the northside's pedestrian shopping area. In the afternoon, cross back to the southside and explore **Temple Bar,** and leave yourself time to visit some of Dublin's pubs. On the final day start with a trip on the DART train to either Bray or Howth for a look at Dublin's coastline and return either by Sandycove and the **James Joyce Martello Tower** or by the architecturally exquisite **Casino** at Marino. Back in the city, have tea at Bewley's and catch a musical performance at the **Olympia Theatre.**

IF YOU HAVE 5 DAYS

Start with **Trinity College** and go on to the **National Museum,** with a walk to Fitzwilliam Square for a look at some of the best-kept Georgian houses and doors. Proceed from here to **St. Stephen's Green** and on to **St. Patrick's Cathedral,** founded in 1190. A living history of Dublin can be seen at medieval **Dublinia,** across the street from ancient **Christ Church Cathedral.** Spend day three exploring the northside of the city center: Cross the Liffey via O'Connell Bridge and walk up **O'Connell Street,** stopping to visit the **General Post Office,** on your way to the **Dublin Writers Museum** and the **Hugh Lane Municipal Gallery of Modern Art.** Visit the **Pro-Cathedral,** the only Catholic cathedral in Dublin, and stroll with Dubliners shopping down Henry, Moore, and Mary streets. On your third day, explore **Temple Bar** and continue westward, jumping across the Liffey to the **Four Courts,** then crossing back to visit the **Royal Kilmainham Hospital** and **Kilmainham Gaol.** Return via the **Guinness Brewery** and **Dublin Castle.** On your fourth day explore the southern outskirts of the city, accessible by DART train, including the suburban areas of Dalkey and Sandycove (where you can visit the **James Joyce Martello Tower**), and the busy ferry port of **Dun Laoghaire.** Visit the **Chester Beatty Library,** with its many Chinese and Turkish exhibits. Before returning to the city center, take a stroll along the 5 km/3 mi beach of **Sandymount Strand.** On the last day tour the northern outskirts of Dublin from **Glasnevin Cemetery** and the **National Botanic Gardens** across to the **Casino** in Marino and the quaint village of **Howth.**

The Georgian Heart of Dublin

If there's one travel poster that signifies "Dublin" more than any other place, it's the one that pictures 50 or so Georgian doorways—door after colorful door, all graced with lovely fanlights upheld by columns. A building boom began in Dublin in the early 18th century, as the Protestant ascendancy constructed town houses for themselves and civic structures for their city in the style that came to be known as Georgian, for the four successive British Georges who ruled from 1714 through 1830. The Georgian architectural rage owed much to architects like James Gandon and Richard Castle. They and others were influenced by Andrea Palladio (1508–80), whose *Four Books of Architecture* were published in the 1720s in London and helped to precipitate the revival of his style that swept through England and its colonies. We begin at Trinity College, although you can pick up anywhere that's convenient to where you're staying.

A Good Walk

Start at **Trinity College** ①, exploring the quadrangle as you head to the Old Library to see the Book of Kells. Trinity can easily eat up at least an hour or more of your time, so when you come back out the front

gate, you can either stop in at the **Bank of Ireland** ②, the one-time home
of the Irish Parliament, or make an immediate left and head up **Grafton
Street** ③, the pedestrian spine of the southside. If Grafton Street's
shops whet your appetite for more browsing or shopping, turn right
down Wicklow Street then left up South William Street to **Powerscourt
Townhouse Centre** ④, which with its choice of cafés is a good place to
take a break. The **Dublin Civic Museum** ⑤ is next door to Powerscourt,
across the alley on its south flank. If you're doing well on time and
want to explore the shopping streets farther east, jog via the alley one
block east to Drury Street, from which you can access the Victorian
George's Street Covered Market ⑥. Whether or not you make this excursion, you should head back to Grafton Street, where **Bewley's
Café** ⑦, a Dublin institution, is another good place for a break. Grafton
Street ends at the northwest corner of **St. Stephen's Green** ⑧, Dublin's
most popular public gardens; they absolutely require a stroll-through.
Newman House ⑨ is on the south side of the green. Amble back across
the green, exiting onto the northeast corner, at which sits the grand
Shelbourne Hotel ⑩, a wonderful place for afternoon tea or a quick
pint at one of its two pubs. Visit the **Huguenot Cemetery** ⑪ and continue across Merrion Row (art enthusiasts should detour to the **RHA
Gallagher Gallery** ⑫) and down Merrion Street along **Merrion Square** ⑬
to **Number Twenty-Nine** ⑭. Cut back through the square to visit the
refurbished **Government Buildings** ⑮, the **Natural History Museum** ⑯,
Leinster House ⑰ and/or the **National Gallery of Ireland** ⑱. The last
leg of this walk is up Kildare Street to the **National Library** ⑲, passing
the back of Leinster House to the **National Museum** ⑳ (stop in at the
Genealogical Office ㉑ if you're doing research about your ancestors).
Other nearby sites include **Mansion House** ㉒, the **Royal Irish Academy** ㉓,
and **St. Ann's Church** ㉔. Continue back down Dawson Street and you
will be back practically to where you started, at the side entrance to
Trinity College.

TIMING
Dublin is so compact you could race through this walk in two hours,
if you don't linger anywhere or set foot in one of the museums. But
there are treasures galore at Trinity, the National Gallery, and the National Museum; the green tranquillity of St. Stephen's Green and Merrion Square; and many of Dublin's finest sites along the way (not to
mention dozens of the city's most historic pubs)—so if you can, this
is a good walk to do over the course of an entire day, or even two.

Sights to See

❷ **Bank of Ireland.** Across the street from the west facade of ☞ Trinity
College stands one of Dublin's most striking buildings: now the Bank
of Ireland, but once the original home of the Irish Parliament. The building was begun in 1729 by Sir Edward Lovett Pearce, who designed the
central section; three other architects would ultimately be involved in
its construction. A pedimented portico fronted by six massive Corinthian
columns dominates its grand facade, which follows the curve of Westmoreland Street as it meets College Green, once a Viking meeting
place and burial ground. Three years after the Parliament was abolished in 1800 under the Act of Union, which brought Ireland under
the direct rule of Britain, the building was bought for £40,000 by the
Bank of Ireland. Inside, hurricane-shape rosettes adorn the coffered ceiling in the pastel-hued, colonnaded, clerestoried **main banking hall,** once
the Court of Requests where citizens' petitions were heard. Just down
the hall is the original **House of Lords,** with tapestries depicting the
Battle of the Boyne and the Siege of Derry, an oak-paneled nave, and
a 1,233-piece Waterford glass chandelier; ask a guard to show you in.
Visitors are welcome during normal banking hours; a brief guided tour

is given every Tuesday at 10:30, 11:30, and 1:45. Accessed via Foster Place South, the small alley on the bank's east flank, the **Bank of Ireland Arts Center** frequently exhibits contemporary Irish art and has a permanent exhibition devoted to "The Story of Banking." ⊠ *2 College Green,* ☏ *01/677–6801; arts center* ☏ *01/671-1488.* ⊘ *Weekdays 10–4; Thurs. until 5; arts center Tues.–Fri. 10–4, Sat. 2–5, Sun. 10–1.*

❼ Bewley's Oriental Cafés. The granddaddies of the capital's cafés, Bewley's has been supplying Dubliners with coffee and buns since 1842 and now has four locations. Bewley's trademark stained-glass windows were designed by Harry Clarke (1889–1931), Ireland's most distinguished early-20th-century artist in this medium (you can see more of his work at Cork City's University Chapel [☞ Chapter 6]). They all make fine places in which to observe Dubliners of all ages and occupations, the aroma of coffee is irresistible, and the cafés' dark interiors—with marble-top tables, bentwood chairs, and dark-mahogany trim—evoke a more leisurely Dublin. The first floor of the Grafton Street location houses a small museum devoted to Bewley's history and is the starting point for two historic walking tours (☞ Guided Tours *in* Dublin A to Z, *below*). ⊠ *78 Grafton St.,* ☏ *01/677–6761 (all locations except Great George's St.).* ⊘ *Sun.–Thurs. 8 AM–1 AM, Fri.–Sat. 7:30 AM–4 AM;* ⊠ *13 S. Great George's St.,* ☏ *01/679–2078.* ⊘ *Mon.–Sat., 7:45 AM–6 PM, Fri.–Sat. reopen 10:30 PM–4 AM;* ⊠ *12 Westmoreland St.* ⊘ *Mon.–Sat. 7:30 AM–9 PM, Sun. 8:30 AM–9 PM;* ⊠ *40 Mary St.* ⊘ *Mon.–Sat., 7 AM–6 PM, Thursday until 9 PM.*

❺ Dublin Civic Museum. Built in 1765–71 as an exhibition hall for the Society of Artists, this building later was used as the City Assembly House, precursor of City Hall. The museum's small, esoteric collection includes Stone Age flints, Viking coins, old maps and prints of the city, and the sculptured head of British admiral Horatio Nelson, which used to top Nelson's Pillar, beside the General Post Office on O'Connell Street (☞ *below*); the column was toppled by an explosion in 1966 on the 50th anniversary of the Easter Uprising. The museum often holds exhibitions relating to the city. ⊠ *58 S. William St.,* ☏ *01/679–4260.* ▭ *Free.* ⊘ *Tues.–Sat. 10–6, Sun. 11–2.*

....

NEED A BREAK? One of Dublin's hottest haunts for the caffeine-addicted, **Kaffe Moka** (⊠ 39 S. William St., ☏ 01/679-8475) has three hyper-stylish floors and a great location in the heart of the city center.

....

㉑ Genealogical Office. The reference library here is a good place to begin your ancestor-tracing efforts. If you're a total novice at genealogical research, you can meet with an advisor (£25 for an hour consultation) who can help get you started. It also houses the **Heraldic Museum,** where displays of flags, coins, stamps, silver, and family crests highlight the uses and development of heraldry in Ireland. ⊠ *2 Kildare St.,* ☏ *01/661–8811. Genealogical Office:* ⊘ *Weekdays 10–12:30, 2–4:30. Heraldic Museum:* ▭ *Free.* ⊘ *Mon.–Wed, 10–8:30, Thurs.–Fri. 10–4:30, Sat. 10–12:30. Guided tours by appointment.*

❻ George's Street Covered Market. This Victorian covered market fills the block between Drury Street to the west and South Great George's Street to the east. It's changed little, despite a restoration. You'll find two dozen or so stalls selling books, prints, fashion, and trinkets. ⊠ *S. Great George's St.* ⊘ *Mon.–Sat. 9–6.*

....

NEED A BREAK? One of Dublin's most ornate traditional taverns, the **Long Hall Pub** (⊠ 51 S. Great George's St., ☏ 01/475-1590) has Victorian lamps, a

28

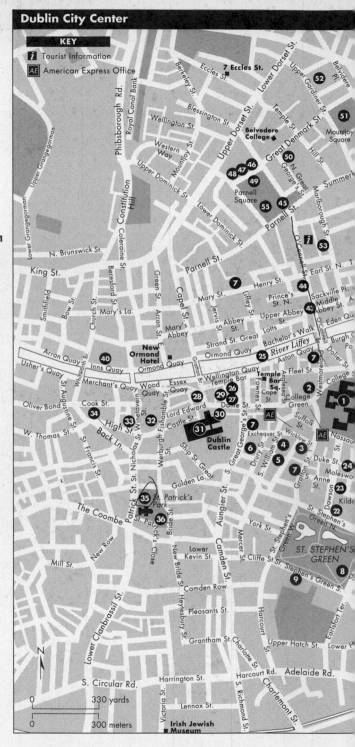

Dublin City Center

KEY

ℹ️ Tourist Information
AE American Express Office

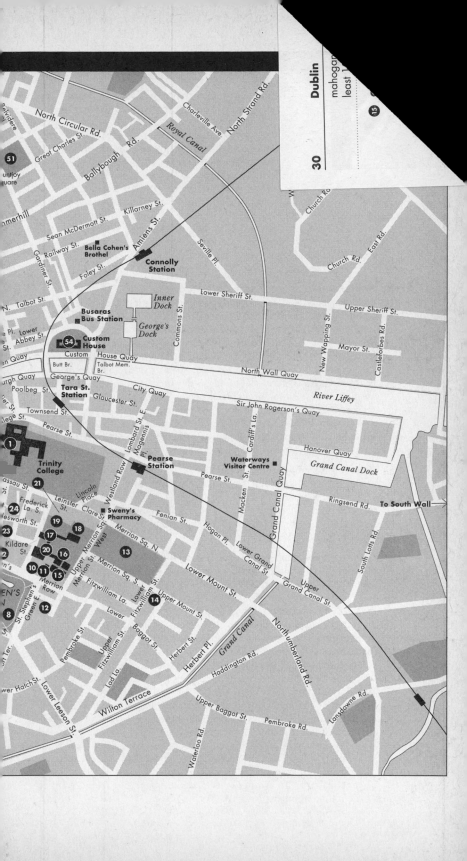

...y bar, mirrors, chandeliers, and plasterwork ceilings, all at ...00 years old. The pub serves sandwiches, beers, and whiskeys.

Government Buildings. Following a major restoration in the early 1990s, these buildings became the offices of the Department of the *taoiseach* (the prime minister, pronounced *tea*-shuck) and the *tánaiste* (the deputy prime minister, pronounced tawn-*ish*-ta). Originally designed as the College of Science in the early 1900s by Sir Aston Webb, a London architect, the building housed the University College Dublin Faculty of Engineering until 1989. Fine examples of contemporary Irish furniture and carpets now decorate the offices. A stained-glass window, known as "My Four Green Fields," was originally made by Evie Hone for the 1939 World Trade Fair in New York. It depicts the four ancient provinces of Ireland: Munster, Ulster, Leinster, and Connacht. The government offices are accessible only via guided tours given on Saturday, though they are dramatically illuminated every night. ⊠ *Upper Merrion St.,* ☎ *01/668–9333.* ⊠ *Free.* ☉ *Sat. 10:30–3:30.*

★ ③ **Grafton Street.** It's no more than 200 yards long and about 20 feet wide, but brick-lined Grafton Street, open only to pedestrians, can make a claim to be the most humming street in the city, if not in all of Ireland. It is one of Dublin's vital spines: the most direct route between the front door of Trinity College and Stephen's Green, and the city's premier shopping street, home to Dublin's two most distinguished department stores: **Brown Thomas** and **Marks & Spencer** (☞ Shopping, *below*). Both on Grafton Street itself and on the smaller alleyways that radiate off it, there are also dozens of independent stores and some of Dublin's most popular watering holes (☞ Pubs *in* Nightlife and the Arts, *below*), including a branch of ☞ **Bewley's Oriental Cafés.** In summertime buskers from all over the country and the world line both sides of the street, pouring out the sounds of drum, whistle, pipe, and string.

⑪ **Huguenot Cemetery.** One of the last such burial grounds in Dublin, this cemetery was used in the late 17th century by French Protestants who had fled persecution in their native land. The gates to the cemetery are rarely open, but you can view its grounds from the street. It stands on the northeast corner across from the square. ⊠ *27 St. Stephen's Green N.*

⑰ **Leinster House.** Built in 1745, Leinster House was the first structure in Ireland by Richard Castle, a follower of Palladio, who was to design some of the country's most important Palladian country houses (☞ Powerscourt House and Russborough *in* Chapter 3). Commissioned by the duke of Leinster, it was the largest private residence in Dublin and almost singlehandedly helped to ignite the Georgian style that dominated Dublin for 100 years. The building has two facades: the one facing Merrion Square is designed in the style of a country house; the other, on Kildare Street, is a town house. This latter facade was a major inspiration for Irishman James Hoban's designs for the White House in Washington, DC. Today it is the seat of Dáil Éireann (the House of Representatives, pronounced dawl erin) and Seanad Éireann (the Senate, pronounced shanad erin), which together constitute the Irish Parliament. When the Dáil is not in session, tours can be arranged weekdays; when the Dáil is in session, tours are available only on Mondays and Fridays. The Dáil visitors' gallery is included in the tour, although it can be accessed on days when the Dáil is in session and tours are not available. To arrange a visit, contact the public relations office at the phone number provided. ⊠ *Kildare St.,* ☎ *01/678–9911 ext. 3166 or 3066.*

㉒ **Mansion House.** Home to the mayor of Dublin, the Mansion House dates from 1710, when it was built for Joshua Dawson, who later sold the property to the government on condition that "one loaf of double refined sugar of six pounds weight" be delivered to him every Christmas. In 1919 the Declaration of Irish Independence was adopted here. The house underwent exhaustive restorations in 1996–97 and is not currently open to the public. Dawson Street (named for the house's original tenant) is the site of the annual and popular **August Antiques Fair.** ⊠ *Dawson St.*

★ ⑬ **Merrion Square.** Created between 1762 and 1764, this tranquil square a few blocks to the east of ☞ **St. Stephen's Green** is lined on three sides by some of Dublin's best-preserved Georgian town houses, many of which have brightly painted front doors over which sit intricate fanlights. Even when its flower gardens are not in bloom, the vibrant, mostly evergreen grounds, dotted with sculpture and threaded with meandering paths, are worth a walk-through. During the famine years of 1845–47, soup kitchens were established here to feed starving refugees. The square has been the home of several distinguished Dubliners, including Oscar Wilde's parents, Sir William and "Speranza" Wilde (No. 1), Irish national leader Daniel O'Connell (No. 58), and authors W. B. Yeats (Nos. 52 and 82) and Sheridan LeFanu (No. 70). Visitors can walk past the houses and read the plaques on the house facades, which identify the former inhabitants. Until 50 years ago, the square was a fashionable residential area, but today most of the houses are offices. At the south end of Merrion Square, on Upper Mount Street, stands **St. Stephen's Church.** Known locally as the "pepper canister" church because of its spire, the structure was inspired in part by Wren's churches in London. ⊠ *Merrion Sq.* ☉ *Daily sunrise–sunset.*

OFF THE
BEATEN PATH

WATERWAYS VISITOR CENTRE – A 15-minute walk down Pearse Street east of Trinity College, this imaginative information center details the history of Ireland's extensive, once vital canal system. Developed 200 years ago, the canals—the **Grand** (south of the Liffey) and the **Royal** (north of the Liffey)—connect Dublin with the Rivers Shannon and Barrow and the interior Lakelands (☞ Robertstown *in* Chapter 3). They have long since been replaced by roads for commercial activity, but they are currently undergoing redevelopment as recreational waterways. The visitor center is built on stilts on an islet of the canal system; cross the gangplank and immerse yourself in the working models, including a lock, and the descriptions of the flora and fauna that are an integral part of the canals. ⊠ *Grand Canal Quay,* ☏ *01/677-7510.* ⊡ *£2.* ☉ *June–Sept., daily 9:30–6:30; Oct.–May, Wed.–Sun. 12:30–5.*

SOUTH WALL – Even farther east of the city center than the Waterways Visitor Centre, South Wall is a long breakwater that stretches 1½ km/ 1 mi out into Dublin Bay from the Ringsend power station. The wall is punctuated at its end by **Poolbeg Lighthouse.** On a nice day, it's a wonderful place for a walk and affords stunning views of Bull Island to the north, Dublin to the west, and the entirety of the bay. It's too far to walk to the wall from the city center, and public transportation runs sporadically, so your best bet is to come out here if you have a car.

★ ⑱ **National Gallery of Ireland.** The first in a series of major civic buildings on the west side of Merrion Square, the National Gallery is one of Europe's finest smaller art museums, with more than 3,000 works. An 1854 Act of Parliament provided for the establishment of the museum, which was helped along by William Dargan (1799–1867), who was responsible for building much of Ireland's railway network in the 19th century (he is honored by a statue on the front lawn). The 1864 building was designed by Francis Fowke, who was also responsible for London's Victoria & Albert Museum. More art than ever before is on display following the completion in 1996 of a four-year renovation and expansion. Unlike Europe's largest art museums, which are almost guaranteed to induce Stendhal's syndrome, the National Gallery can be thoroughly covered in a morning or afternoon without inducing exhaustion.

The museum has a major collection of paintings by Irish artists from the 17th through 20th centuries, including works by Roderic O'Conor (1860–1940), Sir William Orpen (1878–1931), William Leech (1881–1968), and Jack B. Yeats (1871–1957), the brother of W. B. Yeats and by far the best-known Irish painter of this century. Yeats painted portraits and landscapes in an abstract expressionist style not dissimilar from that of the later Bay Area Figurative painters of the 1950s and 1960s. His *The Liffey Swim* (1923) is particularly worth seeing for its Dublin subject matter (the annual swim is still held, usually on the first weekend in September).

The collection also claims exceptional paintings from the 17th-century French, Dutch, Italian, and Spanish schools. Among the highlights that every first-time visitor should strive to see are Caravaggio's *The Taking of Christ* (1602), Velázquez's *Kitchen Maid with the Supper at Emmaus* (c. 1618, a copy of which hangs in Chicago's Art Institute), Rembrandt's *Rest on the Flight into Egypt* (1647), Poussin's *The Holy Family* (1649) and *Lamentation over the Dead Christ* (c. 1655–60), Vermeer's *Lady Writing a Letter with Her Maid* (c. 1670), and somewhat later than these, Goya's *Portrait of Doña Antonia Zárate* (c. 1810). The French Impressionists are represented with paintings by Monet, Sisley, and Pissarro. The northern wing of the gallery, with an atrium installed in 1995–96, houses the British collection and the Irish National Portrait collection, and the amply stocked **gift shop** is a good place to pick up books on Irish artists you're unlikely to find back home. You may see the early stages of construction on nearby Clare Street for an addition slated to be completed in 2000. ✉ *Merrion Sq. W,* ☎ *01/661–5133.* 🎟 *Free.* 🕙 *Mon.–Wed., Fri., and Sat. 10 –5:15; Thurs. 10–8:15; Sun. 2–5.*

NEED A BREAK? **Fitzer's** (✉ Merrion Sq. W., ☎ 01/661–4496), the National Gallery's self-service restaurant, is a find—one of the city's best spots for an inexpensive (all dishes less than £7), top-rate lunch. The 16–20 daily menu items are prepared with an up-to-date take on new European cuisine. It's open Thursday until 8 and Sunday 2—5 in addition to Monday–Saturday lunch.

⑲ **National Library.** The **main Reading Room** of the National Library opened in 1890 to house the collections of the Royal Dublin Society. Beneath its dramatic domed ceiling, countless authors have researched and written their books over the years. Virtually every book ever published in Ireland is kept here, as well as an unequaled selection of old maps and an extensive collection of Irish newspapers and magazines— more than 5 million items in all. The collection contains first editions of every major Irish writer, including books by Jonathan Swift, Oliver Goldsmith, and James Joyce, and Ireland's four recipients of the Nobel Prize for Literature: W. B. Yeats (1923), George Bernard Shaw (1925), Samuel Beckett (1969), and Seamus Heaney (1995). ✉ *Kildare St.,* ☎ *01/661–8811.* 🎟 *Free.* 🕙 *Mon. 10–9, Tues. and Wed. 2–9, Thurs. and Fri. 10–5, Sat. 10–1.*

⑯ **Natural History Museum.** Mounted mammals and birds and skeletons of Ireland's extinct, prehistoric giant deer are among the highlights of this museum, next door to the ☞ **Government Offices.** ⌧ *Merrion Sq. W,* ☎ *01/677-7444.* 🖅 *Free.* ⏱ *Tues.–Sat. 10–5, Sun. 2–5.*

★ ⑳ **National Museum.** Situated on the other side of Leinster House from the National Library, Ireland's National Museum houses a varied, comprehensive collection of Irish artifacts from 6000 BC to the present. The museum is organized around a grand rotunda and elaborately decorated, with mosaic floors, marble columns, balustrades, and fancy ironwork. The museum has the largest collection of Celtic antiquities in the world, including an astonishing array of gold jewelry, carved stones, and weapons. The Treasury collection, including some of the museum's most renowned pieces, is open permanently. Among the priceless relics on display are the 8th-century **Ardagh Chalice,** a two-handle silver cup with gold filigree ornamentation; the bronze-coated, iron **St. Patrick's Bell,** the oldest surviving example (5th–8th centuries) of Irish metalwork; the 8th-century **Tara Brooch,** an intricately decorated piece made of white bronze, amber, and glass; and the 12th-century, bejeweled oak **Cross of Cong,** covered with silver and bronze panels. Another room is devoted to the 1916 Easter Uprising and the War of Independence (1919–21); displays here include uniforms, weapons, banners, and a piece of the flag that flew over the General Post Office during Easter Week, 1916. A recent addition to the museum's collection is a permanent Viking exhibition upstairs, which features a full-size Viking skeleton, swords, and leather works recovered in Dublin and surrounding areas. In contrast to the ebullient late-Victorian architecture of the main museum building, the design of the **National Museum Annexe** is purely functional; it houses temporary shows of Irish antiquities. The 18th-century ☞ **Collins Barracks,** the most recent addition to the museum, houses the museum's collection of glass, silver, costumes, furniture, and other decorative arts. ⌧ *Kildare St.; Annexe: 7–9 Merrion Row;* ☎ *01/677–7444.* 🖅 *Free.* ⏱ *Tues.– Sat. 10–5, Sun. 2–5.*

⑨ **Newman House.** Catholic University was established in this building in 1850, with Cardinal John Henry Newman as its first rector. James Joyce describes turn-of-the-century life at this university in *A Portrait of the Artist as a Young Man.* University College, which no longer uses these houses, restored them to their original, 18th-century splendor. No. 85, the smaller of the two, has exuberant baroque plasterwork inside, while the style of No. 86 is quite different, containing rococo plasterwork, floral swags, and musical instruments. Built in 1765, they are furnished and decorated in period style. At the back of Newman House lie **Iveagh Gardens,** a delightful hideaway with statues and sunken gardens that's one of Dublin's best-kept secrets (you can enter via Earlsfort Terrace and Harcourt Street). The Commons Restaurant (☞ Dining, *below*) is in the basement. ⌧ *85–86 St. Stephen's Green,* ☎ *01/475–7255.* 🖅 *£1.* ⏱ *June–Sept., Tues.–Fri. 10–4:30, Sat. 2– 4:30, Sun. 11–2.*

⑭ **Number Twenty-Nine.** Everything in this carefully refurbished 18th-century home, known simply as Number Twenty-Nine, is in keeping with the elegant lifestyle of the Dublin middle class between 1790 and 1820, the height of the Georgian period, when the house was owned by a wine merchant's widow. From the basement to the attic, in the kitchen, nursery, servant's quarters, and the formal living areas, the National Museum of Ireland has re-created the period's style with authentic furniture, paintings, carpets, curtains, paint, wallpapers, and even bellpulls. ⌧ *29 Lower Fitzwilliam St.,* ☎ *01/702–6165.* 🖅 *Free.* ⏱ *Tues.–Sat. 10–5, Sun. 2–5.*

❹ Powerscourt Townhouse Centre. The steps on either entrance to Powerscourt lead up to an imaginative shopping arcade installed in and around the covered courtyard of a 1771 house. The stores here include high-quality Irish crafts shops and numerous food stalls (☞ Shopping, *below*). The mall exit leads to the Carmelite **Church of St. Teresa's** and **Johnson's Court.** Beside the church, a pedestrian lane leads onto Grafton Street. ⊠ *S. William St.*

⑫ RHA Gallagher Gallery. The Royal Hibernian Academy, an old Dublin institution, is now housed in one of the city's newer spaces, a large, well-lit building. The gallery holds adventurous exhibitions of the best in contemporary art, both from Ireland and abroad. ⊠ *Ely Pl. off St. Stephen's Green,* ☎ *01/661–2558.* ☞ *Free.* ☉ *Mon.–Wed., Fri., and Sat. 11–5; Thurs. 11–9; Sun. 2–5.*

㉓ Royal Irish Academy. Adjacent to the ☞ **Mansion House,** the country's leading learned society houses important manuscripts in its 18th-century library, including a large collection of ancient Irish manuscripts such as the 11th–12th century *Book of the Dun Cow* and the library of the 18th-century poet Thomas Moore. ⊠ *19 Dawson St.,* ☎ *01/ 676–2570.* ☞ *Free.* ☉ *Weekdays 10:30–5.*

★ **⑩ Shelbourne Hotel.** The ebullient, redbrick, white-wood-trimmed facade of the Shelbourne has commanded "the best address in Dublin" from the green's north side since 1824. In 1921 the Irish Free State's constitution was drafted in a first-floor suite here. The most financially painless way to soak up the hotel's old-fashioned luxury and genteel excitement is to stop in for afternoon tea in the elegantly green-wall-papered **Lord Mayor's Lounge** (£9 per person, including sandwiches and cakes) or for a drink in one of its two bars, the **Shelbourne Bar** and the **Horseshoe Bar,** both of which are thronged with businesspeople and politicos after the workday ends. (☞ Lodging, *below*). ⊠ *St. Stephen's Green,* ☎ *01/676–6471.*

㉔ St. Ann's Church (Church of Ireland). St. Ann's plain, neo-Romanesque, granite exterior, put up in 1868, belies the church's rich, Georgian interior, designed in 1720 by Isaac Wills. Among the highlights of the interior are polished-wood balconies, ornate plasterwork, and shelving in the chancel put up in 1723 and still in use for the distribution of bread to the poor of the parish. ⊠ *Dawson St.,* ☎ *01/676–7727.* ☞ *Free.* ☉ *Weekdays 10–3 and Sun. for services.*

★ **❽ St. Stephen's Green.** Dubliners call it simply Stephen's Green, and green it is (year-round)—a verdant, 27-acre city-center square that was an open common until 1663. After a long period of decline, it became a private park in 1814—the first time in its history that it was closed to the general public. Its fortunes changed again in 1880, when Sir Arthur Guinness, later Lord Ardiluan (a member of the Guinness brewery family), paid for it to be laid out anew. Flower gardens, formal lawns, a Victorian bandstand, and an ornamental lake that is home to many waterfowl are all within the park's borders, connected by paths that guarantee strolling here or just passing through will offer up unexpected delights (be sure to look out for palm trees). Among the park's many statues are a memorial to Yeats and another to Joyce by Henry Moore, and the *Three Fates,* a dramatic group of bronze female figures watching over man's destiny. In the 18th century the walk on the north side of the green was referred to as the Beaux Walk because most of Dublin's gentleman's clubs are in town houses here. Today it is dominated by the ☞ **Shelbourne Hotel.** ☞ *Free.* ☉ *Daily sunrise–sunset.*

IRISH JEWISH MUSEUM – Though Ireland has never boasted a large Jewish population (it hovers around 1,800 today), in the late 19th century and early 20th century it did become home to roughly 5,000 European Jews fleeing the pogroms of Eastern Europe. Opened in 1985 by Israeli President Chaim Herzog (himself Dublin-educated), the museum houses a restored synagogue and a display of photographs, letters, and personal memorabilia culled from Dublin's most prominent Jewish families, though the exhibits trace the Jewish presence in Ireland back to 1067. In homage to Leopold Bloom, the Jewish protagonist of Joyce's *Ulysses*, every Jewish reference in the novel has been identified. The museum is off Victoria Street near the northern shore of the Grand Canal, a 20-minute walk or so from St. Stephen's Green. ⊠ *3–4 Walworth Rd.,* ☎ *01/453-1797.* ☉ *Oct.–Apr., Sun. 10:30–2:30; May–Sept., Tues., Thurs., Sun. 11–3:30. Also by appointment.*

★ ❶ **Trinity College.** Ireland's oldest and most famous college is the heart of college-town Dublin. The campus is a must for every visitor. Trinity College, Dublin (familiarly known as TCD) was founded by Queen Elizabeth I in 1592 on the site of the confiscated Priory of All Hallows. For centuries Trinity was the preserve of the Protestant church. A free education was offered to Catholics—provided that they accepted the Protestant faith. As a legacy of this condition, until 1966 Catholics who wished to study at Trinity had to obtain a dispensation from their bishop or face excommunication. Today more than 70% of Trinity's students are Catholics, an indication of how far away those days seem to today's generation. Among the distinguished alumni of the college are Jonathan Swift, Thomas Moore, Sheridan LeFanu, George Berkeley (who gave his name to the northern California city), Oscar Wilde, John Millington Synge, Bram Stoker, and Samuel Beckett. Trinity served as a stand-in for an English university in the 1983 movie *Educating Rita.*

Trinity's grounds cover 40 acres. Most of its buildings were constructed in the 18th and early 19th centuries. The extensive **West Front,** with a classical pedimented portico in the Corinthian style, faces College Green and is directly across from the ☞ **Bank of Ireland;** recently restored, it was built between 1755 and 1759, possibly the work of Theodore Jacobsen, architect of London's Foundling Hospital. The design is repeated on the interior, so the view is the same both from outside the gates and from the quadrangle inside. On the lawn in front of the inner facade are **statues** of orator Edmund Burke and dramatist Oliver Goldsmith. Like the West Front, **Parliament Square,** the cobblestoned quadrangle that lies just beyond this first patch of lawn, also dates from the 18th century. On the right of the square, you'll find the **theater,** or **Examination Hall,** which houses an impressive organ retrieved from an 18th-century Spanish ship and a gilded, oak chandelier from the old House of Commons; concerts are sometimes held here. The **chapel,** which stands on the left of the quadrangle, has stucco ceilings and fine woodwork. Both the theater and the chapel were designed by Scotsman William Chambers in the late 18th century. The looming **Campanile,** or bell tower, erected in 1853, dominates the center of the square.

★ Ireland's largest collection of books and manuscripts is housed in **Trinity College Library.** Its principal treasure is the **Book of Kells,** generally considered the most striking manuscript ever produced in the Anglo-Saxon world. Once thought to be lost, the book is a splendidly illuminated version of the Gospels. Leading Kells scholars now believe that the book originated on the island of Iona in Scotland, where followers of St. Columba lived until the island came under siege in the early-to-mid-9th century. They fled to Kells, County Meath (☞ Chapter 3), bringing the book with them. The 680-page book was rebound in four volumes in 1953, two of which are usually displayed at a time, so you typically see no more than four original pages. (Some wags have taken to calling it the "Page of Kells.") However, all of the most lavishly illustrated pages are reproduced in the extensive exhibit dedicated to the history, artistry, and conservation of the book, through which you must pass to see the originals. At peak hours you may have to wait in line to enter the library; it's less busy early in the day.

The **Old Library,** aptly known as the **Long Room,** is a staggering 213 ft long and 42 ft wide. It contains approximately 200,000 of the 3 million volumes in Trinity's collection in its 21 alcoves. Originally the room had a flat plaster ceiling, but in 1859–60 the perennial need for more shelving resulted in a decision to raise the level of the roof and add the barrel-vaulted ceiling and the gallery bookcases. Since the 1801 Copyright Act, the college has received a copy of every book published in Britain and Ireland, and a great number of these publications must be stored in other parts of the campus and beyond. The carved Royal Arms of Queen Elizabeth I, above the library entrance, is the only surviving relic of the original college buildings. The **Trinity College Library Shop** sells books, clothing, jewelry, and postcards. ☎ *01/608–2308.* 🖃 *£3.50.* ⊘ *Mon.–Sat. 9:30–4:45; June–Sept., Sun. 9:30–4:30, Oct.– May, Sun. noon–4:30.*

Trinity College's stark, modern, Arts and Social Sciences Buildings, with an entrance on Nassau Street, houses the **Douglas Hyde Gallery of Modern Art,** which concentrates on contemporary art exhibitions and has its own bookstore. ☎ *01/677–2941, ext. 1116.* 🖃 *Free.* ⊘ *Mon.–Wed. 11–6, Thurs. 11–7, Fri. 11–6, Sat. 11–4:45.*

The **New Berkeley Library,** the main student library at Trinity, was built in 1967 and named after the philosopher and alumnus George Berkeley. The small open space in front of the library contains a spherical brass sculpture designed by Arnaldo Pomodoro. The library is not open to the general public. ✉ *College Green,* ☎ *01/677–2941.* ⊘ *Grounds daily 8 AM–10 PM.*

In the Thomas Davis Theatre in the arts building, the **"Dublin Experience"** is a 45-minute audiovisual presentation devoted to the history of the city over the last 1,000 years. ☎ *01/608–1688.* 🖃 *£2.75; in conjunction with Old Library, £5.* ⊘ *May–Oct., daily 10–5; shows every hr on the hr.*

Temple Bar

More than anywhere else in Dublin, it is Temple Bar that represents the dramatic changes and ascending fortunes of Dublin in the 1990s. Named after one of the streets of its central spine, the area was targeted for redevelopment in 1991–92 after a long period of neglect, having survived widely rumored plans to turn it into a massive bus depot and/or a giant parking lot, depending on whom you talk to. Temple Bar took off—*fast*—into Dublin's version of New York's SoHo, Paris's Bastille, London's Notting Hill: a thriving mix of high and alternative culture distinct from every other part of the city. Dotting the area's narrow cobblestone streets and pedestrian alleyways are award-winning new apartment buildings (with rents now going sky-high), vintage clothing stores, postage-stamp-size boutiques selling £200 sunglasses and other expensive gewgaws, art galleries galore, a hotel resuscitated by U2, hip restaurants, pubs, clubs, and European-style cafés, and a smattering of cultural venues. It all adds up to what the *Irish Times,* in a 1996 headline, called the "Temple of Boom."

Temple Bar's regeneration was no doubt abetted by that one surefire real estate asset: location, location, location. The area is bordered by Dame Street to the south, the Liffey to the north, Fishamble Street to the west and Westmoreland Street to the east. In fact, Temple Bar is so perfectly situated between everywhere else in Dublin that it's difficult to believe this neighborhood was once largely forsaken. It's now sometimes called the "playing ground of young Dublin," and for good reason: on weekend evenings and daily in the summer it teems with young students not only from ☞ **Trinity College**, at its eastern edge, but from throughout Europe—who fly into Dublin for the weekend, drawn by its pubs, clubs, and lively craic. Some who have witnessed Temple Bar's rapid gentrification and commercialization complain that it's fast losing its artistic soul, but there's still no denying that this is one the best places in Dublin to get a handle on the city in the '90s.

A Good Walk

Start at O'Connell Bridge and walk down Aston Quay, taking in the terrific view west down the River Liffey. Alleys and narrow roads to your left lead into Temple Bar, but hold off turning in until you get to **Ha'penny Bridge** ㉕, a Liffey landmark that's a pedestrian freeway during rush hour. Turn right and walk through Merchant's Arch, the symbolic entry into Temple Bar (see if you can spot the surveillance cameras up on the walls), which leads you onto the area's long spine, named Temple Bar here but also called Fleet Street (to the east) and Essex Street (both east and west, to the west). You're right at Temple Bar Square, one of the two largest plazas in Temple Bar. Just up on the right are two of the area's leading art galleries, the **Temple Bar Gallery** (at Lower Fownes St.) and another block up, the **Original Print Gallery** and **Blackchurch Print Studios** (☞ Art Galleries *in* Nightlife and the Arts, *below*). Turn left into Eustace Street. If you have children, you'll want to check out **The Ark** ㉖ children's cultural center, on your right. Across the street from The Ark, you may want to stop in at the **Temple Bar Information Centre** (☞ Visitor Information *in* Dublin A to Z, *below*) and pick up a handy *Temple Bar Guide* to augment our coverage. Farther down Eustace Street is the **Irish Film Centre** ㉗, Temple Bar's leading cultural venue and a great place to catch classic or new indie films. In the summer, the IFC organizes Saturday night outdoor screenings in Meeting House Square, behind the Ark, accessed via Curved Street. Dublin's leading photography gallery, the **Gallery of Photography** ㉘, is also here. From here, walk a few steps west to the narrow cobbled Sycamore Street; turn right and walk to Dame Street. The **Olympia Theatre** ㉙ is immediately to your right. Head for the corner of Parliament Street, where you can stop for a break or pick up the next tour.

TIMING
You can easily breeze through Temple Bar in an hour or so, but if you've got the time, plan to spend a morning or afternoon here, drifting in and out of its dozens of stores and galleries, relaxing at a café over a cup of coffee or at a pub over a pint, maybe even seeing a film if you're looking for a break from sightseeing.

Sights to See

ᶜ♨ ㉖ **The Ark.** If you're traveling with children and you're looking for something fun to do, be sure to stop by the Ark, Ireland's first purpose-built children's cultural center housed in a former Presbyterian church. Its theater opens onto Meeting House Square for outdoor performances during the summer. A gallery and workshop space host ongoing activities. ⊠ *Eustace St.,* ☎ *01/670–7788.* ⌸ *Free.* ☉ *Mon.–Fri. 9:30– 4, Sat. 10–4.*

38

Dublin West

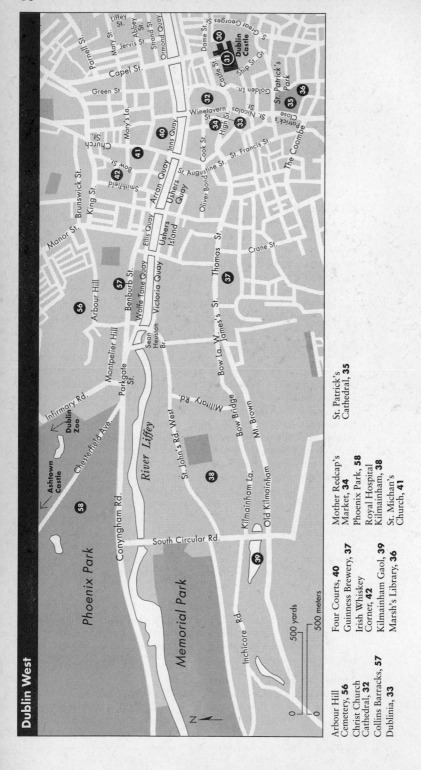

Arbour Hill
Cemetery, **56**
Christ Church
Cathedral, **32**
Collins Barracks, **57**
Dublinia, **33**

Four Courts, **40**
Guinness Brewery, **37**
Irish Whiskey
Corner, **42**
Kilmainham Gaol, **39**
Marsh's Library, **36**

Mother Redcap's
Market, **34**
Phoenix Park, **58**
Royal Hospital
Kilmainham, **38**
St. Michan's
Church, **41**

St. Patrick's
Cathedral, **35**

28 **Gallery of Photography.** Opened in 1995 in an innovative building in Temple Bar's Meeting House Square, Dublin's premier photography gallery has a permanent collection of turn-of-the-century Irish photography and also puts on monthly exhibits of contemporary Irish and international photographers. Every Saturday night from June through August, a screen incorporated into its facade is unfurled for a free outdoor film screening organized by the ☞ **Irish Film Center.** The bookstore is the best place in the city to browse for photography books and pick up arty photography postcards. ⊠ *Meeting House Sq. S,* ☎ *01/ 671–4654.* ☉ *Free.* ☎ *Varies with exhibitions.* ☉ *Mon.–Sat. 11–6.*

25 **Ha'penny Bridge.** This heavily trafficked footbridge crosses the Liffey at a prime spot: Temple Bar is on the south side, and the bridge provides the fastest route to the thriving Mary and Henry street shopping areas to the north (☞ Shopping, *below*). Until early in this century, a half-penny toll was charged to cross it. Yeats was one among many Dubliners who found this too high a price to pay—more a matter of principle than of finance—and so made the detour via O'Connell Bridge.

27 **Irish Film Centre (IFC).** The opening of the IFC in a beautifully restored former Quaker meeting house in 1992 helped to launch the revitalization of Temple Bar. Two comfortable art-house cinemas that show revivals and new independent films; the Irish Film Archive; a bookstore for cineasts; and a bar make this one of the neighborhood's most vital cultural institutions. ⊠ *6 Eustace St.,* ☎ *01/679–5744.* ☎ *Free.* ☉ *Weekdays 9:30–late, weekends 11–late.*

★ **29** **Olympia Theatre.** Recognized as one of the best places anywhere in Europe to see live musical acts, the Olympia is Dublin's second oldest and one of its busiest theaters. Built in 1879, this classic Victorian music hall has a gorgeous, red, wrought-iron facade. Conveniently, two pubs are situated through doors directly off the back of the theater's orchestra section. The Olympia's longstanding Friday and Saturday series, "Midnight at the Olympia," has brought a wide array of musical performers to Dublin, and the theater has also seen many notable actors strut its stage, including Alec Guinness, Peggy Ashcroft, Noël Coward, and even Laurel and Hardy. In November 1996, when Van Morrison played Dublin, he chose to perform here rather than in a bigger venue. If you have a chance to catch a favorite performer (or to discover someone new), go!—you're unlikely to regret it. ⊠ *72 Dame St.,* ☎ *01/677– 7744.*

| NEED A BREAK? | By day **Thomas Read's** (⊠ 123 Parliament St., at Dame St., ☎ 01/ 677–1487) is a European-style café, by night, it's a pub. Its large windows overlooking City Hall and a busy corner in Temple Bar make it a great spot for people-watching. The menu includes bagels, tasty pastries, and baguette sandwiches. The coffees are particularly good. |

Dublin Castle, Christ Church Cathedral, and West Dublin

Dublin is so compact that to separate out the following sites from those covered in our two other city-center southside tours is to potentially mislead by suggesting that this area is at some remove from the heart of the city center. In fact, this tour's starting point, City Hall, is just across the street from Thomas Read's, and Christ Church Cathedral is a very short walk farther west. However, the westernmost sites covered here—notably the Royal Hospital and Kilmainham Gaol—*are* at some distance—more so than may be comfortable if you're not an enthusiastic walker, so you may want to drive or catch a cab or a bus out to them.

A Good Walk

Begin with a brief visit to **City Hall** ㉚, then walk up Cork Hill to the Castle Street entrance to **Dublin Castle** ㉛, whose highlights are only visitable via a guided tour. Leave via the same gate, turn left and walk up Castle Street to **Christ Church Cathedral** ㉜. At the southeast corner of the cathedral, connected via an old bridge, **Dublinia** ㉝ offers a chance to experience life in medieval Dublin. Another block farther west, **Mother Redcap's Market** ㉞ is worth a visit, as is **St. Patrick's Cathedral** ㉟, reached via Nicholas Street, which begins opposite Dublinia. Enthusiasts of old books should pay a visit to **Marsh's Library** ㊱, just next door to St. Patrick's. You can then stroll through the old artisan redbrick dwellings in the Liberties, home to the heaviest concentration of the city's antiques stores, to Thomas Street and the **Guinness Brewery** ㊲. At this point, architecture and modern art buffs should proceed farther west to the **Irish Museum of Modern Art,** housed in the **Royal Hospital Kilmainham** ㊳, and **Kilmainham Gaol** ㊴. If you don't elect to head this way, turn back down Thomas Street, crossing the Liffey at Bridge Street, which on its north side becomes Church Street. On your left is the **Four Courts** ㊵, just up on the left is **St. Michan's Church** ㊶, and a quick jog over to Bow Street (via Mary's Lane) is the **Irish Whiskey Corner** ㊷.

TIMING

Leave yourself a few hours, especially if you want to visit the Guinness Brewery and the Irish Museum of Modern Art at the Royal Hospital. Keep in mind that if you want to cover the easternmost sites—Dublin Castle, City Hall, Christ Church Cathedral and environs—you can easily append these sites onto a tour of Temple Bar.

Sights to See

★ ㉜ **Christ Church Cathedral.** The first Christianized Danish king built a wooden church at this site in 1038. Construction on the present Christ Church—the flagship of the Church of Ireland and one of two Protestant cathedrals in Dublin (the other is ☞ St. Patrick's just to the south)—was begun in 1172 by Strongbow, a Norman baron and conqueror of Dublin for the English crown, and went on for 50 years. By 1875 the cathedral had deteriorated badly; a drastic renovation to the exterior gave it much the look it has today. Remains from the 12th-century building include the north wall of the nave, the west bay of the choir, and the fine stonework of the transepts, with their pointed arches and supporting columns. Strongbow himself is buried in the cathedral beneath an impressive effigy. The vast, sturdy **crypt,** with its 12th- and 13th-century vaults, is Dublin's oldest surviving architecture and the building's most notable feature. ✉ *Christ Church Pl. and Winetavern St.,* ☎ *01/677–8099.* ☉ *Mon.–Sat. 10–5:30, Sun. between church services.*

㉚ **City Hall.** Prominently situated facing the Liffey from Cork Hill at the top of Parliament Street, this grand Georgian municipal building (1769–79), once the Royal Exchange, marks the southwestern corner of Temple Bar. Today it is the seat of the Dublin Corporation, the elected body that governs the city. Twelve columns encircle the domed central rotunda, which has a fine mosaic floor and 12 frescoes depicting Dublin legends and ancient Irish historical scenes. Just off the rotunda is a gently curving staircase, a typical feature of most large Dublin town houses. ✉ *Cork Hill,* ☎ *01/679–6111.* ✍ *Free.* ☉ *Weekdays 9–1, 2:15–5.*

㉛ **Dublin Castle.** Seat and symbol of the British rule of Ireland for seven and a half centuries, Dublin Castle figured largely in Ireland's turbulent history earlier this century. (Neil Jordan's film *Michael Collins* captured the castle's near-indomitable status.) After extensive renovations, it is now used mostly for Irish and EU governmental purposes. The sprawling **Great Courtyard** is the reputed site of the Black Pool (Dubh Linn, pronounced *doov*-lin) from which Dublin got its name, though today it is lined with stretch limos and security guards. In the Lower Castle Yard, the **Record Tower,** the earliest of several towers on the site, is the largest remaining relic of the original Norman buildings, built by King John between 1208 and 1220. Guided tours are offered around the principal **State Apartments** (on the southern side of the Upper Castle Yard), formerly the residence of the English viceroys. Now used by the president of Ireland to host visiting heads of state and EU ministers, they are lavishly furnished with rich Donegal carpets and illuminated by Waterford glass chandeliers. The largest and most impressive of these chambers, **St. Patrick's Hall,** with its gilt pillars and painted ceiling, is used for the inauguration of Irish presidents. The **Round Drawing Room,** in Bermingham Tower, dates from 1411 and was rebuilt in 1777; a number of Irish leaders have been imprisoned in the tower, from the 16th century to the early 20th century. The blue oval **Wedgwood Room** contains Chippendale chairs and a marble fireplace.

Also on the grounds of the castle is the **Church of the Holy Trinity** (formerly called Chapel Royal), designed in 1814 by Francis Johnston, who also designed the original ☞ **General Post Office** building on O'Connell Street. Carved oak panels and stained glass depicting viceroys' coats of arms grace the interior. Look up to view the elaborate array of fan vaults that decorates the ceiling. On the outside more than 100 carved heads adorn the walls. St. Peter and Jonathan Swift preside over the north door; St. Patrick and Brian Boru over the east. One-hour guided tours of the castle are offered every half hour, but the rooms are closed when in official use, so phone first. The easiest way in to the castle today is via the **Cork Hill Gate,** just west of City Hall. ✉ *Castle St.,* ☎ *01/ 677–7129.* 🎫 *State Apartments £2 including tour.* ☉ *Weekdays 10– 5; weekends 2–5.*

🖑 ㉝ **Dublinia.** In the old Synod Hall (formerly a meeting place for bishops of the Church of Ireland), attached via a bridge to ☞ **Christ Church Cathedral,** this is an entertaining and informative reconstruction of everyday life in medieval Dublin. The main exhibits use high-tech audiovisual and computer techniques; there are also a scale model of what Dublin was like around 1500, a medieval maze, and a fine view from the tower. Prints by the 18th-century artist/architect James Malton line the walls of the coffee shop. ✉ *St. Michael's Hill,* ☎ *01/679–4611.* 🎫 *Exhibit and cathedral £3.95.* ☉ *Apr.–Sept., daily 10–5; Oct.–Mar., Mon.–Sat. 11–4, Sun. 10–4:30.*

㊵ **Four Courts.** Today the seat of the High Court of Justice of Ireland, the Four Courts are James Gandon's second Dublin masterpiece, built between 1786 and 1802, close on the heels of his ☞ **Custom House,** downstream on the same side of the River Liffey. The Four Courts replaced a 13th-century Dominican abbey that earlier stood here. In 1922, during the Irish Civil War, the Four Courts was almost totally destroyed by shelling, and the adjoining Public Records Office was gutted, with many of its priceless legal documents destroyed, including innumerable family records; restoration to the building's original style took 10 years. Today the stately Corinthian portico and the circular central hall are worth viewing. Its distinctive copper-covered dome atop a colonnaded rotunda makes this one of Dublin's most instantly recognizable buildings; the view from the rotunda is terrific. ⊠ *Inns Quay,* ☎ *01/ 872–5555.* ✆ *Daily 10:30–4.*

★ ㊲ **Guinness Brewery.** Founded by Arthur Guinness in 1759, Ireland's all-dominating brewer—in fact, the largest stout-producing brewery in the world—is situated on a 60-acre spread to the west of Christ Church Cathedral. Not surprisingly, it is the most popular tourist destination in town. The brewery itself is closed to the public, but the 19th-century **Hop Store,** part museum and part gift shop, puts on an 18-minute audiovisual presentation. The show ends with the curtain rising on the kind of old-fashioned pub—with mahogany decor, mirrors, and snugs—that has become hard to find in modern Dublin. Visitors receive two complimentary glasses (or one pint) of the famous black stout. A gift shop sells the best of Guinness memorabilia: posters, bar towels, beer mats, and garments. ⊠ *Crane St.,* ☎ *01/453–3645.* ✆ *£3.* ✆ *Apr.– Sept., Mon.–Sat. 9:30–5, Sun. 10:30–4:30; Oct.–Mar., Mon.–Sat. 9:30–4, Sun. noon–4.*

㊷ **Irish Whiskey Corner.** Jameson's Whiskey Distillery was built here in 1791. After local distilleries merged in 1966 to form Irish Distillers, part of the old Jameson's complex was converted into the new group's head office, and one of the bonded warehouses was turned into a whiskey museum. Visitors can watch a short audiovisual history of the industry, which actually had its origins 1,500 years ago in Middle Eastern perfume making. Mementos of whiskey making on display include antique posters and a large scale model of an old distillery; you can also view a reconstruction of a former warehouse, where the colorful nicknames of former barrel makers are recorded. There's a compulsory guided tour, audiovisual show, and a complimentary tasting; four attendees are invited to taste different brands of Irish whiskey and compare them against bourbon and Scotch. (If you have a large group and everyone wants to do this, phone in advance to arrange it.) ⊠ *Bow St.,* ☎ *01/872–5566.* ✆ *Tour £3.* ✆ *Tours: May–Oct., weekdays 11, 2:30, 3:30, Sat. 2:30, 3:30, Sun. 3:30; Nov.–Apr., weekdays 3:30. Also by appointment.*

㊴ **Kilmainham Gaol.** Even farther west than the Royal Hospital, this is a grim, forbidding structure where leaders of the 1916 Easter Uprising, including Patrick Pearse and James Connolly, were held before being executed in the prison yard. In the 19th century, other inmates here were the revolutionary Robert Emmet and Charles Stewart Parnell, a leading politician (☞ Avondale House *in* Chapter 3). You can visit the cells, a chilling sight, while the guided tour and a 30-minute audiovisual presentation relate a graphic account of Ireland's political history over the past 200 years from a nationalist viewpoint. ⊠ *Inchicore Rd.,* ☎ *01/453–5984.* ✆ *£1.50.* ✆ *May–Sept., daily 9:30–6; Oct.–Apr., weekdays 9:30–5, Sun. 10–6.*

㊱ **Marsh's Library.** A short walk west from St. Stephen's Green and accessed through a tiny but charming cottage garden lies a gem of old Dublin: the city's—and Ireland's—first public library, founded and endowed in 1701 by Narcissus Marsh, the Archbishop of Dublin, then open to "All Graduates and Gentlemen." The two-story, brick, Georgian building has been practically unchanged inside since it was built. It houses a priceless collection of 200 manuscripts and 25,000 16th- to 18th-century books. Many of these rare volumes are locked inside cages, as are any readers who wish to look at them. The cages were to discourage students who, often impecunious, may have been tempted to make the books their own. The library has recently been restored with great attention to its original architectural details, especially in

the book stacks. ⊠ *St. Patrick's Close off Patrick St.,* ☎ *01/454–3511.*
⊙ *Mon., Wed.–Fri. 10–12:45 and 2–5, Sat. 10:30–12:45.*

③④ **Mother Redcap's Market.** This charming covered market sells everything
from linen, old vinyl LP's, antiques, and secondhand books to palm readings and Irish crafts. ⊠ *High St.* ☒ *Free.* ⊙ *Fri.–Sun. 11–6.*

★ ③⑧ **Royal Hospital Kilmainham.** A short ride by taxi or bus from the city
center, this is regarded as the most important 17th-century building in
Ireland. Completed in 1684 as a hospice for 300 disabled and veteran
soldiers, it is a replica of Les Invalides in Paris. It survived into the 1920s
as a hospital, but after the founding of the Irish Free State in 1922, the
building fell into disrepair. Over the last 15 years, a huge restoration
program has returned the entire edifice to what it once was. The structure consists of four galleries around a courtyard with a grand dining
hall, 100 ft long by 50 ft wide. The architectural highlight is the hospital's Baroque **chapel,** distinguished by its extraordinary plasterwork
ceiling and fine wood carvings. "There is nothing in Ireland from the
17th century that can come near this masterpiece," raves cultural historian John FitzMaurice Mills. Today the Royal Hospital houses the
Irish Museum of Modern Art, opened in 1991. The museum displays
works by non-Irish, 20th-century greats like Picasso and Miró but concentrates on the work of Irish artists. Richard Deacon, Richard Gor-
man, Dorothy Cross, Sean Scully, Matt Mullican, Louis Le Brocquy,
and James Colman are among the contemporary Irish artists represented.
The self-serve Café Musée has soups, sandwiches, and other light fare.
⊠ *Kilmainham La.,* ☎ *01/671–8666.* ☒ *Royal Hospital free, but individual shows may have separate charges; Museum of Modern Art
permanent collection free, small charge for special exhibitions.* ⊙
*Royal Hospital Tues.–Sat. 10–5:30, Sun. noon–5:30, tour every ½ hr;
Museum of Modern Art Tues.–Sat. 10–5:30, Sun. noon–5:30; museum
tours Wed., Fri. 2:30, Sat. 11:30.*

④① **St. Michan's Church.** Built in 1685 on the site of an older, 11th-cen-
tury Danish church, this Anglican church, architecturally undistinguished except for its 120-ft bell tower, features an 18th-century organ,
supposedly played by Handel, and the Stool of Repentance, the only
one still in existence in the city; parishioners who were termed "open
and notoriously naughty livers" used it to do public penance. St.
Michan's main claim to notoriety, however, is down in the vaults,
where the totally dry atmosphere has preserved a number of corpses
in a remarkable state of mummification. They lie in open caskets, and
strong-hearted visitors can shake hands with a former religious cru-
sader or nun. Most of the preserved bodies are thought to have been
Dublin tradespeople. ⊠ *Church St.,* ☎ *01/872–4154.* ☒ *£1.20.* ⊙ *Apr.–
Oct, weekdays 10–12:45 and 2–4:45, Sat. 10–12:45; Nov.–Mar.,
Mon.–Sat. 10–12:45.*

③⑤ **St. Patrick's Cathedral.** The largest cathedral in Dublin and also the
national cathedral of the Church of Ireland, St. Patrick's is the second
of the capital's two Protestant cathedrals (the other is ☞ **Christ
Church**). Legend has it that St. Patrick baptized many converts at a
well on the site of the cathedral in the 5th century. The original building, dedicated in 1192 and early English Gothic in style, was an unsuccessful attempt to assert supremacy over Christ Church Cathedral.
At 305 ft, it is the longest church in the country. In the 17th century,
Oliver Cromwell, dour ruler of England and no friend of the Irish, had
his troops stable their horses in the cathedral. It wasn't until the 1860s
that restoration work to repair the damage was begun, financed by Sir
Benjamin Guinness, of the brewing family. The most famous of St.
Patrick's many illustrious deans was Jonathan Swift, author of *Gul-*

liver's Travels, who held office from 1713 to 1745. **Swift's tomb** is in the south aisle; a corner at the top of the north transept commemorates him. Other memorials include the 17th-century **Boyle Monument,** with its numerous painted figures of family members, and the **monument to Turlough O'Carolan,** the last of the Irish bards and one of the country's finest harp players. To the immediate north of the cathedral is a small park, with statues of many of Dublin's literary figures and the small well said to have been used by St. Patrick. ✉ *Patrick St.,* ☎ *01/475–4817.* 🎫 *£1.20.* ⏲ *May.–Oct., weekdays 9–6, Sat. 9–5, Sun. 10–11, 12:30–3; Nov.–Apr., weekdays 9–6, Sat. 9–4, Sun. 10:30–11, 12:30–3.*

Northside City Center

Today the northside—a mix of densely thronged shopping streets and run-down sections of once genteel homes—is a less appealing part of town to spend time as a visitor than the southside of the city, but it still absolutely warrants a walk for three reasons: its two major cultural institutions, the number of sites of significance with ties to Irish Republicanism, and its busy streets. During the 18th century, most of the upper echelons of Dublin society lived in the Georgian houses around Mountjoy Square and shopped along Capel Street, which was lined with fine furniture and silver stores. The construction of Merrion Square on the southside (completed in 1764) and nearby Fitzwilliam Square (completed in 1825) decisively and permanently changed the northside's fortunes. The city's fashionable social center crossed the Liffey, and although some of the northside's illustrious inhabitants clung to their houses, this area gradually became more run-down. The northside's fortunes may be beginning to change, though. Once-derelict swaths of houses, especially on and near the Liffey, are being rehabilitated, and a large new shopping center opened on Mary Street in late 1996. Still, the redevelopment that has swept through Temple Bar is only in its early stages here, but precisely because it's a place on the cusp of transition, it's an interesting part of town to visit.

A Good Walk

Begin at O'Connell Bridge, heading north up **O'Connell Street** ㊸ and stopping to admire the monument to Daniel O'Connell, then continue north to the **General Post Office** ㊹ (known as the GPO), a major sight in the Easter Uprising of 1916. O'Connell leads to the southeastern corner of Parnell Square. Heading counterclockwise around the square, you'll pass in turn the **Gate Theatre** ㊺ and **Abbey Presbyterian Church** ㊻ before coming to the **Dublin Writers Museum** ㊼ and the **Hugh Lane Municipal Gallery of Modern Art** ㊽, both on the north side of the square; these are the two sites where you should plan to spend the most of your time on the northside. Either before you go in or after you come out, you might want to visit the solemn yet serene **Garden of Remembrance** ㊾.

From here, you have two choices: either to continue exploring the cultural sights that lie to the northeast of Parnell Square and east of O'-Connell Street, or to head to Moore, Henry, and Mary streets for a flavor of middle-class Dublin that you don't get on the spiffier southside. If you decide to continue your cultural explorations, jump two blocks northeast of Parnell Square to the **James Joyce Cultural Centre** ㊿, then head farther northeast to the once glamorous **Mountjoy Square** (51). From here, turn south, stopping in at the **St. Francis Xavier Church** (52) on Gardiner Street. Head back west to Marlborough Street (parallel to and between Gardiner and O'Connell streets) to visit the **Pro-Cathedral** (53). Continue down to the quays and jog a block east to the **Custom House** ⑤, recently opened to the public. If you decide to shop with the locals, leave Parnell Square via the southwestern corner, stopping first to check out the chapel at the **Rotunda Hospital** ⑤. Moore Street is your first left off Parnell Street and leads directly to Henry Street. Just follow the crowds from here.

TIMING

The northside has fewer major attractions than the southside of the city and, overall, is less picturesque. As a result, you're unlikely to want to stroll as leisurely here. If you zipped right through this walk, you could be done in less than two hours. But the two major cultural institutions covered here—the Dublin Writers Museum and the Hugh Lane Municipal Gallery of Modern Art—both easily deserve several hours, so it's worth doing this walk only if you have the time to devote to them. Also, a number of additional sights connected with James Joyce and *Ulysses*—covered in ☞ **"ReJoyce! A Walk through *Ulysses* and James Joyce's Dublin"**—are in the vicinity, so if you're a devoted Joycean, you should consult that essay before setting out on this walk.

Sights to See

㊻ Abbey Presbyterian Church. Completed in 1864, this church on the northeast corner of Parnell Square is popularly known as Findlater's Church, after Alex Findlater, a noted Dublin grocer who endowed it. A soaring spire marks the exterior; the inside has a stark Presbyterian atmosphere, despite stained-glass windows and ornate pews. For a bird's-eye view, take the small staircase that leads to the balcony. ⊠ *Parnell Sq.*

㊿ Custom House. Extending 375 ft on the north side of the Liffey, this is the city's most spectacular Georgian building, the work of James Gandon, an English architect who arrived in Ireland in 1781, when construction commenced here (it continued for 10 years). The central portico is linked by arcades to the pavilions at either end. A statue of Commerce tops the graceful copper dome; statues on the main facade are based on allegorical themes. Republicans set the building on fire in 1921, but it was completely restored and now houses government offices. The building opened to the public in mid-1997 after having been closed for many years, and with it came a new exhibition that traces the building's history and significance. ⊠ *Custom House Quay,* ☎ *01/878–7660.* ⊡ *£2.* ☉ *Weekdays 10–5, weekends 2–5.*

★ ㊼ Dublin Writers Museum. A restored 18th-century town house on the north side of Parnell Square that was once the home of John Jameson, of the Irish whiskey family, is now one of Dublin's best cultural sights. Rare manuscripts, diaries, posters, letters, limited and first editions, photographs, and other mementoes commemorate the life and works of the nation's greatest writers (and there are *many* of them, so leave plenty of time) including Joyce, Shaw, Wilde, J. M. Synge, Lady Gregory, Yeats, Beckett, and many others. Readings are periodically held in the upstairs drawing rooms, gorgeously decorated with paintings and bas-relief wall decorations. The bookshop and café make this an ideal place to spend a rainy afternoon. If you lose track of time and stay until closing time, you might want to dine at Chapter One, a highly regarded restaurant in the basement (☞ Dining, *below*). ⊠ *18 Parnell Sq. N,* ☎ *01/872–2077.* ⊡ *£2.75.* ☉ *Mon.–Sat. 10–5, Sun. 11:30–6.*

㊾ Garden of Remembrance. Opened in 1966, 50 years after the Easter Uprising, the garden, located within Parnell Square, commemorates all those who died fighting for Irish freedom. A large plaza is at the garden's entrance; steps lead down to the fountain area, graced with a sculpture by contemporary Irish artist Oisín Kelly based on the mytho-

logical Children of Lír, who were turned into swans. ⊠ *Parnell Sq.*
☺ *Daily 9–5.*

④⑤ Gate Theatre. The Gate has been one of Dublin's most important theaters since its founding in 1928 by Micháel MacLiammóir and Hilton
Edwards, who also founded Galway City's An Taibhdhearc as the national Irish-language theater (☞ Chapter 7). Many innovative productions by Irish playwrights have been staged here, and Dublin
audiences have encountered foreign playwrights and actors here for
the first time, including Orson Welles and James Mason, who both performed here early in their careers. Today the theater regularly stages
the major repertory of European drama and is particularly committed
to producing the work of young Irish dramatists. ⊠ *Cavendish Row,*
☎ *01/874–4045.*

④④ General Post Office. The GPO is one of the great civic buildings of
Dublin's Georgian era, but its fame derives from the role it played during the Easter Uprising. Here, on Easter Monday, 1916, the Republican forces, about 2,000 in number, and under the guidance of Patrick
Pearse and James Connolly, stormed the building and issued the Proclamation of the Irish Republic. After a week of shelling, the GPO lay in
ruins; 13 rebels were ultimately executed. Most of the original building was destroyed, though the facade—designed by the neoclassical architect Francis Johnston in the early 1800s—survived (you can still see
the scars of bullets on the its pillars). Rebuilt and subsequently reopened
in 1929, it is still a working post office, with an attractive two-story
main concourse. A bronze sculpture depicting the dying Cuchulainn,
a leader of the Red Branch Knights in Celtic mythology, sits in the front
window. The 1916 Proclamation and the names of its signatories are
inscribed on the green marble plinth. ⊠ *O'Connell St.,* ☎ *01/872–
8888.* ☺ *Mon.–Sat. 8–8, Sun. 10:30–6.*

★ **④⑧ Hugh Lane Municipal Gallery of Modern Art.** Built originally as a town
house for the earl of Charlemont in 1762, the Hugh Lane Gallery was
named after a nephew of Lady Gregory (Yeats's aristocratic patron;
☞ Coole Park *in* Chapter 7) who drowned on the *Lusitania,* which
was sunk by the Germans off the coast of County Cork in 1915. Lane
collected both Impressionist paintings and 19th-century Irish and
Anglo-Irish works. A complicated agreement with the National Gallery
in London stipulates that a portion of the 39 French paintings amassed
by Lane shuttle back and forth between London and here. Until 1999,
you can see Courbet's *The Diligence in the Snow,* Manet's *La Concert
aux Tuileries,* Degas's *Beach Scene,* and Vuillard's *The Mantelpiece,*
but not the painting that is widely regarded as the masterpiece of the
collection, Renoir's *The Umbrellas,* which won't be back in Dublin until
1999. Paintings by Degas, Bonnard, and Corot are permanently on display.

Between the ☞ **National Gallery of Ireland**'s collection of Irish paintings and the superlative works here, you can quickly become familiar
with Irish 20th-century art if you aren't already. The Irish artists represented here include Roderic O'Conor, to whom an entire room has
been newly devoted; Paul Henry, well known for his views of the west
of Ireland; William Leech, including his *Girl with a Tinsel Scarf* (c. 1912)
and *The Cigarette*; and the most famous of the group, Jack B. Yeats
(W. B.'s brother). The museum has a dozen of his paintings, including
Ball Alley (c. 1927) and *There Is No Night* (1949). There's also strikingly displayed stained-glass work by early-20th-century Irish master
artisans Harry Clarke and Evie Hone. ⊠ *Parnell Sq. N,* ☎ *01/874–
1903.* ▣ *Free.* ☺ *Tues.–Fri. 9:30–6, Sat. 9:30–5, Sun. 11–5.*

50 James Joyce Cultural Centre. Recently opened to the general public, this restored, 18th-century Georgian town house, once the dancing academy of Professor Denis J. Maginni, is a center for Joycean studies and events related to the author. It has an extensive library and archives, exhibition rooms, a bookstore, and a café. Along with the ☞ **Joyce Museum** in Sandycove, the center is the main organizer of "Bloomstime," which marks the week leading up to June 16's Bloomsday celebrations. ⊠ *35 N. Great George's St.,* ☎ *01/878–8547.* ◪ *£2.50.* ◷ *Mon.–Sat. 9:30–5, Sun. 12:30–5.*

51 Mountjoy Square. Built in the mid-18th century, this square was once surrounded by elegant, terraced houses, but today only the northern side remains intact. The once-derelict southern side has recently been restored and converted into apartments. Irishman Brian Boru, who led his soldiers to victory against the Vikings in the Battle of Clontarf in 1014, was said to have pitched camp before the confrontation on the site of Mountjoy Square. Playwright Sean O'Casey once lived here at No. 35 and used the square as a setting for *The Shadow of a Gunman.*

43 O'Connell Street. Dublin's most famous thoroughfare, 150 feet wide, was previously known as Sackville Street, but its name was changed in 1924, two years after the founding of the Irish Free State. After the devastation of the 1916 Easter Uprising, the street had to be almost entirely reconstructed, a job that took until the end of the 1920s. The main attraction of the street, **Nelson's Pillar,** a Doric column towering over the city center and a marvelous vantage point, was blown up in 1966, the 50th anniversary of the Easter Uprising. The large **monument** at the south end of the street is dedicated to Daniel O'Connell (1775–1847), "The Liberator," and was erected in 1854 as a tribute to the orator's achievement in securing Catholic Emancipation in 1829. Seated, winged figures represent the four "Victories,"—courage, eloquence, fidelity, and patriotism—all exemplified by O'Connell. Ireland's four ancient provinces—Munster, Leinster, Ulster, and Connacht—are identified by their respective coats of arms. **O'Connell Bridge,** the main bridge spanning the Liffey (wider than it is long) marks the street's southern end. As you cross the Liffey, look for the **Millennium Clock** buried in the water on the west side of the bridge. The clock, known to Dubliners as "the time in the slime," was installed in 1996 and is counting down the days, hours, minutes, and seconds, until the next millennium.

NEED A BREAK?

There are a number of good alternatives for a break on the northside: One of Dublin's oldest hotels, the **Gresham** (⊠ Upper O'Connell St, ☎ 01/874–6881) is a pleasant old-fashioned spot for a morning coffee or afternoon tea. **Conway's** (⊠ Parnell St. near Upper O'Connell St., ☎ 01/873–2687), founded in 1745, is reputed to be Dublin's second-oldest pub. Among its antique furnishings is a real gem: a 130-year-old, eight-day grandfather clock. For a real Irish pub lunch, stop in at **John M. Keating** pub (⊠ 14 Mary St./23 Jervis St., ☎ 01/873–1567), at the corner of Mary and Jervis streets. Head upstairs where you can sit at a low table and chat with locals as you warm up with a bowl of soup and nibble on a sandwich.

53 Pro-Cathedral. Dublin's principal Catholic cathedral was built between 1815 and 1825. Although the severely classical church design is on a suitably epic scale, the building was never granted full cathedral status, nor has the identity of its architect ever been discovered; the only clue is in the church ledger, which lists a "Mr. P." as the builder. The church's facade, with a six-pillared portico, is based on the Temple of Theseus in Athens; the interior is modeled after the Grecian-Doric

REJOYCE! A WALK THROUGH JAMES JOYCE'S DUBLIN AND *ULYSSES*

JAMES JOYCE'S genius for fashioning high art out of his day-to-day life brought him literary immortality and makes him, even today, the world's most famous Dubliner. He set all of his major works—*Dubliners, A Portrait of the Artist as a Young Man, Ulysses,* and *Finnegan's Wake*—in the city where he was born and spent the first 22 years of his life, and although he spent the next 36 in self-imposed exile, he never wrote about anywhere else. Joyce knew and remembered Dublin in such detail that he claimed that if the city were destroyed, it could be rebuilt in its entirety from his written works.

Joyceans flock to Dublin annually on June 16 to commemorate **Bloomsday,** the day in 1904 on which Leopold Bloom wanders through the city in *Ulysses.* Why *this* day? It had been an important one for Joyce—when he and his wife-to-be, Nora Barnacle, had their first date. Today Bloomsday has evolved into "Bloomstime," with events taking place in the days leading up to the 16th, then all day and well into the night. Even if you don't make it to Dublin on Bloomsday, you can still roam its streets, sniffing out Bloom's—and Joyce's—haunts.

Begin in the heart of the northside, on **Prince's Street,** next to the ☞ **GPO,** where the office of the old and popular *Freeman's Journal* newspaper (published 1763–1924) was located before it was destroyed during the 1916 Easter Uprising. Bloom was a newspaper advertisement canvasser for the *Journal.* Leopold and Molly Bloom's fictional home stood at **7 Eccles Street,** north of Parnell Square. On Great Denmark Street, **Belvedere College** (☎ 01/677–

4795) is housed in a well-preserved, 18th-century mansion. Between 1893 and 1898, Joyce studied here under the Jesuits. A few steps away, the ☞ **James Joyce Cultural Centre** is the hub of Bloomsday celebrations. Also on the northside are the site of **Bella Cohen's Brothel** (✉ 82 Railway St.), in an area that in Joyce's day contained many such houses of ill-repute. Across town on the western side of the northside, the **New Ormond Hotel** (✉ Upper Ormond Quay, ☎ 01/872–1811) was an afternoon rendezvous spot for Bloom. Plaques in the Siren Suite Ballroom and Malachy's Bar note their Joycean connections.

Across the Liffey, walk up Grafton Street to ☞ **Davy Byrne's Pub,** then proceed to the ☞ **National Library**—where Bloom has a near meeting with Blazes Boylan, his wife's lover, and looks for a copy of an advertisement—via **Molesworth Street.** No establishment mentioned by Joyce has changed less since his time than **Sweny's Pharmacy** (✉ Lincoln Pl.), at the back of Trinity College, which still has its black-and-white exterior and an interior crammed with potions and vials.

A number of key Joyce sites lie outside the city center. On February 2, 1882, Joyce was born in the genteel southern suburb of Rathgar, at **41 Brighton Square,** where he spent the first two years of his life. (Bus 15A and Bus 15B make the 5-km/3-mi journey.) Other sites are covered elsewhere in our guide: **Sandymount Strand** and the **James Joyce Martello Tower** (☞ County Dublin—Southside, *below*) and **One Martello Terrace** (☞ Bray *in* Chapter 3).

style of St.-Philippe du Roule of Paris. A Palestrina choir, in which the great Irish tenor John McCormack began his career, sings in Latin here every Sunday at 11. ✉ *Marlborough St.,* ☎ *01/874–5441.* ✆ *Free.* ⊙ *Daily 8–6.*

⑤⑤ Rotunda Hospital. Founded in 1745 as the first maternity hospital in Ireland or Britain, the hospital was designed on a grand scale by architect Richard Castle (1690–1751), with a three-story tower and a copper cupola. It is now most worth a visit for its **chapel,** with elaborate plasterwork executed by Bartholomew Cramillion in 1757–58, appropriately honoring motherhood. The ☞ **Gate Theater** is housed in an extension. ✉ *Parnell St.,* ☎ *01/873–0700.*

⑤② St. Francis Xavier Church. One of the city's finest churches in the classical style, the Jesuit St. Francis Xavier's was begun in 1829, the year of Catholic Emancipation, and was completed three years later. The building is designed in the shape of a Latin cross, with a distinctive Ionic portico and an unusual coffered ceiling. The striking, faux-marble high altarpiece, decorated with lapis lazuli, came from Italy. The church appears in James Joyce's story "Grace." ✉ *Upper Gardiner St.,* ☎ *01/836–3411.* ✆ *Free.* ⊙ *Daily 8–6.*

Phoenix Park and Environs

Far and away Dublin's largest park, Phoenix Park is a vast green arrowhead-shape oasis north of the Liffey, a 20-or-so-minute walk from the city center. A handful of other cultural sites near the park are also worth visiting, but to combine a visit to any of them with any of our other walks would be a bit difficult. The Custom House and the Irish Whiskey Corner, at the end of our Dublin Castle, Christ Church, and West Dublin tour [☞ *above*], are the sites closest to these (and the Guinness Brewery, across the river, also is fairly close), so if you do make it to any of those, be sure to evaluate whether you have enough time to append a visit to one or another of these sites. Otherwise, plan to make a special trip out here, either walking or via car or cab.

A Good Walk

Beginning at the Custom House, walk down the quays on the north side of the Liffey until you come to Blackhall Place. Walk up to Arbour Hill and turn left: the **Arbour Hill Cemetery** ⑤⑥ will be on your left. Directly across Arbour Hill are the **Collins Barracks** ⑤⑦, now a branch of the National Museum (the main entrance is on Benburb Street on the south side). On its east side Benburb becomes Parkgate Street, and it's just a short stroll farther down to the **Phoenix Park** ⑤⑧'s main entrance.

TIMING

Phoenix Park is *big*; exploring it on foot could easily eat up the better part of a day. If you're looking for a little exercise, head here: Jogging, horseback riding, and bicycling are the ideal ways to explore the park more quickly than you can simply strolling (☞ Outdoor Activities and Sports, *below*).

Sights to See

⑤⑥ Arbour Hill Cemetery. A total of 14 Irishmen were executed by the British following the 1916 Easter Uprising. They were all buried here, including Patrick Pearse, who led the rebellion, his younger brother Willie, who played only a minor role in the uprising, and James Connolly, a socialist and labor leader wounded in the battle. Too weak from his wounds to stand, Connolly was tied to a chair and then shot. The burial ground is a simple but formal area, with the names of the dead leaders carved in stone beside an inscription of the proclamation they issued during the uprising. ⊠ *Arbour Hill.* ☞ *Free.* ☉ *Mon.–Sat. 9–4:30, Sun. 9:30–noon.*

❺❼ Collins Barracks. Until recently, this was the oldest purpose-built military barracks in the world still in use. Now it is home to the ☞ **National Museum**'s collection of glass, silver, costumes, furniture, and other decorative arts. ⊠ *Benburb St.* ☎ *01/677–7444.* ☞ *Free.* ☉ *Tues.– Sat. 10–5, Sun. 2–5.*

★ ☾ ❺❽ Phoenix Park. Europe's largest public park, extending about 3 mi along the Liffey's north bank, encompasses 1,752 acres of verdant green lawns, woods, lakes, and playing fields. It is a jogger's paradise, but Sunday is the best time for everyone to visit: Games of cricket, soccer, polo, baseball, hurling—a combination of lacrosse, baseball, and field hockey—or Irish football are likely to be in progress. Old-fashioned gas lamps line both sides of **Chesterfield Avenue,** the main road that bisects the park for 4 km/2½ mi, named for Lord Chesterfield, a lord lieutenant of Ireland, who laid out the road in the 1740s. To the right as you enter the park, the **People's Garden** is a charming and colorful flower garden that was designed in 1864.

Among the park's major monuments are the **Phoenix Column,** erected by Lord Chesterfield in 1747, and the **198-ft obelisk,** built in 1817 to commemorate the Duke of Wellington, the Irish general who defeated Napoleon for the British. (Wellington was born in Dublin but, true to the anti-Irish prejudice so prevalent in 19th-century England, balked at the suggestion that he was Irish: "If a man is born in a stable, it doesn't mean he is a horse," he is reputed to have said.) A tall, **white cross** marks the spot from which Pope John Paul II addressed more than a million people during his 1979 visit to Ireland. Often, wild deer can be seen grazing in the many open spaces of the park, especially near here.

You're guaranteed of seeing wildlife at the **Dublin Zoo,** the third-oldest public zoo in the world, founded in 1830, and situated a short walk beyond the People's Garden. Many animals from tropical climes are housed in barless enclosures, while Arctic species swim the lakes close to the reptile house. The zoo is one of the few places in the world where lions will breed in captivity. Some 700 lions have been bred here since the 1850s, including the famous MGM film lion. The children's corner features goats, guinea pigs, and lambs. ⊠ *Phoenix Park,* ☎ *01/ 677–1425.* ☞ *£5.* ☉ *Daily 9:30–dusk.*

Both the president of Ireland and the U.S. ambassador have official residences in the park (the president's is known as Aras an Uachtarain), but neither building is open to the public. The Garda Siochana (police) has its headquarters in the park; a small **Garda Museum** contains many relics of Irish police history, including old uniforms. ⊠ *Phoenix Park,* ☎ *01/677–1156, ext. 2250.* ☞ *Free.* ☉ *Weekdays 9–5; call to confirm.*

Also within the park is a **visitor center,** housed within the 17th-century fortified **Ashtown Castle;** it has information about the park's history, flora, and fauna. ⊠ *Phoenix Park,* ☎ *01/677–0095.* ☞ *£1.50.* ☉ *Mar.–May, daily 10–1 and 2–5; June–Sept., daily 9:30–6:30; Oct., daily 2–5; Nov.–Feb. by appointment.*

NEED A
BREAK?

Just before the entrance to Phoenix Park, **Ryan's Pub** (⊠ 28 Parkgate St., ☎ 01/677–6097) is one of Dublin's last genuine, late-Victorian-era pubs. Its dark-mahogany bar counters and old-fashioned lamps and snugs, changed little since its last remodeling in 1896, will give you a good dose of Dublin past, before or after a trip to the park.

DINING

By Vincent Jamison, with contributions from Georgina Campbell

If you arrive in Dublin thinking you're going to eat potatoes, potatoes, and more potatoes, be prepared to have your preconceptions overturned—and to be enthralled and very happily sated in the process. Why? Because Ireland is in the throes of a food revolution, and some of Dublin's chefs are leading the charge. At the heart of the changing food scene are two contrasting—but not opposing—developments: the internationalization of Irish food on the one hand, and the pursuit of an authentically Irish food on the other.

Dublin's restaurateurs are a main reason for the move toward a more internationally inflected fare. Many have trained in top restaurants in France, Switzerland, and Germany; others have worked in New York and Chicago; some have been much farther afield—to Thailand, Hong Kong, and Australia. Not surprisingly, they've come back with new ways of thinking about food—from spices to cooking techniques—and they're not afraid to adapt what they've learned elsewhere to local produce and regional dishes. Some of the chefs get good results by developing a style that reflects a rapprochement between east and west; others succeed through a classical style that could be called Franco-Irish; and still others take their influence from Italy, California, or the traditions of Anglo-Irish fare.

European-style cafés (☞ A Thousand Pubs *in* Pleasures and Pastimes, *above*) and brasserie-style restaurants are the latest arrivals—and Dublin can't seem to get enough of either. At press time (summer 1997), a Planet Hollywood was slated to open before 1998 dawns, while a local restaurateur is planning a 400-seat sports bar is Temple Bar.

Seafood is a common specialty in Dublin—not necessarily the traditional cockles and mussels, but wild salmon and oysters from the clear Atlantic waters of the west coast; deep-sea fish trawled off the shores of Donegal and in the Irish Sea; and lobsters, crabs, and, yes, even sea urchins gathered in rockier coastal waters. Fresh produce, much of it organically grown, is being treated so imaginatively that even the old Irish stalwarts such as potatoes, onions, and carrots have new life. Lamb, beef, and pork and bacon still provide the backbone for many signature dishes, but there is also great interest in venison, quail, and other game—both wild and farmed. There are dozens of excellent cheeses, most produced by small artisan cheese makers. If one of these farmhouse varieties appears on a menu, make a point of trying it.

For space and editorial considerations, we rarely (there are a few exceptions) review hotel restaurants and fast-food joints. Although some hotel restaurants have improved their fare to compete with the more sophisticated stand-alone establishments, many still lag behind. You'll find the usual international fast-food chains here—McDonald's (its Grafton Street outlet is one of the world's busiest), Burger King, Kentucky Fried Chicken, Chicago Pizza—as well as a slew of local chains, including Pizzaland, Abrakebabra and Beshoff's stylish fish 'n' chippers.

Dubliners dine out frequently, and they do so with the enthusiasm and savoir faire of diners in any world-class city. In a town where you never know what will come out of which kitchen next, reviews by local, high-profile dining critics are read eagerly and discussed with an air of anticipation. Regardless of where you eat, tap into this thriving scene: Ask your waiters questions, talk to the chef, compare notes with fellow travelers. Participation will surely add even more flavor to your dining experience.

BREAKFAST

Most Irish hotels and B&Bs still serve a formidable full Irish breakfast, with cereals and juice, followed by main dishes of eggs, bacon, black pudding, and sausage, or even fish courses like smoked haddock or grilled Dover sole. Large hotels are increasingly offering an even broader choice of breakfast, with everything from a simple Danish and coffee to a small steak and eggs or an extensive buffet with lots of fruit, yogurt, and all-you-can-eat versions of the traditional Irish breakfast. Because breakfast is usually included in the cost of the room, it makes sense to make full use of it, but be sure to check breakfast times in advance. It is usually 8 to 10, but some hotels serve from 7 to 11; if you want to get an earlier start, ask for room service.

LUNCH

Lunch, like breakfast, can be a big meal—bigger than you may be ready for after a full breakfast. You may want to skip a full three-course lunch, especially if you're planning to have a full evening meal. To keep things on the light side, order a single dish for lunch, or an array of starters from the à la carte menu. This won't be possible at some restaurants, as they offer only a fixed-price table d'hôte menu for lunch. Pubs and European-style cafés are more flexible at lunchtime, and some serve excellent food; we've highlighted the best places for the sort of light fare that would be perfect for lunch in the "Need a Breaks?" that pepper our exploring coverage, above, but there are others—do review our major dining section, below, and the list of pubs in Nightlife and the Arts, *below*.

DINING HOURS

Dining hours are much the same as they are elsewhere in Europe, with the main rush at lunchtime from 1 to 2 and at dinner from 8 to 9, although more and more Dubliners are dining out after 8 PM for dinner—and are referring to the evening meal as supper. Some hotels serve afternoon tea and scones, but the old-fashioned "high tea," which tended to be a salad with cold meats, is more or less defunct. If you want to eat earlier, many restaurants have early-bird, pre-theater, or tourist menus (and some have post-theater menus later in the evening). Some begin as early as 5:30 PM, but typically they run from 6:30 to 7:30. A few restaurants serve food all day, with final orders close to midnight. Many restaurants close for a few days around Christmas and Easter, and others are closed on bank holidays.

WHAT TO WEAR

People dress up for dinner at top restaurants, but a jacket for men is usually sufficient. Ties are rarely essential. Good casual wear is often quite acceptable.

PRICES

For price ranges *see* Chart 1(A) *in* On the Road with Fodor's. Value-added tax (VAT) will automatically be added to your bill—a 12.5% tax on food, a 25% tax on drinks. Before paying, check to see if service has been included. If it is included, it can be paid with a credit card, but if it's not, it is more considerate to the staff to pay the main bill by credit card but leave the tip (10%–15%) in cash.

Many restaurants have recognized that they are priced out of the reach of some diners and offer early-bird and/or pre- and post-theater menus with set prices and specific times.

South City Center: Ballsbridge, Donnybrook, and Stillorgan

$$$$ ✕ **Le Coq Hardi.** For many years John Howard has been running one
★ of Dublin's best restaurants in a Georgian house in Ballsbridge. Meeting the challenge posed by newer restaurants and younger chefs, he continues to refine and reinvent his own cooking. Service is friendly and relaxed in the plush, comfortable, and quietly elegant dining room. The wine cellar holds many of the world's great wines—including Howard's own favorite, the first-growth *grand cru classe,* Chateau Latour. A ramekin holds appetizer "smokies"—smoked haddock with a sauce of tomato, double cream, and cheese. One of Howard's signature dishes—a little old-fashioned, perhaps, but still popular—is Coq Hardi chicken, stuffed with potatoes and mushrooms, wrapped in bacon before going into the oven, and finished off with a dash of Irish whiskey. The cheese boards are among the best in the country, while desserts tend to be rich and sumptuously classical French. ⊠ *35 Pembroke Rd., Ballsbridge,* ☏ *01/668–9070. Reservations essential. AE, DC, MC, V. Closed Sun.*

$$$ ✕ **Beaufield Mews.** A 10-minute taxi ride from the city center, this 18th-century coach house with stables still has its original cobbled courtyard and is even said to be haunted by a friendly monk. Inside it's all black beams, old furniture, and bric-a-brac, including stable artifacts. The most desirable tables overlook the courtyard or the garden, or are, less predictably, "under the nun" (the nun in question is a 17th-century portrait). While the main attraction is the atmosphere, the food is based on fresh ingredients, and you'll find old favorites like roast duckling à l'orange but also fresh wild-salmon steaks simply grilled or poached and served with hollandaise sauce. The menu also includes game in season—venison and pheasant are specialties—and homemade ice cream. ⊠ *Woodlands Ave., Stillorgan,* ☏ *01/288–6945. Reservations essential. AE, DC, V. Closed Sun., Mon. No lunch.*

$$$ ✕ **Ernie's Restaurant.** High-quality ingredients, attention to detail, and consistency are the hallmarks of this long-established restaurant only a few minutes by taxi from the city center. Built around a large tree and fountain, the restaurant has a welcoming atmosphere, with blue Irish-linen tablecloths and sparkling crystal on the tables; it's also well known for the late Ernie Evans's large collection of paintings of the west of Ireland. The seasonal menu always has a variety of catches of the day—grilled sole with spring onion and thyme butter and poached wild salmon on a bed of creamed potato, for instance—as well as four or five meat and poultry entrées such as roasted rack of Wicklow lamb with a caramelized onion tarte Tatin (a variation of the traditional upside-down apple tart). A seasonal vegetarian platter is also a regular menu item. The homemade desserts are fresh takes on classics, like the honey and ginger-nut ice cream with a chocolate and almond wafer and the strawberry and mango tartlet with vanilla sauce. ⊠ *Mulberry Gardens, Donnybrook,* ☏ *01/269–3300. AE, DC, MC, V. Closed Sun., Mon. and 1 wk at Christmas. No lunch Sat.*

$$$ ✕ **Patrick Kavanagh Room at the Hibernian Hotel.** Named for the Irish
★ poet (whose statue you can find on the nearby banks of the Grand Canal), this eatery is easily one of the most distinguished restaurants affiliated with a hotel in Dublin (☞ Lodging, *below*). You can relax before dinner and browse over the menu in the cozy, plush sitting room before moving on to the elegant terra-cotta, cream, and green dining room and conservatory beyond. The accomplished chef, David Foley, turns out sophisticated, complex cuisine. A terrine of duck liver parfait with a plum mango chutney and a red fruit vinaigrette, or twice-cooked goat cheese soufflé with Parmesan and a tomato fondue are representative

starters. Among the stellar entrées, you might choose confit of duck leg served with eggplant, roast peppers, and zucchini with *tapenade* (a caper-anchovy-olive condiment); sole stuffed with crab mousse, deep-fried vegetables, and a red pepper and scallion sauce; or roast fillet of beef with fennel sautéed in olive oil, smoked bacon, and shallot casserole. The desserts are no less elaborate: pears with a champagne sabayon, and timbale of winter berries in a Cointreau jelly. ✉ *Eastmoreland Pl., Ballsbridge,* ☎ *01/668–7666. AE, DC, MC, V. No lunch Sat.*

$$$ ✗ **Roly's Bistro.** Since opening in 1992, this big, two-story brasserie-
★   style restaurant has become one of the capital's most fashionable eating places. It's run by a well-known restaurateur, Roly Saul, and award-winning chef Colin O'Daly. The crowd, the buzz, the quality of the food, and, above all, the surprisingly reasonable prices make it a small wonder that Roly's Bistro has been a runaway success since the doors opened. Set lunch menus are surprisingly long on choice at the price, while the evening à la carte menu offers a very wide selection, typically ranging from a wild mushroom soup with sorrel, or crab with pink grapefruit served cold to start, through main courses like roast guinea fowl with grapes and lime sauce, rabbit and pigeon pie with red cabbage, or shellfish bake (an aromatic combination of scallops, prawns, and mussels with tomato and basil). Desserts can be both comforting *and* elegant, like the crème brûlée with homemade praline ice cream served in a glass beside it. ✉ *7 Ballsbridge Terr., Ballsbridge,* ☎ *01/668–2611. Reservations essential. AE, MC, V.*

$$ ✗ **China-Sichuan Restaurant.** China's Sichuan Province established
★   this restaurant and its government continues to supply the ingredients and chefs. Widely recognized as one of Ireland's most authentic ethnic restaurants, it is in an ordinary terraced building, about a 15-minute drive from the city center. The focal point is a giant, ceramic, water-lily fountain. Traditional scarlet lanterns and velvet-covered booths set in private areas help create an intimate ambience. Recommended specialties include duck skin stuffed with seafood, and whole steamed sole. Desserts are unexceptional. ✉ *4 Lower Kilmacud Rd., Stillorgan,* ☎ *01/288–4817. Reservations essential. Jacket and tie. AE, MC, V. Closed Sun.*

$$ ✗ **Furama.** Hong Kong native Rodney Mak owns this mainstream Chinese restaurant, which has a pleasant, lacquered polish to it, with comfortable banquettes and good service. Mak's chef is from Malaysia, and he cooks in an eclectic Pan-Asian style. There are a number of good Chinese soups, including chicken and sweet corn chowder, and a won ton with savory dumplings. Spicy *satay* beef (small skewers of grilled beef), and spicy chicken Szechuan are two good meat dishes. For the adventurous, there's frogs' legs in a garlic and black bean sauce. Whole black sole on the bone steamed with ginger and scallion then filleted at the table is representative of Mak's strength with steamed fish. They also serve lobster in the shell from the tank, in three stir-fried styles. Mak also owns a good, Western-style restaurant, Brooks, which is just two doors away. ✉ *Eirpage House, Donnybrook,* ☎ *01/283–0522. AE, DC, MC, V. No lunch Sat.*

$–$$ ✗ **Marrakesh.** Up a flight of stairs near Roly's Bistro in Ballsbridge, this small spot serves authentic food from Morocco—one of the world's most underrated cuisines. Akim Beskri cooks in clay *tagines* (stew pots), the traditional method of desert tribesmen. The tagines' ingredients are a delicate balance of vegetables; meat or poultry; olives, garlic, and preserved lemons; and spices, usually including cumin, ginger, pepper, saffron, and turmeric. They also do a full-blown couscous royale (with beef, lamb, chicken, and spicy sausage), *harira* (a traditional soup with chickpeas), and *mechoui* (a slow-cooked roast side of lamb). Margaret and Akim Beskri also operate La Cave, a popular city-center wine bar. ✉ *11 Ballsbridge Terr., Ballsbridge* ☎ *01/660–5539. AE, DC, MC, V. No lunch.*

City Center (Southside)

$$$$ ✗ **Patrick Guilbaud.** Everything is French here, including the eponymous owner, his chef, the maître d' and the two Michelin stars that have made it Ireland's highest-rated and leading restaurant. Guillaume Le Brun's cooking is a fluent expression of modern French cuisine—not particularly flamboyant, but coolly professional. Expect superb foie gras, confit of Landaise duck in a delicate phyllo pastry, roe deer with junipers—and also some homage to Irish dishes, from Connemara lobster in season to braised pig's trotters. At press time (summer 1997), the restaurant was slated to move in the fall to the new deluxe Hotel Merrion (☞ Lodging, *below*). ✉ *Hotel Merrion, Upper Merrion St.,* ☎ *01/676–4192. AE, DC, MC, V. Closed Sun., Mon., and Dec. 24–Jan. 14.*

$$$$ ✗ **Peacock Alley.** Ireland's most bravura chef-owner is Conrad Gal-
★ lagher, who ran away from school at 12 to be a cook in County Donegal. By 18 he was sous chef at the Plaza in New York, and at 19 *chef de cuisine* at the Waldorf-Astoria's Peacock Alley, whose name he has borrowed. Elegantly set white-linen-covered tables in the modern, sky-lighted, deep-blue-and-green room set the stage for the dazzling fare. Gallagher builds up the food on the plate and dabs multicolor oils and garnishes with painterly precision. His strikingly inventive dishes include an appetizer of smoked salmon with basmati rice, pear, preserved ginger, soy sauce and quesadilla; an intensely flavored roast chestnut soup; deep-fried crab cakes with *katifi* (shredded phyllo pastry); daube of pot-roasted beef; and pan-seared red snapper with puree of pumpkin. His critics claim he has too many flavors on the plate and an excessively extravagant approach, but when he gets it right, he is an extraordinary cook. The strong wine list, excellent service, and lively atmosphere all contribute to making a meal here an experience of Dublin in the thriving '90s at its best. ✉ *47 S. William St.,* ☎ *01/662–0760. Reservations essential. AE, DC, MC, V.*

$$$$ ✗ **Thornton's.** Chef-owner Kevin Thornton is as restrained and clas-
★ sical in his approach as Conrad Gallagher is flamboyant, yet like Gallagher, he is a naturally gifted chef. In a renovated house with pine floors on the north bank of the Grand Canal, the space is coolly understated; the service is French and quite formal. Thornton's cooking style is light, and his dishes are small masterpieces of structural engineering. In season, he marinates legs of partridge, then debones and reforms the bird with the deboned breasts presented as a crown. Desserts are meticulously prepared and range from an elegant fig ice cream to chocolate mousse to blackberry nougat with orange confit. Although slightly off the beaten path (it's a 20-minute walk or short car ride southwest of St. Stephen's Green) and nowhere near as flashy as some of its competitors, this is nonetheless one of Ireland's best restaurants today. ✉ *1 Portobello Rd.,* ☎ *01/454–9067. Reservations essential. AE, DC, MC, V. Closed Sun. No lunch.*

$$$–$$$$ ✗ **The Commons Restaurant.** This large elegant room is in the base-
ment of historic Newman House (☞ The Georgian Heart of Dublin, *above*). The patio doors open onto a paved courtyard for summer aperitifs or alfresco lunches. The award-winning restaurant has changed chefs three times in as many years, but it continues to offer a light treatment of classical French themes. Grilled turbot with colcannon, steamed ravioli of salmon, breast of guinea fowl with sauerkraut, and filet of beef with a smoked bacon polenta are among the entrées. Rhubarb and ginger soufflé might turn up on the dessert menu. Beyond the patio

56

Dublin Dining

gate lie Iveagh Gardens, a quiet, lovely gem of a park. ⊠ *85–86 St. Stephen's Green,* ☎ *01/478–0530. AE, DC, MC, V. Closed Sun. and bank holidays. No lunch Sat.*

$$$ ✕ **Cooke's Café.** Johnny Cooke has turned this Parisian-style bistro into a cool spot for visiting movie stars. Cooke is influenced by eclectic Italian-Californian styles, which he serves up with flair on large white Wedgwood plates in a room that has been sponge-painted in pale gold. He does a crab salad with spinach, coriander, mango salsa, and lime dressing; lobster grilled with garlic herb butter; and in season, a roasted game plate with pungent flavors of wild mallard and teal, sliced venison and wood pigeon, and a chanterelle mushroom-thyme cream sauce. Try one of the excellent cakes prepared by Cooke's own bakery across the street. The outdoor seating on nice summer days is a consolation for the slow service during the busiest times. Upstairs is the new Rhino Room (☞ *below*). ⊠ *14 S. William St.,* ☎ *01/679–0536. Reservations essential. AE, DC, MC, V.*

$$$ ✕ **La Stampa.** Huge Regency mirrors, little bronze cupids, busts of
★ Roman emperors, candelabra, fake flowers, and large skylights are just some of the neoclassical elements of La Stampa's wonderful, large dining room, centrally located between Trinity College and St. Stephen's Green. Chef Paul Flynn changes menus frequently but works primarily in an eclectic, international style—at his best, he cooks with real style. You might start with risotto of field mushrooms and crispy bacon, a roasted parsnip and apple soup made with a homemade stock, or potted ham with mustard vinaigrette and charcoal-grilled *ciabatta* (a small, flat Italian loaf). For a main course, Flynn might do Japanese-style tempura of brill with sesame potatoes and black bean vinaigrette, ragout of monkfish with Thai spices, or supreme of chicken with tabbouleh, hummus, and spiced eggplant. Service is good, and there is an air of fun about the place. ⊠ *35 Dawson St.,* ☎ *01/677–8611, AE, DC, MC, V. No lunch Sat.*

$$$ ✕ **L'Ecrivain.** Chef-owner Derry Clarke's sense of humor is sometimes
★ tested by tipsy patrons who fall over a life-size sculpture of the writer Brendan Behan on their way out of his elegant French restaurant. Smart paintings of Beckett and other Irish writers hang on the walls. The food is serious—disciplined and restrained, with the emphasis on fresh Irish produce, especially seasonal ingredients cooked with care and imagination. Starters may include grilled goat cheese with eggplant and charcoal-grilled Mediterranean vegetables. Cured, marinated lamb with prune stuffing is superb. The table d'hôte menus, especially at dinner, provide variety and good value. Try one of the unusual first-course salads followed, perhaps, by game in season. Desserts, given special care, include crème brûlée, a splendid staple. ⊠ *109a Lower Baggot St.,* ☎ *01/661–1919. AE, DC, MC, V. Closed Sun.*

$$$ ✕ **The Grey Door.** Just off Fitzwilliam Square and a five-minute walk from St. Stephen's Green, this former Russo-Scandinavian restaurant in an elegant Georgian town house has been repositioned as an Irish eatery. The interior is a celebration of Irish craftsmanship, with wooden floors, stylish lighting, handmade tableware; even the logo—of Celtic circles borrowed from neolithic tombs—is quintessentially Irish. Starters include *brotchan rí* (salmon and leek broth), Irish potato and bacon torte, and Irish nettle and watercress soup. Pot-roasted guinea fowl, Kildare lamb with boxty potato, and fillet of hake with mussel stew continue the Irish spirit into the main courses. Vegetarian main dishes include large flat mushrooms stuffed with three toppings, including goat's cheese. In the basement, a less formal restaurant, Pier 32 ($$), has live music most nights. ⊠ *23 Upper Pembroke St.,* ☎ *01/676–3286. AE, DC, MC, V. Closed Sun. No lunch Sat.*

$$$ ✕ **Locks.** Claire Douglas's restaurant on the north shore of the Grand Canal (down the road from Thornton's, [☞ *above*]) sticks to a fairly straightforward treatment of international food, served up in a relaxed atmosphere. It's popular with businesspeople and southside locals. Starters may include a pasta with chicken and mild curry sauce, leeks and mussels in garlic with buttered bread crumbs, or a Thai beef salad. Steak and kidney pie, lemon sole and crabmeat with a mussel sauce, and *feuillete* (puff pastry) of seafood with a prawn sauce are among the superior main courses. Desserts like pear fool in a tall goblet, or a small chocolate and toffee cake, will remind you of classic dishes from another era. ✉ *1 Windsor Terr., Portobello,* ☎ *01/454–3391. AE, DC, MC, V. Closed Sun. No lunch Sat.*

$$$ ✕ **Old Dublin.** Scandinavian and Russian influences appropriately turn up on the menu at this well-established spot, named after the surrounding area east of Dublin Castle which goes back to Viking times. A series of cozy but elegant low-ceiling rooms are decorated with pristine white linens, well-upholstered chairs, and candlelit tables, and they're further warmed by glowing fires. Lunch is table d'hôte, but the dinner menu is cleverly organized with extras on the main menu broadening the choices. Specialties include traditional borscht served with mushroom-filled piroshki and blini served with chopped onion, dill cucumber, sour cream, and a choice of salted salmon, herrings, mushroom salad, or prawns. Familiar dishes such as chicken Kiev and beef Stroganoff are interspersed with surprises such as planked sirloin Hussar, a steak baked between two oak planks, served on an oak platter with salad and sweet pickle. Tempting sweets follow, or there's a good cheese board. ✉ *90–91 Francis St.,* ☎ *01/454–2028,* ℻ *01/454–1406. AE, DC, MC, V. Closed Sun. No lunch Sat.*

$$ ✕ **Imperial Chinese Restaurant.** In a city developing a wide choice of ethnic restaurants, this has long been the preferred choice among many of Dublin's Chinese, especially at lunchtime on Sundays. Behind the elegant facade just off Grafton Street, the two floors are decorated with deep-blue carpets, warm-pink walls, a fountain, and an arch, which breaks up the main ground-floor seating area and gives the place a more intimate feel. The specialty of the house is dim sum, available at lunchtime only, although there are a number of interesting set menus as well. ✉ *12a Wicklow St.,* ☎ *01/677–2580. AE, MC, V.*

$$ ✕ **Rajdoot.** After 31 years in business, this spacious room is polished in its execution of Northern Indian, Nepalese, and Rajasthani dishes. Service is attentive, almost to a fault. You can eat informally at low tables in the reception area or on banquettes in the more formal dining area just behind. The walls have interesting wooden carvings and Indian prints. Starters include tandoori quail or vegetarian staples such as *pakoras* (chickpea fritters with onions, potato, and cabbage in a spicy deep-fried batter). The marinated, lightly spiced, tender chunks of chicken in the shish kebab are served with a long, thin slice of nan bread, hot and sweet chutneys, tomatoes, and capsicum. Duck Jaipur and jumbo prawns with chili garlic are other highlights. ✉ *26–28 Clarendon St.,* ☎ *01/679–4274. AE, DC, MC, V. Closed Sun.*

$$ ✕ **The Rhino Room.** In late spring 1997, Johnny Cooke opened this more ★ casual, less expensive spot upstairs from his buzzing Cooke's Café (☞ *above*). High neo-Gothic windows, black leather banquettes, and a sparkling oak floor set the stage for the Mediterranean-American fare, most of which has been prepared on the open kitchen's charcoal grill. Butter and cream sauces have been banished from the menu, so expect olive oil with the focaccia and ciabatta that kick things off. As you're ordering, you can sample one of the 24 wines by the glass Cooke offers. Grilled beef dishes star, such as the dry, aged 8 ounce fillet with salsa verde, sun-dried tomatoes, and pine nuts. For dessert, fresh Irish raspberries with black cherry crème brûlée is a good choice. ⊠ *14 S. William St.,* ☎ *01/670–5260. AE, DC, MC, V. Closed Sun.*

$–$$ ✕ **La Mère Zou.** Eric Tydgadt is Belgian and his wife Isabelle is from Paris, so it's not surprising that their small basement restaurant is Continental in emphasis. The lunch menu includes six king-size plates; one of them, "La Belge," has a 6-ounce charcoal-grilled rump steak with French fries, and a salad with salami, country ham, chicory, and mayonnaise. In the evening, the dishes are more elaborate, with ragout of venison or medallions of monkfish. ⊠ *22 St. Stephen's Green,* ☎ *01/ 661–6669. AE, DC, MC, V. Closed Jan. 1–10. No lunch weekends.*

$–$$ ✕ **Side Door.** The five-star Shelbourne Hotel (☞ Lodging, *below*) ably offers a variation on the usual *tres cher* hotel dining room (though it has one of those too: 27 The Green) and the uninspired coffee shop. This well-designed budget restaurant has oak floors, cream walls, and art deco wood tables and chairs. You can start off with a bowl of Thai soup, a grilled chicken risotto, or Mediterranean vegetable pizza. Main dishes include supreme of chicken marinated in honey, or charcoal-grilled rib eye of beef. Designer beers and a good wine list nicely complement the food. ⊠ *27 St. Stephen's Green,* ☎ *01/676–6471. AE, DC, MC, V.*

$ ✕ **Burdock's.** In the heart of Viking Dublin, next door to the Lord Edward Pub, Dublin's most famous take-out fish-and-chipper remains steadfastly old-fashioned. Join the inevitable queue and eat on the steps of St. Patrick's Cathedral—the traditional place to consume a Burdock's meal. Be sure to pick up plenty of napkins! ⊠ *Werburgh St.,* ☎ *01/454–0306. No credit cards. Closed Sun.*

$ ✕ **Gotham Café.** This stylish little place just off Grafton Street is very much in tune with the vogue in Dublin for buzzing restaurants with strong Italian–New York leanings. Zipped-up pasta is typically served with a hot chili sauce and Creole sausage; a dozen gourmet pizzas are inventively done with toppings named after hot neighborhoods in other cities: the Tribeca has prawns, roasted peppers, zucchini, cilantro, mozzarella, and hot sauce. ⊠ *8 S. Anne St.,* ☎ *01/679–5266. MC, V.*

$ ✕ **Il Primo.** A few hundred yards from St. Stephen's Green, this lively two-story Italian restaurant has a bare-bones decor, with bare boards and tables, old-fashioned, simple but comfortable wooden-armed office chairs, stainless-steel cutlery, and paper napkins. But the lovely, large, modern crystal wine glasses give a hint of the good things to come: Owner Dieter Bergman is a wine importer, and his Italian wine list is exceptional. Generous middle-of-the-road Irish-Italian cuisine changes seasonally. Typical offerings include a starter of warm spinach salad, wilted in a balsamic vinegar dressing and shallots and served with Parma ham and new potatoes. Among the main courses, a delicious creamy risotto with chunky chicken breasts, a scattering of chicken livers, and wild mushrooms is a standout. ⊠ *Montague St., off Harcourt St.* ☎ *01/478–3373. AE, DC, MC, V. Closed Sun.*

$ ✕ **Juice.** A slick vegetarian restaurant? In *Dublin?* It's true: Opened in early 1996, Juice serves upscale vegetarian fare (some of it is vegan, or dairy-free, and most of it organic) in a large, deep, airy dining room with brushed stainless steel and dark wine-colored lacquer walls. Chef Deb Davis's menu offers a platter of homemade dips and pestos to start—including butter-bean and black olive pâté and spinach and pistachio pesto—served with bread and crudités. The main courses include a tasty spinach and ricotta cheese cannelloni, made with fresh pasta filled with spinach, mushroom, hazelnuts, and ricotta cheese, baked in a creamy tomato and herb sauce. The breads, baked with organic flour, are outstanding. ⊠ *Castle House, S. Great George's St.,* ☎ *01/475–7856. MC, V.*

$ ✕ **Kilkenny Kitchen.** Housed in the Kilkenny Shop (☞ Shopping, *below*), which specializes in superlative Irish craftsmanship and overlooks Trinity College, this self-service restaurant showcases wholesome home cooking in the traditional Irish style. The menu includes a house quiche (combining Irish bacon, herbs, and fresh vegetables), a good traditional Irish stew, casseroles, and an imaginative selection of salads. Homemade scones, bread, and cakes, as well as Irish farmhouse cheeses are all good bets. Lunchtime is busy; expect to share a table. ✉ *6 Nassau St.,* ☎ *01/677–7066. AE, DC, MC, V. Closed Sun.*

$ ✕ **Milano.** The open, gleaming stainless-steel kitchen off this well-designed room turns out a tempting array of flashy pizzas. You can expect to find thinner pizza crust than in the U.S., with combinations like tomato and mozzarella, ham and eggs, Cajun with prawns and tabasco, spinach and egg, or ham with anchovies. The wine list, mostly Italian, can make this a surprisingly upmarket session for a pizza chain, part of the British-owned Pizza Express group. Last orders are taken at midnight, so keep this in mind if you're looking for a late-night bite. ✉ *38 Dawson St.,* ☎ *01/670–7744. AE, MC, V.*

$ ✕ **Mitchells Cellars.** This perennially popular lunch spot just off St. Stephen's Green is situated in the vaulted basement of a revered wine merchant. The quarry-tiled floor, whitewashed walls, red-and-white lamp shades hanging over pine tables, and waitresses neatly dressed in navy and white are all virtually unchanged since the early '70s, as is the menu. Still, a bustling crowd continues to pack the place, drawn to its Country French home cooking—fare that includes soups and pâtés, quiche lorraine and salads, beef braised in Guinness, and chocolate-and-brandy meringue. There's also usually something interesting on the wine list at the right price. Get here early or expect a line. ✉ *21 Kildare St.,* ☎ *01/662–4724. Reservations not accepted. AE, DC, MC, V. Closed Sun., Sat. June–Aug. No dinner.*

$ ✕ **Pasta Fresca.** Situated just off Grafton Street on one of the city center's most interesting thoroughfares, this stylish little Italian restaurant and delicatessen squeezes a surprising number of people into a fairly small area. Antipasto *misto* (assorted sliced Italian meats) makes a good appetizer—or go for a single meat like prosciutto (Italian cured ham), or carpaccio *della casa* (wafer-thin slices of beef fillet, with fresh Parmesan, olive oil, lemon juice, and black pepper). The main courses consist mainly of Pasta Fresca's own very good versions of well-known dishes such as spaghetti *alla bolognese,* cannelloni, and lasagna *al forno.* The pasta is freshly made each day. You'll find lines at lunchtime. ✉ *3–4 Chatham St.,* ☎ *01/679–2402. MC, V. Closed Sun.*

$ ✕ **Yamamori.** Ramen noodle bars offer a staple diet for budget travelers to Japan, but this is the first in Ireland. The meals-in-a-bowl offer a splendid slurping experience, and although you will be supplied with a small Chinese-style soup spoon, the best approach is with the traditional *ohashi* (chopsticks), which allow you to hoist the noodles and leave you to drink the soup. They also do a variety of sushi, which can make an evening meal considerably more expensive than a lunchtime bowl of noodles. ✉ *71 S. Great George's St.,* ☎ *01/475–5001. AE, MC, V.*

City Center (Northside)

$$ ✕ **Chapter One.** Housed in the vaulted, stone-walled basement of the engrossing Dublin Writers Museum, just down the street from the Hugh Lane Municipal Gallery of Modern Art (☞ *above*), this is one of the most notable restaurants in northside Dublin. Dishes include Dublin Bay prawns with Japanese sushi rice, pear, and a sweet soy chili sauce; grilled black sole with poached ravioli stuffed with salmon mousse; and pork with a confit of spiced pork belly. The rich bread and butter pudding and the apple and pecan crumble are two stellar desserts. ⊠ *18–19 Parnell Sq.,* ☏ *01/873–2266. AE, DC, MC, V. Closed Sun. No lunch Sat., no dinner Mon.*

$$ ✕ **Fisherman's Wharf.** This waterfront spot is slightly off the beaten path, next to the northside's Connolly Station and surrounded by the modernist facades and gray-tinted windows of the International Financial Services Centre. But when the sun shines on the lagoon and old docking area just outside, you couldn't wish to be anywhere else for an alfresco lunch or dinner. Not surprisingly, the family of fish importers that owns this restaurant concentrates on seafood. Typical fare includes panfried prawns with an herb dressing, seafood chowder, seafood croquettes, and swordfish fillets seared and served on a bed of mixed pepper confit and chili butter. If you're not in the mood for seafood, you can also find a mille-feuille of lamb's liver with leeks and a chive apple puree. ⊠ *International Financial Services Centre, off Amiens St.,* ☏ *01/670–1900. AE, DC, MC, V. Closed Sun.*

Temple Bar

$$$ ✕ **Les Frères Jacques.** The restaurant in this late-Victorian corner
★ house next door to the Olympia Theatre brings a little bit of Paris to the edge of Dublin's Temple Bar. Nostalgic prints of Paris and Deauville hang on the green-papered walls, while French waiters, dressed in white Irish linen and black bow ties, exude a Gallic charm without being excessively formal. Expect traditional French cooking that nods to the seasons. You'll find a good choice of game in season. Seafood (depending on fresh fish available at the market) is a major attraction, and lobster, from the tank, is a specialty, typically roasted and flambéed with Irish whiskey. Also recommended is the *magret de canard* (roast breast of duck served with a ginger and grapefruit sauce). Sophisticated desserts, such as Chocolate Marquise, laced with rum and served with two sauces, provide a suitably dramatic ending. A piano player who performs Friday and Saturday evenings and the occasional weeknights can usually be persuaded to play your favorite Irish or French tune. ⊠ *74 Dame St.,* ☏ *01/679–4555. AE, DC, MC, V. Closed Sun. and holidays. No lunch Sat.*

$$ ✕ **Eden.** The young owners of several of Dublin's new café-style bars,
★ including Thomas Read's and the Globe, have followed those successes with a hot brasserie-style restaurant with an open kitchen and high wall of glass looking out onto one of Temple Bar's main squares. Patio-style doors lead to an outdoor eating area—a major plus in a city with relatively few alfresco dining spots. Chef Eleanor Walsh's menu is reasonably priced, with main dishes such as a vegetarian buckwheat pancake filled with garlic, spinach, and mature cheddar; duck leg confit with lentils; and grilled breast of corn-fed chicken. Desserts include rhubarb crème brûlée and a selection of homemade ice creams and sorbets. ⊠ *Meeting House Sq.,* ☏ *01/670–5372. Reservations essential. AE, MC, V. No lunch Mon.–Fri.*

$$ ✕ **Elephant & Castle.** One of Temple Bar's most popular and established eateries, Elephant & Castle serves up traditional American food—charcoal-grilled burgers, salads, omelets, sandwiches, and pasta. The American brunch served on Sundays is always packed. Bare tables fill its two rooms, one of which has a long wooden banquette that runs the length of one wall; the crowds and the absence of soft surfaces means the noise level can be high. When the service is good, the turnover tends to be quick, although you may be inclined to linger, as its formula—an atmosphere that's both bustling *and* relaxed, generous portions of food that's unfussy *and* well-prepared—make it a casual Dublin standout.

New Yorkers take note: Yes, this is a cousin of the restaurant of the same name in Greenwich Village. ✉ *18 Temple Bar,* ☎ *01/679–3121. Reservations not accepted. AE, DC, MC, V.*

$$ ✕ **Jaskos.** A French restaurant chain of the same name has opened this large, all-day bistro in the room which formerly held the nearby Olympia Theatre's props, and where "The Soldier's Song," the Irish national anthem, was composed. If you're looking for comforting food at reasonable prices, this is a good bet. The extensive menu includes *planches* (wooden trays) with things like jumbo shrimps and salad. Among the other standouts are diced foie gras with fresh oysters, a dozen escargots with Pernod and garlic butter, monkfish with a banana beurre blanc, and a rib-eye steak with blue-cheese sauce. ✉ *64 Dame St.,* ☎ *01/679–7767. AE, DC, MC, V.*

$$ ✕ **La Med.** Dublin's dozens of new bistro-style restaurants are a sign not only of the city's changing economic fortunes, but also of the craze for all things European. La Med's Parisian owner-manager has created a clean, two-story room overlooking the Liffey on one side and Temple Bar on the other. Its all-day policy means you can get coffee at 11 AM, a well-varied lunch menu at midday, a tapas menu with little pizzas and crostini late in the afternoon, and a full-fledged dinner in the evening. Among the classic main dishes are a substantial bouillabaisse, a pastry tart of creamed leek and onion gratin, fried calamari with aioli, and a seafood platter with a selection of mussels, crab claws, prawns, and cockles served with salad. More expensive dishes include charcoal-grilled sirloin, roasted monkfish Basquaise, which comes with garlic whipped potato and a *piperade* (a light tomato pepper sauce), and couscous served with a variety of vegetables and lamb. ✉ *22 Essex St. E.,* ☎ *01/670–7358. AE, MC, V.*

$$ ✕ **Le Vigneron.** Just behind the Central Bank, this two-story, combination informal bistro and more formal restaurant is one of Temple Bar's better restaurants, and it's open all day. The French bistro menu sticks to the classics, with French onion soup and *saucisson chaud Lyonnais* (traditional French sausage and potato, with white wine and mustard dressing). Desserts follow suit, with tarte Tatin and chocolate mousse. The wine list, which specializes in the relatively little-known Languedoc region, has lots of bottles at better prices than elsewhere. ✉ *6 Cope St.,* ☎ *01/671–5900 or 01/671–5740. AE, DC, MC, V. Bistro closed holidays. No lunch weekends in restaurant.*

$–$$ ✕ **Trastevere.** Walls of glass and a bright Italianate interior with terracotta tiles make this attractive restaurant in Temple Bar Square a good place for lunch, dinner, a snack, or simply an espresso. Food ranges from simple crostini to warm prawn salads, various pastas, and charcoal-grilled chicken. From outside, you can watch the chef at work through a large glass window. This is a good choice for a warm summer day, when the buskers are playing away in the square. ✉ *Temple Bar Sq.,* ☎ *01/670–8343. AE, DC, MC, V.*

$ ✕ **Bad Ass Café.** Sinéad O'Connor used to wait tables at this lively spot in a converted warehouse between the Central Bank and Ha'penny Bridge (a "Rock n Stroll" tour plaque notes O'Connor's past here). Old-fashioned cash shuttles whiz around the ceiling of the barnlike space, which has bare floors and is painted in primary colors inside and out. A wall of glass makes for great people-watching. Although the food—mostly pizzas and burgers—is unexceptional, the Bad Ass can be a lot of fun and is popular with appetites of all ages. Children will enjoy the special Kidz Bizz menu. ✉ *9–11 Crown Alley,* ☎ *01/671–2596. AE, MC, V.*

$ ✕ **Chameleon.** Run by a young couple, Carol Walsh and Vincent Vis, this informal, two-story Indonesian restaurant is on a Temple Bar side street off the south quays of the Liffey. Coconut and peanut are the dominant flavors in six rijsttafel menus, with 20 or more items arranged around a large plate of spiced rice. Typical Indonesian dishes include shrimp croquette; chicken satay; Chinese noodles with pork, bean sprouts, ginger, and garlic; and green beans with butter beans in coconut milk. ⊠ *1 Fownes St. Upper,* ☎ *01/671–0362. MC, V. Closed Mon., Tues., 1 wk in Nov. No lunch.*

$ ✕ **Pierre's.** Although competition in the area is growing by the day, this spartan, franchised Temple Bar restaurant is holding its own. It makes up in wholesome nutrition anything it may lack in decor. Enjoy the aromas emanating from the open kitchen, and start, perhaps, with a homemade soup, such as traditional leek-and-barley, or a huge bowl of steamed mussels with a richly flavored sauce of melted butter and garlic. ⊠ *2 Crow St.,* ☎ *01/671–1248. AE, MC, V.*

LODGING

"An absolute avalanche of new hotels" is how the *Irish Times,* in an April 1997 article, characterized Dublin's hotel boom. It's unlikely that there have ever been more new hotels under construction at one time in the capital than there are now, while at the same time, at least half of the existing hotels that we review below are in the throes of expanding. Many of those that aren't wish they could—as the demand for rooms continues to be unabated. New lodging establishments are being built in all areas of the city, including a fair number in Ballsbridge, an inner "suburb" that's a 20-minute walk from the city center. At press time (summer 1997), a number of these had yet to be completed and will have to wait for our 1999 edition. Why all the new hotels now? The boom in construction is a response both to Dublin's thriving business climate and its draw for visitors whose only business is fun. Europeans have discovered the city as a convenient, happening weekend getaway. What this means is that for all the new supply of rooms, rates are still high at the best hotels by the standards of any major European or American city (and factoring in the exchange rate means a hotel room can take a substantial bite out of any traveler's budget). Service charges range from 15% in expensive hotels to zero in moderate and inexpensive ones. Be sure to inquire at the time of booking.

Many hotels offer a weekend, or "B&B" rate that is often 30%–40% cheaper than the ordinary rate; some hotels also offer a midweek special that provides discounts of up to 35%. These rates are available throughout the year but are harder to get during high season. Ask about them when booking a room (they are available only on a prebooked basis), especially if you plan a brief or weekend stay. If you've rented a car and you're not staying at a hotel with secure parking facilities, it's worth considering a location out of the city center, such as Dalkey or Killiney, where the surroundings are more pleasant and you won't have to worry about stashing your car on city streets (parking can be difficult to find).

Dublin does have a decent choice of less expensive accommodations— including many moderately priced hotels offering basic but agreeable rooms. Many bed-and-breakfast establishments, long the mainstay of the economy end of the market, have upgraded their facilities and now provide rooms with their own bathrooms or showers, as well as multichannel color televisions and direct-dial telephones, for around £20 a night per person. B&Bs tend to be in suburban areas—generally a 10-minute bus ride from the center of the city. This is not in itself a great drawback, and savings can be significant.

If you'd like to go a less conventional route than a hotel or B&B, you should look into renting an apartment or house, with facilities for you to cook your own meals. Apartments and houses tend to be well decorated and furnished, offering you total freedom to come and go as you please; most provide maid service responsible for daily cleaning. Bord Fáilte (pronounced board fallcha) publishes a complete self-catering guide; these recommended properties can be booked through any Tourist Information Office (TIO; ☞ Visitor Information *in* Dublin A to Z, *below*). For lodging prices, *see* Chart 2(A) *in* On the Road with Fodor's. For additional lodging information, *see* Lodging *in* the Gold Guide.

Airport and Environs

$$$ ⬚ **Forte Posthouse.** The only hotel at Dublin Airport, this low-rise, red-brick structure with a plain exterior was recently refurbished. Its rooms are basic but spacious. The Bistro Restaurant serves fish and meat entrées, as well as a selection of vegetarian dishes; Sampans serves Chinese cuisine at dinner only. There's live music in the bar on weekends. Guests have access to a nearby health club. ⊠ *Dublin Airport,* ☎ *01/844–4211,* ℻ *01/844–6002. 189 rooms with bath. 2 restaurants, bar, room service, shops, free parking. AE, DC, MC, V.*

$$ ⬚ **Doyle Skylon.** This modern, five-story hotel with a concrete-and-glass facade is on the main road into Dublin city center from the airport. The generous-size rooms are plainly decorated in cool pastel shades; double beds and a pair of easy chairs are virtually the only furniture. A glass-fronted lobby with a large bar and the Rendezvous Room restaurant dominate the public areas. The cooking is adequate but uninspired, with dishes such as grilled steak, poached cod, and omelets. ⊠ *Upper Drumcondra Rd., Dublin 9,* ☎ *01/837–9121,* ℻ *01/837–2778. 92 rooms with bath. Restaurant, bar, free parking. AE, DC, MC, V.*

South City Center—Ballsbridge

$$$$ ⬚ **Berkeley Court.** The most quietly elegant of Dublin's large modern hotels, Berkeley Court has a glass-and-concrete exterior designed in a modern, blocklike style. Inside, the vast white-tiled and plushly carpeted lobby has roomy sofas and antique planters. The large bedrooms are decorated in golds, yellows, and greens, with antiques or reproductions of period furniture; bathrooms are tiled in marble. Five luxury suites, each with its own Jacuzzi, have recently been added. The Berkeley Room restaurant offers table d'hôte and à la carte menus; the more informal Conservatory Grill, with large windows, serves grilled food and snacks. Guests have access to a health club a short drive away. ⊠ *Lansdowne Rd., Dublin 4,* ☎ *01/660–1711,* ℻ *01/661–7238. 158 rooms with bath, 30 suites. 2 restaurants, bar, barbershop, beauty salon, exercise room, shops, free parking. AE, DC, MC, V.*

$$$ ⬚ **Doyle Burlington.** Dublin's largest hotel, popular with American tour groups and Irish and European business travelers, is about five minutes by car from the city center. Its impersonal, 1972 glass-and-concrete facade belies a friendly and attentive staff. Public rooms are well decorated, especially the large bar, with mahogany counters and hanging plants that enhance the conservatory-style setting. The generous-size bedrooms, decorated with the usual modern plush in neutral tones, have large picture windows. A 144-room concierge level was added in mid-1997. At night Annabel's nightclub and the seasonal Irish cabaret are both lively spots. Although the Burlington has no sports and health facilities, the Doyle hotel group (☞ Doyle Skylon, *above,* and Doyle Tara, *below*) has an exclusive arrangement that allows guests to use the

RiverView Sports Club in nearby Clonskeagh for £5 a visit; it's outfitted with a full range of exercise equipment, swimming pool, sauna, and tennis and squash courts. ⊠ *Upper Leeson St., Dublin 4,* ☎ *01/660–5222,* FAX *01/660–8496. 524 rooms with bath. 2 restaurants, 3 bars, shops, cabaret May–Oct., nightclub, free parking. AE, DC, MC, V.*

$$$ ⌶ **Herbert Park Hotel.** Opened in mid-1996, the Herbert Park sits adjacent to a park of the same name and beside the River Dodder. The large lobby has floor-to-ceiling windows and a slanted glass roof. The spacious bar, terrace lounge, and restaurant are done in a Japanese-inspired decor. Relaxing shades of blue and cream predominate in the nicely sized bedrooms, which are brightened up by green, red, or white bedspreads; all have individually controlled air conditioning, a large desk, and two telephone lines. Some rooms look onto Herbert Park, while eight are specially designed for people with disabilities. A spacious balcony encircles the entire fifth floor but at press time (summer 1997) it was not yet open to guests. ⊠ *Ballsbridge, Dublin 4,* ☎ *01/667–2200,* FAX *01/667–2595. 150 rooms with bath, 3 suites. Restaurant, bar, exercise room, free parking. AE, MC, V.*

$$$ ⌶ **Hibernian.** An early 20th-century Edwardian nurses' home was
★   converted into this small luxury hotel in 1993. The distinctive red-and-amber brick facade has been retained, and every room is a different shape. Although they're relatively small, the rooms are decorated in light pastel shades with deep-pile carpets and comfortable furniture. The public rooms, done in cheerful chintz and stripes, include a period-style library and a new sun lounge—both comfortable spaces to relax before or after a dinner in the hotel's intimate restaurant (☞ Dining, *above*). Most city-center attractions are a 10- or 15-minute walk away. ⊠ *Eastmoreland Pl. off Upper Baggot St., Dublin 4,* ☎ *01/668–7666 or 800/414243,* FAX *01/660–2655. 40 rooms with bath. Restaurant, bar, parking (fee). AE, DC, MC, V.*

$$$ ⌶ **Jurys** and **The Towers.** These adjacent, seven-story hotels, a short cab ride from the center of town, are both popular with businesspeople and vacationers. They both have more atmosphere than most comparable modern hotels, though the Towers has an edge over Jurys, its older (it dates from 1962), larger, less expensive companion. Jurys has large, plainly decorated bedrooms with light walls and brown drapes; furnishings are functional but uninspired. The Towers' bedrooms are a third larger than those of Jurys, decorated in blue and gold with built-in, natural wood furniture; the large beds and armchairs are blissfully comfortable. All the suites in both hotels have their own sitting rooms and kitchenettes. Towers guests have access to a lounge and well-stocked reading room. All shop and restaurant facilities are located in Jurys: Raglans Restaurant is the main, formal dining room; the Coffee Dock serves light fare daily from 5 AM to 4 AM; the plush, clubby Library Lounge is a great place for a drink or afternoon tea; and the Dubliner Pub is a traditional Irish pub with lots of nooks and crannies. ⊠ *Ballsbridge, Dublin 4,* ☎ *01/660–5000,* FAX *01/660–5540. Jurys: 300 rooms with bath, 3 suites; the Towers: 100 rooms with bath, 4 suites with kitchenettes. Restaurant, coffee shop, 2 bars, indoor/outdoor pool, hot tub, shop, cabaret May–Oct. AE, DC, MC, V.*

$$ ⌶ **Lansdowne.** This small Ballsbridge hotel has recently undergone total
★   refurbishment. The cozy bedrooms are all decorated in the Georgian style with deep floral-patterned decor. Photos of sports personalities hang on the walls of the Green Blazer bar in the basement, a popular haunt for local businesspeople and fans of the international rugby matches held at nearby Lansdowne Road; you can get a bite to eat here all day. Next to the bar is Parker's Restaurant, which specializes in seafood and grilled steaks. ⊠ *27 Pembroke Rd., Dublin 4,* ☎ *01/668–*

2522, ⅎ 01/668–5585. *39 rooms with bath, 2 suites. Restaurant, bar, free parking. AE, DC, MC, V.*

$ ▥ **Ariel Guest House.** This redbrick, 1850 Victorian guest house is one
★ of Dublin's finest, conveniently located a few steps from a DART stop and a 15-minute walk from St. Stephen's Green. Rooms in the main house are lovingly decorated with Victorian and Georgian antiques, Victoriana, and period wallpaper and drapes. Thirteen rooms added to the back of the house in 1991 are more spartan, but all are immaculately kept. A Waterford-crystal chandelier hangs over the comfortable leather and mahogany furniture in the gracious, fireplace-warmed drawing room. Breakfast is served in the airy, glass-enclosed dining room. Owner Michael O'Brien and manager Marion Garry are extraordinarily helpful and gracious hosts. ⊠ *52 Lansdowne Rd., Dublin 4,* ☎ *01/668–5512,* ⅎ *01/668–5845. 28 rooms with bath. Dining room, free parking. MC, V.*

$ ▥ **Mount Herbert Guest House.** Budget-minded visitors from all over the world flock to this sprawling guest house, made up of a number of large Victorian-era houses. The hotel overlooks some of Ballsbridge's fine rear gardens and is right near the main rugby stadium. The simple rooms are painted in light shades with little furniture besides the beds, but all of them have bathrooms and 10-channel TVs. In mid-1997 45 rooms were added in the first all-new extension in many years. Guests can relax in the lounge; a large restaurant, overlooking the back garden and children's play area, serves three meals a day, with unpretentious dinners of steaks and stews. There is no bar on the premises, but there are plenty to choose from nearby. ⊠ *7 Herbert Rd., Dublin 4,* ☎ *01/668–4321,* ⅎ *01/660–7077. 195 rooms with bath. Restaurant, gift shop. AE, DC, MC, V.*

City Center (Southside)

$$$$ ▥ **Conrad Dublin International.** A subsidiary of Hilton Hotels, the Conrad is firmly aimed at the international business executive. The seven-story redbrick and smoked-glass building is well located just off St. Stephen's Green. Gleaming, light marble graces the large, formal lobby. Upstairs the rather cramped bedrooms offer uninspiring views of the adjacent tower blocks. The rooms are painted in sand colors and pastel shades of green, nicely outfitted with natural wood furniture, and graced with Spanish marble in the bathrooms. Suites are more spacious, with stylish, dark furniture in the sitting area. A note to light sleepers: The air-conditioning/heating systems can be noisy. The hotel has two restaurants: The airy Plurabelle, which serves informal lunches and evening meals, and the more enclosed, formal Alexandra Room, decorated with heavy wood paneling and drapes, which serves elaborately prepared fish, fowl, and meat dishes. The main bar, Alfie Byrne's, named in honor of Dublin's lord mayor for most of the 1930s, attempts to re-create the traditional Irish pub atmosphere in spite of its high-powered clientele. ⊠ *Earlsfort Terr., Dublin 2,* ☎ *01/676–5555,* ⅎ *01/676–5424. 191 rooms with bath, 9 suites. 2 restaurants, bar, exercise room, free parking. AE, DC, MC, V.*

$$$$ ▥ **Merrion.** Dublin's newest hotel, the Merrion, is also aspiring to become the capital's most luxurious. Set in four exactingly restored Georgian town houses dating from the 1760s, the hotel is centrally located across from Government Buildings, halfway between St. Stephen's Green and Merrion Square. The Merrion is built around two brand-new gardens laid out by Irish garden designer Jim Reynolds. Leading Dublin restaurateur Patrick Guilbaud (☞ Dining, *above*) moved his eponymous restaurant here. At press time (summer 1997), Fodor's had not visited the hotel prior to its projected September open-

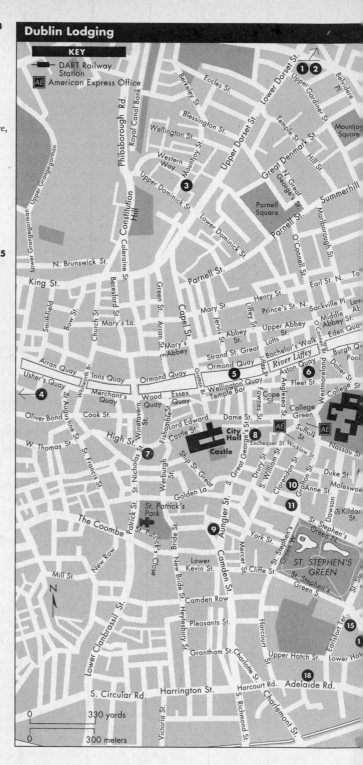

Dublin Lodging

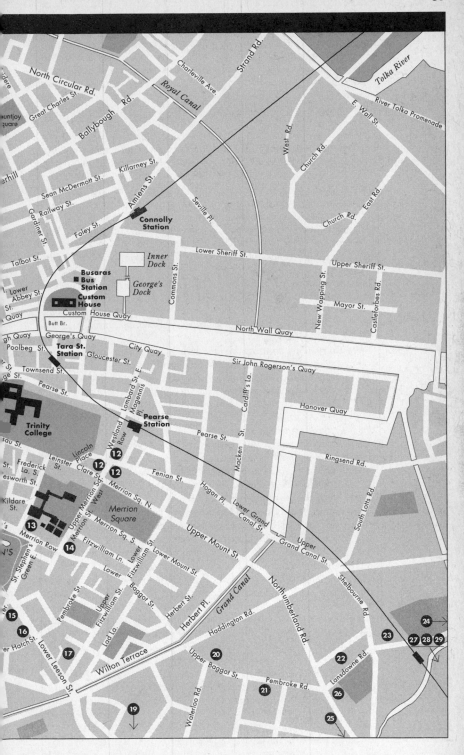

ing; we will review it more fully in our 1999 edition. ⊠ *Upper Merrion St., Dublin 2,* ☎ *01/603–0600,* FAX *01/603–0700. 145 rooms with bath. 2 restaurants, 2 bars, in-room modem lines, in-room safes, minibars, no-smoking floor, no-smoking rooms, room service, in-room VCRs, indoor pool, barbershop, beauty salon, massage, steam room, laundry service and dry cleaning, concierge, business services, meeting rooms, free parking.*

$$$$ 🏨 **Shelbourne.** Old-fashioned luxury prevails at this magnificent show-
★   place—one of Europe's grand old hotels, which has presided over St. Stephen's Green since 1824 (☞ The Georgian Heart of Dublin, *above*). Each room is unique; all have fine, carefully selected furniture and luxurious drapes, with splendid antiques in the older rooms. Those in front overlook the green and the Dublin Mountains in the distance, but rooms in the back, without a view, are quieter. The impressive suites have separate sitting rooms and dressing areas; the largest, with a mini-network of interconnecting rooms, is named in honor of the late Princess Grace of Monaco, who visited in the 1960s and 1970s. Downstairs the public rooms are awhirl with life: The restaurant, 27 The Green, is one of the most elegant rooms in Dublin; Lord Mayor's Lounge, off the lobby, is a perfect rendezvous spot and offers a lovely afternoon tea—a real Dublin tradition; the two bars overflow with prosperous local businesspeople and politicos. ⊠ *27 St. Stephen's Green, Dublin 2,* ☎ *01/ 676–6471,* FAX *01/661–6006. 168 rooms with bath, 22 suites. 2 restaurants, 2 bars, indoor pool, hot tub, sauna, health club, limited free parking. AE, DC, MC, V.*

$$$$ 🏨 **Westbury.** This comfortable, modern hotel has an excellent location in the heart of southside Dublin, right off the city's buzzing shopping mecca, Grafton Street. Both guests and elegantly dressed Dubliners take afternoon tea in the spacious mezzanine-level main lobby, furnished with antiques. Alas, the utilitarian rooms—painted in pastel color schemes—don't share the lobby's elegance. More inviting are the suites, which combine European decor with tasteful Japanese screens and prints. The flowery Russell Room serves formal lunches and dinners; the downstairs Sandbank, a seafood restaurant and bar, has decor resembling a Joycean-period establishment. ⊠ *Grafton St., Dublin 2,* ☎ *01/ 679–1122,* FAX *01/679–7078. 206 rooms with bath, 8 suites. 2 restaurants, shops, free parking. AE, DC, MC, V.*

$$$ 🏨 **Davenport, Mont Clare, and Alexander.** The Davenport's gorgeous, bright yellow neoclassical facade was built in the 1860s to front a church, but a 1993 conversion remade the building into this hotel, terrifically located just behind Trinity College, around the corner from Merrion Square, and down the street from the Government Offices. Beyond the hotel's four-story lobby, few indications of the building's former purpose remain. The reasonably spacious guest rooms and larger suites are well fitted in tasteful deep colors and functional furniture. The hotel restaurant, Lanyon's, serves breakfast, lunch, and dinner amid traditional Georgian decor. In the comfortable President's Bar, you can see how many heads of state you can identify in the photos that cover the walls. The Davenport's sister hotel, the **Mont Clare,** is right across the road; its 78 rooms and two suites were also recently refurbished. In mid-1997, the all-new **Alexander** opened next door, with 100 rooms and three suites. All hotels are fully air-conditioned. ⊠ *Lower Merrion St., Dublin 2,* ☎ *01/661–6800,* FAX *01/661–5663. 118 rooms with bath, 2 suites. Restaurant, bar, free parking. AE, DC, MC, V.*

$$ 🏨 **Central Hotel.** Established in 1887, this grand, old-style redbrick hotel is in the heart of the center city, steps from Grafton Street, Temple Bar, and Trinity College. It has recently undergone a graceful restoration and refurbishment. Guest rooms have high ceilings and practical but

tasteful furniture; although all have showers, not all have baths, so inquire when booking. Adjacent to the hotel is Molly Malone's Tavern, a lively hotel-bar with plenty of regulars who come for the atmosphere and the live, traditional Irish music played on Friday and Saturday nights. The spacious guests' bar and restaurant are on the first floor; the latter serves breakfast, lunch, and dinner. ⊠ *1–5 Exchequer St., Dublin 2,* ☎ *01/679–7302,* ℻ *01/679–7303. 67 rooms with bath, 3 suites. Restaurant, 2 bars. AE, DC, MC, V.*

$$ ⊞ **Drury Court Hotel.** A two-minute walk from Grafton Street and just around the corner from some of the city's best restaurants, this small, centrally located hotel opened in March 1996. The bedrooms are decorated in subtle shades of green, gold, and burgundy and have fully tiled bathrooms. The parquet-floored rathskeller dining room serves breakfast and dinner; lunch is served in the casual Digges Lane Bar, frequented by many young Dubliners. ⊠ *28–30 Lower Stephens St., Dublin 2,* ☎ *01/475–1988,* ℻ *01/478–5730. 30 rooms with bath, 2 suites. AE, DC, MC, V.*

$$ ⊞ **Stephen's Hall All-Suite.** Dublin's only all-suite hotel is in a tastefully modernized Georgian town house just off Stephen's Green. The suites, considerably larger than the average hotel room, include one or two bedrooms, a separate sitting room, a fully equipped kitchen, and bath. They are comfortably equipped with quality, modern furniture. Morel's Restaurant serves breakfast, lunch, and dinner and is popular with nonguests as well. ⊠ *14–17 Lower Leeson St., Dublin 2,* ☎ *01/661–0585,* ℻ *01/661–0606. 37 suites. Restaurant, 2 bars, free parking. AE, DC, MC, V.*

$ ⊞ **Avalon House.** Many young independent travelers rate this cleverly restored Victorian redbrick former medical school the most appealing of Dublin's hostels. A 5–10-minute walk from some of the city's best music venues, the hostel has a mix of dormitories, bedrooms without baths, and bedrooms with bath. The dorm rooms and en suite quads all have loft areas that offer more privacy than you'd typically find in a multibedded room. The Avalon Café serves food until 10 PM but is open as a common room for guests after hours. At press time (summer 1997), a 120-bed extension made up of 2- and 4-bedded rooms with bath was slated to open in June 1998. ⊠ *55 Aungier St., Dublin 2,* ☎ *01/475–0001,* ℻ *01/475–0303. 5 4-bedded rooms with bath, 5 4-bedded rooms without bath, 4 twin rooms with bath, 4 single rooms without bath, 22 twin rooms without bath, 5 12-bedded dorms, 1 10-bedded dorm, 1 26-bedded dorm. Café. AE, MC, V.*

$ ⊞ **Jurys Christchurch Inn.** Expect few frills at this functional budget hotel, part of a new Jurys minichain that offers a low, fixed room rate for up to three adults or two adults and two children. (The Jurys Custom House Inn [⊠ Custom House Quay, Dublin 1, ☎ 01/607–5000, ℻ 01/829–0400], at the International Financial Services Centre, operates according to the same plan.) The biggest plus: the pleasant location, facing Christ Church Cathedral and within walking distance of most city center attractions. The rather spartan rooms are decorated in pastel colors with utilitarian furniture. A bar offers a pub lunch, and the restaurant serves breakfast and dinner. ⊠ *Christchurch Pl., Dublin 8,* ☎ *01/454–0000,* ℻ *01/454–0012. 184 rooms with bath. Restaurant, bar, parking (fee). AE, DC, MC, V.*

$ ⊞ ★ **Kilronan House.** A five-minute walk from St. Stephen's Green, Deirdre and Noel Comer's guest house is a longstanding favorite with vacationers—thanks in large measure to the friendly welcome they receive. The large, late-19th-century terraced house, with a white facade, was carefully converted, and the decor and furnishings are updated each year. Richly patterned wallpaper and carpets grace the bedrooms, while orthopedic beds (rather rare in Dublin hotels, let alone guest houses) help to guarantee a restful night's sleep. Homemade breads are served at the full Irish breakfast. If you have a dog back home whom you're pining after, you'll appreciate Homer, the yellow Labrador who enthusiastically welcomes guests. ⊠ *70 Adelaide Rd., Dublin 2,* ☎ *01/ 475–5266,* FAX *01/478–2841. 14 rooms with bath. MC, V.*

$ ☒ **Number 31.** Two Georgian mews strikingly renovated in the early
★ '60s as the private home of Sam Stephenson, Ireland's leading modern architect, are now connected via a small garden to the grand town house they once served. Together they now form a marvelous guest house a short walk from St. Stephen's Green. Mary and Brian Bennett, the warmly gracious proprietors, serve made-to-order breakfasts at refectory tables in the balcony dining room. The white-tiled sunken living room, with its black leather sectional sofa and modern artwork that includes a David Hockney print, will make you think you're in California, not Dublin. ⊠ *31 Leeson Close, Dublin 2,* ☎ *01/676–5011,* FAX *01/676–2929. 18 rooms with bath. AE, MC, V.*

City Center (Northside)

$ ☒ **Dublin International Youth Hostel.** Housed in a converted convent, Dublin's major hostel has a total of 420 beds divided between private rooms and dorm rooms with 8, 12, 15, or 22 beds. Bath facilities are communal for all guests, even those staying in private rooms. This is a spartan, low-cost alternative to hotels; nonmembers of the international youth hosteling organization can stay for a small extra charge. Continental breakfast is included in the rate. The hostel is north of Parnell Square, near the Mater Hospital. ⊠ *51 Mountjoy St., Dublin 1,* ☎ *01/830–1766,* FAX *01/830–1600. 2 twin rooms, 3 3-bedded rooms, 2 4-bedded rooms, 9 6-bedded rooms, and 8-, 12-, 15-, and 22-bed dorms. Restaurant. MC, V.*

Temple Bar

$$$$ ☒ **The Clarence.** It seems there's no one in Ireland who doesn't know about the Clarence—an 1852 Temple Bar hotel that used to be a favorite place to stay in the capital with clergy and folks up from the provinces. But since mid-1996, when the hotel reopened after an $8-million renovation, guests are much likelier to bump into celebrity friends of co-owners Bono and The Edge of U2 than Father O'Casey from Cork. The hotel is understated to the point of austerity. Stone floors, unadorned oak wainscotting, and a leather-lined elevator set the tone downstairs, where the Octagon Bar and the Tea Room Restaurant (the most sumptuous public space in the hotel) are popular Temple Bar watering holes. Guest rooms are decorated in a soothing earth-tone palette accented with deep purple, gold, cardinal red, and royal blue highlights. With the exception of the penthouse suite, the rooms are small by any standards, but *very* comfortable beds dressed with the most expensive white sheets you've probably ever slept between, sparkling bathrooms, and from the front rooms, views of the Liffey do compensate. The laissez-faire service seems to take its cue from the minimalist decor, so if you like to be pampered, stay elsewhere. The most over-the-top hotel room in the city is the duplex penthouse, which will set you back £1,450 a night—breakfast not included. ⊠ *6–8 Wellington Quay, Dublin 2,* ☎ *01/670–9000,* FAX *01/670–7800. 46 rooms with bath, 4 suites. Restaurant, bar, laundry service, meeting rooms, free parking. AE, DC, MC, V.*

$$ ☒ **Temple Bar.** In 1993 this hotel opened in a former bank building just around the corner from Trinity College in Temple Bar, the neighborhood. The art-deco lobby's imaginative decor includes a large, old-fashioned, cast-iron fireplace, natural-wood furniture, and lots of

plants. Off the lobby are a small cocktail bar and the bright, open, glass-roofed Terrace Restaurant, which serves sandwiches, pastas, omelets, and fish dishes all day. Busker's Bar, a popular Temple Bar watering hole, serves a pub lunch and an early dinner; the Whiskey Corner resembles a traditional Irish pub. Mahogany furniture and autumn green and rust colors are in the bedrooms, nearly all of which have double beds. At press time (summer 1997), 24 new rooms were slated to open in early 1998. ⌷ *Fleet St., Dublin 2,* ☎ *01/677–3333,* ℻ *01/677–3088. 108 rooms with bath. Restaurant, 2 bars, parking (fee). AE, DC, MC, V.*

South County Dublin Suburbs

$$$ ⌷ **Doyle Tara.** On the main coast road five minutes from the Dun Laoghaire ferry terminal and 6½ km/4 mi from the city center, this unpretentious, informal seven-story hotel is also near the Booterstown Marsh Bird Sanctuary (☞ County Dublin—Southside *in* Side Trips, *below*). An extension was recently built onto the main building with a slightly more modern decor. The best rooms are in the original section and face Dublin Bay. The restaurant, attractively refurbished with rustic woodwork, serves grilled fish, steaks, and omelets. The hotel service is very personable. ⌷ *Merrion Rd., Dublin 4,* ☎ *01/269–4666,* ℻ *01/269–1027. 113 rooms with bath. Restaurant, bar, shops. AE, DC, MC, V.*

$$$ ⌷ **Royal Marine.** This 1870 seaside hotel has been totally overhauled in recent years, and its public areas, bar, and restaurant have been completely modernized. The comfortable, capacious bedrooms have also been refurbished with contemporary decor; the eight suites with four-poster beds and separate sitting rooms preserve the lofty ceilings of the original building. Ask for a room at the front of the hotel, facing a gorgeous view of Dun Laoghaire harbor. ⌷ *Marine Rd., Dun Laoghaire, Co. Dublin,* ☎ *01/280–1911,* ℻ *01/280–1089. 96 rooms with bath, 8 suites. Restaurant, 2 bars. AE, DC, MC, V.*

$$ ⌷ **Fitzpatrick Castle Hill.** With its sweeping views over Dun Laoghaire
★ and Dublin Bay, the Fitzpatrick is worth the 13-km/8-mi drive from the city center. The original part of the hotel is a 19th-century stone castle, with a substantial modern addition that houses the guest rooms. A mid-1997 addition added another 20 rooms. Many of the rooms are furnished with antiques and four-poster beds and have large bathrooms. The hotel is convenient to golfing, horseback riding, and fishing; the fitness facilities include an 82-ft heated pool. The views from Killiney Hill, behind the hotel, are spectacular; the seaside village of Dalkey and Killiney Beach are both within comfortable walking distance. ⌷ *Killiney, Co. Dublin,* ☎ *01/284–0700,* ℻ *01/285–0207. 113 rooms with bath. Restaurant, bar, indoor pool, sauna, steam room, health club, baby-sitting, meeting rooms, free parking. AE, DC, MC, V.*

$ ⌷ **Bewleys at Newlands Cross.** On the southwest outskirts of the city, this new four-story hotel is a good option if you're planning to head out of the city (especially to points in the Southwest and West) early and don't want to deal with the morning traffic rush. The hotel is emulating the formula recently made popular by Jurys Inns, in which rooms—here each have a double bed, a single bed, and a sofa bed—are a flat rate for up to three adults or two adults and two children. The large ground floor café—decorated in the rich red upholstery that's a trademark of the Bewley's café chain from which the hotel originates—serves breakfast, lunch, and an à la carte dinner. There is a also a small residents' lounge. ⌷ *Newlands Cross, Naas Rd., Dublin 22,* ☎ *01/464–0140,* ℻ *01/464–0900. 126 rooms with bath. Café, free parking. AE, MC, V.*

NIGHTLIFE AND THE ARTS

Dublin has always had its thriving pubs, but virtually overnight the rest of the world seems to have discovered that it's one of the best cities in all of Europe in which to spend a night on the town. Its pubs and clubs overflow with young cell-phone-toting Dubliners and Europeans who descend on the capital for weekend getaways. The city's 900-plus pubs are the main source of entertainment. Many in the city center offer musical performances—from rock to jazz and traditional Irish music. A number of newspapers have informative listings: *The Irish Times* has a daily guide to what's happening in Dublin and in the rest of the country, as well as complete film and theater schedules. *The Evening Herald* lists theaters, cinemas, and pubs offering live entertainment. *In Dublin* is a fortnightly guide to all film, theater, and musical events around the city. *The Event Guide,* a fortnightly free paper that lists music, cinema, theater, art exhibitions, and dance clubs, can be found in pubs and cafés around the city. In peak season, consult the free Bord Fáilte leaflet "Events of the Week."

The Arts

Theater is the dominant performing art in Dublin, but it's by no means the only one. A handful of cinemas, an opera company, classical music, and galleries supplement the wealth of theater you can see, as well as the city's vibrant pub life.

Art Galleries

Temple Bar Gallery. A flagship of the Temple Bar redevelopment project, this gallery exhibits the work of emerging Irish photographers, painters, sculptors, and other artists in monthly rotating shows. ✉ *5– 9 Temple Bar,* ☎ *01/671–0073.* ☉ *Mon.–Sat. 10–6, Sun. 2–6.*

Original Print Gallery. An ultramodern building by the same award-winning Dublin architect who designed Temple Bar Gallery, this gallery specializes in handmade, limited editions of prints by Irish artists. Also in the building, the **Black Church Print Studio** (☎ 01/677–3629) exhibits prints. ✉ *4 Temple Bar,* ☎ *01/677–3657.* ☉ *Mon.–Sat. 10:30– 5:30, Sat. 11–5, Sun. 2–6.*

Classical Music and Opera

National Concert Hall (✉ Earlsfort Terr., ☎ 01/475–1666), just off St. Stephen's Green, is Dublin's main theater for classical music of all kinds, from symphonies to chamber groups.

Opera Ireland (✉ John Player House, 276–288 S. Circular Rd., Dublin 8, ☎ 01/453–5519) performs at the Gaiety Theatre (☞ *below*); it will be performing Verdi's *Falstaff* and Offenbach's *Tales of Hoffman* April 18–26, 1998. Its fall performances, usually given in late November–early December, had not been announced at press time (summer 1997).

Opera Theatre Company (✉ 18 St. Andrew St., Dublin 2, ☎ 01/679–4962), Ireland's only touring opera company, will perform *Così fan tutte* in Dublin on February 11–12, as well as in Galway (Feb. 1), Sligo (Feb. 3), Derry, (Feb. 5), Athlone (Feb. 14), and Cork (Feb. 19).

Royal Hospital Kilmainham (✉ Military Rd., ☎ 01/671–8666) presents frequent classical concerts.

Film

Dublin has two dozen cinema screens in the city center and boasts large, multiscreen cinema complexes in several of its suburbs, which show a selection of current releases made in Ireland and abroad.

Irish Film Centre (✉ 6 Eustace St., ☎ 01/677–8788; ☞ Exploring Temple Bar, *above*) shows classic and new independent films.

Screen Cinema (✉ 2 Townsend St., ☎ 01/671–4988), between Trinity College and O'Connell Street Bridge, is a popular three-screen art-house cinema.

Rock and Contemporary Music

Olympia Theatre (✉ 72 Dame St., ☎ 01/677–7744; ☞ Exploring Temple Bar, *above*) puts on its "Midnight from the Olympia" shows every Friday and Saturday from midnight–2 AM, with everything from rock to country.

Theater

Abbey Theatre (✉ Lower Abbey St., ☎ 01/878–7222), the home of Ireland's national theater company, stages mainstream, mostly Irish traditional plays. Its sister theater at the same address, the **Peacock**, offers more experimental drama. W. B. Yeats and his patron, Lady Gregory, opened the theater in 1904, which became a major center for the Irish literary renaissance—the place that first staged works by J. M. Synge and Sean O'Casey, among many others. The original theater burned down in 1951, but it reopened with a modern design in 1966.

Andrew's Lane Theatre (✉ 9–11 Andrew's La., ☎ 01/679–5720) and the **Tivoli** (✉ Francis St., ☎ 01/453–5998) present experimental productions.

Gate Theatre (✉ Cavendish Row, Parnell Sq., ☎ 01/874–4045; ☞ Northside City Center, *above*), an intimate 371-seat theater, produces the classics and contemporary plays by leading Irish writers. *A Streetcar Named Desire* is slated for April–May 1998.

Gaiety Theatre (✉ S. King St., ☎ 01/677–1717) is the home of Opera Ireland (☞ *above*) when it's not showing musical comedy, drama, and revues.

Olympia Theatre (✉ 72 Dame St., ☎ 01/677–7744; ☞ Exploring Temple Bar, *above*) is Dublin's oldest and premier multipurpose theatrical venue. In addition to its high-profile musical performances, it has seasons of comedy, vaudeville, and ballet.

Project Arts Centre (✉ 39 E. Essex St., ☎ 01/671–2321) is an established fringe theater.

Nightlife

Dublin has undergone a small nightlife revolution in the last few years. Many of its old-fashioned discos have been eclipsed by sophisticated, internationally known dance clubs. Dubliners typically head for the pubs after the workday ends. Things really start to take off around 10 PM. Pubs officially close at 11 PM in winter, 11.30 PM in summer, but pub-goers put off leaving as long as they can. At clubs with late-night licenses, things don't start to wind down until around 4 AM.

Pubs

SOUTH CITY CENTER: BALLSBRIDGE, DONNYBROOK, AND STILLORGAN

Byrnes (✉ Galloping Green, Stillorgan, ☎ 01/288–7683) has the airy atmosphere of an old-fashioned country pub, even though it's only 8 km/5 mi from the city center. It's one of the few pubs that haven't been renovated. Old prints enhance the decor.

Dubliner Pub (✉ Jurys Hotel, Ballsbridge, ☎ 01/660–5000) was recently remade as an old-fashioned Irish pub; it's a busy meeting place at lunch and after work.

Kiely's (✉ Donnybrook Rd., ☎ 01/283–0208), at first glance, appears to be just another modernized pub, but go up the side lane, and you'll find a second pub, Ciss Madden's, in the same building. Even though it was built in 1992, it's an absolutely authentic and convincing reconstruction of an ancient Irish tavern, right down to the glass globe lights and old advertising signs.

Kitty O'Shea's (✉ Upper Grand Canal St., ☎ 01/660–9965) is decorated with pre-Raphaelite-style stained glass, complementing its lively, sports-oriented atmosphere. Its sister pubs are in Brussels and Paris, but this is the original.

O'Brien's (✉ Sussex Terr., ☎ 01/668–2594), beside the Burlington Hotel, is a little, antique gem of a pub, scarcely changed in 50 years, with traditional snugs.

CITY CENTER

Brazen Head (✉ Bridge St., ☎ 01/677–9549), Dublin's oldest pub (the site has been licensed since 1198!), has stone walls and open fires that have changed little over the years. It's renowned for traditional-music performances and for lively sing-along sessions on Sunday evenings.

Café-en-Seine (✉ 40 Dawson St., ☎ 01/677–4369) is a recent conversion to a Parisian-style "locale," with a wrought-iron balcony, art-deco furniture, and a vaulted ceiling. Café au lait and alcoholic drinks are served all day until closing.

Cassidy's (✉ 42 Lower Camden St., ☎ 01/475–1429) was where President Bill Clinton dropped in for a pint of stout during his visit to Dublin.

Davy Byrne's (✉ 21 Duke St., ☎ 01/671–1298) is a must-visit for Joyceans (☞ "ReJoyce! A Walk through Ulysses and James Joyce's Dublin," *above*). In *Ulysses,* Leopold Bloom stops in here for a glass of burgundy and a Gorgonzola cheese sandwich. He then leaves the pub and walks to Dawson Street, where he helps a blind man cross the road.

Dockers (✉ 5 Sir John Rogerson's Quay, ☎ 01/677–1692) is a trendy quayside spot east of city center, just around the corner from Windmill Lane Studios, where U2 and other noted bands record; at night the area is a little dicey, so come during the day.

Doheny & Nesbitt (✉ 5 Lower Baggot St., ☎ 01/676–2945), a traditional spot with snugs, dark wooden decor, and smoke-darkened ceilings, has hardly changed over the decades it has been open.

Doyle's (✉ 9 College St., ☎ 01/671–0616), a small, cozy pub, is a favorite with journalists who hop over from the *Irish Times* just across the street.

The Globe (✉ 11 S. Great George's St., ☎ 01/671–1220), one of the hippest café-bars in town, draws arty, trendy Dubliners who sip espresso drinks by day and jam it to standing-room capacity by night. There's live jazz on Sundays.

Horseshoe Bar (✉ Shelbourne Hotel, 27 St. Stephen's Green, ☎ 01/676–6471) is a popular meeting place for Dublin's businesspeople and politicians, though it has comparatively little space for drinkers around the semicircular bar.

Kehoe's (✉ 9 S. Anne St., ☎ 01/677–8312) is popular with Trinity students and academics.

McDaid's (✉ 3 Harry St., ☎ 01/679–4395) attracted boisterous Brendan Behan and other leading writers in the 1950s; its wild literary reputation still lingers, although the bar has been discreetly modernized, and the atmosphere is altogether quieter.

Mother Redcap's Tavern (✉ Back La., ☎ 01/453–8306) is an authentic re-creation of a 17th-century Dublin tavern, with stone walls from an old flour mill, beams, and plenty of old prints of the city, as well as trendy Victorian posters.

Neary's (✉ 1 Chatham St., ☎ 01/677–7371), which has an exotic Victorian-style interior, was once the haunt of music-hall artists, as well

Dublin Pubs

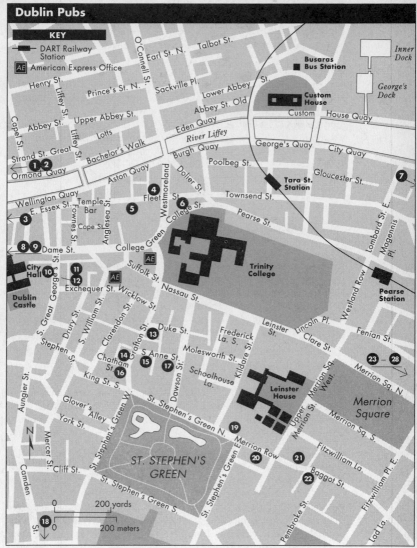

KEY

- ◼ DART Railway Station
- 🅰🅴 American Express Office

Brazen Head, **3**
Byrnes, **23**
Café-en-Seine, **17**
Cassidy's, **18**
Davy Byrne's, **13**
Dockers, **7**
Doheny & Nesbitt, **21**
Doyle's, **6**
Dubliner Pub, **24**
Foxes, **25**
The George, **10**
The Globe, **12**
Horseshoe Bar, **19**

Kehoe's, **15**
Kiely's, **26**
Kitty O'Shea's, **27**
McDaid's, **14**
Mother Redcap's Tavern, **8**
Neary's, **16**
O'Brien's, **28**
O'Donoghue's, **20**
Oliver St. John Gogarty, **5**
Out on the Liffey, **1**
Palace Bar, **4**
Ryan's Pub, **2**

Stag's Head, **11**
Thomas Read's, **9**
Toner's, **22**

as of a certain literary set including Brendan Behan. Join the actors and actresses from the adjacent Gaiety Theatre for a good pub lunch.

O'Donoghue's (⊠ 15 Merrion Row, ☎ 01/676–2807), a cheerful, smoky hangout, offers impromptu musical performances that often spill out onto the street.

Ryan's Pub (⊠ 28 Parkgate St., ☎ 01/677–6097) is one of Dublin's last genuine, late-Victorian-era pubs and has changed little since its last (1896) remodeling. Its dark mahogany counters, old-fashioned lamps, and snugs create a marvelously restful setting.

Stag's Head (⊠ 1 Dame Ct., ☎ 01/679–3701) dates from 1770 and was rebuilt in 1895; theater people from the nearby Olympia turn up around the unusual counter, fashioned from Connemara red marble.

Toner's (⊠ 139 Lower Baggot St., ☎ 01/676–3090), though billed as a Victorian bar, actually goes back 200 years, with an original flag-stone floor to prove its antiquity, as well as wooden drawers running up to the ceiling, a relic of the days when bars doubled as grocery shops. Oliver St. John Gogarty accompanied W. B. Yeats here, in what was purportedly the latter's only visit to a pub.

LESBIAN AND GAY

The George (⊠ 89 S. Great George's St., ☎ 01/478–2983), Dublin's two-floor main gay pub, draws an almost entirely male crowd; its night-club stays open until 2:30 AM nightly except Tuesday.

Out on the Liffey (⊠ 27 Ormond Quay, ☎ 01/872–2480), opened in mid-1996, is Dublin's second gay pub; it draws a mixed crowd of both men and women.

COUNTY DUBLIN—SOUTHSIDE

Foxes (⊠ Glencullen, Co. Dublin, ☎ 01/295–5647), 12 km/8 mi from the city center, sits 1,000 ft up in the Dublin Mountains and is approached by a winding and steeply climbing road that turns off the main Dublin–Enniskerry road at Stepaside. It's packed with ancient artifacts and character. They serve lunch and dinner, and there's traditional Irish music in the evenings.

TEMPLE BAR

Oliver St. John Gogarty (⊠ 57 Fleet St., Temple Bar, ☎ 01/671–1822) is a lively bar that attracts all ages and nationalities and overflows during the summer. On most nights there is traditional Irish music upstairs.

Palace Bar (⊠ 21 Fleet St., ☎ 01/677–9290), scarcely changed over the past 60 years, is tiled and rather barren looking, but popular with journalists and writers (the *Irish Times* is nearby). The walls are hung with cartoons drawn by the illustrators who used to spend time here.

Thomas Read's (⊠ 123 Parliament St., at Dame St., ☎ 01/677–1487) is a European-style bar-café on the edge of Temple Bar that serves atyp-ical pub grub and excellent coffee.

Irish Cabaret

BALLSBRIDGE/SOUTH CITY CENTER

Burlington Hotel (⊠ Upper Leeson St., ☎ 01/660–5222) is a high-class lounge that features a well-performed Irish cabaret, with dancing, music, and song.

Jurys Hotel (⊠ Ballsbridge, ☎ 01/660–5000) stages a cabaret show similar to that at the Burlington Hotel (☞ *above*).

NORTH DUBLIN

Abbey Tavern (⊠ Howth, Co. Dublin, ☎ 01/839–0307) offers a rip-roaring cabaret with rousing, traditional Irish songs.

Castle Inn (✉ Christ Church Pl., ☎ 01/475–1122) is really just a huge pub that has traditional Irish music and dancing with dinner in a medieval-style banquet hall.

Irish Music and Dancing

Comhaltas Ceoltóiri Éireann (✉ 35 Belgrave Sq., Monkstown, ☎ 01/280–0295) offers boisterous summer evenings of genuine Irish music and dancing.

Dance Clubs

The Da Club (✉ 3–5 Clarendon Market, ☎ 01/670–5116), in the refurbished Dublin Arts Club, has become one of the most popular spots in town. Despite its small capacity, it has a large variety of nightly entertainment—from comedy acts to live bands to dance clubs—often running concurrently, as it has two floors. The venue attracts a bright young bohemian crowd. There are full bar facilities.

Leeson Street—just off St. Stephen's Green and known as "the strip"—is a main nightclub area from pub closing time to 4 AM, although it has lost its gloss in recent years. Dress at these places is informal, but jeans and sneakers are not welcome. Most of these clubs are licensed only to sell wine, and the prices can be exorbitant (up to £20 for a mediocre bottle); the up side is that most don't charge to get in.

Lillie's Bordello (✉ Grafton St, ☎ 01/679–9204) is a popular spot for the trendy, professional crowd, and it's a favorite hangout for rock and film stars.

The Pod (✉ Harcourt St., ☎ 01/478–0166) is Dublin's most renowned dance club, especially among the younger set. Entry is judged as much on clothing as on age; it helps to look either trendy or rich.

The Red Box (✉ Old Harcourt Street Station, Harcourt St., ☎ 01/478–0166), adjacent to the Pod and the Chocolate Bar, can pack in more than 1,000 people and surround them with state-of-the-art sound and light. It regularly hosts Irish and international rock acts as well as celebrity DJs from Europe and the U.S. As with most Dublin rock venues, The Red Box has full bar facilities.

The Kitchen (✉ East Essex St., ☎ 01/677–6359), one of the newest nightclubs in Dublin, is in the cavelike basement of the Clarence Hotel (☞ Lodging, *above*); its popularity, primarily with an under-30 crowd, owes much to its owners, Bono and the Edge of U2.

Temple Bar Music Centre (✉ Curved St., ☎ 01/670–9202)—a music venue, rehearsal space, television studio, and pub rolled into one—buzzes with activity every day of the week. A number of music programs have been made here featuring Van Morrison, U2, Sharon Shannon, and Mark Knopfler. Live acts range from rock bands to ethnic music to singer-songwriters.

OUTDOOR ACTIVITIES AND SPORTS

Although you may not be readily able to find a place to work out, there are still plenty of ways to get out and move about. You can explore a beach; cheer on a hometown team; or walk, run, horseback-ride or bike through Phoenix Park. Diehard daily exercisers, take heart: Dublin's dearth of fitness facilities is rapidly being remedied by many hotels.

Beaches

On the north side of Dublin city lies **Bull Island,** created over the years by the action of the tides and offering an almost 3-km-/2-mi-long stretch of fine sand. Bus 130 from Lower Abbey Street stops by the walkway to the beach (☞ County Dublin—Northside *in* Side Trips, *below*). The main beach for swimming on the south side of Dublin is at **Killiney** (13 km/8 mi south of the city center), a shingly beach stretching for 3 km/2 mi. The DART train station is right by the beach; the stop is called Killiney. Near Dublin city center, **Sandymount Strand** is a long expanse of fine sand where the tide goes out nearly 3 km/2 mi, but it is not suitable for swimming or bathing because the tide races in so fast. The strand also can be reached easily by the DART train.

Participant Sports

If it's essential that you get in a daily workout, you should be able to while you're in Dublin, although it will probably take some careful planning. For all its recent changes, the city hasn't yet embraced health clubs and fitness centers. If it's important that you have access to one, your best bet is to stay at one of the four hotels of the Doyle Hotel Group (☞ Burlington Hotel and Doyle Tara *in* Lodging, *above*), which has an exclusive arrangement with one of Dublin's best private facilities. Also check the service information we provide for each hotel for particular fitness amenities; if you find a hotel you'd like to stay at but we don't note any, you should call to inquire, as many of the hotels that are currently expanding are adding these amenities, and others may follow suit.

Bicycling

Cycling is not recommended in the city center as traffic is heavy and most roads don't have shoulders, much less bike lanes. Phoenix Park and some suburbs (especially Ballsbridge, Clontarf, and Sandymount), however, are pleasant for cycling once you're off the main roads. To the immediate south of Dublin, the Dublin and Wicklow Mountains provide plenty of challenging terrain (☞ Chapter 3). Care should always be taken in securing your bicycle when it's left unattended.

Bicycles can be rented for around £35 a week, with an equivalent amount charged for deposit. Nearly 20 firms in the Dublin region rent bicycles; TIOs have a full list. Some of the best firms include **Joe Daly** (✉ Lower Main St., Dundrum, ☎ 01/298–1485); **McDonald's** (✉ 38 Wexford St., ☎ 01/475–2586); **C. Harding** (✉ 30 Bachelor's Walk, off O'Connell St., ☎ 01/873–2455), and **Mike's Bike Shop** (✉ Dun Laoghaire Shopping Center, ☎ 01/280–0417).

Bowling

Bowling is a popular sport in Dublin; two kinds are played locally. The sedate, outdoor variety is played at **Herbert Park** (✉ Ballsbridge, ☎ 01/660–1875). The city has seven indoor bowling centers: **Dundrum Bowl** (✉ Ballinteer Rd., Dundrum, ☎ 01/298–0209); **Leisure-plex Coolock** (✉ Malahide Rd., ☎ 01/848–5722; ✉ Village Green Center, Tallaght, ☎ 01/459–9411); **Stillorgan Bowl** (✉ Stillorgan, ☎ 01/288–1656); **Metro Bowl** (✉ 149 Strand Rd., ☎ 01/855–0400); **Superdome** (✉ Palmerstown, ☎ 01/626–0700) and **Bray Bowl** (✉ Quinsboro Rd., ☎ 01/286–4455).

Golf

The Dublin region is an idyllic place for golfers, with 30 18-hole courses and 15 nine-hole courses, and several more on the way. For detailed information about Dublin's championship courses, including **Portmarnock, St. Margaret's,** and **Royal Dublin,** *see* Chapter 10. Other major 18-hole courses include the following: **Deer Park** (✉ Howth, ☎ 01/832–2624) has appealing water views. **Edmonstown** (✉ Rathfarnham, ☎ 01/493–1082) is close to the Dublin Mountains. **Elm Park** (✉ Donnybrook, ☎ 01/269–3438) has a rural ambience despite its south-city-suburb location. **Foxrock** (✉ Torquay Rd., ☎ 01/289–3992) is in an exclusive residential area. **Newlands** (✉ Clondalkin, ☎ 01/459–2903) is an inland course west of Dublin. **Sutton** (✉ Sutton, ☎ 01/832–3013) is a seaside course north of Dublin. **Woodbrook** (✉ Bray, ☎ 01/282–4799), south of Dublin city center, has stunning mountain views and sea breezes.

Horseback Riding

Dublin's environs offer excellent horseback riding. Stables on the city outskirts give immediate access to suitable riding areas. In the city itself, Phoenix Park provides superb, quiet riding conditions away from the busy main road that bisects the park. About 20 riding stables in the greater Dublin area have horses for hire by the hour or the day, for novices and experienced riders; a few also operate as equestrian centers and offer lessons. Major stables in the area include **Deerpark Riding Center** (✉ Castleknock Rd., Castleknock, ☎ 01/820–7141) and **Brittas Lodge Riding Stables** (✉ Brittas, ☎ 01/458–2726). Outside Dublin, Counties Dublin, Kildare, Louth, Meath, and Wicklow all have unspoiled country territory ideal for horseback riding (☞ Chapter 3).

Jogging

Traffic in Dublin is heavy from early morning until late into the night and it's getting worse, so if you're used to jogging the streets back home, you'll have to dodge vehicles and stop for lights. (Remember to *always* look to your right *and* your left before crossing a street.) If you're staying in Temple Bar or on the western end of the city and you can run 9 km/5 mi, head to Phoenix Park, easily the nicest place in the city for a jog. If you're on the southside, Merrion Square, St. Stephen's Green, and Trinity College are all good places for short jogs, though be prepared to dodge pedestrians; if you're looking for a longer route, ask your hotel to direct you to the Grand Canal, which has a pleasant path you can run along as far east as the Grand Canal Street Bridge.

Swimming

Dublin has 12 public pools, but only two can be recommended to visitors: **Townsend Street** (✉ Townsend St. off Tara St., ☎ 01/677–0503) and **Williams Park** (✉ Rathmines, ☎ 01/496–1275). Privately owned pools open to the public for a small fee are located at **Dundrum Family Recreation Center** (✉ Meadowbrook, Dundrum, ☎ 01/298–4654), **Fitzpatrick's Killiney Castle Hotel** (✉ Killiney, ☎ 01/285–0328), **St. Vincent's** (✉ Navan Rd., ☎ 01/838–4906), and **Terenure College** (✉ Templeogue Rd., ☎ 01/490–7071). For hardier spirits there is year-round sea swimming at the **Forty Foot Bathing Pool** in Sandycove (☞ Side Trips, *below*).

Tennis

Tennis is one of Dublin's most popular participant sports, and some public parks have excellent tennis facilities that are open to visitors. Among the best are **Bushy Park** (✉ Terenure, ☎ 01/490–0320), **Herbert Park** (✉ Ballsbridge, ☎ 01/668–4364), and **St. Anne's Park** (✉ Dollymount, ☎ 01/833–8898). Several private tennis clubs are open to visitors, such as **Kilternan Tennis Centre** (✉ Kilternan Golf and Country Club Hotel, Kilternan, ☎ 01/295–3729); **Landsdowne Lawn Tennis Club,** (✉ Londonbridge Rd., Dublin 4, ☎ 01/668–0219); and **West Wood Lawn Tennis Club** (✉ Leopardstown Racecourse, Foxrock, Dublin 18, ☎ 01/289–2911). For more information, contact **Tennis Ireland** (✉ 22 Argyle Sq., Donnybrook, Dublin 4, ☎ 01/668–1841).

ectator Sports

Gaelic Games

The traditional games of Ireland, including Gaelic football and hurling, attract a huge following, with roaring crowds cheering on their county teams. Games are held at **Croke Park,** the main stadium, just north of the city center. For details of matches, contact the **Gaelic Athletic Association** (⊠ Croke Park, ☎ 01/836–3222).

Horse Racing

Horse racing is one of the great sporting loves of the Irish; nothing attracts the crowds like a race meeting. The sport is closely followed and betting is popular, but the social side of attending racing is also important to Dubliners. The main course in Dublin is **Leopardstown** (☎ 01/289–3607), an ultramodern course on the southside. In the greater Dublin region, other courses include **Fairyhouse** (⊠ Co. Meath, ☎ 01/ 825–6167) and the **Curragh** (☎ 045/441205; ☞ Chapter 3), southwest of Dublin.

Rugby

International rugby matches are staged during the winter and spring at the vast **Lansdowne Road Stadium.** Local matches are played every weekend, also during the winter and spring. For details, contact the **Irish Rugby Football Union** (⊠ 62 Lansdowne Rd., ☎ 01/668–4601).

Soccer

Although soccer, called football in Europe, is the country's latest bigtime sport following some impressive international wins, facilities for watching it are not so ideal; they tend to be small and out of date. **Lansdowne Road,** the vast rugby stadium, is the main center for international matches. For details, contact the **Football Association of Ireland** (⊠ 80 Merrion Sq. S, ☎ 01/676–6864).

SHOPPING

Dublin's central shopping area, from O'Connell to Grafton streets, is the best place in Ireland for concentrated general and specialty shopping, at prices competitive with those in most European countries. Department stores that stock universally known fashion designers and housewares stand beside small, owner-managed boutiques that make shopping in the city a personalized and pleasurable experience. Prices can be higher in the smaller shops, but the department stores are less likely to stock specifically Irish crafts. Shopping in central Dublin can mean pushing through crowds, especially in the afternoons and on weekends. Most large shops and department stores are open Monday–Saturday 9–6. Although nearly all department stores are closed on Sundays, some smaller specialty shops stay open. Shops with later closing hours are noted below. You're particularly likely to find sales during the months of January, February, July, and August.

Shopping Streets

Dublin's dozen or so main shopping streets each have a different character, and it's only by visiting all of them that you can really appreciate just how wide a range of things are for sale here. The main commercial streets north of the river have chain stores and lackluster department stores that tend to be less expensive and less design-conscious than their counterparts in the city center on the other side of the Liffey.

City Center (Northside)

O'Connell Street. One of Dublin's largest department stores, Clery's, faces the GPO across the city's main thoroughfare—more downmarket than southside city streets but still worth a walk. On the same side of the street as the post office is Eason's, a large book, magazine, and stationery store.

Henry Street. Running westward from O'Connell Street, this is the street where middle-class Dublin shops. Arnotts department store is the anchor; a host of smaller, specialty stores sell CDs, footwear, and fashion. Henry Street's continuation, Mary Street, has a branch of Marks & Spencer and the new Jervis Shopping Centre (☞ *below*).

City Center (Southside)

Grafton Street. Dublin's bustling pedestrian-only main shopping street has two upscale department stores, Marks & Spencer and Brown Thomas. The rest of the street is taken up by smaller shops, many of them branches of international chains such as The Body Shop and Bally Shoes, as well as many British chains. Smaller streets off Grafton Street, especially **Duke Street, South Anne Street,** and **Chatham Street,** have worthwhile crafts, clothing, and designer housewares shops.

Francis Street. The Liberties, the oldest part of the city, is the hub of Dublin's antiques trade. This street and surrounding areas, such as the Coombe, have plenty of shops where you can browse. If you're looking for something in particular, dealers will gladly recommend the appropriate store to you.

Nassau Street. Dublin's main tourist-oriented thoroughfare has some of the best-known stores selling Irish goods, but you won't find many locals shopping here. Still, if you're looking for classic Irish gifts to take home, you should be sure at least to browse here.

Dawson Street. Just east of Grafton Street between Nassau Street to the north and St. Stephen's Green to the south, this is the city's primary bookstore avenue, with both Waterstone's and Hodges Figgis (☞ Books, *below*).

Temple Bar. Dublin's hippest neighborhood is dotted with small, precious boutiques—mostly intimate, quirky shops that traffic in a small selection of *tres* trendy goods, from vintage wear to some of the most avant-garde Irish clothing you'll find anywhere in the city.

Specialty Shopping Centers

City Center (Northside)

Ilac Center (✉ Henry St.) was Dublin's first large, modern, shopping center, with two department stores, hundreds of specialty shops, and several restaurants. The stores are not as exclusive as at some of the other centers, but there's plenty of free parking.

Jervis Shopping Centre (✉ Jervis and Mary Sts.), opened in late 1996, is Dublin's newest city center shopping mall; it brought with it the major British chain stores.

City Center (Southside)

Powerscourt Townhouse Centre (✉ S. William St.), the former town home of Lord Powerscourt and built in 1771, has an interior courtyard that has been refurbished and roofed over; a pianist often plays on the dais at ground-floor level. Coffee shops and restaurants share space with a mix of antiques and crafts stores, including the **HQ Gallery,** the main gallery of the Irish Craft Council and one of the finest places in Dublin to buy contemporary crafts.

Royal Hibernian Way (✉ Off Dawson St. between S. Anne and Duke Sts.) is on the former site of the two-centuries-old Royal Hibernian Hotel, a coaching inn that was demolished in 1983. The stylish shops are small

Dublin Shopping

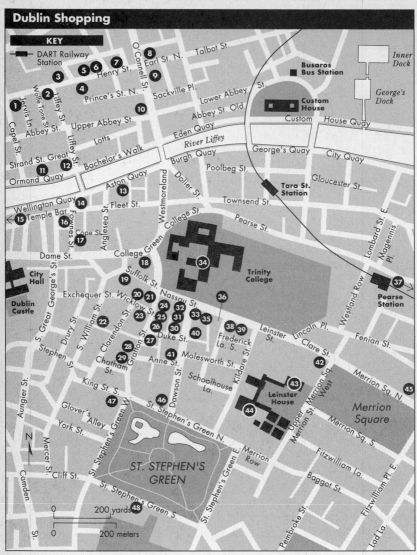

in scale and include a branch of Leonidas, the Belgian chocolate firm.
St. Stephen's Green Centre (✉ Northwest corner of St. Stephen's Green), Dublin's largest and most ambitious shopping center, resembles a giant greenhouse, with ironwork in the Victorian style. On three floors overlooked by a vast clock, the 100 mostly small shops sell a variety of crafts, fashions, and household goods.
Tower Design Centre (✉ Pearse St., ☎ 01/677–5655), east of the heart of the city center (near the Waterways Visitor Centre; ☞ The Georgian Heart of Dublin, *above*), has more than 35 separate crafts firms in a converted 1862 sugar-refinery tower. On the ground floor, visitors can stop at workshops devoted to heraldry and Irish pewter; the other six floors feature hand-painted silks, ceramics, hand-knit items, jewelry, and fine-art cards and prints.

South County Dublin Suburbs

Blackrock (✉ Blackrock, Co. Dublin) is technically outside of Dublin's city center, but it deserves special mention as one of the most customer-friendly shopping centers around. It's built on two levels, looking onto an inner courtyard, with the giant Superquinn Foodstore, cafés, and restaurants. Blackrock can be reached conveniently on the DART train line; it has its own stop.

Department Stores

Arnotts (✉ Henry St., ☎ 01/872–1111) has a wide variety of clothing, household, and sporting goods filling three complete floors; the smaller Grafton Street branch (✉ Grafton St., ☎ 01/872–1111) stocks only new fashion and footwear.
A-Wear (✉ Grafton St., ☎ 01/671–7200; ✉ Henry St., ☎ 01/872–4644) is a line of shops specializing in fashion for men and women. Many of the items are seasonal and closely follow the ever-changing styles. A steady stream of clothing is supplied by leading Irish designers, including John Rocha.
Brown Thomas (✉ Grafton St., ☎ 01/679–5666), Dublin's most exclusive department store, stocks the leading designer names in clothing and cosmetics and a wide variety of stylish accessories. They also carry clothing by Irish designers.
Clery's (✉ O'Connell St., ☎ 01/878–6000) was once the city's most fashionable department store and is still worth a visit, despite its rapidly aging decor. It has four floors of all types of merchandise—from fashion to home appliances—and caters to a distinctly modest, traditional sense of style.
Dunnes Stores (✉ St. Stephen's Green Center, ☎ 01/478–0188; ✉ Henry St., ☎ 01/872–6833; ✉ Ilac Shopping Center, Mary St., ☎ 01/873–0211) is Ireland's largest chain of department stores. All stores stock fashion, household, and grocery items and have a reputation for value and variety.
Eason's (✉ O'Connell St., ☎ 01/873–3811; ✉ Ilac Shopping Center, Mary St., ☎ 01/872–1322) is known primarily for its wide variety of books, magazines, and stationery; its larger O'Connell Street branch now sells tapes, CDs, records, and videos, and other audiovisual goodies.
Marks & Spencer (✉ Grafton St., ☎ 01/679–7855; ✉ Henry St., ☎ 01/872–8833), perennial competitor to Brown Thomas, recently moved down Grafton Street; it stocks everything from fashion (including lingerie) to tasteful, unusual groceries.

Specialty Shops

Antiques

Antiques and Collectibles Fairs (☎ 01/670–8295) take place at Newman House (✉ 85–86 St. Stephen's Green) every second Sunday throughout the year.

Books

Bibliophiles won't have any difficulty weighing down their suitcases with books: Ireland, after all, has produced four Nobel literature laureates in just under 75 years. If you're at all interested in modern and contemporary literature, be sure to leave yourself time to browse the bookstores, as you're likely to find books available here you can't find back home. Best of all, thanks to an enlightened national social policy, there's no tax on books, so if you only buy books, you don't have to worry about getting VAT slips.

Books Upstairs (✉ 36 College Green, ☎ 01/679–6687) carries an excellent range of special-interest books including gay and feminist literature, psychology, and self-help books.

Cathach Books (✉ 10 Duke St., ☎ 01/671–8676) sells first editions of Irish literature and many other books of Irish interest.

Dublin Bookshop (✉ 24 Grafton St., ☎ 01/677–5568) is an award-winning, family-owned bookstore.

Fred Hanna's (✉ 29 Nassau St., ☎ 01/677–1255) sells old and new books, with a good choice of books on travel and Ireland.

Greene's (✉ Clare St., ☎ 01/676–2544) carries an extensive range of secondhand volumes.

Hodges Figgis (✉ 56–58 Dawson St., ☎ 01/677–4754), Dublin's leading independent, stocks 1½ million books on three floors; there's also a pleasant café on the first floor.

Waterstone's (✉ 7 Dawson St., ☎ 01/679–1415), a large branch of the British chain, has two floors featuring a fine selection of Irish and international books.

Winding Stair (✉ 40 Lower Ormond Quay, ☎ 01/873–3292) has lots of slightly dusty secondhand books and a counterculture-y café that overlooks the Liffey and Southside Dublin.

China, Crystal, Ceramics, and Jewelry

Ireland is synonymous with Waterford crystal, which is available in a wide range of products, including relatively inexpensive items. But other lines are now gaining recognition, such as Cavan, Galway, and Tipperary crystal. **Brown Thomas** (☞ *above*) is the best department store; the best specialty outlets are listed below.

Blarney Woollen Mills (✉ 21–23 Nassau St., ☎ 01/671–0068) is one of the best places for Belleek china, Waterford and Galway crystal, and Irish linen.

Designyard (✉ East Essex St., ☎ 01/677–8453) offers beautifully designed Irish and international tableware, lighting, small furniture, and jewelry.

House of Ireland (✉ 37–38 Nassau St., ☎ 01/671–6133) carries an extensive selection of crystal, jewelry, tweeds, sweaters, and other upscale goods.

Kilkenny Shop (✉ 5–6 Nassau St., ☎ 01/677–7066) specializes in contemporary Irish-made ceramics, pottery, and silver jewelry, and also holds regular exhibits of exciting new work by Irish craftsmen.

McDowell (✉ 3 Upper O'Connell St., ☎ 01/874–4961), a jewelry shop popular with Dubliners, has been in business for more than 100 years.

Tierneys (⊠ St. Stephen's Green Centre, ☎ 01/478–2873) carries a good selection of crystal and china. Claddagh rings, pendants, and brooches are popular buys.

Weir & Sons (⊠ 96 Grafton St., ☎ 01/677–9678), Dublin's most prestigious jewelers, sells a wide range of goods in addition to jewelry and watches, including china, glass, lamps, silver, and leather.

Museum Stores

National Gallery of Ireland Shop (⊠ Merrion Sq. W, ☎ 01/678–5450) has a terrific selection of books on Irish art, plus posters, postcards, note cards, and a wide array of lovely bibelots.

National Museum Shop (⊠ Kildare St., ☎ 01/677–7444, ext. 327) carries jewelry based on ancient Celtic artifacts in the museum collection, contemporary Irish pottery, a large selection of books, and other gift items.

Trinity College Library Shop (⊠ Old Library, Trinity College, ☎ 01/608–2308) sells Irish-theme books, *Book of Kells* souvenirs of all kinds, plus clothing, jewelry, and other lovely Irish-made items.

Music

An increasing amount of Irish-recorded material—including traditional folk music, country and western, rock, and even a smattering of classical music—is now available on records, compact discs, and tapes.

Claddagh Records (⊠ 2 Cecilia St., Temple Bar, ☎ 01/679–3664), **Gael Linn** (⊠ 26 Merrion Sq., ☎ 01/676–7283), and **Celtic Note** (⊠ 12 Nassau St., ☎ 01/670–4157) specialize in traditional Irish-music and Irish-language recordings.

HMV (⊠ 65 Grafton St., ☎ 01/679–5334; ⊠ 18 Henry St., ☎ 01/872–2095) is one of the larger record shops in town.

McCullogh Piggott (⊠ 25 Suffolk St., ☎ 01/677–3138) is the best place in town for instruments, sheet music, scores, and books about music.

Tower Records (⊠ 6–8 Wicklow St., ☎ 01/671–3250) is the best-stocked international chain.

Virgin Megastore (⊠ 14–18 Aston Quay, ☎ 01/677–7361) is Dublin's biggest music store and holds in-store performances by Irish bands.

Sweaters and Tweeds

If you think Irish woolens are limited to Aran sweaters and tweed jackets, you'll be pleasantly surprised by the range of hats, gloves, scarves, blankets, and other goods you can find. If you're traveling outside of Dublin, you may want to wait to make these purchases, but if Dublin is it, you still have plenty of good shops to choose from. The tweed on sale in Dublin comes from two main sources, Donegal and Connemara; labels inside the garments guarantee their authenticity. The following are the largest retailers of traditional Irish woolen goods in the city:

An Táin (⊠ 13 Temple Bar Sq. N, ☎ 01/679–0523) carries hyper-stylish handmade Irish sweaters, jackets, and accessories

Blarney Woollen Mills (⊠ 21–23 Nassau St., ☎ 01/671–0068) has a good selection of tweed, linen, and woolen sweaters in all price ranges.

Cleo Ltd. (⊠ 18 Kildare St., ☎ 01/676–1421) sells hand-knit sweaters and accessories made only from natural fibers; they also design and make their own clothing.

Dublin Woollen Mills (⊠ Metal Bridge Corner, ☎ 01/677–5014) at Ha'penny Bridge has a good selection of hand-knit and other woolen sweaters at competitive prices.

Kevin and Howlin (⊠ 31 Nassau St., ☎ 01/677–0257) specializes in handwoven tweed men's jackets, suits, and hats and also sells tweed fabric.

Monaghan's (⊠ Grafton Arcade, 15–17 Grafton St., ☎ 01/677–0823) specializes in cashmere.

Vintage

Flip (⊠ 4 Upper Fownes St., ☎ 01/671–4299), one of the original stores in Temple Bar, sells vintage and retro clothing from the '50s, '60s, and '70s.

Outdoor Markets

Dublin has a number of open-air markets. **Moore Street,** behind the Ilac center, is open from Mondays to Saturdays, 9–6; stalls lining both sides of the street sell fruits and vegetables. The traditional Dublin repartée here is renowned in the city. Other open markets are only open on weekends. A variety of bric-a-brac is sold at the **Liberty Market** on the north end of Meath Street, open on Fridays and Saturdays, 10–6, and Sundays, noon–5:30. The indoor **Mother Redcap's Market** (☞ Dublin Castle, Christ Church, and West Dublin, *above*), opposite Christ Church Cathedral, is open Fridays, Saturdays, and Sundays, 10–5; come here for antiques and bric-a-brac. Outside the city center, weekend markets take place in Blackrock, Dun Laoghaire, and Rathmines (☞ Side Trips, *below*).

SIDE TRIPS

Once you cross over the Grand Canal, which defines the southern border of the city center, you cross into Ballsbridge and other southern areas of the city and its suburbs. If you do set out for points south and you don't have time to see everything, plan to begin in Ballsbridge. If you have a car, then head to Rathfarnham, directly south of the city. Alternatively, head east and follow the coast road south to Dun Laoghaire (and points even farther south, covered in Chapter 3). Beyond Ballsbridge, these areas are too spread out to cover on foot, and either a car or public transportation (the bus or DART) are the only ways to get around. Whether you head north or south, traveling to and from each of the suburbs will take up most of a day, so you will have to pick and choose the trips you prefer.

County Dublin—Southside

Rathfarnham

Two parks lie in the suburb of Rathfarnham, due south of the city at the edge of the Dublin Mountains. (You can take Bus 47A from Hawkins Street in the city center to both of them, or drive, leaving the city center via Nicholas Street just west of Christ Church Cathedral and following it south through Terenure.) The 18th-century house in

⑤⑨ St. Edna's Park has been turned into a museum commemorating Patrick Pearse, leader of Dublin's 1916 Easter Uprising. In the early years of this century, the house was a progressive boys' school, which Pearse and his brother Willie founded. The museum preserves Pearse family memorabilia, documents, and photographs. A charming lake and nature trails are also on the park's 50-acre grounds. ⊠ *Grange Rd., Rathfarnham,* ☎ *01/493–4208.* ⌷ *Free.* ☉ *Park daily 8:30–dusk, museum Apr.–Sept., daily 10–1 and 2–6; Oct.–Mar., daily 10–1 and 2–5.*

ⓒ ⑥⓪ To get to **Marlay Park,** leave St. Edna's Park via Grange Road and walk up the hill for about 1 km/½ mi, turning left at the T junction and continuing ½ km/¼ mi farther. The park marks the start of the **Wicklow Way,** a popular walking route that crosses the Wicklow Mountains for 48 km/30 mi, through some of the most rugged landscapes in Ireland (☞ Chapter 3). In addition to its woodlands and nature walks, the 214-

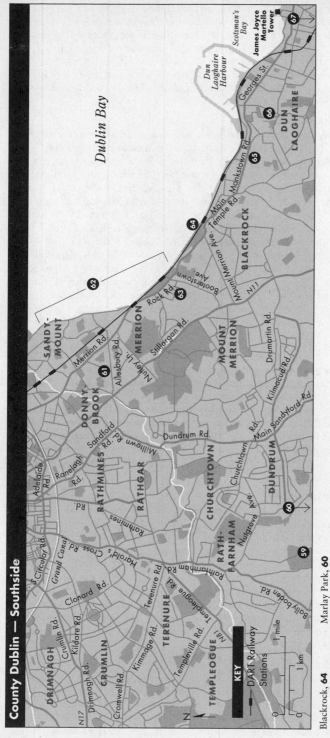

County Dublin — Southside

Blackrock, **64**
Booterstown Marsh
Bird Sanctuary, **63**
Chester Beatty
Library, **61**
Dalkey, **67**
Dun Laoghaire, **66**

Marley Park, **60**
Monkstown, **65**
Sandymount
Strand, **62**
St. Edna's Park, **59**

acre park has a cobbled courtyard, home to brightly plumaged peacocks. Surrounding this courtyard are crafts workshops, where visitors are welcome to watch the craftspeople in the process of bookbinding and making jewelry and furniture. Every Saturday from 3 to 5, kids can take a free ride on the model steam railway. ⊠ *Grange Rd., Rathfarnham,* ☎ *01/493–4059.* 🎟 *Free.* ☉ *Nov.–Jan., daily 10–5; Feb.– Mar., daily 10–6; Apr. and Oct., daily 10–7; May and Sept, daily 10–8; June–Aug., daily 10–9.*

Ballsbridge

Many of Dublin's best hotels and restaurants are in the northern reaches of Ballsbridge, a leafy suburb that is directly across the Grand Canal from the city center. Its major cultural sites, however, are considerably farther south—a bit too far to reach on foot for all but the most ambitious walkers. To visit these sites, take the DART train to Sidney Parade, or Bus 7 or Bus 8 from Burgh Quay (on the south bank of the Liffey, just east of O'Connell Bridge). From the DART station, walk west on Ailesbury Road to Shrewsbury Road, where you'll reach

★ ⑥ the **Chester Beatty Library.** Sir Alfred Chester Beatty (1875–1968), a Canadian mining millionaire, assembled one of the most significant collections of Islamic and Far Eastern art in the Western world, which he then donated to Ireland. Among the library's exhibits are clay tablets from Babylon dating from 2700 BC, Japanese color wood-block prints, Chinese jade books, and Turkish and Persian paintings. The library is slated to close in mid-1998 in preparation for its move to Dublin Castle. ⊠ *20 Shrewsbury Rd., Ballsbridge,* ☎ *01/269–2386.* 🎟 *Free.* ☉ *Tues.–Fri. 10–5, Sat. 2–5; tours Wed. and Sat. at 2:30.*

⑥ To reach **Sandymount Strand,** double back to the Sydney Parade DART station and keep heading west the few blocks to the beach. Stretching for 5 km/3 mi from Ringsend to Booterstown, Sandymount was cherished by James Joyce and his beloved from Galway, Nora Barnacle, and it figures as one of the settings in *Ulysses.* (The beach is "at the lacefringe of the tide," as Joyce put it.) When the tide recedes, the beach extends for 1½ km/1 mi from the foreshore, but the tide sweeps in again very quickly. A sliver of a park lies between the main Strand Road and the beach.

Booterstown

Booterstown lies along Dublin Bay south of Sandymount along the R118. (You can reach it via the DART local train or by car, picking up the R118 from the corner of Lower Merrion Street and Merrion Square.)

⑥ The **Booterstown Marsh Bird Sanctuary** is the largest wildlife preserve in the Dublin area. Curlews, herons, kingfishers, and other fairly rare migratory species come to nest here; information boards along the road describe the birds for visitors. Also on this main road you'll pass **Glena,** the house where Athlone-born John McCormack, one of the best and most popular tenors in the first quarter of this century, died on September 16, 1945. ⊠ *Between the DART line and Rock Rd.,* ☎ *01/454–1786.*

Blackrock

Fine sea views, swimming, and a major shopping center (☞ Shopping, *above*) draw Dubliners down to **Blackrock** (3 km/2 mi south of Booterstown), a bedroom community where James Joyce's parents lived with their large brood for most of 1892. Above the Blackrock DART station, **Idrone Terrace,** lined with restored, old-fashioned lamps, provides a lovely view across the bay to Howth Peninsula.

DINING

$$$ ✕ **Ayumi-Ya Japanese Restaurant.** Eight kilometers/5 miles from the city center, this was Dublin's first Japanese restaurant. Customers have a choice of sitting at regular tables or on the floor, Japanese-style. The wait staff wear kimonos or Japanese-style shirts, and the Japanese proprietor-chef is a qualified dietician who has won numerous awards for her cuisine. Choices include sushi and sashimi, tempura (a deep-fried selection of prawns, vegetables, and fish), beef teriyaki, and teppanyaki, which the chef cooks right at the tables. ✉ *Newpark Centre, Newtownpark Ave., Blackrock,* ☎ *01/283–1767. Reservations essential. AE, DC, MC, V. No lunch Sat., Sun.*

Monkstown

65 One of Dublin's most exclusive suburbs, **Monkstown** (3 km/2 mi south of Blackrock on the R119) boasts two architectural curiosities. John Semple, the architect of Monkstown's **Anglican parish church,** was inspired by two entirely different styles, the Gothic and the Moorish, which he joined into an unlikely hybrid of towers and turrets. Built in 1833 in the town's main square, the church is only open during Sunday services. The well-preserved ruins of **Monkstown Castle** lie about 1 km/⅔ mi south of the suburb; it's a 15th-century edifice with a keep, a gatehouse, and a long wall section, all surrounded by greenery. Monkstown's **Lambert Puppet Theatre** (✉ Clifton La., ☎ 01/280–0974) stages regular puppet shows and has a puppetry museum. To get here, you can take the DART train from the city center to the Monkstown and Seapoint stations.

Dun Laoghaire and Sandycove

66 After the British monarch King George IV disembarked for a brief visit in 1821, **Dun Laoghaire** (pronounced "dun *lear*-ee"; it's 2½ km/1½ mi beyond Monkstown along the R119, the Monkstown Crescent) was renamed Kingstown, but it reverted to its original Irish name 99 years later. Its Irish name refers to Laoghaire, the High King of Tara who in the 5th century permitted St. Patrick to begin to convert Ireland to Christianity. The town was once a Protestant stronghold of the old ruling elite; in some of the neo-Georgian squares and terraces behind the main thoroughfare, **George's Street,** a little of the community's former elegance can still be felt.

Dun Laoghaire has long been known for its great harbor, enclosed by two piers, each 2½ km/1½ mi long. The harbor was constructed between 1817 and 1859, using granite quarried from nearby Dalkey Hill; the west pier has a rougher surface and is less favored for walking than the east pier, which features a bandstand where musicians play during summer. The workaday business here includes passenger-ship and freight-services sailings to Holyhead in north Wales, 3½ hours away (☞ Arriving and Departing by Ferry *in* Dublin A to Z, *below*). Dun Laoghaire is also a yachting center, with the members-only Royal Irish, National, and Royal St. George yacht clubs, all founded in the 19th century, lining the harbor area.

West of the harbor and across from the Royal Marine Hotel and the People's Park, the **National Maritime Museum** is in the former Mariners' church. Its nave makes a strangely ideal setting for exhibits like the French longboat captured during an aborted French invasion at Bantry, County Cork, in 1796. A particularly memorable exhibit is the old optic from the Baily Lighthouse on Howth Head, across Dublin Bay; the herringbone patterns of glass reflected light across the bay until 20 years ago. ✉ *Haigh Terr.,* ☎ *01/280–0969.* 🎟 *£1.* ◷ *May–Sept., Tues.–Sun. 2:30–5:30.*

From the harbor area Marine Parade leads alongside Scotsmans Bay for 1¼ km/¾ mi, as far as the **Forty Foot Bathing Pool,** a traditional bathing area that attracts mostly nude older men. Women were once banned from here, but now hardy swimmers of both genders brave its cold waters.

A few steps away from the bathing pool stands Sandycove's other claim to fame, the **James Joyce Martello Tower.** Originally built in 1804 when Napoleon's invasion seemed imminent, it was demilitarized in the 1860s along with most of the rest of the 34 Martello towers that ring Ireland's coast. In 1904, it was rented to Oliver St. John Gogarty, a medical student who was known for his poetry and ready wit, for £8 a year. He wanted to create a nurturing environment for writers and would-be literati. Joyce spent a week here in September 1904 and described it in the first chapter of *Ulysses,* using his friend as a model for the character of Buck Mulligan. The tower now houses a **Joyce Museum,** founded in 1962 thanks to Sylvia Beach, the Paris-based first publisher of *Ulysses.* The exhibition hall contains first editions of most of Joyce's works. Joycean memorabilia include his waistcoat, embroidered by his grandmother, and a tie that he gave to Samuel Beckett (who was Joyce's onetime secretary). The gunpowder magazine stores the Joyce Tower Library, including a death mask of Joyce taken on January 13, 1941. ⊠ *Sandycove,* ☎ *01/280–8571 or 01/280–9265.* ▱ *£2.* ☉ *Apr.–Oct., Mon.–Sat. 10–1 and 2–5, Sun. 2–6; Nov.–Mar. by appointment.*

DINING

$$$–$$$$ ✕ **Morels Bistro.** Alan O'Reilly has a stylish, first-floor restaurant over the Eagle House pub on the north side of Dun Laoghaire. The summery Mediterranean colors, striking paintings—large and specially commissioned—and curvaceous (albeit uncomfortable) metal chairs at classically white-clothed tables, all create a dashing impression. The eclectic menus might start with baked crab cakes on a bed of diced peppers, drizzled with lemon oil and coriander pesto, or a focaccia tart with wood pigeon, wild mushrooms, caramelized onion, and goat cheese. Exceptionally tender grilled beef with a selection of crisply cooked root vegetables is a terrific entrée. Delicious desserts include a rich chocolate cake, served warm with a melted chocolate sauce and vanilla ice cream. ⊠ *18 Glasthule Rd., Dun Laoghaire, Co. Dublin,* ☎ *01/230–0210, AE, MC, V. No lunch Mon.–Sat.*

$$$ ✕ **Brasserie Na Mara.** The first railway in Ireland, which opened in 1834, was built from Westland Row (now Pearse Station) in Dublin to Dun Laoghaire. Much of the original station's entrance and booking hall has been converted into this restaurant, formerly specializing in fish (*na mara* means "of the sea" in Gaelic), relaunched as a brasserie (they kept the name but jettisoned the emphasis on seafood). Tall Georgian windows overlook the busy Dun Laoghaire ferryport. The menu highlights international dishes with a modern twist, such as beef fillet with red onion confit, grilled cod fillet with crab mousse, and Thai cassoulet of monkfish. Lime-flavored crème brûlée with seasonal fruits wraps things up. ⊠ *Dun Laoghaire Harbour, Co. Dublin,* ☎ *01/280–6767. Reservations essential. AE, DC, MC, V. Closed Sun. and 1 wk at Christmas.*

$ ✕ **Caviston's.** Stephen Caviston and his family have been dispensing fine fare for years from their fish counter and delicatessen in Sandycove. The fish restaurant next door is a lively and intimate place, with appetizers such as a phyllo pastry basket with prawns and twice-baked Gorgonzola soufflé with a green salad. Typical entrées include panfried scallops served in the shell with a Thermidor sauce, and steamed Dover sole with mustard sauce. The Cavistons will also halve a lobster and serve it with a simple butter sauce, all for an exceptionally good price. ⊠ *59 Glasthule Rd., Dun Laoghaire,* ☎ *01/280–9120. MC, V. Closed Sun., Mon., and Dec. 23–Jan. 2. No dinner.*

Dalkey

From the James Joyce Tower at Sandycove, it's an easy walk or very quick drive 1 km/⅔ mi south to **Dalkey.** Along Castle Street, the town's main thoroughfare, you'll observe substantial stone remains, resembling small, turreted castles, of two 15th- and 16th-century fortified houses. During the summer small boats make the 15-minute crossing from Coliemore Harbour to **Dalkey Island,** covered in long grass, uninhabited except for a herd of goats, and graced with its own Martello tower. From Vico Road, beyond Coliemore Harbour, you'll have astounding bay views (similar to those near Italy's Bay of Naples) as far as Bray in County Wicklow (☞ Chapter 3). On Dalkey Hill is **Torca Cottage,** home of the Nobel Prize–winning writer George Bernard Shaw from 1866 to 1874. You can return to Dalkey Village by Sorrento Road.

County Dublin—Northside

Dublin's northern suburbs remain predominantly working-class and largely residential, but they do offer a few places worth an extra trip. As with most suburban areas, walking may not be the best way to get around. A car is recommended, but not essential. Buses and trains service most of these areas, the only drawback being that to get from one suburb to another by public transport means returning back through the city center. Even if you're traveling by car, visiting all these sights will take a full day, so plan your trip carefully before setting off.

Glasnevin

To reach the suburb of Glasnevin, drive from the north city center by Lower Dorset Street, as far as the bridge over the Royal Canal. Turn left, go up Whitworth Road, by the side of the canal, for 1 km/⅔ mi; at its end, turn right onto Prospect Road and then left onto the Finglas road, the N2. You may also take Bus 40 or Bus 40A from Parnell Street, next to Parnell Square, in the north city center. **Glasnevin Cemetery,** on the right-hand side of the Finglas road, is the best-known burial ground in Dublin, with the graves of many distinguished Irish leaders, including Eamon De Valera, a founding father of modern Ireland and a former Irish taoiseach and president. Other notables interred here include late-19th-century poet Gerard Manley Hopkins and Sir Roger Casement, an Irish rebel hanged for treason by the British in 1916. The cemetery is freely accessible all day.

On the northeastern flank of Glasnevin Cemetery, the **National Botanic Gardens** date from 1795 and have more than 20,000 different varieties of plants, a rose garden, and a vegetable garden. The main attraction is the **Curvilinear Range,** 400-ft-long greenhouses designed and built by a Dublin ironmaster, Richard Turner, between 1843 and 1869, and fully restored in 1995. (Turner was also responsible for the Palm House in Belfast's Botanic Gardens [☞ Chapter 9].) A complete replanting of the greenhouses is currently nearing completion. The Palm House, with its striking double dome, was built in 1884 and houses orchids, palms, and tropical ferns. Visitors here can stroll along the Tolka River. ⊠ *Glasnevin Rd.,* ☎ *01/837–4388.* ☜ *Free.* ☉ *Apr.–Sept., Mon.–Sat. 10–6, Sun. 11–6; Oct.–Mar., Mon.–Sat. 10–4:30, Sun. 11–4:30.*

Marino Casino

One of Dublin's most exquisite, yet also most underrated, architectural landmarks, the **Marino Casino** is a small-scale, Palladian-style sum-

County Dublin — Northside

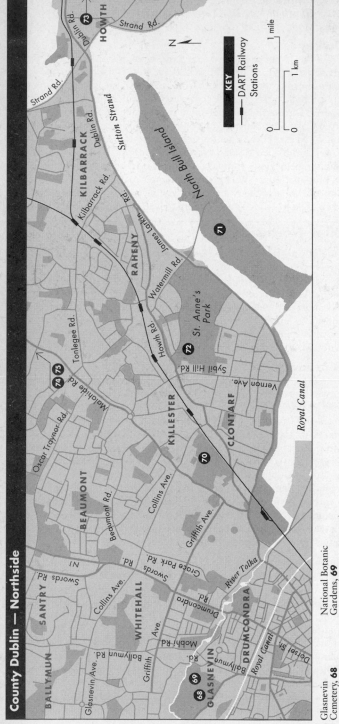

KEY

—— DART Railway
Stations

0   1 km

0   1 mile

HOWTH

Strand Rd.

Dublin Rd.

Strand Rd.

Sutton Strand

KILBARRACK

Dublin Rd.

Kilbarrack Rd.

North Bull Island

RAHENY

James Larkin Rd.

Watermill Rd.

Howth Rd.

St. Anne's Park

Sybil Hill Rd.

Vernon Ave.

KILLESTER

CLONTARF

Royal Canal

Toniegee Rd.

Malahide Rd.

Oscar Traynor Rd.

BEAUMONT

Beaumont Rd.

Collins Ave.

Griffith Ave.

Grace Park Rd.

Swords Rd.

SANTRY

BALLYMUN

Swords Rd.

N1

Collins Ave.

Glasnevin Ave.

Ballymun Rd.

Griffith Ave.

WHITEHALL

Mobhi Rd.

Drumcondra Rd.

River Tolka

DRUMCONDRA

Royal Canal

Dorset St.

GLASNEVIN

Ballymun Rd.

Glasnevin
Cemetery, **68**
Howth, **73**
Malahide Castle, **74**
Marino Casino, **70**

National Botanic
Gardens, **69**
Newbridge House, **75**
North Bull Island, **71**
St. Anne's Park, **72**

merhouse (the secondary definition of the word *casino*), built between 1762 and 1771 from a plan by William Chambers. On the former estate of Lord Charlemont (☞ Hugh Lane Municipal Gallery of Modern Art, *above*), the casino was saved when the estate's grand mansion was demolished in 1921. The ornate fireplaces and period furnishings of the 16 rooms are now fully restored. Outside, four stone lions adorn the terrace, while on the roof, gracious urns hide the chimneys. To get here, take the Malahide road from Dublin's north city center for 4 km/2½ mi. You can also take Bus 20A or Bus 24 to the Casino from Cathal Brugha Street in the north city center. It makes a good stop on the way to Malahide, Howth, or North Bull Island. ⊠ *Malahide Rd., Marino,* ☎ *01/833–1618.* ☞ *£2.* ☉ *June–Sept., daily 9:30–6:00.*

North Bull Island

A 5-km-/3-mi-long island created in the last century by the action of ⓗ the tides, **North Bull Island** is one of Dublin's wilder places, a nature conservancy with vast beach and dunes. The island is linked to the mainland via a wooden causeway that leads to **Bull Wall,** a 1½-km/1-mi walkway that stretches as far as the **North Bull Lighthouse.** To reach the island by car from Dublin's north city center, take the Clontarf road for 4 km/2½ mi to the causeway. The island is also accessible via a second, northerly causeway which gives access to **Dollymount Strand.** (The two routes of entry do not meet at any point on the island.) It is reached from the mainland via the James Larkin Road. A small visitor center is largely devoted to the island's bird life. ⊠ *Off the northerly causeway,* ☎ *01/833–8341.* ☞ *Free.* ☉ *Mar.–Oct., Mon.–Wed. 10:15–1, 1:30–4, Thurs. 10:15–1, 1:30–3:45, Fri. 10:15–1, 1:30–2:30, weekends 10–1, 1:30–5:30. Nov.–Feb., same hrs except 4:30 closing time weekends.*

ⓦ Back on the mainland directly across from North Bull Island is **St. Anne's Park,** a public green with extensive rose gardens (including many prize hybrids) and woodland walks; it is freely accessible all day. ⊠ *James Larkin Rd. and Mt. Prospect Ave.*

Howth

★ ⓧ A fishing village set at the foot of a long peninsula, **Howth** (derived from the Norse *hoved,* meaning head; it rhymes with "both") was an island inhabited as long ago as 3250 BC. Between 1813 and 1833, Howth was the Irish terminus for the sea crossing to Holyhead in north Wales, but it was then superseded by the newly built harbor at Kingstown (now Dun Laoghaire; ☞ *above*). Today, a new marina graces its harbor, which supports a large fishing fleet. Both arms of the harbor pier form extensive walks. (To get here from Dublin, either take the DART train, which takes about 30 minutes; Bus 31B from Lower Abbey Street in the city center; or, by car, take the Howth Road from the north city center for 16 km/10 mi.) Separated from Howth Harbour by a channel nearly 1½ km/1 mi wide, **Ireland's Eye** has an old stone church on the site of a 6th-century monastery and an early-19th century Martello tower. In calm weather, local boatmen make the crossing to the island.

At the King Sitric Restaurant on the East Pier (☞ Dining, *below*), a 2½-km/1½-mi cliff walk begins, leading to the white **Baily Lighthouse,** built in 1814. In some places, the cliff path narrows and drops sheerly to the sea, but the views out over the Irish Sea are terrific. Some of the best views in the whole Dublin area await from the parking lot above the lighthouse, looking out over the entire bay as far south as Dun Laoghaire, Bray, and the north Wicklow coast. You can also see much of Dublin.

Until 1959, a tram service ran from the railway station in Howth, over Howth Summit and back down to the station. One of the open-topped Hill of Howth trams that plied this route is now the star at the **Transport Museum,** a short, 800-yard walk from the Howth's DART station. Volunteers have spent several years restoring the tram, which stands alongside other unusual vehicles, including old horse-drawn bakery vans. ⊠ *Howth Village,* ☎ *01/848–0831 or 01/847–5623.* ⌕ *£1.50.* ☉ *Easter–Sept., daily 10–5:30; Oct.–Easter, weekends and public holidays 2–5:30.*

Next door to the Transport Museum and accessible from the Deer Park Hotel, the **Howth Castle Gardens** were laid out in the early 18th century. The many rare varieties of its fine rhododendron garden are in full flower April–June; there are also high beech hedges. The rambling castle, originally built in 1654 and considerably altered in the intervening centuries, is not open to the public, but you can access the ruins of a tall, square, 16th-century castle and a Neolithic dolmen. ⊠ *Deer Park Hotel, Howth, Co. Dublin,* ☎ *01/832–2624.* ⌕ *Free.* ☉ *Daily 8–dusk.*

DINING

$$$ ✕ **Abbey Tavern.** The original stone walls, flagged floors, blazing turf fires, and old gaslights of the ancient building that houses this Old World tavern all contribute to the historic atmosphere. The upstairs restaurant serves traditional Irish and Continental cuisine and specializes in fish dishes. Sole Abbey (filleted and stuffed with prawns, mushrooms, and herbs) is a house specialty, and fresh Dublin Bay prawns can be cooked to order. Traditional Irish music is offered in a different part of the building. The restaurant is a five-minute walk from the DART station; call for directions. ⊠ *Abbey St., Howth,* ☎ *01/839–0307. Reservations essential. AE, DC, MC, V. No dinner Sun. Oct.–Mar. No lunch Apr.–Sept.*

$$$ ✕ **King Sitric.** This well-known seafood restaurant is one of Howth's main attractions. It's in a Georgian house on the harbor front, with the yacht marina and port on one side, and with sea views from the upstairs seafood bar, where informal lunches are served in summer. Lobster, caught just yards away in Balscadden Bay, is the big treat; it's best at its simplest, in butter sauce. Crab is equally fresh, dressed with mayonnaise or Mornay sauce. ⊠ *East Pier, Howth, Co. Dublin,* ☎ *01/823–6729. Jacket and tie. AE, DC, MC, V. Closed Sun.*

$$ ✕ **Adrian's.** When Adrian Holden's daughter Catriona is in the kitchen, this unpretentious waterfront restaurant in Howth really starts to sing. Six varieties of spiced seafood from the nearby fishing pier are featured. The Holdens will also cook fresh fish in virtually any style you ask— deep-fried in a batter, with ginger or other Asiatic spicing, in a cream or Thermidor sauce, or grilled with a little lemon or lime. ⊠ *3 Abbey St., Howth,* ☎ *01/839–0231. AE, DC, MC, V.*

Malahide

★ ☾ ⓞ On the coast north of Howth, Malahide is chiefly known for **Malahide Castle,** a picture-book castle occupied by the Anglo-Irish and aristocratic Talbot family from 1185 until 1976, when it was sold to the Dublin County Council. The great expanse of parkland around the castle includes a botanical garden with more than 5,000 species and varieties of plants, all clearly labeled. The castle itself is a combination of styles and periods; the earliest section, the three-story tower house, dates from the 12th century. The medieval great hall is the only one in Ireland that is preserved in its original form, while the National Portrait Gallery features many fine portraits of the Talbot family and 18th- and 19th-century Irish notables. Other rooms are well-furnished with authentic

18th-century pieces. Also in the castle is the **Fry Model Railway Museum,** with rare, handmade models of the Irish railway. The castle's self-service restaurant serves good homemade food all day. To get here by car, drive from the north city center on the R107 for 14½ km/9 mi; by train, catch the hourly train from Connolly Station, which takes about 20 minutes; or board Bus 42 to Malahide which leaves from Beresford Place behind the Custom House (service runs every 15 minutes; the ride takes about 40 minutes). ⊠ *Co. Dublin,* ☎ *01/846–2184.* 🎫 *£2.50.* ⊙ *Apr.–Sept., weekdays 10–6, Sat. 11–6, Sun. 2–6; Oct.–Mar., weekends 2–5.*

If you're driving, continue from Malahide through Swords on the coastal road (the R106) for 8 km/5 mi, turning off the N1 road as signposted to **Newbridge House** in Donabate. You can also travel from Malahide to Donabate by train, which takes about 10 minutes. From the Donabate train station, the walk to the Newbridge House grounds takes 15 minutes. Built between 1740 and 1760 for Charles Cobbe, Archbishop of Dublin, Newbridge was owned by the Cobe family until 1985, when it, along with most of its furnishings, were purchased by the state. One of the finest Georgian interiors in Ireland, the **Red Drawing Room** is hung with dozens of paintings and decorated with many fine antiques. The **kitchens** of the house still have their original utensils. Crafts workshops and some examples of old-style transportation, such as coaches, are in the courtyard. Beyond the walled garden are 366 acres of parkland and a restored 18th-century animal farm. **Tara's Palace,** a dollhouse that was made to raise funds for children's charities, is also here; it has 25 rooms, all fully furnished in miniature. The exterior of the dollhouse is based on the facades of three great Irish houses—Carton, Castletown, and Leinster. The **coffee shop** here is renowned for the quality and selection of its homemade goods. ⊠ *Donabate, Co. Dublin,* ☎ *01/843–6534.* 🎫 *House: £2.75, farm £1.* ⊙ *Apr.–Sept., Tues.–Fri. 10–5, Sat. 11–6, Sun. and bank holidays 2–6; Oct.–Mar., weekends and bank holidays 2–5.*

DINING

$$$ ✕ **Bon Appetit.** Owner-chef Patsey McGuirk brought a loyal following from his previous city-center restaurant of the same name when he moved, in 1989, to this substantial Georgian terraced building. The striking floral decor in warm shades of pink creates a cozy, traditional atmosphere, an impression heightened by the staff of black-jacketed waiters. The traditional Continental menu includes such entrées as escargots and mushrooms in garlic-and-cream sauce, and a generous selection of desserts. Especially recommended are Sole McGuirk (filleted, stuffed with prawns and turbot, and baked with white wine and cream); and Duckling Montmorency (with black cherries and a cherry-brandy and orange sauce). ⊠ *9 James's Terr., Malahide,* ☎ *01/845–0314. Jacket and tie. AE, DC, MC, V. Closed Sun. No lunch Sat.*

$$$ ✕ **Siam Thai Restaurant.** One of Ireland's few Thai restaurants is on ★ a quiet lane near Malahide's marina development. A well-balanced selection of aromatic dishes make a good choice to start, typically including chicken satay with a crunchy peanut dip; whole prawns in a crisp, spicy coating; fresh and juicy spring rolls; and crisp, little, deep-fried wonton "money-bags" with a seafood filling; all accompanied by a light, spicy dip. ⊠ *Gas Lane, Malahide, Co. Dublin,* ☎ *01/845–4698. AE, DC, MC, V. Closed Sun.*

DUBLIN A TO Z

Arriving and Departing

By Bus

Dublin Bus (☎ 01/873–4222) operates a shuttle service between Dublin Airport and the city center with departures outside the arrivals gateway; pay the driver inside the coach. The single fare is £2.50. Service runs from 7:30 AM to 11 PM, at intervals of about 30 minutes, to as far as **Busaras** (☎ 01/830–2222), Dublin's main bus station, located just behind the Custom House on the northside. Journey time from the airport to the city center is normally 30 minutes, but it may be longer in heavy traffic.

By Car

Renting a car in Dublin is extremely expensive, with high rates and a 12½% local tax. Gasoline is also expensive by U.S. standards, at around 60p a liter. Peak-period car-rental rates begin at around £200 a week for the smallest models, like a Ford Fiesta. Dublin has many car-rental companies, and it pays to shop around and to avoid "cowboy" outfits. (☞ Car Rentals, *below*).

By Ferry

Irish Ferries (✉ Merrion Row, ☎ 01/661–0511) and **Stena Sealink** (✉ Ferryport, Dun Laoghaire, ☎ 01/204–7777 or 204–7700) offer regular car and passenger service to Dublin from Wales (Holyhead). Irish Ferries sails directly into Dublin port. Stena Sealink docks in Dublin port (3½ hour service to Holyhead) and in Dun Laoghaire (**High Speed Service,** known as "HSS," which takes 99 minutes). Prices and departure times vary according to season, so call either company to confirm. In summer reservations are strongly recommended. Dozens of taxis wait to take you into town from both ports, or you can take DART or a bus to the city center.

By Plane

Dublin Airport (☎ 01/844–4900), 10 km/6 mi north of the city center, serves international and domestic airlines.

FROM THE U.K.

Five airlines now serve destinations in Ireland from 19 British airports; major carriers are Aer Lingus, Ryanair, and British Midland Airways. There are daily services to Dublin from all major London airports; Aer Lingus operates 12 flights from Heathrow Airport, with British Midland operating an additional 10 flights; Ryanair operates several flights from Luton and Stanstead airports, and Virgin Atlantic Cityjet flies from London City Airport. In addition, flights to Dublin leave from Birmingham, Bristol, East Midlands, Liverpool, Luton, Manchester, Leeds/Bradford, Newcastle, Edinburgh, and Glasgow. For reservations and information in Dublin, contact **Aer Lingus** (☎ 01/844–4747), **Ryanair** (☎ 01/844–4411), or **British Midland** (☎ 01/704–4259).

FROM THE U.S.

The two airlines with regularly scheduled flights from the United States to Dublin are **Aer Lingus** (☎ 01/844–4747), which flies direct from New York, Boston, and Chicago to Dublin, and **Delta** (☎ 01/844–4166 or 01/676–8080), which flies direct from Atlanta to Dublin and operates jointly with some of Aer Lingus's flights.

FROM ELSEWHERE IN EUROPE

Major European carriers, such as Air France, Lufthansa, Sabena, SAS, and Alitalia run direct services to Dublin from most European capital cities and major regional airports, especially those in Germany.

Aer Lingus (☎ 01/844–4747) operates flights from Dublin to Cork, Kerry, Shannon, Galway, Knock in County Mayo, and Sligo.

By Taxi

A taxi is a quicker alternative than the bus to get from the airport to Dublin center. A line of taxis waits by the arrivals gateway; the fare for the 30-minute journey to any of the main city-center hotels is about £12 plus tip (tips don't have to be large but they are increasingly expected). It's advisable to ask about the fare before leaving the airport.

By Train

There are no train services from Dublin Airport to the city center. The main train stations in Dublin are **Heuston Station** (✉ End of Victoria Quay) and **Connolly Station** (✉ Amiens St.). The former provides train services to the South and West; the latter provides services to the North and Northwest. Contact the **Irish Rail Travel Centre** (✉ 35 Lower Abbey St., ☎ 01/836–6222) for information.

Getting Around

Traveling around Dublin by public transportation is comparatively easy, although a car is useful for getting to the outlying suburbs. If you're just planning to visit city-center Dublin, definitely plan to do it without a car.

By Bus

Dublin has an extensive network of buses—most of them are green double-deckers. Timetables (£2.50) are available from the **Dublin Bus** office (✉ 59 Upper O'Connell St., ☎ 01/873–4222 [staffed daily 8:30–5:30]) and give details of all routes, times of operation, and price codes. Fares begin at 55p and have to be paid to the driver, who will accept inexact change. Change transactions and the city's heavy traffic can slow service down considerably. Some bus services run on cross-city routes, including the smaller "Imp" buses, but most buses start in the city center. Buses to the north of the city begin in the Lower Abbey Street/Parnell Street area, while those to the west begin in Middle Abbey Street and in the Aston Quay area. Routes to the southern suburbs begin at Eden Quay and in the College Street area. A number of services are links to DART stations, and another regular bus route connects the two main provincial railway stations, Connolly and Heuston. If the destination board indicates AN LÁR, that means that the bus is going to the city center.

By Car

The number of cars in Ireland has grown exponentially in the last few years, and nowhere has their impact been felt more than in Dublin, where the city's complicated one-way streets are congested during the morning and evening rush hours and often during much of the rest of the day. If you can, avoid driving a car except to get you into and out of the city, and be sure to ask your hotel or guest house for clear directions to get you out of the city.

By Taxi

Official licensed taxis, metered and designated by roof signs, do not cruise. Taxi stands are located beside the central bus station, at train stations, O'Connell Bridge, St. Stephen's Green, College Green, and near major hotels; the Dublin telephone directory has a complete list. The initial charge is approximately £2 with an additional charge of about £1.50 a mile thereafter. The fare is displayed on a meter (make sure it's on). Alternatively, you may phone a taxi company and ask for a cab to meet you at your hotel, but this may cost up to £4 extra. Hackney cabs, which also operate in the city, have neither roof signs or meters, and will sometimes respond to hotels' requests for a cab. Negotiate the fare before your journey begins. Although the taxi fleet in Dublin is large, the cabs are nonstandard and some cars are neither spacious nor in pristine condition. Local taxi companies include **VIP Taxis** (☎ 01/478–3333), **Metro** (☎ 01/668–3333), and **Mercs and Perks** (☎ 01/831–7446).

By Train

An electric railway system, the **DART** (Dublin Area Rapid Transit; ☎ 01/836–6222) connects Dublin with Howth to the north and Bray to the south on a fast, efficient line. There are 25 stations on the route, which is the best means of getting to seaside destinations such as Howth, Blackrock, Dun Laoghaire, Dalkey, Killiney, and Bray. The service starts at 6:30 AM and runs until 11:30 PM; at peak periods, 8–9:30 AM and 5–7 PM, trains arrive every five minutes. At other times of the day, the intervals between trains are 15 to 25 minutes. Tickets can be bought at stations, but it is also possible to buy weekly rail tickets, as well as weekly or monthly "rail-and-bus" tickets, from the **Irish Rail Travel Centre** (✉ 35 Lower Abbey St., ☎ 01/836–6222). Individual fares begin at 65p and range up to £1.10. There are heavy penalties for traveling the DART without a ticket. Train services run from Heuston Station (✉ End of Victoria Quay) to Kildare Town west of Dublin via Celbridge, Sallins, and Newbridge, and from Connolly Station (✉ Amiens St.) to more distant locations like Malahide, Maynooth, Skerries, and Drogheda to the north of Dublin, and Wicklow and Arklow to the south.

Contacts and Resources

B&B Reservation Agencies

For a small fee, **Bord Fáilte** will book accommodations anywhere in Ireland through their central reservations system; for credit card reservations, phone 01/605–7777. B&Bs can be booked at local visitor information offices when they are open; however, even these reservations will go through the central reservations system. For more information, *see* Lodging *in* the Gold Guide.

Car Rentals

A dozen car rental companies have desks at Dublin Airport; all the main national and international firms also have branches in the city center. Some reliable firms are: **Avis** (✉ Hanover St., ☎ 01/677–4010; ✉ Dublin Airport, ☎ 01/844–4466). **Budget** (✉ 151 Lower Drumcondra Rd., ☎ 01/837–9802; ✉ Dublin Airport, ☎ 01/844–5919). **Dan Dooley** (✉ 42–43 Westland Row, ☎ 01/677–2723; ✉ Dublin Airport, ☎ 01/844–5156). **Hertz** (✉ Leeson St. Bridge, ☎ 01/660–2255; ✉ Dublin Airport, ☎ 01/844–5466). **Murray's Rent-a-Car** (✉ Baggot St. Bridge, ☎ 01/668–1777; ✉ Dublin Airport, ☎ 01/844–4179).

Embassies

Embassies are open weekdays 9–1 and 2–5. **U.S.** (✉ 42 Elgin Rd., ☎ 01/668–8777). **Canadian** (✉ 65 St. Stephen's Green, ☎ 01/478–1988). **British** (✉ 31 Merrion Rd., ☎ 01/205–3700). **Australian** (✉ Fitzwilton House, Wilton Terr., ☎ 01/676–1517).

Emergencies

For **gardai** (police), **ambulance,** or **fire,** dial 999.

DOCTORS AND DENTISTS

Dublin's **Eastern Help Board** (☎ 01/679–0700) can provide the names of doctors. The **Dublin Dental Hospital** (✉ 20 Lincoln Pl., ☎ 01/662–

0766) has emergency facilities and lists of dentists offering emergency care.

HOSPITALS
Beaumont (☎ 01/837–7755). **St. Vincent's** (✉ Elm Park, ☎ 01/269–4533). **Mater** (✉ Eccles St., ☎ 01/830–1122). **St. James's** (☎ 01/453–7941).

PHARMACY
Hamilton Long (✉ 5 Upper O'Connell St., ☎ 01/874–8456) is open Monday–Wednesday and Saturday 8:30–6., Thursday 8:30–8, and Friday 8:30–7.

Guided Tours
BEYOND THE CITY
Bus Éireann (☎ 01/836–6111) offers day tours to country destinations such as Glendalough out of Busaras, the main bus station.

ORIENTATION
Dublin Bus (☎ 01/873–4222) offers three- and four-hour tours of the city center that include Trinity College, the Royal Hospital Kilmainham, and Phoenix Park. The one-hour City Tour, with hourly departures, allows visitors to hop on and off at any of the main sites. Tickets are available from the driver or Dublin Bus. From mid-April through September Dublin Bus runs a continuous guided open-top bus tour (£8) that allows you to hop on and off the bus as often as you wish and visit some 15 sights along its route. The company also conducts a north-city coastal tour, going to Howth, and a south-city tour, traveling as far as Enniskerry.

Gray Line Tours (☎ 01/661–9666) runs city-center tours that cover the same sights as the Dublin Bus itineraries (☞ *above*).

TRAIN AND CARRIAGE TOURS
DART Train: Guided tours of Dublin using the DART system are organized by **Views Unlimited** (✉ 8 Prince of Wales Terr., Bray, ☎ 01/286–0164 or 01/286–2861).

Horse-Drawn Carriage: Horse-drawn carriage tours are available around Dublin and in Phoenix Park. For tours of the park, contact the **Department of the Arts, Culture and the Gaeltacht** (☎ 01/661–3111). Carriages can be hired at the Grafton Street corner of St. Stephen's Green, without prior reservation.

WALKING TOURS
Historical and Literary Tours: Historical Walking Tours of Dublin (☎ 01/845–0241), run by Trinity College history graduate students, are excellent two-hour tour introductions to Dublin. The Bord Fáilte–approved tour assembles at the front gate of Trinity College mid-May–mid-October, daily at 11, noon, and 3, with an extra tour on Sunday at 2; and mid-October–mid-May on weekends at noon. The cost is £5. An **Old Dublin Medieval Walking Tour** (☎ 01/496–0641 or 01/677–6761) leaves from the museum in Bewley's Café's Grafton Street branch June–September, daily at 2:30. A **Georgian/Literary Walking Tour** also leaves from Bewley's June–September daily at 11. Each tour lasts approximately two hours and costs £5. **Trinity Tours** (☎ 01/608–2320) offers walks of the Trinity College campus on weekends from March 17 (St. Patrick's Day) through mid-May and from mid-May–September daily. The ½-hour tour costs £4.50 and includes admission to the Book of Kells (☞ Trinity College *in* The Georgian Heart of Dublin, *above*); tours start at the college's main gate.

Musical Tours: Dublin Tourism (☞ Visitor Information, *below*) has a booklet to its self-guided **"Rock n Stroll" Trail,** which covers 16 sites with associations to performers such as Bob Geldof, Christy Moore, Sinéad O'Connor, and U2. Most of the sites are in the city center and Temple Bar. The **Musical Pub Crawl** (☎ Discover Dublin, 20 Lower Stephens St., Dublin 2, ✉ 01/478–0191) begins at **Oliver St. John Gogarty's** (✉ Fleet St., Temple Bar) and moves on to three other pubs. Led by two professional musicians who perform songs and tell the story of Irish music, the tour is given May–October, Monday–Thursday and weekends at 7:30 PM; the cost is £6.

Pubs: Colm Quilligan (☎ 01/454–0228) offers highly enjoyable evening walks of the literary pubs of Dublin, where "brain cells are replaced as quickly as they are drowned." The *Dublin Literary Pub Crawl* is a 122-page guide to those Dublin pubs with the greatest literary associations; it's widely available in Dublin bookstores.

Lost and Found
Dublin Bus: Contact its headquarters (✉ 59 Upper O'Connell St., ☎ 01/873–4222).

Railways and DART: Contact **Iarnrod Éireann/Irish Rail** (✉ Travel Centre, 35 Lower Abbey St., ☎ 01/836–6222).

Opening and Closing Times
Dublin is gradually becoming a 24-hour city, even though the bus and DART train services close down for the night at 11:30. (A few lines run until dawn on the weekends.) Many taxis run all night, but the demand, especially on weekends, can make for long lines at the taxi stands. Many clubs on the Leeson Street strip and elsewhere stay open until 4 AM or later. Sunday, once a day of sabbatical rest in Dublin, is now often bustling, with some stores open (☞ *below*).

Banks are open weekdays 10–4 and remain open on Thursdays until 5. All stay open at lunchtime. Most branches have ATMs that accept bank cards and MasterCard and Visa credit cards (☞ Money *in* the Gold Guide). **Museums** are normally open Tuesday–Saturday and also Sunday afternoon; they are usually closed on Monday. **Post offices** are open weekdays 9–1 and 2–5:30, and Saturdays 9–12:30. Main post offices are open Saturday afternoons, too (look for green signs that say "An Post"). The General Post Office (GPO) on O'Connell Street, which has foreign exchange and general delivery facilities, is open Monday–Saturday 8–8, and Sunday 10:30–6:30. To send a postcard to the U.S. costs 38p, to the U.K. 28p.

Pubs open Monday–Saturday at 10:30 AM and 12:30 PM on Sundays. They must close at 11 PM in winter and 11:30 PM in summer, but most pubs take another hour to empty out, as patrons drag out their last drink as long as they can. For a memorable glimpse into a ritual repeated all over Ireland every night, hold out in a pub as long as you can and watch the patrons ignore the bartenders pleading with them to leave. **Stores** are open Monday–Saturday 9–5:30 or 9–6, and Thursdays until 8. Smaller city-center specialty stores open on Sunday as well, usually 10–6. Most department stores are closed on Sunday.

Safety
What crime there is in Dublin is often drug-related. Sidestreets off O'Connell Street can be dangerous, especially at night. When you park your car, *do not* leave any valuables inside, even under a raincoat on the back seat or in the trunk; be especially careful parking around the Guinness Brewery and the Irish Whiskey Corner (☞ Dublin Cas-

tle, Christ Church Cathedral, and West Dublin, *above*), neither of which are in great neighborhoods.

Travel Agencies
American Express (⊠ 116 Grafton St., ☎ 01/677–2874). **Thomas Cook** (⊠ 118 Grafton St., ☎ 01/677–1721).

Visitor Information
The main **Dublin Tourism** information office is on Suffolk Street, just off Grafton Street (☎ 01/605–7799, FAX 01/605–7787, ☉ July–Sept., Mon.–Sat. 8:30–6, Sun. 11–5:30; Oct.–June, daily 9–6). **Bord Fáilte**, the Irish Tourist Board has its own visitor information offices in the entrance hall of its **headquarters** (⊠ Baggot St. Bridge, ☎ 01/602–4000; FAX 01/602–4100, ☉ Weekdays 9:15–5:15); at **Dublin Airport** (☉ Daily 8 AM–10 PM); and at the **Ferryport, Dun Laoghaire**, (☉ Daily 10–9). A suburban tourist office in **Tallaght** is open March–December, daily 9:30–5.

The **Temple Bar Information Centre** (⊠ 18 Eustace St., ☎ 01/671–5717, FAX 01/677–2525) produces the easy-to-use, annually updated *Temple Bar Guide,* which provides complete listings of the area's hundreds of stores, pubs, restaurants, clubs, galleries, and other cultural venues.

3 Dublin Environs

The Boyne Valley and Counties Wicklow and Kildare

The counties immediately north, south, and west of the capital constitute the Pale, an area that was strongly influenced by English rule since the days of the Normans but is also enormously rich in Irish history from as far back as prehistoric times. The sights are dazzling: Celtic crosses and fine churches; the astonishing, ancient passage graves at Newgrange; the "monastic city" of Glendalough; and Castletown, Russborough and Powerscourt Houses, exemplars of the Irish take on the Palladian country house.

O**NLY AN HOUR OR TWO FROM DUBLIN,** you are deep in the countryside. Here (as in other parts of Ireland), the ancestral homes of the dwindling members of the Anglo-Irish ascendancy dot the landscape, and lords and baronets down on their luck have turned hoteliers and welcome guests to castle holidays with adaptable grace. History is rich both north and south of Dublin. The rugged, scenic Wicklow Mountains—to some tastes Ireland's finest—lie tantalizingly close to the capital on its southern edge. Wicklow's evocative monastic settlement at Glendalough, many later abbeys and churches, castles, and several of Ireland's grandest houses and gardens sit amid scenic wooded valleys. Some of the country's most evocative neolithic ruins—including the famous passage graves at Newgrange—lie to the north in the Boyne Valley, where layer upon layer of history penetrates down into earlier, unknowable ages. Flat, pastoral lands define County Kildare and County Meath, both rich in historical remains. Drogheda, a fascinating town settled by the Vikings in the early 10th century, bestrides the River Boyne in County Louth. The Dublin environs also have an impressive eastern coastline that stretches from Counties Wicklow to Louth, punctuated by delightful harbor towns and fishing villages. The coast is virtually unspoiled for its entire length.

Updated by
Sylvia
Thompson

Pleasures and Pastimes

Dining

Dining out in the area is still essentially a casual affair, but the innovations and experimentation of Dublin's top restaurateurs is influencing the cooking at the finer dining establishments outside the capital. As in the Southwest (☞ Chapter 6), chefs hereabouts have a deep respect for fresh, locally grown and raised produce. You will find everything from gourmet Continental-style meals to a hearty ploughman's lunch. For price ranges *see* Chart 1(A) *in* On the Road with Fodor's.

Lodging

The counties of Wicklow and Kildare offer the traveler excellent accommodations, even if the choice may not be vast. If you have only a night or two outside Dublin, try to stay at least one night in one of the area's country-house or manor-house hotels, where some of Ireland's finest hosts welcome guests into sometimes glorious, sometimes rustic, almost invariably comfortable homes. Old-style hotels in Counties Meath and Louth are showing signs of improvement—becoming ever more popular. Bed-and-breakfasts, as elsewhere in Ireland, are always a good option. For price ranges *see* Chart 2(B) *in* On the Road with Fodor's.

Prehistoric and Monastic Sites

The Boyne valley, which straddles the county of Louth and runs through the flat heartland of Meath, is home to 10% of all prehistoric monuments in Ireland. Foremost among these is **Neolithic Newgrange,** passage graves built between 2800 and 2400 BC. The **Hill of Tara,** one of the focal points for the ancient high kings of Ireland, was where disputes between clans were settled; new laws were passed; and, eventually, Christianity was proclaimed from the summit by St. Patrick. The advent of Christianity led to the construction of the monastery of **Glendalough** in County Wicklow, founded by one of St. Patrick's followers, St. Kevin. Later in the 12th century, the monastery of **Mellifont** was founded, the first Cistercian house in Ireland. Not far north of Mellifont are the ruins of another monastic site, **Monasterboice,** where two of the finest high crosses in Ireland stand in the shadow of a 9th-century round tower.

Walking, Hiking, and Biking

Whether you're a novice or a veteran, Wicklow's gentle, rolling hills are a terrific place to begin an Irish walking vacation. Devoted hikers come from all over the world to walk the 137-km/85-mi **Wicklow Way,** the first long-distance trail to open in Ireland and one of the best. Consider participating in one of the walking festivals held at Easter, in May, and in autumn. Biking is also an excellent way to see the area. (☞ Contacts and Resources *in* Dublin Environs A to Z, *below*).

Exploring Dublin Environs

Dublin Environs comprise three basic geographical regions: the mountainous county of Wicklow, which lies to the south of Dublin and contains some of the most breathtaking scenery in the Emerald Isle; the Boyne Valley to the north of Dublin, with its abundant ruins of Celtic Ireland stretching from Counties Meath to Louth; and, southwest of Dublin, the flat pastoral plains of County Kildare, which stretch from the foothills of the Dublin and Wicklow Mountains (they're the same mountains; the two names represent the claims *both* counties make on them) on Kildare's eastern fringe to the Midlands to the west (☞ Chapter 4).

Given their proximity to Dublin, each of the places in the Dublin Environs region can be visited on a day trip from the city. This chapter is organized into three different trips, each of which makes a reasonable—albeit sight-filled—day trip. Keep in mind that it's easy to lose an hour or so making unexpected detours, chatting with locals, and otherwise enjoying the unexpected. The itinerary below covers the highlights of the area. If you have less than three days, use parts of each day's suggested itinerary to plan your day. Two last notes: First, it is unreasonable to plan on getting both to regions north and south of Dublin in the same day. And second, a car is essential to visit most sights.

Numbers in the text correspond to numbers in the margin and on the Dublin Environs map.

Great Itineraries

IF YOU HAVE 3 DAYS

Heading south from Dublin, make a quick stop first in the coastal town of **Bray** ⑱. (If you haven't already explored the towns along Dublin Bay north of Bray but south of Dublin, consult the Side Trips section in Chapter 2 to decide whether or not to visit the County Dublin sights we cover in that section on your way farther south.) Your next stop should be nearby **Powerscourt House, Gardens, and Waterfall** ⑲. Follow the road through **Roundwood** ⑳ and on to **Glendalough** ㉒. Jumping south again, browse for wool fabric and apparel at the oldest mill in Ireland at **Avoca** ㉕, then, for something totally different, make the quick trip over to historic **Avondale Forest Park and House** ㉔, ending your day in ▨ **Wicklow Town** ㉓. The following day, head back toward Glendalough and cross over the thrillingly scenic Wicklow Gap, passing through the quiet village of Hollywood (no relation to its American namesake). From here tour Kildare with stops at the **National Stud and Japanese Gardens** ㉞ and **Castletown House** ㉗ in Celbridge. Spend the night either in nearby ▨ **Straffan** ㉘ or back in ▨ **Dublin** (☞ Lodging *in* Chapter 2). On your third day, head to Counties Meath and Louth, north of Dublin, via the large town of **Trim** ① to the **Hill of Tara** ②. Then head for **Newgrange** ⑤, home to the most important passage tombs in Europe. Follow the road north to **Monasterboice** ⑩, where one of the finest high crosses in all of Ireland awaits, then head on to **Dundalk** ⑭ before enjoying the **Cooley Peninsula Drive** ⑮. Return via historic **Drogheda** ⑧ to Dublin.

When to Tour Dublin Environs

Spring and summer are the seasons when the wild mountains of Wicklow and the flat pasturelands of Kildare are at their best. However, rainfall can be high in March and April. If you're planning to tour the towns and historic sites, winter might be a good time to avoid the crush; bring warm clothing and boots and be prepared for some light snow on the hills.

NORTH OF DUBLIN IN THE BOYNE VALLEY

The area known as the Boyne Valley comprises a wide arc of fertile land with more than 100 prehistoric monuments. Newgrange, Knowth, and Dowth—the most acclaimed of the sites—are all beside the River Boyne. Also well worth the visit are the sites of the Hill of Tara, Mellifont Abbey, the high crosses of Monasterboice, and the towns of Drogheda, Trim, and Navan. Our tour begins at Trim, the locale closest to Dublin, and works its way north. Keep in mind that Omeath and the scenic Cooley Peninsula at the end of this tour are on the border of Northern Ireland, so if you make it this far north, consult Chapter 9, and in particular our coverage of the Mountains of Mourne, which are just across Carlingford Lough.

Trim

❶ *51 km/32 mi northwest of Dublin.*

Trim, situated on the River Boyne, has some of the finest medieval ruins in Ireland. In 1359, on the instructions of King Edward III, the town was walled and its fortifications strengthened; in the 15th century several parliaments were subsequently held here. Oliver Cromwell massacred most of its inhabitants when he captured the town in 1649. The largest Anglo-Norman fortress in Ireland, **Trim Castle** dominates present-day Trim from its 2½ acre site, which slopes down to the river's placid waters. Built by Hugh de Lacy in 1173, the castle was soon destroyed and then rebuilt from 1190 to 1200. The ruins include an enormous keep with 70-ft-high turrets flanked by rectangular towers. The outer castle wall is almost 500 yards long, and five D-shape towers survive. The castle remains are freely accessible at all times. Facing the river is another ruin, that of the **Royal Mint,** an indication of Trim's political importance in the Middle Ages.

Overlooking Trim from a ridge opposite the castle, the **Yellow Steeple,** dating from 1368, is a remnant of the 13th-century Augustinian abbey of St. Mary's. Much of the tower was destroyed in 1649 to prevent its falling into Cromwell's hands, and today, only the striking, 125-ft-high east wall remains. The Church of Ireland **St. Patrick's Cathedral** (✉ Loman St.) dates from the early 19th century, but the square tower belongs to an earlier structure built in 1449. The Trim **visitor center** tells the story of the arrival of the Normans and of medieval Trim. ✉ *Mill St.,* ☎ *046/37227.* ✄ *£2.50.* ⊙ *May–Sept., Wed.–Sun. 9:30–5, Oct.–Apr. by appointment.*

If you know your ancestors are from County Meath, take advantage of the family-history tracing service at the **Meath Heritage and Genealogy Center.** ✉ *Mill St.,* ☎ *046/36633.* ✄ *Free.* ⊙ *Mon.–Fri. 9–5.*

Several places just east and south of Trim are also of interest. At **Newtown** (1¼ km/¾ mi east of Trim on the banks of the River Boyne) lie the ruins of what was the largest cathedral in Ireland, built beginning in 1210 by Simon de Rochfort, the first Anglo-Norman bishop of

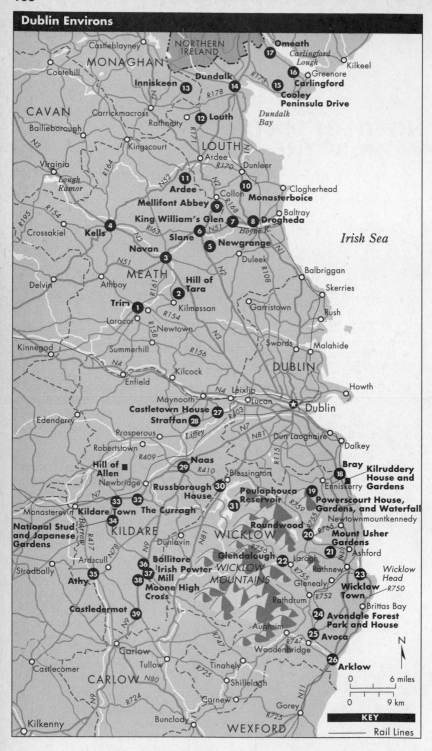

Dublin Environs

Castleblayney

NORTHERN IRELAND

MONAGHAN

Cootehill

17 Omeath
Carlingford Lough
Kilkeel

Greenore

16 Carlingford

15 **Cooley Peninsula Drive**

Inniskeen **13** **Dundalk** **14**

R178

CAVAN

Carrickmacross

Baileborough

Rathnelly

12 **Louth**

Dundalk Bay

N3

Kingscourt

LOUTH

Ardee

Virginia

R164

R170

Dunleer

Lough Ramor

R195 R154

11 **Ardee**

Collon

Clogherhead

10

Mellifont Abbey **9**

Monasterboice

Crossakiel

Kells **4**

King William's Glen

R163

7

Baltray

8 **Drogheda**

Slane **6** N51

Irish Sea

Delvin

Navan

3

Duleek

Boyne R.

Balbriggan

MEATH

N51

N2

Skerries

Athboy

Hill of Tara

R108

Garristown

Rush

Kinnegad

Trim **1**

2

Kilmessan

R154

Newtown

Swords

Malahide

N4

R158

Summerhill

R156

N3

DUBLIN

Enfield

Kilcock

Leixlip

Howth

Maynooth

Lucan

N4

Castletown House **27**

☆ **Dublin**

Edenderry

Straffan **28**

R403

Liffey

Prosperous

N7

Dun Laoghaire

Robertstown

R409

Naas **29**

N81

R115

Dalkey

Hill of Allen

Russborough House **30**

Blessington

Bray

18 **Kilruddery House and Gardens**

Newbridge

R410

31

Poulaphouca Reservoir

Enniskerry

N7

33 **32**

Kildare Town **The Curragh**

Powerscourt House, Gardens, and Waterfall

19

R75p

National Stud and Japanese Gardens

34

KILDARE

Roundwood

Newtownmountkennedy

Monasterevin

Dunlavin

WICKLOW

20

R765

Mount Usher Gardens

R417

N78

Ardscull

N81

Glendalough

21

Ashford

Stradbally

35

Ballitore **36**

Irish Pewter Mill **37**

WICKLOW MOUNTAINS

22

Laragh

Rathnew

Wicklow Head

23

Moone High Cross **38**

R755

R750

Athy

Glenealy

Wicklow Town

Castledermot

39

Rathdrum

R752

Brittas Bay

24

Avondale Forest Park and House

Aughrim

25 **Avoca**

Carlow

R747

Woodenbridge

N

Tullow

26 **Arklow**

Castlecomer

CARLOW N80

Tinahely

0 —— 6 miles

Shillelagh

0 —— 9 km

R724

Carnew

Kilkenny

Bunclody

Gorey

R725

KEY

WEXFORD

—— Rail Lines

Meath. At **Laracor** (3 km/2 mi south of Trim on the R158), there is a wall left of the rectory where Jonathan Swift (1667–1745), the satirical writer, poet, and author of *Gulliver's Travels,* was rector from 1699 until 1714, when he was made dean of St. Patrick's Cathedral in Dublin. Nearby are the walls of the cottage where Esther Johnson, the "Stella" who inspired much of Swift's writings, once lived. One of the most pleasant villages of south County Meath, **Summerhill** (8 km/5 mi southeast of Laracor along the R158) has a large square and a village green with a 15th-century cross. Just south of Summerhill is **Cnoc an Linsigh,** an attractive area of forest walks with picnic sites, ideal for a half-day's meandering. Many of the lanes that crisscross this part of County Meath provide delightful driving between high hedgerows and afford occasional views of the lush pastoral countryside.

Hill of Tara

❷ *14½ km/9 mi west of Trim, 33 km/21 mi northwest of Dublin.*

One of Ireland's most important ancient sites, the Hill of Tara was the symbolic seat of the High Kings of Ireland, and it has inspired many of the greatest Irish legends. Archaeologists have discovered evidence that the hill was occupied over many different eras. The earliest building, a hill fort, is believed to date from the Iron Age, and it is surrounded by multiple ring forts (some of which were ruined in the 19th century by religious zealots from England who believed they would find the Ark of the Covenant here). During the hill's reign as a royal seat, which lasted to the 11th century, a great *feis* (national assembly) was held here every three years, when laws were passed and tribal disputes were settled. Tara's influence waned with the arrival of Christianity; the last king to live here was Malachy II, who died in 1022.

Like so many of the most prominent sites of the pagan, pre-Christian era, Christianity remade Tara in its own image. Today a modern statue of St. Patrick stands here, as does a pillar stone that may have been the coronation stone of the early kings. In the graveyard of the adjacent Anglican church, you'll find a pillar with the worn image of a pagan god and a Bronze Age standing stone. However, the main attraction of the Hill of Tara is its height: It stands more than 300 ft above sea level, and from its top on a clear day, you can see across the flat central plain of Ireland, with the mountains of east Galway rising nearly 160 km/100 mi away. In the mid-19th century, the nationalist leader Daniel O'Connell staged a mass rally that is said to have drawn more than a million people (nearly a third of Ireland's population today). In an old Church of Ireland church on the hillside, the **interpretative center** tells the story of Tara and its legends. ⊠ *Hill of Tara,* ☎ *046/25903.* ⚏ *£1.* ☉ *May–mid-June and mid-Sept–Oct, daily 10–5; mid-June–mid-Sept., daily 9:30–6:30.*

Navan

❸ *10 km/6 mi northwest of the Hill of Tara, 48 km/30 mi north of Dublin.*

A busy market and mining town with evidence of prehistoric settlements, Navan lies at the crucial juncture of the Rivers Blackwater and Boyne. It took off in the 12th century, when Hugh de Lacy, Lord of Trim, had the place walled and fortified, making it a defensive stronghold of the English Pale in eastern Ireland. The Catholic **St. Mary's Church,** built in 1839, features a late-18th-century wood carving of the Crucifixion, the work of a local artist, Edward Smyth, who at the time was the greatest sculptor Ireland had produced since the Middle Ages. On

Fridays, the **Fair Green,** beside the church, is the site of a bustling out-door market. ⊠ *Trimgate St., Navan.* ☉ *Daily 8–8.*

Kells

❹   *16 km/10 mi northwest of Navan.*

In the 9th century, a group of monks from Iona in Scotland took refuge at Kells (Ceanannus Mór) after being expelled by the Danes. St. Columba had founded a monastery here 300 years earlier. Shortly before the arrival of the Scots, the monks here wrote and illustrated the Book of Kells, the Latin version of the four Gospels and one of Ire-land's greatest medieval treasures. (It should be noted that the most current scholarly thought on the book's origins is that the Scottish monks brought it with them.) During the Cromwellian wars it was removed to Trinity College, Dublin, for safekeeping, where it remains. A large exhibit is now devoted to it in the Old Library, and a few pages at a time are on view (☞ Exploring Dublin *in* Chapter 2). A facsimile copy of the Book of Kells is on display in the Church of Ireland **St. Columba's,** in Kells. Four elaborately carved high crosses stand in the church graveyard, while the stump of a fifth is in the marketplace; during the 1798 uprising against British rule, it was used as a gallows.

St. Columba's House, a small, two-story, 7th-century church measur-ing about 24 ft square and nearly 40 ft high, with a steeply pitched, stone roof, is similar in appearance to St. Kevin's Church at Glendalough (☞ County Wicklow's Coast and Mountains, *below*) and Cormac's Chapel at Cashel (☞ Chapter 5). Adjacent to St. Columba's House is the nearly 100-ft-high **round tower,** in almost perfect condition, dat-ing from before 1076. Unusually, its top story has five windows, each pointing to an ancient entrance to the medieval town.

Dining and Lodging

$ ✕🏠 **Lennoxbrook.** This fine, 200-year-old-plus farmhouse is run by Pauline Mullan, whose children are the fifth generation of the family to occupy the house. A casual, friendly mood prevails throughout the house. Upstairs, the four rooms are furnished with finely patterned wall-paper and period furniture. Lamb raised in the area, as well as local produce, is often on the menu at dinner (£10 extra). The house, 5 km/3 mi north of Kells on the N3 road from Dublin to Cavan, is convenient to Newgrange; the Mullans also can provide a gate key to the prehis-toric forts, passage graves, and other remains dating from 2000 BC on the Loughcrew Hills, a 15-minute drive away. ⊠ *Co. Meath,* ☎ *046/ 45902. 4 rooms share 2 baths. Dining room. No credit cards.*

Newgrange

★ ❺   *11⅓ km/7 mi east of Navan.*

Newgrange is one of the most spectacular prehistoric tombs in Europe. Built in the 4th millennium BC, which makes it roughly 1,000 years older than Stonehenge, Newgrange is constructed with some 250,000 tons of stones, the nearest source of which are the Wicklow Moun-tains south of Dublin. How the people who built this tumulus trans-ported the stones here remains a mystery. The mound above the tomb measures more than 330 ft across and is 36 ft high at the front. White quartz stones were used for the retaining wall; egg-shape gray stones are studded at intervals. The passage grave may have been the world's earliest observatory. It is so carefully constructed that on the day of the winter solstice, the rays of the rising sun hit a roof box above the lintel at the entrance to the grave. The rays then shine for about 20 minutes down the passageway that leads to the interior, and illuminate the burial chamber. Visitors to the interior of this Bronze Age tomb may see the effect re-created artificially. The geometric designs on some stones at the center of the burial chamber continue to baffle experts. Access to Newgrange is solely via **Brú na Bóinne** ("palace of the Boyne"), the recently opened Boyne Valley visitor center. ☎ 041/ 24488. ⛒ £3. ⊙ *June–mid-Sept., daily 9–7; May, and mid-Sept.–end Sept., daily 9–6:30; Mar., Apr, and Oct., daily 9:30–5:30; Nov.–Feb. daily 9:30–5.*

The prehistoric sites of **Dowth** and **Knowth** have been under excavation since 1962, and although **Dowth** is still closed to the public, the partially excavated site at **Knowth** is open. It is far larger and more diversified than the more famous Newgrange tomb, with a huge central mound and 17 smaller ones. About one-third of the site has been excavated and can be visited via the visitors center. You can also watch archaeologists at work on the rest of the site. The earliest tombs and carved stones here date from the Stone Age (3000 BC), although the site was in use up until the early 14th century. In the early Christian era (4th–8th centuries AD) it was the seat of the High Kings of Ireland. ✉ *Knowth, Co. Meath,* ☎ 041/24488. ⛒ £2. ⊙ *June–mid-Sept., daily 9–7; May and mid Sept.–end of Sept., daily 9–6:30; Mar., Apr, and Oct., daily 9:30–5:30; Nov.–Feb., daily 9:30–5.*

Slane

⑥ *2½ km/1½ mi north of Newgrange, 46 km/29 mi northwest of Dublin.*

The small, Georgian village of Slane was built around a crossroads in the 18th century. The **Conyngham Arms Hotel** (☎ 041/24155), at the crossroads in Slane, is an agreeable, family-run establishment that serves a buffet from noon to 2:30 and a bar menu throughout the day. The 16th-century building known as the **Hermitage** was constructed on the site where St. Erc, a local man who was converted to Christianity by St. Patrick, led a hermit's existence. **Slane Castle,** beautifully situated overlooking a natural amphitheater, was badly damaged in a 1991 fire, and it is currently completely closed to the public. Back in 1981, Slane's owner, the Anglo-Irish Lord Henry Mountcharles, staged the first of what have been some of Ireland's largest rock concerts; U2, still only one album old, had second billing to Thin Lizzy that year. Most of rock's greatest names have performed since, including Bob Dylan, Bruce Springsteen, David Bowie, and the Rolling Stones; REM's 1995 show holds the record for attendance: 70,000.

The 500-ft-high **Slane Hill,** where St. Patrick proclaimed the arrival of Christianity in 433 by lighting the Paschal Fire, is just north of Slane town. From the top of the hill, you'll have sweeping views of the Boyne Valley. On a clear day, the panorama stretches from Trim to Drogheda, a vista extending for 40 km/25 mi.

A humble, stone, slate-roof cottage, now the **Ledwidge Cottage and Museum** (about 1 km/⅔ mi east of Slane, on the road to Drogheda), formerly belonged to Francis Ledwidge (1887–1917), a farm laborer who wrote lyric poetry. Just as he was beginning to win acknowledgment for his work, he joined the British Army and was killed on a battlefield in Flanders in World War I. His cottage has now been furnished as it was in his time, a tribute to his short life. ☎ 041/24285. ⛒ £1. ⊙ *Apr.–Sept., daily 9–1, 2–7; Oct.–Mar., daily 9–1, 2–4.*

King William's Glen

❼ *7½ km/4½ mi east of Slane.*

On the northern bank of the River Boyne, King William's Glen is where a portion of King William's Protestant army hid before the Battle of the Boyne (1690), which they won by surprising the Catholic troops of James II, who were on the southern side. The nearby site of the battle is marked with an orange and green sign. Many of the Protestant-Catholic conflicts in present-day Northern Ireland can be traced to the immediate aftermath of this battle. Part of the battle site is also incorporated in the nearby **Townley Hall Estate,** which offers forest walks and a nature trail.

Drogheda

❽ *6½ km/4 mi east of King William's Glen, 45 km/28 mi north of Dublin.*

One of the most enjoyable historic towns on the east coast of Ireland, Drogheda was colonized in 911 by the Danish Vikings. Two centuries later, the town was taken over by Hugh de Lacy, the Anglo-Norman lord of Trim (☞ *above*) who was responsible for fortifying many locales up and down the River Boyne. At first, two separate towns existed on the northern and southern banks of the river. In 1412, already heavily walled and fortified, Drogheda was unified, making it the largest English town in Ireland. Today, large 18th-century warehouses line the northern bank of the Boyne. Towering over the river is the great length of the **railway viaduct.** Built around 1850 as part of the railway line from Dublin to Belfast, it is still used and is a splendid example of Victorian engineering; because of its height above the river, the viaduct remains the most prominent landmark in the town.

The center of the town, around West Street, is the historic heart of Drogheda. The bank building on the corner of West and Shop streets, called the **Tholsel,** is an 18th-century, square granite edifice with a cupola; it used to house the town hall. **St. Laurence's Gate,** the only survivor from Drogheda's original 10 gates in its town walls, has two four-story drum towers and is one of the most perfect examples in Ireland of a medieval town gate.

The Gothic Revival, Roman Catholic **St. Peter's Church** (⊠ West St.) houses the preserved head of St. Oliver Plunkett. Primate of all Ireland, he was martyred at Tyburn in London in 1681; his head was pulled from the execution flames. Built in a severe, 18th-century style within an enclosed courtyard, the Anglican **St. Peter's** (⊠ Fair St.) is rarely open except for Sunday services; if the church is closed, it's worth a peek for its setting and the fine views over the town from the churchyard.

The great **Mound of Millmount** (⊠ Just off Dublin Rd. south of Drogheda) was built comparatively recently—two centuries ago—but the mound is said to be atop an 11th-century BC burial place. The gateway to the top of the mound is usually open during the day; if you go to the top, you'll have more expansive views across Drogheda.

The **Millmount Museum** shares space in a renovated British Army barracks with crafts workshops, including a pottery and picture gallery and studio. Relics of eight centuries of Drogheda's commercial and industrial past are on display, including painted banners of the old trade guilds; a circular, willow and leather coracle (the traditional fishing boat on the River Boyne); and many instruments and utensils from domestic and factory use. Rather surprisingly, the museum does not have many mementos of the most infamous episode in Drogheda's history, when the English leader Oliver Cromwell sacked the town in 1649, killing 3,000 people. ⊠ *Millmount Museum,* ☎ *041/33097.* ⊡ *£1.50.* ☉ *Apr.–Oct., Tues.–Sat. 10–5:30, Sun. 2:30–5:30; Nov.–Mar., Wed. and weekends 10–5:30; crafts shops Mon.–Sat. 9:30–5.*

En Route   From Drogheda's center, take the minor road north (R167) that follows the northern bank of the River Boyne for 11 km/7 mi to **Baltray,** which still closely resembles an 18th-century Irish fishing village. From Baltray, continue north another 8 km/5 mi to the fishing village of **Clogherhead.** Take a walk above the local harbor to the heights of Clogher Head for outstanding views north to the Mountains of Mourne (☞ Chapter 9) and south to Skerries.

Dining and Lodging

$$ ✕ **Buttergate.** Traditional Irish dishes are served at lunch and dinner, while tasty "light bites" are available throughout the day. If plans to extend the small conservatory go ahead, the splendid view over the town and the River Boyne will make this one a must-visit while you're in Drogheda. It's next to the Millmount Museum. ⊠ *Millmount,* ☎ *041/ 34759. MC, V.*

$$ ✕🏠 **Boyne Valley Hotel and Country Club.** Once owned by a Drogheda brewing family, this 19th-century mansion sits on 16 acres and is approached via a 1-km/⅔-mi drive. Bedrooms in the main house have recently been renovated; the newer wing of the hotel has double rooms, all with contemporary furnishings. A large conservatory houses a bar and overlooks the grounds, while a large hall is decorated with antiques and comfy chairs. The Cellar Restaurant specializes in fresh fish. In 1996 a fitness center with a 20-meter indoor pool and extensive facilities was added. ⊠ *Dublin Rd., Drogheda, Co. Louth,* ☎ *041/ 37737,* ℻ *041/39188. 37 rooms with bath. Restaurant, bar, indoor pool, hot tub, sauna, steam room, 18-hole golf course, 2 tennis courts, health club. AE, DC, MC, V.*

Mellifont Abbey

❾ *11 km/7 mi north of Newgrange, 8 km/5 mi west of Drogheda.*

On the eastern bank of the River Mattock (which creates a natural border between Counties Meath and Louth here) lie the remains of Mellifont Abbey, the first Cistercian monastery in Ireland. Founded in 1142 by St. Malachy, Archbishop of Armagh, it was inspired by St. Bernard of Clairvaux's monastery, which St. Malachy had visited. Among the most substantial ruins are the two-story chapter house in the 12th-century English-Norman style, once a daily meeting place for the monks; it now houses a collection of medieval glazed tiles. Four walls of the octagonal lavabo, or washing place, still stand, as do some arches from the Romanesque cloister. At its peak Mellifont presided over almost 40 other Cistercian monasteries throughout Ireland, but they were all suppressed by Henry VIII in 1539 after his break with the Catholic church. ⊠ *Mellifont Abbey, Collon,* ☎ *041/26459.* ⊡ *£1.50.* ☉ *May–mid-June and mid-Sept.–Oct., daily 10–5; mid-June–mid-Sept., daily 9:30–6:30.*

Dining

$$$ ✕ **Forge Gallery Restaurant.** In a converted forge in Collon, north of Slane on the N2, this well-established restaurant is decorated in warm rose and plum tones and antique furniture, while an old fireplace throws comforting warmth and light. The cuisine mixes French provincial with a strong hint of traditional Irish cooking. Two popular specialties are salmon and crab in phyllo pastry, and prawns and scallops

in a cream and garlic sauce. Be sure to try one of the seasonal home-made soups. Paintings in the reception area, done by local artists, are for sale. ⊠ *Collon, Co. Louth,* ☎ *041/26272. Reservations essential on weekends. MC, V. Closed Sun. and Mon. and mid-Jan–end Jan.*

Monasterboice

❿ *8 km/5 mi north of Drogheda, 17 km/11 mi northeast of Slane.*

Ireland has more carved stone high crosses than any other European country; an outstanding collection of them is in the small, secluded village of Monasterboice. Dated to 923 AD, the **Muireadach Cross** stands nearly 20 ft high and is considered to be the best-preserved example of a high cross anywhere in Ireland. Its elaborate panels depict biblical scenes, including Cain slaying Abel; David and Goliath; and a centerpiece of the Last Judgment. (Figurative scenes are not a characteristic of earlier high crosses, like those found in Ahenny, County Clare, which are elaborately ornamented but without figures.) From the adjacent **round tower**, 110 ft high, the extent of the former monastic settlement at Monasterboice is apparent. The key to the tower door is held at the nearby gate lodge.

Ardee

⓫ *14½ km/9 mi north of Monasterboice.*

The market town of Ardee, formerly at the northern edge of the Pale, has a broad main street and two 13th-century castles. **Ardee Castle** (the one with square corners) was converted into a courthouse in the 19th century. **Hatch's Castle** (with rounded corners) is presently closed to the public. **St. Mary's Church of Ireland** on Main Street incorporates part of a 13th-century Carmelite church burned by Edward Bruce in early 1316.

All that remains of the **"Jumping Church"** at Kildemock (3 km/2 mi southeast of Ardee) are the foundations and one gable wall, but legend has it that this wall—which now sits 2½ ft inside the original foundations—jumped inward to keep out the grave of an excommunicated man who was buried within the walls of the church.

Dining

$$ ✕ **Gables House and Restaurant.** Just off the Dublin–Derry road (the N2), not far from the Dundalk junction, this family-run spot has traditional decor, with antique mahogany furniture, deep-burgundy velvet curtains, and oil paintings by local artists. Polished tables, silver cutlery, linen napkins, lace coasters, and gleaming lead crystal glasses add elegance. Expect generous portions and a French-influenced cooking style. The catch of the day is often monkfish, halibut, or even shark. The Gables Medley, made up of cheesecake, profiteroles and home-made ice cream, is a satisfying way to get a sugar rush. ⊠ *Dundalk Rd., Ardee,* ☎ *041/53789. AE, MC, V. No dinner Sun.*

Louth

⓬ *11½ km/7 mi north of Ardee.*

St. Patrick, Ireland's patron saint, was reputed to have built his first church in the hilltop village of Louth in the 5th century, and to have made St. Mochta (d. 534) the first bishop of Louth. Still standing at the center of the village is the excellently preserved **St. Mochta's House,** an oratory dating from the 10th century, which has a beautiful, high-pitched stone roof that can be reached by a stairway. The house is freely accessible, but visitors should watch out for cattle in the surrounding field.

Inniskeen

🔞 *6½ km/4 mi north of Louth.*

On the road from Dundalk and just over the Louth county boundary in Monaghan, Inniskeen is a small farming town that acts as a social hearth for the area's far-flung community. Patrick Kavanagh (1906–69), the area's most famous poet, is commemorated at the **Inniskeen Folk Museum,** housed in a converted church next to a round tower. Born and raised here, Kavanagh immortalized the town in his early poem "Inniskeen Road," before becoming one of Ireland's leading poets. He was brought back to the village for burial. ☎ *042/78109.* ✉ *Donations accepted.* ⊙ *May–Sept., Sun. 3–6, or by appointment.*

Dundalk

🔞 *14½ km/9 mi east of Inniskeen, 80 km/50 mi north of Dublin.*

Dundalk, the main town of County Louth (Ireland's smallest county), dates from the early Christian period, around the 7th century. The area near the town is closely connected with Cuchulainn (pronounced Coo-hoo-lin)—"a greater hero than Hercules or Achilles," as Frank McCourt, in *Angela's Ashes,* recalls his father claiming (see page 21 of McCourt's memoir for his father's memorable version of the story). Today, Dundalk is a thriving frontier town—only 9½ km/6 mi from the Northern Ireland border—with many fine historic buildings. On Mill Street, the **bell tower** of a Franciscan monastery with Gothic windows dates from the 13th century. The Catholic **St. Patrick's Cathedral** stands in Dundalk's town center; it was built between 1835 and 1847, when the Gothic revival was at its height, and is modeled on the 15th-century King's College Chapel, at Cambridge, in England, with its buttresses and mosaics lining the chancel and the side chapel walls. The fine exterior was built in Newry granite, and the high altar and pulpit are of carved Caen stone. ✉ *Town center, Dundalk.* ⊙ *Daily 8–6.*

The **Market House,** the **Town Hall,** and the **Courthouse** are other examples of the town's 19th-century heritage; the last is most impressive of the three, built in the 1820s in a severe Greek Revival style, with Doric columns supporting the portico. The Courthouse stands north of St. Patrick's Cathedral.

The Church of Ireland's **St. Nicholas** on Market Square incorporates a 15th-century tower. The church was rebuilt in 1707 and has a large, early-19th-century transept. In the graveyard lies the tomb of Agnes Galt, sister of Robert Burns, the 18th-century Scottish poet. ✉ *Market Sq., Dundalk.* ⊙ *During services only.*

Opened in 1994, the **Dundalk County Museum** is dedicated to preserving the history of the dying major local industries, such as beer brewing, cigarette manufacturing, shoe and boot making, and railway engineering. ✉ *Joycelyn St., Dundalk,* ☎ *042/27056.* ✉ *£2.* ⊙ *Tues.–Sat. 10:30–5:30, Sun. 2–6.*

On the seaward side of Dundalk, extensive **salt marshes** and mud flats lie on the edge of Dundalk Bay. This area is one of the largest bird sanctuaries in Ireland: Species such as Brent geese, curlews, and oystercatchers are regular visitors.

In Ballymascanlon (6½ km/4 mi north of Dundalk), behind the Ballymascanlon Hotel (☞ Dining and Lodging, *below*), you'll find the Neolithic **Proleek Dolmen,** a huge, mushroomlike stone structure that dates from the third millennium BC. Its capstone weighs nearly 50 tons.

Dining and Lodging

$$ ✕🖾 **Ballymascanlon Hotel.** On 130 acres just north of Dundalk, this converted Victorian mansion has long had a fine reputation for comfort and good cuisine. Rooms are large and furnished with reproduction period pieces; a wing with 20 new bedrooms and a well-outfitted fitness center was added in 1996. The restaurant serves Irish and French cuisine and specializes in fresh seafood entrées, such as lobster in season; vegetarian plates are also available. ⊠ *Dundalk, Co. Louth,* ☎ *042/71124,* 𝔽𝔸𝕏 *042/71598. 55 rooms with bath. Restaurant, 2 bars, indoor pool, hot tub, sauna, steam room, 18-hole golf course, 2 tennis courts, health club. AE, DC, MC, V.*

Cooley Peninsula Drive

⑮ *Beginning in Dundalk, 80 km/50 mi north of Dublin, 35 km/22 mi north of Drogheda.*

If you have a car and three or four free hours, the scenic drive around the Cooley Peninsula (a 64-km/40-mi round-trip beginning and ending in Dundalk) has some of the finest views of the east coast of Ireland. Beyond the Carlingford Lough on the north side of the peninsula, the Mountains of Mourne rise in the distance. From **Gyles Quay,** a small coastal village with a clean, safe beach, you'll have excellent views southward along the County Louth coast to Clogher Head. A road winds east around the Cooley Peninsula to **Greenore,** a town built in Victorian times as a ferryboat terminal. Today it has become a port for container traffic.

Carlingford

⑯ *5 km/3 mi east of Greenore.*

The small, medieval fishing town of Carlingford still has some striking thatched cottages, but what makes it particularly attractive is its natural setting: the mountains of the Cooley Peninsula back right up to the town, the Carlingford Lough lies at its feet, and the Mountains of Mourne rise only 5 km/3 mi away across the lough.

A massive, 13th-century fortress that rises up over the entrance to Carlingford Lough, **King John's Castle** has an unusual feature: Its west gateway is only wide enough to admit one horseman. At present, of the historic buildings in the town, only the castle is freely accessible to the public. Other remnants from the area's medieval days include a tower from the town wall and one of its gates, which later became the town hall; the 15th-century **Mint Tower House,** with mullioned windows; and **Taaffe's Castle,** a 16th-century, fortified town house.

Omeath

⑰ *6½ km/4 mi northwest of Carlingford.*

The northernmost town on Cooley Peninsula, Omeath was until recently the last main *Gaeltacht* (Irish-speaking) village in this part of Ireland (most extant Gaeltacht villages are in the Southwest and the West). On the eastern side of the village, you'll find open-air **stations of the cross** at the monastery of the Rosminian Fathers. Jaunting cars (traps pulled by ponies) take visitors to the site from the quayside, which has stalls selling all kinds of shellfish from the nearby lough, including oysters and mussels. A ferry service runs from the quay to Warrenpoint, across the lough in Northern Ireland.

A narrow road climbs the mountains behind Omeath; as you climb higher, the views become ever more spectacular, stretching over the Mountains of Mourne in the north and as far south as Skerries, 32 km/20 mi north of Dublin. This narrow road leads back to Dundalk.

COUNTY WICKLOW'S COAST AND MOUNTAINS

Make your way to the fourth or fifth story of almost any building in Dublin that faces south and you'll see off in the distance—though amazingly, not *that* far off in the distance—the green, smooth hills of the Dublin and Wicklow Mountains. On a clear day the mountains are even visible from some streets in and around the city center. If your idea of solace is green hills (and if you're blessed with blue sky), and your visit to Ireland is otherwise limited to Dublin, County Wicklow—or Cill Mhantain, as it is known in Irish—should be on your itinerary.

Not that the secret isn't out: Rugged and mountainous with dark, wooded forests, Central Wicklow is a popular picnic area with Dubliners. It also cradles one of Ireland's earliest Christian retreats: Glendalough. Nestled in a valley of dense woods and placid lakes, Glendalough and environs can seem (at least during the off-season) practically untouched since its heyday a thousand years ago. The same granite mountains that have protected Glendalough all these years run into the sea along the east coast, which is home to several popular sandy beaches. Our tour takes you from Dublin down to Arklow, sticking to the east side of the Wicklow Mountains. For the few Wicklow sights on the western side of the mountains, *see* the County Kildare and Western County Wicklow tour, *below*. A quick note about getting here: It takes stamina to extract yourself from the unmarked maze of the Dublin exurbs (your best bet is to take the N11, which becomes the M11, and then again the N11), but once you've accomplished that feat, this gorgeous, mysterious terrain awaits.

Bray

18 *22 km/14 mi south of Dublin, 8 km/5 mi east of Enniskerry.*

One of Ireland's oldest seaside resorts, Bray is a trim seaside village known for its dilapidated summer cottages and sand-and-shingle beach, which stretches 2 km/1⅓ mi. When the weather is good, hordes of Dubliners flock to Bray's oceanfront boardwalk to push baby carriages and soak up the sun. (It's the terminus of the DART train from Dublin, so it's easy to get here without a car.) In Bray's old courthouse on Lower Main Street, opposite the Royal Hotel, the **heritage center** in the town hall houses many artifacts from Bray's history, including old photographs and household items. ⊠ *Bray,* ☎ *01/286–8205.* ☞ *Free.* ☉ *Mon., Fri., and Sat. 10–5.*

One Martello Terrace (☎ 01/286–8407), at the harbor, is Bray's most famous address. James Joyce (1882–1941) lived here between 1887 and 1891 and used the house as the setting for the Christmas dinner in *A Portrait of the Artist as a Young Man* (☞ Close-Up: ReJoyce! A Walk through *Ulysses* and James Joyce's Dublin *in* Chapter 2). Today the house is privately owned by an Irish Teachta Dála (member of parliament, known informally as a "TD"). The phone number we list rings into her constituency office, and someone there should be able to help you arrange a visit; they recommend calling on Thursdays, 10 AM–1 PM. Although the residence has been renovated, the dining room portrayed in Joyce's novel still maintains the spirit of his time.

Killruddery House and Gardens are immediately off the Bray–Grey-stones road just south of Bray. The rare, 17th-century, precisely laid-out gardens have fine beech hedges, Victorian statuary, and a parterre of lavender and roses. ✉ *Killruddery,* ☎ *01/286–2777.* 🎫 *£1.* ⊙ *May, June, Sept. daily 1–5; by appointment at other times.*

Dining

$$$ ✕ **Tree of Idleness.** This Greek-Cypriot restaurant, a 10-minute walk
★ from Bray's DART train station, is a pleasant dining spot on the ground floor of a Victorian house along the seafront. It specializes in classic dishes and tasty, hearty portions. Roast lamb stuffed with feta cheese and olives is highly recommended. The extensive wine list includes Greek and Cypriot house wines. ✉ *Seafront, Bray, Co. Wick-low,* ☎ *01/286–3498. AE, DC, MC, V. Closed Mon., last wk. Aug., and first wk. Sept. No lunch.*

Outdoor Activities and Sports

The mountains bordering Bray to the south are laced with uncrowded hiking and mountain-bike trails. One of the best is a well-marked trail that leads from the beach to the 10-ft-tall cross that crowns the spiny peak of **Bray Head,** rising 791 ft from the sea. The semidifficult, 1-hour climb affords stunning views of Wicklow Town and Dublin Bay.

Powerscourt House, Gardens, and Waterfall

✋ ⑲ *25 km/16 mi south of Dublin, 32 km/20 mi north of Glendalough.*

Easily one of the prettiest villages in all of Ireland, **Enniskerry** is built around a sloping central triangular square and surrounded by the wooded Wicklow Mountains. The main reason to visit the area around Enniskerry is the Powerscourt estate. The grounds were originally granted to Sir Richard Wingfield, the first viscount of Powerscourt, by King James I of England in 1609. Richard Castle, the architect of Russborough House (☞ *below*), designed Powerscourt House in a grand Palladian style, and it was constructed between 1731 and 1740. Alas, the house burned down in 1974 immediately following a long period of restoration. It's now undergoing an extensive re-restoration; the original ballroom on the first floor is the only room in the house that gives a sense of the house's former life.

Laid out first from 1745 to 1767, following the completion of the house, and radically redesigned from 1843 to 1875, Powerscourt Gardens are considered among the finest in Europe. The redesign was the work of the eccentric, boozy Daniel Robertson, who liked to be tootled around the gardens-in-progress in a wheelbarrow while nipping at his bottle of sherry; he was inspired by the Villa Butera in Sicily. The gardens comprise sweeping terraces, antique sculptures, and a circular pond and fountain flanked by winged horses. There is a celebrated view of the Italianate patterned ramps, lawns, and pond across the beautiful, heavily wooded Dargle Valley to the noble profile of Sugar Loaf Mountain. The grounds include many specimen trees, an avenue of monkey puzzles, a parterre of brightly colored summer flowers, and a Japanese garden. The kitchen gardens, with their modest rows of flowers, are a striking antidote to the classical formality of the main sections. The gardens also offer a self-serve restaurant, crafts center, garden center, and a children's play area. (Enniskerry can also be reached directly from Dublin by taking the No. 44 bus from the Dublin quays area.) ✉ *En-niskerry,* ☎ *01/286–7676.* 🎫 *£2.80.* ⊙ *Mar.–Oct., daily 9:30–5:30; Nov.–Feb., 10:30–dusk.*

One of the most inspiring sights to the writers and artists of the Romantic generation, **Powerscourt Waterfall** (5 km/3 mi south of the gardens), at a height of nearly 400 ft, is the highest falls in the British Isles. ✉ *Enniskerry.* ⊡ *£1.50.* ☉ *Feb.–Oct., daily 9:30–7; Nov.–Jan, daily 10:30–dusk. Closed two wks following Christmas.*

Dining

$ ✕ **Poppies Country Cooking.** Like something out of a fairy tale, Pop-
★ pies is an adorable café and a perfect breakfast, lunch, or late-after-
noon tea spot (it's open until 6 on weekdays, 7 on weekends). With
only a dozen or so tables, it's cozy, with a low, pine-paneled ceiling,
floral wallpaper and matching cloth lamp shades, and pine farmhouse
furniture. After grabbing a table, amble over to the display case, which
has all the day's offerings. Potato cakes, shepherd's pie, lasagna, veg-
etarian quiche, a variety of house salads (you can order a sampler plate),
and the day's soup are the usual fare. The homemade desserts—caramel
squares, lemon meringue pie, pavlova—are terrific. You'll be tempted
to sit here for hours writing postcards and daydreaming about what
it would be like to be a regular. ✉ *The Sq., Enniskerry,* ☏ *01/282–
8869. No credit cards.*

Roundwood

⓴ *18 km/11 mi south of Enniskerry.*

At 900 ft above sea level and set amid spectacular scenery, Roundwood
is the highest village in Ireland. The Sunday-afternoon market held in
the village hall, where cakes, jams, and other homemade goods are sold,
livens up what is otherwise a sleepy place. From the broad main street,
by the Roundwood Inn (☞ Dining, *below*), a minor road leads west
for 8 km/5 mi to two lakes, **Lough Dan** and **Lough Tay,** lying deep be-
tween forested mountains like Norwegian fjords.

Dining

$$$ ✕ **Roundwood Inn.** This 17th-century inn, furnished in a traditional
★ style, with wooden floors, dark furniture, and diamond-shape windows,
is best known for good, reasonably priced bar food (1$)—homemade
broth, Irish stew, Galway oysters, or smoked Wicklow trout—eaten
at sturdy tables beside an open fire. The restaurant offers a combination of Continental and Irish cuisines, reflecting the traditions of the
German proprietor, Jurgen Schwalm, and his Irish wife, Aine. Local
produce figures prominently on the menu, especially roasts like rack
of Wicklow lamb, prime Irish beef, and local game in winter. Wiener
schnitzel is a house specialty. ✉ *Roundwood,* ☏ *01/281–8107. Reservations essential. MC, V. Restaurant closed Sun. dinner and Mon. except public holidays.*

Mount Usher Gardens

㉑ *14½ km/9 mi southeast of Roundwood.*

Situated on more than 20 acres on the banks of the River Vartry,
Mount Usher Gardens were first laid out in 1868 by Edward Walpole,
who owned a Dublin textile firm. Succeeding generations of the Walpole
family further planted and maintained the grounds, which have more
than 5,000 species, including eucalypti, azaleas, camellias, and rhododendrons, and which make the most of the riverside locale: water is
visible from nearly every place in the gardens, while bridges span the
river. A cluster of crafts shops (including a pottery workshop), a bookstore, and the self-serve restaurant stand at the entrance. The twin villages of Ashford and Rathnew are both nearby to the south and east,
and Newtownmountkennedy is to the north. ✉ *Ashford,* ☏ *0404/40116.*
⊡ *£3.* ☉ *Mar. 17–Oct., daily 10:30–6.*

Dining and Lodging

$$$$ ✕🖅 **Tinakilly House.** William and Bee Power have lovingly restored this Victorian-Italianate mansion, built in the 1870s by Captain Robert Halpin (1836–94), who laid the first transatlantic cable lines as captain of *The Great Eastern,* then the biggest ship in the world. (He's honored with a statue in Wicklow Town [☞ *below*].) Woods used originally in the house's construction, such as mahogany and pitch pine, have been meticulously replaced. The lobby has mementos of Captain Halpin and his nautical exploits, including paintings and ship models; impeccable Victorian antiques fill the house. Some bedrooms have four-poster beds, Jacuzzis, sitting areas, and views of the Wicklow landscape, the Irish Sea, or the lovely gardens on the 7-acre grounds. The French-influenced Irish cuisine in the dining room emphasizes seafood, game, and meat dishes, plus fresh vegetables from the garden; brown and fruit breads are baked daily. ✉ *Rathnew, Co. Wicklow,* ☎ *0404/ 69274,* Ⅸ *0404/67806. 41 rooms with bath. Restaurant, bar, tennis court, horseback riding. AE, DC, MC, V.*

$$ ✕🖅 **Hunter's Hotel.** One of Ireland's oldest coaching inns, first opened in the early 1700s, sits in a lovely rural setting on the banks of the River Vartry, only 1 km/⅗ mi east of Rathnew Village. Period prints, beams, and antiques lend an Old World feel enjoyed by both locals and guests. All bedrooms have delicate flower-print wallpaper and are superbly furnished with Victorian-style pieces. The good-size bathrooms were all updated in 1996. The restaurant serves traditional country-house cuisine using homegrown vegetables, Wicklow lamb, and fresh local seafood. In the summer, afternoon tea with homemade scones and jams is served in the magnificent garden that stretches down to the river. Sunday lunch regularly attracts diners down from Dublin. ✉ *Rathnew, Co. Wicklow,* ☎ *0404/40106,* ⅨX *0404/40338. 16 rooms with bath. Restaurant, bar. AE, DC, MC, V.*

Glendalough

★ ㉒ *19 km/12 mi west of Rathnew, 54 km/34 mi south of Dublin.*

One of Ireland's premier monastic sites, Glendalough is nestled in a lush, quiet valley deep in the rugged Wicklow Mountains. Set around two lakes, evergreen and deciduous trees, and acres of windswept heather, Glendalough flourished as a monastic center from some time in the 5th century until 1398, when English soldiers plundered the site, leaving the ruins that you see today. (The monastery survived earlier 9th- and 10th-century Viking attacks.) Glendalough's most famous resident was St. Kevin (Coemghein, or "fair begotten" in Irish), a descendant of the royal house of Leinster, who came here to live as a hermit and was an abbot at the monastery in 550. The **visitor center** is a good place to orient yourself and pick up a useful pamphlet. Many of the ruins are clumped together just beyond the visitor center, but some of the oldest surround the Upper Lake, where the scenery is really spectacular and the crowds thin out; signed paths direct you. Most ruins are open all day and are freely accessible.

Probably the oldest building on the site, dating from St. Kevin's time, is the **Teampaill na Skellig** (Church of the Oratory), on the south shore of the **Upper Lake.** A little to the east is **St. Kevin's Bed,** a tiny cave in the rock face, about 30 ft above the level of the lake, where St. Kevin lived his hermit's existence. It is not easily accessible; you approach the cave by boat, but climbing the cliff to the cave can be dangerous and is not recommended. At the southeast corner of the Upper Lake is **Reefert Church,** also dating from the 6th century, whose ruins consist of a nave and a chancel. The saint also lived in the adjoining, ru-

ined beehive hut with five crosses, which marked the original boundary of the monastery. There's a superb view of the valley from here.

The ruins by the edge of the **Lower Lake** are the most important of those at Glendalough. The **gateway,** beside the Glendalough Hotel, is the only surviving entrance to an ancient monastic site anywhere in Ireland. An extensive graveyard lies within, with hundreds of elaborately decorated crosses, as well as a perfectly preserved, six-story **round tower.** Built in the 11th or 12th century, it stands 100 ft high, with an entrance 25 ft above ground level.

The largest building at Glendalough is the substantially intact, 7th- to 9th-century **Cathedral,** where you'll find the nave (small for a large church, only 30 ft wide by 50 ft long), chancel, and ornamental oolite limestone window, which may have been imported from England. South of the cathedral is the 11-ft-high Celtic **St. Kevin's Cross.** Made of granite, it is the best-preserved such cross on the site. **St. Kevin's Church** is an early, barrel-vaulted oratory with a high-pitched stone roof.

A note about getting here directly from Dublin: You can take the **St. Kevin's** bus service (☞ Getting Around *in* Dublin Environs A to Z, *below*). Or, if you're driving from Dublin, head south from Christ Church Cathedral, staying on the main road until you reach Rathfarnham village. From there follow the R115, which leads you to Glencree—a beautiful stone village set in a valley—and then on to the Sally Gap. The extra time this takes (versus the main N11/M11/N11) is well worth it, for the R115 is one of Ireland's most spectacularly scenic routes; it passes through eye-popping landscape, including awesome, austere mountaintop passes where, as far as the eye can see, you *don't* see anything but the mountains. Don't do this drive if you're in a hurry, and don't look for a lot of signage—just concentrate on the glorious views. ⊠ *Glendalough,* ☎ *0404/45325.* ☜ *£2.* ⊙ *Mar.–May, Sept.–Oct., daily 9:30–5:30; June–Aug., daily 9–6; Nov.–Feb., Tues.–Sun. 10–4:30; last admission 15 mins. before closing.*

Dining and Lodging

$$ ✕☲ **Glendalough Hotel.** Purists object to how close this old-fashioned, early-19th-century hotel lies to the ruins at Glendalough, but to others it's a convenience. (A 30-bedroom extension completed in 1997 suggests the latter group is the larger.) How close is it? Some of the bedrooms, decorated in quiet, pastel colors, and the main restaurant, a long room with grand windows, overlook the monastery and the wooded mountain scenery; the burble of running water from the Glendassan River audibly enhances the experience. Helpings are hearty on the restaurant's simple menu; the pub is the only one for miles around. ⊠ *Glendalough,* ☎ *0404/45135.* ⅢX *0404/45142. 44 rooms. Restaurant, bar, fishing. AE, DC, MC, V. Closed Jan.*

Wicklow Town

❷ *26 km/16 mi east of Glendalough, 51 km/32 mi south of Dublin.*

At the entrance to the attractive, tree-lined Main Street of Wicklow Town—its name, from the Danish *wyking alo,* means "Viking meadow"—lie the extensive ruins of a 13th-century Franciscan friary. The friary was closed down during the 16th-century dissolution of the monasteries in the area, but its ruins give a sense of Wicklow's stormy past, which began with the unwelcome reception given to St. Patrick on his arrival in 432 AD; inquire at the nearby priest's house (⊠ Main St., ☎ 0404/67196) to view the ruins. The old town jail, just above Market Square, is currently being converted into a major **heritage cen-**

ter (⊠ Wicklow Town, ☎ 0404/67324, Ext. 126), where visitors can trace their genealogical roots in the area.

The **harbor** is Wicklow Town's most appealing area. Take Harbour Road down to the pier; a bridge across the River Vartry leads to a second, smaller pier, at the northern end of the harbor. From this end, follow the shingle beach, which stretches for 5 km/3 mi; behind the beach is the broad Lough, a lagoon noted for its wildfowl. Immediately to the south of the harbor, perched on a promontory that has good views of the Wicklow coastline, is the ruin of the **Black Castle.** This structure was built in 1176 by Maurice Fitzgerald, an Anglo-Norman lord who arrived with the English invasion of Ireland in 1169. The ruins (freely accessible) extend over a large area; with some difficulty, you can climb down to the water's edge.

Between one bank of the River Vartry and the road to Dublin stands the Protestant **St. Lavinius Church,** which incorporates a variety of earlier elements and unusual details: a Romanesque door, 12th-century stonework, fine pews, and an atmospheric graveyard. The church is topped off by a copper, onion-shape cupola, added as an afterthought in 1771. ⊠ *Wicklow Town.* ☞ *Free.* ⏰ *Daily 10–6.*

Dining and Lodging

$ ✕ **Pizza del Forno.** With its red-and-white-check tablecloths, low lighting, and pizza oven blazing away, this is a great vantage for people-watching on Main Street. Inexpensive pizzas, pasta, steaks, and vegetarian dishes appeal to a wide array of appetites. ⊠ *Main St., Wicklow Town,* ☎ *0404/67075. AE, MC, V. Closed Christmas–mid-Feb.*

$$ ✕▦ **Old Rectory Country House.** Once a 19th-century rectory, this small,
★   charming Greek Revival country house stands on a hillside just off the main road from Dublin on the approach to Wicklow Town. Owners Paul and Linda Saunders have a splendid touch. Dark marble fireplaces, bright colors, original oil paintings, and antique and contemporary furniture decorate the house; the light, spacious guest rooms are done in white and pastel shades with antique Victorian furniture. Linda's award-winning "Green Cuisine" makes use of fresh ingredients, especially seafood and organic vegetables. She specializes in salads and desserts, often made or garnished with edible flowers and herbs. ⊠ *Wicklow Town, Co. Wicklow,* ☎ *0404/67048,* ☒ *0404/69181. 5 rooms with bath. Restaurant. AE, MC, V. Closed Christmas–Feb.*

Avondale Forest Park and House

㉔ *17 km/11 mi west of Wicklow Town.*

Just outside the quaint village of Rathdrum, on the west bank of the Avondale River, the 523-acre **Avondale Forest Park** was, in 1904, the first forest in Ireland to be taken over by the state. There's a 5½-km/3½-mi walk along the river, and pine and exotic tree trails. **Avondale House,** on the grounds of the park, resonates with Irish history. The house was the birthplace and lifelong home of Charles Stewart Parnell (1846–91), one of Ireland's leading politicians in the 19th century, a campaigner for democracy and land reform. His career clattered to a halt after he fell in love with a married woman, Kitty O'Shea. When her husband instituted divorce proceedings in 1890, the revelation of Parnell's affair during court hearings ruined his political career, and he died a year later under the strain of the controversy. ("The greatest men fail, or seem to have failed," Wilde said of Parnell.) The house, built in 1779, was acquired by John Parnell, great-grandfather of Charles Stewart, in 1795. It has been flawlessly restored, with the re-

ception and dining rooms on the ground floor filled with Parnell memorabilia, including some of his love letters to Kitty O'Shea and political cartoons portraying his efforts to secure home rule for Ireland. ☎ *0404/46111.* ▱ *£2.75, parking £2.* ۞ *May–Sept., daily 10–6; Oct.–Apr., 11–5..*

Avoca

㉕ *6½ km/4 mi south of Avondale Forest Park.*

The small hamlet of Avoca is set amid heavily forested hills at the confluence of the Rivers Avonbeg and Avonmore. Beneath a riverside tree here, the Irish Romantic poet Thomas Moore (1779–1852) composed his 1807 poem "The Meeting of the Waters." There are some pleasant forest walks nearby, with scenic views of the valley. The oldest handweaving mill in Ireland, **Avoca Handweavers,** offers a short tour of the mill, which is still in operation. The store sells a wide selection of its own superb fabrics and woven and knit apparel, some of which are difficult to find elsewhere. ☎ *0402/35105.* ▱ *Free.* ۞ *Shop daily 9:30–5:30, mill weekdays 8–4:30.*

Three kilometers/2 miles south of Avoca is another attractive village, **Woodenbridge,** situated at a bubbling meeting of the Rivers Aughrim and Avoca.

Arklow

㉖ *11 km/7 mi south of Avoca, 8 km/5 mi south of Woodenbridge.*

Arklow's long, bustling main street winds its way down a gently sloping hill. Bread lovers and those with a sweet tooth should stop in at **Stone Oven Bakery** (✉ 65 Lower Main St., ☎ 0402/39418) at the bottom of the hill. The German-born baker, Egon Friedrich, turns out sourdough breads and delicious sweet treats, including hazelnut-chocolate triangles; they can prepare simple cheese and bread sandwiches to go or which you can eat in their tiny, slightly haphazard café. Down on the waterfront at the **Arklow Pottery Factory** (well signed throughout the town), you can take guided tours and shop for crafts. ☎ *0402/32401.* ۞ *Weekdays 9:30–5, weekends 10–5.*

The **Maritime Museum,** in the public library building near the railway station, traces Arklow's distinguished seafaring tradition; exhibits include old photographs, some original boats, and the logs of long-dead captains. To get here, take a left at St. Peter's Church as you're heading out of town in the direction of Gorey and Wexford. ✉ *St. Mary's Rd.,* ☎ *0402/32868.* ▱ *£1.50.* ۞ *May–Sept., Mon.–Sat. 10–1 and 2–5; Oct.–Apr., weekdays 10–1 and 2–5.*

Ⓒ Immediately north of Arklow, **Brittas Bay,** with its white, sandy beaches, quiet coves, and rolling dunes, is popular in summer with vacationing Dubliners, and is perfect for adventurous kids.

Coolattin Wood, about 25 km/16 mi to the southwest of Arklow, is one of the last original native woods left in Ireland, with impressively tall oak trees. The timber for the roof of Dublin's St. Patrick's Cathedral came from here.

COUNTY KILDARE
AND WEST WICKLOW

With it's gently sloping hills and grass-filled plains, County Kildare is the horse capital of Ireland. For first-time visitors, the National Stud just outside Naas offers a fascinating glimpse into the world of horse breeding. The Japanese Gardens, adjacent to the National Stud, are among Europe's finest, while Castletown House, in Celbridge to the north, is one of Ireland's foremost Georgian treasures. Our tour makes Dublin your starting point, but you may want to pick up this leg from Glendalough (☞ *above*). The spectacular drive across the Wicklow Gap, from Glendalough to Hollywood, makes for a glorious entrance into Kildare. One last note: Consult Chapter 5 if you make it as far south as Castledermot (the southernmost point in this tour), since Carlow and environs are only 10 km/6 mi farther south.

OFF THE **MAYNOOTH** – Before heading to Castletown House, make a quick de-
BEATEN PATH tour slightly farther west to Maynooth (24 km/15 mi west of Dublin), a
tiny Georgian town. Here you'll find **St. Patrick's College,** a center for the training of Catholic priests and one of Ireland's most important lay universities. The visitor center chronicles the college's history. ☎ 01/ 628–5222. ☉ May–Sept, Mon.–Sat. 11–5, Sun. 2–6, guided tours every hr.

At the entrance to St. Patrick's College lie the ruins of **Maynooth Castle,** largely destroyed in 1647. The castle keep, the oldest part, dates from the 13th century, and the keep and the great hall are still in reasonable condition. The key can be obtained from Mrs. Saults at 9 Parson Street. ☒ Free.

Castletown House

❷ *20 km/13 mi southwest of Dublin, 6½ km/4 mi south of Maynooth.*

In the early 18th century, a revival of the architectural style of Andrea Palladio (1508–80) swept through England, where architects built dozens of houses reinterpreting a style already 150 years old. The rage swept through Ireland among the Anglo-Irish aristocracy; *see also* Russborough House, *below* for another fine example nearby, and for references to others. Arguably the largest and finest example of an Irish Palladian-style house is Castletown, begun in 1722 for William Conolly (1662–1729), the Speaker of the Irish House of Commons and then the country's wealthiest man (he made his fortune in forfeited estates after the Battle of the Boyne). Conolly first hired the Italian architect Alessandro Galilei, who designed the facade of the main block, then in 1724, the young Irish architect Sir Edward Lovett Pearce, to complete the house; he added the colonnades and side pavilions. Conolly's death brought construction to a halt; it wasn't until his great nephew, Thomas Conolly, and his wife, Lady Louisa (née Lennox), took up residence in 1758 that work on the house picked up again. Throughout the 1760s and '70s, Lady Louisa oversaw the alteration and redecoration of the house.

Because of current restoration work inside, some rooms may be closed (at press time [summer 1997], the dining room is closed), but there are many splendid features, including hall plasterwork by the Lafranchini brothers, Swiss-Italian craftsmen who were active in Dublin in the mid-18th century. The ground-floor **Print Room** is the only 18th-century example in Ireland of this elegant fad. Like oversize postage stamps in a giant album, black-and-white prints were glued to the walls by fashionable young women who unwittingly anticipated the universal impulse among teenagers to cover their bedroom walls with posters. Upstairs at the rear of the house, the **Long Gallery,** almost 80 ft by 23 ft, is the most notable of the public rooms. In the 1770s it was redecorated in Pompeian style and three Venetian Murano glass chandeliers were hung. The house was rescued in 1967 by Desmond Guinness (of the brewing family), then the President of the Irish Georgian Society, and it is now the property of the Irish state. It's a good idea to phone ahead before visiting, as opening times may change due to continuing restoration work. ⊠ *Celbridge, Co. Kildare,* ☎ *01/628–8252.* ⊠ *£2.50.* ⊙ *Apr.–Sept., weekdays 10–6, Sat. 11–6, Sun. and bank holidays 2–6; Oct, Mon.–Sat. 10–5, Sun. and bank holidays 2–5; Nov.–Mar., Sun. and public holidays 2–5.*

Dining and Lodging

$$$$ ✕⊞ **Moyglare Manor.** Set on 16 pastoral acres dotted with sheep and cows, reached via a ⅘-km/½-mi tree-lined drive, this majestic Georgian manor house is just a half-hour drive (29 km/18 mi) west of Dublin. Owner Nora Devlin has exuberantly decorated the house with her renowned antiques collection; fresh flowers further enliven the decor. Velvet chairs, oil paintings, and thickly draped windows are in the drawing room, while the grand bedrooms have four-poster canopy beds, roomy wardrobes, marble fireplaces, and comfortable, chintz armchairs. Lamp-shaded wall sconces add a romantic touch to the formal dining room, where a traditional French menu is served. Rich desserts match the spirit of the house. There is horseback riding nearby— a bonus if you're an equestrian. ⊠ *Maynooth, Co. Kildare,* ☎ *01/628– 6351,* FAX *01/628–5405. 17 rooms with bath. Restaurant, 2 bars. AE, DC, MC, V.*

Straffan

㉘ *7 km/4½ mi south of Celbridge, 25½ km/16 mi west of Dublin.*

Attractively situated on the banks of the River Liffey, Straffan is home to the Kildare Hotel and Country Club (☞ Dining and Lodging, *below*), where Arnold Palmer designed The K Club, one of Ireland's most renowned 18-hole golf courses (☞ Chapter 10). The only one of its kind in Ireland, the **Straffan Butterfly Farm** has a tropical house with exotic plants, butterflies, and moths. Mounted and framed butterflies are available for sale. ⊠ *Co. Kildare,* ☎ *01/627–1109.* ⊠ *£2.50.* ⊙ *May–July, daily 12–5:30.*

The **Steam Museum** covers the history of Irish steam engines, handsome machines used in Ireland industrially as well as agriculturally, in such operations as churning butter and threshing corn. There's also a collection of model locomotives. Engineers are present on "live steam days"; phone in advance to confirm. ⊠ *Lodge Park,* ☎ *01/627–3155.* ⊠ *Live steam days £4, other times £3.* ⊙ *Easter–Sept., Tues.–Sun. 2–6; Jun.–Aug., Mon.–Sat.. 2–6, Sun. and bank holidays, 2:30– 5:30.*

En Route County Kildare has two major canal systems that connect Dublin with the Rivers Shannon and Barrow and the interior Lakelands. Sixteen kilometers/10 miles west of Straffan, **Robertstown** sits on the **Grand Canal** (the other major canal is the **Royal**, which heads to the northeast from Dublin), where you can take scenic walks and, during the summer, barge trips. Built in the early 19th century to accommodate passengers on the canal, the **Grand Canal Hotel** (☎ 045/870005) offers candlelit dinners and musical entertainment.

Dining and Lodging

$$$$ ✕⊞ **Kildare Hotel and Country Club.** Manicured gardens and the
★ renowned Arnold Palmer–designed K Club golf course (☞ Chapter 10) surround this mansard-roofed, French, former residence that dates from the 1870s. The spacious, very comfortable guest rooms are decorated with antiques and have large windows that overlook either the

Liffey or the golf course. Chef Michel Flamme serves an unashamedly French menu at the Byerly Turk Restaurant (named after a famous racehorse). A representative three-course meal: roast duck confit with mixed beans, followed by guinea fowl with cream of *girolles* (dried mushrooms) and fruit tartlets on crème anglaise. ⊠ *Co. Kildare,* ☎ *01/627–3333,* ℻ *01/627–3312. 45 rooms with bath. 2 restaurants, 2 bars, indoor pool, 18-hole golf course, 4 tennis courts, horseback riding, fishing. AE, DC, MC, V.*

$$$ ✕🗊 **Barberstown Castle.** With a 13th-century castle keep at one end, an Elizabethan central section, and a large Georgian country house at the other, Barberstown effortlessly blends 750 years of Irish history. Turf fires blaze in beautifully ornate fireplaces in the three sumptuously furnished lounges. Bedrooms are elegantly furnished with reproduction pieces; some have four-poster beds. A suite in the courtyard with a double room, twin room, and shared bath would suit families. The restaurant—half Georgian, half medieval (the latter part is in the ground floor of the castle keep)—serves creatively prepared fare; at dinner you can choose several starters from the tasting menu. ⊠ *Straffan, Co. Kildare,* ☎ *01/6288157,* ℻ *01/6277027. 31 rooms with bath. Restaurant, bar. AE, DC, MC, V.*

Naas

㉙ *13 km/8½ mi south of Straffan, 30 km/19 mi southwest of Dublin.*

The seat of County Kildare and a thriving market town in the heartland of Irish thoroughbred country, Naas is full of pubs where trainee jockeys discuss the merits of their various stables. The **Punchestown Racecourse** (⊠ 3 km/2 mi from Naas) has a wonderful setting amid rolling plains, with the Wicklow Mountains (16 km/10 mi away) forming a spectacular backdrop. Although horse races are held regularly here, the most popular event is the April Steeplechase Festival (☞ Festivals and Seasonal Events *in* Chapter 1).

Russborough House

㉚ *16 km/10 mi southeast of Naas.*

One of the highlights of the western part of County Wicklow, Russborough House is among the finest of the Palladian-style villas built throughout Ireland by the Anglo-Irish ascendancy in the first half of the 18th century. (Castletown House [☞ *above*], Emo Court [☞ Chapter 4], and Castle Coole [☞ Chapter 9] are the other brightest stars in this constellation.) In 1741, a year after Joseph Leeson inherited a vast fortune from his father, a successful Dublin brewer, he commissioned Richard Castle (architect of Leinster House [☞ Exploring Dublin *in* Chapter 2] and Powerscourt [☞ *above*]) to build this palatial house, and he worked on it until his death (after which Francis Bindon took over). They pulled out all the stops: Russborough is a confident, majestic house, with a silver-gray Wicklow granite facade that extends for more than 700 ft, encompassing a seven-bay central block, off which radiate two semicircular loggias connecting the flanking wings.

Baroque exuberance reigns in the house's main rooms, especially in the lavishly ornamented plasterwork ceilings executed by the Lafranchini brothers (they also worked at Castletown House). After a long succession of owners, Russborough was bought in 1952 by Sir Alfred Beit, the nephew of the German co-founder (with Cecil Rhodes) of the De Beers diamond operation, and it now belongs to Lady Beit, his widow. In 1988, after two major robberies, the finest works in the Beits' art collection, then considered one of the finest private collections in Europe, were donated to the National Gallery of Ireland (☞ Exploring Dublin *in* Chapter 2). However, works by Gainsborough, Guardi, Reynolds, Rubens, and Murillo remain, as well as bronzes, silver, and porcelain. The views from Russborough's windows takes in the foothills of the Wicklow Mountains as well as a small lake in front of the house; the extensive woodland on the estate is open to visitors. ⊠ *Off the N81, Blessington,* ☎ *045/865239.* ☎ *£3, upstairs bedrooms £1.50.* ☉ *June–Aug., daily 10:30–5:30; Easter, Apr., and Oct., Sun. and bank holidays 10:30–5:30; May and Sept., Mon.–Sat. 10:30–2:30, Sun. and bank holidays 10:30–5:30.*

Poulaphouca Reservoir

㉛ *33 km/21 mi west of Glendalough.*

Known locally as the **Blessington Lakes,** Poulaphouca (pronounced "pool-a-*fook*-a") Reservoir is a large meandering artificial lake that provides Dublin's water supply minutes from Russborough House. You can drive around the entire perimeter of the reservoir on minor roads; on its southern end lies Hollywood Glen, which is a particularly beautiful natural spot.

The small market town of **Blessington,** with its wide main street lined on both sides by tall trees and Georgian buildings, lies on the western shore of the lakes and is one of the most charming villages in the area. Founded in the later 17th century, it used to be a stop on the Dublin–Waterford mail-coach service in the mid-19th century; until 1932, a quaint steam train ran from here to Dublin, along the side of the main road.

Just beyond the southern tip of the Poulaphouca Reservoir (13 km/8 mi south of Blessington on the N81), you will spot a small sign for the **Piper's Stones.** A short walk from the road, this Bronze Age stone circle was probably used in a ritual connected with worship of the sun.

Dining and Lodging

$$$$ ╳▥ **Rathsallagh House.** Set amid 530 acres of parkland, Rathsal-
★ lagh—low-slung, ivy-covered, Queen Anne stables converted to a farmhouse in 1798—awaits at the end of the long drive that winds through the golf course. Kay and Joe O'Flynn, oversee a stellar staff and an impeccably run operation. The comfortable guest rooms, most with seating areas, are decorated in different colors; bathrooms are well appointed (some have extra-large tubs). Downstairs, the two drawing rooms are decorated with enveloping couches and chairs and fresh flower arrangements; large windows, fireplaces, and lots of lamps make for good light to read or relax by day or night. In the elegant wood-paneled dining room, sconces with silk-covered lamp shades, an open fireplace, and candles softly illuminate the beautifully set tables. Spring or carbonated water served in a crystal pitcher is left at your table and refilled as often as necessary. Kay's outstanding haute Irish dinner menu changes daily and gives pride of place to homegrown vegetables and hearty roasts of local lamb and beef. Specialties include a cheese soufflé and warm salad of pigeon breast. The route to the house is well signposted (49 km/31 mi southwest of Dublin) and is not far from where the N756 meets the N81, but call ahead for precise directions. ⊠ *Near Dunlavin, Co. Wicklow,* ☎ *045/403112,* ℻ *045/403343. 17 rooms with bath. Restaurant, bar, indoor pool, massage, sauna, 18-hole golf course, tennis court, croquet, DC, MC, V.*

Outdoor Activities and Sports

There are splendid views of the Blessington Lakes from the top of **Church Mountain,** which you reach via a vigorous walk through **Woodenbo-**

ley Wood, at the southern tip of Hollywood Glen. Follow the main forest track for about 20 minutes and then take the narrow path that heads up the side of the forest to the mountaintop.

The Curragh

32 *8 km/5 mi southeast of Naas.*

The broad plain of The Curragh, bisected by the main N7 road, is the biggest area of common land in Ireland, encompassing about 31 square km/12 square mi, and is devoted mainly to grazing. It's also Ireland's major racing center, home to **Curragh Racecourse** (☎ 045/441205), where the Irish Derby and other international horse races are run (☞ *Festivals and Seasonal Events in* Chapter 1).

The **Curragh Main Barracks,** a large camp where the Irish Army trains, has a small museum. One of its prize relics is the armored car once used by Michael Collins, the former head of the Irish Army who, in December 1921, signed the Anglo-Irish Treaty designating a six-county North to remain in British hands, in exchange for complete independence for Ireland's remaining 26 counties. Collins was assassinated in 1922; his life was dramatized in Neil Jordan's 1996 film. The car can be seen with permission from the commanding officer. ☎ *045/445000; ask for the command adjutant.*

OFF THE BEATEN PATH	**HILL OF ALLEN** – If time permits, detour 8 km/5 mi northwest of Newbridge to the 676-ft-high Hill of Allen, one of the few high points on the surrounding plain and thus a wonderful vantage. It has a special place in Irish mythology: It was the site of one of three royal palaces in Leinster some 1,500 years ago; Fionn Mac Cumhaill, the hero of many Irish folk tales, also lived here.

Kildare Town

33 *5 km/3 mi from the Curragh, 51 km/32 mi southwest of Dublin,*

Horse-breeding is the basis of Kildare's thriving economy. Right off Kildare's main market square, the **Silken Thomas** (☎ 045/522232) re-creates an old-world atmosphere with open fires, dark wood decor, and leaded lights; it's a good place to stop for lunch before exploring the sights here. **St. Brigid's Cathedral** (Church of Ireland) is where the eponymous saint founded a religious settlement in the 5th century. The present cathedral, with its stocky tower, is a restoration of a building that dates from the 13th century. It was partially rebuilt about 1686, but restoration work wasn't completed for another 200 years. The stained-glass west window of the cathedral depicts three of Ireland's greatest saints: Brigid, Patrick, and Columba. ⊠ *Off Market Sq.* ≊ *Free.* ☉ *Daily 10–6.*

The 108-ft-high **round tower,** in the graveyard of St. Brigid's Cathedral, is the second highest in Ireland and dates from the 12th century. Extraordinary views across much of the Midlands await those energetic enough to climb the stairs to the top. ☎ *045/441654.* ≊ *60p.* ☉ *May–Sept., daily 10–1, 2–5.*

34 If you're a longtime horse aficionado or just curious, the **National Stud,** a main center of Ireland's racing industry, is well worth a visit. Founded in 1900 by Colonel William Hall-Walker (later Lord Wavertree), a brewing heir, and transferred to the Irish state in 1843, the Stud is home to breeding stallions who are groomed, exercised, tested, and bred within the neat white buildings, which are set around immaculately kept green lawns. Spring and early summer, when mares will have new foals, are the best times to visit. Walker believed in astrology, and he built the stallion boxes with lantern roofs that allow the moon and stars to work their magic on the occupants. Also on the grounds, the **National Stud Horse Museum** recounts the history of the horse in Ireland. Its most outstanding exhibit is the skeleton of Arkle, the Irish racehorse that won outstanding victories in races in Ireland and England during the late 1960s. The museum also contains medieval evidence of horses, such as bones from 13th-century Dublin, and some early examples of equestrian equipment. ☎ 045/521617. ▧ *£5 (includes entry to the Japanese Gardens).* ⊘ *Feb.–Nov., daily 9:30–6.*

★ ㉞ Adjacent to the National Stud, the **Japanese Gardens** were created between 1906 and 1910 by the Stud's founder, Colonel Hall-Walker, and laid out by a Japanese gardener, Tassa Eida, and his son Minoru. The gardens are recognized as among the finest in Europe, although they're something of an east-west hybrid rather than authentically Japanese. The Scots pine trees, for instance, are an appropriate stand-in for traditional Japanese pines, which signify long life and happiness. The gardens symbolically chart the human progression from birth to death (the focus is on a man's journey, not a woman's). A series of landmarks are situated on a meandering path: the Tunnel of Ignorance (no. 3) represents a child's lack of understanding, the Engagement and Marriage bridges (nos. 8 and 9) span a small stream, and from the Hill of Ambition (no. 13), you can look back over your past joys and sorrows. It ends with the Gateway to Eternity (no. 20), beyond which lies a Buddhist meditation sand garden. It's a worthwhile destination any time of the year, though it's particularly glorious in spring and fall. ✉ *South of Kildare Town about 2½ km/1½ mi, clearly signposted to left of market square,* ☎ *045/ 521617.* ▧ *£5 (includes entry to the National Stud).* ⊘ *Feb.–Nov., daily 9:30–6.*

Athy

㉟ *24 km/15 mi south of Kildare Town, 33½ km/21 mi south of Naas.*

The River Barrow widens considerably at Athy, an industrial town; though it has seen better days, a recent designation as a heritage town may help spiff things up. Overlooking the river, by the bridge, 16th-century **White's Castle,** now a private house, was built by the earl of Kildare to defend this strategic crossing. The modern pentagonal **Catholic church** (1963–65) has a striking interior with Stations of the Cross by George Campbell, a noted Irish artist; statues; and a crucifix on the high altar by local artist Brid ni Rinn. ▧ *Free.* ⊘ *Daily 8–6.*

Ballitore

㊱ *8 km/5 mi east of Athy, 26 km/16 mi south of Naas.*

In the 18th and 19th centuries, Ballitore was a Quaker settlement. An old schoolhouse has been converted into a small **Quaker Museum.** Among the pupils at the school was Edmund Burke (1729–97), the orator and political philosopher who was close to Samuel Johnson and Sir Joshua Reynolds. Burke was born in Dublin of a Catholic mother and Protestant father; after studying at Trinity he went to London in 1750. His essay *A Philosophical Inquiry into the Origin of Our Ideas of the Sublime and Beautiful* (1756) was a pioneering psychological study of aesthetic theory that is still read today. ☎ 045/31109. ▧ *£1.* ⊘ *Sporadically, usually Sun. afternoon.*

An old mill has been converted into the **Crookstown Heritage Centre,** a museum of the flour-milling and baking industries. Built in 1840, its presence helped reduce the effects of the Great Famine in this area. You can get a quick bite in its coffee shop. ☎ *0507/23222.* 🍴 *£2.* ⊘ *Apr.–Sept., daily 10–7; Oct.–Mar., Sun. 2–5:30.*

③⑦ From Ballitore take the main N9 road south for 3 km/2 mi to Timolin, where the **Irish Pewter Mill** pays splendid tribute to an old Irish craft; it incorporates showrooms, a factory, and a museum. Jugs, plates, and other pewter items are for sale. ☎ *0507/24164.* ⊘ *May–Sept., weekdays 9:30–5, weekends 11–4.*

South Kildare is home to several well-preserved high crosses, set amid monastic ruins. One-and-a-half kilometers/1 mile beyond Timolin on the N9, take the signposted right turn at the Moone Post Office and
③⑧ continue for 3 km/2 mi to the **Moone High Cross,** an ancient Celtic cross that stands 17½ ft high, with 51 sculptured panels showing scriptural scenes.

Dining

$ ✕ **Moone High Cross Inn.** Down the road from the Moone High Cross, this old pub is packed with a cornucopia of local artifacts, newspaper clippings, and old photographs—all fascinating browsing while you nosh on the eclectic bar food that includes a good steak, salmon, and bacon and cabbage. Save room for the homemade apple pie. On sunny days, you can sit outside and admire the old signs in the beer garden. ✉ *Bolton Hill, Moone,* ☎ *0507/24112. MC, V. Closed Jan.*

Castledermot

③⑨ *8 km/5 mi south of Moone.*

On the left-hand side of the village of Castledermot, you'll find an almost perfectly preserved 10th-century **round tower** together with two 10th-century **high crosses,** equally well preserved, on the grounds of the local church. From the church gate, you can walk back to the main road along the footpath that is totally enclosed by trees. On the right-hand side of the road in the village, the substantial ruins of a Franciscan friary, mostly dating from the 14th century, are freely accessible.

Lodging

$$$ 🏰 **Kilkea Castle.** Built in 1180 as a defensive Anglo-Norman castle, Kilkea was the longtime home of the FitzGerald family; it was modified in the 17th century and later restored. Eleven rooms are in the castle itself; the rest are set around an adjacent courtyard (those in the castle are more luxuriously furnished). The restaurant is now in what was the great hall of the castle; dishes are based on fresh, seasonal produce—some of it from the old walled gardens laid out below. The hotel has an extensive sports complex, including an 18-hole golf course and clubhouse. ✉ *Castledermot, near Athy, Co. Kildare,* ☎ *0503/45156,* 🖷 *0503/45187. 36 rooms with bath. Restaurant, 2 bars, indoor pool, hot tub, sauna, steam room, 18-hole golf course, 2 tennis courts, archery, health club, fishing. AE, DC, MC, V.*

DUBLIN ENVIRONS A TO Z

Getting Around

By Bus

Bus services link Dublin with main and smaller towns in the environs. All bus services for the region depart from Busaras, the central bus station, at Store Street. For bus inquiries, contact **Bus Éireann** (☎ 01/836–6111). **St. Kevin's** (☎ 01/281–8119), a private bus service, runs daily from Dublin (outside the Royal College of Surgeons on St Stephen's Green) to Glendalough, stopping off at Bray, Roundwood, and Laragh en route.

Buses leave Dublin Monday–Saturday at 11:15 AM and 6 PM (7 PM on Sundays); buses leave Glendalough Monday–Saturday at 7:15 AM and 4:15 PM (5:30 PM on Sundays). One-way fare: £5, round-trip: £8.

By Car

The easiest and best way to tour Dublin's environs is by car, because many sights are not served by public transportation, and what service there is, especially to outlying areas, is infrequent. If you need to rent a car, *see* Car Rentals, *in* Dublin A to Z *in* Chapter 2.

To get to destinations in **County Wicklow,** the N11/M11 is the fastest and most clearly marked route. The two more scenic routes to Glendalough are the R115 to the R759 to the R755, or the R177 to the R755.

To get to destinations in the **Boyne Valley,** follow the N3, along the east side of Phoenix Park, out of the city and make Trim and Tara your first stops. Alternatively, leave Dublin via the N1/M1 to Belfast. Try to avoid the road during weekday rush hours (8 AM–10 AM and 5 PM–7 PM); stay on it as far as Drogheda and start touring from there.

To get to destinations in **County Kildare,** follow the quays along the south side of the Liffey (they are one-way westbound) to St. John's Road West (the N7); in a matter of minutes, you're heading for open countryside. Avoid traveling this route during the evening peak rush hours, especially on Friday, when Dubliners are themselves making their weekend getaways.

By Train

Iarnród Éireann trains run the length of the east coast, from Dundalk to the north in County Louth, to Arklow along the coast in County Wicklow. Trains make many stops along the way; there are stations in Drogheda, Dublin (the main stations are **Connolly Station** [✉ Amiens St.] and **Pearse Station** [✉ Westland Row]), Bray, Greystones, Wicklow, and Rathdrum. From Heuston Station (✉ Victoria Quay and St. John's Road W), the Arrow, a new commuter train service, runs westward to Celbridge, Naas, Newbridge, and Kildare Town. Contact Iarnród Éireann (✉ Irish Rail, ☎ 01/836–6222) for schedule and fare information.

Contacts and Resources

B&B Reservation Agencies

For a small fee, **Bord Fáilte** will book accommodations anywhere in Ireland through their central reservations system. B&Bs can be booked at local visitor information offices when they are open; however, even these reservations will go through the central reservations system. For more information, *see* Lodging *in* the Gold Guide.

Car Rentals

See Car rentals *in* Dublin A to Z *in* Chapter 2.

Emergencies

Police, fire, and **ambulance** (☎ 999 toll-free).

Guided Tours

Bus Éireann (☎ 01/836–6111) runs guided bus tours to many of the historic and scenic locations throughout the Dublin environs daily during the summer. Visits include trips to Glendalough in Wicklow; Boyne Valley and Newgrange in County Louth; and the Hill of Tara, Trim, and Navan in County Meath. All tours depart from Busaras Station, Dublin; information is available by phone Monday–Saturday 8:30–7, Sunday 10–7.

Gray Line (☎ 01/661–9666), a privately owned touring company, also runs many guided bus tours throughout the Dublin environs between May and September.

BICYCLING

Glendalough Mountain Bike Treks (✉ 29 Castle Court, Booterstown, Co. Dublin, ☎ 01/289–8705 or 087/596278) organize one-day and overnight excursions from Dublin to the Wicklow Mountains April through October. For overnight trips they arrange accommodations in hostels and B&Bs; they can also provide bikes and helmets.

HORSEBACK RIDING

Wicklow Trail Rides (✉ Grainne Sugars, Calliaghstown Riding Center, Ratcoole, Co. Dublin, ☎ 01/4589236, FAX 01/4588171) takes experienced adult horseback riders on weeklong rides through the Wicklow Mountains (May–September), with overnight stays in country homes and guest houses. Instructional holidays for children and adults at the riding center are also available.

WALKING AND HIKING

County Wicklow sponsors three annual walking festivals. The two-day **Rathdrum Easter Walking Festival** (☎ 0404/46262) includes hill walks of varying lengths over Easter weekend. The first weekend of May, the **Wicklow Mountains May Walking Festival** (☎ 0404/66058) is centered around Blessington. The **Wicklow Mountains Autumn Walking Festival** (☎ 0404/66058) is based in the Glenmalure area.

Visitor Information

For information on travel in the Dublin environs and for help in making lodging reservations, contact one of the following Tourist Information Offices (TIOs): **Dublin Tourism** and **Bord Fáilte** (☞ Visitor Information *in* Dublin A to Z, Chapter 2). **Dundalk** (☎ 042/35484, FAX 042/38070). **Mullingar** (☎ 044/48650, FAX 044/40413). **Trim** (☎ 046/37227, FAX 046/31595).

Mullingar is the head office of tourism covering the counties of Wicklow, Louth, Meath, and Kildare. During the summer, temporary TIOs are open throughout the environs, in towns such as Arklow and Wicklow Town, in County Wicklow; Drogheda and Dundalk in County Louth; and Kildare Town in County Kildare.

4 The Midlands

Counties Offaly, Roscommon, Longford, Cavan, Monaghan, Westmeath, the north of Tipperary, and the south of Leitrim

Unspectacular and unsung, the flat plains of the Midlands form the geographical heart of Ireland. There's water at every turn in this landscape of wide lakes and fast rivers, including the mighty Shannon, Ireland's central artery and the longest river in the British Isles. Among the highlights are Clonmacnoise, Ireland's most important monastic ruins; historic towns with industries such as lace-making and crystal; the gardens of Birr Castle; and some of Ireland's finest Anglo-Irish houses—Strokestown House, Castle Leslie, and Emo Court.

By Alannah
Hopkin

RISH SCHOOLCHILDREN WERE ONCE TAUGHT to think of their country as a saucer with mountains around the edge and a dip in the middle. The dip is the Midlands—or the Lakelands, as it is also sometimes referred to—and this often overlooked region comprises seven counties: Cavan, Laois (pronounced "leash"), Westmeath, Longford, Offaly, Roscommon, and Monaghan, in addition to North Tipperary.

A fair share of Ireland's 800 bodies of water speckle this lush countryside. Many of the lakes formed by glacial action some 10,000 years ago are quite small, especially in Cavan and Monaghan. Anglers who come to the area have learned to expect a lake to themselves, and many return year after year to practice the sport. Because of all the water, much of the landscape lies under blanket bog, a unique ecosystem that's worth exploring. The River Shannon, one of the longest rivers in Europe and the longest in the British Isles, bisects the Midlands from north to south, piercing a series of loughs (lakes): Lough Allen, Lough Ree, and Lough Derg. The Royal Canal and the Grand Canal cross the Midlands from east to west, ending in the Shannon north and south of Lough Ree. Stretches of both canals have been developed for recreational purposes.

The main roads from Dublin to the south and the west cross the area—and came to eclipse the Shannon and the canals as transportation arteries—but there is also a network of minor roads linking the more scenic areas. You'll find more conventionally attractive hill and lake scenery in the forest parks of Killykeen and Lough Key. The towns themselves—including Nenagh, Roscommon, Athlone, Boyle, Mullingar, Tullamore, Longford, and Cavan—are not among Ireland's most distinctive, but they are likely to appeal to people hungry for a time when the pace of life was slower and every neighbor's face was familiar. A Midland town's main hotel is usually the social center, a good place from which to experience life as the locals do. You might witness a wedding reception (generally a boisterous occasion for all age groups), a First Communion supper, a meeting of the local Lions Club, or a gathering of the neighborhood Weight Watchers group. By now you've probably realized: Night owls and thrill-seekers should probably head elsewhere.

The Midlands are, last but not least, dotted with some of Ireland's most impressive heritage properties from disparate eras: Strokestown Park House, Birr Castle Gardens, Emo Court and Gardens, Castle Leslie, and the magnificent monastic ruins of Clonmacnoise on the banks of the Shannon.

Pleasures and Pastimes

Dining

Most of the restaurants are simple eateries, ranging in price from inexpensive ($) to moderate ($$), and are often attached to a family hotel. Mullingar, in the center of the Midlands, is the beef capital of Ireland, and the many lakes and rivers of the region provide an abundance of fresh salmon and trout. And since no place in Ireland is more than an hour and a half from the sea, you can also expect to find fresh ocean fish. The approach to cooking may often be conventional, but the ingredients will always be first-rate. For price ranges, *see* Chart 1(A) *in* On the Road with Fodor's.

Lodging

Accommodations in the area are simple but offer good value. The choice will usually be between a small-town hotel offering a reasonable standard of simple comfort or a scenically located, country-house bed-and-breakfast, perhaps overlooking a small lake or river. Either way, informality is the order of the day. For price ranges, *see* Chart 2(B) *in* On the Road with Fodor's.

Outdoor Activities and Sports

BICYCLING

One of the best ways to immerse yourself in the Midlands is to tour the region on a bicycle. Although the area may not offer the spectacular scenery of the more hilly coastal regions, its level terrain means a less strenuous ride. The twisting roads are generally in good condition, and there are good picnic spots in the many state-owned forests just off the main roads. Bord Fáilte recommends two long tours: one of the Athlone-Mullingar-Roscommon area and another of the Cavan-Monaghan-Mullingar region. Whenever possible, try to avoid the major trunk roads that bisect the region.

BOATING

With 485 km/300 mi of navigable rivers and numerous island-studded lakes in the region, a boat is the best way to see the Midlands at a leisurely pace and from an unusual and memorable angle. Several companies rent out charter boats of varying sizes for vacations on the water. Most of these vessels hold from six to eight people, and all are operated by the parties who rent them, meaning everyone can be captain for a day.

FISHING

Anglers from all over the world are attracted to the region's River Shannon and its system of lakes. Beam, rudd, tench, roach, perch, and hybrids are the main varieties, while pike roam select waters. Monaghan, Cavan, Boyle, and the small lakes to the east and west of Lough Derg are the best coarse fishing areas, while brown-trout lakes and rivers can be found around Birr, Banagher, Mullingar, and Roscommon. For pike, you'll find the most fruitful areas around Cavan, Clones, Cootehill, Castleblaney, Kingscourt, Carrick-on-Shannon, Boyle, Belturbet, and Butlersbridge. The Midlands region hosts several angling festivals, with prize money and fringe events such as sing-alongs, dart games, and card competitions. Castleblaney has a tournament in March; Carrickmacross and Ballinsasloe, in May; Athlone, in July and October; and Cootehill, in September.

GOLF

While the parkland courses of the Midlands may lack the spectacular challenge of Ireland's more famous scenic and coastal courses, they have a quiet charm all of their own. On weekdays, at least, you are unlikely to have any trouble booking a tee time. Six 18-hole courses have opened in the Midlands in recent years, considerably reducing the pressure on facilities. Greens fees are generally moderate at around £12.

HIKING AND WALKING

Forest park trails (at Killykeen, Lough Key, and Dun a Ri forest parks) and narrow country roads invite visitors to tour parts of the Midlands on foot. One impressive walking trail to the east of Birr, called the Slieve Bloom Way, runs through the Slieve Bloom Mountains on a 50-km/31-mi circular route; its attractions include deep glens, rock formations, waterfalls, and views from mountain peaks.

Exploring the Midlands

Our coverage of the Midlands is organized into three different tours: Portarlington–Castlepollard, Longford–Clones, and Boyle–Nenagh. The first two tours can easily be strung together for an extended visit in the Midlands, as they chart a course almost due north from the initial starting point in Portarlington, County Laois. Because our third tour covers sights west of those in the first two tours, keep them in mind if you're flying into Shannon and beginning your explorations of Ireland in the western half of the country. In fact, because the Midlands border virtually every major county of Ireland, there are three places in this chapter where you should be alert to other nearby locales we cover in other chapters: The easternmost sites in the Midlands (Emo Court and Coolbanagher) are within a few miles of the westernmost sites in Dublin Environs (☞ Chapter 3); the westernmost sites in the Midlands (Boyle and Lough Key Forest Park) are just across the border from County Sligo (☞ Chapter 8); and the northernmost sites and towns of the Midlands are just across the border from Northern Ireland (☞ Chapter 9).

Numbers in the text correspond to numbers in the margin and on the Midlands map.

Great Itineraries

The Midlands is a relatively small region, but part of its attraction lies in the temptation to spend time off the beaten path following a loose itinerary. Ten days would allow for a leisurely exploration of the region by bicycle. Car drivers could cover the same route in five days with plenty of time to improvise. Three days would be enough to sample the central area of the region, which is probably more sensible than driving long distances on small roads in an effort to see everything.

IF YOU HAVE 3 DAYS

Heading east from Shannon Airport, turn off the N7 Limerick–Dublin road for ☒ **Birr** ㉗, a quiet, Georgian town, built around its magnificent Castle and Gardens. Then take the nearby **Bord na Mona Bog Rail Tour** ㉕ near Shannonbridge, a good introduction to the flora and fauna of Ireland's many bogs. While you're in the area, stop at **Clonmacnoise** ㉔, Ireland's most important monastic settlement, which overlooks the River Shannon, and return to Birr for the night. The next day head toward ☒ **Longford** ⑨ to get another view of bog culture at the **Corlea Trackway Exhibition Centre.** Next head for **Strokestown** ㉑ and its namesake house, where the award-winning museum documents the causes and effects of the 1845–51 Great Irish Famine. Try to find time to tour the house and gardens as well. Spend the night back in Longford. Book yourself a visit to **Carrigglas Manor,** a romantic Tudor-Gothic house built just outside Longford in 1837 that has Jane Austen associations. If the weather is good, take some fresh air in **Lough Key Forest Park** ⑳ near **Boyle** ⑲, from where you will be well positioned to explore the West or Northwest (☞ Chapters 7 and 8).

IF YOU HAVE 5 DAYS

Heading from Dublin or from points east in Wicklow and Kildare, start off at **Emo Court and Gardens** ①, the only large-scale country house designed by James Gandon, the architect responsible for much of Georgian Dublin; the lovingly restored house was recently given to the nation. Move northward to the Gothic Revival Charleville Castle outside **Tullamore** ③, then on to **Kilbeggan** ④, where you can learn all about whiskey-making at the Kilbeggan Distillery. If you have time, stop in at **Belvedere House Gardens** ⑤, which have a beautiful lakeside setting. Stay in or around ☒ **Mullingar** ⑥ for the night. In the morning on day two, briefly explore Mullingar, then head north on the scenic R 394 to **Castlepollard** ⑦ and the nearby and massive Tullynally Castle and Gardens, the ancestral home of Antonia Fraser, the prolific and highly regarded biographer of the English aristocracy. Crystal aficionados will want to stop in **Cavan** ⑪, while nature buffs can easily

The Midlands

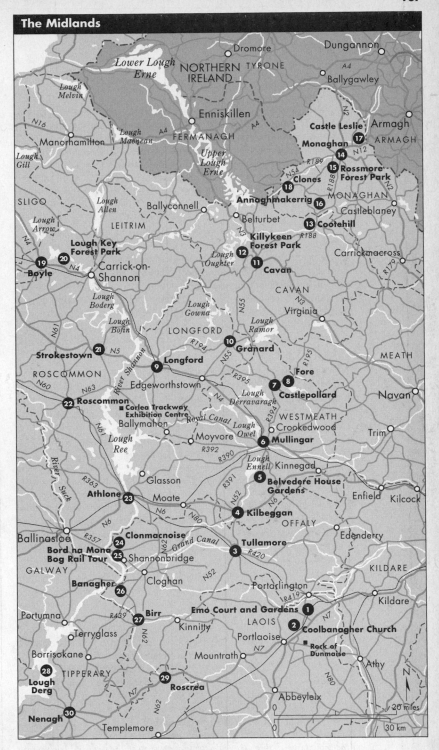

Dromore

Dungannon

Lower Lough Erne

NORTHERN IRELAND

TYRONE

Ballygawley

Lough Melvin

Enniskillen

A4

Lough Macnean

FERMANAGH

Castle Leslie **17**

Armagh

Monaghan **14**

ARMAGH

N2

N12

N16

Manorhamilton

A4

Upper Lough Erne

R189

Rossmore Forest Park **15**

Lough Gill

SLIGO

Lough Arrow

LEITRIM

Lough Allen

Ballyconnell

Clones **18**

Annaghmakerrig

16

MONAGHAN

N54

N3

R188

Castleblaney

N4

Belturbet

Cootehill **13**

Carrickmacross

19 **20**

Lough Key Forest Park

Carrick-on-Shannon

Lough Oughter

Killykeen Forest Park

12

R188

R179

Boyle

N4

11

Cavan

CAVAN

N3

Virginia

Lough Boderg

Lough Gowna

Lough Ramor

N55

MEATH

Lough Bofin

LONGFORD

Granard **10**

Navan

Strokestown **21**

N5

Longford **9**

River Shannon

R194

Fore **8** **7**

Castlepollard

ROSCOMMON

N61

N60

Edgeworthstown

N55

R395

Lough Derravaragh

R194

R195

N63

Roscommon **22**

N4

WESTMEATH

Crookedwood

Trim

Corlea Trackway Exhibition Centre

Ballymahon

Royal Canal

Lough Owel

Mullingar **6**

N61

Lough Ree

Moyvore

R392

R390

Kinnegad

N52

N6

Enfield

Kilcock

River Suck

R363

Glasson

Lough Ennell

R391

Belvedere House Gardens **5**

Athlone **23**

Moate

N6

N80

Kilbeggan **4**

OFFALY

Edenderry

Ballinasloe

R357

N6

Clonmacnoise **24**

Grand Canal

Tullamore

3

R420

KILDARE

Bord na Mona Bog Rail Tour **25**

Shannonbridge

N52

Portarlington

Kildare

GALWAY

Banagher **26**

Cloghan

R419

N7

Portumna

R439

Birr **27**

Kinnitty

Emo Court and Gardens **1**

LAOIS

2 Coolbanagher Church

Terryglass

N62

Portlaoise

Rock of Dunmaise

Athy

Borrisokane

N7

N80

28

Lough Derg

TIPPERARY

Roscrea **29**

Abbeyleix

Mountrath

N

N7

N62

30

Nenagh

Templemore

0 — 20 miles

0 — 30 km

spend the afternoon exploring the water-laced **Killykeen Forest Park** ⑫.
Spend the night in ⊞ **Cootehill** ⑬, an old-fashioned, friendly County
Cavan town popular with the many anglers who frequent this area.
Begin your third day visiting ⊞ **Castle Leslie** ⑰, beautifully situated on
the shores of Glaslough (the Green Lough) and home to the talented
and mildly eccentric Leslie family. If you're ready for some downtime,
you can extend your visit and stay the night. Alternatively, you can either jump across the border and explore the southernmost sights in
Northern Ireland (☞ Chapter 9), or head southwest, making a brief
stop at **Rossmore Forest Park** ⑮ on your way to the border town of ⊞
Clones ⑱, a lace-making center. On your fourth day, skip down to ⊞
Longford ⑨, where the nearby **Carrigglas Manor**, a romantic Tudor-
Gothic house, has associations with Jane Austen (and where you can
stay the night). Not far to the west lies **Strokestown** ㉑ and its namesake house; its museum devoted to the Great Irish Famine is not to be
missed, and the house and newly restored gardens are also worth a look.
The **Corlea Trackway Exhibition Centre** merits a quick stop. ⊞ **Athlone** ㉓
is a convenient place to spend the night—from here you're well positioned for an early morning visit to **Clonmacnoise** ㉔, the most important early Christian monastic site in Ireland. Stop at the **Bord na Mona
Bog Rail Tour** ㉕ near Shannonbridge on your way to **Banagher** ㉖, where
you can either take a two-hour Shannon cruise (a great trip in good
weather) or drive around **Lough Derg** ㉘. Depending on your time, end
up in either ⊞ **Birr** ㉗, ⊞ **Roscrea** ㉙, or ⊞ **Nenagh** ㉚; from any of these
towns you're not far from Shannon Airport and points to the west and
southwest.

When to Tour the Midlands

The Midlands are a good year-round touring choice because, unlike
the more popular touring destinations in the West and Southwest,
restaurants, accommodations and the major attractions remain open.
The area tends to be quiet at all times of the year, with the exception
of boating resorts on the Shannon and its loughs, which are generally
heavily booked by Irish vacationers in July and August.

THE EASTERN MIDLANDS

The eastern fringe of the Midlands is not far from Dublin—about an
hour's drive—and a visit to the area could easily be grafted onto a tour
of Dublin Environs (☞ Chapter 3). Our eastern tour begins at Portarlington, the village in the chapter closest to Dublin, and moves
northwest to Castlepollard and environs, stopping just short of Longford, the jumping-off point for the Northern Midlands.

Portarlington

72 km/45 mi southwest of Dublin.

If you enjoy large-scale, domestic architecture, drive to Portarlington,
which until recently had a sizable bilingual (English/French) population of Huguenot origin. Just 7⅓ km/4½ mi south of Portarlington sits
★ ❶ **Emo Court and Gardens,** one of the finest large-scale country houses
near Dublin open to the public. (If you elect to skip over much of the
Midlands, at least try to tack on a visit to Emo, especially if you're in
Counties Kildare or Wicklow [☞ Chapter 3].) Begun in 1790 by James
Gandon, architect of the Custom House and the Four Courts in Dublin,
Emo (the name derives from the Italian version of the original Irish name
Imoe) is thought to be Gandon's only domestic work on as grand a
scale as his Dublin civic buildings. Construction continued on and off

for 70 years, as family money troubles followed the untimely death of the Emo's first patron and owner, the first Earl of Portarlington.

In 1996, after nearly 30 years of loving restoration, Emo's English-born owner, Mr. Cholmeley Dering Cholmeley-Harrison, donated the house to the Irish nation. (He had his work cut out for him: The Jesuits who owned the house from 1930–69 had radically altered it.) The ground-floor rooms have now been beautifully restored and decorated. Among the highlights are the **entrance hall,** with its trompe l'oeil in the apses on each side, and the **library,** with an Italian marble mantle carved with putti frolicking among grapevines. But the showstopper, and one of the finest rooms in Ireland, is the domed **rotunda**—in fact the work of one of Gandon's successors, the Irish architect William Caldbeck—inspired by the Roman Pantheon. The rotunda's blue-and-white coffered dome is supported by marble pilasters with gilded, Corinthian capitals. Emo's 55 acres of grounds include a 20-acre lake, lawns planted with yew trees, a small garden (the Clocker) with Japanese maples, and a larger one (the Grapery) with rare trees and shrubs. ⊠ *Emo, Co. Laois,* ☎ *056/ 21450; ask for Anne Teehan or Paddy Friel; or 0502/26573 Mon. and Fri. 11:30–2 and erratic hrs at other times.* ⊡ *Gardens free, house £2.* ☉ *Gardens daily 10:30–5:30; house mid-June–mid-Sept. daily 10–6.*

❷ **Coolbanagher Church,** the familiar name for the exquisite Church of St. John the Evangelist, was, like Emo, designed by James Gandon. On view inside are Gandon's original 1795 plans; there's also an elaborately sculpted 15th-century font from an earlier church that once stood nearby, and adjacent is Gandon's mausoleum for Lord Portarlington, his patron at Emo. The church is open daily in the summer; during other months, ask around in the tiny village for a key, or call the rectory (☎ 0502/24143), which is a 10-minute drive away. ⊠ *1½ km/1 mi south of Emo Court on R419.* ☉ *May–Oct., daily 9–6.*

Dining and Lodging

$ ✕⊡ **Roundwood House.** Just off the N7 at the foot of the Slieve Bloom
★ mountains, this is a warm, relaxed, classically beautiful 1730s house. Behind the symmetrical Palladian facade lies a simple interior, with family antiques and Persian rugs on well-worn wooden floors in the study, drawing room, and other common rooms. You can stay in one of the large rooms in the main house or in a smaller, cozy room in the original house, which dates from 1650 is just beyond an herb garden at the back. There are 18 acres of woodland to explore and more strenuous hill walks in the Slieve Blooms. Hosts Frank and Rosemarie Kennan are likely to share a table with you at dinner. ⊠ *Mountrath, Co. Laois,* ☎ *0502/32120,* ⨊ *0502/32711. 10 rooms with bath. Dining room. AE, DC, MC, V.*

Tullamore

❸ *27 km/17 mi northwest of Portarlington.*

Tullamore, the county seat of Offaly, is a big country town situated on the Grand Canal. The main reason to pass through Tullamore is **Charleville Forest Castle** (1½ km/1 mi outside Tullamore on N52 to Birr), a castellated, Georgian–Gothic Revival manor house set on about 30 acres of woodland walks and gardens. This magnificent building dates from 1812 and is a fine example of the work of the architect Francis Johnston, who was responsible for many of Dublin's stately Georgian buildings. Guided tours of the interior are available. ⊠ *Co. Offaly,* ☎ *0506/21279.* ⊡ *£2.50.* ☉ *May, weekends and holidays 2–5; June– Sept., Wed.–Sun. 11–5; Oct.–Apr., groups of four or more by appointment.*

Outdoor Activities and Sports

BOATING

A river cruiser for a floating holiday can be rented from **Celtic Canal Cruisers Ltd.** (⊠ 24th Lock, Co. Offaly, ☎ 0506/21861).

GOLF

Tullamore Golf Club (⊠ Brookfield, Co. Offaly, ☎ 0506/21439) is an 18-hole, parkland course.

Kilbeggan

④ *11 km/7 mi north of Tullamore.*

Kilbeggan is known mainly for the **Kilbeggan Distillery,** which was established in 1757 to produce a traditional Irish malt whiskey. It closed down in 1954 and was reopened in 1987 by Cooley Distillery, which now makes its whiskey in County Louth but brings it here to be matured in casks. The distillery has been restored as a museum of industrial archaeology illustrating the process of Irish pot-whiskey distillation and the social history of the workers' lives. ⊠ *Co. Westmeath,* ☎ *0506/ 32134.* ☞ *£2.* ⊘ *Apr.–Oct., daily 9–6; Nov.–Mar., daily 10–4.*

⑤ **Belvedere House Gardens** (19 km/12 mi north of Kilbeggan) is remarkable for a beautiful setting on the northeast shore of Lough Ennel. Terraced gardens descend in three stages to the waters of the lake and provide a panoramic view of its islands. The estate also contains a walled garden with many varieties of trees, shrubs, flowers, and parkland landscaped in the 18th-century style. ⊠ *Co. Westmeath,* ☎ *044/40861.* ☞ *£1.* ⊘ *Apr.–Oct., daily noon–6.*

Mullingar

⑥ *24 km/15 mi northeast of Kilbeggan.*

Mullingar, County Westmeath's major town, is a busy commercial and cattle-trading center on the Royal Canal, midway between two large, attractive lakes, Lough Owel and Lough Ennel. This is an area of rich farmland, and the town is known as Ireland's beef capital; farmers all over Ireland describe a good young cow as "beef to the ankle, like a Mullingar heifer." The buildings in Mullingar date mostly from the 19th century.

The large, Renaissance-style **Catholic Cathedral of Christ the King** was completed in 1939. Finely carved stonework decorates the front of the cathedral, and the spacious interior has mosaics of St. Patrick and St. Anne by the Russian artist Boris Anrep. ⊘ *Daily 9–5:30.*

Mullingar's **Military Museum in Columb Barracks** is home to a surprisingly wide array of artifacts that includes weapons from the two World Wars; long, canoelike boats of oak from the 1st century AD that have been found in the surrounding lakes; and uniforms and other articles of the old IRA, including a pistol said to have been the property of Michael Collins, who was Chief of Staff in the War of Independence and the Civil War. ⊠ *Columb Barracks,* ☎ *044/48391.* ⊘ *By appointment only.*

Dining and Lodging

$$$ ✕⊞ **Crookedwood House.** This large, 200-year-old rectory overlook-
★   ing Lough Derravaragh is 13 km/8 mi north of Mullingar on the R394 Castlepollard road. Proprietors Noel and Julie Kenny added a wing of spacious bedrooms ($$) in 1995; their dining room is particularly notable—Noel is recognized as a leading Irish chef. Dinner begins in a comfortable sitting room, where orders are taken and drinks served,

and moves on to three interconnecting low-beamed rooms with white-washed walls. Starters may include grilled breast of wood pigeon on a warm white salad, or marinated smoked salmon with crème fraîche, crepe and chive dressing; main courses might feature a trio of salmon, sole, and scallops with lobster sauce, a hunter's plate (venison and wild duck on a bed of red cabbage, with juniper and red wine sauce), or such vegetarian daily specials as *rösti* (potato pancake) with creamed mushrooms. ✉ *Mullingar, Co. Westmeath,* ☎ *044/72165,* FAX *044/72166. 8 rooms with bath. Restaurant. AE, DC, MC, V. Closed 2 wks in Nov. No lunch Tues.–Sat., no dinner Sun.*

Outdoor Activities and Sports

GOLF

Delvin Castle Golf Club (✉ Delvin, Co. Westmeath, ☎ 044/64315) is a 9-hole course. **The Heath Golf Club** (✉ Portlaoise, Co. Laois, ☎ 0502/46533) is a challenging, 18-hole, parkland course. **Mullingar Golf Club** (✉ Belvedere, Mullingar, Co. Westmeath, ☎ 044/48629) is an 18-hole, parkland course.

HORSEBACK RIDING

Mullingar Equestrian Centre (✉ Athlone Rd., Co. Westmeath, ☎ 044/48331) offers riding on the shores of Lough Derravaragh and lessons at all levels. The Centre also organizes residential riding holidays.

Castlepollard

❼ *21 km/13 mi north of Mullingar.*

Castlepollard is an unusually pretty village of multihued, 18th- and 19th-century houses laid out around a large triangular green. The biggest (literally!) nearby attraction is **Tullynally Castle and Gardens** (1½ km/1 mi down the road to Granard), the largest castle in Ireland still lived in as a family home. How big is it? The total circumference of the building's masonry adds up to nearly ¼ mi—an astonishing agglomeration of towers, turrets, and battlements that dates from the first early fortified building, circa 1655, up through the mid-19th century, when additions in the Gothic Revival style went up one after another. Two wings designed by Sir Richard Morrison in 1840 that joined the main block to the stable court had dramatically different purposes: one was given over entirely to luxurious quarters for the Dowager Countess; the other housed 40 *indoor* servants. Think of Tullynally the next time you pay your heating bill: it was one of the first houses in the British Isles to have central heating.

Tullynally—the name, literally translated, means "Hill of the Swans"—has been the home of 10 generations of the literary Pakenham family and the seat of the earls of Longford. Among the living Pakenhams are the current earl of Longford, Frank Pakenham, the prison reformer and anti-pornography campaigner; his wife Elizabeth and his daughter Antonia Fraser, both historical biographers; and his brother Thomas, a historian. In addition to a fine collection of portraits and furniture, the house contains an immense kitchen furnished with many fascinating 19th-century domestic gadgets, including a marmalade cutter and an oversize contraption designed to take the buttermilk out of the freshly churned butter. The grounds also include a landscaped park and formal gardens. ✉ *Co. Westmeath,* ☎ *044/61159.* ☞ *Castle and gardens £3.50, gardens only £2.* ☉ *Gardens: May–Oct., daily 10–5; castle rooms: July 16–Aug. 15, guided tours daily 2:30–6 and by appointment for groups.*

Fore

⑧ *5 km/3 mi east of Castlepollard.*

The simple village of Fore is dominated by the remains of **Fore Abbey. St. Fechin's Church,** dating from the 10th century, has a massive, cross-inscribed lintel stone. Nearby are the remains of a 13th-century Benedictine **abbey,** whose imposing square towers and loophole windows resemble a castle rather than an abbey.

THE NORTHERN MIDLANDS

This tour starts in Longford and works its way north, leaving the ancient kingdom of Leinster for Ulster's two most southerly counties, Cavan and Monaghan. (Ulster's four other counties, which now constitute Northern Ireland, are covered in Chapter 9.) The land north of Cavan is characterized by small, round hills called drumlins, and is known as "drumlin country."

Longford

⑨ *37 km/24 mi northwest of Castlepollard, 124 km/77 mi northwest of Dublin.*

Longford, the county seat of County Longford, is a typical little market-town community. Jane Austen fans should consider making a visit to **Carrigglas Manor,** 5 km/3 mi northeast of Longford on the R194 to Granard. The romantic, Tudor-Gothic house, built in 1837 by Thomas Lefroy, offers a glimpse into gracious country living in 18th-century surroundings. His descendants, who still reside here, like to note that as a young man in England, Lefroy was romantically involved with the novelist Jane Austen. Just why they never married is a mystery, but it is believed that she based the character of Mr. Darcy in *Pride and Prejudice* on Mr. Lefroy. The house features some good plasterwork, and many of its original, mid-19th-century furnishings. A magnificent stable yard, belonging to an earlier house on the site, was designed in 1790 by James Gandon, architect of Dublin's Custom House and Four Courts. Visitors to the stable yard and gardens also have access to a small **costume museum,** which displays mostly 18th-century apparel found in the house. Visitors who want to tour the house must make advance reservations; it is also possible to stay overnight (☞ *below*). ✉ *Co. Longford,* ☎ *043/45165.* ✆ *Stable yard, gallery, and shop free; gardens and museum £2.50.* ⊙ *Stable yard, gardens and museum daily 11–6; house, by appointment only, early June–early Sept., Thurs.–Mon. 2–6.*

OFF THE BEATEN PATH — **CORLEA TRACKWAY AND EXHIBITION CENTRE** – Twenty-three kilometers/14 miles southwest of Longford, this center is situated on a 20-acre site of specially preserved bog land. Displays include part of an Iron Age timber trackway dating from 147 BC that was found underneath the bog during turf-cutting activities. The history of the bog is explained in audiovisual and showcase displays. ✉ *Kenagh, Corlea,* ☎ *043/ 22386.* ✆ *£2.50.* ⊙ *June–Sept., daily 9:30–6:30.*

Dining and Lodging

$$ ✕▭ **Carrigglas Manor.** Jeffry and Tessa Lefroy, today's owners of this historic house, like to stress that they are not running a hotel, but are rather welcoming visitors as private guests. Bedrooms are impeccably decorated with fine antiques, but have baths, not showers, and no television or telephones. There is no bar, but guests may help themselves from a drinks tray in the library. Simpler, cottage-style accommodation is available in the stable yard ($). Dinner, eaten with the Lefroys beneath portraits of their ancestors, is prepared in traditional country-house style. ⊠ *Longford, Co. Longford,* ☎ *043/45165,* FAX *043/ 41026. 6 rooms, 4 with bath. Dining room. MC, V. Closed Nov.–Apr.*

Granard

⑩ *18 km/11 mi northeast of Longford.*

The market town and fishing center of Granard stands on high ground near the Longford–Cavan border. The **Motte of Granard** at the southwest end of town was once the site of a fortified Norman castle. In 1932, a statue of St. Patrick was erected here to mark the 15th centenary of his arrival in Ireland. (At least a dozen statues of the patron saint, all virtually identical, were put up that year; see how many others you can spot on your travels.)

Outdoor Activities and Sports
County Longford Golf Club (⊠ Glack, Co. Longford, ☎ 043/46310) is an 18-hole, parkland course.

Cavan

⑪ *30 km/19 mi north of Granard, 114 km/71 mi northwest of Dublin.*

A small, quiet, undistinguished town serving the local farming community, Cavan has two main streets parallel to one another: Main and Farnham streets. With its pubs and shops, Main Street is like many others in similar Irish towns; Farnham has some Georgian houses, churches, and a courthouse. **Cavan Crystal** is an up-and-coming rival to Waterford in the cut-lead-crystal line; the company offers guided factory tours and access to their factory shop. This is a good opportunity to watch skilled craftspeople at work if you can't make it to Waterford. At press time (summer 1997), a major new building is underway; it will house a visitor center, a glass museum, a restaurant, and a coffee shop and is slated to open in early 1998. ⊠ *Cavan Town,* ☎ *049/31800.* ⌖ *Free.* ☉ *Guided tour mid-Mar.–Dec., weekdays at 9:30, 10:30, 11:30.*

⑫ Eleven kilometers/7 miles north of Cavan, the **Killykeen Forest Park** lies among the beautiful, mazelike network of lakes called Lough Oughter. Within the park's 600 acres are a number of signposted walks and nature trails, stables offering horseback riding and boats and bicycles for rent. Twenty-eight fully-outfitted 2- and 3-bedroom cottages are available for weeklong, weekend, or mid-week stays; everything is provided except towels. Rates vary according to season; call for details. ⊠ *Cavan,* ☎ *049/32541.* ⌖ *Free, parking £1.50.* ☉ *Feb.– Dec., daily 9–5.*

Dining and Lodging
$$$$ ✕☎ **Slieve Russell Hotel and Country Club.** This magnificent hotel on
★ 300 acres 26 km/16 mi west of Cavan makes a convenient break on the Dublin–Sligo journey. Water burbles in the circular fountain before the palatial, neoclassical facade; the spacious lobby gleams with polished marble. The 101 deluxe bedrooms have a Jacuzzi, super-king-size beds, and chunky, art deco–style furniture. The sports and spa facilities are outstanding, but for many guests the golfing and excellent freshwater and trout fishing are the main attractions. White linens and wrought-iron chandeliers grace the formal Conall Cearnach restaurant; its extensive menu includes a variety of traditionally prepared seafood dishes, such as black sole on the bone or salmon hollandaise. The Brackley Buttery is more informal. ⊠ *Ballyconnell, Co. Cavan,* ☎ *049/26444,* FAX *049/26474. 141 rooms with bath, 10 suites. 2*

restaurants, 2 bars, 2 indoor pools, sauna, steam room, 9- and 18-hole golf courses, 4 tennis courts, health club, horseback riding, Ping Pong, squash, fishing. AE, DC, MC, V.

$$ ✕⊞ **Cabra Castle.** This sprawling, gray-stone castle with its crenellated battlements and Gothic windows could have been designed in Hollywood. In fact, it was built in 1699 as the centerpiece of a 1,000-acre estate, most of which now belongs to the Dun a Ri National Park. If you want the full treatment, ask for a "castle room," furnished with bigger and more elaborate Victorian antiques than the others. The Victorian-Gothic theme is carried through the bar and the restaurant with varying degrees of success; if you like that sort of thing, be sure to look at the castle gallery, which has hand-painted ceilings and leaded windows. ⊠ *Kingscourt, Co. Cavan,* ☎ *042/67030,* FAX *042/67039. 40 rooms with bath. Restaurant, bar, 9-hole golf course, horseback riding, fishing, bicycles. AE, DC, MC, V.*

Outdoor Activities and Sports

There are two courses at the **Slieve Russell Hotel** (⊠ Ballyconnell, Co. Cavan, ☎ 049/26444); a 9-hole, par-three, parkland course and an 18-hole, championship course. Visitors are welcome at the 18-hole **County Cavan Golf Club** (⊠ Arnmore House, Cavan, ☎ 049/31283).

En Route   Beyond Cavan you enter the heart of the **northern Midlands,** with lakes both large and small on either side of the road. County Cavan and County Monaghan each have at least 180 lakes. The countryside is distinguished by its drumlins—small, steep hills consisting of boulder clay left behind by the glacial retreat 10,000 years ago. The boulder clay also filled in many of the pre-glacial river valleys, causing the rivers to change course and create shallow lakes, which provide excellent fishing.

Cootehill

⓭ *26 km/16 mi northeast of Cavan.*

One of the most underestimated small towns in Ireland, Cootehill has a lovely setting on a wooded hillside in the heart of County Cavan. Its wide streets, with their intriguing old shops, are always busy without being congested. Most of its visitors are anglers from Europe, the United Kingdom, and the rest of Ireland.

Only pedestrians are allowed through the gates of **Bellamont Forest,** which lead, after about a mile of woodlands, to the exquisite, hilltop **Bellamont House,** designed in 1728 by Edward Lovett Pearce, architect of the Dublin's Bank of Ireland. Small but perfectly proportioned, it has been virtually unaltered since it was built; it is considered one of Ireland's finest Palladian-style houses. It is now a private home but is occasionally opened to the public. If you are interested, inquire locally or at the Tourist Information Office (TIO) in Cavan. Walk up the main street of Cootehill to "the top of the town" (past the White Horse Hotel), and you will see the entrance to the forest.

Dining and Lodging

$ ✕⊞ **Riverside House.** The unpretentious, genuine, old-fashioned Irish hospitality at Joe and Una Smith's farm is appreciated by both serious anglers and nonsporting guests. (The lodging is signposted 1 km/⅔ mi outside town off the R188 Cavan road.) A substantial Victorian house on 100 acres overlooks the River Annalee. All rooms have peaceful views and are individually decorated with modest antiques and family hand-me-downs. Bring your boots if you want to explore around this working dairy farm. ⊠ *Co. Cavan,* ☎ *049/52150,* FAX *049/52150. 6 rooms, 4 with bath. Dining room, boating, fishing. MC, V.*

Outdoor Activities and Sports

Rossmore Golf Club (⊠ Rossmore Park, near Cootehill, Co. Monaghan, ☎ 047/81316) is an 18-hole, parkland course. **Nuremore Hotel** (⊠ Carrickmacross, Co. Monaghan, ☎ 042/61438) has an 18-hole, championship golf course.

Monaghan

⑭ *24 km/15 mi north of Cootehill.*

A former British garrison town, Monaghan is built around a central square known as the Diamond. The town's old **Market House,** elegantly constructed of limestone in 1792, is now the tourist office (☞ Visitor Information *in* Midlands A to Z, *below*). Nearby is the award-winning **County Museum,** which traces the history of Monaghan from earliest times to the present through archeological finds, traditional crafts, artwork, and a variety of other historical artifacts. ⊠ *Hill St.,* ☎ *047/82928.* 🎫 *Free.* ☉ *June–Sept. 1, Tues.–Sat. 11–5; Oct.–May, Tues.–Sat. 11–1 and 2–5.*

⑮ Just outside town (on the R189 Newbliss road), fresh air in pleasant surroundings are to be had at **Rossmore Forest Park,** 691 acres of low hills and small lakes with pleasant, forest walks through rhododendron groves and signposted nature trails that are freely accessible.

⑯ At **Annaghmakerrig** (5 km/3 mi southwest of Newbliss), a small forest park with a lake is the site of **Annaghmakerrig House,** home of the Shakespearian stage director Sir Tyrone Guthrie until his death in 1971. He left it to the nation as a residential center for writers, artists, and musicians. It is not officially open to the public, but anyone with a special interest in the arts or in its previous owner can ask to be shown around, and visitors can wander around and picnic on its grounds. ⊠ *Near Newbliss, Co. Monaghan,* ☎ *047/54003.*

Dining and Lodging

$$$ ✕▨ **Nuremore Hotel and Country Club.** This Victorian country house
★ is now a luxury hotel with excellent sporting facilities, including its own trout lake. There are open fires in the large lounge, which is furnished with plump armchairs and Victorian tables. The bedrooms are decorated with mahogany Victorian furniture and coordinated color schemes. The restaurant serves a hybrid French–Irish cuisine in formal surroundings amid a dusky-pink decor. It is 81 km/50 mi from both Dublin and Belfast, making it a popular weekend retreat for city-dwellers, and 27 km/17 mi southeast of Cootehill. ⊠ *Carrickmacross, Co. Monaghan,* ☎ *042/61438,* 𝔉𝔄𝔛 *042/61853. 69 rooms with bath. Restaurant, bar, indoor pool, sauna, steam room, 18-hole golf course, 2 tennis courts, health club, horseback riding, squash, fishing. AE, DC, MC, V.*

Castle Leslie

⑰ *11 km/7 mi northeast of Monaghan.*

Leave Monaghan on the N12 and follow it out of town to Castle Leslie, originally a medieval stronghold, which has been the seat of the Leslie family since 1664. The castle sits on the shores of deep, beautiful **Glaslough,** which means "green lake," whose waters are mirrorlike on sunny days. The present house was built around 1870 in a mix of Gothic and Italianate styles—Sir John Leslie, who built it, had spent years in Italy and picked up many ideas, including the colonnaded loggia, said to have been copied from Michelangelo's cloister at Santa Maria degli Angeli in Rome. The mildly eccentric Leslie family is known for its literary and artistic leanings—when Jonathan Swift stayed here, he wrote in the guest book: "Glaslough with rows of books upon its shelves/written by the Leslies about themselves." It has many notable relations by marriage, including the Duke of Wellington, who defeated Napoléon at Waterloo, and Sir Winston Churchill. Wellington's death mask is preserved at Castle Leslie, as is Churchill's baby dress, along with an impressive collection of Italian works of art, including a chimneypiece by Andrea Della Robbia bursting with winged angel's heads, bunches of lemons, sprays of leaves, ribbons, and scrolls. There are 14 acres of gardens with miniature golf and croquet; home-baked teas are served in the tearoom and conservatory. ⊠ *Co. Monaghan,* ☎ *047/88109.* ☞ *£3, including tour.* ⊙ *May–Aug., daily 2–6; tour on hr and other times by appointment.*

Dining and Lodging

$$–$$$ ✕☱ **Castle Leslie.** If the tour isn't enough to satisfy your curiosity about what it's like to live in an Irish country house, you can now stay the night here. Some of the furniture and paintings predate the existing house, dating all the way back to 1660. The large bedrooms have pleasant parkland views and are decked out in Victorian splendor with a wealth of antiques; most beds are either canopied, four-poster, or half-tester. Pre-dinner drinks are served in the drawing room by a roaring log fire. A four-course menu of Continental cuisine with five choices of starter and main course is served by candlelight. Starters may include crispy duck confit with pickled red cabbage or Parma ham and melon, while braised partridge in season, coq au vin, or salmon with sesame and ginger vinaigrette typify the entrées. ⊠ *Glaslough, Co. Monaghan.* ☎ *047/88109,* ㉫ *047/88256. 14 rooms with bath or shower. Dining room, fishing, boating. MC, V.*

Clones

⑱ *24 km/15 mi west of Monaghan.*

Just 1 km/½ mi from the Northern Ireland border, Clones (pronounced "clo-*nez*") was the site, in early Christian times, of a monastery founded by St. Tighearnach, who died here in AD 458. An Augustinian abbey replaced the monastery in the 12th century, and its remains can still be seen near the 75-ft **round tower** on Abbey Street. In the central diamond of the town stands a 10th-century, Celtic high cross, with carved panels representing scriptural scenes. Nowadays Clones, a small, agricultural market town, is one of two lace-making centers in County Monaghan—the other is Carrickmacross. Local rectors' wives, in an attempt to bring in some income, took up the craft introduced in the 19th century. Crocheting and small raised dots are two hallmarks of Clones lace. A varied selection is on display around the town and can be purchased at the **Clones Lace Centre.** ⊠ *Co. Monaghan,* ☎ *047/ 51051.* ☞ *Free.* ⊙ *Mon. and Wed.–Sat. 10–6.*

Dining and Lodging

$$$ ✕☱ **Hilton Park.** To find this large, stately, early Georgian country house,
★ look for a large set of black gates with silver falcons 5 km/3 mi outside Clones on the R183 Ballyhaise road. It has three private lakes on its 500-acre grounds, which include 50 acres of gardens and parkland, a working sheep farm, and an organic market garden. Next door is Clones Golf Club. Johnny and Lucy Madden, the friendly hosts, run their house with stylish informality. All rooms are individually decorated with antiques and have lovely views; some have four-poster beds. Dinner—freshly prepared produce from their market garden and local meat and fish—is available for residents. ⊠ *Clones, Co. Monaghan,*

☎ 047/56007, ⒻⒶⓍ 047/56033. *5 rooms, 3 with bath. Dining room, lake, 9-hole golf course, croquet, boating, fishing. MC, V. Closed Oct.–Mar.*

Outdoor Activities and Sports

Clones Golf Club (✉ Hilton Park, Clone, Co. Monaghan) is a 9-hole course on limestone that is dry year-round.

NORTH TIPPERARY AND THE WEST MIDLANDS

Our Midlands tour concludes with the area's western fringe, picking up in the town of Boyle in County Roscommon. (If you do make it this far, be sure to consult Chapter 8; locales covered there are a short distance from Boyle and environs.) The tour skirts the Lough Key, Lough Ree, Lough Derg, and the River Shannon and, depending how you travel south, takes you through the hilly landscape of unspoiled County Leitrim—it, too, dappled with clean, cool lakes, beloved of anglers for its peaceful, fish-filled waters. Despite a liberal sprinkling of villages, County Leitrim is almost uninhabited (though it is the home of one of Ireland's leading writers, John McGahern). Between the area's many bodies of water, much of the land is bog, a fragile ecosystem that rewards closer investigation. The towns are small and generally undistinguished, with the exceptions of Birr and Strokestown, both of which were laid out by architects and designed to complement the "big houses" that share their names. The tour then brings you southward, to northern County Tipperary.

Boyle

⑲ *190 km/118 mi northwest of Dublin.*

An old-fashioned town on the Boyle River midway between Lough Gara and Lough Key, Boyle makes a good starting point for visits to the nearby Curlew Mountains. In the center of town is **King House,** built about 1730 by the local King family, who moved 50 years later to larger quarters at Rockingham in what is now Lough Key Forest Park (☞ *below*); that house burned down in 1957. The King family originally came from Staffordshire, England, and worked aggressively to establish themselves as local nobility. (Edward King, an ancestor of the Kings who settled here, drowned in the Irish Sea in 1636; he was the subject of Milton's poem *Lycidas*). From 1788 to 1922 the house was owned by the British Army and used as a barracks for the Connaught Rangers, known as the fiercest regiment of the British Army (Wellington called them the "Devil's Own"). By the time the county government took it over in 1989, the house had fallen into disrepair; local farmers had kept coal and cattle in the house, so you can imagine what the place must have looked like. After extensive renovations, the house was opened to the public in 1995, with exhibits on the Connaught Rangers, the Kings of Connaught, and the history of the house. A coffee shop, popular with locals, serves traditional Irish breakfasts and hearty lunches, both with plenty of homemade baked goods on the menu. ✉ *Boyle,* ☎ *079/63242.* ▧ *£2.50.* ☉ *May–Sept., daily 10–6; Apr. and Oct., weekends 10–6; last tour at 5.*

The main reason to visit Boyle is the ruins of the **Cistercian abbey** (on the N4). The church was begun in the late 12th century when the Romanesque style still prevailed, but as construction went on, the then-hot Gothic style made it to Ireland, evident in arches on the north side. A 16th- to 17th-century gatehouse, through which you enter the abbey, has a small exhibition. The ruins are freely accessible.

⑳ Lough Key Forest Park (☎ 079/62214), part of what was once the massive Rockingham Estate, is 3 km/2 mi northeast of Boyle. Now a popular base for campers, backpackers, walkers, and anglers, the park consists of 840 acres on the shores of the lake and contains a bog garden, a deer enclosure, a cypress grove and some ruins from Rockingham days, including the remains of a stable block, church, icehouse, and temple; boats can be hired on the lake. There is also a restaurant. Parking is £2, and the park is freely accessible.

En Route   If you take the N4 south out of Boyle on your way to Strokestown, you'll pass briefly into County Leitrim and through its largest town, **Carrick-on-Shannon,** a surprisingly busy place considering that its population is fewer than 2,000 people. The town has plenty of lively bars, and you can rent a boat here to tour the Shannon. South of Carrick, labyrinthine back lanes meander across the broad Shannon and the lakes—Boderg, Bofin, and Kilglass—that straddle the river.

Strokestown

㉑   *28 km/17 mi south of Boyle.*

Like many villages near a "big house," Strokestown was designed to complement the house. The widest main street in Ireland—laid out to rival the Ringstrasse in Vienna—leads to three Gothic arches that mark the entrance to the grounds of **Strokestown Park House.** Home to the Pakenham Mahon family from 1660 to 1979, the house once sat on 27,000 acres and was the second largest estate in Roscommon, after the King family's Rockingham. The house has a complicated architectural history that, to some degree, mirrors the histories of other Anglo-Irish houses. The oldest parts of the house date to 1696; Palladian wings were added in the 1730s to the original block, and the house was extended again in the early 19th century. The house's contents are a rich trove specific to the site, as the contents were never liquidated in the auctions that similar houses experienced. The interior is full of curiosities, such as the gallery above the kitchen, which allowed the lady of the house to supervise domestic affairs from a safe distance. Menus were dropped from the balcony on Monday mornings with instructions to the cook for the week's meals. One wing houses lavish stables with vaulted ceilings and Tuscan pillars. There is also a distillery and a fully equipped nursery. The gardens, which are undergoing an ambitious restoration plan that will include the widest and longest herbaceous borders in Ireland, opened in 1995. The award-winning **Irish Famine Museum,** housed in the stable yards, documents in detail the disastrous Famine (1845–50) and the subsequent mass emigration. ⊠ *Strokestown, Co. Roscommon,* ☎ *078/33013.* 🖃 *House £3, museum £3, garden £2.50.* ☉ *Easter–Oct., Tues.–Sun. 11–5:30.*

Roscommon

㉒   *43 km/27 mi south of Boyle, 19⅓ km/12 mi south of Strokestown.*

Roscommon is the capital of County Roscommon, where sheep- and cattle-raising is the main occupation. It's a pleasant little town with a number of solid stone buildings, including the **Bank of Ireland** in the former courthouse, and the former **county jail.** On the southern slopes of a hill in the lower part of town sit the remains of **Roscommon Abbey.** In the abbey's principal ruin, a church, eight sculpted figures representing gallowglasses, or medieval Irish professional soldiers, stand at the base of the choir. The ruins are freely accessible. To the north of Roscommon Town are the weathered remains of **Roscommon Castle,** a large Norman stronghold first built in the 13th century.

Outdoor Activities and Sports

Bikes can be rented from **Brendan Sheerin** (⊠ Main St., Boyle, Co. Roscommon, ☎ 079/62010) and **Leo Hunt** (⊠ Main St., Roscommon, Co. Roscommon, ☎ 0903/26299).

Athlone

㉓ *29 km/18 mi southeast of Roscommon, 127 km/79 mi west of Dublin, 121 km/75 mi east of Limerick.*

Athlone originated as a crossing point of the Shannon (which is at its midpoint here), at first as a ford, and later marking the boundary between the old provinces of Leinster (to the east) and Connacht (to the west). It is the main shopping hub for the surrounding area and an important road and rail junction, but it contains little of great interest to the visitor. You might make a go of it, though, by exploring the sign-posted town trail that takes you through Athlone's recently christened "Left Bank" (behind the castle [☞ *below*]), where many of the buildings date from at least 200 years ago.

Athlone Castle is the site most worth visiting in Athlone. Situated right beside the River Shannon, at the southern end of Lough Ree, it was built in the 13th century. After their defeat at the Battle of the Boyne in 1691, the Irish retreated to Athlone and made the river their first line of defense. The castle, which has been substantially altered and repaired, was extensively renovated in 1991, the 300th anniversary of this rout. It remains an interesting example of a Norman stronghold and houses a small museum of artifacts relating to Athlone's eventful past. Admission includes access to an interpretative center depicting the siege of Athlone in 1691, the flora and fauna of the Shannon, and the life of the tenor John McCormack (1884–1945), an Athlone native and probably the finest lyric tenor Ireland has ever produced. ⊠ *Town Bridge, Athlone, Co. Westmeath,* ☎ *0902/72107* ⊑ *£2.20.* ☉ *May–Sept., daily 10–5; Oct.–Apr. by appointment.*

Dining and Lodging

$$$ ✕ **Le Château.** Candlelit tables are set with Irish crystal, white linen, and fine bone china at this second-floor restaurant in Athlone's colorful Old Quarter. Owner-chef Stephen Linehan relies on fresh local ingredients. Try his combination of hot and cold oysters as a starter, or a warm salad of duck confit with orange segments. Main courses include medallions of veal with smoked bacon, garlic, and herbs, or roast peppered monkfish with fresh herb sauce. For deserts try the lemon tart, or in summer, fresh strawberry vol-au-vents with homemade ice cream. The menu comes in three languages (reflecting the number of visitors to Athlone on Shannon cruisers who stop and eat here.) ⊠ *Abbey La., Co. Westmeath,* ☎ *0902/94517. AE, MC, DC, V. No lunch.*

$$$ ✕ **Wineport Restaurant.** About 5 km/3 mi north of town on the shores
★ of Lough Ree, this pleasantly informal restaurant, in a wooden boathouse adorned with memorabilia from the original Lough Ree Yacht Club, has earned several prestigious awards since its debut in 1993. The menu changes every eight weeks; starters include smoked and grilled eel from Lough Ree served with spiced apple and lemon cream. Roast organic venison (from a nearby farm) served in a juniper marinade is a popular year-round main course, and in spring and summer you may try roast rack of lamb served in white wine jus with a timbale of mussels and herb stuffing. There are always vegetarian specials, and the desserts are every bit as unusual as the main courses. ⊠ *Glasson, Co. Westmeath,* ☎ *0902/85466. AE, DC, MC, V. No dinner Sun.*

$$$ ✕🏠 **Hodson Bay Hotel.** Instead of staying in Athlone's unremarkable
★ town center, head 4 km/2½ mi out of town on the N63 to this four-
story mansion on the shores of Lough Ree. Once an 18th-century
family home, the hotel is adjacent to Athlone's golf course and has its
own marina. All guest rooms are coordinated in deep pastel shades with
well-designed wooden furniture. The bar overlooks the lake, as does
L'Escale Restaurant, a romantic, candlelit room with tables set with
pink linens. The menu offers imaginative Irish cooking with a French
accent: veal steak with orange and tarragon butter, or Atlantic sea-
food in lobster, cream, and brandy sauce are typical main courses. ✉
Roscommon Rd., Athlone, Co. Westmeath, ☎ *0902/92444,* FAX *0902/
92688. 100 rooms with bath. 2 restaurants, bar, indoor pool, sauna,
18-hole golf course, 2 tennis courts, health club, horseback riding, fish-
ing, meeting rooms. AE, DC, MC, V.*

Outdoor Activities and Sports

BICYCLING

Rent bikes from **M. R. Hardiman** (✉ Irishtown, Athlone, Co. Westmeath,
☎ 0902/78669).

BOATING

MV *Avonree* is a riverboat that travels up the Shannon to nearby
Lough Ree. The ride is 1½ hours, and light refreshments are available.
✉ *The Strand, Athlone,* ☎ *0902/92513.* 🎫 *£5.* ☉ *Sailings July–Sept.,
Thurs.–Tues. at 11, 2:30, and 4; Wed. at 4:30.*

A river cruiser for a floating holiday can be rented by the week from
Athlone Cruisers Ltd. (✉ Jolly Mariner Marina, Athlone, Co. Westmeath,
☎ 0902/72892) or **S. G. S. Marine** (✉ Ballykeeran, Athlone, Co. West-
meath, ☎ 0902/85163).

GOLF

Mount Temple Golf Club (✉ Campfield Lodge, Moate, Co. Westmeath,
☎ 0902/81545) is a 9-hole, parkland course 19 km/12 mi east of
Athlone. **Athlone Golf Club** (✉ Hodson Bay, Athlone, Co. Westmeath,
☎ 0902/92073 or 0902/92235) is a lakeside, 18-hole, parkland course.
Glasson Golf & Country Club (✉ Glasson, Athlone, Co. Westmeath,
☎ 0902/85120) is an 18-hole, parkland course bordered on three
sides by Lough Ree and the River Shannon.

Clonmacnoise

★ ㉔ *20 km/13 mi south of Athlone, 93 km/58 mi east of Galway.*

Many ancient sites dot the River Shannon, but the foremost of these
is Clonmacnoise, early Christian Ireland's foremost monastic settlement
and, like Chartres, a royal site. The monastery was founded by St. Cia-
ran between 543 and 549 at a location that was not as remote as it
now appears to be—near the intersection of two of what were then
Ireland's most vital routes: the Shannon River, running north–south,
and the Eiscir Riada, running east–west. Like Glendalough, Celtic Ire-
land's other great monastic site, Clonmacnoise benefitted from isola-
tion—surrounded by bog, accessible only via one road or the Shannon.

The monastery was founded on an esker, or natural gravel ridge, over-
looking the Shannon, and a marshy area known as the Callows, which
today is protected habitat for the corncrake. Numerous buildings and
ruins remain. The small **Cathedral** dates as far back as the 10th cen-
tury but has additions dating to as recently as the 15th century. It was
the burial place of kings of Connaught and of Tara and of Rory
O'Conor, the last High King of Ireland, buried here in 1198. The two
round towers include **O'Rourke's Tower,** which was struck by light-

ning and subsequently rebuilt in the 12th century. There are **eight smaller churches.** The smallest is thought to be the burial place of St. Ciaran; the only one not built within the monastery walls is the Nun's Church, about ½-mi east. The **high crosses** have now been moved into the visitor center to protect them from the elements (copies stand in their original places); the best preserved of these being the **Cross of the Scriptures,** also known as **Flann's Cross.** Some of the treasures and manuscripts originating from Clonmacnoise are now housed in Dublin; most are at the National Museum, while the 12th-century *Book of the Dun Cow* is at the Royal Irish Academy Library (☞ Chapter 2).

Clonmacnoise survived raids by feuding Irish tribes, Vikings, and Normans for almost exactly 1,000 years, until 1552, when the English garrison from Athlone reduced it to ruin. Since then it has remained a prestigious burial place. Among the ancient stones are many other graves of local people dating from the 17th to the mid-20th century, when a new graveyard was consecrated on adjoining land. Archaeologists have recently discovered the remains of the oldest bridge yet discovered in Ireland, dating from AD 804. The bridge is under the Shannon adjacent to the Clonmacnoise ruins; one of the upright timbers of the bridge can be seen at low tide below the most westerly bank of the earthwork enclosing the castle. ⊠ *Co. Offaly,* ☎ *0905/74195.* 🎟 *£2.50.* ☯ *Mid-June–Sept., daily 9–7; Oct.–May, daily 10–6 or dusk.*

Bord na Mona Bog Rail Tour

★ ㉕   *9½ km/6 mi south of Clonmacnoise.*

As you pass through the small town of Shannonbridge, on either side of the road you'll notice vast stretches of chocolate-brown bog lands and isolated industrial plants for processing this area's natural resource. Under the jurisdiction of Bord na Mona, the same government agency that makes commercial use of other bog lands, the area is worth exploring.

Bog is used in peat-fired, electricity-generating stations, compressed into briquettes for domestic hearths, and made into moss peat and plant containers for gardeners. Ireland's liberal use of a resource that is scarce elsewhere in Europe provoked an indignant reaction from botanists and ecologists in the 1980s, which resulted in the setting aside of certain bog areas for conservation. Among these are the **Clara Bog** and **Mongan's Bog** in County Offaly, both relatively untouched, raised pieces of land with unique flora, and the **Scragh Bog** in County Westmeath. Because of the preservative qualities of peat, it is not unusual to come across bog timber 5,000 years old, or to dig up perfectly preserved domestic implements from more recent times—not to mention the occasional cache of treasure. Deer, badgers, and wild dogs inhabit the bog lands, along with a rich bird and plant life.

If you would like to have a close look at a bog, take a ride on the Bord na Mona Bog Rail Tour, which leaves from Uisce Dubh. A small, green-and-yellow diesel locomotive pulls one coach across the bog at an average of 24 kph/15 mph per hour while the driver provides commentary on a landscape unchanged for millennia. There are more than 1,200 km/745 mi of narrow-gauge bog railway, and the section on the tour, known as the Clonmacnoise and South Offaly Railway, is the only part accessible to the public. ⊠ *Uisce Dubh, near Shannonbridge, Co. Offaly,* ☎ *0905/74114.* 🎟 *£3.50.* ☯ *Tour Apr.–Oct., daily on the hr 10–5.*

Banagher

㉖   *21 km/13 mi southeast of Shannonbridge.*

A small but lively village on the shores of the River Shannon, Banagher has a marina that makes a popular base for water-sports fans. Anthony Trollope, who came to Ireland as a Post Office surveyor in 1841, lived and wrote his first book, *The Macdermots of Ballycloran*, here. Charlotte Brontë spent her honeymoon here. **Flynn's** (⊠ Main St., ☎ 0509/51312), a light and spacious Victorian-style bar in the center of town, offers a lunch menu of generously filled sandwiches, salad platters, a roast meat of the day, chicken, fish, or burgers and chips. It's a popular spot with the boating crowd and can be busy on weekends.

If you happen to be in Banagher on a Thursday or a Sunday, you can take a two-hour **Shannon cruise** on the *River Queen*, an enclosed launch that seats 54 passengers and has a full bar on board. ⊠ *Silver Line Cruisers Ltd., The Marina, Banagher, Co. Offaly,* ☎ *0509/51112.* ☜ *£3.50.* ☉ *June–mid-Sept., Thurs. 3, Sun. 2:30 and 4:30, weather permitting.*

Birr

㉗   *12 km/8 mi southeast of Banagher, 130 km/80 mi west of Dublin.*

Birr is a quiet, sleepy place with tree-lined malls and modest, Georgian houses. It was recently designated as a heritage town. The town's roots go back to the 6th century, but it was much later, in the mid-18th century, that the town was given its modern-day appearance, as a Georgian building boom took hold.

★   All roads in Birr lead to the gates of **Birr Castle Demesne,** a Gothic Revival castle (built around an earlier 17th-century castle that was damaged by fire in 1823) that is still the home of the earls of Rosse. It is not open to the public, but you can visit the surrounding 150 acres of gardens. The present earl and countess of Rosse continue the family tradition of making botanical expeditions for specimens of rare trees, plants, and shrubs from all over the world. The formal gardens contain the tallest (32 ft) box hedges in the world. In spring, you can see a wonderful display of flowering magnolias, cherries and crab apples, and naturalized narcissi; in autumn, the maples, chestnuts, and weeping beeches blaze red and gold. The grounds are laid out around a lake and along the banks of two adjacent rivers; above one of these stands the castle. The grounds also contain **Ireland's Historic Science Centre,** an exhibition on astronomy, photography, and engineering, housed in the stable block. The giant (72-inch) reflecting telescope, built in 1845, remained the largest in the world for the next 75 years and has recently been restored. Allow at least two hours to see all that's here. ⊠ *Rosse Row, Birr, Co. Offaly,* ☎ *0509/20336.* ☜ *£3.50.* ☉ *Apr.–Oct., daily 9–6.*

Dining and Lodging

$$$$ ✕▥ **Tullanisk House.** Set in its own deer park, this 18th-century dower
★   house for Birr Castle has been carefully restored; it offers elegant accommodation in the atmosphere of a private home. Rooms vary in size, but owner-hosts Susie and George Gossip have decorated them all with character (books and magazines are everywhere). Open fires, board games, and table tennis are available on wet days, and there are 700 acres of woodland behind the house. Dinner (for which reservations are essential) is served on family china and silverware by candlelight in the classic Georgian dining room. All guests sit at the host's table and share the same menu, which features fresh local produce cooked,

usually by George, in classic country-house style, with game a specialty during winter. ⊠ *Co. Offaly,* ☎ *0509/20572,* ☏ *0509/21783. 7 rooms, 5 with bath. Dining room, Ping-Pong. MC, V.*

$$$ ✕🖬 **Kinnitty Castle.** Situated 16 km/10 mi east of Birr at the foot of the Slieve Bloom mountains, Kinnitty is an exuberant, turreted Gothic Revival edifice, rebuilt in 1927 of ashlar granite. Everything is on a large scale, including the bedrooms, which have large four-poster beds, intricately carved chairs, and heavy old beams incorporated into the bathrooms. The dining room has enormously tall windows and a dark wood floor; the menu features starters such as grilled goat's cheese with pine kernels or oven-roasted quail stuffed with foie gras. Typical main courses are panfried loin of lamb with its own sweetbreads or ragout of lobster from the tank, finished with Sevruga caviar. ⊠ *Kinnitty, Birr, Co. Offaly,* ☎ *0509/37318,* ☏ *0509/37284. 18 rooms with bath. Restaurant, bar, tennis court, horseback riding, Ping-Pong, fishing. AE, MC, V.*

$ ✕🖬 **Dooly's.** This 250-year-old, black-and-white coaching inn is tucked away in a corner of Birr's central square. A log fire burns in the front lobby, which is decorated in the Georgian style. Rooms have all been refurbished and modernized and have pastel-colored, floral drapes and bedspreads with plain, dark-pastel walls. The bar and coffee shop are busy all day long; there is a more relaxed atmosphere in the Emmet Restaurant. The five-course table-d'hôte dinner menu, an excellent value, may feature medallions of beef flamed in whiskey and onions or fresh Corrib salmon steak poached in pink peppercorns and white wine. ⊠ *Emmet Sq., Birr, Co. Offaly,* ☎ *0509/20032,* ☏ *0509/21332. 18 rooms with bath. Restaurant, coffee shop, bar, horseback riding, fishing. AE, DC, MC, V.*

Lough Derg

㉘ *16 km/10 mi west of Birr on the R489.*

Between Portland and Portumna the River Shannon widens into 32,000 acres of unpolluted water, known as Lough Derg, a popular center for water sports, including waterskiing, yachting, and motor cruising. Fishermen flock here as well for pike- and coarse-angling. There are excellent woodland walks around the shore of the Lough. (Be sure not to confuse this Lough Derg with the lake of the same name in County Donegal, a well-known pilgrimage site, covered in Chapter 8.) The well-signposted, scenic **Lough Derg Drive** (approximately 90 km/50 mi) encircles the lake, passing through a number of pretty waterside villages, from Portumna in the north to Killaloe in the south. **Terryglass,** on the eastern shore of Lough Derg and well signposted on the R439 from Birr, is popular with water-sports enthusiasts and anglers, as well as regular vacationers seeking an away-from-it-all destination; it is considered one of the prettiest villages in Ireland.

Dining and Lodging

$$ ✕🖬 **Ballycormac House.** This 300-year-old farmhouse, owned by Herb and Christine Quigley, former residents of Washington, D.C., is 11 km/7 mi southwest of Birr. The snug, low-beam cottage has open fireplaces and antiques. Bedrooms are warm and cozy. Accomplished cooks (on winter weekends they offer cooking classes), the Quigleys grow their own herbs and vegetables in the gardens on the 20-acre property. They describe their cooking style as modern eclectic; the evening meal is served to guests only. During summer, Irish lamb may be butterflied American-style and grilled, and in winter pheasant is braised and served with sloe gin, orange, and cranberries. Vegetarians should notify the hosts in advance. Horseback riding and golf holidays can also be arranged.

✉ *Aglish, Borrisokane, Co. Tipperary,* ☎ *067/21129,* ℻ *067/21200.*
5 rooms with bath. Dining room. DC, MC.

$ 🏠 **Riverrun House.** Typical of the very best of the newer B&Bs around
the country, this rambling farmhouse-style building in the middle of
the village combines country stylishness with practicality. Clean, clut-
ter-free rooms have duvet-covered king-size beds, framed botanical prints,
one or two pieces of antique country pine, and throw rugs on stripped
pine floors. The sunlit breakfast room has simple, oilcloth-covered tables and a large antique pine dresser. Dinner isn't served, but the village has two pub restaurants. A stream runs through the pretty,
south-facing garden, and small children are made especially welcome.
✉ *Terryglass, Nenagh, Co. Tipperary,* ☎ *067/22125,* ℻ *067/22187.*
6 rooms with bath. Dining room, tennis court, bicycles. AE, MC, V.

$ 🏠 **Tir na Fiúise.** Host Niall Heenan and his friendly sheep dog Ben pre-
side over this off-the-beaten-path farmhouse (the name means "land
of fuschia") that offers guests an authentic experience of farm life. The
100 acres, currently undergoing conversion to organic methods, offer
plenty of opportunities to get acquainted with Irish farming life: You
can help with hay making or turf cutting in season, take a farm or bog
walk, admire the sheep and free-range pigs, or just relax by a blazing
fire. The simple, bright rooms offer great country views. Breakfast is
served until noon and includes, besides the usual, homemade yogurt,
hot prunes in honey sauce, and fresh grapefruit. Terryglass, 2 km/1.3
mi away, is a lively village with a choice of pub-restaurants. ✉ *Terry-*
glass, Borrisokane, Co. Tipperary, ☎ ℻ *067/22041. 4 rooms with bath.*
Boating, fishing, bicycles. MC, V. Closed Nov.–Easter.

Outdoor Activities and Sports
The 18-hole, parkland course at **Birr Golf Club** (✉ The Glens, Birr, Co.
Offaly, ☎ 0509/20082) is highly recommended by discerning golfers.

Roscrea

29 *19 km/12 mi south of Birr.*

The main Dublin–Limerick road, passing through Roscrea, a charming town steeped in religious history, cuts right through a 7th-century
monastery founded by St. Cronan. It also passes the west facade of a
12th-century Romanesque church that now forms an entrance gate to
a modern Catholic church. Above the structure's round-headed doorway is a hood molding enclosing the figure of a bishop, probably St.
Cronan.

With your back to St. Cronan's, turn left and then right into Castle
Street to visit **Damer House,** a superb example of an early 18th-cen-
tury town house on the grand scale. It was built in 1725 within the
curtain walls of a Norman castle, at a time when homes were often
constructed beside or attached to the strongholds they replaced. During most of the 19th century, the house was used as a barracks; it was
subsequently rescued from decay by the Irish Georgian Society. The
house has a plain, symmetrical facade and a magnificent carved-pine
staircase inside; on display are exhibitions of local historical interest.
The 13th-century stone castle is surrounded by a moat and consists of
a gate tower, curtain walls and two corner towers. The house is home
to the **Roscrea Heritage Centre.** ✉ *Roscrea,* ☎ *0505/21850.* 🎫 *£2.50.*
🕐 *Mid-May–Sept., daily 9:30–6; Oct.–early May, weekends 10–5.*

Outdoor Activities and Sports
Roscrea Golf Club (✉ Demyrale, Co.. Tipperary, ☎ 0509/21130) is an
18-hole, parkland course with views of the Slieve Bloom Mountains.

Nenagh

③⓪ *35 km/21 mi west of Roscrea, 35 km/22 mi west of Limerick.*

Nenagh was originally a Norman settlement; it grew to a market town in the 19th century. Standing right in the center of Nenagh, the **Castle Keep** is all that remains of the town's original settlement. Originally one of five round towers linked by a curtain wall, and measuring 53 ft across the base, it rises to 100 ft, with 19th-century castellations at the top. The gatehouse and governor's house of Nenagh's old county jail now form the **Nenagh Heritage Centre,** which has permanent displays of rural life in the recent past before mechanization, as well as temporary painting and photography exhibits. ☎ *067/32633.* ☞ *£2.* ☉ *Easter–Oct., weekdays 9:30–5, Sun. 2:30–5; Nov.–Easter, weekdays 9:30–5.*

Dining and Lodging

$$$$ ✕⊡ **St. David's.** This gray stone Victorian fishing lodge, now a small,
★ elegant, impeccably run hotel, sits on 17 acres of gardens, woodland, and neatly manicured lawns sloping down to the shore of Lough Derg. The Austrian owner-host-chef, Bernhard Klotz, brings a Continental flair to the decor with massive cut-flower arrangements that adorn the lounge and conservatory. Rooms are large and luxurious, furnished with canopied beds, brocade curtains, and mahogany antiques. The Victorian-style dining room has an open fire and serves a table d'hôte menu of classic French and Italian cuisine using local and homegrown produce. ⊠ *Puckane, Nenagh, Co. Tipperary,* ☎ *067/24145,* ⅁⅄ *067/24388. 10 rooms with bath. Restaurant, bar, horseback riding, boating, fishing. AE, MC, V. Closed mid-Jan.–mid-March.*

Outdoor Activities and Sports

BOATING

Shannon Sailing (⊠ Dromineer, ☎ 067/24295) offers cruises of scenic Lough Derg by water bus and also hires out cruisers and sailboards.

GOLF

Nenagh Golf Club (⊠ Beechwood, Co. Tipperary, ☎ 067/31476) is a typical Midlands course: green, flat, and not too busy.

THE MIDLANDS A TO Z

Arriving and Departing

By Bus

Bus Éireann (☎ 01/836–6111) runs an express bus from Dublin to Mullingar in 1½ hours, with a round-trip fare of £9. Buses depart three times daily. A regular-speed bus, leaving twice daily, makes the trip in two hours.

By Car

Mullingar (the regional capital), Longford, and Boyle are on the main N4 route between Dublin and Sligo. It takes one hour to drive from Dublin to Mullingar (55 km/34 mi), and two hours from Mullingar to Sligo. To get from Mullingar to the Southwest, you can take the N52 to Nenagh where it meets the N7, and follow that into Limerick—a trip (150 km/94 mi) of about two hours. The R390 from Mullingar leads you west to Athlone, where it connects with the N6 to Galway. The drive (120 km/75 mi) takes about 2½ hours.

By Plane

The principal international airport serving the Midlands is **Dublin Airport** (☎ 01/844–4900). **Sligo Regional Airport** (☎ 071/68280) has daily flights from Dublin on Aer Lingus. Car rental facilities are available at Dublin Airport. For more information on these airports, *see* Arriving and Departing *in* Chapters 2 and 8.

By Train

A direct-rail service links Mullingar to Dublin, with three trains every day making the 1½-hour journey. It costs £7.50 one-way and £12.50 round-trip. Contact **Irish Rail** (☎ 01/836–6222) for information.

Getting Around

By Bus

The express buses leaving Dublin (☞ Arriving and Departing by Bus, *above*) make stops at Mullingar (1½ hrs), Longford (2¼ hrs), Carrick-on-Shannon (3 hrs), Boyle (3¼ hrs), and Sligo (4¼ hrs). There is also a daily bus from Mullingar to Athlone, and an express service connecting Galway, Athlone, Longford, Cavan, Clones, Monaghan, and Sligo. Details of all bus services are available from Bus Éireann depots at the following locations: **Athlone Railway Station** (☎ 0902/72651), **Cavan Bus Office** (☎ 049/31353), **Longford Railway Station** (☎ 043/45208), **Monaghan Bus Office** (☎ 047/82377), **Sligo Railway Station** (☎ 071/69888), and **Bus Éireann** (Dublin, ☎ 01/836–6111).

By Car

Most of the winding roads in the Midlands are uncongested, although you may encounter an occasional animal or agricultural machine crossing the road, and Mullingar, the cattle-trading town, can become badly congested. If you're driving in the north of Counties Cavan and Monaghan, be sure to avoid "unapproved" roads crossing the border into Northern Ireland. The approved routes into Northern Ireland connect the towns of Monaghan and Aughnacloy, Castlefinn and Castlederg, Swalinbar and Enniskillen, Clones and Newtownbutler, and Monaghan and Rosslea. Those driving a rented car should make sure it has been cleared for cross-border journeys.

By Train

Trains from Mullingar, departing twice daily every weekday and Sunday, stop at Longford (35 min), Carrick-on-Shannon (1 hr), Boyle (1¼ hrs), and Sligo (2 hrs).

Contacts and Resources

B&B Reservation Agencies

For a small fee, **Bord Fáilte** will book accommodations anywhere in Ireland through their central reservations system. B&Bs can be booked at local visitor information offices when they are open; however, even these reservations will go through the central reservations system. For more information, *see* Lodging *in* the Gold Guide.

Car Rentals

There are a handful of car rental firms in the Midlands. **Hamill's Rent-a-Car** (✉ Dublin Rd., Mullingar, Co. Westmeath, ☎ 044/48682). **Gerry Mullin** (✉ North Rd., Monaghan, ☎ 047/81396). **O'Reilly & Sons** (✉ Dublin Rd., Longford, ☎ 043/46494).

Emergencies

Police, fire, and **ambulance** (☎ 999 toll-free). For medical and ambulance service, contact Mullingar's **General Hospital** (☎ 044/40221).

PHARMACY

Weir's Chemist (✉ Market Sq., Mullingar, ☎ 044/48462).

Outdoor Activities and Sports

FISHING

General information about fishing can be obtained in most hotels, B&Bs, and bars. Contact the Irish Tourist Board for more details on angling tournaments (☞ Visitor Information, *below* for local offices, and the Gold Guide). For information on necessary licenses and permits, contact the **Eastern Regional Fisheries Board** (⊠ Balnagowan Mobhi Boreen, Dublin 9, ☎ 01/837–9209).

Visitor Information

Five Midlands TIOs are open all year: **Clonmacnoise** (⊠ Clonmacnoise, ☎ 0905/74134). **Longford** (⊠ Main St., ☎ 043/46566). **Mullingar** (⊠ Dublin Rd., ☎ 044/48650, FAX 044/40413). **Portlaoise** (⊠ James Fintan Lawlor Ave., ☎ 0502/21178). **Roscommon** (⊠ The Square, ☎ 0903/26342).

Another six Midlands TIOs are open seasonally: **Athlone** (⊠ Church St., ☎ 0902/94630), open April–October. **Birr** (⊠ Emmet Sq., ☎ 0509/20110), open May–September. **Boyle** (⊠ Bridge St., ☎ 079/62145), open April–September. **Carrick-on-Shannon** (⊠ River Quay, Co. Leitrim, ☎ 078/20170). **Cavan** (⊠ Farnham St., ☎ 049/31942), open April–September. **Monaghan** (⊠ Market House, ☎ 047/81122), open April–September. For off-season inquiries about Boyle, Cavan, and Monaghan, consult the Sligo TIO (☞ Visitor Information *in* The Northwest A to Z *in* Chapter 8).

5 The Southeast

Counties Wexford, Carlow, Kilkenny, Tipperary, and Waterford

Although the Southeast doesn't have Ireland's wildest scenic landscape, it does have plenty to offer—things all Ireland, and the world, enjoys. Kilkenny, briefly Ireland's capital, is its most medieval city. Tipperary's Golden Vale is home to the country's most fertile farmland. Counties Wexford and Waterford are leading summer destinations for natives in the know. Opera cognoscenti flock to Wexford's annual festival for rarities performed nowhere else. And long before Kleenex and Xerox turned their brand names into the thing itself, Waterford set a standard for cut crystal that all the world knows by name.

THE SOUTHEAST WILL SURPRISE VISITORS who expect all of Ireland to be rugged and wild. It isn't, especially in the Southeast, an area characterized inland by fertile river valleys and lush, undulating pastureland, and a coast that alternates between long, sandy beaches and rocky bays backed by low cliffs. The Southeast has the mildest, sunniest, and also the driest weather in Ireland, with as little as 30 inches of rainfall per year—compared to an average of 80 inches on parts of the west coast. The combination of sunshine and sandy beaches makes the Southeast's coast a popular vacation area with Irish families, but except for the resort of Tramore, it is relatively undeveloped. Its main attractions remain the natural beauty of its landscape and its small and charming fishing villages.

Updated by
Alannah
Hopkin

Both coastal and inland areas have a long, interesting history. There is evidence of settlements from some 9,000 years ago in the Slaney Valley near Wexford. The Kings of Munster had their ceremonial center on the Rock of Cashel, which in the 7th century became an important monastic center and bishopric. There were other thriving early Christian monasteries at Kilkenny, Ardmore, and Lismore.

The quiet life of early Christian Ireland was disrupted from the 9th century onward by a series of Viking invasions. The Vikings liked what they found here—a pleasant climate; rich, easily cultivated land; and a series of safe, sheltered harbors—so they stayed and founded the towns of Wexford and Waterford. (Waterford's name comes from the Norse Vadrefjord, Wexford's from Waesfjord.) Less than two centuries later, the same cities were conquered by Anglo-Norman barons and turned into walled strongholds. The Anglo-Normans and the Irish chieftains soon started to intermarry, but the process of integration halted with the Statute of Kilkenny in 1366, for the English feared that if such intermingling continued they would lose whatever control over Ireland they had.

The next great crisis was Oliver Cromwell's Irish campaign of 1650 which, in attempting to crush Catholic opposition to the English parliament, brought widespread slaughter. The ruined or extensively rebuilt condition of most of the region's early churches is a result of Cromwell's desecrations. His outrages are still a vivid part of local folk memory, but not as vivid as the 1798 Rebellion, an ill-timed and unsuccessful bid for a united Ireland inspired by the French Revolution. The decisive "battle" took place at Vinegar Hill near Enniscorthy, where some 20,000 rebels, armed only with pikes, were cut down by British cannon fire. Songs commemorating these events of almost 200 years ago, such as "The Rising of the Moon" and "The Croppy Boy," are still sung in local bars.

Carlow Town, Kilkenny City, Enniscorthy, and Wexford Town together provide an introduction to Irish history. All have remnants of their successive waves of invaders—Celt, Viking, and Norman. Wexford's narrow streets are built on one side of a wide estuary, and it has a delightful maritime atmosphere. Waterford, although less immediately attractive than Wexford, is also built on the confluence of two of the region's rivers, the Suir and the Barrow. It offers a richer selection of Viking and Norman remains, some good Georgian buildings, and also the world-renowned Waterford Glass Factory, open to visitors.

Kilkenny City, an important ecclesiastic and political center up to the 17th century, is now a lively market town whose streets still contain many remains from medieval times, most notably the beautiful St. Canice's Cathedral and a magnificent 12th-century castle.

The road between Rosslare and Ballyhack passes through quiet, atypical, flat countryside dotted with thatched cottages. Beyond Tramore, flat, sandy beaches give way to rocky Helvick Head and the foothills of the Knockmealdown Mountains at Dungarvan. Among the inland riverside towns, Carrick-on-Suir and Clonmel each have a special, quiet charm. In the far southwest of County Waterford, near the Cork border, Ardmore offers up early Christian remains on an exposed headland, while not far away, up the wooded splendor of the Blackwater Valley, the tiny cathedral town of Lismore has a hauntingly beautiful fairy-tale castle.

Anglers will scarcely believe the variety of fishing and scenery along the Rivers Barrow, Nore, and Suir, and especially in the Blackwater Valley area. County Tipperary is the location of the Rock of Cashel, a vast, cathedral-topped rock rising up above the plain and one of Ireland's most stunning ancient sights. The ancient seat of the kings of Munster, Cashel is also, according to legend, where St. Patrick converted the High King of Ireland to Christianity.

Pleasures and Pastimes

Festivals and the Arts

There are two major arts festivals in the area: Kilkenny Arts Week, held in late August, features classical music, theater, and art exhibits; and the Wexford Opera Festival, where each year in late October and early November three rare operas are given full-scale productions with internationally renowned casts. (☞ Nightlife and the Arts *in* Kilkenny City and Wexford Town, *below.*)

Dining

The restaurants in this region are generally small and informal. Seafood—especially Wexford mussels, crab, and locally caught salmon—appears on most menus, along with local lamb, beef, and game in season. Food will usually be prepared in a simple, country-house style, but be prepared for some pleasant surprises, as there are some ambitious Irish chefs at work in the area in both restaurants and hotels. For price ranges, *see* Chart 1(A) *in* On the Road with Fodor's.

Lodging

The southeast coast is popular with Irish families during the months of July and August, when it is advisable to book in advance, especially at places right on the coast. For price ranges *see* Chart 2(B) *in* On the Road with Fodor's.

Outdoor Activities and Sports

BICYCLING

The Southeast is a relatively unchallenging area for cyclists, with the only seriously hilly parts in the Knockmealdown and Comeragh mountains to the south of the region. If you enjoy bird life and sea vistas, try planning a coastal route: Between Arklow and Wexford it is predominantly flat with long expanses of sandy beaches. The Hook Peninsula between Wexford and Waterford has a network of small, quiet roads, many of them leading to tranquil fishing villages. Traveling from Waterford to Dungarvan via Dunmore East and Tramore offers a variety of scenery combining cliff-top rides with stretches of long, sandy beaches.

GOLF

Some of Ireland's best parkland courses can be found in the Southeast, and there is also a championship links course at Rosslare. Mount Juliet, near Kilkenny, has been publicly acclaimed by Nick Faldo as one of Europe's best. It is one of six 18-hole courses to open in the area in recent years. *See* Chapter 10 for more details.

HIKING

Two hiking trails cross the region, and the scenery on both trails is interestingly varied with wooded hills, rich farmland, and several rivers. The South Leinster Way begins in the County Carlow town of Kildavin and makes its way southwest over Mt. Leinster and the River Barrow, terminating in Carrick-on-Suir. A second trail, the Munster Way, picks up where the first ends and leads through the Vee Gap in the Knockmealdown Mountains and on to Clogheen.

HORSEBACK RIDING

If you have any equestrian skills at all, you will probably want to ride some of the fine horses bred in this part of Ireland. Inland, the terrain is mainly arable farmland, while the long, sandy beaches of the coast are regularly used as gallops. Most establishments offer riding by the hour—hourly rates vary from £9 to £12—and many stables offer hunting packages to the more experienced rider; rates are available on request.

SPECTATOR SPORTS

The people of the Southeast are a sporting lot, and on any given day you're likely to find the stand at the races or the hurling matches overflowing. Greyhound racing is extremely popular here, and Irish dogs are considered to be among the best in the world. Races are held at night, and there is usually a bar and a restaurant within the stadium. Horse races are also held regularly in the area at small, informal meetings. Ask locally about Gaelic football and hurling venues. These skillful and fast-moving games can often be watched for free, or for the nominal entrance price at one of the five GAA Grounds in the area.

Exploring the Southeast

The Southeast is geographically a large region (a car is essential for getting around here), stretching from the town of Carlow near the border of County Wicklow (☞ Chapter 3) in the north to Ardmore near the border of County Cork (☞ Chapter 6) in the south. Outside of the months of July and August, when the Irish themselves head here for their own vacations, the region is relatively free of traffic, making it ideal for leisurely exploration. Wexford, Waterford, and Kilkenny all have compact town centers best explored on foot, and they also make good touring bases.

Numbers in the text correspond to numbers in the margin and on the Southeast, Kilkenny City, Wexford Town, and Waterford City maps.

Great Itineraries

IF YOU HAVE 3 DAYS

Three days is enough time for a greatest-hits itinerary of the Southeast, though it won't leave you much time for meandering along the back roads. Start in the south of the region by taking the main Cork–Wexford road (the N25) and heading north to visit the cliff-top early Christian monuments at **Ardmore** ㊽. Travel on through **Dungarvan** ㊻ to **Lismore** ㊾, a small pretty village on the Blackwater River with a very large castle. From Lismore drive on along a scenic route known as the Vee Gap to ⌶ **Cahir** ㊿. On the next day, spend the morning visiting the **Rock of Cashel** in the market town of **Cashel** ㊾. Drive on via Urlingford on the main N8 to **Kilkenny City** ④–⑪ and explore its medieval cathedral and its newly restored castle. Drive through **Leighlinbridge** ② to the riverside village of ⌶ **Graiguenamanagh** ⑬. On the following morning head for the coast again and have a look at the old

Viking port of **Wexford** ⑰–㉗. Drive on down this pretty stretch of coast through the pretty waterside villages of **Kilmore Quay** ㉚ and **Ballyhack** ㉛ and cross by car ferry to ☒ **Waterford City** ㉜–㊸, another old Viking settlement on the estuary of the Rivers Suir and Nore-Barrow. Waterford is on the main Cork–Wexford road.

IF YOU HAVE 5 DAYS

Five days allows for a leisurely sampling of the different regions within the Southeast, with time to get to know its three biggest towns, Kilkenny, Wexford, and Waterford. Start in the middle of the region in **Kilkenny City** ④–⑪ and explore the medieval city center with its castle and cathedral on foot. Cross the River Barrow at **Leighlinbridge** ② and drive down to ☒ **Graiguenamanagh** ⑬, an unspoiled and hilly riverside village. On the following morning drive west to **Jerpoint Abbey** ⑫, a ruined Cistercian monastery in a stone-built village on the River Nore. Follow the River Nore southward to **New Ross** ⑭, a busy river port. Follow signposts for the **John F. Kennedy Arboretum** ⑮, which is near the cottage at **Dunganstown** where the president's great-grandfather was born. Then pick up the main road to **Wexford** ⑰–㉗, a Viking settlement on the estuary of the River Slaney. Just outside town, at **Ferrycarrig**, is **The Irish National Heritage Park** ㉘. Spend the night in attractive ☒ **Wexford,** which has narrow streets full of character. If wildlife interests you, don't miss **Curracloe Strand,** a 9-km/6-mi sandy beach just to the north of the town.

On the next day, take the small coast road through **Kilmore Quay** ㉚ and **Ballyhack** ㉛ past thatched cottages and narrow lanes to the port of **Waterford City** ㉜–㊸. A large collection of Viking artifacts, recently discovered, is on display in a building near the Norman stronghold, Reginald's Tower. Continue south on the lovely coast road through **Dunmore East** ㊹, a fishing village with several thatched cottages, to the seaside resort of **Tramore** ㊺, which has another long, sandy beach. Pick up the main coast road to **Ardmore** ㊽, where the early Christians built a cliff-top monastery and round tower. Return to ☒ **Dungarvan** ㊻, a cheerful little fishing town, for the night. On the next day follow the Blackwater Valley up to **Lismore** ㊾, which has one of Ireland's prettiest castles. Follow the scenic route known as the Vee Gap through the Knockmealdown Mountains past Mount Melleray, home to an order of contemplative monks who welcome visitors. Continue to **Cahir** ㊿ at the foot of the Galtee mountains where you can visit another kind of castle, this time Norman. Spend the afternoon exploring the **Rock of Cashel,** symbol of both Celtic and Christian Ireland, in the market town of **Cashel** ㊽.

When to Tour the Southeast

The Southeast is a good area of Ireland to visit off-season for a number of reasons: Restaurants and accommodations will be open between March and November, months when many places in the more touristy, western regions close down. And then there's the weather: significantly less rain falls here than elsewhere, making this a good choice if you're visiting in the spring and autumn. Remember that in July and August, the Irish themselves descend on the coastal resorts, so if you do head for the beaches of the Southeast in the summer, be sure to reserve your accommodations well in advance.

CARLOW TOWN, KILKENNY CITY, AND WEXFORD TOWN

This tour covers a region rich in historical and maritime attractions. From Carlow Town's small county seat you travel through the farmlands of the Barrow Valley to Kilkenny City, pausing to explore the historic city center on foot. From Thomastown, just outside Kilkenny, another cross-country drive follows the River Nore to New Ross, where it meets the River Barrow, and proceeds to John F. Kennedy's ancestral home and the Arboretum planted in his memory. The tour ends in the old Viking port of Wexford Town.

Carlow Town

❶ *83 km/52 mi south of Dublin.*

Carlow Town was established by the Anglo-Normans in the 12th century. Its position on the border of the English Pale—the area around Dublin that was dominated by the English from Elizabethan times on—made it an important strategic center and hence the scene of many bloody battles and sieges. Today Carlow is a modern market town on the banks of the River Barrow, with a population of about 11,700 employed in such industries as sugar-beet refining, flour milling, and malting.

The Roman Catholic **Cathedral of the Assumption** is one of Carlow Town's most prominent sights. Completed in 1883, the Gothic-style cathedral is notable for its stained-glass windows and a magnificently sculpted marble monument on the tomb of its builder, Bishop James Doyle (1786–1834), a champion of Catholic emancipation; the monument was carved by the Irish sculptor John Hogan (1800–58). ⊠ *Tullow St.,* ☎ *0503/31227.* ⊘ *Daily 10–8.*

The ruins of the 13th-century **Carlow Castle** can be found near the bridge on the grounds of Corcoran's Mineral Water Factory. This castle withstood a siege by Cromwell's troops in 1650, only to be destroyed accidentally in 1814 when a Dr. Philip Middleton attempted to renovate the castle for use as a mental asylum. While setting off explosives to reduce the thickness of the walls, he managed to demolish all but the west wall and its two flanking towers. (Despite what the story might suggest, Middleton was not himself to be a patient.)

The **County Museum** is housed in Carlow's town hall, whose exhibits include a reconstructed blacksmith's forge and a preindustrial kitchen. ⊠ *Centaur St.,* ☎ *0503/31759.* ☞ *£1.* ⊘ *Tues.–Sun. 2:30–5:30.*

The famous **Browne's Hill Dolmen** is reached by taking a 3-km/2-mi detour on the road to Tullow (R725) east of Carlow Town. This stone monument dates from 2000 BC and, with a capstone weighing in at 100 tons, is considered the largest in Ireland. Nineteenth-century historians thought that dolmens were Druidic altars, while the peasantry believed them to be giants' graves. They are, in fact, megalithic tombs dating from the Stone Age (circa 3000–2000 BC). The dolmen is accessible through a field gate along the road; there is no entrance fee.

Outdoor Activities and Sports

GOLF

Carlow Golf Club (⊠ Deerpark, Co. Carlow, ☎ 0503/31695), 3 km/2 mi north of the town on the Dublin road, is set in a wild deer park; it remains open all year.

HORSEBACK RIDING

Carrigbeg Stables (⊠ Carrigbeg, Bagenalstown, Co. Carlow, ☎ 0503/21962) offers riding by the hour or the day.

SPECTATOR SPORTS

Celtic football and hurling matches are held at **Carlow GAA Grounds** (⊠ Dr. Cullen Park, Co. Carlow, ☎ 0503/32414).

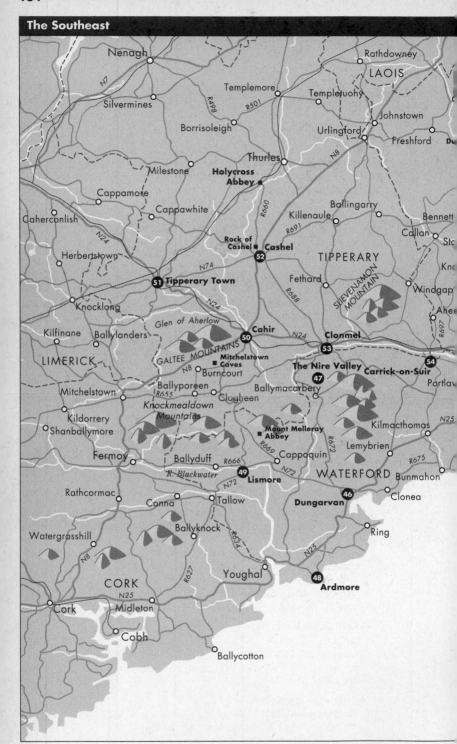

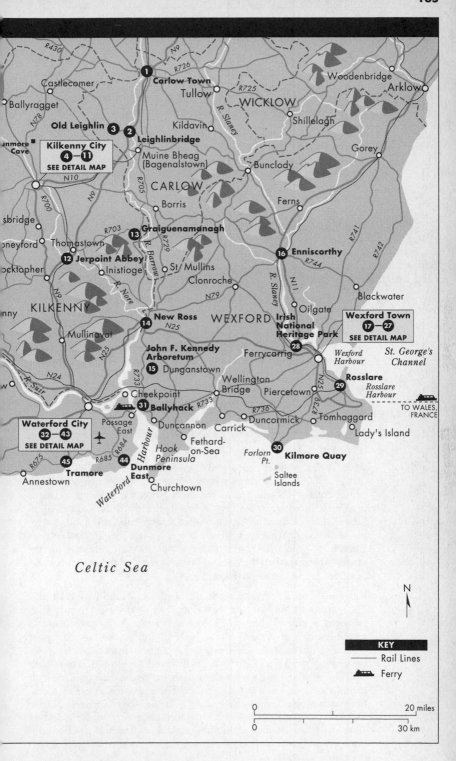

Castlecomer

Ballyragget

Carlow Town
1

Tullow

Woodenbridge

Arklow

R430

N9

R726

WICKLOW

Shillelagh

R725

Old Leighlin
3 **2**

Kildavin

R78

Leighlinbridge

Muine Bheag
(Bagenalstown)

Bunclody

Gorey

Kilkenny City
4 — 11
SEE DETAIL MAP

unmore
Cave

N10

CARLOW

Ferns

R741

R700

N9

R705

Borris

R703
13 Graiguenamanagh

Enniscorthy
16

R744

R742

Jerpoint Abbey
12

Thomastown

oneyford

bridge

Inistioge

St/ Mullins

R729

R. Barrow

R. Nore

Clonroche

N79

Enniscorthy

R. Slaney

ocktapher

KILKENNY

N9

Mullinavat

New Ross
14
N25

WEXFORD

Oilgate

N11

Irish
National
Heritage Park
28

Wexford Town
17 — 27
SEE DETAIL MAP

Blackwater

N25

John F. Kennedy
Arboretum
15 Dunganstown

R733

Ferrycarrig

Wexford
Harbour

St. George's
Channel

N24

R. Suir

Cheekpoint

Wellington
Bridge

Piercetown

Rosslare
29

Rosslare
Harbour

N25

Waterford City
32 — 43
SEE DETAIL MAP

Passage
East

31 Ballyhack
R733

Duncormick

Tomhaggard

TO WALES,
FRANCE

Duncannon

Carrick

R736

Lady's Island

R675

R685

R684

44

Dunmore
East

Fethard-
on-Sea

Forlorn
Pt.

30 Kilmore Quay

45 Tramore

Annestown

Hook
Peninsula

Churchtown

Saltee
Islands

Waterford Harbour

Celtic Sea

N

0   20 miles

0   30 km

Leighlinbridge

❷ *10 km/6 mi south of Carlow Town on N9.*

In Leighlinbridge, the first bridge over the River Barrow was built in 1320. On the east bank of Leighlinbridge lie the ruins of **Black Castle,** built in 1181, one of the earliest Norman fortresses constructed in Ireland and the scene of countless battles and sieges over the centuries. Only one ruined 400-year-old tower stands today.

Dining

$$ ✕ **Lord Bagenal Inn.** This famous old pub beside the River Barrow is today a bar-restaurant with open fires and warm lighting. The bar menu consists of a basic selection of steaks, poultry, and fresh fish. The French-style restaurant's menu changes weekly and is considerably more sophisticated. A typical menu might include a homemade soup, avocado with prawn dressing, tournedos steak, or poached or grilled salmon steak served with hollandaise or lime butter sauce. The award-winning wine list offers many finds. ⊠ *Main St., Co. Carlow,* ☏ *0503/21668. DC, V. No dinner Sun., Mon.*

Old Leighlin

❸ *5¾ km/3 mi west of Leighlinbridge, signposted to the right off the N9.*

Worth a quick stop, the tiny village of Old Leighlin is the site of a monastery founded in the 7th century by St. Laserian. It was rebuilt in the 12th century as St. Laserian's Cathedral and enlarged in the 16th century. Worth noticing here are the Gothic doorway, some curiously carved 16th-century grave slabs, and St. Laserian's cross and holy well.

Kilkenny City

❹ *24 km/15 mi southwest of Leighlinbridge on N10, 121 km/75 mi southwest of Dublin.*

The finest example of a medieval town in Ireland, Kilkenny City (population 10,000) is an impressively preserved, 900-year-old Norman citadel attractively situated on the River Nore, which forms the moat of its magnificently restored castle. In the 6th century, St. Canice (a.k.a. "the builder of churches") established a large monastic school here; the town's name reflects Canice's central role: Kil Cainneach means Church of Canice. Kilkenny's medieval look wasn't established for another 400 years, when the Anglo-Normans fortified the city with a castle, gates, and a brawny wall.

Kilkenny holds a special place in the history of Anglo-Irish relations. The infamous 1366 Statute of Kilkenny, intended to strengthen English authority in Ireland by keeping the heirs of the Anglo-Norman invaders from becoming absorbed into the Irish way of life, was an attempt at apartheid. Intermarriage became a crime punishable by death. Irish cattle were barred from grazing on English land. Anglo-Norman settlers could lose their estates for speaking Irish, for giving their children Irish names, or for dressing in Irish clothes. The native Irish were forced to live outside town walls in shantytowns. Ironically, the process of Irish and Anglo-Norman assimilation was well underway when the statute went into effect; perhaps if this intermingling had been allowed to continue, Anglo-Irish relations in this century might have been more harmonious.

By the early 17th century, the Irish Catholics had grown impatient with such repression; they tried to bring about reforms with the Confederation of Kilkenny, which governed Ireland from 1642 to 1648, with Kilkenny as the capital. Pope Innocent X sent money and arms. Cromwell responded in 1650 by overrunning the town and sacking the cathedral, which he used to stable his horses.

The center city is small and, despite the large number of historic sights, easily covered in less than three hours. One of the most pleasant cities south of Dublin, Kilkenny City is home to more than 50 pubs, many of them on Parliament and High streets, which support a lively music scene. Some of the pubs, as well as many of the town's shops, have old-fashioned, highly individualized, brightly painted facades. (The Victorian tradition of painting storefronts had nearly died out in many towns, but since the 1980s Kilkenny has led in its revival.) Kilkenny City is also a center for well-designed crafts, especially ceramics and sweaters; the premier venue is the Kilkenny Design Centre.

❺ St. Canice's Cathedral, on the corner of Dean Street and Parliament Street, is the best place to begin a walking tour of Kilkenny City. In spite of Cromwell's defacements, this is still one of the finest cathedrals in Ireland, and it is Ireland's second-largest medieval church, after St. Patrick's Cathedral in Dublin. The bulk of the 13th-century structure (restored in 1866) is in the early English style. Within the massive walls is an exuberant Gothic interior, given a somber grandeur by the extensive use of a locally quarried black marble. Many of the memorials and tombstone effigies represent distinguished descendants of the Normans, some depicted in full suits of armor. Look for a female effigy in the south aisle wearing the old Irish or Kinsale cloak; the 12th-century black marble font at the southwest end of the nave; and St. Ciaran's Chair in the north transept, also made of black marble, with 13th-century sculptures on the arms.

The biggest attraction on the grounds is the 102-ft **round tower,** built in 847 and all that remains of the monastic development reputedly begun in the 6th century, around which the town developed. If you have the energy to climb the tower's 167 steps, the 360° view from the top is tremendous. Next door is **St. Canice's Library,** containing some 3,000 16th- and 17th-century volumes. ⊠ *Dean St.* 🖾 *Free; tower £1.* ⊘ *Cathedral: Easter–Sept., Mon.–Sat. 9–6, Sun. 2–6; Oct.–day before Easter, Mon.–Sat. 10–1 and 2–4, Sun. 2–4; Tower: daily 9–1 and 2–6.*

❻ The ruins of the **Black Abbey** south of St. Canice's Cathedral belong to a 13th-century friary, named after the black capes of the Dominican friars. It has recently been restored as a Dominican church. A museum displaying a number of historical artifacts is next door in the presbytery. 🖾 *Free.* ⊘ *Daily 9–1, 2–6.*

Across the street from the Courthouse (two blocks east of the Black
❼ Abbey ruins), **Rothe House,** dating primarily from 1594, with 1610 additions, is a restored home of a wealthy Tudor merchant. The house is now the headquarters of the **Kilkenny Archaeological Society,** which has a motley collection of Bronze Age artifacts, ogham stones, and coal-mining gear. There's also a genealogical research facility that can help you trace your ancestors. ⊠ *Parliament St.,* ☎ *056/22893.* 🖾 *£2.* ⊘ *Apr.–Sept., Mon.–Sat. 10:30–5, Sun. 1–5; Oct.–Mar., Mon.–Sat. 1–5, Sun. 3–5.*

❽ Kyteler's Inn (⊠ Kieran St., ☎ 056/21064), the oldest in town, is in the cellar of a building notorious as the place where Dame Alice Kyteler, an alleged witch, was accused of poisoning her four husbands. The restaurant retains its 14th-century stonework and exposed beams. Its menu features an à la carte dinner, including plainly cooked Irish steak, salmon, and chicken. Lunch is served at tables in the bar. How-

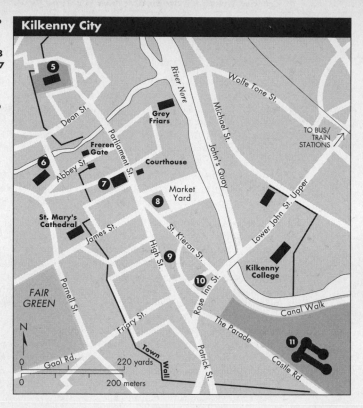

ever, the owners can't resist serving witch's broth—really just a home-made vegetable soup.

⑨ The **Tholsel,** or town hall, which was built in 1761 on Parliament Street, stands near the site of the medieval Market Cross.

⑩ The **Tourist Information Office (TIO),** as well as CityScope, a sound-and-light show on 17th-century Kilkenny, is housed in the **Shee Alms House** (off the east side of High Street). The building was founded in 1582 by Sir Richard Shee as a hospital for the poor and served in that capacity until 1895. ✉ *Rose Inn St.,* ☎ *056/51500.* ☞ *CityScope £1.* ⊙ *May–Sept., Mon.–Sat. 9–6, Sun. 11–5; Oct. and Apr., Mon.–Sat. 9–5; Nov.–Mar., Tues.–Sat. 9–5; CityScope on the ½ hr.*

★ **⑪** Founded in 1172 and dominating the south end of town, **Kilkenny Castle** served for more than 500 years, beginning in 1391, as the seat of the Butler family—later designated earls and dukes of Ormonde—one of the more powerful clans in Irish history. In 1967 the 6th Marquess of Ormonde handed over the present building, which dates largely from 1820, to the state; since then it's been through a series of restorations. The gray stone building, with two turreted wings and numerous chimneys poking over the battlements, stands amid rolling lawns beside the River Nore in 49 acres of landscaped parkland. Most impressive is the 150-ft-long, aptly named **Long Gallery,** a refined airy hall that contains a collection of family portraits, frayed tapestries, and a skylit, decorated ceiling made up of carved oak beams adjoined with Celtic lacework and adorned with brilliantly painted animal heads. The **Butler Gallery** houses a collection of modern art and frequently changing exhibitions. ✉ *The Parade, Kilkenny,* ☎ *056/21450.* ☞ *£3; grounds and Butler Gallery free.* ⊙ *Apr.–May, daily 10:30–5; June–Sept.,* *daily 10–7; Oct.–Mar., Tues.–Sat. 10:30–12:45 and 2–5, Sun. 11–12:45 and 2–5.*

Dunmore Cave, a natural limestone cavern containing weird rock formations, lies about 11 km/7 mi north of Kilkenny on the N78 (follow signposts for Castlecomer and Athy). The cave is mentioned in the ancient Book of Leinster as the dwelling place of Lord of the Mice, a giant cat killed by a female warrior named Aithbel. In the late 19th century, the bones of some 44 individuals, 25 of them children, were found here; they were probably seeking refuge from a Viking attack. Like many other Irish caves, Dunmore was considered the entrance to hell until well into the 17th century. Nowadays the cave is equipped with pathways, catwalks, and bridges to enable you to explore the eerie beauty of its formations in safety. ✉ *Dunmore,* ☎ *056/67726.* 🎫 *£2.* ☉ *Mid-Mar.–mid-June, Tues.–Sat. 10–5, Sun. 2–5; mid-June–mid-Sept., daily 10–7; Oct.–mid-Mar., weekends 10–5.*

Dining and Lodging

$$$ ✕ **Ristorante Rinuccini.** Kilkenny City's premier Irish/Italian restaurant is in the basement of a Georgian town house opposite Kilkenny Castle. In early evening a harpist sets the mood in the intimate, softly lit dining room, which has red tablecloths and rustic ladder-back chairs. Owner Antonio Cavaliere's menu includes homemade pastas like penne with a smoked salmon, cream, and wine sauce; and spaghetti with fresh crabmeat, garlic, olive oil, and chili. Humanely raised Irish veal is served in a variety of traditional ways. ✉ *1 The Parade, Co. Kilkenny,* ☎ *056/61575. AE, DC, MC, V.*

$$ ✕🏠 **Lacken House.** Owner-chef Eugene McSweeney and his wife Breda run this Georgian restaurant-with-rooms on the edge of Kilkenny. The nicely outfitted rooms are decorated in pretty Laura Ashley fabrics. Traditional furnishings in the cellar restaurant maintain the period character of the house. Uniformed waitresses serve international dishes made with fresh local ingredients. Salmon from the nearby Nore is the star of the menu in dishes: it is served as a fillet with a galette of potato and celeriac served with sage butter sauce. For dessert try the homemade ice creams. ✉ *Dublin Rd., Co. Kilkenny,* ☎ *056/61085,* FAX *056/62435. 8 rooms with bath. Restaurant, bar. AE, DC, MC, V. Restaurant closed Sun., Mon.*

$$$ 🏠 **Newpark Hotel.** Set back from the road in the rural suburbs of Kilkenny City, this hotel is a popular base for businesspeople, tour groups, and independent travelers. At its core is a Victorian house, now surrounded by modern extensions. All the bright guest rooms are decorated in soft, pastel colors and have floral-patterned drapes; those in the rear have the best views. The public spaces in the hotel are done in a country style and are accented with comfortable pine furnishings. ✉ *Castlecomer Rd., Co. Kilkenny,* ☎ *056/22122,* FAX *056/61111. 84 rooms with bath. 2 restaurants, pool, steam room, 2 tennis courts, health club, horseback riding, fishing. AE, DC, MC, V.*

$$ 🏠 **Butler House.** This elegant Georgian house, an integral part of the
★ Kilkenny Castle complex, once belonged to the earls of Ormonde. It is now open to guests under the management of the Kilkenny Civic Trust. The best approach is through the crafts workshops opposite the castle and into its old-style, walled back garden. Rooms have a modern sensibility, with oatmeal-color carpets, off-white bedspreads, large potted plants, and contemporary prints. Ask for a room with a bow window overlooking the garden and castle; those facing Patrick Street are noisier and generally smaller. The restaurant is open for lunch year-round and for dinner June through September. ✉ *16 Patrick St., Co.*

Kilkenny, ☎ *056/65707,* FAX *056/65626. 14 rooms with bath. Restaurant. AE, DC, MC, V.*

Nightlife and the Arts

1998 marks the 25th anniversary of the **Kilkenny Arts Week** (☎ 056/63663), which runs for nine days around the third week of August. Classical music, film, theater, literary events, and visual arts exhibits take place throughout Kilkenny.

Outdoor Activities and Sports

BICYCLING

Bikes can be rented through **J. J. Wall** (✉ 88 Mandlin St., Co. Kilkenny, ☎ 056/21236) when the weather is good for exploring the quiet countryside around Kilkenny.

GOLF

Kilkenny Golf Club (✉ Glendine, Co. Kilkenny, ☎ 056/65400), 2 km/1.25 mi northeast of town, is an 18-hole, par-71, mainly flat course.

SPECTATOR SPORTS

The 1336 Statutes of Kilkenny expressly forbid the ancient Irish game of hurling, today one of this area's most popular sports. Gaelic football and hurling matches are held at **Kilkenny GAA Grounds** (✉ Nowlan Park, Co. Kilkenny, ☎ 056/22481). At **Kilkenny Greyhound Racetrack** (✉ St. James's Park, Co. Kilkenny, ☎ 0504/21013), evening meetings are held where betting is the main attraction. **Gowran Park** (✉ Co. Kilkenny, ☎ 056/26126) holds horse races regularly.

Shopping

Kilkenny is a byword for good, modern design. The town's leading outlet, the **Kilkenny Design Centre** (✉ Kilkenny Castle, ☎ 056/22118), in the old stable yard opposite the castle, sells a range of goods that combine traditional crafts with modern design, including ceramics, jewelry, sweaters, handwoven textiles, and so on. **The Sweater Shop** (✉ High St., ☎ 056/63405) carries a good range of knitwear. **P. T. Murphy** (✉ 85 High St., ☎ 056/21127) specializes in heraldic jewelry. **Richard Duggan and Sons Ltd., The Monster House** (✉ High St., ☎ 056/22016) is a small department store with a good selection of Irish crystal and other souvenirs. **Nicholas Mosse Pottery** (✉ Bennettsbridge, ☎ 056/27105) stocks an attractive array of hand-decorated spongeware. **Chesneau Leather Goods** (✉ Old Creamery, Bennettsbridge, ☎ 056/27456) uses high-quality leather and solid-brass fittings in bags and purses that are exported worldwide. **Stoneware Jackson Pottery** (✉ Bennettsbridge, ☎ 056/27175) makes distinctive, hand-thrown tableware. **Rudolf Heltzel** (✉ 10 Patrick St., ☎ 056/21497) is known for the striking modern designs of gold and silver jewelry. You can see glass being blown at the **Jerpoint Glass Studio** (✉ Stoneyford, ☎ 056/24350)—where the glass is heavy but modern and uncut—and then pick up a bargain in the factory shop.

Jerpoint Abbey

⑫ *14½ km/9 mi south of Kilkenny on R700.*

Thomastown is a pretty, stone-built village on the River Nore. A short detour 2 km/1 mi to the south of Thomastown on the N9 lies Jerpoint Abbey, a ruined Cistercian monastery that dates from about 1180. The tombs and the restored Romanesque cloisters decorated with affecting human figures and are definitely worth a visit. Guides are available from mid-June to mid-September. ☎ *056/21755.* 🎫 *£2.* ☉ *Apr.–mid-June and mid-Sept.–mid-Oct., Tues.–Sun. 10–1 and 2–5;*

mid-June–mid-Sept., daily 9:30–6:30; otherwise, obtain key from on-site caretaker.

Dining and Lodging

$$$$ ✕🍽 **Mount Juliet.** Within the walls of this 1,400-acre estate on the River
★   Nore (17 km/11 mi south of Kilkenny City on the N9) lies this imposing, three-story Georgian mansion. Behind its symmetrical, gray stone facade, many of the house's original features are intact, including finely stuccoed ceilings and marble mantelpieces. The two major activities here are horseback riding on the extensive trails within the estate, and golfing on the Jack Nicklaus–designed parkland championship course. The Lady Helen McAlmont Restaurant, a stately room in Wedgwood blue and white, its tables adorned with crystal, silverware, and fine linen, serves haute cuisine with Franco-Irish touches from succulent local produce. Bedrooms are large and individually decorated, with mahogany furniture, super-king-size beds, and original fireplaces. ⊠ *Co. Kilkenny,* ☎ *056/24455,* FAX *056/24522. 53 rooms with bath. 2 restaurants, 2 bars, indoor pool, sauna, 18-hole golf course, tennis court, archery, croquet, horseback riding, fishing. AE, DC, MC, V.*

$ ✕🍽 **Berryhill.** A charming, creeper-clad 1789 house perched high on
★   a ridge overlooking the River Nore and the picturesque village of Inistioge (just southeast of Thomastown), this is a warm, comfortable family home on a working sheep farm. Guests can enjoy the bright, airy drawing room, with its baby grand piano and a drinks trolley with an "honesty book." Rooms are generous-size suites, decorated on animal themes—there's the frog (with veranda), pig, and elephant. Guests can roam the fields and enjoy private fishing. Fresh trout is often a breakfast option, served at the dining-room table in front of a big open fire. Dinner, country-house style, can be prebooked. ⊠ *Inistioge, Co. Kilkenny,* ☎ FAX *056/58434. 3 suites with bath. Croquet, fishing. MC, V. Closed Nov.–Mar., except when guests rent all 3 rms.*

Outdoor Activities and Sports

GOLF
For detailed information about **Mount Juliet Golf Club** (⊠ Co. Kilkenny, ☎ 056/24455), the regular host of the Irish Open, *see* Chapter 10.

HORSEBACK RIDING
The excellent facilities at **Mount Juliet** (⊠ Co. Kilkenny, ☎ 056/24455) are open to nonresidents.

Graiguenamanagh

⑬   *15 km/9 mi northeast of Thomastown on R703.*

Graiguenamanagh is a pretty, unspoiled village on the banks of the River Barrow at the foot of Brandon Hill. In the 13th century the early English-style church of **Duiske Abbey** was the largest Cistercian church in Ireland. The choir, the transept, and part of the nave of the original abbey church have been incorporated into the new Catholic church. Purists will be disappointed by the modernization, which was carried out between 1973 and 1983, although various medieval building techniques were used. The roof, for instance, is made of unseasoned Irish oak joined only with dowels and wedges. This is good walking country; ask locally for directions to the summit of **Brandon Hill** (1,694 ft), a 7-km/4½-mi hike.

Dining and Lodging

$ ✕🍽 **Waterside.** All the rooms and the restaurant in this 19th-century
★   stone corn mill have views of the picturesque River Barrow, on which it sits. The rooms have patchwork quilts and fully tiled bathrooms. The restaurant, which occupies the whole ground floor of the old mill

building, has exposed pitch-pine beams, prettily decorated windows, and candles and crisp white linens on the tables. Seasonal menus feature the finest local ingredients, including salmon, duck, and lamb. Waterside is 27 km/17 mi southeast of Kilkenny, and it's popular with hikers and those who value the nearby riding and golf. ⊠ *The Quay, Co. Kilkenny,* ☎ *0503/24246,* FAX *0503/24733. 14 rooms with bath or shower. 2 restaurants, 2 bars, fishing. MC, V.*

New Ross

⑭   *17 km/11 mi south of Graiguenamanagh on R705.*

New Ross is a busy inland port on the banks of the River Barrow. Even though it is one of the oldest towns in County Wexford, settled in the 13th century on an ancient monastic site, only the most dedicated history buffs will be tempted to stop and explore the steep narrow streets above its unattractive docks. The major attraction in New Ross is a cruise up the River Barrow on the **Galley Cruising Restaurant** (☎ 051/421723). You can take in the peaceful farmlands along the riverbank while sampling lunch, afternoon tea, or dinner. The emphasis is on fresh local produce and seafood. The restaurant is open Easter–October only.

Ballylane Farm is just a short detour 3 km/2 mi from New Ross on the Wexford N25 road. These 200 acres provide an opportunity to experience a working farm firsthand and to add greatly to your appreciation of the Irish countryside as a working environment. Maps and information sheets are supplied to guide you through fields and woodlands where you can observe a wide variety of farm animals and local wildlife. ⊠ *New Ross,* ☎ *051/425666.* ☞ *£2.50.* ☉ *Mid-Mar.–Apr., weekends 10–6; May–Oct., daily 10–6; group tour by appointment.*

⑮   The **John F. Kennedy Arboretum** is clearly signposted from New Ross on the R733, which follows the banks of the Barrow southward for about 5 km/3 mi. The cottage where the president's great-grandfather was born may be found in Dunganstown. Kennedy relatives are still living in the house. About 2 km/1¼ mi down the road at Slieve Coillte is the entrance to the arboretum, which features more than 600 acres of forest, nature trails, and gardens, as well as an ornamental lake. The grounds contain some 4,500 species of trees and shrubs and serve as a resource center for botanists and foresters. The top of the park offers fine panoramic views. ⊠ *Dunganstown,* ☎ *051/388171.* ☞ *£2.* ☉ *May–Aug., daily 10–8; Sept. and Apr., daily 10–6:30; Oct.–Mar., daily 10–5.*

Shopping
The **Butlersland Craft Centre** (⊠ New Ross, ☎ 051/422612) is on the main N25 2 km/1¼ mi east of New Ross and stocks an extensive range of Irish craft products, including clothing, cut glass, wood crafts, and jewelry.

Enniscorthy

⑯   *19 km/12 mi northeast of New Ross on N79.*

Enniscorthy, a thriving market town with a rich history, is on the main road between Dublin and Wexford, to the south of the popular resort of Gorey. Built on the steeply sloping banks of the River Slaney, the town is dominated by **Enniscorthy Castle,** constructed by a Norman knight in 1199 and once leased to the English poet Edmund Spenser, author of *The Faerie Queene,* who first came to Ireland in 1580 as secretary to the lord deputy of Ireland (Spenser's prose defense of Lord Grey of Wilton's repressive policies was published posthumously in 1633,

34 years after his death). The castle was the site of fierce battles against Oliver Cromwell in the 17th century and during the Uprising of 1798. Its square-towered keep now houses the **County Wexford Museum,** which contains thousands of historical items, including a reconstructed dairy and displays of pottery and military memorabilia from the 1798 and 1916 uprisings. The curator is often eager to provide commentary on the exhibits. ⊠ *Castle Hill,* ☎ *054/35926.* ⌐ *£2.* ⊙ *Apr.–mid-Sept., Mon.–Sat. 10–6, Sun. 2–5; mid-Sept.–Mar., daily 2–5.*

On the east side of town is **Vinegar Hill,** where the most important battle in the uprising of 1798 took place. In the battle that marked the end of that uprising, on June 21 some 20,000 rebels, armed only with pikes and agricultural implements, made a last desperate stand against the continuous bombardment of the British Army's cannon fire.

St. Aidan's Cathedral stands on a commanding site overlooking the Slaney. This Gothic-revival building was built in the mid-19th century under the direction of Augustus Welby Pugin, the architect of the Houses of Parliament in London.

Outdoor Activities and Sports

GREYHOUND RACING

The Showgrounds (⊠ Co. Wexford, ☎ 054/33172) have greyhound racing on Mondays and Thursdays at 8 PM, with bar and catering facilities available.

HORSEBACK RIDING

Boro Hill House Equestrian Centre (⊠ Clonroche, Co. Wexford, ☎ 054/44117) offers residential riding holidays and hunting breaks as well as daily and hourly riding. The center is fully equipped with indoor and outdoor arenas, forest trails, and a cross-country course.

Shopping

Kiltrea Bridge Pottery (⊠ Kiltrea Bridge, Caime, ☎ 054/35107) specializes in large, hand-thrown terra-cotta pots suitable for both indoor and outdoor planting. **Carley's Bridge Pottery** (⊠ Carley's Bridge, ☎ 054/35312) is worth visiting for its selection of handcrafted pottery work.

Wexford Town

⑰ *24 km/15 mi south of Enniscorthy on N11, 142 km/88 mi south of Dublin.*

Wexford is an ancient place defined on maps by the Greek cartographer Ptolemy as long ago as the 2nd century AD. Its Irish name is Loch Garman, but the Vikings called it Waesfjord—the harbor of the mud flats—which became Wexford in English. Wexford became an English garrison town after it was taken by Oliver Cromwell in 1649. (The Anglo-Norman conquest of Ireland began in County Wexford in 1169, so the British presence has deep roots, and Wexford has been an English-speaking county for centuries.)

The River Slaney empties into the sea at Wexford Town. The harbor has silted up since the days when the Viking longboats docked here; nowadays only a few small trawlers fish out of here. Wexford Town's compact center is set on the south bank of the Slaney, with its main street running parallel to the quays on the riverfront. It can be explored on foot in an hour or two. Allow at least half a day in the area if you also intend to visit the Heritage Park at nearby Ferrycarrig, and a full day if you also want to take in Johnstown Castle Gardens and its agricultural museum or walk on the nature reserve at Curracloe Beach to the north of the town. The town is at its best in late October, when the Wexford Opera Festival (☞ *below*) engenders a carnival atmosphere that affects all walks of life.

⑱ The **TIO** on the waterfront at Crescent Quay is a good place to start exploring Wexford Town on foot and to find out about guided walking tours organized by local historians. Standing in the center of Crescent **⑲** Quay, the large bronze **statue of Commodore John Barry** (1745–1803) commemorates the man who came to be known as the "Father of the American Navy." Born in 1745 in nearby Ballysampson, Barry settled in Philadelphia at age 15, became a brilliant naval fighter during the War of Independence (thus avenging his Irish ancestors), and trained many young naval officers who went on to achieve fame for themselves. **Main Street** (one block inland from the quays), a narrow thoroughfare, is the major shopping street of the town, with a pleasant mix of old-fashioned bakeries, butcher shops, stylish boutiques, and a share of Wexford's more than 90 pubs—friendly places that exude provincial Irish charm.

From most points in town you can see, rising above the rooftops, the graceful spires of two elegant examples of 19th-century Gothic architecture, known as the **twin churches,** because their exteriors are identical, their foundation stones were laid on the same day, and their spires **⑳** both reach a height of 230 ft. The **Church of the Immaculate Concep- ⑳** **tion** is on Rowe Street. The **Church of the Assumption** may be found on Bride Street.

㉒ The **Franciscan Church** (✉ School St.) has a ceiling worth noting for **㉓** its fine, locally crafted stucco work. The **Wexford Bull Ring** (✉ Quay St., back toward quays) was once the scene of bullbaiting, a cruel medieval sport that was popular among the Norman nobility. This arena was also the site of another, far more tragic event in 1649, when Cromwell's soldiers massacred 300 panic-stricken townspeople who had gathered here to pray as the army stormed their town. The birthplace of Oscar Wilde's mother, Jane Francis Elgee (who wrote as "Speranza"), was in the old rectory on Main Street near the Bull Ring. Her son definitely got from her his gift as an epigrammatist.

㉔ The red sandstone **Westgate Tower** was the largest of five fortified gateways in the Norman and Viking town walls, and it is the only one to remain standing. The early 13th-century tower has been sensitively restored. Keep an eye out as you wander around this part of town for other preserved segments of the old town walls. Westgate Tower houses the **Wexford Experience,** an introduction to Wexford's history. This audiovisual presentation lasts for about 30 minutes and is supplemented by seasonal exhibitions. ☎ *053/46506.* 🎫 *£1.* ◷ *May–Sept., Mon.–Sat. 10–6, Sun. 2–6; Oct.–Apr., Mon.–Sat. 11–5.*

㉕ The ruins of the 12th-century **Selskar Abbey** (south of Westgate Tower) still stand. Here the first treaty between the Irish and the Normans was signed in 1169.

A few last addresses are worth noting as you wander the town's narrow, winding streets. **Oliver Cromwell's temporary residence** was at 29 Main Street South. The **birthplace of William Cody,** father of the famous American showman "Buffalo" Bill Cody, may be found on King Street. The Cornmarket was the site of the 19th-century poet **Thomas Moore's home.**

㉖ The **Wexford Wildfowl Reserve** on the north bank of the Slaney is a short walk across the new bridge from the main part of town. Thirty percent of the world's Greenland white-fronted geese spend their winters on the mud flats, known locally as slobs, which also draw ducks,

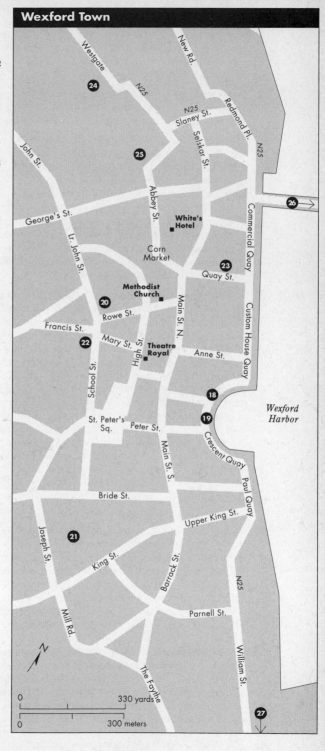

Wexford Town

swans, and other waterfowl. Screened blinds and an observation tower are provided for bird-watchers, and a collection of the various species who live on the slobs has been established at the reception center. The reserve is signposted off R741, 4 km/2½ mi north of Wexford. ⊠ *North Slob, Wexford Harbour,* ☎ *053/23129.* ⚑ *Free.* ☉ *Apr. 16–Sept., daily 9–6; Oct.–Apr. 15, daily 10–5.*

🖑 **Curracloe Strand,** 11 km/7 mi northeast of Wexford Town, runs for 9 km/6 mi, and besides being a popular swimming place in summer is also home to many migratory birds in the winter.

㉗ The signpost for **Johnstown Castle Gardens** may be reached by following the N25 for 5 km/3 mi in the direction of Rosslare. The castle itself, a massive, Victorian-Gothic building in gray stone, is now an agricultural college, but the attractive and well-maintained grounds, with ornamental lakes and more than 200 different trees and shrubs, are open to the public. The main attraction is the **Irish Agricultural Museum,** housed in the quadrangular stable yards. Extensive displays are devoted to rural transportation, farming, and the activities of the farmyard and the farmhouse, with a special exhibit on dairying. The museum also contains an important collection of Irish country furniture. ☎ *053/42888.* ⚑ *£2.* ☉ *Mon.–Sat. 9–12:30 and 1:30–5, Sun. 2–5.*

★ 🖑 ㉘ The **Irish National Heritage Park** at Ferrycarrig, 5 km/3 mi from Wexford Town on the N25, is one of the most successful and enjoyable attractions to be opened in Ireland in recent years. This 35-acre, open-air theme park beside the River Slaney should not be missed. In about an hour and a half, a guide takes you through 9,000 years of Irish history—from the first evidence of humans on this island, at around 7000 BC, to the Norman settlements of the mid-12th century. Full-scale replicas of typical dwelling places illustrate the changes in beliefs and lifestyles. Highlights of the tour include a prehistoric homestead, a *crannóg* (lake dwelling), an early Christian *rath* (fortified farmstead), a Christian monastery, a horizontal water mill, a Viking longhouse, and a Norman castle. There are also examples of pre-Christian burial sites and a stone circle. Most of the exhibits are "inhabited" by students in appropriate dress who will answer questions. The unspoiled riverside site includes several nature trails. ⊠ *Ferrycarrig,* ☎ *053/20733.* ⚑ *£3.50.* ☉ *Mid-Mar.–Oct., daily 10–7; last admission at 5.*

Dining and Lodging

$$ ✕ **The Granary.** Good restaurants now abound in WexfordTown, but you will be well looked after here by co-owners Paddy Hatton and his wife, Mary, a Ballymaloe-trained chef. The restaurant is opposite the Westgate in the heart of historic Wexford. It was originally a grain store, and the heavy beams and pillars have been retained. The extensive menu offers a good range of local seafood including scallops in their shells with a white wine sauce. In winter, pigeon breast with juniper and cranberry sauce is a popular choice. ⊠ *Westgate, Co. Wexford,* ☎ *053/23935. AE, DC, MC, V. Closed Sun.*

$ ✕ **Oak Tavern.** About 2 km/1¼ mi from Wexford Town and just a few hundred meters from the gates of the Irish National Heritage Park on the Enniscorthy Road, the pub-restaurant in this Old World inn is a good place to stop on your way back into town. In cold weather, warm yourself beside log fires that blaze in the lounge; in good weather relax on the riverside terrace. ⊠ *Ferrycarrig,* ☎ *053/20922. AE, MC, V.*

$$$ ✕▥ **Ferrycarrig.** If you want to stay out of Wexford town center, this modern low rise is 3 km/2 mi outside town (on the N11 Enniscorthy road) on the bank of the River Slaney. Rooms are identically furnished,

with relaxing, pastel blue or pink color schemes and light-wood trim; they all overlook the well-kept riverside gardens. The Conservatory Restaurant is highly regarded locally for its fine cuisine and high standard of service. A singer and pianist entertain at dinner, which is worth lingering over. Typical dishes include boned guinea fowl with a fresh cranberry and orange sauce, or poached turbot in a tomato and cucumber *vin blanc* sauce, surrounded by fresh mussels. ⊠ *Ferrycarrig Bridge, Co. Wexford,* ☎ *053/20999,* 𝔽𝔸𝕏 *053/20982. 39 rooms with bath. 2 restaurants, 2 bars, horseback riding, fishing. AE, DC, MC, V.*

$–$$ ✕🖬 **Horetown House.** About 20 minutes' drive from Wexford, this three-story, rambling Georgian house is furnished in the old-fashioned style with family hand-me-downs, and it is fast becoming one of the few places of its kind that has not been done up by interior decorators. Children are made welcome, and good-value riding packages are a specialty. The stone-flagged Cellar Restaurant is more sophisticated than the house, serving a set, five-course dinner with dishes such as Wexford mussels in garlic, wild venison in mushroom sauce, and excellent salmon and steaks. The nightlife consists of a chat with the Young family beside the drawing-room fire, so don't head here if you're one for bright lights, big city. ⊠ *Foulksmills, Co. Wexford,* ☎ *051/565771,* 𝔽𝔸𝕏 *051/565633. 12 rooms, 4 with bath. Restaurant, horseback riding. DC, MC, V.*

$$ 🖬 **White's Hotel.** Housed in an historic 19th-century building fronted by a modern conservatory, this property is a friendly, convivial place conveniently located in the heart of town. Its recently refurbished, old-fashioned passageways, brass trim, and red-velvet decor combine with candlelight and roaring log fires to create a warm ambience. The country-style guest rooms are furnished with Victorian reproductions. Rooms found in the new addition to the hotel are more spacious. ⊠ *George's St., Co. Wexford,* ☎ *053/22311,* 𝔽𝔸𝕏 *053/45000. 82 rooms with bath. Restaurant. bar, sauna, steam room, health club. AE, DC, MC, V.*

$ 🖬 **McMenamin's Town House.** Early breakfast by arrangement and an exceptional degree of comfort for its price range make this four-story, Victorian villa, a short walk from the railway station in the town center, an ideal stopover en route to or from the Rosslare ferries. Book months rather than weeks in advance if you want a room here during the Opera Festival. The bedrooms are spacious, warm, and immaculately clean, with glorious, large pieces of highly polished Victorian furniture and antique beds, including a mahogany half-tester. There are about eight choices at breakfast, including fresh fish of the day. Don't leave without tasting Kay and Seamus McMenamin's homemade whiskey marmalade. ⊠ *3 Auburn Terr., Co. Wexford,* ☎ 𝔽𝔸𝕏 *053/46442. 6 rooms with bath. MC, V. Closed Dec. 18–29.*

Nightlife and the Arts

Touring companies and local productions can be seen in Wexford at the **Theatre Royal** (⊠ High St., ☎ 053/22400). Hands down, the **Wexford Opera Festival** (☎ 053/22144), held during the last two weeks of October and dribbling into November, is the town's leading cultural event. More than 30 years old, the festival puts on seldom-performed works with top talent from all over the world. As of press time (summer 1997), the operas for the 1998 season have not been announced, but the three operas slated for 1997—Mercadate's *Elena da Feltre,* Dargonizhski's *Rusalka,* and Respighi's *La Siamma*—are representative of the rarity of the operas performed here. Along with an ever-expanding fringe, the festival supplies a variety of musical events from 11 AM to midnight.

Outdoor Activities and Sports

BICYCLING

If you'd like to explore the long, sandy coast of this area at a leisurely pace, bicycles can be hired at **The Bike Shop** (⊠ 9 Selskar St., Co. Wexford, ☎ 053/22514).

HORSEBACK RIDING

Ballingale Farm (⊠ Taghmon, Co. Wexford, ☎ 053/34387) has facilities for both children and adults, including a cross-country course. **Horetown Equestrian Centre** (⊠ Horetown House, Foulksmills, Co. Wexford, ☎ 051/565771) specializes in residential riding holidays with cross-country riding and will teach you how to play polo-crosse. **Sheimalier Riding Stables** (⊠ Forth Mountain, Taghmon, Co. Wexford, ☎ 053/39251) offers riding by the hour.

SPECTATOR SPORTS

Horse races are held regularly at the **Wexford Racecourse** (⊠ Bettyville, Co. Wexford, ☎ 053/42307).

Shopping

The **Wool Shop** (⊠ 39 S. Main St., ☎ 053/22247) is the place to go for Aran sweaters. **John Hore's** (⊠ 31 S. Main St., ☎ 053/22200) specializes in handmade Irish linen. At **Nostalgia** (⊠ Paul's Quay, ☎ 053/46754) you can find your own small slice of Ireland's past.

COASTAL DRIVE FROM WEXFORD TOWN TO ARDMORE

This tour follows mainly minor roads along the prettiest parts of the coast in Counties Wexford and Waterford, pausing midway to explore Waterford City on foot.

Rosslare

㉙ *18 km/11 mi southwest of Wexford Town off N25 on the R470.*

The village of Rosslare is a seaside resort with a long, sandy beach, while Rosslare Harbour, 8 km/5 mi south of the village, is one of Ireland's busiest ports and the terminus for car ferries from Fishguard, Pembroke, Le Havre, and Cherbourg.

Dining and Lodging

$$$ ✕🖾 **Kelly's.** Situated right on a sandy beach, this traditional weekend
★ retreat has been owned and run by the Kelly family since 1895. Its extensive recreational facilities are a big draw. Guest rooms are done in comfortable, rustic decor, and those facing the front have lovely sea views. Waterford glass chandeliers hang in the restaurant, but the friendly service swiftly relaxes the ambience. The menu features fresh local produce served in classic French style. Main courses may include panfried medallions of venison with forest mushrooms, Barbary duck with mango and applesauce, or medallions of monkfish with chervil sabayon. ⊠ *Rosslare, Co. Wexford,* ☎ *053/32114,* 🆁🆇 *053/32222. 99 rooms with bath. Restaurant, indoor-outdoor pool, sauna, steam room, 18-hole golf course, 2 indoor tennis courts, 2 outdoor tennis courts, croquet, health club, horseback riding, jogging, squash, beach, fishing, cabaret. AE, DC, MC, V. Closed Dec.–Feb. 28.*

$ 🖾 **Tuskar House Hotel.** Found in a quiet area near the ferry port, this small, family-run hotel promises simple pleasures: comfortable rooms with good views of the sea (especially from the rear), decorated with functional, modern furniture in a bright, cheery palette; some have balconies. Public rooms have lots of polished pine, glass, and greenery. Seafood is a specialty at the restaurant. ⊠ *St. Martin's Rd., Rosslare Harbour, Co. Wexford,* ☎ FAX *053/33363. 30 rooms with bath. Restaurant, bar. AE, DC, MC, V.*

Nightlife and the Arts
Portholes Bar at the **Hotel Rosslare** (Rosslare Harbour, ☎ 053/33110) is a popular spot for lively, traditional Irish music most evenings during the summer.

Outdoor Activities and Sports
Rosslare Golf Club (⊠ Rosslare Strand, Co. Wexford, ☎ 053/32203) is a 27-hole, par-72, championship links. A mixture of links and parkland can be found at the Southeast's newest course, the 18-hole, par-72 **St. Helen's Bay** (⊠ Kilrane, Co. Wexford, ☎ 053/33669).

Kilmore Quay

30 *22 km/14 mi south of Rosslare on R739.*

A quiet, old-fashioned, seaside village of thatched and whitewashed cottages noted for its fishing industry, Kilmore Quay is also popular with recreational anglers and bird-watchers. From the harbor there is a pleasant view to the east from the harbor over the flat coast that stretches for miles. During the last two weeks in July, the village hosts a lively **seafood festival** (☎ 053/29922) with a parade, seafood barbecues, and other events.

The **Saltee Islands,** Ireland's largest bird sanctuary, is a popular offshore day trip from Kilmore Quay. (From mid-May to the end of July, look for boats at the village waterfront to take you to the islands.) In late spring and early summer, several million seabirds nest among the dunes and on the rocky scarp on the south of the islands. Even if you are not an ornithologist, it's worth making the trip at these times to observe the sheer numbers of gulls, kittiwakes, puffins, guillemots, cormorants, and petrels.

The **Kilmore Quay Maritime Museum** is onboard the lightship *Guillemot.* The boat, built in 1923, is the last Irish lightship to be preserved complete with cabins and engine room, and it contains models and artifacts relating to the maritime history of the area. ☎ *053/29655.* ⊠ *£1.* ☉ *May–Sept., daily noon–6; Oct.–Apr. by appointment.*

Shopping
Country Crafts (⊠ Kilmore Quay, ☎ 053/29885) overlooks the harbor of Kilmore Quay and has a mixture of Irish-made crafts, antique pine furniture, and paintings by local artists.

En Route On leaving Kilmore Quay, make your way northwest on the R736, then head west through Duncormick and on to Wellington Bridge. Past the bridge, head toward Fethard-on-Sea on the R733, following signs for the **Ring of Hook** drive. This is a strange and atypical part of Ireland, where the land is exceptionally flat and the narrow roads are straight. Except during July and August, when the many sandy beaches attract vacationing families, the roads are virtually empty, and the tiny hamlets appear eerily deserted. But the area has its own special charm, a peace and quiet enhanced by small, thatched cottages with tiny but carefully tended gardens.

The Ring of Hook leads to **Duncannon,** a small resort with a good sandy beach and a delightful nautical atmosphere, on the north side of Waterford Harbour. Its history is marked by the visits of two kings: James II beat a hasty retreat out of Ireland through Duncannon port after his defeat at the Battle of the Boyne in 1690, and his successor, William III, also spent some days here before leaving for England.

Ballyhack

★ **③** *34 km/21 mi west of Kilmore Quay.*

On the upper reaches of Waterford Harbour, the pretty village of Ballyhack, with its square castle keep, wooden buildings, thatched cottages, and green, hilly background, is much admired by painters and photographers. The castle was once owned by the Knights Templars of St. John of Jerusalem, who held the ferry rights by royal charter; traditionally, they were required to keep a boat at Ballyhack to transport injured knights to the King's Leper Hospital at Waterford. Nowadays a small car ferry plies the same route in a five-minute crossing to Passage East.

Dunbrody Abbey may be reached by taking a short detour 5 km/3 mi north of Ballyhack on the R733 New Ross road. This ruined Cistercian abbey dates from the late 12th century and flourished until about 1539 when Henry VIII instigated the dissolution of the monasteries. Next to the Dunbrody Abbey lies **Dunbrody Castle,** property of the Marquess of Donegall, with a fledgling 1,500-tree yew-hedge maze, tea shop, gift shop, and a small museum. ⊠ *Campile,* ☎ *051/388603.* 🖼 *Free; parking £1 cars, 50p bikes.* ☉ *Apr., May, and Sept., daily 10–6; July–Aug., daily 10–7.*

Dining

$$ ✕ **Neptune Restaurant.** When Pierce and Valerie McAuliffe reopened their restaurant in spring 1997 after a winter break, they had refurbished their tiny waterside restaurant—a ferry ride across the River Nore between Counties Waterford and Wexford—and come up with a new concept: by day cooking school; by night, restaurant. On Tuesday–Thursday mid-June through mid-September, from noon to 2, they're offering "A Taste of Ireland" cooking demonstrations for £20 per person, including lunch and wine. The dinner menu still specializes in fresh local salmon, crab, and other seafood. Salmon is served grilled with herb butter, with hollandaise sauce, or cooked in a hot Thermidor sauce. The hot crab Behat (white crabmeat oven-baked in vegetable sauce with French mustard and cheese) is a regular item on the menu, which also caters to meat eaters. ⊠ *Ballyhack Harbour, New Ross, Co. Wexford,* ☎ *051/389284. AE, DC, MC, V. Closed Dec.–Mar. No lunch Fri.–Mon. No dinner Sun.; no dinner Mon. in Apr.–May and Sept.–Oct.*

Waterford City

㉜ *5 km/3 mi west of Ballyhack by ferry and road (R683), 62 km/39 mi southwest of Wexford Town, 158 km/98 mi southwest of Dublin.*

The largest town in the Southeast, Waterford, like Wexford Town to the east, was founded by the Vikings in the 9th century and taken over by Strongbow, the Norman invader, in 1170. The city resisted Cromwell's 1649 attacks—his phrase "by Hook or by Crooke" refers to his two siege routes, one via Hook Head, the other via Crooke Village on the estuary—but did not prosper again 1783, when George and William Penrose set out to create "plain and cut flint glass, useful and ornamental," and thereby set in motion a glass-manufacturing industry without equal. The best Waterford glass was produced from the late 1780s to the early 19th century. This early work, examples of which can be found in museums and public buildings all over the country, is characterized by a unique, slightly opaque cast that is absent from the modern product.

Waterford has better preserved city walls than anywhere in Ireland but Derry (☞ Chapter 8). Initially, the slightly run-down commercial center doesn't look too promising. You'll need to park your car and proceed on foot to discover the heritage that the city has made admirable efforts over the past decade to preserve. The compact town center can be visited in a couple of hours. Allow at least another hour if you intend to take the Waterford Crystal factory tour.

The **city quays**—at the corner of Greyfriar's Street and Custom House Parade—is a good place to begin a tour of Waterford City. (The TIO is also down there, at No. 41 The Quay.) The city quays stretch for nearly a mile along the River Suir and were described in the 18th century as the best in Europe. The **Waterford Heritage Centre** on Greyfriar's Street is home to some of the 75,000 historical artifacts excavated from beneath the city in the mid-1980s. Parts of Viking houses are displayed alongside samples of leather work, bone carvings, pottery, and ornate jewelry. ⊠ *Greyfriar's St.,* ☎ *051/871227.* ☜ *£2.* ☉ *June–Sept., daily, 10–5. Oct.–May, weekdays 10–5.*

Admission to the Heritage Centre also gives access to the massive, pepper-pot-shape **Reginald's Tower,** a waterside landmark on the east end of Waterford's quays that marks the apex of a triangle containing the old walled city of Waterford. Built by the Vikings for the city's defense in 1003, it has 80-ft-high, 10-ft-thick walls; an interior stairway leads to the top. The tower served in turn as the residence for a succession of Anglo-Norman kings, including Henry II, John, and Richard II; a mint for silver coins; a prison, and an arsenal. It is said that Strongbow's marriage to Eva, the daughter of Dermot MacMurrough, took place here in the late 12th century, thus uniting the Norman invaders with the native Irish. It has recently been restored to its original medieval appearance and furnished with appropriate 11th–15th-century artifacts.

One of Waterford's finer Georgian buildings, **City Hall,** on the Mall, dates from 1788 and was designed by John Roberts, a native of the city. On the way you'll pass some good examples of domestic Georgian architecture—tall, well-proportioned houses with typically Irish, semicircular fanlights above the doors. The arms of Waterford hang over the city hall's own entrance, which leads into a spacious foyer that originally was a town meeting place and merchants' exchange. The building contains two lovely theaters, an old Waterford dinner service, and an enormous 1802 Waterford glass chandelier, which hangs in the Council Chamber (a copy of the chandelier hangs in Independence Hall in Philadelphia). The **Theatre Royal** (☞ Nightlife and the Arts, *below*) is the setting for the annual Festival of Light Opera in October. ⊠ *The Mall,* ☎ *051/873501.* ☜ *Free.* ☉ *Weekdays 9–1 and 2–5.*

The Bishop's Palace is another building that is among the most imposing of the remaining Georgian town houses. Only the foyer is open to the public. ⊠ *Alongside city hall on Mall.* ☜ *Free.* ☉ *Weekdays 9–5.*

As you turn into Colbeck Street, you'll see one of the remaining portions of the **old city wall;** there are sections all around the town center. The site of **St. Olaf's Church** (⊠ St. Olaf's St.) may be reached by taking a left at the top of Colbeck Street and then an immediate right. St. Olaf's was built, as the name implies, by the Vikings in the mid-11th century. All that remains of the old church is its original door, which has been incorporated into the wall of the existing building (a meeting hall). The ruined tower of **Blackfriars Abbey** (⊠ High St.), reached via St. Olaf's Street and High Street, belonged to a Dominican abbey founded in 1226 and returned to the crown in 1541 after

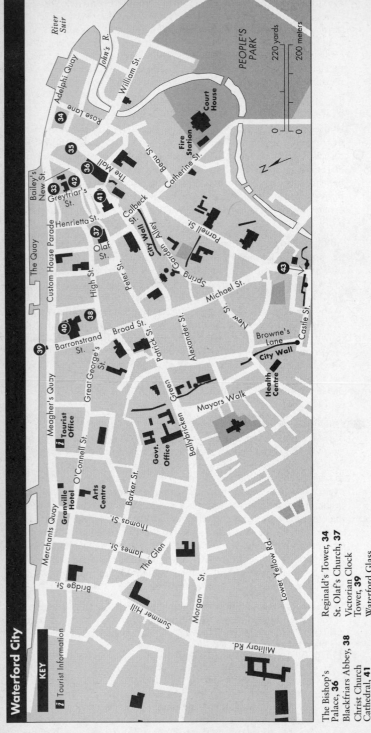

Waterford City

KEY

ℹ️ Tourist Information

River Suir

John's R.

Adelphi Quay

Rose Lane

William St.

PEOPLE'S PARK

Court House

34

35

Bailey's New St.

The Mall

36

42

33

Greyfriar's St.

41

Fire Station

Beau St.

Catherine St.

Colbeck St.

Henrietta St.

37

City Wall

Garden Alley

Spring Garden

Parnell St.

Custom House Parade

The Quay

Olaf St.

High St.

Peter St.

Michael St.

43

40

38

Barronstrand St.

Broad St.

New St.

Patrick St.

Alexander St.

Browne's Lane

Castle St.

City Wall

39

Meagher's Quay

ℹ️ **Tourist Office**

Great George's St.

Green

Ballybricken

Mayors Walk

Health Centre

O'Connell St.

Govt. Office

Barker St.

Merchants Quay

Granville Hotel

Arts Centre

Thomas St.

James St.

The Glen

Bridge St.

Summer Hill

Morgan St.

Lower Yellow Rd.

Military Rd.

220 yards

200 meters

0

N

The Bishop's Palace, **36**
Blackfriars Abbey, **38**
Christ Church Cathedral, **41**
City Hall, **35**
French Church, **42**
Holy Trinity Cathedral, **40**

Reginald's Tower, **34**
St. Olaf's Church, **37**
Victorian Clock Tower, **39**
Waterford Glass Factory, **43**
Waterford Heritage Centre, **33**

(39) the dissolution of the monasteries. It was used as a courthouse until Cromwellian forces destroyed it in the 17th century. The **Victorian Clock Tower** on Merchant's Quay (visible as you look down Barronstrand Street to the quays) was built in 1864 with public donations. Although it has no great architectural merit, it serves as a reminder of the days when Waterford was a thriving, bustling port. (Now, as elsewhere in Ireland, Waterford's workforce is more likely to be employed in high-tech and service industries than on the waterfront.)

(40) The Roman Catholic **Holy Trinity Cathedral** (⌧ Barronstrand St. be-tween High St. and clock tower) has a simple facade and a richly (some would say garishly) decorated interior with high, vaulted ceil-ings and ornate, Corinthian pillars. Surprisingly, it was built in the late 18th century, when Catholicism was barely tolerated, on land granted

(41) by the Protestant city fathers. The Church of Ireland **Christ Church Cathe-dral** (⌧ Henrietta St. near High St.), like Holy Trinity, was designed by John Roberts (who also did City Hall) with a Renaissance-style fa-cade more ornate than its Catholic sister. An unusual memento mori is inside: the high-relief effigy of James Rice depicts him wrapped in his shroud in a state of decay, with frogs and bugs climbing out of his

(42) corpse. The roofless ruins of the **French Church** (⌧ Greyfriar's St.), a 13th-century Franciscan abbey, may be seen across Cathedral Square. The church, also known as Greyfriars, was given to a group of Huguenot refugees (hence the "French") in 1695. A splendid east window remains amid the ruins.

If the weather is favorable you might consider a **cruise** along Water-ford's harbor and the wide, picturesque estuary of the River Suir. A luxury river cruiser serving lunch (£13), tea (£6), and dinner (from £20) departs from the quay beside Reginald's Tower and tours for two to three hours. Tickets can be purchased at the Tourism Information Of-fice. ⌧ *Galley Cruises,* ☎ *051/421723.* ☉ *Tours June–Aug., daily, weather permitting.*

★ (43) The city's most popular attraction is the **Waterford Glass Factory**, about 2 km/1¼ mi from the TIO. (Take the N25 Waterford–Cork road south from the quay, or ask at the tourist office about the regular bus service.) When the factory opened in 1783, it provided English roy-alty with a supply of ornate handcrafted flatware, chandeliers, and dec-orative pieces. Over the years, its clientele and product line diversified, and today the United States is the biggest market. The worthwhile tour of the factory takes you through the specialized crafts of blowing, cut-ting, and polishing glass—all carried out against a noisy background of glowing furnaces and ceaseless bustle. An extensive selection of crys-tal is on view (and for sale) in the showroom. To reserve a place in a 60-minute tour, which includes an optional 18-minute audiovisual show, call the factory or the tourist office. ⌧ *Cork Rd., Kilbarry,* ☎ *051/373311.* ▣ *£3.50.* ☉ *Nov.–March, weekdays 9–5, tours 9:30–3; Apr.–Oct. daily 8:30–6, tours 8:30–4.*

Dining and Lodging

$$$ ✕ **Dwyers of Mary Street.** In an old Royal Irish Constabulary barracks
★ (the original bars are still on the downstairs windows), this French-in-fluenced spot has a menu that changes every two weeks and a lovely pink, green, and cream color scheme. Original paintings grace the walls, and antiques are mixed with modern touches, such as Bauhaus chairs. A typical meal might begin with garlic prawns in a *rösti* nest, followed by boned quail with apples and sultana (raisin) stuffing and seasonal vegetables. Finish with the brown bread ice cream (homemade ice creams are one of chef and co-owner Martin Dwyer's specialties).

⊠ *8 Mary St., Co. Waterford,* ☎ *051/877478. AE, DC, MC, V. Closed Sun. No lunch.*

$ ✕ **Olde Stand Steak and Seafood.** Amid old paintings, city maps, and a handcrafted wooden bar, nibble on oysters with brown bread or seafood chowder as a snack or lunch at the bar. The menu in the main restaurant is mostly steaks (5 different cuts, from 8 to 14 ounces) and seafood—including salmon, monkfish, and shellfish. There's usually a trio of vegetarian dishes available, as well. ⊠ *45 Michael St.,* ☎ *051/ 879488. AE, DC, MC, V.*

$ ✕ **Reginald Restaurant and Pub.** Here 20th-century locals—drawn by the snacks and the lunchtime bar food—mix and mingle in a setting that includes a section of the city's 9th-century Viking wall (if only it could talk!). The dinner menu includes fresh monkfish and steamed mussels as well as chicken, veal, and steak dishes. ⊠ *The Mall,* ☎ *051/ 855087. AE, MC, V.*

$$$$ ✕🏨 **Waterford Castle.** If coming to the Emerald Isle didn't take you far enough away, this 17th-century stone castle (with 19th century additions) on its own 310-acre island in the River Suir may do the trick. (The island is 3 km/2 mi outside Waterford City and can be reached only by car ferry.) The Great Hall and the drawing room have fine oak paneling, ornate, antique furniture, and tapestries. The luxuriously decorated guest rooms have four-poster beds. Some bathrooms have original tile work and all have reproduction claw-foot tubs. Plush is the word in the Munster Room restaurant, with its ornate, plastered ceiling, oak furniture, and deep-burgundy Donegal carpet, where the fare tends to country-style dishes like poached salmon, asparagus served in puff pastry, and bread-and-butter pudding. ⊠ *The Island, Ballinakill, Co. Waterford,* ☎ *051/878203,* FAX *051/879316. 19 rooms with bath. Restaurant, indoor pool, 18-hole golf course, 2 tennis courts, health club, croquet, fishing. AE, DC, MC, V.*

$ ✕🏨 **Diamond Hill Country House.** On a quiet cul-de-sac off the Waterford–Rosslare road, just 3.2 km/2 mi from Waterford City, sits this creeper-covered, modern guest house. Rose and Terry Masterson have won several awards for both their fine Irish breakfasts and the lovely gardens. Tweed fabrics, tapestries, and plenty of greenery dominate in the public spaces. Bedrooms are bright and airy and are filled with modern furniture. ⊠ *Slieverue, Co. Waterford,* ☎ *051/832855,* FAX *051/ 832254. 10 rooms with shower. Dining room, wine bar. AE, MC, V.*

$$$ 🏨 **Jurys Hotel.** This modern, five-story hotel sits on 38 acres of quiet parkland high above the River Suir, though it is just 1 km/½ mi from the center of Waterford. There's a large marble and brass-trimmed foyer and comfortable lobby seating areas. All the rooms have panoramic views of the city and surrounding countryside and are done in bright, pleasant colors, with modern, functional furniture. ⊠ *Ferrybank, Co. Waterford,* ☎ *051/832111,* FAX *051/832863. 98 rooms with bath. Restaurant, bar, indoor pool, sauna, 2 tennis courts, health club, fishing. AE, DC, MC, V.*

Nightlife and the Arts

Culture buffs won't want to miss the **Garter Lane Arts Centre** (⊠ 22a O'Connell St., ☎ 051/855038), the largest such cultural center in Ireland. Call ahead for a schedule of upcoming concerts, exhibits, and theater productions at the center. The **Waterford International Festival of Light Opera** (☎ 051/375437), the only competitive event of its kind, is a great draw for amateur musical societies from throughout Ireland and Great Britain. The festival runs for 17 nights every September at the **Theatre Royal** (⊠ City Hall, The Mall, ☎ 051/874402).

We'll give you a $20 tip for driving.

See the real Europe with Hertz.

It's time to see Europe from a new perspective. From behind the wheel of a Hertz car. And we'd like to save you $20 on your prepaid Affordable Europe Weekly Rental. Our low rates are guaranteed in U.S. dollars and English is spoken at all of our European locations. Computerized driving directions are available at many locations, and Free Unlimited Mileage and 24-Hour Emergency Roadside Assistance are standard in our European packages. For complete details call 1-800-654-3001. Mention PC #95384 So, discover Europe with Hertz.

Offer is valid at participating airport locations in Europe from Jan.1 – Dec.15, 1998, on Economy through Full size cars. Reservations must be made at least 8 hours prior to departure. $20 will be deducted at time of booking. Standard rental qualifications, significant restrictions and blackout periods apply.

Pick up the phone.

Pick up the miles.

MCI — Calling Card

415 555 1234 2244
J.D. SMITH

WorldPhone

Use your MCI Card® to make an international call from virtually anywhere in the world and earn frequent flyer miles on one of seven major airlines.

Enroll in an MCI Airline Partner Program today. In the U.S., call **1-800-FLY-FREE.** Overseas, call MCI collect at **1-916-567-5151.**

1. To use your MCI Card, just dial the WorldPhone access number of the country you're calling from.
   (For a complete listing of codes, visit www.mci.com.)
2. Dial or give the operator your MCI Card number.
3. Dial or give the number you're calling.

# Austria (CC) ♦	022-903-012		# Netherlands (CC) ♦	0800-022-91-22
# Belarus (CC)			# Norway (CC) ♦	800-19912
From Brest, Vitebsk, Grodno, Minsk	8-800-103		# Poland (CC) ÷	00-800-111-21-22
From Gomel and Mogilev regions	8-10-800-103		# Portugal (CC) ÷	05-017-1234
# Belgium (CC) ♦	0800-10012		Romania (CC) ÷	01-800-1800
# Bulgaria	00800-0001		# Russia (CC) ÷ ♦	
# Croatia (CC) ★	99-385-0112		To call using ROSTELCOM ■	747-3322
# Czech Republic (CC) ♦	00-42-000112		For a Russian-speaking operator	747-3320
# Denmark (CC) ♦	8001-0022		To call using SOVINTEL ■	960-2222
# Finland (CC) ♦	08001-102-80		# San Marino (CC) ♦	172-1022
# France (CC) ♦	0-800-99-0019		# Slovak Republic (CC)	00-421-00112
# Germany (CC)	0130-0012		# Slovenia	080-8808
# Greece (CC) ♦	00-800-1211		# Spain (CC)	900-99-0014
# Hungary (CC) ♦	00▼800-01411		# Sweden (CC) ♦	020-795-922
# Iceland (CC) ♦	800-9002		# Switzerland (CC) ♦	0800-89-0222
# Ireland (CC)	1-800-55-1001		# Turkey (CC) ♦	00-8001-1177
# Italy (CC) ♦	172-1022		# Ukraine (CC) ÷	8▼10-013
# Kazakhstan (CC)	8-800-131-4321		# United Kingdom (CC)	
# Liechtenstein (CC) ♦	0800-89-0222		To call using BT ■	0800-89-0222
# Luxembourg	0800-0112		To call using MERCURY ■	0500-89-0222
# Monaco (CC) ♦	800-90-019		# Vatican City (CC)	172-1022

Is this a great time, or what? :-)

MCI

T & H Doolan's Bar (⊠ 32 George's St., ☎ 051/872764) hosts good, traditional Irish music most summer nights and on weekends year-round.

Outdoor Activities and Sports

GOLF

Waterford Castle Golf Club (⊠ The Island, Ballinakill, Co. Waterford, ☎ 051/871633) is an 18-hole, par-72 course that claims to be Ireland's only true island course. **Faithlegg Golf Club** (⊠ Faithlegg House, Checkpoint, Co. Waterford, ☎ 051/382241), is an 18-hole, par-72 course set in mature landscape on the banks of the River Suir.

HORSEBACK RIDING

Horses are available by the hour at **Kilotteran Equitation Centre** (⊠ Kilotteran, Co. Waterford, ☎ 051/384158).

SPECTATOR SPORTS

Gaelic football and hurling can be seen at the **Waterford GAA Grounds** (⊠ Walsh Park, Co. Waterford, ☎ 051/358219).

Shopping

While in Waterford, definitely pay a visit to the world-famous **Waterford Glass Factory** (⊠ Cork Rd., Kilbarry, ☎ 051/373311; ☞ *above*). The showroom displays an extensive selection of both Waterford crystal and Wedgwood china. The best selection of crystal in Waterford City itself is on show at **Joseph Knox** (⊠ 3 Barronstrand St., ☎ 051/875307). For crystal and china, check out the shopping arcade at **Broad Street Centre** (⊠ Broad St., no phone) where you'll notice an emphasis on tweeds, knitwear, and crystal.

En Route   Our tour now heads down to the coast to the seaside villages of Dunmore East and Tramore. Alternatively, if you're willing to slightly postpone your exploration of coastal villages, you may want to head inland to Carrick-on-Suir, from which point you can head back down to the seaside towns of Dungarvan and Ardmore, or north to Clonmel and other County Tipperary destinations.

Dunmore East

㊹ *16 km/10 mi east of Waterford via 683 and R684.*

Home to an attractive lighthouse, Dunmore East is a quaint, one-street fishing village of thatched cottages at the head of Waterford Harbour. Plenty of small beaches and cliff walks are nearby, and you get a wonderful view of the estuary from the hill behind the village.

Dining

$$–$$$ ✕ **Ship Restaurant.** Fresh, local seafood is the emphasis at this simply furnished restaurant on the ground floor of a 19th-century house overlooking the bay. The food is an imaginative mixture of French and Irish influences. Start off, perhaps, with deep-fried pastry parcels stuffed with fresh crabmeat, or panfried prawns with a lemon, verbena, and thyme mousseline. Entrées include grilled or panfried black sole, or mosaic of sea trout, brill, and crabmeat with champagne sauce. Desserts, such as a chocolate boat filled with white-chocolate mousse on a raspberry coulis, are tempting, and there's a good selection of Irish farmhouse cheeses. ⊠ *Co. Waterford,* ☎ *051/383141 or 051/383144. AE, MC, V. Closed Sun. and Mon. Nov.–Mar. No lunch Sept.–May.*

Tramore

㊺ *11 km/7 mi south of Waterford City on R685.*

☺   Tramore has a 5-km/3-mi-long **beach** that is a popular escape for families from Waterford and other parts of the Southeast, as the many va-

cation homes and camper parks show. It is Ireland's biggest seaside resort, and a dream come true for young children, but it is not to everybody's taste. One part of the seafront is taken over by a 50-acre
amusement park, a miniature railway, and a boating lake, while the upper
half of town is rather more quiet and reserved. At the western end of
the beach, the sand gives way to rocky cliffs guarded by the Metal Man,
a giant cast-iron figure that stands on top of a great pillar. It's said that
if a young woman hops on one foot around the base of the pillar three
times, she will be married within a year. This custom, which is still observed in a lighthearted way, can be traced back to a stone that stood
on the spot centuries ago and was used in ancient Celtic fertility rites.

Dining

$ ✕ **Esquire.** Originally built in 1937 as a "Gentleman's Bar," this quiet
retreat retains an air of gentility. Paul Horan, the internationally trained
owner-chef, applies his skills to fresh local produce. A full à la carte
menu with such dishes as smoked salmon, Irish peppered steak with
brandy, and vegetarian specials is served in the restaurant, while a sim-
pler—and faster—bar-food menu is also available. ⊠ *Cross Market
St.,* ☎ *051/386237. MC, V.*

Outdoor Activities and Sports

GOLF

Tramore Golf Club (⊠ Newtown Hill, Co. Waterford, ☎ 051/386170)
is an 18-hole, championship course overlooked by the Comeragh
Mountains.

SPECTATOR SPORTS

Horse races are held regularly at **Tramore Racecourse** (⊠ Co. Waterford, ☎ 051/381574).

En Route   Eleven kilometers/7 miles west of Tramore on the R675, you join the
coast again at **Annestown,** a smaller, quieter resort town with a good,
sandy beach. Eight kilometers/5 miles beyond this is the former cop-
per-mining center of **Bunmahon,** now a fishing village popular with vacationers. This area offers a pleasant coastal drive with good
views—unusual rock formations in the cliffs interspersed with sand
dunes—as well as various rare flowers and birds. You will find attractive,
easily accessible beaches at **Stradbally** and **Clonea.**

Dungarvan

46 *42 km/26 mi southwest of Tramore on R675.*

Gradually the lowlands of Wexford and eastern Waterford, with their
covering of soft grasses, give way to heath and moorland; the bog is
created and maintained by the wetter climate of the hillier western Waterford countryside. You will see the mountains responsible for this
change in climate rising up behind Dungarvan, the largest coastal
town in County Waterford. This bustling fishing and resort spot is situated at the mouth of River Colligan, which empties into Dungarvan
Bay here. It is a popular base for climbers and hikers.

Dungarvan has several waterside bars with a relaxed, nautical atmosphere. You can feast on local seafood at **The Moorings** (⊠ Davitt's
Quay, ☎ 058/41461). **Merry's** (⊠ Lower Main St., ☎ 058/41974), once
a 17th-century wine merchant's establishment, is a reasonably priced
restaurant with plenty of Old World atmosphere and decorated with
unusual bygones.

Nightlife and the Arts

The **Seanachie Pub** (⊠ Ballymacart, Ring, ☎ 058/46285) is an award-
winning place that features traditional music and dancing in the court-

yard on Sundays during the summer. There is a *ceili* (Irish dance) held nightly during the summer at the Irish-language college, **Colaiste na Rinne** (☎ 058/46104) at Ring, an Irish-speaking village 7 km/5 mi south of Dungarvan.

Outdoor Activities and Sports

BICYCLING

If you are tempted to explore the coast of the Dungarvan area and the nearby Nire Valley by bike, bicycles can be rented at **Tony O'Mahony** (✉ 14 Sexton St., Abbeyside, Co. Waterford, ☎ 058/43346).

FISHING

To rent a skippered boat for deep-sea fishing contact Cormack Walsh at the **Sea Angling Service** (✉ 42 Lower Main St., Co. Waterford, ☎ 058/43514).

GOLF

West Waterford Golf Club (✉ Coolcormack, Co. Waterford, ☎ 058/43216) is an 18-hole, par-72, parkland course playable year-round.

THE NIRE VALLEY, THE BLACKWATER VALLEY, AND COUNTY TIPPERARY

This tour takes you inland, through some of Ireland's most lush pasturelands, to some of its most romantic sites. The Nire Valley, in the mountains between Dugnravan and Clonmel, is a newly popular area for hiking and outdoor pursuits. The Blackwater Valley is renowned for its beauty, its peacefulness, and its excellent fishing. Some of the finest racehorses in the world are raised in the fields of Tipperary, which is also the county in which you will find the magnificent monastic remains on the Rock of Cashel.

The Nire Valley

47 *29 km/18 mi northwest of Dungarvan on R672, 16 km/10 mi southeast of Clonmel.*

A visit to the Nire Valley—one of Ireland's lesser-known wilderness walking areas—is an optional detour on the way from Dungarvan to the Blackwater Valley, and is worthwhile only if you have time to take a walk in this fairly remote spot. But if you do, this little pocket of land that time forgot will enchant you. The valley of the River Nire starts in the village of **Ballymacarbery** and runs along the base of the Comeragh Mountains. Both forest and mountain walks pass through quiet country where sheep far outnumber people. **Knocknagriffin,** the highest peak in the Comeraghs at 2,476 ft, with views back to Waterford on the coast and inland to Tipperary Town, is easily accessible to a moderately fit walker. Walking instructions and maps are provided locally by **Nire Valley Tourist Information** (☎ 052/36455).

Dining and Lodging

$ ✕🝙 **Hanora's Cottage.** The cottage, one of Ireland's premier B&Bs,
★   was built in the heart of the Nire Valley by owner Seamus Wall's great-grandparents, John and Hanora, in the late 19th century. The guest rooms are a generous size by cottage standards and are prettily decorated with chintz curtains and spreads. Nearby golf, riding, and walking are the main activities here (guided walks are offered every Saturday), while the less energetic simply unwind in front of the open fire, which still has the bellows wheel and creel (for hanging pots) from the original cottage kitchen. The evening meal is prepared by the Wall's son Eoin, a promising young chef, and packed lunches are provided using

Seamus's famous home-baked brown bread. ✉ *Ballymacarbery, Co. Waterford,* ☎ *052/36134,* ℻ *052/36540. 8 rooms with bath. Dining room. MC, V.*

Outdoor Activities and Sports

Explore the Nire Valley on horseback by joining a guided hack from **Melody's Riding Stables** (✉ Ballymacarbery, near Clonmel, Co. Tipperary, ☎ 052/36147).

Ardmore

48 *24 km/15 mi south of Dungarvan on N25.*

Ardmore is a delightful village on its own peninsula at the base of a tall cliff, and it's far more restrained in tone than Tramore. Ardmore has ancient roots: in the 5th century, St. Declan is reputed to have disembarked here from Wales 30 years before St. Patrick arrived in Ireland. Ardmore's monastic remains are found on the top of the cliff. The ruined, 12th-century **Cathedral of St. Declan** has some ogham stones inside, and weathered but interesting biblical scenes carved on its west front. The saint is said to be buried in **St. Declan's Oratory,** a small early Christian church that has been partially reconstructed. The 97-★ ft-high **round tower,** one of 70 round towers remaining in Ireland, is in exceptionally good condition and has one of the most spectacular settings. Round towers were built by the early Christian monks as watchtowers and belfries but came to be used as places of refuge for the monks and their valuables during Viking raids. This is the reason the doorway is 15 ft above ground level: Once inside, the monks could pull the ladder into the tower with them.

Lismore

49 *40 km/25 mi northwest of Ardmore on N72.*

The enchanting little town of Lismore is built on the banks of the Blackwater, a river famous for its trout and salmon. Today, with a population of only 920, Lismore is a sleepy village, popular with anglers and romantics. From the 7th to the 12th century, however, it was an important monastic center, founded by St. Carthac (or Carthage), and it had one of the most renowned universities of its time. The only reminders of those days are the village's two cathedrals, a Roman Catholic one from the late 19th century, and the Church of Ireland St. Carthage's, which dates from 1633 and incorporates fragments of an earlier church. The latter cathedral also has some interesting tombs and effigies.

As you cross the bridge entering Lismore, you will be struck by a dramatic view of the magnificent **Lismore Castle,** a vast, turreted gray stone ★ building atop a wooded rock that overhangs the river. There has been a castle here since the 12th century, but the present structure, built by the sixth duke of Devonshire, dates from the mid-19th century. The castle still remains in the same family, and was for many years the Irish home of Fred Astaire's sister, Adele, who married the duke of Devonshire. The upper and lower gardens, open to the public, consist of woodland walks, including an unusual yew walk said to be more than 800 years old, and an impressive display of magnolias, camellias, and shrubs. ☎ *058/54424.* ✑ *£2.50.* ☉ *May–Sept., daily, 1:45–4:45.*

En Route Leave Lismore, heading east on the N72 for 6½ km/4 mi for Cappoquin, a well-known coarse-angling center, and pick up the R669 north into the **Knockmealdown Mountains.** Your route is signposted as the Vee Gap road, the Vee Gap being its summit, from which you get superb views of the Tipperary plain, the Galtee Mountains in the northwest, and a peak called Slievenamon in the northeast. If the visibility is good, you should be able to see the Rock of Cashel, ancient seat of the kings of Munster, some 32 km/20 mi away. Just before you enter the Vee Gap, look for a 6-ft-high mound of stones on the left side of the road. It marks the grave of Colonel Grubb, a local landowner who liked the view so much that he arranged to be buried here standing up so that he could look out on the scene for all eternity.

You might like to break your journey and visit the **Mount Melleray Abbey.** The monastery was founded in 1832 by the Cistercian Order in what was then a barren mountainside wilderness. Over the years the order has succeeded in transforming the site into more than 600 acres of fertile farmland. The monks maintain strict vows of silence, but visitors are permitted into most areas of the abbey. It is also possible to stay in the guest lodge by prior arrangement; from Easter on through the summer, book two weeks in advance. ☎ 058/54404, ℻ 058/52140. ✉ *Free.* ⊙ *Daily 9–6.*

Cahir

㊿ *37 km/23 mi north of Lismore on N8.*

Cahir (pronounced "care") is a small market town on the River Suir, at the crossroads of the busy N24 and N8 roads. **Cahir Castle,** Cahir's main attraction, is a massive limestone structure dating from 1164 and built on rock in the middle of the river. There are regular guided tours and an audiovisual display in the lodge. ☎ 052/41011. ✉ *£2.* ⊙ *Apr.–June and late Sept.–mid-Oct., daily 10–6; June–mid-Sept., daily 9–7:30; late Oct.–Mar., daily 10–1 and 2–4:30.*

Dining and Lodging

$ ✕ **Castle Court Hotel.** If you're looking for a quick bite before or after visiting the castle, forego the overpriced eating spots right around the castle and head a block up the hill for the best bar food in town. The square Georgian building has an elegant and comfortable bar with polished mahogany and well-upholstered seats. Choose from the daily hot specials—bacon and cabbage or seafood bake, for example—or order from the extensive sandwich menu. ✉ *Church St.,* ☎ *052/41210. AE, DC, MC, V.*

$ ✕🏨 **Bansha Castle.** In the heart of quiet, wooded country backed by the Glen of Aherlow (about 8 km/5 mi from Cahir on the N24 Tipperary road) sits this early 20th-century stone house, which incorporates a Norman-style round tower. The atmosphere is relaxed and friendly: The family cat occupies the best fireside armchair in the chintzy but unfussy drawing room. Large rooms, all with great views, are simply furnished with plain carpets and mahogany reproduction pieces. Good home cooking using locally grown organic produce is served in the dining room (guests dine at separate tables). A plethora of nearby outdoor activities includes walking, golf, salmon and trout fishing, and horseback riding at a stable across the road. ✉ *Bansha, Co. Tipperary,* ☎ *062/54187,* ℻ *062/54294. 6 rooms, 4 with bath. Dining room. No credit cards.*

$ ✕🏨 **Kilcoran Lodge Hotel.** This handsome, sprawling, 19th-century former hunting lodge sits amid beautiful countryside 6 km/4 mi outside Cahir beneath the Galtee Mountains. It's conveniently located on the main Cork–Dublin (N8) road. Rooms facing the front have the best views of the beautiful, heather-covered slopes. Guest rooms have Victorian-style furnishings and comfortable beds. The furnishing in the public areas is discreet and stately, and the entire hotel wears the ambience of a country manor house. Overall, it is a good value. ✉ *Co.*

Tipperary, ☎ 052/41288, FAX 052/41994. 23 rooms with bath. Restaurant, bar, indoor pool, health club. AE, DC, MC, V.

Outdoor Activities and Sports

Explore the Galtee mountains and the Glen of Aherlow on horseback with the **Bansha Equestrian Centre** (✉ Bansha, Co. Tipperary, ☎ 062/54194).

OFF THE BEATEN PATH

MITCHELSTOWN CAVES – Make your way first to Ballyporeen (from Cahir, take the R670 and after 7 km/4 mi turn right to the R665 at a T-junction), a one-horse town in the foothills of the Knockmealdown Mountains. A signpost to the right by the town church will direct you to Mitchelstown Caves. Follow this road for 5 km/3 mi. You'll end up at one of the finest subterranean limestone formations in Ireland, created by the motion of water against the rock over millions of years. Some of the caves are massive, extending for miles. Although only a part of the system is open to the public, it is still an impressive and uncommercial sight. *☎ 052/67246. £2.50. Daily 10–6.*

En Route

To your left as you drive from Cahir to Tipperary Town on N24 is the **Glen of Aherlow,** a lovely 10-mi-long wooded stretch skirting the River Aherlow and its tributaries between the Galtee Mountains to the south and the Slievenamuck Hills to the north. The highest summit in the Galtees is the 3,018-ft Galtymore Mountain.

Tipperary Town

(51) *22 km/14 mi southwest of Cahir on N24.*

Tipperary Town, a dairy-farming center at the head of a fertile plain known as the Golden Vale, is a good starting point for climbing and walking in the hills around the Glen of Aherlow. Racehorses are County Tipperary's most famous export. Try to catch a horse race in the southeast if you can: It makes an enjoyable and inexpensive day out.

Outdoor Activities and Sports

Tipperary Town's racetrack is situated 5 km/3 mi west of town and is called, somewhat confusingly, **Limerick Junction Race Course** (✉ Limerick Junction, Co. Tipperary, ☎ 062/52766).

Cashel

(52) *17 km/11 mi northeast of Tipperary Town on N74.*

Cashel is a market town on the busy Cork–Dublin road, which, in spite of the incessant heavy traffic running through it, retains some interesting Victorian shop fronts on its **Main Street,** with four-part windows divided by timber pilasters. The town has a lengthy history as a center of royal and religious power. From roughly AD 370 until 1101, it was the seat of the kings of Munster, and it was probably at one time a center of Druidic worship. Here, according to legend, St. Patrick arrived in about AD 432 and baptized King Aengus, who became Ireland's first Christian ruler. One of the many legends associated with this event is that St. Patrick plucked a shamrock to explain the mystery of the Trinity, thus giving a new emblem to Christian Ireland.

★ The **Rock of Cashel** is one of Ireland's most visited sites, but it is no less worthwhile for its popularity. The rock itself, which is a short walk to the north of the town, rises as a giant, circular mound 200 ft above the surrounding plain; it is crowned by a tall cluster of gray monastic remains. Legend has it that the devil, flying over Ireland in a hurry, took a bite out of the Slieve Bloom Mountains to clear his path (the gap, known as the Devil's Bit, can be seen to the north of the rock) and spat it out here in the Golden Vale. Take some time to linger here, sitting on the grass admiring the view of the plains of Tipperary, and absorbing the atmosphere of its pagan and Christian pasts.

The best approach to the rock is along the **Bishop's Walk,** a 10-minute hike that begins just outside the drawing room of the Cashel Palace Hotel (☞ *below*) on Main Street. (Ask for directions at the reception desk.) As you enter the monastic site, you'll see ahead a rough stone with an ancient cross; this is where, according to legend, St. Patrick baptized King Aengus. (Patrick was old then and drove his staff into the earth to support himself. After the ceremony, it was discovered that the staff had passed through the king's foot and the grass was soaked with blood. Aengus didn't complain, as he thought that this suffering was part of the initiation rite.) The stone at this site was also the Coronation Stone of the Munster kings; it dates from as early as the 4th century.

Actually, the stone that you see upon arrival is a replica; the real one is on display in the new **museum** across from the entrance. Although the museum with its 15-minute audiovisual display is an innovation that some find inappropriate and unnecessary, it does provide enthusiastic young guides, who will ensure that you do not miss the many interesting features of the buildings atop the Rock of Cashel.

The shell of **St. Patrick's Cathedral** is the largest building on the summit. The 13th-century cathedral was originally built in a flamboyant variation on Romanesque style, but it was destroyed by fire in 1495. The restored building was desecrated during the 16th century in a particularly ugly incident, in which hundreds of townspeople who had sought sanctuary in the cathedral were burned to death when Cromwell's forces surrounded the cathedral with turf and set it afire. There is a series of sculptures in the north transept representing the Apostles and other saints and the Beasts of the Apocalypse. Look for the octagonal staircase turret that ascends beside the **Central Tower** to a series of defensive passages built into the thick walls. From the top of the Central Tower, you'll have a wonderful view of the surrounding plains and mountains. Another passage gives access to the **round tower,** a well-preserved building 92 ft high.

The entrance to **Cormac's Chapel,** the best-preserved building on top of the Rock, is behind the south transept of the cathedral. The chapel was built in 1127 by Cormac Macarthy, king of Desmond and bishop of Cashel (combination bishop-kings were not unusual in the early Irish church). Note the high corbeled roof, modeled on the traditional covering of early saints' cells (as at Glendalough [☞ Chapter 3] and Dingle [☞ Chapter 6]); the typically Romanesque, twisted columns around the altar; and the unique carvings around the south entrance. ⊠ *Rock of Cashel,* ☎ *062/61437.* ☐ *£2.50.* ⊙ *Mid-Mar.–June, daily 9:30–5:30; June–Sept., daily 9–7:30; Oct.–mid-Mar., daily 9:30–4:30.*

The **Bru Boru Heritage Center,** where Irish music, dancing, and culture are studied, lies at the base of the rock. Exhibits on aspects of Irish heritage change seasonally, and you can visit the crafts shop, genealogy center, and restaurant (☞ Nightlife and the Arts, below). ☎ *062/61122.* ☐ *Heritage Center free, evening song and storytelling £5.* ⊙ *Heritage Center June–Oct., daily 9 AM–11 PM, and Nov.–May, daily 9–5; evening song and storytelling mid-June–mid-Sept., Tues.–Sun. 9 PM.*

In the same building as the TIO, the **Cashel of the Kings** heritage center explains the historic relationship between the town and the rock and includes a scale model of Cashel as it looked during the 1600s.

The center also offers guided tours of the town. ⊠ *City Hall,* ☎ *062/ 62511.* ☜ *£1.* ⊙ *Jan.–May and Sept.–Dec., daily 9:30–5; June– Aug., daily 9:30–7.*

The **G. P. A. Bolton Library,** on the grounds of the St. John the Baptist Church of Ireland Cathedral, has a particularly notable collection of 12,000 rare books and manuscripts on display. ⊠ *John St.,* ☎ *062/ 61944.* ☜ *£1.50.* ⊙ *Mar.–Oct., Mon.–Sat. 9:30–5:30, Sun. 2:30–5:30.*

Dining and Lodging

$$$$ ✕ **Chez Hans.** This small, converted Victorian church at the foot of the
★ Rock of Cashel oozes Old World charm: Dark wood and tapestries pro- vide an elegant background for tables dressed in beige linen. Traditional French cuisine with a hint of nouvelle takes advantage of fresh Irish in- gredients. Specialties include roast rack of spring lamb with a fresh herb crust and tarragon sauce; the steaks are always excellent, as is the fish. Owner-chef Hans Matthia has compiled an unusual list of 11 house wines, including two exclusive whites from his sister's vineyard in Germany. ⊠ *Rockside, Co. Tipperary,* ☎ *062/61177. Reservations essential. MC, V. Closed Sun., Mon., and 1st 3 wks of Jan. No lunch.*

$$ ✕ **Spearman Restaurant.** This small, front-parlor restaurant is hidden away in the center of Cashel, behind the TIO. Stained-glass windows, hunting prints on the walls, art deco–style side lights, and tall-back chairs disguise the fact that this was, until recently, a grocery store. Young local chef John Spearman is gaining a high reputation for imaginative, affordable food based on the best of fresh local produce. Start perhaps with a warm salad sprinkled with bacon and blue cheese, or a cream of leek and mushroom soup; follow with stylish entrées such as baked chicken breast with a honey and whole-grain-mustard sauce and poached salmon in a creamy tarragon sauce. ⊠ *97 Main St., Co. Tip- perary,* ☎ *062/61143. AE, DC, MC, V. Nov.–Apr.: Closed Mon. No dinner Sun.*

$$$$ ✕🏨 **Cashel Palace.** Dramatically set at the foot of the Rock of Cashel,
★ this 1730s redbrick-and-stone bishop's palace is an exquisite accom- modation, set back from the street in its own garden. The pine-pan- eled public rooms are dominated by twin marble fireplaces and carved pillars; a striking, intricately carved, red-pine staircase sweeps up- stairs. Four-poster canopy beds, antiques, and spacious bathrooms characterize the luxurious guest rooms; ask for one facing the back so that you can enjoy the breathtaking view of the Rock of Cashel. The menu at the elegant Three Sisters Restaurant relies on game in season, local lamb and beef, and fresh fish imaginatively prepared, while the bistro-style basement Buttery Restaurant serves simple light meals all day. ⊠ *Main St., Co. Tipperary,* ☎ *062/62707,* 𝔽𝔸𝕏 *062/61521. 19 rooms with bath. 2 restaurants, bar, fishing. AE, DC, MC, V.*

$$$ 🏨 **Dundrum House Hotel.** Nestled beside the River Muteen, this mag- nificent, four-story Georgian house (12 km/7½ mi outside busy Cashel) is well worth the trek for the quiet of the countryside. Fourteen high- ceilinged bedrooms take up the main house; the rest are in a three-story wing built during the house's previous incarnation as a convent. All of the rooms have large pieces of early Victorian furniture, lovely views of the surrounding parkland, and relaxing pink-and-green decor. The old convent chapel, stained-glass windows intact, is now a cock- tail bar. Elaborate plaster ceilings, attractive period furniture, and open fires make the spacious dining room and lounge inviting. ⊠ *Dundrum, Co. Tipperary,* ☎ *062/71116,* 𝔽𝔸𝕏 *062/71366. 60 rooms with bath. Restaurant, bar, 18-hole golf course, tennis court, fishing. AE, DC, MC, V.*

Nightlife and the Arts

Folksinging, storytelling, and dance are enjoyed from May through September, Tuesday through Saturday at the **Bru Boru Heritage Center** (☎ 062/61122) at the foot of the Rock of Cashel.

Outdoor Activities and Sports

The natural features of the mature Georgian estate at Dundrum House Hotel have been incorporated into an 18-hole, par-72 course for the **County Tipperary Golf and Country Club** (✉ Dundrum House Hotel, Dundrum, Co. Tipperary, ☎ 062/71116). Visitors are welcome every day.

OFF THE BEATEN PATH

HOLYCROSS ABBEY – Attractively situated on the banks of the River Suir (14 km/9 mi north of Cashel on R660), Holycross is a Cistercian abbey church named after a relic of the True Cross. Incorporating late-12th- and early 15th-century architecture, the abbey has been carefully restored and has some well-preserved stone carvings and window traceries. Part of the buildings are again occupied by priests who conduct pilgrimage services at 3 PM every Sunday from April to August. ✉ *Holycross, near Thurles,* ☎ *0504/43241.* *Free.* ⏲ *Easter–Sept., Mon.–Sat. 10:30–5:30, Sun. 2–5:30.*

Clonmel

(53) *24 km/15 mi southeast of Cashel on R688.*

Clonmel, the county seat of Tipperary, is set on the prettiest part of the River Suir, with wooded islands and riverside walks. With a population of about 12,500, it is one of Ireland's largest and most prosperous inland towns. There has been a settlement here since Viking days; in the 14th century the town was walled and fortified as a stronghold of the Butler family. The novelist Laurence Sterne (1713–68), author of *Tristram Shandy,* was born here, and the English novelist Anthony Trollope (1815–82) served for a time in the post office. O'Connell Street, the main thoroughfare, runs east–west and close to the river. At one end is the **West Gate,** built in 1831 on the site of the medieval one. Among other notable buildings are the **Court House** (designed by Sir Richard Morrison), and the **Franciscan friary** and **St. Mary's Church of Ireland,** both of which incorporate remains of earlier churches and some interesting tombs and monuments.

Clonmel is well known in sporting circles as the home of the Tipperary foxhounds and a greyhound-racing center. It is also the headquarters of the Irish Coursing Club. At greyhound races, the dogs chase an electronic "hare" around a fenced-in, miniature racecourse; at a coursing meet they chase and kill a real hare in an open field. The latter, although an ancient sport with its own rules, is not for the squeamish, and meets are frequently disrupted by animal lovers. Hereabouts you're likely to see sleek, slim greyhounds (some worth thousands of pounds) being exercised on leashes along the road.

Dining and Lodging

$ ✕ **Mulcahy's of Clonmel.** This award-winning bar-restaurant serves a selection of salads, snacks, and hot dishes from 10:30 to 7 in the Carvery Food Bar; from 6 PM an extensive à la carte menu is available in the Melleray Restaurant. ✉ *47 Gladstone St.,* ☎ *052/22825. AE, DC, MC, V.*

$$ ✕🏨 **Minella Hotel.** This bowfront, Georgian manor hotel is found in a quiet neighborhood on the bank of the River Suir. The rooms, which are all in wings separate from the main house, afford fine views of the river, particularly those in the front and in the east wing. "Executive" rooms in the new wing are larger, and some have Jacuzzi baths. The Victorian furnishings are comfortable; walls are decorated with hunting prints. The dining room is oak-paneled and has a good reputation for freshly prepared classic cuisine. ✉ *Coleville Rd., Co. Tipperary,* ☎ *052/22388,* FAX *052/24381. 70 rooms with shower. Bar, restaurant, fishing, bicycles. AE, DC, MC, V.*

Outdoor Activities and Sports

GOLF

Clonmel Golf Club (✉ Lyreanearla, Co. Tipperary, ☎ 052/24050) is an 18-hole course on the slopes of the Comeragh Mountains that welcomes visitors daily.

SPECTATOR SPORTS

Clonmel is at the very heart of sporting Ireland. Hurling and Gaelic football are played on Sundays at the **Clonmel GAA Grounds** (✉ Western Rd., Co. Tipperary, ☎ 052/21806). Horse races are held regularly at **Clonmel Racecourse** (✉ Powerstown Park, Co. Tipperary, ☎ 052/22852). Greyhound races are held at night in a relaxed atmosphere with bar and catering facilities at **Clonmel Greyhound Racetrack** (✉ Davis Rd., Co. Tipperary, ☎ 052/21118).

Carrick-on-Suir

54 *20 km/12 mi east of Clonmel on N24.*

Uncharacteristically for towns in Ireland, Carrick-on-Suir lies partly in County Tipperary and partly in County Waterford. The beautifully restored **Ormonde Castle** is the town's main attraction. A Tudor manor house, one of the best-preserved Tudor buildings in Ireland, is the most interesting part of the castle; it was built in 1584 beside an older castle keep overlooking the river. The town is one of several claiming to be the birthplace of Anne Boleyn, and the house is said to have been built in order to entertain her daughter, Queen Elizabeth I, who never visited here. It contains some good, early stucco work, especially in the 100-ft Long Room, and many arms and busts of the English Queen. ☎ *051/640787.* 🔺 *£1.50.* ☉ *May–mid-Oct., daily 9:30–6:30.*

Dining and Lodging

$ ✕🖳 **Cedarfield House.** A pair of tall, three-story bay windows flanks the entrance to this late-18th-century, whitewashed house owned by a Spaniard, Rafa Alvarez, and his Irish wife, Penny. Inside, a log fire burning in the lobby and a large lounge welcome guests. Their dining room (also with an open fire) serves a table d'hôte three-course dinner with Continental options like hake Basque-style (in a light sauce with parsley and peas), as well as classics such as Barbary duck breast with port and red currant sauce. Rafa imports Spanish wine, which guests can sample in the basement wine bar. The large bedrooms, beautifully furnished with Laura Ashley fabrics and Victorian mahogany antiques, have views over rolling green countryside. ✉ *Waterford Rd., Co. Tipperary,* ☎ *051/640164,* FAX *051/641580. 6 rooms with bath. Dining room. MC, V. Closed Jan 8–29.*

Shopping

The **Tipperary Crystal Shop** (✉ Ballynoran, ☎ 051/641188), a factory outlet that offers free tours of the glass-cutting facility weekdays from mid-March to October, also has a showroom open daily.

THE SOUTHEAST A TO Z

Arriving and Departing

By Car

Waterford City, the regional capital, is easily accessible from all parts of Ireland. From Dublin, take the N7 southwest, change to the N9 in Naas, and continue along this highway through Carlow Town and Thomastown until it terminates in Waterford. The N25 travels east–west through Waterford City, connecting it with Cork in the west and Wexford Town in the east. And from Limerick and Tipperary Town, the N24 stretches southeast until it, too, ends in Waterford City.

By Ferry

The region's primary ferry terminal is found just south of Wexford Town at Rosslare. **Stena Sealink** (☎ 053/33115) sails directly between Rosslare Ferryport and Fishguard, Wales. Pembroke, Wales, can be reached on the B+I Lines (☎ 053/33311), and there are three sailings weekly to France's Le Havre and Cherbourg on Irish Ferries (☎ 053/33158).

By Plane

Waterford Regional Airport (☎ 051/75589) is on the Waterford–Ballymacaw road in Killowen. Waterford City is 9½ km/6 mi from the airport. A hackney cab from the airport into Waterford City will cost approximately £12. **British Airways** (☎ 051/75589 or 1800/626747) schedules flights out of this small regional airport daily to Stanstead, England.

Getting Around

By Bus

Bus Éireann (☎ 01/836–6111 or 051/73401) makes the Waterford–Dublin journey four times daily for about £6. There are three buses daily between Waterford City and Limerick, and three between Waterford City and Rosslare. The Cork–Waterford journey is made twice daily. In Waterford City, the terminal is Plunkett Station.

By Car

For the most part, the main roads in the Southeast are of good quality and are free of congestion. Side roads are generally narrow and twisting, and drivers should keep an eye out for farm machinery and animals on country roads.

By Train

Waterford City is linked by **Irish Rail** (☎ 01/836–6222 or 051/73401) service to Dublin. Trains run from Plunkett Station in Waterford City to Dublin four times daily, making stops at Kilkenny, Thomastown, and Carlow Town. The daily train between Waterford City and Limerick makes stops at Tipperary Town and Clonmel. The train between Rosslare and Waterford City runs twice daily.

Contacts and Resources

B&B Reservation Agencies

For a small fee, **Bord Fáilte** will book accommodations anywhere in Ireland through their central reservations system. B&Bs can be booked at local visitor information offices when they are open; however, even these reservations will go through the central reservations system. For more information, *see* Lodging *in* the Gold Guide.

Car Rentals

The major car rental companies have offices at Rosslare Ferryport, and in most large towns rental information can be found through the local tourism office. Typical car-rental prices start at about £40 per day with unlimited mileage, and they usually include insurance and all taxes. **Budget** has offices in Rosslare Harbour (✉ The Ferryport, ☎ 053/33318) and Waterford City (✉ 41 The Quay, ☎ 051/421670). **Murray's Europcar** has offices in Rosslare Harbour (☎ 053/33634) and Waterford City (✉ Cork Rd., ☎ 051/373144).

Emergencies

Police, fire, and **ambulance** (☎ 999 toll-free). **Waterford Regional Hospital** (✉ Ardkeen, ☎ 051/873321).

Guided Tours

Kilkenny: Walking tours of Kilkenny are arranged by Tynan Tours and operate from Monday through Saturday from the Kilkenny TIO (☎ 056/65929 or 056/51500).

Waterford City: Burtchaell Tours lead a Waterford walk at noon and 2 PM daily from March through September. It leaves from the Granville Hotel. For details and off-season information, call 051/873711.

Wexford Town: Walking tours of historic Wexford Town, arranged by the Old Wexford Society, meet at the Talbot Hotel on Trinity Street and at White's Hotel on George's Street every evening during the summer. For details contact the tour guide, Mr. Sam Coe (☎ 053/41081).

Outdoor Activities and Sports

FISHING

For further information on this and other angling activities in the region, contact the **Southern Regional Fisheries Board** (✉ Anglesea St., Clonmel, Co. Tipperary, ☎ 052/23971).

SPECTATOR SPORTS

Tickets to major Gaelic football and hurling matches are available through the **Gaelic Athletic Association** (✉ GAA, Croke Park, Jones's Rd., Dublin 3, ☎ 01/836–3222). For smaller venues, enquire at local TIOs.

Visitor Information

Carlow Town (✉ Hadden Shopping Center, Tullow St., Co. Carlow, ☎ 0503/31554). **Cashel** (✉ City Hall, Co. Tipperary, ☎ 062/61333, FAX 062/61789). **New Ross** (✉ Harbour Centre, The Quay, Co. Wexford, ☎ 051/21857). **Tipperary City** (✉ 3 James St., Co. Tipperary, ☎ 062/51457). **Kilkenny** (✉ Rose Inn St., ☎ 056/51500, FAX 056/63955). **Rosslare** (✉ Rosslare Ferry Terminal, Kilrane, Rosslare Harbour, Co. Wexford, ☎ 053/33622, FAX 053/33421). **Tramore** (✉ Railway Sq., Co. Waterford, ☎ 051/81572). **Waterford City** (✉ 41 The Quay, Co. Waterford, ☎ 051/875788, FAX 051/877388). **Wexford Town** (✉ Crescent Quay, Co. Wexford, ☎ 053/23111, FAX 053/41743).

6 The Southwest

In and Around Cork and Killarney, the Ring of Kerry, the Dingle Peninsula, and Shannonside

Spectacular's the word for the Southwest, where the superlatives flow like the Rivers Lee and Blackwater through County Cork. Five-star scenery is everywhere, from Kinsale along the coast west to Mizen Head in the far southwest corner, to the glorious mountains and lakes of Killarney. And the food! Thanks to its accomplished chefs and the bounty of farms, fields, lakes, and coast, County Cork has become to the Irish food world what California is to America's. You'll also find a mild climate, the nation's second- and third-largest cities, and large Irish-speaking areas: What more could you ask for?

By Alannah
Hopkin

WE RECEIVE HUNDREDS OF LETTERS a year from visitors who have just returned from a trip to Ireland. These letters can go on for pages, with astonishingly detailed accounts of people met, things done, places stayed, meals eaten. What you learn from reading some of these letters is that many visitors—especially those who are making a second, third, or fourth visit to Ireland—fly into Shannon and never leave the Southwest. Why? There's no one single overriding reason that makes this region such an attractive destination, but instead dozens of great reasons.

First, there's the Southwest's gorgeous natural and rural beauty. South of the city of Cork, the resort town of Kinsale is the gateway to a relatively unspoiled coastline containing Roaring Water Bay, with its many islands, and the magnificent natural harbor, Bantry Bay. Southwest of Bantry are spectacular Cape Clear and Mizen Head. Three peninsulas jut far out into the Atlantic: the Beara in County Cork and the Iveragh and the Dingle in County Kerry (the road known as the Ring of Kerry makes a complete circuit of the Iveragh Peninsula). Also in County Kerry, Killarney's sparkling blue lakes and magnificent sandstone mountains constitute one of the most splendidly romantic landscapes in the whole country (though there is a price: the area in July and August is packed with visitors). Lush green fields bordered by darker green hedgerows blanket the area's gently rolling hills. Miles and miles of pretty country lanes meander through this rich but sparsely populated farmland.

The Southwest also claims Ireland's second and third largest cities—Cork and Limerick. The pace of life here is perceptibly slower than in Dublin—not surprising considering how substantially smaller these cities are from the capital. Even in the Southwest's major cities, to be in a hurry hereabouts is to verge on demonstrating bad manners. It was probably a Kerryman who first remarked that when God made time, he made plenty of it.

As you look over thick, fuchsia hedges at thriving dairy farms or stop off at a wayside restaurant to sample the region's seafood and locally raised meat, it is hard to imagine that some 150 years ago this area was decimated by famine. Thousands perished in the fields and the workhouses, and thousands more took "coffin ships" from Cobh in Cork Harbour to the New World. Between 1846 and 1849 the population of Ireland fell by an estimated 2½ million, or roughly 30 percent (according to the 1841 census, the Irish population was 8,175,124). Many small villages in the Southwest were wiped out.

The region was battered again in the War for Independence and the Civil War that was fought with intensity in and around "Rebel Cork" between 1919 and 1921. Economic recovery only began in the late '60s, which led to a boom in hotel construction and renovation—not always, alas, in the style most appropriate to the area. Around the Shannon estuary you move into "castle country," littered with ruined castles and abbeys as a result of Elizabeth I's attempt to subdue the old Irish province of Munster in the 16th century. Limerick City, too, bears the scars of history from a different confrontation with the English, the Siege of Limerick, which took place in 1691.

Outside of Killarney and Shannon, tourist development remains fairly low-key. The area is trying to absorb more visitors without losing too much of what attracts them in the first place: uncrowded roads, unpolluted beaches and rivers, easy access to golf and fishing, and unspoiled scenery where wildflowers, untamed animals, and rare birds (which have all but disappeared in more industrialized European countries) still thrive.

Pleasures and Pastimes

Dining

The Southwest—especially County Cork—rivals Dublin as Ireland's food-culture epicenter. Cork has astonishing resources: sparkling waters full of a wide array of fish, acre after acre of potato fields, cows galore, wild mushrooms and berries, and much, much more. Cork's dedicated, inventive chefs turn this bounty into a feast—all, it often seems, for your benefit—in food markets (Cork City's English Market, most notably), bakeries, cafés, restaurants, B&Bs, and country houses. In tiny Shanagarry, Darina and Tim Allen train hundreds of chefs every year at their Ballymaloe Cookery School. Outstanding restaurants and the International Gourmet Festival in October draw crowds to Kinsale, the "Gourmet Capital of Ireland." Whether trained at home or abroad, area chefs put a premium on fresh, local (often organically grown) produce. To sample the region's best cuisine, consult our five-day gastronomic tour (☞ Great Itineraries, *below*).

Very few restaurants in Southwest Ireland require a jacket and tie or fancy dinner attire. Unless specified below, you should feel entirely at ease with your own interpretation of "casual but neat." In July and August and on weekends from May to October, the places we've listed are very popular, and it is essential to book a table in advance. Be patient with delays and junior front-of-house staff, who are often culinary arts students obtaining their first work experience. For price ranges, *see* Chart 1(A) *in* On the Road with Fodor's.

Lodging

Some of the most sumptuous country-house hotels in the country are in the Southwest. You'll also find more modest establishments, many in spectacular seaside locations. Though some country houses appear grand, their main aim is to provide a relaxed stay in beautiful surroundings. A good pair of walking boots and a sensible raincoat are more useful here than a formal wardrobe. If you want to dress for dinner, as some people do, feel free. By and large, however, informality is the order of the day. Keep in mind that facilities may be minimal: Only expensive hotels have fitness centers, for instance. At the least, most hotels can organize golf, deep-sea fishing, freshwater angling, and horseback riding. Many B&Bs have introduced private bathrooms and, in the larger towns, televisions and direct-dial phones in rooms. Accommodations in West Cork, Killarney, and Dingle are seasonal: Between November and March, many places close down; outside these months, especially from July to mid-October, hotels are busy, so book well in advance. If your first choice for a hotel is full, ask for a recommendation to similar lodgings nearby. For price ranges, *see* Chart 2(B) *in* On the Road with Fodor's.

Nightlife and the Arts

As elsewhere in rural Ireland, social life centers around the pub; a visit to the "local" is the best way to find out what's going on. Residents have not lost their natural curiosity about "strangers," as visitors are called. You will frequently be asked, "Are you enjoying your holiday?" "Yes" is not a good enough answer: What the locals are really after is your life story. Mid-June through September, you'll find musical entertainment in pubs on most nights; in other seasons, Thursday through Sunday are the busiest times. Dingle is the best place for traditional Irish music; elsewhere, pubs and clubs offer a mix of traditional, Irish,

and folk ballads; country and rock classics; and a touch of New Orleans jazz in Cork and Kinsale. Spontaneous music sessions are common, especially on the Dingle Peninsula; elsewhere, performances
usually begin around 9. Nightclubs are usually attached to hotels or
bars; they are open from 10:30 PM until 1 or 2 AM. Expect to pay a
£5–£8 cover fee.

Outdoor Activities and Sports

BICYCLING

You'll find some of the most spectacular scenery in the country around
Glengarriff, Killarney, and **Dingle.** The length of the hills—rather than
their steepness—is the challenge here, but without the hills there
wouldn't be such great views. A less strenuous option, equally scenic,
but on a smaller scale, is the coast of West Cork between **Kinsale** and
Glengarriff. The **Beara Peninsula** proves very popular with cyclists who
enjoy its varied coastal scenery and relative lack of traffic. Traffic can
be a problem in July and August on the **Ring of Kerry,** where there is
a lack of alternative routes to the one main circuit. Because of the various mountain ranges in the area, rain is never far off, except on the
hottest summer days, so always carry a light, waterproof jacket. The
Irish Tourist Board publication, "Cycling Ireland" (£2), suggests six
bicycling circuits that can be made in the region. For bicycle rentals,
expect to pay about £8 per day, or £32 for seven days, with a £40 refundable deposit.

FISHING

Besides an abundance of facilities for sea angling and a wealth of
salmon and trout rivers, the Southwest has the bonus of scenic surroundings—be it the black-slate cliffs of the coast or the lush vegetation of Killarney and the Ring of Kerry. **Shore fishing** is available all
along the coast, from Cobh in the east to Foynes in the west. The whole
region offers excellent opportunities for **lake and river fishing,** although most anglers head for Waterville or Killarney. Coarse anglers
will find pike at Macroom and coarse-angling facilities at Mallow and
Fermoy. The **deep-sea fishing** season runs from April to October. Boat
rentals cost about £20 per person per day. Boats can be rented at Ballycotton, Cork Harbour in Cobh, Midleton, Passage West, Crosshaven,
Kinsale, Courtmacsherry, Clonakilty, Castletownshend, Valentia Island,
Fenit, and Dingle.

GOLF

Many of the Southwest's 18-hole courses are world-famous, championship clubs set amid wonderful scenery. The leading courses in the
region—**Cork Golf Club, Waterville Golf Links, Killarney Golf and Fishing Club,** and **Tralee Golf Club**—are all covered in depth in Chapter 10.

HIKING

Particularly in the far southwest around Killarney and Dingle, this is
classic hiking country, with spectacular scenery and a feeling of wilderness (even though you're never more than 3 or 4 km/2 or 3 mi from
civilization). On higher ground, fog can come down very quickly, so
take local advice on weather conditions and adjust your schedule accordingly. Two signposted, long-distance walking trails wind through
the region: The 209-km/130-mi **Kerry Way** begins in Killarney and loops
around the Ring of Kerry. The 153-km/95-mi **Dingle Way** loops from
Tralee around the Dingle Peninsula. Both routes consist of paths and
"green roads" (unsurfaced) with some stretches linked by surfaced roads.
In general, these routes, although rough underfoot, are suitable for families, particularly in summer. The 209-km/130-mi **Beara Way** is a
mainly off-road walk around the rugged Beara Peninsula in West Cork.
Other good, off-the-highway walks can be found in Killarney Na-

tional Park; Gougane Barra (northeast of Ballylickey off the R584), Farran (off the N22 about 16 km/10 mi west of Cork City) and Doneraile Forest (off the N20 about 8 km/5 mi north of Mallow) parks in County Cork; and Currachase Forest Park (east of Askeaton off the N69), County Limerick.

Exploring the Southwest

Our coverage of the Southwest is organized into five tours: **Cork City and Environs** (which includes the ever-popular Blarney Castle, home of the Blarney Stone), **East Cork and the Blackwater Valley** (covering Youghal and Ballymaloe), **Kinsale to Glengarriff via Bantry Bay** (Mizen Head, Cape Clear, and other points in the far southwest), the **Ring of Kerry, In and Around Killarney,** the **Dingle Peninsula,** and **North Kerry and Shannonside.** We begin in Cork (under the assumption that you'll approach from points east) and make a clockwise sweep of the area. We end on the northern fringe, crossing over the border from County Kerry into County Limerick, and then briefly into the very southeastern reaches of County Clare in the area immediately around Shannon Airport. If you fly into Shannon, you can easily do the entire sequence of tours in reverse, or pick and choose from those that interest you.

The big must-see attraction in the Southwest, Killarney, requires a full day (partly on foot) to appreciate. Killarney also makes a good base for exploring the Ring of Kerry and the Dingle Peninsula. The main cities in the area—Cork, Tralee, and Limerick—have quiet charm, but they cannot compete with the magnificent scenery farther west. Kinsale is a good starting point for a leisurely exploration of the coast west to Bantry, which can take one day or three, depending on your appetite for unscheduled stops and impromptu exploration. Two national parks, Glengarriff near the sea and Gougane Barra in the mountains, are also well worth visiting.

Numbers in the text correspond to numbers in the margin and on the Southwest, Cork City, and Killarney Area maps.

Great Itineraries

IF YOU HAVE 3 DAYS

Base yourself in 🚉 **Killarney Town** ㊽ for the two nights of this tour. Reserve one day for a leisurely exploration of **Killarney**'s famous lakes and mountains. Visit the **Gap of Dunloe** ㊿ on an organized tour and walk or ride horseback through the gap itself, crossing the lake beyond by rowboat. The next day head for the Ring of Kerry via **Killorglin** ㊼ and enjoy the mix of subtropical vegetation caused by the nearby Gulf Stream and rugged cliffs. You need reasonable visibility for the Ring of Kerry, so if the seaward weather promises mist, head inland instead to **Gougane Barra Forest Park,** where the hermit St. Finbarr had his mountain retreat. Follow the granite-walled **Pass of Keimaneigh** to **Bantry** ㉞. A cliff-top road runs between Bantry and Glengarriff with wonderful views out to sea along the 24-km/15-mi inlet of Bantry Bay. The stretch of road between **Glengarriff** ㉟ and Killarney Town, known as the tunnel road, is one of Ireland's most famous scenic routes, and it comes into Killarney Town past the **Ladies' View** ㊽, little changed since it impressed Queen Victoria's ladies-in-waiting almost 150 years ago.

IF YOU HAVE 5 DAYS FOR A GASTRONOMIC TOUR

Apart from the innovative chefs working in the kitchens of some of Dublin's finest restaurants, Cork is indisputably Ireland's leading food region (☞ Dining, *above*)—with superlative country-house hotels serving food prepared from the freshest local ingredients; the country's lead-

ATLANTIC OCEAN

CLARE

Mouth of the Shannon

Kilkee
Kilrush
Killimer
Tarbert
74 Glin
Ballybunion
Listowel
73
Abbeyfeale

N67
N68
N69
R523

Brandon Bay
Tralee Bay
Tralee
72
71
Blennerville
Castlemaine
Castleisland

Kilmakedar Church Gallarus Oratory
70 Mt. Brandon
Ballydavid
Connor Pass
Kilcummin
DINGLE PENINSULA
R559
N21
N70
R578
R57

Dún an Óir
68 69
Ballyferriter
66 67
Dunquin
65
60 **Dingle Town**
R561
59
Slea Head
61
63 62
Ventry Dunbeg
Annascaul
Inch
N22

Blasket Islands
64
Dingle Bay
Rossbeigh **46**
Glenbeigh Kerry **45**
47 **Killorglin**
Killarney
48 — 58
N72
R562

Caragh Lake
Lake Leane
Muckross

Cahirciveen
44
Ring of
N70
IVERAGH PENINSULA
KERRY *Upper Lake*
KILLARNEY NATIONAL PARK
N22

Valentia Island **42**
Ballinskelligs Bay
39 **Staigue Fort**
R568
N70
R569
37 **Kenmare**
R584

Skellig Islands **43**
41
Waterville
N70
Ring of Kerry
38
Sneem
Parknasilla
Tahilla
R571
Gougane Barra Forest Park

Caherdaniel
40
Kenmare River
BEARA PENINSULA
35 **Glengarriff**
Garnish Island **36**
Ballylickey
R586

Castletown Bere
R572
34 **Bantry**
Dursey Island
Bere Island
Bantry Bay
Durrus

Ballydehob
N71
Skibbereen
Schull
R592
Liss Ard Foundation
30
R596
Castletownshe

Mizen Head Signal Station
Goleen
Crookhaven
Roaring Water Bay
R595
31 **Baltimore**
32
Sherkin Island
33
Cape Clear Island

Celtic Sea

KEY
— Rail Lines
🚢 Ferry

0 _____ 20 miles
0 _____ 30 km

N

ing cooking school; and its self-proclaimed "gourmet capital." If you're a dedicated foodie or you've already done a wider sweep through the country and you want to focus on one region, our 5-day tour, taking in the region's best food, may be for you. Begin in **Cork City** ①–⑱ and stop in at the city's not-to-be-missed **English Market** ⑪. You can stay overnight and also dine at the 🏨 **Arbutus Lodge,** sampling their eight-course "tasting menu," which will introduce you to French-Irish haute cuisine, and choosing from their widely acclaimed wine list. On the next day head out to 🏨 **Ballymaloe House** in **Shanagarry** ㉓, for 50 years the Allen family farm and today run by three generations of the family. The decor is simple but elegant country style, and the emphasis is on fresh local produce and fish from nearby **Ballycotton.** If you plan carefully, you may be able to fit in a one-day cooking class at the **Ballymaloe Cookery School and Gardens,** a mile away, also run by the Allen family. At the least, the gardens, with their wide variety of herbs and edible plants, are a nice way to see food before it hits the table. Next drive northwest to **Mallow** ㉕ in the Blackwater Valley to 🏨 **Longueville House,** another family-run operation, albeit on a grander scale. Proprietor William O'Callaghan's President's Restaurant earns raves as one of the finest in Ireland; he also runs one of Ireland's only vineyards. Next head to **Kenmare** ㊲, where the 🏨 **Sheen Falls Lodge** has 300 acres of semitropical gardens beside the fall of the river Sheen; stroll in the gardens before dining in La Cascade restaurant. The following day drive back toward the pretty waterfront village of **Kinsale** ㉗, where spots like **The Oystercatcher** and the 🏨 **Blue Haven Hotel** have helped earn the town the title of "gourmet capital of Ireland." Return to Cork City the next day.

IF YOU HAVE 7 DAYS

Start at **Bunratty Castle** ㊽, the nearest attraction to Shannon Airport, and a must-see for first-time visitors. Continue on to 🏨 **Limerick City** ㊻ and take a look at either the restored **King John's Castle** or the Irish landscape paintings and Celtic and medieval treasures at the **Hunt Museum.** Spend the night in Limerick; the following day, head south for **Blarney** ⑲, with its castle, where you can kiss the Blarney Stone and browse around Ireland's largest selection of craft shops. Then proceed to 🏨 **Cork City** ①–⑱, where you can make an overnight stop. Take a walk around the city center and enjoy the city's lively nightlife, including pubs, restaurants, and theater. The next day head east up to Cork Harbour to visit **Cobh** ㉑, where the Queenstown Heritage Centre documents the history of Irish emigration. Cross the harbor by ferry and visit 🏨 **Kinsale** ㉗, an historic little port built on hilly slopes, with a star-shape fort dating from 1620 on its large, natural harbor. The town is a fashionable resort with gourmet restaurants and some good crafts shops and art galleries. The following day, drive through scenic West Cork around Bantry Bay and into **Glengarriff** ㉟, where you can take a boat to the subtropical gardens of **Garnish Island** ㊱, just a few minutes offshore. Continue on to **Kenmare** ㊲, a pretty village on a river estuary, and then go on to 🏨 **Killarney Town** ㊽ via a scenic road known as the Windy Gap. Spend the night here and make an early start the next day, either taking a half-day tour of the **Gap of Dunloe** ㊿ or viewing the splendid scenery in the park around **Muckross House** (56). In the afternoon, leave for the Ring of Kerry, driving past **Sneem** ㊳ through subtropical vegetation to 🏨 **Waterville** ㊶ or 🏨 **Caragh Lake** on the west side of the Ring. From **Cahirciveen** ㊹ you can see the Dingle Peninsula across the water, and the stretch of road that you will take to reach 🏨 **Dingle Town** (60), the next overnight stop and the best base for exploring the peninsula. A short drive outside town, you'll find the spectacular cliffs and early Christian remains beyond **Slea Head** (63).

On the final day, drive across the Connor Pass and up to **Tralee** ⑫, which has a lively museum devoted to County Kerry's past, and a steam railway running from nearby **Blennerville** ⑪. From Tralee, return to Limerick City and Shannon Airport on the Adare road (N21) or take the N69 to Tarbert and the ferry into County Clare to reach Galway and the west of Ireland.

When to Tour the Southwest

The weather is most likely to be warm and sunny in July and August, but there is no guarantee against rain. July and August are the busiest months with Irish, British, and Continental tourists heading for the area in large numbers. Visiting in high season means the bars and restaurants of the area will be lively, but also crowded. The best time to visit the Southwest is in the "shoulder seasons"—May through June and September through October, when the weather will still be mild; most if not quite all accommodations and attractions will be open, and crowds can be avoided. Lodging and restaurants outside the main cities are seasonal and choice will be limited between November and mid-March. However, not everything closes down at this time of year, and the roads and scenic spots will be blissfully uncrowded. It may be wet, but it seldom gets cold in this part of the world.

CORK CITY AND ENVIRONS

The major metropolis of the south, Cork is Ireland's second-largest city (population 175,000), but put this in perspective: Roughly half of Ireland's 3.6 million people live in and around Dublin, a city 10 times the size. Small though it may be relative to the capital city, Cork is a spirited, lively place, with a formidable pub scene, some of the country's best traditional music, a respected and progressive university, art galleries, and offbeat cafés.

The city received its first charter in 1185 from Prince John of Norman England, and it gets its name from the Irish word *corcaigh*, which means "marshy place." The original 6th-century settlement was spread over 13 small islands in the River Lee. Major development occurred during the 17th and 18th centuries with the expansion of the butter trade, and many attractive Georgian-style buildings with wide bowfront windows were constructed during this time. As late as 1770, Cork's main streets—Grand Parade, Patrick Street, and the South Mall—were submerged under the Lee. Around 1800, when the Lee was partially dammed, the river was divided into two streams that now flow through the city, leaving the main business and commercial center on an island, not unlike Paris's Ile de la Cité. As a result, the city features a number of bridges and quays, which, although initially confusing, add greatly to the port's unique character. (A word of warning to drivers: They also can contribute to traffic bottlenecks during rush hours.)

"Rebel Cork" emerged as a center of the nationalist Fenian movement in the 19th century. The city suffered great damage during the War of Independence in 1919–21, when much of its center burned. Cork is now fast regaining some of its former glory through sensitive commercial development and an ongoing program of inner-city renewal. In late summer and early autumn, Cork hosts some of Ireland's premier festivals, including October's huge **Cork Jazz Festival,** which draws about 50,000 visitors from around the world; the **Cork Film Festival,** also in October; and a number of others. *See* Festivals and Seasonal Events *in* Chapter 1 *and* Nightlife and the Arts, *below,* for more information.

Cork City

❶ *254 km/158 mi south of Dublin, 105 km/65 mi west of Limerick City.*

Cork's historical sights, though spread out, are still best visited on foot, for the most part; you may want to take a bus to the city's westernmost sights. Patrick Street is the center city's main thoroughfare.

❷ **Patrick's Bridge** is a good place to start a walk around the city. From the bridge, you can look across the river to St. Patrick's Hill, where tall Georgian houses have mostly been converted to doctors' offices. The hill is so steep that steps are cut into the pavement. The tower of **❸** **St. Mary's Pro-Cathedral** dominates in part the slopes of the hilly north city. If you're interested in tracing Cork ancestors, the presbytery at St. Mary's has records of births and marriages dating from 1784. ⊠ *Cathedral Walk.* 🎫 *Free.* ⊙ *Daily 9–6.*

❹ Also in the north city, **St. Anne's Church** has the pepper-pot Shandon Steeple, which has a four-sided clock and is topped with a golden, salmon-shape weather vane. The Bells of Shandon were immortalized in an atrocious but popular 19th-century ballad of that name. If you climb the 120-ft tower, you can have the bells rung out over Cork. ⊠ *Church St.,* 🎫 *£1; with bell tower £1.50.* ⊙ *May–Oct., Mon.–Sat. 9:30–5; Nov.–Apr., Mon.–Sat. 10–3:30.*

Firkin Crane, Cork's former 18th-century butter market, stands beside St. Anne's Church. This round building houses two small performing spaces. Adjacent is the Shandon Craft Market. You can make your way back to the quays along the Lee via the pretty lanes lined with small, tidy houses.

❺ **Patrick Street,** which cuts a graceful curve, lies to the south of Patrick Bridge. If you look up above some of the standardized plate-glass and plastic shop facades here, you'll see examples of the bowfront Georgian windows that are emblematic of old Cork. The street saw some of the city's worst fighting in the years 1919–21, during the War of Independence. Roches Stores is the largest department store in town; Cash's, next door, is the most upscale. Tall ships that once served the butter trade used to load up before heading downstream to the open sea on **Merchant's Quay,** right off Patrick Street. The design of the large shopping center on the site evokes the warehouses of old.

The **bus station** is one block downstream from (west of) Patrick Bridge if you face the river. The Brian Boru Bridge, in front of the bus station, leads to Kent (Rail) Station, which is north of the river two blocks to the right. **Winthrop Street** is a pedestrian mall off Patrick Street. Winthrop leads to Oliver Plunkett Street, a busy, narrow road known **❻** for its fashion boutiques and jewelry stores, and home of the **General Post Office,** a neoclassical building with an elegant, colonnaded facade. The friendly, old **Long Valley** (⊠ Winthrop St., ☎ 021/272144), popular with artists, writers, students, and eccentrics, serves tea, coffee, and pints, as well as enormous sandwiches.

❼ Housed in the 1724 building that was once the city's Custom House, the **Crawford Municipal Art Gallery** is Ireland's most respected provincial art gallery. Its permanent collection includes a number of landscape paintings depicting Cork in the 18th and 19th centuries. Irish painters whose work is particularly worth looking for include William Leech (1881–1968), Daniel Maclise (1806–70), James Barry (1741–1806), and Nathanial Grogan (1740–1807). The Crawford regularly mounts adventurous exhibitions of modern Irish and foreign artists. Its café, run by the Allen family of Ballymaloe (☞ Shanagarry, *below*), is a good

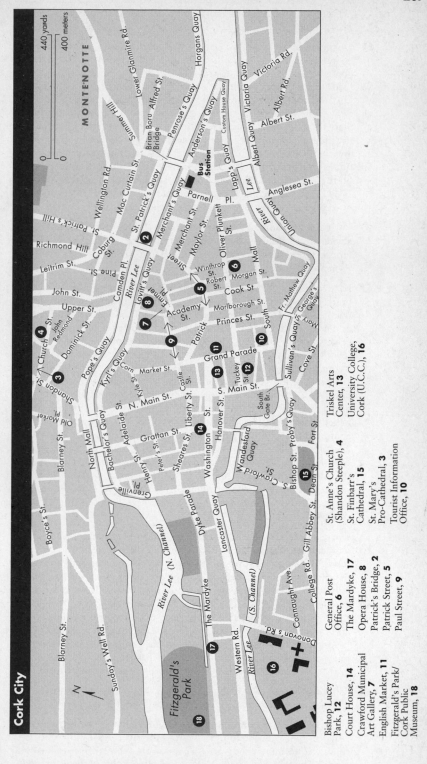

Cork City

MONTENOTTE

440 yards
400 meters

N

Bishop Lucey
Park, **12**
Court House, **14**
Crawford Municipal
Art Gallery, **7**
English Market, **11**
Fitzgerald's Park/
Cork Public
Museum, **18**

General Post
Office, **6**
The Mardyke, **17**
Opera House, **8**
Patrick's Bridge, **2**
Patrick Street, **5**
Paul Street, **9**

St. Anne's Church
(Shandon Steeple), **4**
St. Finbarr's
Cathedral, **15**
St. Mary's
Pro-Cathedral, **3**
Tourist Information
Office, **10**

Triskel Arts
Center, **13**
University College,
Cork (U.C.C.), **16**

place in town for a light lunch or a homemade sweet treat. ⊠ *Emmet Pl.,* ☎ *021/273377.* ⌑ *Free.* ⊙ *Weekdays 9–5, Sat. 9–1.*

⑧ On the left of the Crawford Gallery, the **Opera House** (⊠ Lavitt's Quay), an unfortunate concrete building built in 1965, replaced the ornate old opera house, which was destroyed in a fire. To the west of the Craw-
⑨ ford Gallery, **Paul Street** runs through the heart of the old French Quarter, where Huguenots who fled religious persecution in France settled. Pretty lanes radiate off the street, while the piazza is a popular place for street theater and entertainment. The shops here offer the best in modern Irish design—from Donegal tweeds to handblown glass— and, in an alley north of the piazza, shops sell a good selection of antiques. The best cakes, fruit tarts, and ice cream in Cork are handmade on the premises of **Gingerbread House** (⊠ Paul St. Piazza, ☎ 021/ 276411). Sit at the big refectory tables for a made-to-order sandwich or a roll and coffee, before selecting a slice of the day's baking.

⑩ The Cork City **Tourist Information Office (TIO)** is in the Grand Parade, a wide thoroughfare at the western extreme of Patrick Street. ⊠ *Tourist House, Grand Parade,* ☎ *021/273251,* 🆂 *021/273504.* ⊙ *Weekdays 9–6, Sat. 9–1.*

★ **⑪** Food lovers should head right for the **English Market,** housed in an elaborate, red-and-brown-brick and cast-iron Victorian building. (Its official name is The Princes Street Market, and it's also known locally as the Covered Market.) A turn-of-the-century predecessor to today's urban farmers' markets, the market is a great place to get a sense of Cork's thriving food scene. Among the 140 stalls, keep an eye out for **Maunaclea Farm Cheeses,** run by Martin Guillemot and Anne Marie Jaumaud, who left France for Cork and now sell some of the area's finest cheeses. Local coffee lovers claim **Iago,** Sean Calder-Potts' deli, has the best coffee in town; it also sell sandwiches made from their freshly baked *ciabatta* (a slipper-shaped Italian bread). Olives from Greece, Spain, France, and Italy; olive oil; and olive-oil soap can all be had at **The Olive Stall.** Kay O'Connell's **Fish Stall,** in the market's legendary fresh-fish alley, sells local smoked salmon. **O'Reilly's Trip and Drisheen** sells a Cork specialty, tripe (cow's intestines) and *drisheen* (blood sausage). Upstairs is the Farmgate, an excellent café (☞ Dining and Lodging, *below*). ⊠ *Entrances on Grand Parade and Princes St.* ⊙ *Weekdays 9–5:30, Sat. 9–1.*

Opened in 1985 in celebration of the 800th anniversary of Cork's Nor-
⑫ man charter, **Bishop Lucey Park** is a tiny, green oasis in the center of town. During excavation for the park, workers unearthed portions of the city's original fortified walls, now preserved just inside the arched entranceway. Sculpture by contemporary Cork artists is scattered
⑬ throughout the park. The **Triskel Arts Center,** north of the Bishop Lucey Park and reached by an alleyway off Grand Parade, has a small auditorium that shows films and live theater, a coffee shop, and exhibitions of contemporary arts and crafts. It's a good place to get the pulse of artsy goings-on about town. ⊠ *Tobin St.,* ☎ *021/272022.* ⌑ *Free.* ⊙ *Weekdays 11–6, Sat. 11–5, and during advertised performances.*

⑭ The **Court House** (⊠ Washington and S. Main Sts.) with an imposing Corinthian portico, dates from 1835 and is still in use today.

⑮ South of the River Lee's south channel, **St. Finbarr's Cathedral** may be reached by taking the footpath across the river in Grand Parade and following the quays westward. (This was once the entrance to medieval Cork.) The three spires of the 19th-century Gothic cathedral are visible up ahead on Bishop Street. St. Finbarr established a monastery on this site around AD 650 and is credited as the founder of Cork. The present cathedral, completed in 1879, belongs to the Church of Ireland and houses a 3,000-pipe organ. ✉ *Bishop St.* ☎ *021/963387.* 🎟 *Free.* ◷ *Daily 9–6.*

⑯ The main quadrangle of **University College, Cork** (known as U. C. C., with about 10,000 students) is a fine example of 19th-century university architecture in the Tudor-Gothic style, reminiscent of many Oxford and Cambridge colleges. Several ancient ogham stones are on display, as well as occasional exhibitions of archival material from the old library. The **Honan Collegiate Chapel,** to the east of the quadrangle, was built in 1916 and modeled on the 12th-century, Hiberno-Romanesque style, which is best exemplified by the remains of **Cormac's Chapel** at Cashel (☞ Chapter 5). Most noteworthy about the chapel are its stained-glass windows (1915), some of the finest created by Harry Clarke, widely regarded as Ireland's most distinguished stained-glass craftsmen of the period. The U. C. C.'s Doric porticoed gates are at the corner of Donovan's and Western roads, about a mile up Washington Street and the Western Road. ☎ *021/276871.* 🎟 *Free.* ◷ *Weekdays 9–5.*

⑰ **The Mardyke** is a popular riverside walk where cricket is played on
⑱ summer weekends. Bordered on one side by the Mardyke, **Fitzgerald's Park** contains the **Cork Public Museum,** a Georgian mansion that houses a well-planned exhibit of Cork's history from ancient times to the present day, with a strong emphasis on the city's Republican history. ☎ *021/270679.* 🎟 *Free.* ◷ *Weekdays 11–1 and 2:15–5, Sun. 3–5; closed bank holidays.*

Dining and Lodging

$$$ ✕ **Cafe Paradiso.** This simple, café-style restaurant near the university and across from Jurys Hotel serves Mediterranean-style food, which is so tasty that even dedicated meat eaters forget it's vegetarian. The room is basic, with assorted tables and spindly chairs; the daily special is chalked up on a board, and the food is served on enormous platters. Chef Denis Cotter garners raves for his risottos with seasonal vegetables (such as pumpkin and radicchio), his gougères-choux pastry rings with savory fillings, and his excellent, homemade desserts. ✉ *16 Lancaster Quay, Western Rd., Co. Cork,* ☎ *021/277939. MC, V. Closed Sun.*

$$$ ✕ **The Ivory Tower.** Seamus O'Connell is the adventurous, young owner-chef of this small town-center restaurant. Bare wooden floors and stick-back chairs of the first-floor Georgian dining room are warmed by the original artwork, but the real star here is the brilliantly eclectic menu. O'Connell has cooked in Mexico and Japan and describes his approach as "trans-ethnic fusion." Tagliatelle of flashed squid, wild pheasant tamale, and cajun blackened swordfish with banana ketchup (yes, banana ketchup!) are just some of the surprising—and very accomplished—combinations offered. ✉ *35 Princes St.,* ☎ *021/274665. MC, V. Closed Sun., Mon.*

$ ✕ **Farmgate Café**. On a terrace above the fountain at the Princes Street
★ entrance to Cork's English Market (☞ *above*), this simple restaurant-café is one of the best lunch spots in town. One side of the terrace is open to the market and operates as self-service; the other side is glassed in and served by waiters (reservations advised). A piano player presides at lunchtime most days. A large share of the food prepared here comes from the market below. Tripe and drisheen are always on the menu, while daily specials include less challenging but no less traditional Irish dishes such as corned beef with colcannon and loin of smoked bacon with *champ* (potato mashed with scallions or leeks). There's also a daily savory tart and a pasta and a catch of the day. The terrific baked goods range from healthy carrot cake to a lovely light lemon tart. The

restaurant is open Monday–Saturday, 10:30–5; last food orders are taken at 4 PM. A sister restaurant is in Midleton (☞ *below*). ⊠ *English Market, Cork,* ☎ *021/278134. MC. V.*

$$$$ ✕⊡ **Jurys.** Beside the River Lee, a five-minute walk from the city center, is this modern, two- and three-story structure made of smoked glass and steel. Its large, open lobby-restaurant area features a waterfall and hanging greenery (some of it plastic). Cork's Bar is popular with the locals at lunch and in the early evening. The mezzanine-level Fastnet Restaurant serves an à la carte, international menu with an emphasis on fresh local produce, especially seafood and beef. Bedrooms, plain yet spacious, have quilted spreads, small sofas, and floor-to-ceiling picture windows. The most desirable rooms overlook the interior patio garden and pool. ⊠ *Western Rd., Co. Cork,* ☎ *021/276622,* ℻ *021/274477. 185 rooms with bath. 2 restaurants, 2 bars, pool, sauna, 2 tennis courts, health club, squash court. AE, DC, MC, V.*

$$$ ✕⊡ **Arbutus Lodge.** Declan and Patsy Ryan's two-story, hillside
★   villa—only a five-minute drive from the city center, well signposted from St. Luke's Cross—is the first choice in Cork for those who like the feeling of staying in a fancy, private home. Airy guest rooms are individually decorated with fine antiques and original paintings. The outstanding restaurant, with its large bay window, polished-mahogany sideboards, and plush-velvet chairs, is the perfect setting for a leisurely sampling of the eight-course tasting menu, an introduction to French-Irish haute cuisine. Local meat, fish, and game, lightly sauced and garnished, are highlights. In winter, try roast pheasant with lentils; in summer, baked sea bass with sea-urchin sauce is breathtaking. The wine list is stellar. For an inexpensive lunch, the Gallery Bar, with its panorama of the city, is an ideal lunch spot. ⊠ *Middle Glanmire Rd., Montenotte, Co. Cork,* ☎ *021/501237,* ℻ *021/502893. 16 rooms with bath, 4 suites with bath. Restaurant, bar, tennis court. AE, DC, MC, V.*

$ ✕⊡ **Isaac's.** A warehouse only a short walk from both the bus and rail stations was stylishly rehabbed into this restaurant, hostel, and budget hotel—all three far more pleasant than the words *hostel* and *budget* connote. The reception area's notice board is the best place in town to get the lowdown on concerts, travel bargains, and offbeat activities. Cheerful guest rooms are attractively functional with lots of primary colors; if you want a private room with bath, specify this when reserving. Rates include Continental breakfast at the hotel's cafeteria. Modern art hangs on the walls of the popular brasserie-style restaurant, which has well-spaced, oilcloth-covered tables. The eclectic east-meets-Mediterranean menu offers fare such as bruschetta with oyster mushrooms, tapenade and grilled spring onions; and salmon cakes bound with mashed potatoes and served with chive mayonnaise. Whatever your budget, this one is worth trying. ⊠ *48 MacCurtain St., Co. Cork,* ☎ *021/500011 or 021/503805,* ℻ *021/506355. 48 private rooms, 10 with bath, 18 dorms with 4–16 beds (200 beds in total). Restaurant, cafeteria, Ping-Pong, bicycles. MC, V.*

$$$$ ⊡ **Hayfield Manor.** Cork's newest luxury hotel, opened in 1996, is built
★   to resemble an old country house. It sits beside the university campus, five minutes' drive from the city center. The marble-floored lobby is dominated by a splendid carved wooden double staircase, while a wood-paneled library overlooks the walled patio-garden. The Victorian-style bar serves food until 7 PM. The elegant leisure center is kept exclusively for the hotel's patrons. Rooms are spacious with unobtrusive decor in a vaguely Louis XV style. All bathrooms have lace shower curtains and double sinks. ⊠ *Perrott Ave., College Rd.,* ☎ *021/315600,*

FAX 021/316839. *53 rooms with bath. Restaurant, bar, indoor pool, sauna, health club. AE, DC, MC, V.*

$$$ 🏨 **Fitzpatrick Silver Springs.** On expansive lawns 10 minutes outside town on the Dublin–Rosslare approach road, this large, impersonal, glass-and-concrete hotel (it's from the '60s) is favored by tour buses in summer and business travelers in winter. The main recommendation is its recently added fitness center. The largest rooms, decked out in French-boudoir style in pink-and-gray plush, are in the newest (1988) wing. ⊠ *Tivoli, Co. Cork,* ☎ *021/507533,* FAX *021/507641. 109 rooms with bath. 2 restaurants, 2 bars, pool, sauna, steam room, 9-hole golf course, 3 tennis courts, bowling, 2 squash courts. AE, DC, MC, V.*

$$$ 🏨 **Morrison's Island.** This luxury, modern, all-suite hotel on the riverside is a two-minute walk from Patrick Street. Spacious, modern, one- or two-bedroom suites with kitchen are furnished with handcrafted light-oak furniture. Polished marble floors and warm, terra-cotta walls enhance the stylish, mezzanine-level bar and restaurant overlooking the river. Four penthouses have terrace views of the city and the river. ⊠ *Morrison's Quay, Co. Cork,* ☎ *021/275858,* FAX *021/275833. 40 suites with bath. Restaurant, bar, bicycles. AF, DC, MC, V.*

$$ 🏨 **Rochestown Park.** Set in seven acres of mature gardens in the fashionable suburb of Douglas (5 km/3 mi south of the city), Rochestown has been built around a Victorian manor house that overlooks its own wooded gardens and the estuary of Cork harbor. All the rooms are decorated in a modern style with cotton spreads, wool carpets, and light-oak fixtures. The Douglas Tavern is a popular (self-service) lunch spot with locals. The large health center specializes in thalassotherapy—seaweed wraps and baths. ⊠ *Rochestown Rd., Douglas, Cork,* ☎ *021/ 892233,* FAX *021/892178. 63 rooms with bath. Restaurant, bar, pool, sauna, health club. AE, DC, MC, V.*

$ 🏨 **Jurys Cork Inn.** Opened in 1994, this budget hotel pursues the same policy as its Dublin and Galway counterparts, charging per room, each of which sleeps three adults or two adults and two children. Beside a busy bridge over the River Lee, the inn is a short walk from the city center and bus and rail stations. Rooms are well appointed for the price range: bright and airy with light-wood trim and matching drapes and spreads. ⊠ *Anderson's Quay, Co. Cork,* ☎ *021/276444,* FAX *021/ 276144. 133 rooms with bath. Restaurant, bar. AE, DC, MC, V.*

$ 🏨 **Victoria Lodge.** This exceptionally well-appointed B&B, built originally in the early 20th century as a Capuchin monastery, is a five-minute drive from the town center; it is also accessible by several bus routes. Breakfast is served in the spacious old refectory with its intact polished benches and paneled walls; the common room is now a television lounge. The simple, comfortable bedrooms feature pastel-color chenille spreads, cotton curtains, and mahogany bureaus. ⊠ *Victoria Cross, Co. Cork,* ☎ *021/542233,* FAX *021/542572. 30 rooms with bath. Cafeteria. AE, MC, V.*

Nightlife and the Arts

FESTIVALS AND SEASONAL EVENTS

Ireland's oldest film festival, the **Cork Film Festival** (☎ 021/271711) was established in 1956 and has evolved into one of the country's most important cinema events. New feature-length films from Ireland and abroad and documentaries share the bill with short films, a particular specialty of this festival. It's usually held the second week of October. October 23–26, 1998, the **Cork Jazz Festival** (☎ 021/270463) brings major national and international performers to venues throughout the city.

GALLERIES

Cork Arts Society (⊠ 5 Father Mathew St., off South Mall, ☎ 021/ 277749) has a representative selection of oils and watercolors by local artists, all of which are for sale. Offbeat exhibits can be found at the **Triskel Arts Center** (⊠ Tobin St., off S. Main St., ☎ 021/272022). A selection of younger artists' work can be seen at the **ArtHive** (⊠ Thompson House, MacCurtain St., ☎ 021/505228).

MUSIC AND THEATER

Cork Opera House (⊠ Lavitt's Quay, ☎ 021/270022) is the city's major hall for touring productions and variety acts. Smaller productions are staged at the **Everyman Palace** (⊠ MacCurtain St., ☎ 021/501673), where the ornate, Victorian interior has recently been restored.

PUBS AND NIGHTCLUBS

De Lacy House (⊠ 74 Oliver Plunkett St., ☎ 021/270074) attracts a young crowd for rock and folk gigs. The bar at the **Metropole Hotel** (⊠ MacCurtain St., ☎ 021/508122) is one of the best places for jazz. The **Morrison's Island Hotel** (⊠ Morrison's Island, ☎ 021/275858) is another good spot for jazz. Live music (rock and nostalgia) gets top billing at **Rearden's Mill** (⊠ 25 Washington St., ☎ 021/273351. Traditional musicians gather at **An Spailpin Fanach** (⊠ 28 S. Main St., ☎ 021/277949).

Outdoor Activities and Sports

BICYCLES

Rent a bike to explore the city and its environs at **Kilgrew's Cycle Centre** (⊠ 6 Kyle St., Co. Cork, ☎ 021/276255).

FISHING

Fishing tackle, bait, and licenses, as well as friendly advice on local resources, can be obtained at **T. W. Murray** (⊠ 87 Patrick St., Co. Cork, ☎ 021/271089).

GOLF

Douglas Golf Club (⊠ Douglas, Co. Cork, ☎ 021/891086) is a tree-lined, parkland, 18-hole course in the southern suburbs of the city. **Cork Golf Club** (⊠ Little Island, Co. Cork, ☎ 021/353451; ☞ Chapter 10). **Lee Valley Golf Club** (⊠ Clashanure, Ovens, Co. Cork, ☎ 021/331721) is a par-72, 18-hole, championship course 15 minutes west of the city. **Monkstown Golf Club** (⊠ Parkgarriffe, Monkstown, Co. Cork, ☎ 021/841376) is an 18-hole, par-70, strategically bunkered, parkland course 11 km/7 mi southeast of the city.

HORSEBACK RIDING

Hitchmough Riding School (⊠ Highland Lodge, Monkstown, Co. Cork, ☎ 021/371267) has an indoor arena for all-weather riding. **Pinegrove Riding School** (⊠ White's Cross, near Cork City, Co. Cork, ☎ 021/303857) will provide one- and two-hour hacks in the countryside north of the city.

Shopping

ANTIQUES

Anne MacCarthy (⊠ Paul's Ln., ☎ 021/273755) specializes in china, silver, glass, linen, and lace. **Irene's** (⊠ 22 Marlboro St., ☎ 021/270642) sells antique jewelry. **Mills Antiques** (⊠ 3 Paul's Ln., ☎ 021/273528) carries Irish, English, and European paintings, printings, silver, porcelain, and small furniture. For furniture, paintings, and other large decorative objects try **O'Regan's Antiques** (⊠ 27 Lavitt's Quay, ☎ 021/272902). **Victoria's** (⊠ 2 Oliver Plunkett St., ☎ 021/272752) carries interesting jewelry, Victoriana, and period clothes.

BOOKS

Collins Bookshop (⊠ Carey's Ln., ☎ 021/271346) sells new books. **Mercier Bookshop** (⊠ 18 Academy St., ☎ 021/275040), off Patrick Street, also sells new books. **Lee Bookstore** (⊠ 10 Lavitts Quay, ☎ 021/

272307) sells a wide selection of secondhand and antiquarian books, many of Irish interest, plus Irish prints and engravings.

CLOTHING

Meadows and Byrne (⊠ Academy St., ☎ 021/272324) has some of the best Irish-made fashion and casual wear in the area, as well as a good selection of ceramic tableware and glass. The best tweed comes from Donegal, and the **House of Donegal** (⊠ 6 Paul St., ☎ 021/272447) features a good stock of it. The shop sells both men's and women's ready-to-wear and made-to-measure, which they will ship home to you, and it also carries classic rainwear. For casual weatherproof clothing, try **The Tack Room** (⊠ Unit 3, Academy St., ☎ 021/272704).

DEPARTMENT STORE

Cash's (⊠ 18 Patrick St., ☎ 021/276771) is Cork's leading department store and has a good selection of Waterford glass.

MUSIC

Fans of Irish music should visit **The Living Tradition** (⊠ 40 MacCurtain St., ☎ 021/502040).

SHOPPING CENTER

The **Merchant's Quay Shopping Centre** (⊠ Merchant's Quay, ☎ 021/275466) is the largest indoor mall in downtown Cork.

SPORTING GOODS

For inexpensive rainwear, go to **Penney's** (⊠ 27 Patrick St., ☎ 021/271935). **Matthews** (⊠ Academy St., ☎ 021/277633) has a wide selection of sporting gear. **Great Outdoors** (⊠ 23 Paul St., ☎ 021/276382) caters to most outdoor sports needs.

Blarney

19 *10 km/6 mi northwest of Cork City on R617.*

Blarney is a small community built around a village green. (To get here in the peak season of July and August, or if you're en route to Killarney from Cork City, follow the signposts off the main N22 Killarney road at Carrigrohane to avoid Cork's inner-city traffic jams.) Just to the north of Blarney is **Blarney Castle**—or what remains of it: The ruined central keep is all that's left of this mid-15th-century stronghold. The walls of the castle contain the famed **Blarney Stone**, set in a wall below the castle's battlements; kissing the stone, it's said, endows the kisser with the fabled "gift of gab." It's 127 steep steps to the battlements. To kiss the stone, you must lie down on the battlements, hold on to a guardrail, and lean your head way back. It's good fun and not at all dangerous.

Expect a line from mid-June to September 1; while you wait, you can admire the views of the thickly wooded River Lee valley below and chuckle over how the word "blarney" come to mean what it does: Queen Elizabeth I wanted Cormac MacCarthy, Lord of Blarney, to will his castle to the crown. Lord Blarney consistently refused her request with eloquent excuses and soothing compliments. Exhausted by his comments, the queen reportedly exclaimed, "This is all Blarney. What he says he rarely means."

Visitors can also take pleasant walks around the castle grounds; **Rock Close** contains oddly shaped limestone rocks landscaped in the 18th century and a grove of ancient yew trees that is said to have been the center of Druid worship. ⊠ *Blarney Castle,* ☎ *021/385252.* ⊆ *£3.* ☉ *May and Sept., Mon.–Sat. 9–6:30, Sun. 9–5:30; June–Aug., Mon.–Sat. 9–7, Sun. 9–5:30; Oct.–Apr., Mon.–Sat. 9–sundown, Sun. 9–5:30.*

Two hundred yards from the castle, **Blarney Castle House** was built in 1784 in the style of a Scottish baronial mansion. The three-story, gray-stone building has picture-book turrets and fancy, stepped gables. The interior features Elizabethan and Victorian antiques, a fine stairwell, and numerous family portraits. ☎ *021/385252.* ☜ *£2.50.* ☉ *June–mid-Sept., Mon.–Sat. noon–5.*

Outdoor Activities and Sports

BICYCLES

Bicycles can be rented at **Tony McGrath** (✉ Stoneview, Co. Cork, ☎ 021/385658).

GOLF

Muskerry Golf Club (✉ Carrigrohane, near Blarney, Co. Cork, ☎ 021/385297) is an 18-hole, par-71, parkland course.

Shopping

Blarney has more crafts shops than anyplace else in Ireland. Most of these stores are concentrated on the south and west of the village green, a two-minute walk from the castle. A shopping visit here can be used profitably for price comparison and bargain hunting; in spite of appearances, these shops, in general, will not rip you off. **Blarney Woolen Mills** (☎ 021/385280) has the largest stock and the highest turnover. The mills sell everything from Irish-made high fashion to Aran hand knit items to leprechaun key rings.

Cork Harbour–Fota Island and Cobh

Fota Island, 19 km/12 mi from Cork City; Cobh, 24 km/15 mi from Cork City on N25.

To explore Cork Harbour, follow the signposts for Waterford on the N25 along the northern banks of the River Lee. Alternatively, a suburban rail service from Kent Station (☎ 021/506766 for timetable) has stops at Fota Island and Cobh (pronounced "Cove"), and it offers better harbor views than the road.

Just outside Cork City on the opposite side of the River Lee, **Blackrock Castle** (☎ 021/357414) is a turreted, 16th-century fortification, rebuilt in the 19th century in gray stone with crenellations. A picture-perfect riverside castle, it now houses a restaurant and bar. Shortly after you get a glimpse of Blackrock, the road leaves the river. The turning for Fota Island and Cobh (R624) is clearly signposted off the N25 on the right-hand side about 8 km/5 mi outside town. Turn right again at the gate lodge of the huge estate on Fota Island.

☙ ⑳ **Fota Demesne** encompasses a magnificent arboretum (freely accessible) and the 70-acre **Fota Wildlife Park,** an important breeding center for cheetahs and wallabies. It also contains free-ranging monkeys, zebras, giraffes, ostriches, flamingos, emus, and kangaroos. ☎ *021/812678.* ☜ *Wildlife park £3.70; arboretum, gardens, and parking lot £1.* ☉ *Mar. 17–Sept., Mon.–Sat. 10–6, Sun. 11–6; Oct., Sat. 10–6, Sun. 11–6.*

Barryscourt Castle is a 5-km/3-mi detour (clearly signposted outside the gates of Fota House). The 13th-century structure has a courtyard and flanking towers. Guided tours are given June–September. ✉ *Carrigtwohill,* ☎ *021/883864.* ☜ *Free, tour £1.50.* ☉ *Daily 11–6.*

⑳
★ Many generations who left the port of Cork on immigrant ships for the New World left from **Cobh,** a pretty, largely 19th-century fishing port and seaside resort with considerable maritime history. **The Queenstown Project,** in the old Cobh railway station, re-creates the experience of the million emigrants who left the town between 1750 and the

mid-20th century. It also tells the stories of the great transatlantic liners, including the *Titanic*, whose last port of call was Cobh, and the *Lusitania*, which was sunk by a German submarine off this coast on May 7, 1915, with the loss of 1,198 lives. Many of the *Lusitania*'s victims are buried in Cobh, which has a memorial to them on the local quay. ☎ *021/813591.* ⌨ *£3.50.* ⊙ *Feb.–Nov., daily 10–6.*

The best view of Cobh is from **St. Colman's Cathedral,** an exuberant neo-Gothic granite church designed by Pugin in 1868. Inside are granite niches that portray the Roman Catholic church's history in Ireland, beginning with the arrival of St. Patrick. Cork Harbour opens to the sea some 8 km/5 mi from Cobh at **Roches Point.** One-hour harbor tours from Marine Transport are a splendid way to take in Cobh's glorious watery environs. ⊠ *Kennedy Pier,* ☎ *021/811485.* ⌨ *£3.50.* ⊙ *May–Sept., daily at 10, 11, noon, 1:30, and 2:30.*

Outdoor Activities and Sports

GOLF

Fota Island Golf Club (⊠ Fota Island, Carrigtwohill, Co. Cork, ☎ 021/883700) is a par-72, 18-hole course.

WATER SPORTS

Explore Cork Harbour from the water by renting a sailing dinghy from **International Sailing Center** (⊠ 5 E. Beach, Cobh, Co. Cork, ☎ 021/811237).

En Route The **Cork Harbour Crossing** is a car ferry that runs from Carrigaloe near Cobh to Glenbrook near Ringaskiddy, cutting out the traveling through Cork City. This is useful if you are heading for Kinsale and West Cork. It operates continuously from 7:15 AM to 12:45 AM daily and costs £3 per car, 60p for pedestrians.

EAST CORK AND THE BLACKWATER VALLEY

Although most visitors to Cork head west out of the city for the scenic coastal areas between Cork and Glengarriff, the east and the north of the county are also worth exploring. East Cork, and Youghal in particular, is popular with Irish tourists for its long, sandy beaches. The main attraction in North Cork is the Blackwater River, which crosses the county from east to west. It is famous for both its trout and salmon fishing and its surrounding scenery. This tour starts in the far corner of the county at Youghal and works its way west toward the Kerry border.

Youghal

❷ *48 km/30 mi east of Cork City on N25, 74 km/46 mi south of Waterford.*

Situated on the mouth of the Blackwater river, on the border between Counties Cork and Waterford, Youghal (pronounced "yawl") is an ancient walled seaport with a fine, natural harbor. The town was included in a 40,000-acre land grant given to Sir Walter Raleigh by Elizabeth I in the late 16th century. Local legend states that Sir Walter Raleigh planted the first potatoes in Ireland here, a claim disputed by several other locations (and by all accounts he spent little time here). Its long, sandy beach makes it a popular summer day-trip destination for Corkonians. The town itself is now in the throes of some major investment, aimed at updating its appeal.

The **clock tower** (⊠ Main St.), Youghal's main landmark, dates from 1776 and was originally built as a jail. A set of steps beside the clock tower leads up to a well-preserved stretch of the old town walls. From here there is a magnificent panoramic view of the town and the estuary. The **Youghal Heritage Centre** allows you to learn more about the town's long history with an audiovisual presentation. If this whets your appetite, trained guides are available to show you the town; a walking tour takes about an hour and a half. ⊠ *Market Sq.,* ☎ *024/92390.* ☜ *£1, tour £2.50.* ☉ *June–mid-Sept., daily 9:30–7; mid-Sept.–May, weekdays 9:30–5:30.*

At the **Youghal quays,** you may see today's catch being unloaded from one of the small, brightly painted trawlers that fish these waters. The **Moby Dick Lounge Bar** (⊠ Market Sq., ☎ 024/92756) contains memorabilia of the filming here of John Huston's film of Melville's *Moby Dick,* in which Youghal masqueraded as New Bedford, Massachusetts. **St. Mary's Collegiate Church** (under the town walls) dates from the 13th century and contains many interesting monuments, including the tomb of Richard Boyle (1566–1643), who succeeded Sir Walter Raleigh as Mayor of Youghal and became the first earl of Cork. The brightly painted monument commemorates his three wives and 16 children and is similar to one in St. Patrick's' Cathedral in Dublin, which Sir Richard ordered because he was not sure whether he would die in Dublin or Youghal. ⊠ *Emmet Pl.,* ☎ *024/92350.* ☉ *Key available from adjacent lodge.*

Dining and Lodging

$$$ ╳▥ **Aherne's.** In the Fitzgibbon family since 1923, Aherne's has a
★ highly regarded seafood restaurant and bar that draws food lovers from Cork City (it's under an hour's drive). Start with hot creamed oysters or mussels in garlic broth; popular main courses include hot buttered lobster, grilled salmon with fresh fennel, and more elaborate creations such as plaice stuffed with oysters in a red-wine sauce. The inexpensive bar food includes seafood pie topped with mashed potatoes. In their own wing, the 12 bedrooms are furnished with Victorian and Georgian antiques. They all have super-king-size beds; the two newest have dressing rooms. ⊠ *163 N. Main St., Youghal, Co. Cork,* ☎ *024/92424,* ℻ *024/93633. 12 rooms with bath. Restaurant, bar, fishing. AE, DC, MC, V.*

$ ╳▥ **Ballymakeigh House.** Signposted off the N25 9.5 km/6 mi west
★ of Youghal, this is the Irish farmhouse of your dreams. From the conservatory behind the creeper-clad house you can watch the cows ambling home while breakfasting on one of Margaret Browne's fresh strawberry muffins. Reserve by 5 PM for her legendary six-course dinners, which have a set menu of the best local produce available that day; herbs and edible flowers from the Ballymakeigh garden add color to many dishes. The impeccably kept, cozy rooms show the attention to detail you would expect from a former "Housewife of the Year." This is the kind of place where most people end up staying much longer than just one night. ⊠ *Killeagh, Co. Cork,* ☎ *024/95184,* ℻ *024/95370. 7 rooms with bath. Dining room, tennis court, Ping-Pong, bicycles. MC, V.*

Outdoor Activities and Sports

Youghal Golf Club (⊠ Knockaverry, Youghal, Co. Cork, ☎ 024/92787) is a scenic, 18-hole course that overlooks the bay.

Shanagarry

㉓ *27 km/17 mi west of Youghal via N25 and R632.*

Until recently, Shanagarry was a quiet farming village well off the beaten track chiefly known for its Quaker connections. The most fa-

In case you want to see the world.

At American Express, we're here to make your journey a smooth one. So we have over 1,700 travel service locations in over 120 countries ready to help. What else would you expect from the world's largest travel agency?

do more ®

http://www.americanexpress.com/travel

Travel

In case you're running low.

We're here to help with more than 118,000 Express Cash locations around the world. In order to enroll, just call American Express before you start your vacation.

do more

Express Cash

And just in case.

We're here with American Express® Travelers Cheques and Cheques *for Two*.® They're the safest way to carry money on your vacation and the surest way to get a refund, practically anywhere, anytime.

Another way we help you...

do more®

Travelers Cheques

mous Shanagarry Quaker was William Penn (1644–1718), the founder of the Pennsylvania colony, who grew up in **Shanagarry House,** still a private residence in the center of the village. The gates are across from **Shanagarry Castle,** now owned and being restored by the potter and entrepreneur Stephen Pearce (☞ Shopping, *below*). The house's most famous tenant since William Penn was Marlon Brando, who stayed there in the summer of 1995 while filming *Divine Rapture* in nearby Ballycotton.

More recently, **Ballymaloe House** (☞ Dining and Lodging, below), one of Ireland's first country-house hotels, on the eastern edge of the village, has brought a stream of visitors to the area. On the other side of Shanagarry, **Ballymaloe Cookery School and Gardens,** run by Darina and Tim Allen (daughter-in-law and son of Ballymaloe House proprietors Myrtle and Ivan Allen), attracts budding chefs from all over Ireland and, increasingly, from points beyond, to its wealth of cooking classes and programs, which range from one day to 12 weeks. (Its graduates can be found in the kitchens of many Irish restaurants, which often promote the connection.) Darina Allen, one of Ireland's best-known chefs, has recently planted formal herb, fruit, and vegetable gardens, and in late 1996, a Celtic maze (not yet knee-high). Though it now stands in the midst of unplanted fields, a folly decorated inside with an astonishing variety of shells is slated to be the centerpiece of additional gardens. ✉ *Kinioth House, Shanagarry, Co. Cork,* ☎ *021/646785.* ▣ *£3.* ☉ *May–Sept., daily 9–6.*

Five kilometers/3 miles beyond Shanagarry, the pretty fishing village of **Ballycotton** is built on the top of a cliff overlooking an island where large colonies of seabirds breed. There are good cliff walks and a nearby beach.

Dining and Lodging

$–$$ ✕ **Farmgate Restaurant and Country Store.** Owner-chef Máróg O'Brien emphasizes simplicity and top-notch ingredients at this spacious spot. By day, lunch and the homemade cakes make it a popular café. On Saturday evenings, live music and atmospheric lighting turn up the romantic quotient. O'Brien's striking collection of modern art hangs amid the assorted farmhouse pine tables and dressers. Highlights on the menu include free-range duck on the bone, roasted with potato stuffing and served with applesauce. Grilled, poached, or oven-roasted seafood comes with a light sauce made from fish juices and fresh herbs. For dessert, try the chocolate pear tart, light as a feather, or the lightly caramelized bread and butter pudding. Locally grown organic vegetables, area cheeses, and the Farmgate's own homemade baked goods, sauces, jams, and condiments are on sale at the entrance. This is a cousin to the Farmgate Café in Cork, and is about halfway between Cork and Shanagarry. ✉ *Coolbawn, Midleton, Co. Cork,* ☎ *021/632771. MC, V. Closed Sun. No dinner Mon.–Wed.*

$$$ ✕▥ **Ballymaloe House.** One of Ireland's best-known country houses, Ballymaloe has been the home of Myrtle and Ivan Allen for nearly 50 years. Gentle hills rise up behind the house, while farmland surrounds it as far as your eye can see. Each color-themed guest room is elegantly, if simply, decorated (rooms do not have TVs). Myrtle, the doyenne of Irish cooking, presides over the dining room, the walls of which are hung with Ivan's notable Irish art collection. Chef Rory O'Connell presents a daily-changing, six-course, haute Irish menu that relies on fresh fish from nearby Ballycotton, local lamb and beef, and homegrown herbs and vegetables. The superb, mostly local cheeses served before dessert exemplify Myrtle Allen's longstanding practice of supporting small food

purveyors around Cork. Signposted from the main N25 at Midleton, 11 km/7 mi east of Cobh (32 km/20 mi from Cork City), the house can be difficult to find, especially at night, so request exact directions. ⊠ *Shanagarry, Midleton, Co. Cork,* ☎ *021/652531,* ℻ *021/652021. 32 rooms with bath. Restaurant (jacket and tie), bar, outdoor heated pool, tennis court, deep-sea fishing by arrangement. AE, DC, MC, V.*

Shopping

The ceramicist Stephen Pearce makes tableware and bowls in four signature styles—the newest is a gold porcelain—which are available in many Irish crafts shops. He sells a wide selection at his own **Stephen Pearce Emporium** (⊠ Shanagarry, near Cloyne, ☎ 021/646262) where he also stocks an interesting range of Irish-made and exclusively imported crafts.

Fermoy

㉔ *35 km/22 mi north of Cork City on N8, 43 km/27 mi west of Youghal on R634 (Tallow Rd.), which adjoins N72.*

An army town dating mainly from the mid-19th century, Fermoy is a major crossroads on the Dublin–Cork road; the east–west road that passes through town (N72) is an attractive alternative route to Killarney (98 km/61 mi). Its bridge spanning the Blackwater is flanked by two weirs dating from 1689. The town is popular with game fishers.

Dining and Lodging

\$\$ ✕🏠 **Ballyvolane House.** Approaching from Dublin, Castlelyons is signposted off the N8 in Rathcormac, just south of Fermoy. An informal country-house atmosphere pervades this imposing 1728 stone mansion surrounded by extensive gardens, beyond which is a 100-acre dairy farm. Dinner is served at a large table in the elegant dining room; family silver is set on white linens. The rooms are exceptionally big, sitting areas are generous, and decor consists of a rich assortment of antiques and family heirlooms. Both dinner and accommodation must be booked at least 24 hours in advance, but the preplanning is well worth it. ⊠ *Castlelyons, Co. Cork,* ☎ *025/36349,* ℻ *025/36781. 6 rooms with bath. Dining room (wine license only), horseback riding, fishing. MC, V.*

Outdoor Activities and Sports

For local information on salmon and trout angling contact the **Salmon Angler's Association** (Liam McGarry, ⊠ Moorepark, Fermoy, Co. Cork, ☎ 025/31422).

Mallow

㉕ *30 km/19 mi east of Fermoy on N72.*

In the 18th century, Mallow was a popular spa, often mentioned in the same breath as Bath. Today it is an angling center and market town. (It's at the intersection of the Cork–Limerick and Waterford–Killarney roads, within an hour's drive of all four towns.) At the bottom of Mallow's Main Street, the **Clock House** is a half-timbered building dating from 1855 that sits on the site of the Rakes of Mallow Club, the headquarters of the notorious, 18th-century gamblers, drinkers, and fortune hunters remembered in the song "The Rakes of Mallow." Not much remains today of Mallow's glory, but the old **Spa Well** can still be seen in the town center, and there are several interesting facades with overhanging bay windows dating from the 18th and early 19th century on Main Street. The English novelist Anthony Trollope lived at No. 139 for a time, and he hunted regularly with the Duhallow, enhancing the fame of the local pack. The ruins of **Mallow Castle,** which dates from the late 16th century, are at the bottom of the main street behind (freely accessible) ornamental gates. The castle was burnt by the Jacobites in 1689, and its stables were then converted into a house, which is still in use as a private home. From here you can view the white, fallow deer that are unique to Mallow and were originally presented by Elizabeth I.

Castletownroche, 12 km/7 mi east of the Mallow, is the site of **Anne's Grove Gardens,** which were inspired by the ideas of William Robinson, a 19th-century gardener who favored naturalistic planting. Exotic foliage plants border paths winding down to the river; magnificent magnolias and vast numbers of naturalized primulas in spring and hydrangeas in summer are among the plants on view in the rolling countryside. ☎ 022/26145. ⌑ £2.50. ⊘ Mid-Mar.–Sept., Mon.–Sat. 10–5, Sun. 1–6.

Dining and Lodging

$$$ ✕▦ **Longueville House.** The Southwest of Ireland has no shortage of
★ outstanding country-house hotels, but by many accounts Longueville wins highest honors. Limestone quoins frame the facade of the large, elegant Georgian mansion. The three-story central block, dating from 1720, is flanked by two slightly later wings, while a Victorian-era, glass-and-iron conservatory punctuates the east end. The stately drawing rooms, decorated with large, gilt-framed mirrors and oil paintings, overlook the tranquil lawns and rows of oaks of the 500-acre estate, which rolls down to the Blackwater. Bedrooms are comfortable and filled with antiques; the high-ceilinged rooms on the first story at the front are particularly desirable. At the Presidents' Restaurant (named for the portraits of the Republic's presidents that hang here), William O'Callaghan, son of founding proprietors Michael and Jane O'Callaghan, serves food he describes as "true to its origins," and which Vincent Jamison, our Dublin dining critic, calls "some of the finest food in Europe." All of O'Callaghan's food has been grown or raised right on the property, and he also produces a fruity Riesling-like white wine from his own vineyard (until recently the only one in the country). ⌂ Mallow, Co. Cork, ☎ 022/47156, ℻ 022/47459. 20 rooms with bath. Restaurant, bar, fishing. AE, DC, MC, V. Closed Dec. 23–Feb. 28.

Outdoor Activities and Sports

Mallow Golf Club (⌂ Ballyellis, Co. Cork, ☎ 022/21145) is an 18-hole, par-72, parkland course with excellent views of the Blackwater Valley.

Kanturk

26 15 km/9 mi west of Mallow on N72 and R579.

Kanturk lies at the meeting of two rivers, the Allow and the Dalua. It is more of a village than a town, but its interesting, Victorian shop fronts bear witness to its past importance as a market town. **Kanturk Castle** (⌂ 2 km/1¼ mi outside town on the R579 Banteer Road, and freely accessible) was built by a local Macarthy chieftain in 1601, but it was never completed, as his English neighbors complained it was too large for an Irishman. Ornate stone fireplaces and mullioned windows in the five-story shell give some idea of the scope of Macarthy's ambitions.

OFF THE BEATEN PATH **MILLSTREET** – This town 17 km/10 mi southwest of Kanturk has come to international attention because of the **Green Glens Arena** (☎ 029/70039), which started life as the home of the Millstreet International Horse Show for show jumpers, and which has since been used to hold the Eurovision Song Contest, boxing title fights, and concerts by international artists, including Don Williams, Willie Nelson, Kenny Rogers, Tammy Wynette and George Jones, and the Cranberries. As of press time (summer 1997) the 1998 lineup had not been announced, but if you're in the area, call for schedule information. Millstreet is also 32 km/20 mi east of Killarney (☞ *below*).

Dining and Lodging

$$$$ ✕🏨 **Assolas Country House.** This picture-postcard, ivy-covered 17th-
★ century manor possesses the air of a dignified family home more than it does a hotel. Joe and Hazel Bourke have immaculately furnished the house and its bedrooms with period antiques. Dinner begins in front of the blazing log fire in the drawing room, where guests peruse the night's menu over aperitifs. Old Bourke family silver is on the tables in the quiet, red, Queen Anne dining room. Hazel's refined cooking shows off the food's natural goodness. Her culinary skills, as well as the well-manicured gardens, are award-winning. Kanturk is known for its good fishing and hunting, and it is within an hour's drive of Cork, Limerick, and Killarney. ⊠ *Kanturk, Co. Cork,* ☎ *029/50015,* ℻ *029/ 50795. 9 rooms with bath. Restaurant, tennis court, boating, fishing. AE, MC, V. Closed Nov.–mid-Mar.*

$ ✕🏨 **Clonmeen Lodge.** The O'Leary family offers residential riding holidays from their home, a modest redbrick Georgian lodge on the bank of the scenic Blackwater midway between Kanturk and the Green Glens Arena. Non-riding guests are also welcome, with golf, hiking, hunting, and fishing other popular outdoor activities. The dinner menu relies on locally produced meat and fish and is served beside an open log fire (reserve by 3 PM); wine is the only alcohol available. ⊠ *Clonmeen, Banteer, Co. Cork,* ☎ *029/56238,* ℻ *029/56294. 6 rooms with bath. Dining room, horseback riding, fishing. MC, V.*

KINSALE TO GLENGARRIFF VIA BANTRY BAY

This tour takes you on a scenic drive of about 136 km/85 mi around the unspoiled coast of West County Cork. It starts at the historic old port—and now booming seaside town—of Kinsale and meanders through a variety of seascapes to the lush vegetation of Glengarriff. The drive from Kinsale to Glengarriff can take about two hours non-stop, but the whole point of taking this tour is to linger anywhere that takes your fancy. The tour is most enjoyable between May and October, when the weather is still warm enough to explore the area on foot.

Kinsale

★ ㉗ *29 km/18 mi southwest of Cork City on R600.*

Kinsale is a lovely seaside village, made all the more precious by its relative isolation—though it feels it's a world apart, in fact it's less than 30 km (20 mi) from Cork. Situated at the tip of the wide, fjordlike harbor opening out from the River Bandon, the town center is nestled around small streets lined with upscale shops and eateries with colorful, pastel facades. Its steep, narrow streets climb up the slopes of Compass Hill. Tall, slate-roof and unusual slate-front houses have an unmistakable Spanish influence, which can be traced back to the Battle of Kinsale in 1601, when the Irish and Spanish joined forces here to fight the English—and lost. The loss was an important one for the Irish aristocracy, as they soon took off for Europe, leaving behind their lands to English settlers. Kinsale went on to become an important fishing port, as well as a British army and naval base.

Today Kinsale has a number of fine restaurants—it's often referred to as "the gourmet capital of Ireland," a billing it especially lives up to during the first week in October, when it hosts its annual **Gourmet Festival** (☞ Festivals and Seasonal Events *in* Chapter 1). But foodies can't alone claim Kinsale; yacht owners and deep-sea anglers are also big visitors here. A signposted walking tour of the town, with an accompanying booklet (£1 from the Kinsale TIO or Boland's on Pearse Street), will familiarize you with its history.

Cuttings and memorabilia from the wreck of the *Lusitania* (☞ Cobh, *above*) are among the best artifacts in Kinsale's local **museum,** in the town's 17th-century, Dutch-style courthouse. The 1915 inquest into the *Lusitania*'s sinking took place in the **courtroom,** briefly making it the focus of the world's attention; it has been preserved as a memorial. The museum staff will also give you details of free guided walks that take place regularly in the summer, or by appointment for groups. ⊠ *Old Courthouse, Market Pl.,* ☎ *021/772044.* ⊒ *35p.* ☉ *Mon.– Sat. 11–5, Sun. 3–5.*

★ ㉘ On the harbor shore on the east side of the Bandon's estuary, the British built **Charles Fort** in the late 17th century, in the wake of their defeat of the Spanish and Irish forces. One of the best preserved "star forts" in Europe, it encloses some 12 acres on a cliff top (it's similar to Fort Ticonderoga in New York State). In its heyday, it had a population of 2,000, and it was in use until 1920, when it was burned out by the Irish Republican Army. If the sun is shining, take the footpath that is signposted **Scilly Walk;** it winds along the edge of the harbor under tall, overhanging trees and then through the village of Summer Cove. A guided tour is available mid-April through October. ⊠ *3 km/2 mi east of town,* ☎ *021/772684.* ⊒ *£2.* ☉ *Mid-June–mid-Sept., daily 10–6; mid-Apr.– mid-June and mid-Sept.–Oct., Mon.–Sat. 9–5, Sun. 9:30–5:30; Nov.– mid-Apr., weekdays 8–4:30, except public holidays.*

The **Spaniard Inn** (⊠ Scilly, ☎ 021/772436) looks over the town and harbor from a hairpin bend on the road to Charles Fort. Inside, sawdust-covered floors and a big open fire make this onetime fisherman's bar a cozy spot in the winter. In the summer, you can take a pint to the sunny veranda and watch the world go by on land and sea.

Dining and Lodging

$$$$ ✕ **The Oystercatcher.** Owner-chef Bill Patterson has turned a low-beamed, rustic outpost 8 km/5 mi from town into a must-stop on any gastronomic pilgrimage to the Southwest. Rough-hewn tables and chairs, shelves with ironstone platters and teapots, and copper pots on the walls decorate the two joined old stone and stucco fishermen's cottages. There is only a table d'hôte five-course menu—no à la carte— so plan to feast. Oysters turn up in a variety of dishes, from a starter of rock oysters on a bed of angel-hair pasta topped with chili and ginger sauce, to homemade oyster sausage. Pheasant is served with a port wine sauce and walnuts, or try the lobster Thermidor. If you're really adventurous, forego classic desserts like the tangy lemon tart for the old-fashioned savory desserts, such as scrambled eggs with anchovies on toast. ⊠ *Ballinaclashet Cross, Oysterhaven,* ☎ *021/770822. MC, V. Closed Jan.–mid-Mar.; Mon., Tues. Easter–July. No lunch.*

$$$ ✕ **Max's Wine Bar.** Owner Wendy Tisdall impeccably runs this spot— more a small, chic restaurant than a wine bar. A variety of small antique tables with equally varied chairs and benches fill the low-beamed main room, while a small, flower-filled conservatory is at the back. Most menu choices can be ordered as either starters or main courses. Salads, often overlooked at all but the finest Southwest restaurants, are especially good here, as is the homemade soup. Monkfish simmered

in cream and tarragon and salmon in sorrel sauce are among the seafood choices.☒ *Main St.,* ☎ *021/772443. MC, V. Closed Nov.–mid-Feb.*

$$$ ✕⌷ **Blue Haven.** In the heart of Kinsale, this attractively kept, yellow
★   stucco, blue-trimmed town house combines an acclaimed seafood restaurant with a small hotel. Rooms are both in the main house and, thanks to a 1995 acquisition, in the house next door. New rooms have custom-designed, dark-oak furniture, canopied antique beds, and spacious baths; those in the main house, though generally smaller, are cheerfully decorated with paintings by local artists. Inexpensive bar food is served until 9:30 PM in the lounge bar, the patio, and the conservatory, which are all decorated with swagged curtains, hanging plants, and nautical brass. The quiet, pastel-color restaurant overlooks a floodlit garden with a fountain adorned by cherubs. For dinner, you can enjoy fare either traditional—sole on the bone with lemon and parsley butter, or more unusual—medallions of hake coated in a Pernod batter and served with a white butter sauce. ☒ *3 Pearse St., Co. Cork.,* ☎ *021/772209,* 𝖥𝖠𝖷 *021/774–268. 18 rooms with bath. Restaurant, bar, fishing. AE, DC, MC, V.*

$$$ ✕⌷ **Jim Edwards.** One of the most successful pub-restaurants in Ire-
★   land, this spot is renowned for the quality of its steaks and seafood. The restaurant is unpretentiously decorated with dark-wood tables, dark-green place mats, and red carpets and drapes. The staff, under the supervision of the owner and his wife, is friendly and efficient. Portions tend to be exceptionally generous, and children are welcome. Recommended dishes include the fricassee of seafood and the succulent char-grilled local steak fillet. The separate bar serves inexpensive fare. Well-equipped guest bedrooms ($) renovated in 1996 are over the bar. ☒ *Market Quay, Co. Cork,* ☎ *021/772541. 7 rooms with bath. AE, DC, MC, V.*

$$$ ⌷ **Trident.** This modern low rise on the water's edge is popular with visitors who come for deep-sea fishing (mainly all-male, Dutch or English groups). The cinder-block, modern rooms feature large windows overlooking the inner harbor. The Fisherman's Bar is a congenial spot for conversation among the locals and visiting anglers. ☒ *Pier Head, Kinsale, Co. Cork,* ☎ *021/772301,* 𝖥𝖠𝖷 *021/774173. 58 rooms with bath. Restaurant, bar, sauna, health club, Ping-Pong, fishing. AE, DC, MC, V.*

$$ ⌷ **The Moorings.** Only yards from the water's edge in the fishing village of Scilly, this newly built accommodation has a panoramic view across Kinsale harbor, and yet is only a few minutes' walk from Kinsale's town center. Hosts Pat and Irene Jones are full of friendly advice, and won't discourage you if you're tempted to install yourself in the sunny conservatory and simply watch the boats go by. Nicely sized guest rooms all have large, tiled bathrooms, patchwork-quilt spreads, and interesting paintings by local artists. The five rooms on the top floor have tiny balconies with two chairs. ☒ *Scilly, Co. Cork,* ☎ *021/772376,* 𝖥𝖠𝖷 *021/772675. 9 rooms with bath. MC, V.*

$$ ⌷ **Old Bank House.** This tall, Georgian town house is owned and managed by Michael and Marie Riese, a Swiss-Irish couple, with sophisticated flair. The large rooms have tall windows (double-glazed against traffic noise) with classically draped curtains that match the pale-yellow walls. Pretty touches like dried-flower arrangements and discreet modern prints add to the elegance. The honeymoon suite on the third floor has a magnificent harbor view, a large bathroom, and a super-king-size bed. ☒ *Pearse St., Co. Cork,* ☎ *021/774075,* 𝖥𝖠𝖷 *021/774296. 9 rooms with bath. AE, MC, V.*

$$ ▣ **Scilly House.** Native Californian Karin Young has turned this lovely
★ 1760 Georgian house set in an acre of mature gardens into a country
inn, right on the edge of town opposite the Spaniard Inn. All the rooms
have wonderful views of the town, the harbor, and Charles Fort, and
are decorated with colonial furniture and old, American quilts on the
walls alongside Karin's watercolors. Bedrooms are clean and fresh, with
a restrained pink-and-white floral motif. In the evenings, host Bill
Skelly often leads a sing-along around the grand piano in the library.
The restaurant has a license for wine only. ⊠ *Scilly, Co. Cork,* ☎ *021/
772413,* FAX *021/774629. 7 rooms with bath. Restaurant, bar. AE, MC,
V. Closed Nov.–Apr. 1.*

$ ▣ **Kilcaw House.** Value for the money, off-road parking, and the per-
sonal attention of Henry and Christina Mitchell, the enthusiastic own-
ers, all make this newly built (1996) guest house a good choice. In high
season and on busy weekends when the town can be buzzing into the
small hours, Kilcaw's country location—a mile outside town on the
Cork side of the R600—guarantees peace and quiet. An open fire in
the lobby, polished pine floors, and striking colors help to add char-
acter to the farmhouse-style building. Rooms are well-equipped, spa-
cious, and uncluttered, with country pine furniture and throw rugs on
the wooden floors. ⊠ *Pewter Hole Cross, Co. Cork,* ☎ *021/774155,*
FAX *021/278382. 7 rooms with bath. AE, MC, V.*

Nightlife and the Arts

Check out the **Spaniard Inn** (⊠ Scilly, ☎ 021/772436) for live rock
and folk groups. **The Shanakee** (⊠ Market St., no phone) is renowned
in the area for traditional Irish music. The **Bacchus Brasserie** (⊠
Guardwell, ☎ 021/772382) offers dining and dancing to the over-25s.

Outdoor Activities and Sports

BICYCLES

Rent a bike from **Deco Cycles** (⊠ 18 Main St., Co. Cork, ☎ 021/774884)
to explore the picturesque hinterland of Kinsale.

DIVING

Kinsale Dive Centre (⊠ Folk House, Guardwell, Co. Cork, ☎ 021/
772382) will take you on a guided wreck dive and rent all equipment.

FISHING

For deep-sea angling contact **Kinsale Sea Angling Facilities Center** (⊠
Trident Hotel, Pier Head, Co. Cork, ☎ 021/772301).

HORSEBACK RIDING

Skevanish Riding Center (⊠ Innishannon, Co. Cork, ☎ 021/775476)
offers riding by the hour and lessons in an all-weather, indoor arena.
Residential riding holidays in local B&Bs can also be arranged.

WATER SPORTS

The **Oysterhaven Holiday and Activity Center** (⊠ Oysterhaven, near
Kinsale, Co. Cork, ☎ 021/770738) offers rental of all sailboarding equip-
ment, including wet suits. **Castlepark Sea School** (⊠ Castlepark, Co.
Cork, ☎ 021/772927) rents out a variety of sailing dinghies by the hour
or by the day.

Shopping

Victoria Murphy (⊠ Market Quay, ☎ 021/774317) has an interesting
selection of small antiques and antique jewelry. **Kinsale Crystal** (⊠ Mar-
ket St., ☎ 021/774463) is a master cutter's studio that sells 100% Irish,
mouth-blown, hand-cut crystal. **Boland's** (⊠ Pearse St., ☎ 021/772161)
features some unusual items, including exclusive sweaters, designer rain-
wear, and linen shirts. **Keane on Ceramics** (⊠ Pier Rd., ☎ 021/772085)
is a gallery that represents the best of Ireland's ceramic artists. **Giles**

Norman Photography Gallery (⊠ 44 Main St., ☎ 021/774–373) sells unusual black-and-white prints of Irish scenes.

En Route Leave Kinsale through its center by following the quays and drive west along the Bandon River toward the bridge on the R600. The route takes you through **Garretstown Woods** (signposts for Clonakilty on the R600), which are carpeted with wild bluebells in April; then past the edge of Courtmacsherry Bay, running alongside a wide, saltwater inlet that teems with curlew, plover, and other waders. The **Pink Elephant** (⊠ Harbour View, Kilbrittain, ☎ 023/49608) is an irresistible stopping place in good weather—a pink-painted, moderately priced bar and restaurant with sweeping sea views on its own grounds high above Courtmacsherry Bay. The bar serves soup and sandwiches on homemade brown bread; the restaurant features plain home cooking, including local seafood and roasted or grilled meat.

Timoleague

㉙ *19 km/12 mi west of Kinsale on R600.*

The small town of Timoleague marks the eastern end of the **Seven Heads Peninsula,** which stretches around to Clonakilty. A mid-13th-century **Franciscan abbey** at the water's edge is Timoleague's most striking monument. (Walk around the back to find the entrance gate.) The abbey was sacked by the English in 1642, but like many ruins of its kind, it was used as a burial place until recent times. A tower and walls with Gothic-arched windows still stand, and you can trace the ground plan of the old friary—the chapel, refectory, cloisters, and wine cellar. At one time the friars were well-known wine importers.

Timoleague Castle Gardens are right in the village. Although the castle is long gone—it has been replaced by a modest early 20th-century house in gray stone—the original gardens have survived. Palm trees and other frost-tender plants flourish in the mature shrubbery; there are two large, old-fashioned walled gardens, one for flowers and one for fruits and vegetables. ☎ 023/46116. 🎫 £2. ☉ *Easter weekend and June–Aug., daily noon–6.*

Courtmacsherry, the pretty village of multicolor cottages glimpsed across the water, has sandy beaches that make it a popular holiday resort. It can be reached by following the signposts from Timoleague.

Dining and Lodging

$$ ✕ **Casino House.** Midway between Kinsale and Timoleague on the R600 sits this old farmhouse, converted by owner-chefs Michael and Kerrin Relja, a German-Yugoslav couple, into an informal restaurant. Two small dining rooms, one blue and one green, each have their own sitting room with open fire for pre-dinner drinks; the whole place is wittily decorated in an uncluttered style. Highlights of the adventurous menu include the garlic prawn salad or lobster risotto for starters, and roast loin of lamb served with Roman gnocchi and bacon-wrapped beans as a main course. Relja's summer fruits with sabayon is an outstanding seasonal dessert. ⊠ *Coolmain, Kilbrittain, Co. Cork, ☎ 023/49944. MC, V. Closed Feb.–mid March; Wed. Easter–Oct.; weekdays Nov., Dec., and Jan.*

En Route This area is the heart of **West County Cork,** where natives have been called "a nation unto themselves" and small, twisted roads are overhung by tall hedges of *Fuchsia magellanica.* Originally imported as a garden shrub in the mid-19th century, it quickly adapted to the balmy sea air and is widely regarded as a weed used here for hedging—albeit a beautiful one with its delicate, drooping flowers in shades of mauve and red. In June, the hedges are offset by tall, purple foxgloves, and, in August and September, by bright-purple heather.

Many of the shops and businesses in the small market town of **Clonakilty** (9½ km/6 mi from Timoleague on the R600/N71) have abandoned chrome and plastic materials for traditional, hand-painted signs and wooden facades—to very charming effect. The best of the several traditional music pubs in town is **De Barra's** (⊠ 55 Pearse St., ☎ 023/33381). Many fine, sandy beaches are near Clonakilty; the best are at **Inchydoney,** 3 km/2 mi outside of town.

The **birthplace of Michael Collins** (1890–1922) is signposted about 5 km/3 mi west of Clonakilty off the N71 (just past the tiny village of Lissavaird). The ground plan of the simple homestead where the controversial founder of the modern Irish army was born has been reinstated by his nephew, and there is a bronze memorial (it's freely accessible). There is another memorial in the nearest village, **Woodfield,** opposite the pub where Collins is said to have had his last drink on the day he was shot in an ambush.

The N71 briefly joins the sea again at **Rosscarbery,** where you leave the main road by turning left at the signpost for Glandore at the end of the causeway. Glandore and Union Hall are twin fishing villages on either side of the landlocked Glandore Harbour. With its steep hill and pretty church, **Glandore** is a popular spot for visitors from the United Kingdom and Germany. Glandore's influx of affluent visitors and expensive yachts has not been shared in **Union Hall,** where simple fishing trawlers still tie up at the quay. In the area hereabouts, you are truly in the back of beyond, where tiny roads are without route numbers.

Castletownshend (clearly signposted from Union Hall via Rineen) has an unusual number of graciously designed, large, stone houses, mostly dating from the mid-18th century, when it was an important trading center. Its main street runs steeply down a hill to the sea. The sleepy town awakens in July and August, when its sheltered harbor bustles. Sparkling views await from the cliff-top perch of St. Barrahane's Church, which has a medieval oak altarpiece and three stained-glass windows by the early 20th-century Irish artisan Harry Clarke. The low-beamed interior of **Mary Ann's** (☎ 028/36146), one of the oldest bars in the country, is frequented by a very friendly mix of visitors and locals and is a good place for a pint and a sandwich. Writer Edna O'Brien claims that it is her favorite pub in the whole world.

Nightlife and the Arts

St. Barrahane's Church in Castletownshend is the setting for the annual **Festivals of Classical Music** (☎ 028/36193), which showcases local and international chamber musicians. Dates for 1998 are July 23 and 30 and August 6, 13, and 20.

Skibbereen

③⓪ *85 km/53 mi west of Kinsale.*

Skibbereen is the main market town in this neck of Southwest Cork, and it's a good base for the sights nearby. The weekly cattle market (Wednesday) and country market (Friday)—not to mention the plethora of pubs punctuated by bustling shops and coffeehouses—keep the place jumping year-round.

Garden lovers take note: Still partially under construction at press time (summer 1997) but well worth visiting is the **Liss Ard Foundation.** More than 50 acres are planted with various gardens designed to highlight the natural beauty of the landscape in an ecologically sound way. Particularly worthwhile are the 10-acre **Sky Gardens,** designed by American artist James Turrell to celebrate the wonder of light. Allow at least three hours. A guided tour is available upon request. ⊠ *On Castle-townshend road out of Skibbereen.* ☎ *028/22368.* ⌦ *£5.* ☉ *May–Oct., daily 10–dusk; call for hrs Nov.–Apr.*

Dining and Lodging

$$$$ ✕⌂ **Lissard Lake Lodge.** This renovated, lakeside Victorian lodge offers guests something offbeat: a country house without the usual country-house style. Every room does have a view of beautifully landscaped gardens, but there the resemblance to more traditional houses ends. The minimalist decor relies on black and white and natural woods. In the bedrooms, the huge beds have plump, white duvets, while a black pillar contains a TV, VCR, and CD player (CDs and videos can be borrowed from reception). The bathrooms, behind sliding Japanese paper doors, are equipped with stainless-steel sinks and large, white tubs. The one small guest lounge is sparsely furnished even by minimalist standards. Chef and co-owner Claudia Meister oversees dinner. Her dairy-free cooking draws from Mediterranean and Asian cuisines. Starters include roast sea scallops and vegetable spring rolls, while the main course might be fillet of turbot Japanese-style. ⊠ *Skibbereen, Co. Cork,* ☎ *028/40000,* ⅌ *028/40001. 10 rooms with bath. Restaurant (reservations essential); bar, tennis court, fishing. AE, DC, MC, V. Closed mid-Jan.–mid-Feb.*

$ ✕⌂ **West Cork Hotel.** This busy, long-established, family-run hotel in a large Victorian on the River Ilen has recently been redecorated in a stylish Old Colonial ambience. Rooms—all refurbished—offer a high standard of comfort and good value in the price range. The restaurant, famous for its steaks, features both fashionable modern dishes like Louisiana crab cakes, as well as more traditional offerings that include an outstanding mixed grill of bacon, sausage, lamb cutlet, liver, black pudding (blood sausage), and kidney. ⊠ *Bridge St., Skibbereen, Co. Cork,* ☎ *028/21277,* ⅌ *028/22333. 36 rooms with bath. Restaurant, bar, horseback riding, fishing. AE, DC, MC, V.*

Nightlife and the Arts

The **West Cork Arts Center** shows films and occasionally has poetry readings and exhibits of work by local artists. The on-site craft shop also sells items made by area artisans. ⊠ *North St., Skibbereen,* ☎ *028/22090.* ☉ *Mon.–Sat. 10–6.*

Outdoor Activities and Sports

Bicycles to explore West Cork's coast and country can be rented from **N.W. Roycroft** (⊠ Ilen St., Co. Cork, ☎ 028/21235).

Baltimore

③① *13 km/8 mi southwest of Skibbereen on R595.*

The beautiful, crescent-shape fishing village of Baltimore is now a popular sailing center and attracts its share of vacationing families from Ireland and abroad, especially during the peak summer months. The village was sacked in 1631 by a band of Algerian sailors; as a result, watchtowers were installed at the harbor mouth to protect the town.

③② **Sherkin Island,** one of Baltimore's two famous attractions, is a half-mile off the coast, only a 10-minute ferry ride away. Seven ferries are scheduled daily (☎ 028/20125 for times). On the island, you'll find the ruins of **Dun Na Long Castle** and **Sherkin Abbey,** both built around 1470 by the O'Driscoll's, a seafaring clan known as the "scourge of the Irish seas." The island's population today is 90, and there are several safe, sandy beaches and abundant wildlife.

33 Even more impressive than Sherkin Island is **Cape Clear Island,** a 1-by-3-mi island that is part of the West Cork Gaeltacht, or Irish-speaking area. The ferry to the island, which is 4 mi offshore, takes about an hour from Baltimore (£9 round-trip; ☎ 028/39119 for sailing times). It's exciting to watch the skipper thread his way through the many rocks and tiny islands of Roaring Water Bay. You have excellent views of the **Fastnet Rock Lighthouse,** focus of a renowned yachting race. Sparsely populated (about 200 residents), the island has one pub and a few simple B&Bs, but it is otherwise rugged and unblemished (electricity from the mainland was not brought over, via an underground cable, until April 1997), and it can be explored on foot in about an hour. Bird-watchers may want to schedule more time: Cape Clear is the southernmost point of Irish territory, and its observatory, the oldest in the Republic, has racked up all kinds of sightings of rare songbird migrants. Large flocks of oceangoing birds can be seen offshore in the summer.

OFF THE
BEATEN PATH
MIZEN HEAD SIGNAL STATION – If you still have an appetite for lovely coastal villages, take a detour from Skibbereen on the R592 out the Mizen Head Peninsula to Schull, then the R591 on to Goleen and Crookhaven. The scenery here becomes more rugged and beautiful as you travel west, and as you get to Mizen Head itself, the peninsula ends in a series of cliffs. The Mizen Head Signal Station, at the southwesterly point of mainland Ireland, was automated in 1993, and now the lighthouse-keeper's house has a dramatically located, cliff-top visitor center that explains the everyday life of a lighthouse station. The center hosts maritime exhibitions, but many people make the journey simply for the spectacular scenery, which includes a 99-step approach path and its suspension bridge. If you're continuing on to Bantry, plan to drive through Durrus. ✉ *Goleen,* ☎ *028/35225.* ☞ *£2.* ☉ *Mid-Mar.–May and Oct., daily 10:30–5; June–Sept., daily 10–6; Nov.–mid-Mar., weekends 11–4.*

Dining and Lodging

$ ✕🏠 **The Heron's Cove.** You really will see herons outside your window at Sue Hill's idyllic harborside retreat. The well-designed modern house, built on the edge of a secluded sea inlet, is only minutes' walk from Goleen's appealing village center. In summer months part of the house and its terrace becomes an informal restaurant. Fresh local seafood stars on the menu, which also includes lamb, duck, and steak; fresh herb sauces and homemade mayonnaise make subtle accompaniments, and there's a terrific wine list. Off-season (November–March), evening meals are prepared on request for guests only. The exceptionally well-equipped rooms, furnished in part with antiques, offer great views from every window. ✉ *The Harbour, Goleen, Co. Cork,* ☎ *028/35225,* 🗷 *028/35422. 5 rooms with bath. Restaurant, fishing. AE, DC, MC V.*

Outdoor Activities and Sports

Sailing dinghies as well as sailboards can be rented by the hour or by the day from **Baltimore Sailing School** (✉ The Pier, Baltimore, Co. Cork, ☎ 028/20141).

Bantry

34 *25 km/16 mi northwest of Skibbereen on N71.*

Bantry is an unprepossessing town with a large market square at the head of Bantry Bay. A long plaza has recently been constructed that attracts artisans, craftspeople, and musicians in summer. As you enter

Bantry, on the right-hand side of the road you'll see the porticoed entrance to **Bantry House,** one of Ireland's most magnificent houses, beautifully situated overlooking the sea. First built in the early 1700s, then subsequently altered and expanded later that century, the house as it looks today is largely the vision of Richard White, the second earl of Bantry, who entirely redesigned the house and created the Italianate gardens that surround it. On his European grand tours, Richard gobbled up fine art, furniture, and other antiques, including Aubusson tapestries said to have been ordered by Louis XV for the marriage of Marie Antoinette to the Dauphin. Some of the rooms are now a little shabby, but the beauty of the location compensates for the lack of polish. The long climb to the top of the rear garden pays off with what has been called "one of the great views in Ireland." Next to the house is **The Bantry 1796 French Armada Exhibition Center,** a small but worthwhile museum illustrating the abortive attempt by Irish nationalist Wolfe Tone and his French ally General Hoche to land 14,000 troops in Bantry Bay to effect an uprising. ⊠ *Bantry House,* ☎ *027/50047.* 🎫 *House or museum £5.* ☉ *Fall–spring, daily 9–6; summer, daily 9–8.*

The glorious sweep of **Bantry Bay** is on your left as you climb out of town past Ballylickey on the N71. The balladeers celebrate this bay. This is a starker, more magnificent prospect than any encountered so far, and the sparse, windswept vegetation gives an idea of what the wet and windy winters are like on the more exposed part of this coast.

Dining and Lodging

$$$$ ✕ **Blair's Cove House.** In the converted stables of a Georgian mansion overlooking Dunmanus Bay, gleaming silverware, pink tablecloths, and a large, crystal chandelier are set off, jewel-in-the-rough-style, against stone walls and exposed beams. A covered, heated terrace overlooks the rose-filled courtyard and fountain and is used in summer. The cuisine is French-Irish (the owners are French) with an emphasis on fresh local produce. Try rack of lamb cooked on the open, oak-wood grill, or a seafood special such as monkfish in Pernod sauce. The restaurant is licensed to serve wine only. ⊠ *Blair's Cove, Durrus, Co. Cork,* ☎ *027/61127. MC, V. Closed Sun.; Mon. Sept.–June; and Nov. 1–Feb. No lunch.*

$$$$ ✕ **Shiro Japanese Dinner House.** One of the biggest surprises of West
★   Cork's culinary world has been the success of this tiny, 20-seat restaurant, which serves authentic Japanese cuisine in an Edwardian house surrounded by palm trees. The room is decorated with watercolors by the talented hostess, Tokyo-born Kei Pilz. A fixed-price, five-course menu is available with a choice of main dishes such as yakitori and tempura. ⊠ *Ahakista, Durrus, Co. Cork,* ☎ *027/67030. Reservations essential. AE, DC, MC, V. Closed Jan. and Feb. No lunch.*

$$ ✕🏠 **Sea View House.** Set in its own wooded grounds overlooking
★   Bantry Bay, this large, three-story, 19th-century country-house hotel offers excellent value for the money. Owner-manager Kathleen O'Sullivan keeps an eagle eye on what was, until 1980, her private home. Inlaid antique furniture, polished brass, and ornate curtains set a tone of luxury. Bedrooms with sea views have small sofas in the bay windows; others have views of the wooded gardens. Polished tables in the elegant dining room are set with crocheted mats and linen napkins; service is friendly and informal. A set dinner menu emphasizes imaginatively prepared local produce; seafood is a specialty. ⊠ *Ballylickey, near Bantry, Co., Cork,* ☎ *027/50073,* FAX *027/51555. 17 rooms with bath. Restaurant, bar, horseback riding, fishing. AE, DC, MC, V. Closed mid-Nov.–mid Mar.*

Nightlife and the Arts

Between June 28–July 5, 1998, roughly 20 concerts will be held in the library at Bantry House during the **West Cork Chamber Music Festival.** The '98 festival (the third annual) will have a Russian theme, with the Borodin Quartet among the internationally renowned groups slated to perform; for more information, contact organizer Francis Humphrys (☎ 027/61105).

Outdoor Activities and Sports

The present nine holes at the **Bantry Park Golf Club** (⊠ Donemark, Co. Cork, ☎ 027/50579) are a good test of golf, while an additional nine holes overlooking Bantry Bay opened in 1997.

Shopping

Manning's Emporium (⊠ Ballylickey, ☎ 027/51049) is a showcase for locally made farmhouse cheeses, pâtés, and salamis—an excellent place to put together a picnic or just to browse. One of the West's larger independents, **Bantry Bookstore** (⊠ New St., ☎ 027/50064) has six rooms full of new, antiquarian, and secondhand books.

Glengarriff

35 *14 km/8 mi northwest of Bantry on N71, 21 km/13 mi southeast of Kenmare.*

The descent into wooded, sheltered Glengarriff reveals yet another kind of landscape: It is mild enough down here for subtropical plants to thrive. Trails along the shore are covered with rhododendrons, and they afford beautiful views of the nearby inlets, loughs, and lounging seals. You are also back on the beaten path, with crafts shops, tour buses, and boatmen soliciting your business by the roadside.

36 **Garnish Island,** about 10 minutes offshore, features beautiful, formal Italian gardens, shrubberies with rare subtropical plants, and excellent views from the strange Grecian temple. From the island's Martello tower, built at the end of the 18th century, the British watched for attempted landings by Napoleonic forces, including Hoche's ill-fated one. (The boat trip is subject to negotiation—expect to pay about £5 round-trip.) ☎ 027/63040. ⊠ £2.50. ☉ *July and Aug., Mon.–Sat. 9:30–6:30, Sun. 11–7; Apr.–June and Sept., Mon.–Sat. 10–6:30, Sun. 1–7; Mar. and Oct., Mon.–Sat. 10–4:30, Sun. 1–5; last landing 1 hr before closing.*

OFF THE
BEATEN PATH

THE BEARA PENINSULA – The relatively undeveloped Beara Peninsula (pronounced *bar-*a) is one of Ireland's better-kept secrets—the one part of the Southwest that most visitors leave out, opting instead for the Ring of Kerry. For a wonderful, whole-day scenic drive, turn left at Glengarriff and head south on R572 along the peninsula's edge. Much of the road hugs either the coast or the side of the **Slieve Miskish Mountains** and gives phenomenal views across Kenmare Bay to the Sheep's Head Peninsula. Just beyond Castletownbere lie the ruins of **Dunboy Castle and House,** which is open Easter–October, daily 10–7. **Dursey Island,** which is signposted, is a bird-watcher's paradise. It is still inhabited but accessible only by a cable car that can carry three passengers, one cow, or five sheep. The squeamish be forewarned: The journey involves swinging violently 50 ft above the ocean. ⊠ *Dursey Island,* ☎ 027/73016. ⊠ *50p.* ☉ *Mon.–Sat. at 9, 11, 2:30, and 5; July and Aug., also 7 PM and 8 PM; call for Sun. times.*

Return from Dursey Island via tiny **Allihies,** the former site of a huge copper mine, where a detour takes you along a precipitous and breathtaking coastal road to Eyeries, a ghost town–like village overlooking Coulagh Bay, and then up the south side of the Kenmare River to Kenmare (☞ *below*)

THE RING OF KERRY

Running along the perimeter of the Iveragh Peninsula, the dramatic Ring of Kerry is probably the single most popular tourist route in Ireland. Stunning mountain and coastal views are around virtually every turn of the road. There's only drawback: On a sunny day, it seems like half of all the tourists in Ireland that day are there, packed into buses, on bikes, or backpacking along the same two-lane road. Because tour buses ply the Ring counterclockwise, we recommend that independent travelers take it clockwise, starting at Kenmare. This is equally convenient whether you're approaching from Glengarriff (on the N71) or Killarney (also on the N71), which is the traditional—and by some accounts, more practical—starting point. The trip covers 176 km/110 mi on the N70 (and briefly the R562) if you start and finish in Killarney; the journey will be 40 km/25 mi shorter if you only venture between Kenmare and Killorglin. Allow at least one full day to circumnavigate the Ring. And because rain blocks views across the water to the Beara Peninsula in the east and the Dingle Peninsula in the west, pray for sunshine. It makes all the difference.

Kenmare

㊲ *21 km/13 mi northwest of Glengarriff, 34 km/21 mi south of Killarney on N71.*

A small market town at the head of the sheltered Kenmare River estuary, Kenmare was founded in 1670 by Sir William Petty (Cromwell's surveyor general, a multitasking entrepreneur—a sort of proto-Goethe) and today is a popular touring base. Most of its buildings date from the 19th century, when it was part of the enormous Lansdowne Estate, itself assembled by Petty. The **Kenmare Heritage Centre** explains the history of the town and supplies a walking route through the town pointing out places of interest. ☎ *064/41233.* ☜ *£1.* ☉ *Apr.–Oct., Mon.–Sat. 9:30–5:30.*

Dining and Lodging

$$ ✕ **D'Arcy's Old Bank House.** This town-center L-shape room, previously a bank, has been transformed into a restaurant with an open fire, white damask on the tables, and local paintings on the white and terra-cotta walls. Owner-chef Matt D'Arcy's accomplished, classic French menu offers excellent value and features the best of fresh local produce. Try, for example, *supreme de volaille et saumon* (breast of chicken and salmon with a creamy prawn sauce) or *filet de boeuf et champignon en croute* (panfried beef fillet with savory mushrooms in pastry). For dessert his wild heather, honey, and lavender ice cream is a must. ⊠ *Main St., Co. Kerry,* ☎ *064/41589. AE, MC, V. Closed last wk of Jan., 1st wk of Feb., Dec. 24–29, and Mon. and Tues. Oct.– May. No lunch Oct.–May.*

$–$$ ✕ **Packie's.** Owner-chef Maura O'Connell Foley established Kenmare's original first-class restaurant, the Lime Tree, but she has since opted for a quieter life at Packies. The small room has a flagstone floor, an exposed-stone fireplace, and paintings by local artists on the walls. The delicious bistro-style menu includes wild smoked salmon with red onion and caper salsa, or crab claws with garlic butter or olive oil. Classically Irish dishes like casserole of beef with Guinness and mushrooms turn up as well. The selection of Irish farmhouse cheeses is splendid. ⊠ *Henry St., Co. Kerry,* ☎ *064/41508. MC, V. Closed Sun. and Nov.–Easter.*

$$$$ ✕🖽 **Park Hotel.** The Park, an 1897 sprawling stone chateau, is one of
★ Ireland's premier country-house hotels. Set on 11 acres and a two-minute walk to town, the property has views of the Caha Mountains and terraced lawns that sweep down to the bay. A marble fireplace and a tall grandfather clock preside over the thickly carpeted lobby. Owner-manager Francis Brennan is a stickler for detail and has made great efforts to recapture the hotel's heyday. The bedrooms are individually designed with late-Victorian furniture faithful to the house's original period; walnut or mahogany bedroom suites have matching wardrobes, chests of drawers, and headboards. "Superior deluxe" rooms are the smallest, but big by the standards of other places, with armchairs or sofas in the bedroom area. Park Suite rooms have an entrance hall and a separate sitting area; nine larger suites are also available. All bedrooms have finely equipped bathrooms with glossy, Italian-marble tiling. Be sure to sample the modern Irish cuisine of the renowned restaurant, which uses local ingredients in a mélange of Asian and Continental styles. ⊠ *Kenmare, Co. Kerry,* ☎ *064/41200,* F̅A̅X̅ *064/41402. 50 rooms with bath. Restaurant, bar, 18-hole golf course, tennis court, croquet, Ping-Pong, fishing, bicycles. AE, DC, MC, V. Closed Jan.–Apr. 10.*

$$$$ ✕🖽 **Sheen Falls Lodge.** The magnificent setting—300 secluded acres
★ of lawns, semitropical gardens, and forest between Kenmare Bay and the falls of the River Sheen—is easily matched by this rambling, bright-yellow, slate-roof manor house, built by the descendants of Sir William Petty, and the former seat of the earls of Kerry. The public rooms, decorated in warm orange tones, include a mahogany-paneled library with more than 1,000 books, mainly of Irish interest, and a billiard room adjacent to the bar. The bedrooms have a combination of new and antique furnishings; they all offer stunning bay or river views. The restaurant, La Cascade (it overlooks the falls), serves classic French cuisine using local produce such as lobster, salmon, oysters, mussels, quail, pheasant, lamb, and beef. ⊠ *Co. Kerry,* ☎ *064/41600,* F̅A̅X̅ *064/ 41386. 40 rooms with bath. Restaurant, bar, sauna, steam room, tennis court, croquet, health club, horseback riding, fishing, bicycles. AE, DC, MC, V.*

$ 🖽 **Sallyport House.** Just across the bridge on the way into Kenmare, this substantial family home dating from 1932 has been enlarged to serve as a comfortable B&B. The spotless rooms, all with harbor or mountain views, are furnished with a variety of Victorian and Edwardian antiques. Janey Arthur has placed family heirlooms in all rooms; if you are interested in old Irish furniture, ask for a tour. Breakfast is served overlooking the orchard, and in summer you can pick your own apples. Fresh fruit salad and a cheese platter are part of the excellent breakfast. ⊠ *Arthur Family, Co. Kerry,* ☎ *064/42066,* F̅A̅X̅ *064/41752. 5 rooms with bath. No credit cards. Closed mid-Nov.–Apr. 1.*

Nightlife
Try the **Kingdom Bar** (☎ 064/41361) for traditional music.

Outdoor Activities and Sports
Seafari (⊠ Kenmare Pier, Co. Kerry, ☎ 064/83171) has two-hour, scenic, wildlife cruises and also runs the Marine Activities Centre, which offers sea fishing, sailboat day trips, boardsailing, canoeing, waterskiing, and tube rides.

Shopping

Avoca Handweavers (⊠ Moll's Gap, ☎ 064/34720) sells wool clothing and mohair rugs and throws in a wide range of colors and weaves. **Black Abbey Crafts** (⊠ 28 Main St., ☎ 064/42115) specializes in fine Irish-made crafts. **Cleo's** (⊠ 2 Shelbourne St., ☎ 064/41410) stocks Irish-made wool and linen and Irish handknits, which are made to their own striking designs, often drawn from Ireland's past. **Nostalgia** (⊠ 27 Henry St., ☎ 064/41389) has a good selection of antique lace and linen.

Sneem

❸❽ *27 km/17 mi southwest of Kenmare on N70.*

One of the prettiest villages in Ireland (and, it can seem, most popular), filled with houses washed in different colors, Sneem (from the Irish *an tSnaidhm*—the knot) sits around an English-style green on the estuary of the Ardsheelaun River. Look for "the pyramids" (as they are known locally) beside the parish church. These 12-ft-tall, traditional stone structures with stained-glass insets look as though they have been here forever. In fact, the sculpture park was completed in 1990 to the design of the Kerry-born artist, James Scanlon, who has won international awards for his work in stained glass. The road then runs inland for a few miles before emerging at the coast again at Castlecove.

❸❾ **Staigue Fort,** signposted 4 km/2½ mi inland at Castlecove, is one of the finest examples of an Iron Age stone fort in Ireland. Approximately 2,500 years old, this structure, made from local stone, is almost circular and about 75 ft in diameter, with only one entrance, on the south side. Between the Iron Age (from 500 BC to the 5th century AD) and early Christian times (6th century AD), such "forts" were, in fact, fortified homesteads within which several families of one clan and their cattle lived. The walls at Staigue Fort are almost 13 ft wide at the base, 7 ft wide at the top; they still stand at 18 ft on the north and west sides. Within the walls stairs lead to narrow platforms on which the lookouts stood. (Private land must be crossed to reach the fort, and a nominal "compensation for trespass" is often requested by the landowner.)

❹❶ **Caherdaniel** is the next village west on N70. Right beyond Caherdaniel is **Derrynane House,** once the home of Daniel O'Connell (1775–1847), "The Liberator," who campaigned for Catholic Emancipation (the granting of full rights of citizenship for Catholics), which became a reality in 1828. The house with its lovely garden and 320-acre estate now forms **Derrynane National Park.** The south and east wings of the house (which O'Connell himself remodeled) are open to visitors and still contain much of the original furniture and other items associated with O'Connell. ☎ *066/75113.* ☞ *House £2, park free.* ☉ *Jan.–Mar., Nov., and Dec., weekends 1–5; Apr. and Oct., Tues.–Sun. 1–5; May–Sept., Mon.–Sat. 9–6, Sun. 11–7.*

Dining and Lodging

$$$$ ☒ **Parknasilla Great Southern.** A porter in a frock coat and striped gray pants typifies the elegant and slightly stuffy turn-of-the-century atmosphere of this grand old hotel. Previous guests include General de Gaulle, Princess Grace, and George Bernard Shaw, who wrote much of *Saint Joan* while staying here. Although some rooms are a bit plain, they have been tastefully decorated in soft pinks and blues. The sheltered coastal location (3 km/2 mi south of Sneem) and excellent sporting facilities make it an ideal retreat. ⊠ *Parknasilla, near Sneem, Co. Kerry,* ☎ *064/45122,* FAX *064/45323. 85 rooms with bath. Restaurant, bar, pool, sauna, 9-hole golf course, tennis court, horseback riding, wind-*

surfing, boating, waterskiing, fishing, bicycles. AE, DC, MC, V. Closed Jan.–mid-Feb.

Waterville, Valentia Island, and the Skelligs

④ *35 km/22 mi west of Sneem, 5 km/3 mi north of Caherdaniel on N70.*

Like many villages on the Ring, Waterville has a few restaurants and pubs, but little else. It *is* famous for game fishing, its 18-hole championship golf course, and for the fact that Charlie Chaplin and Charles DeGaulle once kept summer homes here. Salmon and trout fishing are excellent at nearby Lough Currane.

Just outside Waterville, a scenic detour is signposted from the main Ring to **Ballinskelligs,** a small, Irish-speaking fishing village with an old monastery, a pub, and a fine sandy beach. In the far northwestern corner of the Ring, **Valentia Island** lies across Portmagee Channel. Some of the romance of visiting an island has been lost since Valentia was connected to the mainland by a road bridge in 1971. The island still gives its name to weather reports, but the station that monitors the Atlantic weather systems has now moved onto the nearby mainland.

★ ㊸ The **Skelligs**—Little Skellig, Great Skellig, and the **Washerwoman's Rock**—is a group of distinctive conical-shape rock islands that may be seen from Valentia Island on a clear day. The largest rock, the Great Skellig, or **Skellig Michael,** rises 700 ft out of the Atlantic. It has the remains of a settlement of early Christian monks, reached by climbing 600 increasingly precipitous steps. In spite of 1,000 years' battering by Atlantic storms, the church, oratory, and beehive-shape living cells are surprisingly well preserved.

The Skellig Experience, situated where the road bridge joins Valentia Island, contains exhibits on local bird life, the history of the lighthouse and keepers, and the life and work of the early Christian monks. There is also a 15-minute audiovisual show that allows you to "tour" the monastery without leaving dry land. If, however, you'd like to see the Skelligs up close (landing is prohibited without a special permit), you can take a 1½-hour guided cruise with author and Skellig expert, Des Lavelle. Little Skellig is the breeding ground of more than 22,000 pairs of gannets, while **Puffin Island** to the north has a large population of shearwaters, storm petrel, and puffins. Photographers will love the boat trip, but sailors are warned that these are choppy waters at the best of times. ⊠ *Valentia,* ☎ *066/76306.* 🎫 *Center £3; cruise negotiable, but expect about £15.* ☉ *Apr.–June and Sept., daily 9:30–5; July and Aug., daily 9:30–7; call to confirm weather-dependent cruise times, or ask at the Killarney TIO.*

Dining and Lodging

$ ✕ **The Smuggler's Inn.** On a 2 km-/1 mi-long sandy beach, Lucille and Harry Hunt's small, family-run guest house has a restaurant with a strong reputation for its seafood. It's an ideal spot for a leisurely lunch or a quick pint and a sandwich. ⊠ *Cliff Rd., Waterville, Co. Kerry,* ☎ *066/ 74330. AE, DC, MC, V. Closed Nov. 3–Feb. 15.*

$$ ✕🏠 **Butler Arms.** The white, castellated towers at the corners of this hotel provide a familiar landmark on the Ring. The building has been in the same family for three generations; it has a regular clientele, predominantly male, who come back year after year for the excellent fishing and golf facilities nearby. It was a favorite base for Charlie Chaplin. Although the accommodations are neither smart nor chic, the rambling old lounges with open turf fires are comfortable places to relax and converse. ⊠ *Waterville, Co. Kerry,* ☎ *066/74144,* 📠 *066/74520. 30* *rooms with bath. Restaurant, 2 bars, tennis court, horseback riding, fishing. AE, DC, MC, V. Closed mid-Oct.–Easter.*

Nightlife
Head for the **Strand Hotel** (☎ 066/74248) for live folk music.

Outdoor Activities and Sports
Waterville Golf Club (✉ Ring of Kerry, Co. Kerry, ☎ 066/74102) is one of the toughest and most scenic courses in Ireland or Britain (☞ Chapter 10).

Cahirciveen

⓬ *18 km/11 mi northwest of Waterville on N70, 27½ km/17 mi southeast of Glenbeigh.*

Cahirciveen (pronounced cah-her-sigh-*veen*) marks the Ring's western fringe, and it is the main market town and shopping center for South Kerry, at the foot of Bentee Mountain. The **Old Oratory** (✉ Main Rd., ☎ 066/72996), a former church that dominates the main street, was built in 1888 to honor the local hero, Daniel O'Connell (☞ Caherdaniel *under* Sneem, *above*); it is now a gift shop and visitor center. Following the tradition in this part of the world, the town's modest, terraced houses are painted in different colors—the brighter the better. The same sign writers who recently transformed Kenmare with their old-fashioned, hand-painted signs have been at work here, too. The **Cahirciveen Heritage Centre** is housed in the converted former barracks of the Royal Irish Constabulary, an imposing, castlelike structure built after the Fenian Rising of 1867 to suppress any further revolts. The center has displays depicting scenes from times of famine in the locality, the life of Daniel O'Connell, and the history of the RIC. ✉ *Barracks, Cahirciveen,* ☎ *066/72777.* ☜ *£2.50.* ☉ *June–Sept., Mon.–Sat. 10–6, Sun. 2–6; Oct.–Mar., weekdays 9:30–5:30.*

En Route   The road from Cahirciveen to Glenbeigh is one of the highlights of the Ring. To the north is Dingle Bay and the jagged peaks of the Dingle Peninsula, which will, in all probability, be shrouded in mist. If they are not, the gods have indeed blessed your journey. The road runs close to the water here, and beyond Kells it climbs high above the bay, hugging the steep side of Drung Hill before descending to Glenbeigh. Note how different the stark character of this stretch of the Ring is from the gentle, woody, Kenmare Bay side.

Glenbeigh

⓭ *27 km/17 mi northeast of Cahirciveen on N70, 11½ km/7 mi west of Killorglin.*

Set on a boggy plateau by the sea, the block-long town of Glenbeigh is a popular holiday base, offering excellent hiking in the **Glenbeigh Horseshoe**, as the surrounding mountains are known, and exceptionally good trout fishing on Lough Coomasaharn. Worth a quick look, the **Kerry Bog Village Museum** is a cluster of reconstructed, fully furnished cottages, which gives a vivid portrayal of the daily life of the region's working class in the early 1800s. ✉ *Beside Red Fox Bar,* ☎ *066/69184.* ☜ *£2.* ☉ *Mar.–Nov., daily 8:30–7; Jan.–Mar. by request.*

⓮ **Rossbeigh,** just north of Glenbeigh, has about 3 km/2 mi of soft-yellow, sandy coastline backed by high dunes. It faces Inch Strand, a similar formation across the water on the Dingle Peninsula (☞ The Dingle Peninsula, *below*). A signpost to the right just outside Glenbeigh points to **Lough Caragh,** another tempting side excursion to a beautiful expanse of water set among gorse-and-heather-covered hills and majestic mountains. The road encircles the lake, hugging the shoreline much of the way.

Dining and Lodging

$$$ ✕⚏ **Caragh Lodge.** Built in the mid-19th century as a fishing lodge, this charming old house by the lake sits in 9 acres of spectacular gardens filled with azaleas, camellias, and magnolias. The three big rooms in the main house are furnished with Victorian and Georgian antiques; rooms in the courtyard and in a garden annex are smaller and have modern, light-oak furniture. Comfortable sitting rooms overlook the lake, as does the dining room. Owner Mary Gaunt supervises the four-course, set dinner menu. Cider-baked ham with Calvados sauce or poached wild salmon with fresh basil sauce are typical of the fare, which features lots of garden-fresh produce. ✉ *Caragh Lake, Killorglin, Co. Kerry,* ☎ *066/69115,* 𝔽𝔸𝕏 *066/69316. 11 rooms with bath. Restaurant (wine license only), tennis court, boating, fishing. AE, DC, MC, V. Closed mid-Oct.–mid-Apr. No lunch.*

$$$ ⚏ **Ard na Sidhe.** ("Sidhe," pronounced sheen, means "hill of the
★ fairies.") This secluded, gabled, Edwardian mansion is built of stone walls, now ivy-covered, punctuated by casement windows set in stone mullions. Attractive, large rooms have coordinated carpets and spreads, and lovely floral drapes on the bay windows; those in the main building are the nicest. Antiques and open fires adorn the traditionally furnished lobby and lounges. The hotel also offers delightful, award-winning lakeside gardens. Guests are entitled to use the sporting facilities at the Europe hotel (☞ Killarney, *below*) and at Dunloe Castle in Killarney. ✉ *Caragh Lake, near Killorglin, Co. Kerry,* ☎ *066/69105,* 𝔽𝔸𝕏 *066/ 69282. 20 rooms with bath. Restaurant, bar, boating, fishing. AE, DC, MC, V. Closed Oct. 11–Apr. 5.*

Outdoor Activities and Sports

Dooks Golf Club (✉ Glenbeigh, Co. Kerry, ☎ 066/68205) is a challenging traditional links on the shore of Dingle Bay (☞ Chapter 10).

Killorglin

47 *14 km/9 mi east of Glenbeigh, 22 km/14 mi west of Killarney.*

The last stop on the Ring before Killarney (or the first, if you're going counterclockwise), the hilltop town of Killorglin is the scene of the **Puck Fair**, three days of merrymaking during the second weekend in August. A large billy goat with beribboned horns, installed on a high pedestal, presides over the fair. The origins of the tradition of King Puck are lost in time. Though some horse, sheep, and cattle dealing still occurs at the fair, the main attractions these days are free outdoor concerts and extended drinking hours. The crowd is predominantly young and invariably noisy, so avoid Killorglin at fair time if you've come for peace and quiet. On the other hand, if you intend joining in the festivities, be sure to book accommodations well in advance.

Dining

$$$ ✕ **Nick's Seafood and Steak.** Owner-chef Nick Foley trained as a veterinary surgeon but prefers life in the kitchen. The old, stone town house has a bar-cum-dining room at street level and a quieter dining room on the floor above. Foley is known for his cockle-and-mussel soup and his steaks. In winter, sample the haunch of Kerry venison in red-wine and juniper sauce. All vegetables are grown locally. ✉ *Main St., Co. Kerry,* ☎ *066/61219. AE, DC, MC, V. Closed Nov.–Easter.*

IN AND AROUND KILLARNEY

One of southwest Ireland's most attractive locales, Killarney is also the most heavily visited city in the region (its proximity to the Ring of Kerry and to Shannon Airport help to ensure this). Light rain is typical of the area around Killarney, but because of the region's topography, it seldom lasts long. Indeed, the showers (you can track the clouds' approach over the lakes) can actually add to the spectacle of the ever-changing scenery. The rain is often followed within minutes by brilliant sunshine and, yes, even a rainbow.

Exploring Killarney

87 km/54 mi west of Cork City on N22, 19 km/12 mi southeast of Killorglin, 24 km/15 mi north of Glengarriff.

The lakes and mountains of Killarney are among the most celebrated—and indisputably the most commercialized—attractions in Ireland. Killarney's heather-clad mountains, lush, subtropical vegetation, and deep-blue lakes dotted with wooded isles have left a lasting impression on a long stream of visitors, beginning in the 18th century with the English travelers Arthur Young and Bishop Berkeley. Visitors in search of the natural beauty so beloved by the Romantic movement began to flock to the Southwest, including writers Sir Walter Scott and William Thackeray. By the mid-19th century, Killarney's stunning scenery was considered as exhilarating and awe-inspiring as anything in Switzerland or England's Lake District. The influx of affluent visitors that followed the 1854 arrival of the railway transformed the lives of Kerry's impoverished natives, and set in motion a snowball of commercialization that continues today.

But the beauty of the surrounding area—an unbeatable combination of wild mountain scenery and lush, subtropical vegetation—persists. The air smells of damp woods and heather moors. Amazingly, the vegetation is splendid at any time of year. The red fruits of the Mediterranean strawberry tree (*Arbutus unedo*) are at their height in October and November. Also at that time, the bracken turns rust, contrasting with the many evergreens. In late April and early May, the purple flowers of the rhododendron *ponticum* put on a spectacular display. (This Turkish import has adapted so well to the climate that its vigorous growth threatens native oak woods, and many of these purple plants are being dug up by volunteers in an effort to control its spread.)

48 You may want to limit time spent in **Killarney Town** itself if discos, Irish cabarets, and singing pubs—the latter a local specialty with a strong Irish-American flavor—aren't your thing. Killarney's nightlife is at its liveliest from May to September; Irish and European visitors pack the town in July and August, while peak season for Americans follows in September and October. At other times of the year, particularly from November to mid-March, when many of the hotels are closed, the town is quiet to the point of being eerie. Given the choice, go to Killarney in April, May, or early October.

★ **49** On your way to the Gap of Dunloe from Killarney, **Aghadoe** (5 km/3 mi outside Killarney on the R562 Beaufort–Killorglin road) is an outstanding place to preview some of the sights to come. Standing beside Aghadoe's 12th-century, ruined church and round tower, be sure to remember to breathe as you watch the shadows creep across the Lower Lake, with Innisfallen Island in the distance and the Gap of Dunloe away to the west.

Killarney Area

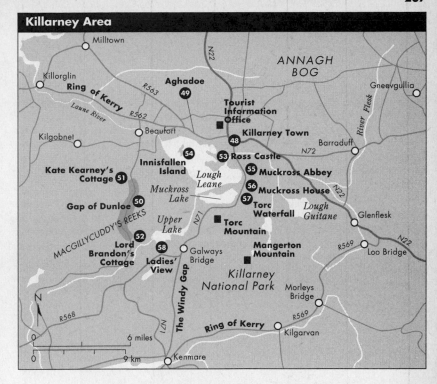

★ ⑩ Massive, glacial rocks form the side of the **Gap of Dunloe,** one of Killarney's primary sights. (The rocks create strange echoes: Give a shout to test it out.) The gap is 7 km/4½ mi west of Killarney on the Beaufort Road, R562, and well signposted. The road through the gap stretches for 6½ km/4 mi—from ☞ **Kate Kearney's Cottage** to ☞ **Lord Brandon's Cottage**—between MacGillicuddy's Reeks, Ireland's highest mountains to the west, and the Purple Mountains. Five small lakes are strung out beside the road. Cars are banned from the gap, but in summer the first 3 km/2 mi are busy with horse and foot traffic, much of which turns back at the halfway point.

To see the entire gap and continue on via boat over Upper Lake and Lough Leane, take an organized tour from your hotel or Killarney town center (☞ Guided Tours *in* The Southwest A to Z, *below*). Whether you walk or ride (on horseback or in a jaunting car), you're given two hours to get to ☞ **Lord Brandon's Cottage,** at the head of the ☞ **Upper Lake,** where you pick up a boat for the 1¼-hour ride that lands at ☞ **Ross Castle;** from here it's a 5-minute walk into town. Most tour companies have a free shuttle service and will pick you up from lodgings within a 5-km/3-mi radius of Killarney town center. (The value of an organized tour is that you avoid ending up with your car at Dunloe and yourself back in Killarney.)

⑪ **Kate Kearney's Cottage** (☎ 064/44116) is a good place to rent a jaunting car (pony and trap) or pony. Kate was a famous beauty who sold illegal *poteen* (moonshine) to visitors from her home, contributing greatly, one suspects, to their enthusiasm for the scenery. Appropriately enough, it's now a pub, and a good place to pause for a glass of Irish coffee.

The **Upper Lake** comes into view at the head of the Gap, with the lonely
⑫ Black Valley stretching into the hills at the right. From **Lord Brandon's Cottage,** a tea shop serving soup and sandwiches (open Easter–Sept.,

daily 10–dusk), a path leads to the edge of the lake, and the journey is continued by rowboat. It is an old tradition for the boatman to carry a bugle and illustrate the echoes. Look out for caves on the left-hand side when passing through the narrow Middle Lake. The boat passes under Brickeen Bridge and into the **Middle Lake,** where 30 islands are steeped in legend, much of which your boatman is likely to recount.

53 At the end of the journey through the Gap of Dunloe, **Ross Castle** is a fully restored 14th-century stronghold. It was the last place in the province of Munster to fall to Oliver Cromwell's forces in 1652. A later dwelling has 16th- and 17th-century furniture. ▩ £2.50. ☉ *May and Sept., daily 9–6; June–Aug., daily 9–6:30; Oct., daily 9–5.*

54 The romantic ruins on **Innisfallen Island** date from the 6th or 7th century. Between 950 and 1350 the *Annals of Innisfallen* were compiled here by monks. (The book survives in the Bodleian Library in Oxford.) You can reach the launch and castle by car. To get to the island, you can rent a rowboat at Ross Castle (£1.50 per hour), or you can join a cruise (£5) in a covered, heated launch.

A half-day trip to Muckross Abbey, Muckross House and Estate, and the Torc Waterfall is another popular excursion from Killarney. Cars are not allowed to tour the grounds of the estate, but you'll find a parking lot at the house. Some people choose to make the whole trip by jaunting car, renting one at the stand near the TIO in Killarney. (The cost of a jaunting car is £15–£28, negotiable with the driver, for up to four people. Get an estimate from the TIO.) To save time and money, drive the 4 km/2½ mi to Muckross Abbey on the N71 Kenmare road, and pick up a jaunting car there. Or, rent a bicycle in town, pack a lunch, and make a day of it.

55 The 15th-century, Franciscan **Muckross Abbey,** like ☞ Ross Castle ruined by Cromwell's British troops in 1652, is still amazingly complete, although roofless. An ancient yew tree rises above the cloisters and breaks out over the abbey walls. Three flights of stone steps allow access to the upper floors and living quarters, where you can visit what was once their dormitory, kitchen, and refectory. ▩ *Free.* ☉ *Daily dawn–dusk.*

56 **Muckross House,** a 19th-century, Elizabethan-style manor now houses the **Kerry Folklife Center,** where bookbinders, potters, and weavers demonstrate their crafts. The informal grounds here are noted for their rhododendrons and azaleas, the water garden, and the outstanding limestone rock garden. In the park beside the house, **The Kerry Country Life Experience** comprises reconstructed farm buildings and outhouses, a blacksmith's forge, a carpenter's workshop, and a selection of farm animals. It is a reminder of the way things were done on the farm before the advent of electricity and the mechanization of farming. ⊠ *About 1½ km/1 mi west of the abbey on the N71,* ☎ *064/31440.* ▩ *Farms or house £3.30, farms and house £4.50.* ☉ *House Sept.–June, daily 9–5:30; July and Aug., daily 9–7; farms mid-March–Apr., weekends 2–6; May and Oct., daily 2–6; and June–Sept., daily 10–7.*

57 The **Torc Waterfall** is about a 10-minute walk from the parking lot. After your first view of the roaring cascade, it's worth the climb up a long flight of stone steps to the second, less-frequented clearing. If the ★ **58** weather is fine, return to your car and drive on west to **Ladies' View,** a panoramic vista of the three lakes and the surrounding mountains. The name goes back to 1905, when Queen Victoria was a guest at Muckross House. Upon seeing the view of the three lakes, her ladies-in-waiting were said to have been dumbfounded by its beauty. The N71 continues to Kenmare, from where you can complete the circuit by taking the shorter but very narrow Windy Gap route, or make a wide sweep via Kilgarvan on the R569 and N22, driving back through Killarney to Aghadoe.

Dining and Lodging

$$$$ ✕ **Fredrick's.** Breathtaking views of Killarney's lakes from the rooftop
★ restaurant of the Aghadoe Heights hotel (☞ *below*) make this the ultimate romantic venue. And, as if that weren't enough, the food is outstanding. Silver candelabra, white linen, and fully upholstered chairs beckon from the tables (ask for one at the front when you book). The English chef prepares a classic French menu, which varies according to season. Starters may include Dingle Bay oysters, or grilled squid with sesame prawns on young leeks. Main courses include classics such as black sole grilled or meunière, or more unusual dishes like medallions of veal with crab soufflé. This is one of the most expensive restaurants in Ireland, but it will provide an unforgettable occasion. ⊠ *Aghadoe Heights, Co. Kerry,* ☎ *064/31766. Jacket and tie. AE, DC, MC, V.*

$$$ ✕ **Strawberry Tree.** There are only eight tables in this tiny, upstairs, town-center restaurant, but its reputation for imaginative cooking has spread far and wide. Rustic stone walls, old wooden floors, blue-and-white linens, and blue-velvet chairs set the stage. Owner-chef Evan Doyle describes his cooking as very rustic and very Irish, and the fact that all the food is bought locally from organic growers and free-range producers comes out in the tasting. Corned beef is served in cabbage parcels lined with parsley sauce, salmon is smoked over apple wood, and pork fillet is stuffed with Clonakilty black pudding. Yer Man's, a wittily decorated, tiny "olde village pub" underneath, has the same owner, and it's a good bet for bar food at lunchtime. ⊠ *24 Plunkett St., Co. Kerry,* ☎ *064/32688. AE, DC, MC, V. Closed Dec. and Jan.*

$$ ✕ **Gaby's Seafood.** The best seafood in town packs Gaby's small din-
★ ing room, with its tiled floors, pine booths, and red-gingham cloths with matching lamp shades. Try the seafood mosaic (seven or eight kinds of fresh fish in a cream-and-wine sauce) or lobster Gaby (shelled, boiled in a cream-and-cognac sauce, and served back in the shell). ⊠ *17 High St., Co. Kerry,* ☎ *064/32519. AE, DC, MC, V. Closed Mon. No lunch Sun.*

$ ✕ **Sheila's.** Simply furnished with stripped-pine tables and red paper place mats, Sheila's has fed the people of Killarney and its visitors for more than 30 years—it was recently handed down from mother to daughter. The unpretentious menu features such Irish specials as corned beef with cabbage and Irish stew (Kerry lamb stewed with barley, carrots, onion, and potatoes). In a town bedeviled by tourist traps, this friendly spot offers excellent value for the money. The restaurant is licensed to serve wine only. ⊠ *75 High St., Co. Kerry,* ☎ *064/31270. AE, DC, MC, V.*

$$$$ ✕🛏 **Aghadoe Heights.** Its location on a bluff (4 km/2½ mi outside town on the Tralee side, signposted off the N22) translates into unforgettable lake views that will long remain with you. Eight acres of grounds ensure absolute peace and quiet. The luxurious interior is a mix of the impeccable—the owner's antiques and paintings adorning the public rooms—and the ostentatious—gilded decor. Two-thirds of the bedrooms have lake views, and all are relatively large with good-size bathrooms, matching floral drapes and spreads, lace-covered cushions, and fitted natural wood furniture. The three suites are exceptionally spacious with romantic views of the lakes and a ruined abbey. ⊠ *Aghadoe Heights, Co. Kerry,* ☎ *064/31766,* FAX *064/31345. 57 rooms with bath. Restaurant, bar, indoor pool, sauna, tennis court, fishing. AE, DC, MC, V.*

$$ ✕🛏 **Beaufort House.** This secluded Georgian house, set in 40 acres of woodland and situated 9 km/6 mi outside Killarney on the R562 Killorglin road, is convenient for both Killarney and the Ring of Kerry. An enthusiastic young couple, Donald and Rachel Cameron, renovated the house in 1994. They like to warn their guests that while they offer peace and privacy, two small children and a dog are also in residence. The hall, library, and drawing room all have open fires. The large, uncluttered rooms are furnished with a variety of antiques. The evening meal, often featuring local lamb or home-caught fish, must be booked 24 hours ahead. Two miles of private salmon and trout fishing are nearby on the River Laune. ⊠ *Co. Kerry,* ☎ *064/44764,* FAX *064/44764. 4 rooms with bath. Fishing. MC, V. Closed Nov.–Easter, except by arrangement.*

$$ ✕▦ **Foley's.** Inside this 19th-century former coaching inn in the center of town, what appears to be a simple, front-parlor restaurant behind a small bar with an open fire is in fact a warren of small rooms decorated with half-paneled walls, stained glass, and Tiffany lamps. Chef-owner Carol Hartnett does the cooking and makes use of local ingredients, including superior Irish cream and butter. Roulade of trout stuffed with prawn mousse and grilled T-bone steak with garlic butter are two typical main dishes. The wine list offers more than 200 selections, and a pianist entertains in summer. All rooms have been decorated with Victorian antiques and old country furniture, including sofas and chaises longues; windows are double-glazed, so the rooms are quieter than you would expect. ⊠ *23 High St., Co. Kerry,* ☎ *064/31217,* FAX *064/34683. 12 rooms with bath. AE, DC, MC, V. Closed Nov.–Apr. 4.*

$$$ ▦ **Europe.** A secluded lakeside location (a five-minute drive from town) and luxurious but unfussy decor gives this modern, five-story hotel the edge over its competitors. Most bedrooms have solid-pine trim, a lake view, and a private balcony. The spacious lounges and lobbies, although a bit impersonal, have picture windows overlooking the lake and mountains, an imaginative display of old, carved timber, and antiques. The sports facilities, including an Olympic-size pool, are among the best and most up-to-date in the area. ⊠ *Killorglin Rd., Fossa, Co. Kerry,* ☎ *064/31900,* FAX *064/32118. 205 rooms with bath. 2 restaurants, 2 bars, pool, sauna, tennis court, horseback riding, fishing, bicycles. AE, DC, MC, V. Closed Nov.–Mar. 15.*

$$ ▦ **Castlerosse.** This modern, lakeside hotel, outside town on the Killorglin road (R562), is near the renowned Killarney Golf Club. Wild red deer often graze its grounds, which run to the shores of Lough Leane and adjoin Killarney National Park. Bedrooms are built around a central garden and have modern, light-oak, built-in furniture and neutral-color decor; about half have a lake view, so if you want one, ask when reserving. A major 1995 refurbishment added a leisure center and a 20-meter pool. ⊠ *Co. Kerry,* ☎ *064/31144,* FAX *064/31031. 110 rooms with bath. Restaurant, bar, indoor pool, sauna, steam room, health club, fishing, bicycles. AE, DC, MC, V.*

$$ ▦ **Killeen House.** Originally built as a rectory with high gables and tall chimneys in 1838, this small, family-run hotel is about eight minutes' drive from town, just beyond the breathtaking Aghadoe Heights viewing point. The hotel is too low to enjoy the view, but it is set in the midst of quiet pastureland with 1½ acres of gardens. The decor is homey rather than elegant, with a friendly bar with more than 6,000 golf balls stuck on the wall (given its proximity to the Killarney Golf and Fishing Club, it's a popular spot with golfers and anglers). All rooms have pastoral views and are decorated with dark, floral spreads, matching drapes, and plain carpets. Four newer "championship" rooms are extra large. ⊠ *Aghadoe, Co. Kerry,* ☎ *064/31711,* FAX *064/31811. 19 rooms with bath. Restaurant, bar. AE, DC, MC, V. Closed Dec.–Feb.*

$ 🖬 **Arbutus.** Run by the friendly Buckley family since it was built more than 60 years ago, this is a good budget hotel in the town center—a short step from the bus and train station and a three-minute walk from the main shopping and dining area. The lobby has an open fire, and the quiet, oak-paneled bar is popular with locals. The rooms in the new second-story section are recommended for the space and recent furnishings. ⊠ *College St., Co. Kerry,* ☎ *064/31037,* FAX *064/34033. 44 rooms with bath. Restaurant, bar. AE, DC, MC, V.*

$ 🖬 **Kathleen's Country House.** Situated on the Tralee road a mile out-
★ side town, this imaginatively designed, two-story guest house incorporates traditional slate walls and roofing and large, modern windows. It was built in 1979 to owner-manager Kathleen O'Regan-Sheppard's exacting specifications; she keeps everything spotlessly clean. The relatively spacious, light, and airy rooms are trimmed in wood and have bright floral comforters and matching curtains. The small second-floor lounge offers pleasant views of the wooded valley and Killarney below. The restaurant serves only fresh produce and organic vegetables and is licensed to serve wine. ⊠ *Madam's Height, Tralee Rd., Co. Kerry,* ☎ *064/32810,* FAX *064/32340. 16 rooms with bath. Restaurant, horseback riding. AE, MC, V.*

$ 🖬 **Lime Court.** Budget accommodations have been springing up along the Muckross road between Killarney and the national park; this one is only a five-minute walk from the town center. The modern building has two large bay windows at the front, with the rooms in an extension behind it, away from the road. Antiques and large potted plants adorn the reception area, while a baby grand piano anchors the spacious lounge. The relatively large guest rooms overlook green fields and are light, airy, and plainly but comfortably furnished with small sitting areas. ⊠ *Muckross Rd., Co. Kerry,* ☎ *064/34547,* FAX *064/34121. 16 rooms with bath. Ping-Pong. MC, V.*

Medieval Banquets

The **Killarney Manor Banquet** offers a five-course meal hosted by "Lord and Lady Killarney" in their 1860, castellated manor house. The food, with a choice of poached salmon or roast Kerry lamb for the main course, is served by waitresses in 19th-century costume. The entertainment here is excellent by any standards, with a team of professional singers and dancers presenting favorite Irish tunes. ⊠ *Loreto Rd.,* ☎ *064/31551.* 🖼 *Entertainment plus 5-course meal and mulled-wine reception £26, entertainment only £9.* ☉ *Apr.–Oct., daily 8 PM: entertainment 8:45–10:45.*

Nightlife and the Arts

Singing bars are popular in Killarney, where a professional leads the singing and encourages audience participation and solos. Try **The Laurels** (⊠ Main St., ☎ 064/31149). **Buckley's Bar** (⊠ College St., ☎ 064/ 31037) has traditional entertainment nightly from June to September. The **Kenmare Rooms** in the East Avenue Hotel (⊠ East Ave., ☎ 064/ 32522) has a live, traditional Irish cabaret Monday to Thursday from May to September. The charge includes admission to Revelles Disco. "Over 21s, Neat Dress Essential," is the rule here. **Scott's Hotel Gardens** (⊠ College Rd., ☎ 064/31060) is a summer hot spot, with big-name cabaret acts, piano bars, and discos. **Gleneagles** (⊠ Muckross Rd., ☎ 064/31870) is another happening place in the summer.

Outdoor Activities and Sports

FISHING

Killarney's lakes and rivers have salmon and brown trout. **O'Neill's** (⊠ Plunkett St., Co. Kerry, ☎ 064/31970) provides fishing tackle, bait, and licenses. To improve your technique contact **Angler's Paradise** (⊠

Loreto Rd., Muckross, Co. Kerry, ☎ 064/33818) where the Michael O'Brien International Fishing School organizes game, coarse, and deep-sea fishing trips by day or by night.

For many people, the two courses at the legendary **Killarney Golf and Fishing Club** (⊠ Mahony's Point, Co. Kerry, ☎ 064/31034) are the chief reason they're in town; for details *see* Chapter 10. **Beaufort Golf Course** (⊠ Churchtown, Beaufort, Co. Kerry, ☎ 064/44440) with a 18-hole, par-71 course is also surrounded by magnificent scenery, and unlike most Irish golf clubs, it has buggy, trolley, and club-rental facilities.

The **Mangerton walking trail** is reached by turning left off the N71 midway between Muckross Abbey and Muckross House (following signposts). The summit of **Mangerton Mountain** (2,756 ft) can be reached on foot in about two hours (less should you choose to rent a pony). **Torc Mountain** (1,764 ft) can be reached off Route N71; it is a satisfying 1½-hour climb. Do not attempt mountain climbing in the area in misty weather, since visibility can quickly drop to zero. The **Kerry Way**, a long-distance walking route, passes through the **Killarney National Park** on its way to Glenbeigh (detailed leaflet from the TIO). For the less adventurous, four safe and well-signposted nature trails of varying lengths are available in the National Park. Try Arthur Young's Walk (4 km/2½ mi); it passes through old yew and oak woods frequented by Sika deer.

Killarney Riding Stables Ltd. (⊠ Ballydowney, Co. Kerry, ☎ 064/31686) offers four- and seven-day treks in Killarney National Park, with accommodation; or half-day treks. **Rocklands Riding Stables Riding School** (⊠ Rockfield, Tralee Rd., Co. Kerry, ☎ 064/32592) rents horses by the hour and half day for trekking in the Killarney National Park and mountains.

Shopping

Shopping in Killarney means crafts and souvenirs, and the most reliable crafts shops in Killarney are on Main Street and High Street; they all carry a standard range of crystal, handknits, T-shirts, sweatshirts, and tweed hats. **Blarney Woolen Mills** (⊠ 10–11 Main St., ☎ 064/33222) has a large selection of crafts, clothing, and souvenirs. **Bricacín Craft Shop** (⊠ 26 High St., ☎ 064/34902) has an interesting collection of crafts including candles, ceramics and handwoven wool, many of which are locally made. **The Sweater Company** (⊠ 3 New St., ☎ 064/35406) carries classic, traditional, and designer knitwear. **Heart and Hand Crafts** (⊠ 13 Main St., ☎ 064/36700) includes silk wall hangings, pine furniture, woodcraft, and iron craft in its selection of crafts. Visit the **Frank Lewis Gallery** (⊠ 6 Bridewell La., beside General Post Office, ☎ 064/34843) for original paintings and sculptures.

THE DINGLE PENINSULA

The Dingle Peninsula stretches for some 30 mi between Tralee (pronounced tra-*lee*) in the east and Slea Head in the west. Small in size yet topographically diverse and brazenly scenic, Dingle's peninsula is composed of rugged mountains and cliffs, interspersed with softly molded glacial valleys and lakes. Along its coast stretch long, sandy beaches and rocky cliffs pounded by the Atlantic Ocean. On the coastal plains, dry-stone walls enclose small, irregular fields, while exceptional prehistoric and early Christian remains are scattered throughout the peninsula. Dingle is also notorious for its heavy rainfall and an impenetrable sea mist that can strike at any time of year. (If it does, sit it out in Dingle Town or the village of Dunquin, and enjoy the friendly bars, cafés, and crafts shops.) At its far western end, west of Dingle Town, the peninsula, like parts of County Kerry, is Gaeltecht: Irish is still spoken on a daily basis, although like most Gaeltacht communities, it is bilingual nowadays, with English as the second language.

The peninsula can be covered in a long day trip of about 160 km/99 mi. (If mist or continuous rain is forecast, postpone your trip until visibility improves.) From Killarney, Killorglin, or Tralee, head for Castlemaine, and take the coast road (the R561 and R559) to the town of Dingle. You'll pass through the sheltered seaside resort of Inch (19 km/12 mi west of Castlemaine, 45 km/28 mi northwest of Killarney), where the head of Dingle Bay is cut off by two sand spits that enclose Castlemaine Harbour. Inch has a long (6½ km/4 mi), sandy beach backed by dunes that are home to a large colony of natterjack toads. Our tour picks up here.

Annascaul

59 *7 km/4½ mi west of Inch.*

Near the junction of the Castlemaine and Tralee roads, Annascaul was an important livestock center until the 1930s. This explains why such a small village has such a wide street—cattle trading was carried out in the streets—and also why it boasts so many pubs for so few residents. Photographers will be tempted to snap **Dan Foley's** (☎ 066/57257) flamboyantly painted pub. Wander in for a pint, and have a chat with Dan, who is also a magician, a farmer, and an expert on local history.

Dingle Town

60 *18 km/11 mi west of Annascaul, 67 km/42 mi west of Killarney, 45 km/28 mi west of Killorglin on R561.*

Backed by mountains and facing a sheltered harbor, Dingle, the chief town of its eponymous peninsula, has a year-round population of 1,400 that more than doubles in the summer months. Although many expect Dingle to be a quaint and undeveloped Gaeltacht village, Dingle in fact offers a wide choice of crafts shops, seafood restaurants, and pubs; still, its main streets—The Mall, Main and Strand streets, and The Wood—can be covered in less than an hour. Celebrity hawks take note: Off-season Dingle is favored as a hideaway by several celebrities, including Julia Roberts, Paul Simon, and Dolly Parton. These and others have their visits commemorated on Green Street's "path of stars."

Dingle's pubs are well known for their music, but among them **O'Flaherty's** (✉ Bridge St., at entrance to town, ☎ 066/51983), a simple, stone-floored bar, is something special and a mecca for traditional musicians. Spontaneous sessions occur most nights in July and August, less frequently at other times. Even without music, this pub provides a good spot to compare notes with fellow travelers.

Since 1985 Dingle's central attraction, apart from its music scene, has been a winsome bottle-nosed dolphin who has taken up residence in the harbor. The Dingle dolphin, or **Fungie,** as he has been named, will play for hours with swimmers (a wet suit is essential) and scuba divers, and he follows local boats in and out of the harbor. It is impossible to predict whether he will stay, but boatmen have become so confident of a sighting that they offer trippers their money back if Fungie does not appear. Boat trips at a cost of £5 leave the pier hourly in July and August between 11 and 6, weather permitting. At other times, call Jimmy Flannery, Sr., at 066/51163.

Dining and Lodging

$$ ✕ **Beginish.** Dingle is an oasis in a culinary desert, although this spot
★ is outstanding by any standard. Muted classical music floats through
the small rooms, carpeted in pale green, with fresh flowers on the blue-
linen tablecloths. The food imaginatively interprets French nouvelle cui-
sine; specialties include brill fillets on leek fondue with white-wine sauce,
and fillet of lamb in phyllo pastry with duxelles. The wine list, with
about 100 choices, includes a good selection of half-bottles. ⊠ *Green
St., Co. Kerry,* ☎ *066/51588. AE, DC, MC, V. Closed Mon. and mid-
Nov.–mid-Mar.*

$ ✕▥ **Doyle's Seafood Bar and Town House.** Sandstone-slate floor, rush-
seat chairs, and pine tables create a casual atmosphere at this center-
city spot. Chef-owner John Doyle prefers to keep the fresh seafood simple:
Fillets of plaice (flounder) stuffed with crab with prawn sauce is about
the fanciest dish. Crab claws beurre blanc and scallops with a chive-
butter sauce are more typical options. Irresistible homemade desserts
round out the menu. Eight very comfortable, moderately priced bed-
rooms are available in the adjoining town house—as long as you don't
mind the pervasive odor of fish! ⊠ *John St., Co. Kerry,* ☎ *066/51174,*
FAX *066/51816. 8 rooms with bath. DC, MC, V. Closed Sun. and mid-
Nov.–mid Mar.*

$ ✕▥ **Greenmount House.** Wonderful views of the town and harbor await
at this modern B&B, a short walk uphill from the town center (turn
right at the roundabout at the entrance to Dingle and right again when
you come to the first T-junction). A modern bungalow connects to a
brand-new extension, where six suites each have a sitting room and
balcony. Rooms in the original house, though smaller, are impeccable
and comfortably decorated with pine beds and floral drapes and
spreads. An outstanding breakfast is served in the conservatory that
connects the two buildings. ⊠ *Mrs. Mary Curran, Greenmount House,
Gortanora, Co. Kerry,* ☎ *066/51414,* **FAX** *066/51974. 12 rooms with
bath. Closed Dec. 22–27.*

$$ ▥ **Skellig.** A five minute walk from town center, the recently refurbished Skellig is a showcase of Irish craft, art, and design. The light-wood-
framed, octagaonal reception area has specially commissioned stained-glass
doors, and original paintings hang in the corridors. The spacious rooms
have modern, pale-wood furniture and drapes and spreads with bold prints;
more than half the rooms have a sea view (if you want one, say so when
reserving). Floor-to-ceiling windows in the Coastguard Restaurant look
out over Dingle Bay; this is the town's only eatery right at the water's
edge and, as you'd expect, the specialty is seafood. Try the steamed fillet of turbot with a cassoulet of prawns or the poached supreme of salmon
with a tomato béarnaise. ⊠ *Co. Kerry,* ☎ *066/51144,* **FAX** *066/51501.
110 rooms with bath. Restaurant, bar, pool, sauna, steam room, exercise room, tennis court. AE, DC, MC, V. Closed mid-Nov.–April 1.*

$ ▥ **Cleevaun Country House.** Set in one acre of landscaped gardens,
this modern, whitewashed, slate-roofed house overlooks Dingle Bay.
Bright, well-equipped bedrooms have the same natural, cottage-pine
wood used throughout the inn. The breakfast menu offers a wide
choice—a nice alternative to the ubiquitous "fry." To get here, follow the signs through Dingle Town toward Slea Head (R559) for 1½
km/1 mi. ⊠ *Lady's Cross, Co. Kerry,* ☎ **FAX** *066/51108. 8 rooms with
bath. MC, V. Closed Dec.–Feb. 15.*

Nightlife

Just about every bar on the Dingle Peninsula, particularly in the town
of Dingle, offers music every night in July and August. **O'Flaherty's**

(☞ *above*) is a fine place for traditional music. For sing-along and dancing, try **An Reált—The Star Bar** (⊠ The Pier, no phone).

Outdoor Activities and Sports

BICYCLES
You're likely to remember a bike ride around Slea Head (☞ *below*) for a long time to come. Bicycles may be rented at **John Moriarty** (⊠ Main St., Co. Kerry, ☎ 066/51316).

HORSEBACK RIDING
Ballintaggart House Hostel and Equestrian Centre (⊠ Co. Kerry, ☎ 066/51454), offers riding by the hour and day and half-day treks on the Dingle Peninsula.

Shopping

Lisbeth Mulcahy at **The Weaver's Shop** (⊠ Green St., ☎ 066/51688) sells outstanding handwoven, vegetable-dyed, woolen wraps, mufflers, and fabric for making skirts. **Louis Mulcahy**'s pottery (⊠ Clogher, near Dingle, ☎ 066/56229) sells tableware, lamps, and decorative bowls and urns. **Cosai** (⊠ Strand St., ☎ 066/52052) sells a variety of Irish-made crafts. Don't miss Dingle's café-bookshop, one of the first in the world, **An Cafe Liteartha** (☎ 066/51388), for new and second-hand books of local interest, and friendly conversation.

Ventry

61 *8 km/5 mi west of Dingle Town on R561.*

The next town after Dingle along the coast, Ventry has a small outcrop of pubs and newsagents and a long, sandy beach with safe bathing and ponies for rent. Between Ventry and Dunquin, you'll find several interesting archaeological sites on the spectacular, cliff-top road along Slea Head.

62 **Dunbeg,** the Iron Age promontory fort, can be seen on the left below the road, after you pass between two tall hedges of fuchsia bushes about 6 km/3½ mi west of Ventry (it's freely accessible; follow the signposts across fields). A fortified stone wall cuts off the promontory, and the landward side is protected by an elaborate system of earthworks and trenches. Within the enclosure is a ruined circular building, with walls up to 22 ft wide. Unlike Staigue Fort on the Ring of Kerry (☞ *above*), this was not a homestead but rather probably a refuge in times of danger.

En Route If you continue west along the coast road beyond Dunbeg, you'll see signs indicating "Prehistoric Beehive Huts"—clocháns in Irish. Built of unmortared stone on the southern slopes of Mt. Eagle, these cells were used by hermit monks in the early Christian period; some 414 exist between Slea Head and Dunquin. Due to the increase in traffic, some local farmers, on whose land these monuments stand, are charging a "trespass fee" of 50p from visitors.

Slea Head

★ **63** *7 km/10 mi west of Dingle Town on R561.*

From the top of the towering cliffs of Slea Head, the view of the Blasket Islands and the Atlantic Ocean is unforgettable—guaranteed to stop you in your tracks. Alas, Slea Head has become so popular that tour buses, barely able to negotiate the narrow road, are causing traffic jams, particularly in July and August. **Coumenole,** the long, sandy strand below, looks beautiful and sheltered, but swimming here is dangerous. This treacherous stretch of coast has claimed many lives in shipwrecks—most recently in 1982 when a large cargo boat, the *Ranga,* foundered on the rocks and sank. In 1588, four ships of the Spanish Armada were driven through the Blasket Sound; two made it to shelter, and two sank. One of these, the *Santa Maria de la Rosa,* was found only recently and is currently being excavated by divers during the summer months.

★ ⑥⑤ The largest of the **Blasket Islands** visible from Slea Head, the **Great Blasket,** was inhabited until 1953. The Blasket islanders were great storytellers and were encouraged by Irish linguists to write their memoirs. *The Islandman,* by Tomás O Crohán, gives a vivid picture of a hard way of life. "Their likes will not be seen again," O Crohán poignantly observed. **The Blasket Centre** explains the heritage of these islanders and celebrates their use of the Irish language with videos and exhibitions. ✉ *Dunquin, Dingle Peninsula,* ☎ *066/56371.* ✉ *£2.* ☉ *Easter–Sept., daily 10–6; July and Aug., 10–7.*

Dunquin

⑥⑤ *9 km/5½ mi west of Ventry on R559.*

Once the mainland harbor for the islanders, Dunquin is at the center of the Gaeltacht, and it attracts many students of Irish language and folklore. David Lean shot *Ryan's Daughter* hereabouts in 1969. The movie gave the area its first major boost in tourism, though it was lambasted by critics—"Gush made respectable by millions of dollars tastefully wasted," lamented Pauline Kael—sending Lean into a dry spell he didn't come out of until 1984's *A Passage to India.* **Kruger's Pub** (☎ 066/56127), Dunquin's main social center, has long been frequented by artists and writers—including Brendan Behan—and it still is; it's also the only eatery for miles and a good place to stop for a bite.

Dunquin's pier (signposted from the main road) is surrounded by cliffs of colored Silurian rock, more than 400 million years old and rich in fossils. Down at the pier you'll see, stored upside down, curraghs, open fishing boats traditionally made of animal hide stretched over wooden laths and tarred, but now usually covered in canvas. Three or four men walk the curraghs out to the sea, holding them aloft over their heads. Similar boats are used in the Aran Islands (☞ Chapter 7), and, when properly handled, they prove extraordinarily seaworthy. If you're interested in going out to the Blaskets, inquire in Dunquin in June, July, and August for boats heading to Great Blasket during the day, depending on the weather. (There's no scheduled ferry service, nor a phone.)

En Route Between Dunquin and Ballyferriter, the road skirts **Clogher Strand**—not a safe spot to swim, but a good place to watch the ocean pounding dramatically on the rocks when a storm is approaching or a gale is blowing. Overlooking the beach is **Louis Mulcahy's pottery studio.** One of Ireland's leading ceramic artists, Mulcahy produces large pots and urns that are both decorative and functional. He has trained several local people to work in the studio, and visitors are welcome to watch the work in progress and to buy items at workshop prices. ✉ *Clogher Strand,* ☎ *066/56229.* ☉ *Daily 9:30–6.*

Ballyferriter

⑥⑥ *5 km/3 mi northeast of Dunquin, 14 km/9 mi west of Dingle on R559.*

Like the other towns at this end of the peninsula, Ballyferriter is a Gaeltacht village, and mainly a holiday spot for vacationers with RVs, many of them German or Dutch. The area around here is great for walking. In 1580, an invasion force of about 600 Spaniards and Italians ⑥⑦ built a new fortress within **Dún an Óir** (about 3 km/2 mi beyond Ballyferriter), originally an Iron Age promontory fort. They came to support the Catholic-Irish against the Protestant-English. The English successfully bombarded the fort from land and sea, and they then slaughtered all survivors, including many innocent local inhabitants. Dún an Óir—which means "fort of gold" in Irish—is now largely obliterated, but folk memory of the massacre is so strong that a memorial was erected on the site in 1980. ⌑ *Free.*

68 One of the best-preserved, early Christian churches in all of Ireland, **Gallarus Oratory** dates from the 7th or 8th century, and ingeniously makes use of corbeling—successive levels of stone projecting inward from both side walls until they meet at the top to form an unmortared roof. The structure is still watertight after more than a thousand years. ⌑ *Free.*

69 **Kilmakedar Church** is one of the finest examples of Romanesque (Early Irish) architecture surviving. Although the Christian settlement dates from the 7th century, the present structure was built in the 12th century. Native builders integrated foreign influences with their own local traditions, keeping the blank arcades and round headed windows, but using stone roofs, sloping doorway jambs, and weirdly sculpted heads. Ogham stones and other interestingly carved, possibly pre-Christian stones are on display in the churchyard. ⌑ *Free.*

70 The summit of **Mt. Brandon** (3,127 ft) is away on the left as you cross the **Connor Pass** from south to north (☞ *below*), and is accessible only to hikers. Do not attempt the climb in misty weather. The easiest way to make the climb is to follow the old pilgrims' path, the Saint's Road; it starts at Kilmakedar Church and rises to the summit from Ballybrack, which is the end of the road for cars. At the summit, you'll reach the ruins of an early Christian settlement. The top can also be approached from a path that starts just beyond Cloghane (signposted left on descending the Connor Pass); the latter climb is longer and more strenuous.

Lodging

$ ⌑ **Granville Hotel.** Rooms in this small, family-run hotel in a converted Georgian house take advantage some of the best scenery on the Dingle peninsula: Ten have sea views and the rest overlook the wild Kerry mountains. The rooms are of all shapes and sizes, and most are simply furnished with modest antiques. Granville attracts independent-minded, outdoor types; hosts Billy and Breege Granville can arrange a trip to the Blasket Islands and advise on local facilities for deep-sea fishing, horseback riding, guided walks, and mountaineering. And it's probably the only hotel in Ireland with a butterfly farm on its grounds. ⌑ *Ballyferriter, Dingle Peninsula, Co. Kerry,* ☎ FAX *066/56116. 14 rooms with bath. Restaurant, bar. DC, MC, V.*

En Route   From Kilmakedar, return to Dingle on the well-signposted main road (R559), then head north across the **Connor Pass,** a mountain route that passes over the center of the peninsula and offers magnificent views of **Brandon Bay, Tralee Bay,** and the beaches of North Kerry, with **Dingle Bay** in the south. It was from Brandon Bay that Brendan the Navigator (AD 487–577) is believed to have set off on his famous voyages in a specially constructed curragh. On his third trip it is possible that he reached Newfoundland or Labrador, then Florida. Brendan was the inspiration for many voyagers, including Christopher Columbus.

Blennerville

71 *60 km/37 mi east of Ballyferriter, 5 km/3 mi west of Tralee on R560.*

Just before you get to Tralee, a five-story **windmill** with black and white sails is the main attraction in Blennerville. The surrounding buildings have been turned into a visitor center, with crafts workshops, an audiovisual history of the windmill, hands-on activities like flour grinding, and an exhibition recalling Blennerville's past as County Kerry's main point of emigration during the Great Famine (1846–51). ☎ 066/ 21064. ⌨ £2.50. ⊘ Apr.–Oct., daily 10–5.

A very popular **steam railway** shuttles back and forth between Blennerville and Tralee, with departures from each terminus every half hour April through September. ☎ 066/27777. ⌨ £2.50.

Tralee

72 *5 km/3 mi east of Blennerville, 50 km/31 mi northeast of Dingle on R559.*

County Kerry's capital and its largest town, Tralee (population 21,000) has neither ruins nor quaint architecture, yet it makes a go at attracting visitors without them. Tralee has long been associated with the popular Irish song "The Rose of Tralee," the inspiration for the annual **Rose of Tralee International Festival.** The last week of August, Irish communities from around the world send young women to join native Irish competitors; one of them is chosen as the "Rose of Tralee." Festival goers, musicians, and entertainers pack the town; a horse race run at the same time contributes to the crowds. Tralee is also the home of **Siamsa Tíre**— the National Folk Theatre of Ireland, which stages dances and plays based on Irish folklore (☞ Nightlife and the Arts, below).

The Kerry County Museum, Tralee's major cultural attraction, traces the history of Kerry's people from 5000 BC to the present using dioramas and an entertaining audiovisual show; there's also a streetcar ride through a life-size reconstruction of Tralee in the Middle Ages. ⊠ *Ashe Memorial Hall, Denny St.,* ☎ *066/27777.* ⌨ *£3.50.* ⊘ *Sept.– July, Mon.–Sat. 10–6; Aug., Mon.–Sat. 10–8.*

☺ Ireland's biggest water complex, **AquaDome** has sky-high water slides, a wave pool, raging rapids, water cannons, and other thrills; adults can seek refuge in the Sauna Dome. ⊠ *Dingle Rd.,* ☎ *066/28899.* ⌨ *£4.* ⊘ *Mid-May–Sept. 1, daily 10–10; Sept. 2–mid-May, weekdays 2–10, weekends 11–8.*

Dining and Lodging

$$ ✕ **Larkin's.** Owner-chef Michael Fitzgibbon specializes in local seafood and other high-quality, Irish produce. The setting is a Georgian town house with a spacious interior decorated with antique pine and contemporary works of art, situated beside the Mount Brandon Hotel and opposite the Siamsa Tíre Folk Theatre. A meal begins by the open fire in the bar, where you choose from a menu that includes daily specials marked up on a blackboard. A baked parcel of mussels in phyllo pastry is a good way to start; entrées include lobster from the tank poached with melted butter, or a sirloin steak flamed in Irish whiskey. Homemade desserts include ice cream, chocolate roulade with raspberry coulis, and seasonal fruit tartlet. A selection of Irish farmhouse cheeses is also available. ⊠ *14 Princes St., Co. Kerry,* ☎ *066/21300. AE, DC, MC, V. No lunch Sat.*

$$$ ▥ **Ballyseede Castle.** Golfers take note: This former Fitzgerald Castle ★ is within easy reach of five of the best courses in the region. Victorian additions complement this 15th-century, three-story castle. Individually decorated rooms have been generously furnished with antiques, and two magnificent drawing rooms with ornamental plasterwork and marble fireplaces complete the picture. Try the Yeats room, which is one of the fanciest. Ballyseede is 3 km/2 mi east of Tralee on the main

Killarney road. ⊠ *Co. Kerry*, ☎ *066/25799*, FAX *066/25287. 12 rooms with bath. Restaurant, bar, horseback riding, fishing. DC, MC, V.*

$$ 🖭 **Abbeygate.** Built in 1995 on the site of Tralee's old marketplace (virtually in the town center, though on a quiet spot behind today's main shopping street), this is an attractive addition to the town's hotels. Nicely sized rooms have country-style wood furniture and large, fully tiled bathrooms. The Old Market Place Pub, a rambling, imaginatively designed bar, seats 500 people and is built in the traditional style with wood floors, open fires, and a cozy atmosphere. There is bar food at lunchtime, and music and dancing nightly from June to September and at least three nights a week at other times. ⊠ *Maine St., Co. Kerry*, ☎ *066/29888*, FAX *066/29821. 100 rooms with bath. Restaurant, 2 bars. AE, DC, MC, V.*

$$ 🖭 **Brandon.** A five-story, modern hotel in the center of town, the Brandon is not especially exciting, but it is the only place in Tralee with a pool and a fitness center, and, unlike some of its competition, it's clean and well run. The decent-size rooms are furnished plainly, with uninspiring urban views. The restaurant is reputable. Rates shoot up during the Rose of Tralee Festival (late August) and the Listowel races (third week in September). ⊠ *Princes St., Co. Kerry*, ☎ *066/23333*, FAX *066/25019. 182 rooms with bath. Restaurant, 2 bars, indoor pool, sauna, steam room, health club, horseback riding, fishing. AE, DC, MC, V.*

Nightlife and the Arts

Try to catch the **National Folk Theater of Ireland** (Siamsa Tíre). Language is no barrier to this colorful entertainment, which re-creates traditional rural life through music, mime, and dance. ⊠ *Godfrey Pl.*, ☎ *066/23055.* 🎫 *£4.* ☉ *Shows July and Aug., Mon.–Sat. 8:30; May, June, and Sept., Tues. and Thurs. 8:30.*

Ballad sessions are more popular here than is traditional Irish music. **Horan's Hotel** (⊠ Clash St., ☎ 066/21933) has disco music and cabaret acts nightly during July and August and on weekends only during the off-season.

Outdoor Activities and Sports

BICYCLES

Bicycles can be rented from **Jim Caball** (⊠ Staughton's Row, Co. Kerry, ☎ 066/21654).

GOLF

You are in the heart of great golfing country in Tralee. For detailed descriptions of **Ballybunion Golf Club** (⊠ Ballybunion, Co. Kerry, ☎ 068/27146) and **Tralee Golf Club** (⊠ West Barrow, Ardfert, Co. Kerry, ☎ 06/36379), *see* Chapter 10.

HORSEBACK RIDING

El Rancho Farmhouse and Riding Stables (⊠ Ballyard, Co. Kerry, ☎ 066/21840) specializes in residential trekking holidays between Tralee and the Dingle Peninsula.

OFF THE BEATEN PATH **BALLYBUNION –** A detour 41 km/25 mi northwest of Tralee on the N69 and the R553 will take you to this seaside resort, famous for its long, sandy beach and championship golf course (☞ Chapter 10).

NORTH KERRY AND SHANNONSIDE

Because of their proximity to Shannon Airport, the gateway to Ireland for transatlantic visitors not flying into Dublin, North Kerry and Shannonside have many more formally organized attractions than the rest of the Southwest. The area's well-restored castles help compensate for the absence of dramatic scenery. Picking up where the Dingle Peninsula tour left off, this tour begins in Listowel, in the northwest of County Kerry, and then jumps across the Kerry–Limerick border, where the first stop is in Glin, on the south side of the Shannon estuary. Limerick City, the Republic's third largest, and those parts of County Clare on the north side of the Shannon round it out. A hint to travelers arriving at Shannon Airport: If you plan to focus on the Southwest, follow the tours outlined in this chapter from back to front.

Listowel

(73) *27 km/16 mi northwest of Tralee on N69.*

A small, sleepy market town, Listowel only really comes alive for its annual horse race during the third week of September. You reach the town from the west by driving along a plain at the base of the Stack's Mountain.

Dining

$–$$$ ✕ **Allo's Bar and Bistro.** Just off Listowel's main square, this rustic bar dates from 1859 and serves the best local produce, freshly prepared. Chefs Armel Whyte and Theo Lynch serve local beef and lamb, but are best known for their imaginative fish recipes, which often feature oysters and lobster, not otherwise widely available hereabouts. Dinner is served Tuesday–Saturday 7–8:15, while the bistro is open Monday–Saturday until 7. No food is served on Sunday, though the bar is open. ✉ *41 Church St.,* ☏ *068/22880. MC, V.*

En Route Leaving Listowel to the northeast on the N69 leads to **Tarbert** (18 km/11 mi), the terminus for the **ferry to Killimer** in West Clare, a convenient 20-minute shortcut if you're heading for the west of Ireland. The **Shannon,** with a length of 273 km/170 mi, is the longest river in Ireland or Britain. The magnificent estuary stretches westward for a further 96 km/60 mi before reaching the sea.

Glin

(74) *5 km/3 mi east of Tarbert on N69, 51 km/32 mi north of Tralee on N69.*

The Fitzgerald family has held the title of Knight of Glin since the 14th century. While they've built numerous structures in the area, the present ★ **Glin Castle,** situated on the banks of the Shannon, dates only from 1785. Between 1820 and 1836 the 25th knight added crenellations and Gothic details to make the house look more like an ancestral home. A delicate plasterwork ceiling, painted in the original red and green, graces the neoclassical hall, which opens onto a splendid "flying" staircase: two risers that join to a single central tongue. The present knight of Glin (the 29th), Desmond Fitzgerald, a Harvard-educated art historian, is an expert on Irish decorative arts (and an outspoken arts advocate), so it's fitting that the house has an exceptional collection of Irish 18th-century mahogany and walnut furniture. ✉ *Co. Limerick,* ☏ *068/34173.* £3. ⏲ *May and June, daily 10–noon and 2–4; other times by appointment.*

Dining and Lodging

$$$$ ✕ **Glin Castle.** The Fitzgerald family home offers a genuine experience of Irish castle living in one of the outstanding private houses of the world (☞ *above*). The house sits on 500 acres encompassing formal gardens, parkland, and a dairy farm. Ballybunion is the nearest golf course. The large rooms, though elegantly furnished with the outstanding Irish furniture for which Glin is renowned, are both intimate and comfortable. Country-house cuisine is served in the dining room, where portraits of Fitzgerald ancestors hang on the red walls. The menu makes use of vegetables and fruit from the walled garden, with locally produced meat and poultry, and freshly caught fish. ✉ *Co. Limerick,* ☎ *068/34112,* ℻ *068/34364. 6 rooms with bath. Tennis court, croquet, horseback riding, boating, fishing. AE, MC, V.*

En Route   Nine kilometers/5½ miles beyond Glin up the N69, **Foynes** was the landing place for transatlantic air traffic in the 1930s and '40s. Flying boats used to land here to refuel before heading on to their European destinations. The town's **museum,** in the terminal of the original Shannon Airport, celebrates Foynes' aviation history; it's a must for devoted flying buffs. ☎ *069/65416.* ⌂ *£3.* ☉ *Mar. 31–Oct., daily 10–6.*

The N69 continues to Limerick through **Askeaton,** where the ruins of a 15th-century Desmond stronghold almost cover a rocky islet on the River Deel. On the bank of the river are the well-preserved ruins of a (freely accessible) 15th-century Franciscan friary.

Castle Matrix, in Rathkeale on R518, dates from 1440, when it was in possession of the earls of Desmond. Confiscated by Elizabeth I, the castle served as a meeting place for the young poets Edmund Spenser and Walter Raleigh in 1589. Raleigh subsequently brought the first potato tubers from North Carolina to Castle Matrix, from where they were distributed throughout south Munster (the old provincial name for the region). In 1962, the late Colonel Sean O'Driscoll, an American architect, bought Castle Matrix and restored it. The library, which serves as the headquarters of the **Irish Heraldry Society,** has an important collection of documents relating to the "Wild Geese," Irish mercenaries who served in European armies in the 17th and 18th centuries. ☎ *069/ 64284.* ⌂ *£3.* ☉ *May 15–Sept. 15, Sat.–Thurs. 11–5.*

Adare

★ ⑦⑤   *19 km/12 mi south of Limerick City on N21, 82 km/51 mi southeast of Tralee on N21.*

A pretty village with several thatched cottages amid wooded surroundings on the banks of the River Maigue, Adare is rich in ruins; on foot, you can locate the remains of two 13th-century abbeys, a 15th-century friary, and the keep of a 13th-century Desmond castle.

Dining and Lodging

$$$ ✕🏠 **Dunraven Arms.** This two-story inn in Adare's picturesque village center, established in 1792, oozes old-world charm. The dark walls of the cozy bar and lounges are hung with paintings and prints of horseback riders (Adare is good hunting country). The bedrooms are comfortably and tastefully decorated with antiques. Try Room 6, where Charles Lindbergh stayed while he worked on the design of Shannon Airport. Rooms in the new (1996) wing are slightly larger; another 12 were slated to open in May 1997 but at press time (summer 1997) had not yet been seen by us. ✉ *Main St., Co. Limerick,* ☎ *061/396–633,* ℻ *061/396–541. 78 rooms with bath. Restaurant, bar, pool, sauna, steam room, health club, horseback riding, fishing. AE, DC, MC, V.*

$$$ ✕🏠 **Mustard Seed at Echo Lodge.** In 1996, after 10 years in the village of Adare, owner-chef Dan Mullane moved his highly regarded restaurant a short drive (13 km/8 mi) west to the village of Ballingarry. Its new home, an 1884 former convent on six acres, has a series of themed guest rooms—black-and-white, carnival, Chinese, and so on, all of which have views over rolling countryside. Mullane is legendary for his attention to detail, and his menu shows it, with its extensive use of herbs and vegetables from Echo Lodge's own organic garden. Free-range duck-

ling, roast lamb, and seafood such as shark steak show up in imaginative preparations, and there are always good vegetarian options. ⊠ *Ballingarry, Co. Limerick,* ☎ *069/68508,* FAX *069/68508. 12 rooms with bath. Restaurant, bar. AE, MC, V. Closed Sun. to nonguests.*

$$$$ ⌶ **Adare Manor.** Until 1988, this Victorian Gothic mansion was the home of the earls of Dunraven. Today it is a showy hotel owned by New Jersey business executive Tom Kane and his wife Judy. Vast stone arches, heavy Flemish wood carvings, and an elaborately decorated ceiling adorn the lordly central hall, off which are a library and drawing and dining rooms. The glorious 36-ft-high, 100-ft-long gallery, wainscotted in oak, is the architectural highlight, though it is used only for special events. The eight "staterooms" in the original house are the most sumptuous, with huge marble bathrooms, comfortable seating areas, and stone-mullioned windows. Most rooms have super-king-size beds and nonworking fireplaces; all have heavy drapes and thick carpets and overlook either the 840 acres of grounds or the Maigue, which runs right beside the hotel. Andrew Lloyd Webber fans will appreciate the piped-in tape loop that wafts through the dining room. Adare's golf course, designed by Robert Trent Jones, is considered one of the best new courses in Ireland (☞ Chapter 10). ⊠ *Adare, Co. Limerick,* ☎ *061/396566,* FAX *061/396124. 64 rooms with bath. Restaurant, 2 bars, indoor pool, sauna, 18-hole golf course, horseback riding, fishing. AE, DC, MC, V.*

Outdoor Activities and Sports

GOLF

Adare Manor Golf Club (⊠ Adare Manor, Co. Limerick, ☎ 061/396204) is an 18-hole, par-69, parkland course (☞ Chapter 10).

HORSEBACK RIDING

The **Clonshire Equestrian Center** (⊠ Adare, Co. Limerick, ☎ 061/396770) has all-weather riding facilities and will also organize trail riding and residential holidays.

Shopping

George and Michelina Stacpoole sell an unusual combination of designer knitwear and antiques (⊠ Main St., ☎ 061/396409). **Adare Gallery** (⊠ Main St., ☎ 061/396898) sells Irish-made jewelry, porcelain, and woodwork, as well as original paintings.

Limerick City

● 16 km/10 mi northeast of Adare, 198 km/123 mi southwest of Dublin.

At the head of the Shannon estuary and the intersection of a number of major crossroads, Limerick is an industrial port and the fourth-largest city in the Republic (population 60,000). The area around the cathedral and the castle is the old part of the city, dominated by mid-18th-century buildings with fine Georgian proportions. Economic investment is helping to spiff up its image as an unattractive city marked by high unemployment and a higher crime rate than elsewhere in the Republic. Frank McCourt's 1996 memoir *Angela's Ashes*—set in Limerick, where McCourt grew up desperately poor—has also helped to pique interest in the city's fortunes today. If you fly into or out of Shannon Airport, you may well pass through here; if you have a few hours to spare, check out the revitalization firsthand. (The answer to the question everyone asks: No, a direct connection is not thought to exist between the city and the facetious five-line verse form known as a limerick—first popularized by the English writer Edward Lear in his 1846 *Book of Nonsense*.)

Like most Irish coastal towns, Limerick was originally a 9th-century Danish settlement, and in 1197, Richard I granted the city's charter. In 1691, after the Battle of the Boyne, the Irish retreated to the walled city, where they were besieged by William of Orange, who made three unsuccessful attempts to storm the city but then raised the siege and marched away. A year later, another of William's armies overtook the city for two months, and the Irish opened negotiations. The resulting Treaty of Limerick was never ratified—it guaranteed religious toler-ance—and 11,000 men of the Limerick garrison joined the French army rather than fight in a Protestant "Irish" army.

In early 1997, the **Hunt Museum** moved from the University of Lim-erick in Plassey to the Old Custom House on the banks of the Shan-non in the city center. The museum has the finest collection of Celtic and medieval treasures outside the National Museum in Dublin. An-cient Irish metalwork, European objets d'art, and a good selection of Irish landscape paintings—including works by Jack B. Yeats—are on view. ✉ *Rutland St.,* ☎ *061/312833.* ✉ *£3.90.* ☉ *Tues–Sat. 10–5, Sun. 2–5.*

Limerick is a predominantly Catholic city, but the Protestant **St. Mary's Cathedral** is the city's oldest religious building. Once a 12th-century palace—pilasters and a rounded Romanesque entrance were part of the original structure—it dates mostly from the 15th century (the black-oak carvings on misericords in the choir stalls are from this pe-riod) and with an extensive 19th-century restoration. A 45-minute son-et-lumière show highlights major episodes from Limerick's history; reservations are not needed. ✉ *Bridge St.,* ☎ *061/416238.* ✉ *Show £2.50.* ☉ *Mid-June–Sept. 15, daily 7 PM and 9:15 PM.*

First built by the Normans in the early 1200s, **King John's Castle** still bears traces on its north side of the 1691 bombardment. If you climb the drum towers (the oldest section), you'll have a good view of the town and the Shannon. Inside, a 22-minute audiovisual slide show il-lustrates the history of Limerick and Ireland; an archaeology center has three newly excavated, pre-Norman houses; and two exhibition cen-ters display 3-D models of Limerick's history from its foundation in AD 922. ✉ *Castle St.* ☎ *061/411201.* ✉ *£3.50.* ☉ *Apr.–Sept., daily 9:30–5; Oct.–Mar., weekends 9:30–5.*

The office of the **Limerick Regional Archives** (✉ Michael St., ☎ 061/410777) is in the Granary, built in 1774 for grain storage. For a small fee, the archives provides a genealogical research service.

On **O'Connell Street,** you'll find the main shopping area, which con-sists mostly of modest chain stores; the street lies a three- or four-minute walk to the south of the Granary. **Cruises Street,** a pedestrian thoroughfare, has Limerick's most chic shops (even though they are chiefly high-street multiples) and an inviting atmosphere (with oc-casional street entertainers). This street is on the opposite side of O'Connell Street from the Arthur's Quay Shopping Centre. This new shopping mall and the futuristic Tourist Information Center are the first fruits of a civic campaign to develop Limerick's Shannon-side quays. Just off O'Connell Street lies the **Dolmen Gallery** (✉ Honan's Quay, ☎ 061/417929), which specializes in exhibits of con-temporary Irish art; it also has a very pleasant restaurant that serves healthy, homemade food.

⑦ Plassey, 5–10 minutes from Limerick on the Ring Road (signposted Dublin N7), is the setting for the University of Limerick, which has a small, nicely landscaped campus.

Dining and Lodging

For lodging convenient to Shannon Airport, *see also* Adare, *above*, and Ennis and Newmarket-on-Fergus *in* Chapter 7.

$–$$ ✕ **Jasmine Palace.** Gourmet dining has never really caught on in Limerick, but the city does abound in Chinese restaurants. Of several reasonably elegant ones in the town center, this second-floor eatery on the main street (opposite the Royal George Hotel) has been there longest, and many would argue that it's the best. Tables are set with pale-blue linen, fresh flowers, and heavy cutlery; chopsticks are also available. The menu is strong on Cantonese and Szechuan specialties. Irish steak is served on a sizzling platter with black bean sauce; the duck and prawn pot is an individual stew pot with pieces of duck and whole king prawns in a rich, spicy sauce. ⊠ *37 O'Connell St., Co. Limerick,* ☎ *061/412484. AE, DC, MC, V.*

$$$$ ✕🖬 **Castletroy Park.** Sitting grandly atop a hill on the outskirts of town
★ (follow signs for the N7 Dublin Road, with views of the university campus and the surrounding countryside, this large, three-story, redbrick and stone hotel is a real gem. The lobby, with its polished wood and Oriental rugs, leads to a large conservatory-cum–coffee shop, overlooking an Italian-style courtyard. The guest rooms, scented with potpourri, are decorated with solid wood furniture, muted floral drapes and spreads, and rag-rolled walls. Well-equipped bathrooms have robes, slippers, and marble basins. Executive rooms have extra-large king-size beds, a large writing desk, two phones, and fax and computer plugs. The fitness center, one of the best around, has a 20-meter pool. You can mix with the locals in the Merry Pedlar Pub and Bistro or enjoy a formal meal in MacLaughlin's restaurant. ⊠ *Dublin Rd., Co. Limerick,* ☎ *061/335566,* 🅵🅰🆇 *061/331117. 107 rooms with bath. 2 restaurants, bar, in-room modem lines, pool, sauna, steam room, health club. AE, DC, MC, V.*

$$ 🖬 **Greenhills.** This friendly, family-run hotel is a modern low rise in a quiet, suburban area where the N18 meets the city-center route. Twenty minutes from Shannon and five minutes from the city center, it makes an excellent touring base. The best and newest rooms are in a quiet wing above the fitness center and are big enough to have a small couch, tables, and chairs. All the rooms are color-coordinated in various styles with dark-wood furniture and tiled bathrooms. Children will love the 17-meter pool, and in high season, they can take part in the hotel's kiddy club. ⊠ *Ennis Rd., Co. Limerick,* ☎ *061/453033,* 🅵🅰🆇 *061/453307. 55 rooms with bath. Restaurant, bar, coffee shop, pool, sauna, steam room, tennis court, children's program. AE, DC, MC, V.*

$ 🖬 **Jurys Inn.** Clean, airy and new (April 1997), unlike some of Limerick's other budget hotels, this is the latest hotel in Ireland's rapidly expanding Jurys chain that rents per room rather than per person. (The "inn," though, is something of a misnomer, as the hotel is large and relatively anonymous.) Rooms are a good size for the price bracket, and have light-wood furnishings. It overlooks an urban stretch of the Shannon now being converted from industrial to leisure use, and it's a short step from the main shopping and business district. ⊠ *Lower Mallow St., Mount Kennett Pl., Co. Limerick,* ☎ *061/207000,* 🅵🅰🆇 *061/400966. 151 rooms with bath. Restaurant, bar. AE, DC, MC, V.*

Nightlife and the Arts

ART GALLERIES

The **Dolmen Gallery** (⊠ Honan's Quay, ☎ 061/417929) shows interesting work by contemporary artists. The **Belltable Arts Center** (⊠ 69 O'Connell St., ☎ 061/319866) has a small auditorium for touring pro-

ductions and exhibition space. **The Limerick City Gallery** (⊠ ▮
☎ 061/310633) has a small, permanent collection of Irish art
notably Jack B. Yeats's *The Chairplanes*) and mounts interesting s
of contemporary art.

PUBS, CABARET, AND DISCOS

Foley's Bar (⊠ Lower Shannon St., ☎ 061/418783) has a ballad or
traditional session every night except Wednesday. Traditional music is
featured at **Nancy Blake's Pub** (⊠ 19 Denmark St., ☎ 061/416443)
on Tuesday and Sunday. **The Locke** (⊠ 3 George's Quay, ☎ 061/
413733), a riverside pub, is one of Limerick's oldest bars, dating from
1724, and has traditional music Sunday, Monday, and Tuesday nights.
Traditional Irish musicians perform in the Merry Pedlar Pub in the
Castletroy Park Hotel (⊠ Dublin Rd., ☎ 061/335566) twice a week,
usually on Wednesday and Sunday nights.

Outdoor Activities and Sports

BICYCLES

Bicycles can be rented from **Emerald Cycles** (⊠ 1 Patrick St., ☎ 061/
416983).

FISHING

Fishing tackle, bait, and licenses can be obtained at **The Cycle Center**
(⊠ Thomond Shopping Center, Roxboro, Co. Limerick, ☎ 061/
44900).

GOLF

Limerick Golf and Country Club (⊠ Ballyneety, Co. Limerick, ☎ 061/
351881) is an 18-hole, par-72, parkland course.

HORSEBACK RIDING

Clarina Riding Center (⊠ Clarina, near Limerick City, Co. Limerick,
☎ 061/353087) offers riding by the hour.

Shopping

The **Arthur's Quay Shopping Centre** (⊠ Arthur's Quay, ☎ 061/419888)
near the TIO is the city's biggest indoor mall. **Lane Antiques** (⊠ 45
Catherine St., ☎ 061/339307) is an old-world gallery selling antiques,
prints, paintings, collectibles, and antiquarian books. **Celtic Bookshop**
(⊠ 2 Rutland St., ☎ 061/401155) specializes in books of Irish interest. **Mahony's Bookshop** (⊠ 120 O'Connell St., ☎ 061/418155) is a
general-interest store.

Bunratty Castle and Folk Park

★ **78** *18 km/10 mi west of Limerick City on N18 (the road to Shannon Airport).*

Likely to be the first Irish castle visitors arriving into Shannon Airport
see, Bunratty Castle and Folk Park is one of those rare attractions that
appeals to all age groups and manages to be both educational and fun.
Bunratty Castle, built in 1460, has been fully restored and decorated
with 15th- to 17th-century furniture and furnishings. The castle gives
a wonderful insight into the life of those times. As you pass under the
walls of Bunratty, look for the three "murder holes," which allowed
defenders to pour boiling oil on attackers below. On the castle grounds,
and every bit as quaint as some first-time visitors expect all of modern Ireland to be, **Bunratty Folk Park** re-creates a 19th-century village
street and has examples of the traditional rural housing of the region.
Exhibits include a working blacksmith's forge; demonstrations of flour
milling, bread making, candle making, thatching, and other traditional skills; and a variety of farm animals in reconstructed small holdings. An adjacent museum of agricultural machinery cannot compete

he furry and feathered live exhibits. Medieval banquets are held
astle twice nightly (☞ *below*). ☎ *061/361511.* ☑ *£4.75.* ☉
May, daily 9:30–5:30 (last entry 4:15); June–Aug., daily 9:30–
last entry 6).

No visit to Bunratty is complete without a drink in **Durty Nelly's** (☎
061/364072), an Old World pub that has inspired imitations around
the world.

Quin

21 km/13 mi north of Bunratty.

79 A 15th-century MacNamara stronghold, **Knappogue Castle** has been
extensively restored and furnished in the 15th-century style. Like Bunratty, it's a venue for medieval-style banquets, and it looks spectacular at night when floodlit. ☒ *Quin,* ☎ *061/368103.* ☑ *£2.40.* ☉
May–Sept., daily 9:30–4:30.

80 The **Craggaunowen Project,** north of Knappogue Castle, is signposted
off the road to Sixmilebridge about 10 km/6 mi from Quin. **Craggaunowen Castle,** a 16th-century tower house, has been restored with
furnishings from the period. Particularly worth seeing are the two
replicas of early Celtic-style dwellings that have been constructed on
the castle grounds. On an island in the lake, reached by a narrow footbridge, is a clay-and-wattle *crannóg,* a fortified lake dwelling; it resembles
what might have been built in the 6th or 7th century when Celtic influence still predominated in Ireland. The reconstruction of a small ring
fort shows how an ordinary farmer would have lived in the 5th or 6th
century, at the time Christianity was being established. Characters
from the past explain their Iron Age (500 BC–AD 450) lifestyle, show
you around their small holding, which is stocked with animals, and
demonstrate crafts skills from bygone ages. It is a strange experience
to walk across the little wooden bridge above reeds rippling in the lake
into Ireland's Celtic past as a jumbo jet passes overhead on its way into
Shannon Airport—1,500 years of history compressed into an instant.
☒ *Kilmurry, Sixmilebridge,* ☎ *061/367178.* ☑ *£3.50.* ☉ *Mid-Mar.–
mid-Apr., Fri.–Sun. 10–5; mid-Apr.–mid-May and mid-Sept.–mid-Oct.,
daily 10–6; mid-May–mid-Sept., daily 9–6.*

Medieval Banquets

If you're a first-time visitor, you may not want to miss the **medieval banquets** held at the Bunratty and Knappogue castles. Do note, though: Both
events cater largely to overseas visitors, many of them on organized tours,
and they're likely to have little appeal for independent travelers in search
of "the real Ireland." But if you're up for it, a warmhearted evening of
Irish hospitality should be taken in the lighthearted spirit in which it is
offered. Medieval banqueting may not be authentic, but it is fun. At Bunratty, you'll be welcomed by Irish colleens in 15th-century dress who bear
the traditional bread of friendship, then led off to a honey-and-mead reception. Before sitting down at the long tables in the candlelighted great
hall, you don a bib: You'll need it, because you'll be eating the four-course
meal medieval-style—with your fingers! Serving wenches take time out
to sing a few ballads or pluck the strings of a harp. Because the banquets
are so popular, book as far in advance as possible. ☎ *Bunratty and Knappogue: 061/360788.* ☑ *4-course meal, wine, mead, and entertainment
£31.* ☉ *Daily, subject to demand, 5:45 and 8:45.*

A ***ceili*** at Bunratty Folk Park is the next best thing if you can't get a
reservation for a banquet; this program features traditional Irish dance
and song and a meal of Irish stew, soda bread, and apple pie. ☎ 061/
360788. ☑ *£26 including wine.* ☉ *May–Sept., daily 5:45 and 9.*

THE SOUTHWEST A TO Z

Arriving and Departing

By Bus

Bus Éireann operates Expressway services from Dublin to Limerick City, Cork City, and Tralee. Add approximately one hour to the journey time by train. Most towns in the region are served by the provincial Bus Éireann network (☎ 01/836–6111, 061/313333, 021/508188, or 066/23566).

By Car

The main driving access route from Dublin is the N7, which goes directly to Limerick City (192 km/120 mi); from Dublin, pick up the N8 in Portlaoise for Cork City (257 km/160 mi). The journey time between Dublin and Limerick runs just under three hours; between Dublin and Cork it takes about 3½ hours.

By Ferry/Bus

Train connections between Rosslare Harbour and Cork City, Limerick City, or Tralee all involve changing at Limerick Junction, so the journey time is usually longer than by car or bus. It is quicker and cheaper, if less comfortable, to use the long-distance buses that service the ferries. **International Express Supabus** leaves London's Victoria Coach Station daily and travels overnight via Bristol to Fishguard, then on to Cork, Killarney, and Tralee. Timetables can be obtained from any National Express Coach Station or by calling Supabus in Luton, England (☎ 1582/404511). An Irish company, **Slattery's** (☎ 171/4821604) runs a bus service from London to Cork and Tralee. The journey to Cork via Rosslare is by bus and ferry, and, at about 16 hours, arduous. (A note about both these phone numbers: Since they are U.K. numbers, if you dial from Ireland, first dial 00 [access code] and 44 [the U.K. country code].)

Swansea–Cork Ferries (☎ 1792/456116) operates a 10-hour crossing between the two ports on a comfortable, well-equipped boat. Supabus (☞ *above*) will get you to the Swansea ferry from anywhere in the United Kingdom.

By Ferry/Car

From the United Kingdom, the Southwest has two ports of entry: Rosslare (in County Wexford) and Cork City. (☞ The Southeast A to Z *in* Chapter 5, for Rosslare ferry details.) From Rosslare Harbour by car, take the N25 to Cork (208 km/129 mi) and allow 3½ hours for the journey. You can pick up the N24 in Waterford for Limerick City (211 km/131 mi), which also takes about 3½ hours.

By Plane

The Southwest has two international airports: Shannon in the West, and Cork on the Southwest coast. **Shannon Airport** (☎ 061/471444), 26 km/16 mi west of Limerick City, is the point of arrival for all transatlantic flights; it also serves some flights from the United Kingdom and Europe. **Cork Airport** (☎ 021/313131), 5 km/3 mi south of Cork City on the Kinsale road, is used primarily for flights to and from the United Kingdom. Regular 30-minute internal flights are scheduled between Shannon and Dublin, Shannon and Cork, and Cork and Dublin. **Kerry County Airport** (☎ 066/64644) at Farranfore, 16 km/10 mi from Killarney, mainly services small planes, but it is gradually increasing its commercial traffic with a daily flight from London via Dublin. *See* Air Travel *in* the Gold Guide for specific information about airlines.

By Bus from Shannon Airport. Bus Éireann (☎ 061/474311) runs a regular bus service to Limerick City between 8 AM and midnight. The ride takes about 40 minutes and costs £3.40.

By Bus from Cork Airport. Bus service runs between the airport and the Cork City Bus Terminal (✉ Parnell Pl., ☎ 021/506066) every 30 minutes, on the hour and the half hour. The ride takes about 10 minutes and costs about £2.

By Taxi. Taxis can be found outside the **main terminal building** at the Shannon and Cork airports. The ride from Shannon Airport to Limerick City costs about £18; from Cork Airport to Cork City costs about £5.

By Train

From **Dublin Heuston Station** (☎ 01/836–6222), the region is served by three direct rail links to Limerick City, Tralee, and Cork City. Journey time from Dublin to Limerick is 2½ hours; to Cork, 2¾; to Tralee, 3¾. For passenger inquiries: in Limerick, ☎ 061/315555; in Cork, ☎ 021/506766; in Tralee, ☎ 066/23522.

Getting Around

By Bus

The provincial bus service, cheaper and more flexible than the train, serves all the region's main centers. Express services are available between Cork City and Limerick City (twice a day) and between Cork and Tralee (high season only), and between Killarney, Tralee, Limerick, and Shannon (once a day; twice in peak season).

If you plan to travel extensively by bus, a copy of the Bus Éireann timetable (50p from bus terminals) is essential. As a general rule, the smaller the town, and the more remote, the less frequent its bus service. For example, Kinsale, a well-developed resort 29 km/18 mi from Cork, is served by at least five buses a day, both arriving and departing; Castlegregory, a small village on the remote Dingle Peninsula, has bus service only on Fridays.

The main bus terminals are at **Cork** (✉ Parnell Pl., ☎ 021/508188); **Limerick** (✉ Colbert Station, ☎ 061/313333); and **Tralee** (✉ Casement Station, ☎ 066/23566).

By Car

A car is the ideal way to explore this region, packed as it is with scenic routes, attractive but remote towns, and a host of out-of-the-way restaurants and hotels that deserve a detour. Roads are generally small, with two lanes (one in each direction). You will find a few miles of two-lane highway on the outskirts of Cork City, Limerick City, and Killarney, but much of your time will be spent on roads so narrow and twisty that it is not advisable to exceed 40 mph.

Getting around the Southwest is every bit as enjoyable as arriving, provided you set out in the right frame of mind—a relaxed one. There is no point in imposing a rigid timetable on your journey when you are visiting one of the last places in Western Europe where you are as likely to be held up by a donkey cart, a herd of cows, or a flock of sheep as by road construction or heavy trucks.

By Train

The rail network, which covers only the inner ring of the region, is mainly useful for moving from one touring base to another. Except during the peak season of July and August, only four trains a day run between Cork (or Limerick) and Tralee. More frequent service is offered between Cork City and Limerick City, but the ride involves changing at Limerick Junction—as does the journey from Limerick to Tralee—to wait for a connecting train. Be sure to ascertain the delay involved in the connection. (For passenger inquiries, *see* Arriving and Departing by Train, *above*.) The journey from Cork to Tralee takes 2¼ hours; from Cork to Limerick, about 2–2½ hours; from Limerick to Tralee, 3–3½ hours.

Contacts and Resources

B&B Reservation Agencies

For a small fee, **Bord Fáilte** (the Irish Tourist Board) will book accommodations anywhere in Ireland through their central reservations system. B&Bs can be booked at local visitor information offices when they are open; however, even these reservations will go through the central reservations system. For more information, *see* Lodging *in* the Gold Guide.

Car Rentals

All the major car rental companies have desks at Shannon and Cork airports.

Shannon Airport: Avis (☎ 061/471094). **Dan Dooley** (☎ 061/471098). **Euro Dollar** (☎ 061/472633). **Hertz** (☎ 061/471369). **Payless Bunratty** (☎ 061/475549). **Murray's Europcar** (☎ 061/471618).

Cork Airport: Avis (☎ 021/281111). **Budget** (☎ 021/314000). **Dan Dooley** (☎ 021/276611). **Euro Dollar** (☎ 021/344884). **Hertz** (☎ 021/965849). **Murray's Europcar** (☎ 021/966736).

Killarney: Avis (☎ 064/36655). **Budget** (☎ 064/34341). **Murray's Europcar** (☎ 064/31237). **Randles** (☎ 064/31237).

Emergencies

Police, fire, and **ambulance** (☎ 999 toll-free).

DOCTOR AND DENTIST

Southern Health Board (✉ Dennehy's Cross, Cork, ☎ 021/545011).

PHARMACIES

Cork: Hamilton Long (✉ 66 Patrick St., Co. Cork, ☎ 021/270548). **Killarney: P. O'Donoghue** (✉ Main St., Co. Kerry, ☎ 064/31813). **Limerick: Roberts James** (✉ 105 O'Connell St., Co. Limerick, ☎ 061/44414).

Guided Tours

Bus Éireann, part of the state-run public-transport network, offers a range of day and half-day guided tours from June to September. They can be booked at the bus stations in Cork or Limerick or at any TIO (☞ Visitor Information, *below*). A full-day tour costs £12; half-day, £7.50, exclusive of meals and refreshments. Bus Éireann also offers open-top bus tours of Cork City on Tuesdays and Saturdays in July and August for £4 .

Tourist Trails, which allow the visitor to follow a signposted route while reading an accompanying booklet (£1), have been set up in Cork City, Limerick City, Youghal, Kinsale, and Killarney Town. Booklets can be purchased at local TIOs. History buffs should inquire at TIOs for details of guided walking tours, which are organized during the summer by local volunteers.

TOUR OPERATORS

Country House Tours (✉ 71 Waterloo Rd., Dublin 4, ☎ 01/688/6463, FAX 01/668/6578) organizes self-driven or chauffeur-driven tours for small or large groups with accommodations in private country houses and castles, and they also cater to special-interest tours, including gardens, architecture, ghosts, and golf.

Valerie Fleury of **Discover Cork** (⊠ Belmont, Douglas Rd., Cork City, Co. Cork, ☎ 021/293873, 🄵🄰🄾 021/291175) can prearrange special-interest tours of the region for small or large groups. Half-day and full-day tours are individually planned for groups of 10 or more to satisfy each visitor's needs.

Kerry Country Rambles (⊠ 53 High St., Killarney, Co. Kerry, ☎ 064/35277) organizes theme walks, archaeology tours, and walking holidays.

Limerick City Tours (⊠ Noel Curtin, Rhebogue, Co. Limerick, ☎ 061/311935) offers inexpensive walking tours of Limerick from June to September (and by arrangement other months).

Shannon Castle Tours (⊠ Bunratty Folk Park, Bunratty, Co. Clare, ☎ 061/360–788) will escort you to an "Irish Night" in Bunratty Folk Park or take you to a medieval banquet at Bunratty or Knappogue Castle (☞ *above*); although the banquet isn't authentic, it is a boisterous occasion that is full of goodwill.

KILLARNEY AREA

Destination Killarney (⊠ Scott's Gardens, Killarney, Co. Kerry, ☎ 🄵🄰🄾 064/32638) is the foremost Killarney tour operator. Besides offering full-day and half-day tours of Killarney and Kerry by coach or taxi, the group will prearrange your visit, lining up accommodations, entertainment, special-interest tours, and sporting activities in one package. A **full-day** (10:30–5) tour costs from £10 to £13 per person, excluding lunch and refreshments. The **Killarney Local Circuit** tour is an excellent **half-day** orientation. The memorable **Gap of Dunloe** tour at £13 includes a coach and boat trip. Add £12 for a horseback ride through the gap. More conventional day trips can also be made to the Ring of Kerry, the Loo Valley, and Glengarriff; the city of Cork and Blarney Castle; Dingle and Slea Head; and Caragh Lake and Rossbeigh.

Gray Line Shannonway Tours (⊠ Limerick TIO, Arthur's Quay, Limerick, Co. Limerick, ☎ 061/413088) organizes full-day and half-day coach tours of Killarney and the Shannon region (mid-June–Sept. only).

Jaunting cars (pony and trap) that carry up to four people can be rented at a stand outside Killarney TIOs. They can also be found at the entrance to Muckross Estate and at the Gap of Dunloe. A ride costs between £12 and £24, negotiable with the driver, depending on time (one–two hours) and route.

The following companies will organize full-day and half-day trips by coach or taxi around Killarney and the Ring of Kerry: **Deros Tours** (⊠ 22 Main St., Killarney, ☎ 064/31251). **Killarney and Kerry Tours** (⊠ Innisfallon, 15 Main St., Killarney ☎ 064/33880). **Castlelough Tours** (⊠ 7 High St., Killarney, ☎ 064/32496).

Outdoor Activities and Sports

FISHING

Your hotel or the local TIO can suggest places that rent boats. The latter will also recommend locations for coarse and game fishing, or contact the **South Western Regional Fisheries Board** (⊠ 1 Nevilles Terr., Macroom, Co. Cork, ☎ 026/41221).

HIKING

Details on Southwest hiking trails are available on free information sheets from the Irish Tourist Board: **Sheet 26C** for the **Kerry Way** and **Sheet**

26G for the **Dingle Way.** Inquire at Cork City's TIO or locally for a map of the **Beara Way** (☞ Visitor Information, *below*).

WATER SPORTS

Because of the demands of Irish insurance laws, boat charter is still in its infancy here, with only one company in business for bareboat charter. For the same reasons, dinghy rentals are not very widespread, and you will need to demonstrate your competence. Sailboards, on the other hand, are relatively easy to rent. Wet suits (also rentable) are essential for sailboarding except on the hottest days in July and August. Rental of sailboarding equipment, including wet suits, starts at about £10 an hour. Sailing dinghies, as well as sailboards, can be rented by the hour (from about £6) or by the day (from about £20). Dinghy and sailboard rental contacts are listed under the towns that provide them.

The average cost of a six-berth yacht between 28 and 35 ft ranges from £120 per person per week (low season) to £200 (high season).

Contact **Sail Ireland Charters** (⊠ Trident Hotel, Kinsale, Co. Cork, ☎ 021/772927, FAX 021/774170) for bareboat charters. For details of residential dinghy sailing courses in the Southwest, contact **Glenans Irish Sailing Club** (⊠ 28 Merrion Sq., Dublin 2, ☎ 01/661–1481).

Visitor Information

Bord Fáilte provide a free information service; their TIOs also sell a selection of tourist literature. For a small fee they will book accommodations anywhere in Ireland.

SUMMER-ONLY OFFICES

TIOs in the following towns are open weekdays 9–6, Sat. 9–1, July–August only: **Bantry** (⊠ Co. Cork, ☎ 027/50229). **Clonakilty** (⊠ Co. Cork, ☎ 023/33226). **Dingle** (⊠ Co. Kerry, ☎ 066/51188). **Kenmare** (⊠ Co. Kerry, ☎ 064/41233). **Kinsale** (⊠ Co. Cork, ☎ 021/772234 or 021/774417, FAX 021/774438). **Youghal** (⊠ Co. Cork, ☎ 024/92390).

YEAR-ROUND OFFICES

The following TIOs are open weekdays 9–6, Sat. 9–1: **Cork City** (⊠ Grand Parade, Co. Cork, ☎ 021/273251, FAX 021/273504). **Killarney** (⊠ Town Hall, Co. Kerry, ☎ 064/31633, FAX 064/34506). **Limerick** (⊠ Arthur's Quay, Co. Limerick, ☎ 061/317522, FAX 061/317939). **Shannon Airport** (⊠ Co. Clare, ☎ 061/471664). **Skibbereen** (⊠ North St., Co. Cork, ☎ 028/21766, FAX 028/21353). **Tralee** (⊠ Ashe Memorial Hall, Denny St., Co. Kerry, ☎ 066/21288).

7 The West

Cliffs of Moher, the Burren, Galway City, the Aran Islands, Connemara, County Mayo

Counties Clare, Galway, and Mayo have a colossal variety of spectacular landscapes. The majestic Cliffs of Moher do constant battle with the stormy Atlantic. The ghostly gray-white limestone expanse of the Burren is a strange, eerie landscape. The Aran Islands are rugged outposts of the tenacious Irish spirit. The "hidden kingdom" of Connemara claims the glorious Twelve Bens, which are reflected in clear blue lakes set amid sepia bog land. Marking its northern boundary stands Croagh Patrick, the mountain of penance, and beyond, Achill Island, Ireland's largest. At the center of all this: Galway, the city that loves to celebrate and, as one of Europe's fastest growing metropolises, has much to.

By Alannah
Hopkin

Updated by
Jennifer Grimes
and Alannah
Hopkin, with
contributions
by Sarah
McQuaid

AS ANY DUBLINER WILL TELL YOU, the West is distinctively different from the rest of Ireland. Within Ireland, the West refers to the region that lies west of the River Shannon; most of this area falls within the old Irish province of Connaught. The coast of this region is situated at the far western extremity of Europe, facing its nearest neighbors in North America across 3,200 km/2,000 mi of Atlantic ocean. While the East, the Southwest, and the North were influenced by either Norman, Scots, or English settlers, the West escaped systematic resettlement and, with the exception of the walled town of Galway, remained purely Irish in language, social organization, and general outlook for far longer than the rest of the country. The land in the West, predominantly mountains and bogs, did not immediately tempt the conquering barons. Oliver Cromwell was among those who found the place thoroughly unattractive, and he gave the Irish chieftains who would not conform to English rule the choice of going "to Hell or Connaught."

It wasn't until the late 18th century, when better transport improved communications, that the West started to experience the so-called foreign influences that had already Europeanized the rest of the country. The West was, in effect, dragged out of the 16th century and into the 19th. Virtually every significant building in the region dates either from before the 17th century or from the late 18th century onward. As in the Southwest, the population of the West was decimated by the Great Famine (1845–50) and by waves of mass emigration that followed until the 1950s. Towns were unknown in pre-Christian Irish society, and even today, 150 years after the famine, many residents still live on small farms rather than in towns and villages. Especially during the wet, wintry months, you can still walk out of your country house, hotel, or B&B in the morning and smell all the nearby turf fires.

Today, the West is, for many, the most typically Irish part of the country. Particularly in western County Galway, you'll find the highest concentration of Gaeltacht (Irish-speaking communities) in all of Ireland, with roughly 40,000 native Irish speakers making their homes here. When the first entirely Irish-language TV station began broadcasting in late 1996, it was from the tiny village of An Spideál, on the north shore of Galway Bay in the heart of the Gaeltacht. Throughout this area, you'll see plenty of signs that are in Irish only: Would you ever suspect that Gaillimh is the Irish for Galway? (☞ Getting Around by car *in* The West A to Z, *below,* for the Irish names of a few major locales.) But wherever you go in the West, you'll not only see, but more importantly *hear,* the most vital way in which traditional Irish culture survives here: traditional musicians play in pubs all over the West, and they are recognized as being the best in the Republic (☞ A Year-Round Fleadh, *below*).

A major factor in the region's recovery from economic depression has been the attraction of visitors to its spectacular scenery. By and large, though, the development that has come with the cultivation of tourism in the West has been mercifully low-key and unobtrusive. Yes, residents of the West have encouraged the revival of such cottage industries as knitting, weaving, and woodworking. But apart from a seaside promenade and fun palace at Salthill, just outside Galway, the area has seen no major investment in public amenities. Alas, this relative unconcern with development cuts both ways: The 5,000-acre Connemara National Park is one of the only protected areas in one of Ireland's most important bog-land areas. The vast majority of bog land in Connemara and County Mayo has already been farmed for its peat, leaving bereft swaths of land lamented by environmentalists.

There may be no better sign of the West's aspiration to both move forward *and* remain tied to its traditions than the thatched cottages, which are popular hereabouts as holiday homes. Some of the traditional whitewashed cottages are truly old, while others are entirely new, built *to resemble* the old. Of course, there's nothing new about the West's greatest virtue for visitors, apart from its glorious scenery and high-flying capital city: its people. No matter how many times you get out of the car for a photo-op—and we guarantee that you're going to *fly* through rolls of film out here—the stories that you're going to tell when you show your friends and family those pictures are going to be about the session of traditional music you stumbled upon in a small pub, the local who pointed you to your own lake in an overlooked corner of Connemara, and the great *craic* ("crack," or good conversation and fun) you're likely to discover wherever you go.

Pleasures and Pastimes

The Arts, Festivals, and Seasonal Events

The Irish love their festivals in the West, and they certainly know how to put them on. The **Cuirt Literary Festival** and the **Galway Oyster Festival** are but two of many annual events hosted by Galwegians, but the highlight of the annual festival calendar is the **Galway Arts Festival**. During the second two weeks in July the town—already ordinarily abuzz—-hosts theater, film, rock, jazz, traditional music, poetry readings, comedy acts, and visual arts exhibitions, plus a joyous parade that, for the first time in 1997, kicked things off rather than brought them to a close (no word yet on 1998). Throughout the year, Galway's renovated **Town Hall Theater** lights up its stage for performances by, among many other groups, the 20-year-old Druid Theatre, whose adventurous productions travel regularly to Dublin and London. Not to be outdone by their neighbor to the south, a smaller but very lively festival in Connemara, the **Clifden Community Arts Week** is held in mid-September, while the **Westport Arts Festival** takes place in the last week of September.

Dining

Because the West has a brief high season—from mid-June to early September—and a quiet off-season, it does not offer as big a choice of small, owner-operated restaurants as other parts of Ireland. Often the best place to eat is a local hotel—Sheedy's Spa View in Lisdoonvarna, for example, which has one of the few excellent chefs in County Clare, or Rosleague Manor in Letterfrack. The dominant style of cuisine in the West might be called "country-house cooking," with an emphasis on classic, but lovingly prepared, dinner-party fare: homemade pâté, a seafood cocktail, tournedos or salmon hollandaise, and chocolate mousse for dessert. Even at Drimcong House, outside Galway City, Gerry Galvin, arguably Ireland's finest chef, prepares fresh local produce in relatively simple ways, albeit with the kind of subtlety that eludes lesser talents—and with an astonishing array of homegrown herbs and vegetables.

Restaurants in the West are less expensive than elsewhere and portions are extremely generous. You'll find it hard to stick to a diet here, and salads and fresh fruit are scarce (though you can always ask for a salad, and virtually always be rewarded with something quite acceptable). The stars on menus in the West are the meat—especially spring lamb, steak, chicken, and duck—and the seafood—especially oysters, salmon, and sea trout. Lobster, crayfish, crab, scallops, and mussels are available throughout the summer. Galway Bay's famous oysters are at their best when there is an "r" in the month; the oyster season officially runs from September to late April.

The majority of restaurants in the West are happy with a "casual but neat" appearance, so dress code is not indicated. Exceptions are the grander ($$$ and $$$$) country-house hotels, where any man in the cocktail bar or dining room after 7 PM should wear a jacket and tie. For price ranges *see* Chart 1(A) *in* On the Road with Fodor's.

Lodging

Some of Ireland's finest country-house and castle hotels, distinguished old and new hotels, and a good choice of inexpensive B&Bs—they're all to be found in the West. Ashford and Dromoland castles are undoubtedly the stars of the region, but less over-the-top places such as Ballynahinch Castle and Cashel House Hotel, both in Connemara, offer similar comfort on a smaller, more intimate scale. The region is short on moderately priced hotels (particularly Galway City), but to compensate, there are wonderful places to stay in the lower price range. One of the great attractions of staying in the West, however much you pay for the night, is the restful atmosphere of so many of the hotels and guest houses, often situated in the middle of a large private estate beside a lake or river, overlooking the sea or distant mountains. Accommodations are busy in July and August, and the best places also get full in May, June, and September, particularly on weekends, so reserve well in advance. As wonderful as many properties are, facilities like tennis courts and indoor pools are scarce, as are television sets in bedrooms, even in upscale hotels. For price ranges *see* Chart 2(B) *in* On the Road with Fodor's.

Outdoor Activities and Sports

FISHING

Some of the best angling in Europe is on the West's rivers, lakes, and seas. **Game fishing** for wild Atlantic salmon, wild brown trout, and sea trout is one of the main attractions of the West. The salmon and brown trout season runs from March through September, closing earlier in some waters. Generally, fishing is at its best between mid-May and mid-June. The **sea trout** season starts in late May and also ends at the end of September; it has been disappointing in some places in recent years due to the infestation of sea lice, but strenuous efforts are being made to ensure a good season in 1998. **Shore fishing** is available all along the coast. Boats can be hired from April to October for deep-sea fishing (about £18 per person per day) from the following ports: Doonbeg, Liscannor, and Ballyvaughan in **County Clare;** Roundstone, Spiddle, Clifden, Cleggan, and Inishbofin Island in **County Galway;** and Westport, Ballina, Belmullet, and Killala in **County Mayo.**

HIKING AND WALKING

If you like challenging hills and relatively rough terrain, the West is excellent hiking country. The unusual, almost lunar landscape of the Burren in County Clare is less demanding than the terrain in Connemara. Here, and in the country to the north of Connemara in South County Mayo, the countryside is sparsely populated and subject to sudden changes in weather—usually associated with the onset of rain. There are only two signposted trails in the area. The **Burren Way** runs from Ballinalacken, just north of Doolin, to Ballyvaughan on the shores of Galway Bay, a distance of about 20 km/12½ mi. The trail runs through the heart of the Burren's limestone landscape, with ever-changing views of the Aran Islands and Galway Bay. The 73-km/45-mi **Western Way** extends from Oughterard on Lough Corrib through the mountains of Connemara and South County Mayo past Killary Harbour to

Westport on Clew Bay; this trail includes some of the finest mountain and coastal scenery in Ireland.

SPECTATOR SPORTS: SAILING AND HORSE RACING

Galway Hookers, solid, heavy, broad-beamed sailing boats with distinctive, gaff-rigged, brownish-red sails can still be seen on the waters of Galway Bay. Enthusiasts maintain a small fleet and hold frequent races on Galway Bay in July and August (☞ Kinvara, *below*). Many small **horse races** are held throughout the year in the West, including trotting races, pony races, beach derbies, and the like. Local Tourist Information Offices (TIOs) can provide details. The main event is the **Galway Races,** beginning immediately following the end of the Galway Arts Festival, at the end of July and beginning of August. This boisterous, full-scale festival attracts a massive crowd and all manner of sideshows, with card sharps, fortune-tellers, rifle ranges, and open-air concerts.

Pubs and Live Traditional Music

No matter how you choose to spend your time in the West, do be sure to visit at least one pub. For whether or not you drink a pint of Guinness or any other alcohol, pubs here are more than just bars—they're the area's vital social centers, places to connect with natives and other travelers, to hear leads about current and local activities, and, above all, places to hear Irish traditional music played live (☞ A Year-Round Fleadh, *below*).

Shopping

Galway City and Ennis are the West's major shopping areas. Their most interesting shops carry crafts, Irish-made clothing, jewelry, books, and antiques. Connemara offers a large concentration of crafts shops; it is the best place in Ireland to buy an Aran sweater—either a traditional, off-white design, or plain, linen and cotton Aran-style knits in jewel-like red, green, or blue. Galway City is the place to buy a Claddagh ring. On the Aran Islands, sally rods are woven into attractive baskets (once used for potatoes or turf); colorful woven belts, known as *críoses,* are hand-plaited from strands of wool. Handwoven woolen or mohair shawls or rugs provide an affordable touch of luxury. Musical instruments, traditionally made furniture, Connemara marble jewelry, modern lead crystal, batik, handmade beeswax candles, tweed place mats, and dried flower arrangements are among the West's many other goods—in addition to tweeds and sweaters, of course.

Exploring the West

Our coverage of the West is organized into three regional tours, which cover this territory from south to north. Our **first tour,** "The Burren and Beyond—West Clare to South Galway," picks up minutes from Shannon Airport and not far from Ennis, the gateway to coastal County Clare. Our **second tour,** "Galway and the Aran Islands," shows you the very best of buzzing, bustling Galway City and takes you out to the three Aran Islands, standing guard at the mouth of Galway Bay. Our **third tour,** "Through Connemara and County Mayo," takes you north of Galway Bay and west of Galway City into the fabled "hidden kingdom" of Connemara and beyond to the highlights of County Mayo: monumental Croagh Patrick, the pretty town of Westport, and the breathtaking Achill Island. Allow at least four days for exploring the region, and seven days if you aim to visit the Aran Islands and Achill Island. Although distances between sites are not great, most of the routes in this chapter use the scenic but slower national secondary routes. Covering 80 km–112 km/50 mi–70 mi per day on these roads is a comfortable target.

Numbers in the text correspond to numbers in the margin and on the West and Galway City maps.

Great Itineraries

IF YOU HAVE 4 DAYS

Assuming you're arriving in the West either via Shannon Airport or by crossing into County Clare via the Killimer–Tarbert ferry, you'll first pass through either **Ennis** ② or **Kilrush** ③. If the weather's good, head for the beach town of **Kilkee** ④. If not, head right for the **Cliffs of Moher** ⑥. Next stop should be the heart of the **Burren** ⑨, though you might want to stop at the **Burren Display Centre** in Kilfenora first to pick up more information about Ireland's strangest landscape. Both **Doolin** ⑦ and ⊞ **Lisdoonvarna** ⑧ are within the Burren and famous for their traditional music. Spend the night either in Lisdoonvarna or in ⊞ **Kinvara** ⑮ or ⊞ **Ballyvaughan** ⑩, both on Galway Bay.

On your second day, head right for ⊞ **Galway City** ⑯–㉚. Spend the morning exploring Galway on foot, poking around its shops, and finding out whether any theater or other performing arts events are on later that night. In the afternoon, take a cruise up the River Corrib or drive out along the north shore of Galway Bay to **Salthill** ㉚ and beyond into the Gaeltacht. Eat an early dinner right in Galway before taking in some theater, or drive out to one of the restaurants just outside town for a more leisurely dinner. Whether or not you go to the theater, try to get to a pub in town for some traditional live music and good craic before heading off to bed.

On your third day, you can kick around Galway for another day. (Galway is easily the liveliest city in Ireland after Dublin, and it's the only large city out in the West, so be sure you've gotten your fill of its buzz before you depart. Particularly if you're here during a festival, there are plenty of special events to keep you busy.) If you do decide to stay based in Galway, you might want to either take the ferry out to the **Aran Islands** ㉛ for the day or make the quick trip south to **Coole Park** ⑬ and **Thoor Ballylee** ⑭, the two southernmost sites in the west of Ireland important to W. B. Yeats (most of the rest are in County Sligo [☞ Chapter 8]). Either way, again spend the night in Galway or at one of the country houses outside town (or perhaps even in a B&B on the Aran Islands, if you make it out there). Alternatively, if you're ready for scenery and a smaller town, head out through the moorlands of Connemara through **Oughterard** ㉜ to the Alpine-like coastal village of ⊞ **Clifden** ㊱, where you'll find gorgeous scenery and a surprisingly good selection of pubs and restaurants. Spend the night here or in a country house, hotel, or B&B in and around ⊞ **Cashel** ㉞ or ⊞ **Letterfrack** ㊲.

If you've spent your third night in Galway, follow the alternative day-three itinerary above, but don't linger too long in Clifden. Push on, as should those who stayed the night in or near Clifden, first to **Connemara National Park,** then just beyond to the **Kylemore Valley's** ㊳ much-photographed **Kylemore Abbey,** which has a breathtaking lakeside location and a better-than-average crafts shop. Continue through **Leenane** ㊴ to ⊞ **Westport** ㊵, the prettiest village in County Mayo, and a good place to spend the night. On the way, you won't be able to miss the distinctive conical shape of **Croagh Patrick,** the penitential mountain that was a refuge of St. Patrick during his years converting Ireland to Christianity. Try to be in Westport on Thursday, when its old-fashioned farmers' market is held. On your fourth day, make the walk up Croagh Patrick or stroll around Clew Bay seeing how many islands you can count. If the weather cooperates, you might want to venture out to **Achill Island** ㊶. At the end of the day, continue on north to Sligo (☞ Chapter 8) or head for a Midlands destination (☞ Chapter 4).

The West

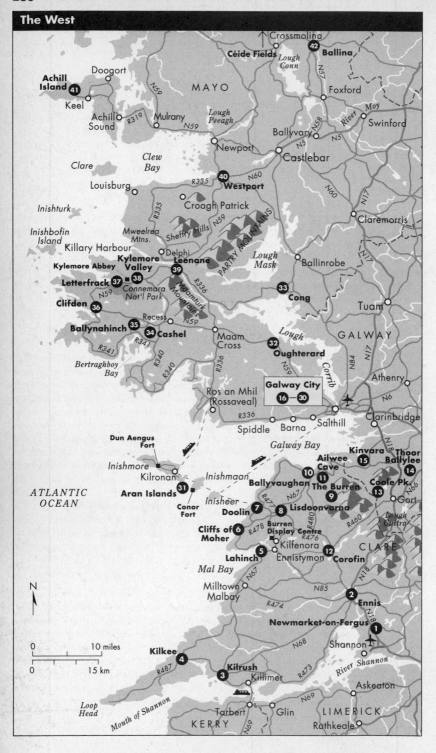

Crossmolina
Céide Fields
Lough Conn
Ballina 42
MAYO
Doogort
Achill Island 41
Keel
Achill Sound
R319
Mulrany
N59
Lough Peeagh
Newport
Foxford
River Moy
Swinford
N57
Ballyvary
N58
N5
N5
Castlebar
Clare
Clew Bay
Louisburg
R335
Westport 40
N60
Claremorris
N60
N17
Croagh Patrick
R335
Inishturk
Mweelrea Mtns.
Sheffry Hills
N59
PARTY MOUNTAINS
Lough Mask
Ballinrobe
N17
Inishbofin Island
Killary Harbour
Delphi
Kylemore Valley
Leenane 39
R336
Lough Mask
Cong 33
GALWAY
Tuam
Kylemore Abbey
Letterfrack 37 38
Connemara Nat'l Park
Maumturk Mountains
N84
Clifden 36
N59
Recess
R336
N59
Maam Cross
Oughterard 32
N59
Lough Corrib
Ballynahinch 35 34 **Cashel**
R341
R341
R340
Oughterard 32
Athenry
N6
Bertraghboy Bay
R341
R340
Ros an Mhil (Rossaveal)
Galway City 16 — 30
Clarinbridge
N18
R336
Spiddle
Barna
Salthill
Galway Bay
ATLANTIC OCEAN
Dun Aengus Fort
Inishmore
Kilronan
Inishmaan
Aran Islands 31
Inisheer
Conor Fort
Ailwee Cave 10
Kinvara 15
Thoor Ballylee 14
Ballyvaughan
11 **The Burren**
Coole Pk. 13
N66
Gort
Doolin 7 8 **Lisdoonvarna** 9
N67
R47
R480
R460
Lough Cutra
Cliffs of Moher 6
R478
Burren Display Centre
R476
Kilfenora
12
CLARE
Lahinch 5
Ennistymon
Corofin
N18
Mal Bay
N67
Milltown Malbay
R474
N85
Ennis 2
N68
Shannon
N18
Newmarket-on-Fergus
1
0   10 miles
0   15 km
N
Kilkee 4
R487
Kilrush 3
Killimer
R473
River Shannon
Askeaton
Loop Head
Tarbert
Glin
N69
LIMERICK
Mouth of Shannon
KERRY
N69
Rathkeale

Our four-day itinerary can easily be expanded into a seven-day trip, with the following modifications: Spend a full two days exploring western County Clare, staying one night in the seaside town of **Lahinch** ⑤ (especially if you're a golfer or traveling with one) and another in any of the towns noted above. Depending on how much time you want in Galway, you might want to make it to **Coole Park** ⑬ and **Thor Ballylee** ⑭ on one of your first two days in the West, rather than taking a bite out of the time you have for Galway and the Aran Islands. Begin your third (rather than your second) day by heading to ⊡ **Galway City** ⑯–㉚. Plan on spending three full days based either right in or just outside of Galway. Spend two of these days in Galway itself and one on a day trip out to the **Aran Islands** ㉛. On your sixth day, follow our alternative day-three itinerary above, ending up either in ⊡ **Clifden** ㊱, ⊡ **Cashel** ㉞, or ⊡ **Letterfrack** ㊲ for the night. Then follow our day-four itinerary above for your seventh day.

When to Tour the West

"Soft weather," as the Irish call on-again, off-again rainy days, is almost always a possibility in the West, but the months of May and October are likelier to be drier than the rest of the year. The Burren is at its best in May, when the wildflowers are in season. April, May, and October are good times for an off-peak visit. In July and August, expect to rub elbows with Irish families taking their holidays here; they're also the best months to hear traditional music. It doesn't take many visitors to overwhelm Galway City's narrow streets, so if you don't love crowds, steer clear in late July, when the Arts Festival and Galway Race take place back-to-back. Many restaurants and accommodations in Connemara and the Burren are seasonal and close from October to Easter, although thanks to a steady rise in demand, the season is definitely extending slightly each year. If you do choose to visit the West between November and March, your choice of places to stay and to eat will be limited, but you do get to feel as though you have the place to yourself. A word of warning, though: During the winter, the weather in the West can be harsh, with gales and rain sweeping in day after day from the Atlantic.

THE BURREN AND BEYOND—WEST CLARE TO SOUTH GALWAY

County Clare claims two of Ireland's unique natural sites: the awesome Cliffs of Moher and the stark, mournful landscape of the Burren, which hugs the coast from Black Head in the north to Doolin and the Cliffs of Moher in the south. Yet western County Clare is widely beloved among native Irish for another natural phenomena significantly less unique than these: its beaches. Though just another Irish beach town to some, Kilkee, to name just one, is a favorite summer getaway, the sort of unassuming place that natives beg you not to put into your guidebook. So whether you're looking for inimitable scenery or just a lovely beach to plunk down on for a few hours and relax in the sun (if you're lucky!), this tour is a good starting point into the natural wonders of the West.

This tour begins at Newmarket-on-Fergus, within minutes of Shannon Airport, and it makes a good jumping-off tour through the west if you've just arrived in Ireland and are planning to head for Galway. It also follows directly from the end of Chapter 6, which concludes 10 km/6 mi down the road, at Bunratty Castle and Folk Park (and the Knappogue Castle, also nearby), so be sure to take a moment to glance at those sights to decide whether to include them as you get underway. This first tour is also the connecting link between County Limerick (and other points in the Southwest) and Galway City. If you're approaching it from the Southwest and you're not going into Limerick City itself, it's easy to pick up the tour from Killimer, reached via the ferry from Tarbert (☞ Arriving and Departing *in* The West A to Z, *below*).

Newmarket-on-Fergus

❶ *13 km/8 mi north of Shannon Airport on N18.*

A small town in County Clare, Newmarket-on-Fergus is chiefly remarkable nowadays as the nearest town to Dromoland Castle Hotel, formerly the home of Lord Inchiquin, chief of the O'Brien clan.

Dining and Lodging

$$$$ ✕🏠 **Dromoland Castle.** A popular first stop with affluent American
★   and French visitors arriving at Shannon Airport, Dromoland is the ancestral home of the O'Briens, the descendants of Brian Boru, High King of Ireland. The massive, turreted, neo-Gothic castle—dating from the 19th century, when it replaced its 16th century predecessor—looks the part, standing regally beside a scenic lake, surrounded by tidily landscaped formal gardens and a golf course. Inside, the grand, plushly carpeted rooms are graced with large ancestral portraits, crystal chandeliers, and oak paneling; hushed, well-dressed guests sit amid all the splendor, sipping tea or drinks. Bedrooms overlook the old Queen Anne stable yard and feature Regency-style furniture and a pleasant pink or green color scheme. The vast suites have ruched drapes on the tall windows, great views over the park, and antiques, many of them Irish-Georgian. Award-winning cuisine is served in the formal, oak-wainscoted dining room. ✉ *Co. Clare,* ☎ *061/368144,* 𝖥𝖠𝖷 *061/363355. 73 rooms with bath. Restaurant, bar, 18-hole golf course, 2 tennis courts, horseback riding, Ping-Pong, fishing, bicycles. AE, DC, MC, V.*

Outdoor Activities and Sports

Dromoland Golf Course (✉ Newmarket-on-Fergus, Co. Clare, ☎ 061/ 368444) is one of the most scenic in the country, set in a 700-acre estate of rich woodland in the grounds of the Dromoland Castle Hotel. It has a natural lake that leaves little room for error on a number of holes.

Ennis

❷ *9½ km/6 mi east of Newmarket-on-Fergus on N18, 37 km/23 mi northwest of Limerick, 138 km/86 mi north of Tralee.*

A major crossroads and a convenient stop between the West and the Southwest, Ennis is the county town of County Clare, a pleasant if physically unremarkable market town that's often bustling. It has always fostered traditional music, especially fiddle playing and step-dancing (a kind of square dance). The **Fleadh Nua** (pronounced fla-nooa) festival in Ennis at the end of May attracts both performers and students of Irish music. Two statues in Ennis bear witness to the role its citizens have played in Irish democracy. On a tall limestone column above a massive pediment in the town center stands a **statue of Daniel O'Connell** (1775–1847), "The Liberator" (☞ Sneem *in* Chapter 6), who was a member of Parliament for County Clare between 1828 and 1831, and instrumental in bringing about Catholic Emancipation. Outside the courthouse (in the town park, beside the River Fergus, on the west side of Ennis) stands a larger-than-life bronze **statue of Eamon De Valera** (1882–1975), who successfully contested the election here in 1917, and thus launched his political career. Although De Valera was born in the United States, his maternal forebears were from County Clare. He was the dominant figure in Irish politics during this century, serving as prime minister for most of the years from 1937 until 1959, when he resigned as leader of Fianna Fáil, the party he founded, and went on to serve as president until 1973.

Dining and Lodging

$$$$ ✕⊞ **Carnelly House.** This 250-year-old Queen Anne–style, redbrick house is an elegant, convenient base for exploring the West (it's 5 km/3 mi south of Ennis, 16 km/10 mi from Shannon Airport). The perfectly proportioned drawing room has elaborate plasterwork decorations. The large, comfortable bedrooms have canopied or four-poster beds and bucolic views over the 100-acre estate. Irish country-house breakfasts and dinners (the latter by prior arrangement) are served at the large mahogany family dining table. Dishes such as rack of lamb with garlic and rosemary, pheasant in port, or poached wild salmon are frequent menu items. Hosts Dermot and Rosemarie Gleeson will fill you in on the beguiling house's colorful history. ⊠ *Clarecastle, Co. Clare,* ☎ *065/28442,* ℻ *065/29222. 5 rooms with bath. Horseback riding, fishing. MC, V.*

$$$ ✕⊞ **Old Ground.** A popular base for Americans, especially golfers, this rambling, creeper-clad hotel in Ennis's town center dates from the early 18th century. Though it has been much added to over the years—the latest addition, in spring 1997, added 25 large, traditionally furnished rooms—it retains an old-world elegance. Older bedrooms have pine headboards, brass bedside lights, and candy-striped wallpaper. Some rooms overlook the busy main street, so try to get one facing the gardens. Be sure to look at the lovely old silver and the large Georgian sideboards in the dining room. ⊠ *Co. Clare,* ☎ *065/28127,* ℻ *065/ 28112. 83 rooms with bath. Restaurant, bar, fishing. AE, DC, MC, V.*

Nightlife

Although Ennis is not as fashionable as, say, Galway, it is one of the West's traditional music hot spots. Below are the pubs where you're likeliest to hear sessions, but keep in mind they don't necessarily take place every night and the scene is constantly changing. Phone ahead to check whether a session is happening.

Ciaran's Bar (⊠ 1 Francis St., ☎ 065/40180). **Cruise's** (⊠ Abbey St., ☎ 065/41800). **Kerins'** (⊠ Lifford, ☎ 065/20582). **May Kearney's Bar** (⊠ 1 Newbridge Rd., ☎ 065/24888). **The Old Ground** (⊠ O'Connell St., ☎ 065/28127). **Paddy Quinn's** (⊠ 7 Market St., ☎ 065/28148). **The Temple Gate** (⊠ The Square, ☎ 065/23300).

Outdoor Activities and Sports

BICYCLING

Cycle into the Burren by renting a bike from **Michael Tierney** (⊠ 17 Abbey St., Co. Clare, ☎ 065/29433).

GOLF

Ennis Golf Club (⊠ Drumbiggle Rd., Co. Clare, ☎ 065/24074) is an 18-hole, parkland course overlooking the town.

HORSEBACK RIDING

Ballyshannon Riding Establishment (⊠ Ballyshannon House, Quin, Co. Clare, ☎ 065/25645) has woodland trail riding and beginners' lessons and will provide riding equipment.

Shopping

The Belleek Shop (⊠ 36 Abbey St., ☎ 065/29607) carries Belleek china, Waterford crystal, and Donegal Parian china, as well as Lladro,

Hummel, and other collectible china. **Flax In Bloom** (✉ 30 Abbey St., ☎ 065/20833) offers women's and teenagers' fashions with an emphasis on Irish design and classic fabrics. **The Sweater Shop** (✉ 41 O'Connell St., ☎ 065/20950) sells designer knitwear. At **Clare Business Center** (✉ Francis St., ☎ 065/20166) you'll find a variety of crafts workshops that sell to the public. **Carraig Donn** (✉ 29 O'Connell St., ☎ 065/28188) stocks Waterford glass and other Irish crystal, Belleek and other fine china, and their own array of knitwear. Stop off at the **Antique Loft** (✉ Clarecastle, ☎ 065/41969) for collectibles and pine and mahogany antiques.

En Route   Ennis is the gateway to western County Clare, the focus of the remainder of this tour, and from here you have three options, which you might want to consider depending on your time, your interests, and the weather: First, you can **head for the coast**—a popular summer playground for many generations of Irish people. Our tour follows this course, so simply continue following it. If you do go this route, take the N68 out to Kilrush. (If you're crossing from County Kerry via the **Tarbert–Killimer** ferry you can join the tour at Kilrush, 5 km/3 mi west of Killimer [☞ Arriving and Departing *in* The West A to Z, *below*].) An interesting side note: The N68 west to Kilrush is a good stretch of relatively straight, two-lane highway passing through a thinly populated region of small farms—typical of those in the West, often between 30 and 100 acres, and some no more than small holdings. In order to make a living, most of these farmers or their spouses (in some cases both) have a second job, such as fishing, running a B&B, or working seasonally. The rest rely on government subsidies, but few of them would trade their lives in western Ireland for more lucrative pursuits elsewhere. Alternatively, if the season or the weather doesn't make the beach or a golf course look too promising, you might consider **heading right for Lahinch** on the N85 (32 km/27 mi from Ennis), bypassing County Clare's far western shores. For a third option, if you're anxious to see the Burren and get to Galway City, you might want to **head right for Corofin,** the southeastern gateway to the Burren (take the N85 to the R476) **and/or Gort** (31 km/19 mi north of Ennis on the N18, 23 km/14½ mi northeast of Corofin on the R460), midway on the main Galway road.

Kilrush

❸   *43 km/27 mi southwest of Ennis on N68.*

A small market town, Kilrush was laid out, like most towns in West Clare, in the mid-19th century, with a large central square, off which radiate the town's main streets. The widest of these leads to the harbor and the docks. This plan makes the town (population 3,000) seem bigger than it actually is. An exhibition entitled **Kilrush in Landlord Times** explains the history of the town from its beginnings in the late 18th century; it's also the starting point for a heritage walk through the town's streets that takes you back to the 19th century. ✉ *Market House,* ☎ *065/51577.* 🎟 *£1.* ☉ *May–Sept., Mon.–Sat. 9:30–5:30, Sun. noon–4.*

Outdoor Activities and Sports
Kilrush Golf & Sports Club (✉ Parknamoney, Ennis Rd., Co. Clare, ☎ 065/51138) has 18 holes and overlooks the Shannon estuary.

Kilkee

❹   *12 km/8 mi west of Kilrush on N68.*

Kilkee is one of the most beloved west coast beach resorts among native Irish people, many of whom have summered here for generations.

Its major draw is its safe bathing—both in the waters along its magnificent, long, sandy beach and in deep rock pools known as Pollock holes, which remain full at low tide (they attract scuba divers as well as swimmers). From Kilkee, you can take an excursion to **Loop Head Lighthouse** on the R487 (about 38 km/24 mi round-trip). Loop Head is the westernmost point of County Clare, situated at the northern tip of the mouth of the Shannon, the very end of its long estuary.

Outdoor Activities and Sports

Kilkee Golf and Country Club (✉ East End, Co. Clare, ☎ 065/56048) overlooks the sea and has some spectacular, cliff-edge holes. Founded in 1896, it was expanded in 1994 to an 18-hole, par 72.

En Route The main route heads north up the coast on N67. Sandy beaches and more Pollock holes can be found by taking a left off the main road at any sign that indicates STRAND and traveling for about 2½ km/1½ mi.

Lahinch

⑤ *47 km/30 mi north of Kilkee on N67, 30 km/18 mi west of Ennis on N85.*

A shortcut joins the main tour on the N67 at Lahinch, another busy resort village beside a long, sandy beach backed by dunes, best known for its links golf courses, and—believe it or not—its surfing. Back in 1972, the European Surfing Finals were held here, putting Lahinch on the world surfing map. Today Tom and Rosemary Buckley's **Lahinch Surf Shop** (✉ The Promenade, ☎ 065/81543), Ireland's oldest (open since 1990), is ground-zero for County Clare surfers.

Dining and Lodging

$$ ✕⌂ **Aberdeen Arms.** This beautifully refurbished, Victorian, seaside hotel
★ is a model of its kind, offering elegance and comfort in a friendly, easygoing setting. Humorous golfing prints hanging on the dark-paneled walls of the bar and grill room appeal to the many golfers who stay here. The newest rooms face the sea and have spectacular skylights and windows. All rooms are large and tastefully decorated with built-in, cream-color melamine closets, plain carpets, and matching cream-floral drapes and spreads; some have Georgian-style tables and chairs. The main dining room offers an excellent and varied menu of French-Irish cuisine, and one of the best breakfasts in the county. ✉ *Co. Clare,* ☎ *065/81100,* FAX *065/81228. 55 rooms with bath. 2 restaurants, 2 bars, sauna, 10 tennis courts, health club, fishing, bicycles. AE, DC, MC, V.*

Nightlife

For traditional music try **O'Dwyer's 19th** (☎ 065/81440).

Outdoor Activities and Sports

The championship course at **Lahinch Golf Club** (✉ Co. Clare, ☎ 065/81003) offers challenging links following the natural contours of the dunes. The 6,613-yard course has hosted many great golfing occasions since it opened in 1892. The **Castle Course** (✉ Co. Clare, ☎ 065/81003), the newer Lahinch course, offers a more carefree round of seaside golf, with shorter holes than the championship course.

Shopping

The Design Lodge (☎ 068/81744) is a small shop that carries Irish-made goods, including sweaters, linen, tweed, and other fine gift items.

En Route From Lahinch, continue on to the Cliffs of Moher. For the first time on this coast, the road narrows and starts to climb. It twists past small, whitewashed farms and green fields with glimpses of the sea on the horizon.

The Cliffs of Moher

★ ⑥ *10 km/6 mi northwest of Lahinch on R478.*

One of Ireland's most breathtaking natural sites, the majestic Cliffs of Moher rise vertically out of the sea in a wall that stretches over a long 8 km/5 mi swath and as high as 710 ft. You can see the stratified deposits of five different rock layers in the cliff face's striations. Numerous seabirds, including a large colony of puffins, make their home in the shelves of rock on the cliffs. On a clear day you can see the Aran Islands and the mountains of Connemara to the north and the lighthouse on Loop Head and the mountains of Kerry to the south. **O'Brien's Tower** is a defiant, broody sentinel built at the cliffs' highest point. The parking area is a favorite spot of performers; in the high season, there's likely to be free entertainment—step dancers, fiddle players, or even a one-man band. The visitor center, a good refuge from passing rainsqualls, has a gift shop and tearoom. ☎ *065/81171.* ▧ *Free.* ☉ *Cliffs and O'Brien's Tower: freely accessible; visitor center: mid-Feb.–Apr., daily 10–5; May, June, and Sept., daily 10–6; July and Aug., daily 9:30–6:30.*

Doolin

⑦ *6 km/4 mi north of the Cliffs of Moher on R479.*

A tiny village consisting almost entirely of B&Bs, hostels, pubs, and restaurants, Doolin is widely said to have three of the best pubs in Ireland for traditional music (☞ Nightlife *and* A Year-Round Fleadh, *below*). But with the worldwide surge of interest in Irish music during the last decade, the village is more of a magnet for German, Dutch, Swedish, and French musicians than it is for young, or even established, Irish artists. On **Doolin Pier,** about 1½ km/1 mi outside the village, local fishermen sell their catch fresh off the boat—lobster, crayfish, salmon, and mackerel. From spring until early fall (weather permitting), a regular ferry service takes visitors for a 30-minute ride to Inisheer, the smallest of the Aran Islands (☞ *below*). ☎ *065/77086.* ▧ *£14.* ☉ *More than 10 sailings daily mid-Mar.–Oct.*

Dining

$$$ ✕ **Bruach na Haille.** The name means "the bank of the river Aille," and the river can be seen from the side windows of this charming cottage restaurant, owned by John and Helen Browne for 20 years. The low-beamed, cozy rooms have flagstone floors, old dressers laden with colorful delft china, and open turf fires. Lobster from Doolin Pier is usually on the menu, along with starters such as warm salad of monkfish or roulade of smoked salmon with horseradish mayonnaise. Main courses may include baked seafood au gratin—cod and shellfish in a rich creamy sauce baked in individual portions. Their sirloin steak with Irish whiskey sauce is renowned. The restaurant is licensed to serve wine only. ⊠ *Roadford,* ☎ *065/74120. AE, DC, MC, V. Closed Nov.–mid-Mar. No lunch.*

Nightlife

Doolin's three pubs famous for their traditional music sessions are **Gus O'Connor's** (☎ 065/74168), **McDermott's** (no phone), and **McGann's** (☎ 065/74133). Gus O'Connor's also serves excellent bar food.

Outdoor Activities and Sports

Cycle along the coast with a rented bike from **Patrick Moloney, Doolin Hostel** (⊠ Co. Clare, ☎ 065/74006).

Shopping

Design Ireland Plus (☎ 065/74309), beside the cemetery and the church, carries only Irish-made goods, including sweaters, modern lead crystal, linen, lace, and tweed. A jeweler's workshop and a resident batik maker are also on the premises.

Lisdoonvarna

8 *5 km/3 mi east of Doolin on R478.*

One of only two spa towns in Ireland (the other is Enniscrone, in western County Sligo), Lisdoonvarna has several sulfurous and iron-bearing springs with radioactive properties, all containing iodine. The town grew up in the late-19th century to accommodate visitors who wished to "take the waters." Its buildings reflect a mishmash of mock-architectural styles: Scottish baronial, Swiss chalet, Spanish hacienda, and American motel. Depending on your taste, it's either lovably kitschy or unappealingly tacky. If you're curious about health cures, the renovated **Lisdoonvarna Spa and Bath House** is worth a visit. Iron and magnesia make the water offered here for drinking taste terrible (as does most spa water). In comparison, the bathing water is pleasant, if enervating. Electric sulfur baths, massage, wax baths, sauna, and a solarium are available at the spa complex, which sits on the edge of town in an attractive parkland setting. ☎ 065/74023. ☜ *Complex free, sulfur baths £5 (book in advance).* ☉ *Early June–early Oct., daily 10–6.*

In July and August, Lisdoonvarna is a favorite getaway for Irish under-30s. It's also the traditional vacationing spot for the West's bachelor farmers, who used to congregate here at harvest time in late September with the vague intention of finding wives. (Irish farmers are notoriously shy with women and reluctant to marry, often postponing the event until their mid- or late-fifties, if ever.) This tradition is now formalized in the **Matchmaking Festival,** held during late September. Middle-aged singles dance to the strains of country-and-western bands, and a talent contest is held to find the most eligible bachelor.

Dining and Lodging

$ ✕🖫 **Ballinalacken Castle.** On a hill 4 km/2½ mi outside Lisdoonvarna, this sprawling Victorian lodge stands on 100 acres of wildflower meadows beside the 16th-century ruins of an O'Brien stronghold. Its bow windows take advantage of glorious panoramic views of the Atlantic, the Aran Islands, and the Connemara hills. Bedrooms come in all different shapes and sizes; some have marble fireplaces and high ceilings. There are six large rooms in a new wing; all have sea views and dark-wood furniture. The furniture in the public rooms is a haphazard mix of hand-me-downs, modern stuff, lovely old Irish oak, and sumptuous, inlaid bureaus. Fresh local seafood and local lamb are featured in the modest restaurant. ✉ *Co. Clare,* ☎ *065/74025,* 𝔽𝔸𝕏 *065/74025. 12 rooms with bath. Restaurant, bar. MC, V. Closed Oct. 5–Mar.*

$ ✕🖫 **Sheedy's Spa View.** Originally a 17th-century farmhouse, this small,
★ friendly hotel is only a short walk from both the town center and the spa wells. It's been in the hands of the Sheedy family since 1855. The rooms are simple, spotlessly clean, and well-cared-for; most have a Georgian-style coffee table and chairs. Patsy Sheedy and her son, Frankie, who studied abroad, serve French-Irish cuisine at their award-winning, moderately priced Orchid Restaurant. Warm crab and smoked haddock potato cakes with a sage and walnut pesto, red pepper, and chili mayonnaise is a hearty starter. Fresh local lobster with garlic butter or panfried sirloin steak with Cajun root vegetables in a wild mushroom and brandy cream are two main courses; local lamb and salmon are other usual options. Pear and apple tarte Tatin (traditional upside-down apple tart) with prune ice cream on a fresh vanilla sauce is elegantly done. ✉ *Co. Clare,* ☎ *065/74026,* 𝔽𝔸𝕏 *065/74555. 10 rooms with bath. Restaurant, bar, tennis court. AE, DC, MC, V. Closed Oct.–Mar.*

Nightlife

Country music and ballad singing are popular in the bars of Lisdoon-varna. For traditional music try the **Roadside Tavern** (☎ 065/74084).

The Burren

★ ⑨   *Extending throughout western County Clare from the Cliffs of Moher in the south to Black Head in the north, as far southeast as Corofin.*

As you travel north toward Ballyvaughan, the landscape becomes rockier and stranger. Instead of the seemingly ubiquitous Irish green, gray becomes the prevailing color. You're now in the heart of the Burren, a 300 square km/116 square mi expanse that is one of Ireland's fiercest landscapes. The Burren is aptly named—it's an Anglicization of the Irish word *bhoireann*, which means "a rocky place"—for stretching off in all directions, as far as the eye can see, fissured limestone (known as *karst*) lies in great, irregular slabs, or pavements, as they're locally called, with deep cracks between them. From a distance, it looks like a lunar landscape, so dry that nothing could possibly grow on it. In the spring (especially from mid-May to mid-June), the Burren becomes a wild rock garden, as an astonishing variety of wildflowers bloom between the cracks in the rocks, including at least 23 native species of orchid. The Burren also supports an incredible variety of wildlife, including frogs, newts, lizards, badgers, stoats, sparrow hawks, kestrels, and dozens of other birds and animals. The wildflowers and other plants are given life from the spectacular caves, streams, and potholes that lie beneath the rough, scarred pavements. With the advent of spring, "turloughs," seasonal lakes that disappear in dry weather, appear on the plateau's surface. Botanists are particularly intrigued by the cohabitation of Arctic and Mediterranean plants—many so tiny you won't see them from your car window, so make a point of exploring some of this rocky terrain on foot. Dozens of signposted walks run through both coastal and inland areas. For a private guided tour, contact Mary Angela Keane (☎ 065/74003; £25 per hour) or Shane Connelly (☎ 065/77168; £10 per person); May and June are peak months for flora, but a tour is worthwhile at any time of year.

In Kilfenora (8 km/5 mi southeast of Lisdoonvarna on the R476), the tiny **Burren Display Centre** has a modest audiovisual display and other exhibits that explain the Burren's geology, flora, and archaeology. ☎ *065/88030.* 🎫 *£2.20.* ☺ *June–Aug., daily 9:30–6; Mar.–May, Sept., and Oct., daily 10–5.*

Also in Kilfenora, beside the Burren Display Centre, the ruins of a small 12th-century church, once the **Cathedral of St. Fachan,** have been partially restored as a parish church. There are some interesting carvings in the roofless choir, including an unusual, life-size skeleton. In a field about 165 ft west of the ruins is an elaborately sculpted **high cross** that is worth examining, even though parts of it are badly weathered.

Nightlife

Vaughan's Pub (☎ 065/88004) in Kilfenora is known for its traditional music sessions.

Ballyvaughan

⑩   *16 km/10 mi north of Lisdoonvarna on N67.*

A pretty little waterside village and a good base for exploring the Burren, Ballyvaughan attracts walkers and artists who enjoy the views of Galway Bay and access to the Burren. Just outside Ballyvaughan, you'll ⑪ see a signpost to the right for the **Ailwee Cave,** the only such chamber in the region accessible to those who aren't spelunkers. This vast, 2-million-year-old cave is illuminated for about 3,300 feet and contains an underground river and waterfall. ☎ 065/77036. ⌨ £3.95. ☺ *Early Mar.–early Nov., daily 10–6 (last tour 5:30); July and Aug., daily 10–7 (last tour 6:30).*

Dining and Lodging

$$$ ✕⌂ Gregan's Castle Hotel. The Haden family runs this quiet, meticulous, large Victorian country house, located at the base of the aptly
★ named Corkscrew Hill (on the N67, midway between Ballyvaughan and Lisdoonvarna). The house is surrounded by award-winning gardens and overlooks Galway Bay and the gray mountains of the Burren (it's 6½ km/4 mi from the beach at Ballyvaughn Bay). All bedrooms are individually furnished with Georgian and Victorian antiques and William Morris wallpaper; older ones have molded-plaster ceilings. The spacious new rooms on the ground floor have private patio gardens but lack the splendid views of the rooms upstairs. The restaurant, rather formal for this part of the world (jacket and tie are required), serves updated French cuisine. You might start with half a dozen oysters (in season) and move on to panfried turbot, steamed asparagus, and a lobster butter sauce. ✉ *Co. Clare,* ☎ *065/77005,* ⨳ *065/77111. 22 rooms with bath. Restaurant, bar, croquet, fishing, bicycles. AE, MC, V. Closed Nov.–Mar.*

$$ ✕⌂ Hyland's Hotel. In the heart of the Burren, this family-run, yellow-and-red coaching inn dates back to the early 18th century. A turf fire greets you in the lobby. Rooms vary in size and shape but all have pine furniture and fresh-looking color-coordinated drapes and spreads. If you like mountain views, ask for a room with a skylight looking out over the Burren. The dining room, cheerfully decorated in country pine with red tablecloths, specializes in simply prepared local produce. The Fisherman's Catch includes salmon, prawns, crab claws, and mussels poached with dill and lime. Homemade ice cream and terrine of triple-chocolate mousse often appear on the dessert menu. There is live music in the bar most nights from June to mid-September and Irish storytelling once a week. ✉ *Co. Clare,* ☎ *065/77037,* ⨳ *065/77131. 30 rooms with bath. Restaurant, bar. AE, MC, V. Closed Jan. 6–Feb.*

$ ✕⌂ Admiral's Rest. You can guess from the nautical bric-a-brac on view that this place belongs to a retired naval man—one John Macnamara, who is an expert on the Burren's wildlife. In a modernized cottage on the coast road between Lisdoonvarna and Ballyvaughan, the restaurant is just across the road from the sea, visible through the large windows. Varnished stone floors, stone-topped tables, *sugán* (rope-seated) chairs, an open, wood-and-turf fire, and posies of wildflowers on the tables make up the rugged decor. Seafood is the mainstay of the menu—simply prepared fare like lobster, mussels, or crab claws in garlic butter—but you can also order grilled T-bone steak, Irish stew, or a spicy vegetarian salad. The restaurant is licensed to serve wine only. Nine inexpensive B&B rooms are available in the bungalow next door. ✉ *Fanore, Co. Clare,* ☎ *065/76105,* ⨳ *065/76161. 9 rooms. AE, MC, V. Closed Nov.–Easter.*

Nightlife

The **Monk's Pub** (☎ 065/77059), near the waterfront, offers a great music session and a friendly welcome.

En Route From Ballyvaughan, it's a 48 km/30 mi trip circumnavigating Galway Bay to Galway City. If you're eager to get there, skip the next two towns and head there directly, first passing through Kinvara (☞ *below*). If you're on a more leisurely pace, continue on our tour by heading back south through the Burren on the R480 and the R476 to Corofin.

Corofin

⑫   *23 km/14½ mi south of Ballyvaughn, 16 km/10 mi east of Kilfenora on the R476.*

If you're searching for your Irish roots, Corofin's **Clare Heritage Center** offers a genealogical service and advice for do-it-yourselfers. Its displays on the history of the West of Ireland in the 19th century cover culture, traditions, emigration, and famine, as it exposes some grim statistics. In 1841, for example, the population of County Clare was 286,394. Fifty years later, famine and emigration had reduced this number to 112,334, and the population continued to decline, reaching an all-time low of 73,597 in 1956. (It is now heading for the 90,000 mark.) ☎ 065/37955. ⊠ *£2.* ⊙ *Apr.–Oct., daily 10–6; Nov.–Mar. (genealogy service only) weekdays 9–5; museum by appointment.*

In a 15th-century castle on the edge of Corofin, the **Dysert O'Dea Castle Archaeology Center** has an exhibition on the antiquities of the Burren. Twenty-five monuments stand within a 1½-km/1-mi radius of the castle; these date from the Bronze Age to the 19th century, and all of them are described at the center. ☎ 065/37722. ⊠ *£2.* ⊙ *May–Sept., daily 10–6.*

Coole Park and Thoor Ballylee

24 km/15 mi northeast of Corofin on N18.

⑬   On the left-hand side just north of the little town of Gort is **Coole Park,** where once stood the home of Lady Augusta Gregory (1859–1932), W. B. Yeats's patron and the co-founder with him of Dublin's Abbey Theater (☞ Chapter 2). Yeats visited here often, as did almost all of the other writers who contributed to the Irish literary revival in the first half of the century, including George Bernard Shaw and Sean O'Casey. Yeats's poem "The Wild Swans at Coole" vividly conveys Coole's pastoral serenity: "The trees are in their autumn beauty,/ The woodland paths are dry,/ Under the October twilight the water/ Mirrors a still sky;/ Upon the brimming water among the stones/ Are nine-and-fifty swans." Douglas Hyde, the first president of Ireland, was also a visitor. The house fell derelict after Lady Gregory's death and was demolished in 1941, and the park is now a national forest and wildlife park. The only reminder of its literary past is the **Autograph Tree,** a copper beech on which many of Lady Gregory's famous guests carved their initials. Picnic tables make this a lovely alfresco lunch spot. ☎ 091/631804. ⊠ *Visitor center £2, park free.* ⊙ *Visitor center mid-Apr.–mid-June and Sept., Tues.–Sat. 10–5, and mid-June–Aug., daily 9:30–6:30; park daily 10–dusk.*

⑭   **Thoor Ballylee,** another site Yeats fans won't want to miss, is signed on the right side of the road just north of Coole Park (it's 5 km/3 mi up the N66). It is one of the only major sites in the west of Ireland associated with the Nobel Prize–winning poet *not* in County Sligo (☞ Chapter 8). In his fifties and newly married, Yeats bought this 14th-century Norman tower as a ruin in 1916 for £35 (Ezra Pound dubbed it, characteristically, "Ballyphallus.") Set beside a whitewashed, thatch-roof cottage, with a tranquil stream running along its other side, the tower's proximity to Lady Gregory's house at Coole Park made it a desirable location, though it required significant work on Yeats's part to make it livable. He lived here intermittently until 1929, writing some of his more mystical writings here, including *The Tower* and *The Winding Stair.* It's now fully restored with Yeats's original decor and furniture. The audiovisual display is a useful introduction to the poet and his times. ☎ 091/631436. ⊠ *£3.* ⊙ *Easter–Sept., daily 10–6.*

En Route   As the N18 runs farther north you'll see fields hedged by dry stone walls made of gray boulders piled on top of one another; mortar is not used in the walls' construction. They are a typical feature of the west of Ireland, as are the long evenings caused by the sun slowly sinking over the Atlantic on the western horizon. As you approach Galway City you will catch an occasional glimpse of the sea on your left. This is Oyster Country, where the famous Galway oyster grows.

Kinvara

⑮   *13½ km/8½ mi east of Ballyvaughan, 15 km/9 mi northwest of Gort on the N67, 25 km/15½ mi south of Galway City.*

Whether you're coming from Ballyvaughn or from Gort, Kinvara is worth a visit. The picture-perfect village has recently been growing as a holiday base, thanks to its gorgeous bay-side locale, great walking and sea angling, and numerous pubs. Kinvara is most well known for its long-standing early August sailing event, **Cruinniú na mBád** (Festival of the Gathering of the Boats), in which traditional brown-sailed Galway hookers laden with turf race across Galway Bay. (Hookers were used until the early part of this century to carry turf, provisions, and cattle across Galway Bay and out to the Aran Islands. A sculpture in Galway's Eyre Square [☞ *below*] honors their local significance.)

On a rock to the north of Kinvara Bay, the 16th-century **Dunguaire Castle** stands commanding the approaches from Galway Bay. It is said to be on the site of a castle built by the King of Connaught in the 7th century. One of its previous owners, Oliver St. John Gogarty, was a surgeon, man of letters, and model for James Joyce's Buck Mulligan, a character in *Ulysses*. Today Dunguaire is used for a literarily themed medieval banquet that honors local writers and others with ties to the West, including Lady Gregory, W. B. Yeats, Sean O'Casey, and Pádraic Ó'Conaire (☞ Eyre Square *in* Galway, *below*). ⊠ *Kinvara, Co. Galway,* ☎ *091/637108.* ⊡ *£2.50; banquets £29.* ☉ *May–Sept., daily 9:30–5:00; banquets at 5:30 and 8:30.*

Dining and Lodging

$ ✕ **Moran's of the Weir.** Signposted off the main road on the south side of Clarinbridge, this waterside thatched cottage, the home of the Moran family since 1760, houses a simply furnished restaurant at the back that serves only seafood. It's *the* place to stop and sample the local oysters, grown on a bed in front of the restaurant—but only if there is an "r" in the name of the month of your travels! If oysters aren't in season, try the seafood special—smoked salmon, crab, prawns, and crab claws with homemade brown bread—or a bowl of garlic mussels. ⊠ *The Weir, Kilcolgan, Co. Galway,* ☎ *091/796113. AE, MC, V.*

$$ ✕🏠 **Merriman Inn.** This whitewashed, thatched inn on the shores of Galway Bay may look traditional; in fact, it's the newest midsize hotel in the West, opened in May 1997. Like its sister hotel, Brennan's Yard in Galway City, the Merriman is decorated with locally made, well-designed furniture as well as original crafts, paintings, and sculpture. The bar and lounge both have open fires and a relaxed, friendly atmosphere. All the guest rooms are well equipped, but not all have views of Galway Bay, so ask for one when booking. Michael Clifford, one of Ireland's leading chefs, presides over the restaurant. He has a reputation (garnered while running his own establishments in Cork City) for fresh interpretations of traditional Irish dishes. Here he serves such items as grilled lamb cutlets with garlic confit, herbs, and crisp shallots and wild Irish salmon with *champ* (mashed potato and scallions) and lemon butter sauce. Pear tarte Tatin and caramelized pancakes filled

with bananas and butterscotch sauce are among the desserts. ⊠ *Kinvara, Co. Galway,* ☎ *091/638222,* FAX *091/637686. 32 rooms with bath. Restaurant, bar, meeting room. AE, DC, MC, V.*

$ ✕⊡ **Burren View Farm.** Situated 5 km/3 mi west of Kinvara on the edge of Galway Bay, this simple B&B, relatively isolated on a working sheep and cattle farm, has a million-dollar view. Stone-walled fields dotted with sheep surround the yellow-painted, two-story house. The breakfast room, sun lounge, and front bedrooms look out across a wide sea inlet to the gray expanse of the Burren. Rooms are plain and homely, but clean and well-maintained. Mrs. O'Connor will provide wholesome evening meals, Irish or Continental style, on request. ⊠ *Doorus, Kinvara, Co. Galway,* ☎ *091/637142,* FAX *091/638131. 5 rooms, 2 with bath. Dining room, tennis court, fishing.*

Nightlife and the Arts

The first weekend in May, Kinvara hosts the annual **Cuckoo Fleadh** (☎ 091/637145). You can hear traditional music most nights at the **Winkles Hotel** (⊠ The Square, ☎ 91/637137).

GALWAY CITY AND THE ARAN ISLANDS

Galway is often said to be a state of mind as much as it is a specific place. The largest city in the West today (population 60,000 and growing) and the ancient capital of the province of Connaught, Galway is "the place where the clocks seem to run without the urgencies of elsewhere," as the writer Cormac MacConnell has put it. Galway has also always been the chief trading post for the Aran Islands, those "fragments of Connemara flung offshore," to again quote MacConnell. Although the islands receive upward of 100,000 visitors per year (most of them between June and August), a voyage out to the islands is still, for many visitors to Ireland, among their most unforgettable experiences—and a good opportunity to enhance your understanding of Irish folkways and Gaelic culture.

Galway City

🔟 *27 km/12½ mi north of Kinvara, 219 km/136 mi west of Dublin, 105 km/65 mi north of Limerick.*

The secret is out: Galway is hot, hot, hot. As almost any Galwegian will tell you, theirs is the fastest-growing city in all of Ireland. And if that doesn't impress you, how about this: it's the fastest-growing city *in all of Europe.* It's an astonishing fact—and once you arrive, you have to wonder: Where can this city possibly grow? For even though Galway is the largest city in the West, its heart is *tiny*—a warren of streets so compact that if you spend more than a few hours here, you'll soon be strolling its streets with the sort of easy familiarity you thought you'd only ever feel in your hometown.

For many Irish people, Galway is a favorite weekend getaway, the liveliest place in the Republic, the city of festivals. Good roads and rail links with the capital make it the number one destination within Ireland for jaded Dubliners. It's also a university town: University College Galway (or UCG as it's locally known) is a center for Gaelic culture (Galway marks the eastern gateway to the West's large Gaeltacht). A fair share of UCG's 9,000 students study the Irish language, while hundreds of students enrolled in colleges and universities in the United States, Italy, and elsewhere in Europe take a semester abroad here. These students make Galway a sort of Irish frontier-town of youth culture. On many weekends, and especially many festival weekends, you'll see as many pierced and Adidased teenagers and twentysomethings here as you'd find at a Phish concert.

But its students aren't its only avant garde. Galway has long attracted writers, artists, and musicians. The latter keep the traditional music pubs lively year-round—the de facto centers of culture in a town that has no major cultural sites and institutions apart from UCG. Its two small but internationally acclaimed theater companies draw a steady stream of theater people. This cosmopolitan, bohemian populace and its left-coast geography make Galway something like the San Francisco of Ireland.

And although you're not conscious of it when you're in the center of town, Galway is—like its California counterpart—spectacularly situated, on the north shore of Galway Bay, where the River Corrib flows from Lough Corrib out into the sea. If you're lucky, you may get a Galwegian to sing you his or her rendition of the song "Galway Bay," memorably crooned by Bing Crosby. Barely a 10-minute walk or 5-minute drive out of town, Grattan Road, which runs along the bay's northern shore out to the nearby seaside village of Salthill, offers spectacular vistas across the vividly blue bay to the south shore's Black Head and beyond, to the three Aran Islands (☞ *below*).

By what magic does Galway look the way it does? The founders of Galway were Anglo-Normans who arrived in the mid-13th century and fortified their settlement against "the native Irish," as local chieftains were called. Galway became known as the City of the Tribes because of the dominant role in public and commercial life of the 14 families who founded it. Their names, still common in Galway and elsewhere in Ireland, recur regularly in any account of Irish history and culture: Athy, Blake, Bodkin, Browne, D'Arcy, Dean, Font, French, Kirwan, Joyce, Lynch, Morris, Martin, and Skerret. Particularly in and around its main pedestrian-oriented street—the name of which changes from Williamsgate to William to Shop to High to Quay, the city's medieval heritage is everywhere apparent: in the intimate two- and three-story stucco buildings, the windy streets and narrow passageways, the cobblestones underfoot. In the early 1980s, Galway was the first city in Ireland to revive the old Irish tradition of hand-painted wooden shop signs with Gaelic lettering. Modern sculptures, floral hanging baskets, and window boxes are further signs of Galway's deep-seated civic pride.

The question facing Galway today is this: What price success? Galway's growth and popularity mean that at its busiest moments, pedestrians jam-pack its narrow, one-way streets, spilling off its even narrower sidewalks. If there's a city that doesn't sleep in Ireland, this is it. In fact, if you want to be guaranteed of a quiet night's sleep, either ask for a room in the back of your center-city hotel or stay outside of town. First-time visitors here during late July's annual Galway Races week may be surprised to find that helicopters have become a not uncommon form of transportation, shuttling revelers from the races to parties and back again. There's something emblematic about whirring helicopters and galloping horses, bound together in the same fate, the modern machines and the ancient prancers moving the crowds to great heights, both figuratively and literally. Galwegians and their guests cheer on these emblems of present and past, and in this probably guarantee their own future.

A Good Walk

Orient yourself at **Eyre Square** ⑰, part of whose central square is occupied by **Kennedy Park.** Before you really get going, you may want to stop in at the **Tourist Information Office** ⑱ just off the southeast corner of the square. At the top (north side) of Eyre Square, turn left down Williamsgate Street. This is the spine of old Galway. Its name changes four times before it reaches the River Corrib—it is successively called **William Street, Shop Street, High Street,** and **Quay Street.** If you have any postcards to mail, you may want to stop at the General Post Office, on the left-hand side of Eglinton Street, the first right off Williamsgate Street. At the corner of William and Shop streets, **Lynch's Castle** ⑲ is one of Galway's oldest buildings. Continue down Shop Street to the pedestrian way just beyond Abbeygate Street; here **Lynch Memorial Window** ⑳ and **Collegiate Church of St. Nicholas** ㉑ are adjacent to one another. Joyce fans might want to make the 30-second detour across Lombard/Market Streets to Bowling Green, site of the **Nora Barnacle House** ㉒.

It's a minute's walk from the church to **Tiġ Neaċhtain** ㉓ (Naughton's in English, pronounced *knock*-tons), a pub (popular with locals) at the corner of Cross Street and Quay/High Street. This corner is the very heart of old Galway's main historic and commercial district: Nearly all the city's best restaurants, bars, boutiques, art galleries, and crafts, antiques, and bookstores line the narrow, winding streets and alleys in this vicinity. Nothing is more than a five-minute walk from anything else. If this area is bursting at the seams, one block to the east of Shop Street/High Street, between Abbeygate and Cross streets, Middle Street is a significantly less trafficked, up-and-coming, and still somewhat undiscovered thoroughfare that has a number of worthwhile stores, restaurants, and the national Irish-language theater.

The **Spanish Arch** ㉔ and the **Galway City Museum** ㉕ are adjacent, right on the river's east bank, across from the Jurys Inn parking lot. Just beyond Jurys (☞ *below*) but before crossing the Wolf Tone Bridge, turn right onto the pedestrian path that parallels the river. Follow it past the William O'Brien Bridge to the **Salmon Weir Bridge** ㉖ (you'll need to jog off the path onto Abbeygate Street just short of the bridge to gain access to it). Right before you as you cross the bridge is the **Cathedral of Our Lady Assumed into Heaven and St. Nicholas** ㉗ (known locally simply as "the Cathedral"). A five-minute-or-so walk down University Road brings you to **University College Galway** ㉘. For a pretty walk back to the center of town, turn right onto Canal Road and follow it back to the intersection of Dominick Street, Fairhill, and Raven Terrace. From here it's a brief jog to Claddagh Quay, which will take you out to the **Claddagh** ㉙. If you're out this far, you may want to continue on to **Salthill** ㉚; otherwise, head back to the center of town.

TIMING
You could easily do this walk in a morning or afternoon (less the walk out to Salthill), although if you browse in stores, chat with locals, or stop off for a pint or a cup of tea, you could stretch it out into a *very* leisurely all-day excursion. You may want to plan your day so you hit what most interests you and leave time to explore along the bay, get out to Salthill, or take a bay cruise.

Sights to See

㉗ **Cathedral of Our Lady Assumed into Heaven and St. Nicholas.** On an island forming the west bank of the River Corrib beside the Salmon Weir Bridge, Galway's largest Catholic church was dedicated by Cardinal Cushing of Boston in 1965. The cathedral was built on the site of the old Galway jail; a white cross embedded into the pavement of the adjacent parking lot marks the site of the cemetery that stood beside the jail.

㉙ **Claddagh.** On the west bank of the Corrib estuary, this district was once an Irish-speaking fishing village outside the walls of the old town.

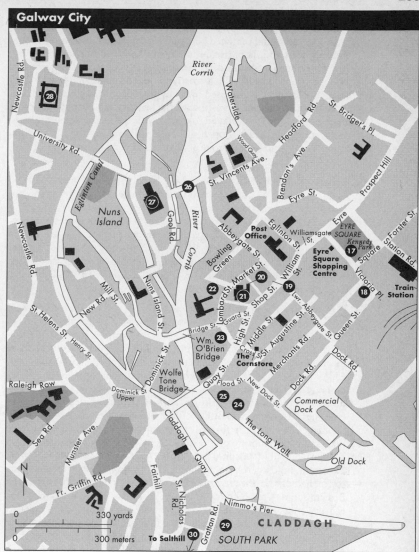

Cathedral of Our
Lady Assumed into
Heaven and St.
Nicholas, **27**

Claddagh, **29**

Collegiate Church of
St. Nicholas, **21**

Eyre Square, **17**

Galway City
Museum, **25**

Lynch's Castle, **19**

Lynch Memorial
Window, **20**

Nora Barnacle
House, **22**

Salmon Weir
Bridge, **26**

Salthill, **30**

Spanish Arch, **24**

Tig Neaċtain, **23**

Tourist Information
Office, **18**

University College
Galway (UCG), **28**

The name is an Anglicization of the Irish *cladach*, which means marshy ground. It retained its own strong, separate identity until the 1930s, when its traditional thatched cottages were replaced by a conventional housing plan and its particular character and traditions were largely lost. One thing has survived: the Claddagh ring, composed of two hands clasped around a heart with a crown above it (symbolizing love, friendship, and loyalty), is still used by many Irish people as a wedding ring. Traditionally, the ring is worn with the heart facing into you if you're married or otherwise unavailable, and with the heart facing outward (indicating your heart is open) if you're still looking for Mr. or Mrs. Right. Reproductions in gold or silver are favorite souvenirs of Galway.

㉑ **Collegiate Church of St. Nicholas.** Built by the Anglo-Normans in 1320 and enlarged in 1486 and again in the 16th century, the church contains many fine carvings and gargoyles dating from the late Middle Ages, and it is one of the best-preserved medieval churches in Ireland. Legend has it that Columbus prayed here on his last stop before setting off on his voyage to the New World. On Saturday mornings, a **street market,** held in the pedestrian way beside the church, attracts two dozen or so vendors and hundreds of shoppers. ⊠ *Lombard St.* ☜ *Free.* ☉ *Daily 8–dusk.*

⑰ **Eyre Square.** The largest open space in center-city Galway on the east side of the Corrib, Eyre Square encompasses a hodgepodge of monuments and concrete and grassy areas. In the center is **Kennedy Park,** a patch of lawn named in honor of John F. Kennedy, who spoke from this patch of ground when he visited the city in June 1963. At the north end of the park, a 20-ft steel **sculpture** standing in the pool of a fountain represents the brown sails seen on Galway hookers, the area's traditional sailing boats (☞ Kinvara, *above*). Seated beside this sculpture is the genial stone **figure of Pádraic Ó'Conaire,** a pioneer of the Irish-language revival at the turn of the century who was born in Galway (his birthplace fronting on the docks is marked with a plaque). When he died in a Dublin hospital in 1928, his only possessions were his pipe (which he holds here), his tobacco, and an apple. Now the entrance to Kennedy Park, the **Browne Doorway** was taken in 1905 from the Browne family's town house on Upper Abbeygate Street; it has the 17th-century coats of arms of both the Browne and Lynch families, called a "marriage stone," because when the families were joined in marriage their coats of arms were, too. Keep an eye out for similar if less elaborate versions of the entranceway as you walk around the old part of town. The **bronze cannons** were presented at the end of the Crimean War to the Connaught Rangers, a legendary regiment of the British Army made up of Irish men recruited from the west of Ireland (☞ King House *in* Boyle *in* Chapter 4).

㉕ **Galway City Museum.** Next door to the Spanish Arch (☞ *below*), the city's civic museum contains an array of materials relating to local history: old photographs, antiquities (the oldest is a stone axe head carbon-dated to 3500 BC), and other historical gewgaws. A new museum slated to be built behind the existing museum is scheduled to open in 2000. ⊠ *Spanish Arch,* ☎ *091/567641.* ☜ *£1.* ☉ *Mid-March–Sept., daily 10–1 and 2:15–5:15; Oct.–mid-March, Tues.–Thurs. 10–1 and 2:15–5:15.*

⑲ **Lynch's Castle.** Now a branch of the Allied Irish Banks, this is the finest remaining example in Galway of a 16th-century fortified house—fortified because the neighboring Irish tribes persistently raided the village, whose commercial life excluded them. Decorative details on its stone lintels are usually found only in southern Spain. Like the Spanish Arch (☞ *below*), it serves as a reminder of the close trading links that once existed between Galway and Spain. ⊠ *Shop St.*

㉓ Lynch Memorial Window. Embedded in a stone wall above a built-up Gothic doorway, the window marks the spot where, according to legend, James Lynch FitzStephen, mayor of Galway in the early 16th century, condemned his son to death after he had confessed to murdering a Spanish sailor who had stolen his girlfriend. When no one could be found to carry out the execution, Judge Lynch hanged his son himself, ensuring that justice prevailed, before retiring into seclusion.

㉒ Nora Barnacle House. On June 16, 1904, James Joyce (1882–1941) had his first date with Nora Barnacle, who would become his wife. He later chose to set *Ulysses* on this day, now known universally as Bloomsday (☞ Close-Up: ReJoyce! *in* Chapter 2)—"a recognition of the determining effect upon his life of his attachment to her," as Joyce's biographer Richard Ellman has said. Nora was born here, the daughter of a poor baker; today it has a modest collection of photographs, letters, and memorabilia, and a small gift shop. ⊠ *4 Bowling Green,* ☎ *091/564743.* ▣ *£1.* ⊙ *Mid-May–mid-Sept., Mon.–Sat. 2–5; off-season by appointment.*

★ ㉖ Salmon Weir Bridge. The bridge itself is nothing special, but in season—from mid-April to early July—shoals of salmon are visible from its deck, as they lie in the clear river water before making their way upstream to the spawning grounds of Lough Corrib. It is a memorable sight.

㉚ Salthill. Just 3¼ km/2 mi west of Galway, Salthill is a lively, hugely popular fun-and-games seaside resort with its own fun palace. Its promenade is the traditional place "to sit and watch the moon rise over Claddagh, and see the sun go down on Galway Bay"—in the words of the city's most famous song.

㉔ Spanish Arch. Built in 1584 to protect the quays where Spanish ships unloaded cargoes of wines and brandies, the arch now stands in the parking lot opposite Jurys Inn. It's easily (and often) mistaken for a pile of weathered stones, yet it's another reminder of Galway's—and Ireland's—past links with Spain (☞ Kinsale *in* Chapter 6).

㉓ Tig Neachtain. You can hear traditional music every night at this popular pub, which stands at a busy little crossroads in the heart of the old town. Grab a spot at one of its old-fashioned, partitioned snugs at lunchtime for an inexpensive selection of imaginative bar food. It's a good place to mingle with local actors, writers, artists, musicians, and students, although it can get sardine-can crowded. ⊠ *17 Cross St.,* ☎ *091/566172.*

⑱ Tourist Information Office. Just off Eyre Square, around the corner from the bus and train station and the Great Southern Hotel, this is the place to make reservations and find out about the latest happenings in and around town. ⊠ *1 Victoria Pl.,* ☎ *091/563081.* ⊙ *Weekdays 9–6, Sat. 9–1.*

㉘ University College Galway (UCG). Across the River Corrib, in the northwestern corner of the city, UCG was opened in 1846 to promote the development of local industry and agriculture, but today it's a center for Irish-language and Celtic studies. The Tudor-Gothic–style quadrangle, completed in 1848, is worth a visit, though much of the rest of the campus is architecturally undistinguished. Its library boasts an important archive of Celtic-language materials, and, in July and August, it also hosts courses in Irish studies for overseas students.

Dining and Lodging

$$$ ✕ **Casey's Westwood Lodge.** Owner-chef John Casey has earned a rep-
utation for imaginative, carefully prepared food at this edge-of-town
spot. The lodge is clearly visible from the N59 Clifden road, set back
among trees behind its parking area. Interconnected, high-ceiling din-
ing rooms are decorated in green and pink. Choose from starters that
are playful variations on familiar Irish dishes, such as crab and potato
cakes with leek and blue-cheese sauce, or home-cured spiced beef with
salad and chutney. Some main courses are Irish-inspired, like filet of
beef on a bed of colcannon with honey and thyme sauce. The dessert
list ranges from banana crème brûlée to Westwood's own bread-and-
butter pudding. ✉ *Newcastle Rd., Co. Galway,* ☎ *091/521442. AE,
MC, V.*

$$$ ✕ **Drimcong House.** A 300-year-old lakeside house north of Galway
★   City is the home of one of Ireland's most highly regarded restaurants.
Its chef-owner, Gerry Galvin, is something of a Renaissance man,
widely known for his extraordinarily inventive cooking. Galvin's wife
Marie supplies the kitchen with herbs and vegetables organically grown
on their own land, some of which you may have never encountered
before. The evening begins around the fireplace in the parlor, where
after ordering a cocktail you pore over the week's handwritten menu.
You have a choice of ordering 5, 4, or 3 courses, or a 5-course vegetarian menu. The half-dozen or so appetizers might include a ravioli
of oysters and smoked eel or confit of duck leg with parsnip and
potato mash. The entrées, unfussy and simple, are exactingly executed. Panfried loin of lamb is served in consommé with herb dumplings;
grilled salmon is served with a watercress and radish salad with an an-
chovy dressing. Desserts, such as a hot apple croûte with praline ice
cream and custard sauce, sparkle. The elegant, understated dining
room is decorated with prints and original paintings by contemporary
Irish artists; the service is exceptional. You're virtually guaranteed an
unforgettable experience. To get here, take the N59 Oughterard/Clif-
den road 13 km/8 mi north from Galway just through the village of
Moycullen; the driveway is up on the right. ✉ *Moycullen, Co. Galway,* ☎ *091/555115. Reservations essential. AE, DC, MC, V. Closed
Sun., Mon., and Dec. 25–mid-Mar. No lunch.*

$$$ ✕ **Kirwan's Lane Creative Cuisine.** A newly revamped alley at the river
end of Quay Street is home to Mike O'Grady's stylish modern restau-
rant. Blue-stained wooden tables, narrow floor-to-ceiling windows, and
a quarry-tiled floor set the stage for an sophisticated, fashionable
menu. Mille-feuille of fresh crab comes with peach chutney, while
Connemara black pudding is served on a compôte of sweet apple, cham-
pagne beurre blanc, and oysters. Main courses are updates of hearty
bistro-style dishes like loin of lamb with bacon mashed potato, glazed
shallots and rosemary, or fillet of salmon on a bed of sweet and sour
fennel, crispy beetroot and star anise. ✉ *Kirwan's Lane, Galway,* ☎
091/568266. AE, DC, MC, V. Closed Sun.

$$$ ✕ **Nimmo's.** Swiss chef Stephan Zeltner, who established himself on
the Galway scene with a small restaurant above Naughton's pub, has
now moved to a riverside location in an old stone building with a sep-
arately-run wine bar downstairs. The long, spacious second-floor room
has well-spaced tables set with white linen and original paintings on
the walls. He prepares robust food, exemplified by starters like quail
and mushroom stew or a shellfish ragout with smoked salmon. Panfried chicken breast with duck foie gras or noisettes of venison with
apple and Calvados are typically substantial entrées. Fish of the day
is based on market availability. ✉ *Spanish Arch, Galway,* ☎ *091/563565.
AE, DC, MC, V. Closed Sun. No lunch.*

$$ ✗ **De Burgos.** Once a grain store, this labyrinthine rathskeller restaurant has whitewashed stone walls and vaulted stone ceilings that complement the elegant art deco–style furniture and the pink and black linens. De Burgos was the name of one of the influential Norman families (the Blakes) that settled in Galway in the 13th century, and the historical link shows up in the French-influenced menu. Seafood is always available—noisettes of monkfish with tomato-and-chive *coulis* (thick, pureed sauce), for instance, or steamed supreme of cod with prawn sauce. Medallions of venison come with a red-wine sauce finished with red-currant jelly and cream. A simpler, less expensive, bar-food menu is served in the bar-reception area. ☒ *15–17 St. Augustine St., Galway,* ☎ *091/562188. Reservations advised. AE, DC, MC, V. Closed Sun.*

$$ ✗ **Malt House.** Hidden away in an alley off High Street in the center of old Galway, Barry and Therese Cunningham's bustling pub-restaurant has long been popular with both locals (who often celebrate special occasions here) and visitors for good food served in informal surroundings. You can either eat in the bar itself or in the fancier main room (beamed ceilings, white, rough-cast walls, and chintz curtains) just off the bar. Entrées are divided into "from the sea" and "from the land." Fresh prawns panfried in garlic butter is a popular seafood option, while the sirloin steak with green peppercorn sauce and the rack of lamb with a parsley crust should please landlubbers. At lunchtime a range of lighter dishes is also available, including crabmeat and potato cakes with a light mustard sauce. ☒ *Olde Malte Arcade, High St., Galway,* ☎ *091/563993. AE, DC, MC, V. Closed Sun. Oct.–Apr.*

$–$$ ✗ **McDonagh's Seafood Bar.** The McDonagh's are one of Galway's most entrepreneurial families (☞ Hotel Spanish Arch, *below,* next door, was opened in late 1996 by Easter McDonagh), and this spot is a longtime town landmark. After a major mid-1997 renovation, it's now partly a fish-and-chips bar and partly a "real" fish restaurant, while the fresh fish shop from which the business grew has moved to separate quarters. If you've yet to try fish and chips, this is the place to start: cod, whiting, mackerel, haddock, or hake is deep-fried in a light batter and served with a heap of freshly cooked chips. Or try Galway oysters au naturel, or a bowl of mussels steamed in wine and garlic. The restaurant has a wide choice of classic seafood, including a fine seafood special: a platter of hot lobster, scallops, crab claws, and prawns. The restaurant is licensed to serve wine only. ☒ *22 Quay St., Galway,* ☎ *091/565001. AE, MC, V. No lunch Sun. Oct.–Apr.*

$ ✗ **Bridge Mills.** A 400-year-old former grain mill situated right beside the River Corrib has been renovated into a minimall and this restaurant, which dominates the ground floor. Pine tables and stick-back chairs contrast nicely with the mill's heavy stone walls. You can sit outside beside a bubbling stream and watch local fishermen pulling salmon out of the river. During the day, the fare includes freshly made salads and sandwiches and hot daily specials, with desserts like fresh fruit tarts and homemade crepes. The evening menu is more substantial: roast rack of lamb with mustard and tarragon, 10-ounce sirloin steaks, and vegetarian specials like spinach and ricotta cannelloni. ☒ *O'Brien's Bridge, Galway,* ☎ *091/566231. AE, MC, V. No dinner Oct.–mid-May.*

$$$$ ⌂ **Glenlo Abbey.** Five minutes outside the city on the N59 Clifden road, set well back from the road with views over Lough Corrib, and surrounded by its own golf course, Glenlo is Galway's newest luxury hotel, opened in 1992. Built in 1740, it was previously a private home, not a monastery as the name implies. The lobby resembles a gentleman's club, with its solid parquet floors, large, leather Chesterfield sofas, and old, leather-bound books. The spacious bedrooms are in a new wing and have Georgian-style furniture in mahogany veneer and super-king-size beds. The bathrooms have marble walls; some have whirlpool baths. The elegant and rather hushed French Room serves Irish and international cuisine in formal, Regency-style surroundings. ⊠ *Bushy Park, Co. Galway,* ☎ *091/526666,* ℻ *091/527800. 44 rooms with bath. Restaurant, 2 bars, sauna, 9-hole golf course, tennis court, fishing.*

$$$ 🏨 **Ardilaun House.** This lovely, 19th-century house lies at the end of
★ a tree-lined avenue in a quiet suburb, midway between the city center and the Salthill promenade—about five minutes' drive from both. Open fires, fresh flower arrangements, and Regency-style furniture characterize the quiet public rooms overlooking the gardens. The individually designed bedrooms are decorated with a pink, gray, or green color scheme and Irish-made mahogany furniture with brass trim. All the fully tiled bathrooms have heated towel racks and marble sinks. For views of the bay, book a top-floor, even-numbered room. Other rooms, which are just as pleasant, overlook the flower garden, shrubberies, and a fountain. ⊠ *Taylor's Hill, Co. Galway,* ☎ *091/521433,* ℻ *091/521546. 89 rooms with bath. Restaurant, 2 bars, sauna, health club. AE, DC, MC, V.*

$$$ 🏨 **Galway Great Southern.** Built in 1845 to coincide with the arrival of the railway, and grandly situated on the southeastern side of Eyre Square, this is still the best address in town. A pianist tinkles away in the large lobby, which, like the two bars, is a popular gathering spot. All the guest rooms are decorated in tastefully muted, color-coordinated schemes, with Georgian-style tables and chairs, though they vary in size. The large, deluxe rooms in the original building have tall ceilings and windows and are particularly elegant, though those at the front directly above the bar can be loud late into the night. Rooms at the back are newer; those in the back on the fifth floor have views of Galway Bay, as does the swimming pool. French-Irish cuisine is served at the formal Oyster Room. ⊠ *Eyre Sq., Co. Galway,* ☎ *091/564041,* ℻ *091/566704. 115 rooms with bath. Restaurant, 2 bars, indoor pool, sauna. AE, DC, MC, V.*

$$ 🏨 **Brennan's Yard.** Beside the historic Spanish Arch and an easy walk from Galway's shops and restaurants, this tall, four-story stone building in the dockland area has been strikingly converted into a pleasant modern hotel. The large windows in the bar look across the sea to the Claddagh (☞ *above*), as do some of the bedrooms—ask for a sea view when booking. The rooms are not large and have quite small windows because of the age of the building, but they are very well designed, color-coordinated in dark pastels, and individually furnished with antique pine and paintings by local artists. ⊠ *Lower Merchant's Rd., Co. Galway,* ☎ *091/568166,* ℻ *091/568262. 24 rooms with bath. Restaurant, bar. AE, DC, MC, V.*

$$ 🏨 **Hotel Spanish Arch.** Opened in late 1996 on a busy stretch of Quay Street, Easter McDonagh's small hotel is effusively designed in an updated Victorian style. Historical artifacts that have been incorporated into the hotel's decor include elaborate wooden paneling in the large, airy bar and a 16th-century Carmelite convent wall in the small, tucked-away restaurant. The rooms are all nearly identical except for their individualized, fully color-coordinated schemes, with plush curtains, bedspreads, and carpets. You should be sure to request a room in the back, as those in the front can be noisy, first with late-night revelers, then with the early-morning street cleaners and garbage trucks. ⊠ *Quay St., Co. Galway,* ☎ *091/569600,* ℻ *091/569191. 20 rooms with bath. Restaurant, bar. AE, DC, MC, V.*

$ ⚏ **Cregg Castle.** Set on a 165-acre wildlife preserve about 15 km/9 mi north of Galway on the N17 (turn left for Corrandulla just beyond Claregalway), this 17th-century castle is pleasantly informal. The Brodericks, the owners, all play instruments, and traditional sessions often take place around the huge, log-and-turf fire in the Great Hall. Due to the castle's age, the bedrooms vary in shape and size and are decorated mainly with sturdy Victorian bygones. Breakfast is served until noon around an antique dining table that seats 18 people. The restaurant is licensed to serve wine only; reservations for dinner should be made by 3 PM. ⊠ *Corrandulla, Co. Galway,* ☎ FAX *091/791434. 10 rooms, 5 with bath. Closed Nov.–Feb.*

$ ⚏ **Jurys Galway Inn.** At the foot of Galway's busy main Quay Street, right on the banks of the Corrib, this newly built, four-story hotel offers good-quality, budget accommodation. Each room is big enough for three adults or two adults and two children, and Jurys fixed-price policy applies to all of them. The light, airy rooms have modern pine fittings, plain carpets and walls, double-glazed windows, and fully equipped bathrooms. Those overlooking the river are quieter than those in front. The atmosphere unavoidably tends toward anonymous-international, but it's centrally located and the level of comfort is high for the price range. ⊠ *Quay St., Co. Galway,* ☎ *091/566444,* FAX *091/568415. 128 rooms with bath. Restaurant, bar, parking (fee). AE, DC, MC, V.*

$ ⚏ **Norman Villa.** Dee and Mark Keogh's Victorian town house, mid-
★ way between the city center and the seaside promenade of Salthill, is ideally located, away from the bustle but within easy walking distance of both places. Brightly painted walls, Victorian brass beds with Irish linen sheets, varnished floorboards, working wooden shutters, and fun, off-beat paintings and artifacts make for lively, pleasant decor. Vegetarians are readily accommodated at breakfast. ⊠ *86 Lower Salthill, Co. Galway,* ☎ FAX *091/521131. 5 rooms with bath. Parking. No credit cards. Closed Jan. 10–31.*

Nightlife and the Arts

Because of its small size and concentration of pubs and restaurants, Galway can seem even livelier at 11 PM than it is at 11 AM. On weekends when there are a lot of students and other revelers in town, Eyre Square and environs can be rowdy late at night after pub-closing time. On the plus side, if you've been staying out in the countryside and you're ready for a little nightlife, you're certain to find plenty of it here.

FESTIVALS AND SEASONAL EVENTS

The **Galway Arts Festival** (☎ 091/583800), the city's premier annual event, spans the last two weeks in July and includes drama, film, music, children's events, and a huge parade. The **Galway Races** at Ballybrit Race Course (to the north of town off the N17) start the day after the arts festival ends for a week of mad revelry. At the end of September, the **Galway International Oyster Festival** (☎ 091/527282) indulges visitors with the "food of the gods." Mid-April's **Cuirt Literary Festival** (091/565886) brings in leading Irish and international writers for a week of readings and other events.

PUBS AND OTHER NIGHT SPOTS

The best area for traditional music is the Quay Street–Shop Street area between Eyre Square and the Spanish Arch. You will usually find a session after about 9 PM at **The Quays** (⊠ Quay St., ☎ 091/561777), **Neáchtain's** (⊠ 17 Cross St., ☎ 091/561720), **Taaffe's** (⊠ 19 Shop St., ☎ 091/564066), **Crane's** (⊠ 2 Sea Rd., ☎ 91/587419), and the **Cottage Bar** (⊠ Lower Salthill, ☎ 091/526754). **Le Graal** (⊠ 38 Lower Dominick St., ☎ 091/567614), licensed to sell wine only, is a bar-brasserie that metamorphoses into a lively late nightspot. **Aras na Gael** (⊠ 45

A YEAR-ROUND FLEADH

DUBLIN MAY BE the political capital of Ireland, but Galway is the center of its traditional-music universe, a place where you can hear this music all through the year, whether or not there's a *fleadh*, or traditional music festival, on. ☞ **Galway City** and its environs have given birth to some of the most durable names in Irish music: De Danann, Arcady, singers Dolores and Seán Keane, and the mercurial accordion genius Mairtín O'Connor. Seán Ryan, acknowledged master of the tin whistle, has been playing every Sunday at the ☞ **Crane Bar** for nearly 20 years. The hottest sessions these days take place at the ☞ **Cottage Bar** in Lower Salthill, where up-and-coming young musicians are drawn by the cozy atmosphere and the fine acoustics. In the city itself, there's still plenty of music to be found at old reliables such as ☞ **Neaćhtain's,** ☞ **Taaffe's,** and ☞ **Aras na Gael.**

EIRE 32

RIALTAS NA hÉIREANN 1922 1997

South of Galway the fishing village of ☞ **Kinvara** hosts the annual **Cuckoo Fleadh,** a small but growing festival that's five years old in 1998. Resident musicians like De Danann alumni Jackie Daly and Charlie Piggott play regularly at **Winkles Hotel,** where, in 1989, a very young and relatively unknown accordion player got together with a few friends for a casual recording session. The resulting album, *Sharon Shannon,* went platinum virtually overnight, becoming the most successful traditional music recording ever released. Today, Shannon, who grew up on a farm outside Corofin, County Clare, and got her first accordion when she was 11, is one of Ireland's leading trad Irish musicians.

Down the road, the lively market town of ☞ **Ennis**—where Shannon took lessons from local maestro Frank Custy—has lately come into its own, attracting a growing cadre of musicians—the Custys, Siobhán and Tommy Peoples, Josephine Marsh, P. J. King, flute player Kevin Crawford, and most recently, accordion whiz kid Murt Ryan, just arrived from Tipperary. Sessions take place at an ever-changing roster of pubs; ☞ **May Kearney's,** ☞ **Ciaran's,** and most notably ☞ **Cruise's** are all hot venues. This last pub boasts an adjacent concert venue where a few years ago a group of local musicians recorded a lovely live album, *The Sanctuary Sessions.* Still available through stores specializing in traditional music, the album is an excellent introduction to Irish music, with the featured artists including most of the above-mentioned musicians as well as banjo player Mary Shannon and the wonderful Galway singer Seán Tyrrell. In May, Ennis is home to the ☞ **Fleadh Nua** festival—celebrating its 25th year in 1998—with concerts, competitions, workshops, and *ceilís* (Irish dancing and song).

— By Sarah McQuaid

A PANTHEON OF TRADITIONAL IRISH INSTRUMENTS

Irish music is a living, evolving tradition, and the types of instrument on which it is played is increasing. Among the recent arrivals are the mouth organ, Jew's harp, viola, 5-string banjo, synthesizer, and saxophone. At the average session, however, you might find some or all of the following:

Accordion. Most traditional musicians play a button accordion, with two rows of buttons that produce a different tone depending on whether the bellows are pulled or pushed. Sharon Shannon, Mairtín O'Connor, Jackie Daly, Joe Burke, and Seamus Begley are among the most well-known button accordionists.

Banjo. Irish players generally use four-string tenor banjos, most of which were made in America in the 1930s, when it was a popular jazz instrument. They're often richly decorated with gold or silver plating, mother-of-pearl inlay, and elaborate carving on the wooden parts.

Bodhran. This drum is made of goatskin stretched across a round wooden frame; it's played with a wooden stick called a beater or tipper.

Bouzouki. A flat back and 8 or 10 strings characterize the bouzouki played by most Irish musicians. Some use the term "cittern" or "Irish bouzouki" to distinguish it from the Greek bouzouki, which has 6 strings and a round back.

Concertina. Especially popular with Clare musicians, the concertina comes in two varieties: Anglo and English. The former, in which a different note is produced depending on whether the bellows is pulled or pushed (as with the button accordion) is most typical.

Fiddle. This is the most popular melody instrument in Irish music. Among the great fiddle players are Frankie Gavin of De Danann, Mairead Ni Mhaonaigh and Ciaran Tourish of Altan, Tommy Peoples, and Nollaig Casey.

Flute. Wooden flutes from the 19th century, with six finger holes and anywhere from zero to eight keys, are in great demand among traditional musicians. Matt Molloy is the acknowledged king of the flute players.

Guitar. Formerly disparaged by arch-traditionalists, the guitar is gaining respectability, especially since a number of musicians are using it to play melody rather than just backup chords. When used in Irish music, the instrument is often tuned DADGAD rather than the standard EADGBE.

Tin Whistle. Occasionally referred to as a penny whistle, most are made of metal, although plastic and wooden whistles are appearing more often. Whistles come in various keys ranging from B flat (lowest) to G (highest) with D being most common.

Uilleann Pipes. Uilleann (pronounced "illun") literally means "elbow," referring to the use of the elbow to pump the bellows that fills the bag, as distinct from the Scottish highland pipes which are filled by a blow pipe held in the mouth. The full set of pipes includes the bellows, bag, a chanter that plays the melody, drones that generate continuous low notes, and regulators that can be pressed to produce chords. The better-known pipers include Davy Spillane, Declan Masterson, Ronan Browne and Finbar Furey.

—By Sarah McQuaid

Lower Dominick St., ☎ 091/526509) is one of the few Irish-speaking pubs in the city center.

The **Town Hall Theatre** (✉ Courthouse Sq., Woodquay, ☎ 091/569777), opened in 1995 in the city's former town hall, is lit virtually every night of the year.

The renowned **Druid Theatre** company (✉ Chapel La., ☎ 091/568617) is well-respected for its adventurous and accomplished productions, mainly of 20th-century Irish and European plays. The players perform regularly at the Royal Shakespeare Company's small stage in London; when they're home, they usually appear at the Town Hall. At press time (summer 1997), they had just announced a **John Millington Synge Festival** for June or July 1998, in which they will stage new productions of all seven Synge plays, including his best known, "The Playboy of the Western World" (1907).

An Taibhdhearc (✉ Middle St., ☎ 091/562024), pronounced "Awn Tie-vark," was founded in 1928 by Hilton Edwards and Micháel Macliammóir as the national Irish-language theater. It continues to produce first-class shows, mainly of Irish works in both the English and the Irish languages.

Macnas (✉ Fisheries Field, Salmon Weir Bridge, ☎ 091/561462) is an internationally renowned, Galway-based troupe of performance artists who have brought street theater to new levels. Their participation in the Galway Arts Festival's annual parade is always much anticipated.

High-quality work by local artists can be found at **Kenny's Bookshop & Art Gallery** (☞ Shopping, *below*). The art gallery at **University College Galway** (☎ 091/524411) puts on a number of shows each year.

Outdoor Activities and Sports

Set off to explore the Galway area, especially its coast, by renting a bike from **Celtic Cycles** (✉ Queen St., Victoria Pl., Eyre Sq., Co. Galway, ☎ 091/566606).

You can get fishing licenses, tackle, and bait at **Freeny's** (✉ High St., Co. Galway ☎ 091/562609). **Murt's** (✉ 7 Daly's Pl., Woodquay, Co. Galway, ☎ 091/561018) can also handle your fishing needs.

The **Galway Golf Club** (✉ Blackrock, Salthill, Co. Galway, ☎ 091/522033) is an 18-hole, par-71 course with excellent views of Galway Bay, the Burren, and the Aran Islands. Some of the fairways run close to the ocean. **Galway Bay Golf and Country Club** (✉ Renville, Oranmore, Co. Galway, ☎ 091/790500) is a new par-72, parkland course designed by Christy O'Connor, Jr., on the shores of Galway Bay.

A **Corrib Cruise** from Wood Quay (behind the Town Hall Theatre at the Rowing Club) is a lovely way to spend a fine afternoon; it lasts 1½ hours and travels 8 km/5 mi up the River Corrib and about 6 km/3½ mi around Lough Corrib. You can also rent the boat for an evening. ☎ *091/568903.* ▱ *£5.* ⊙ *May–Sept., daily 2:30 and 4:30.*

There are nine courts at the **Galway Lawn Tennis Club** (✉ Threadneedle St., Salthill, Co. Galway, ☎ 091/522353) available to nonmembers at £4 per hour.

WATER SPORTS

Galway Sailing Center (⊠ Renville, Oranmore, Co. Galway, ☎ 091/794527) offers dinghy sailing and board sailing on Lough Corrib or on coastal waters. Instruction is also available.

Shopping

For a brief overview of Galway's shopping scene, *see* A Good Walk, *above.*

BOOKSTORES

Kenny's Bookshop (⊠ High St., ☎ 091/562739) has five floors of books of Irish interest, mainly secondhand and antiquarian, as well as prints, maps, and a small art gallery. **Charlie Byrne's Bookshop** (⊠ The Cornstore, Middle St., ☎ 091/561766) sells a large, varied selection of used books and remainders.

CLOTHING, CRAFTS, AND GIFTS

Design Ireland Plus (⊠ The Cornstore, Middle St., ☎ 091/567716, ⊠ Grainstore, Lower Abbeygate St., ☎ 091/566620) has an excellent range of contemporary Irish-made crafts and clothing. **Faller's Sweater Shop** (⊠ 25 High St. and ⊠ 35 Eyre Sq., ☎ 091/561255) has the choicest selection of Irish-made sweaters, competitively priced. **Meadows & Byrne** (⊠ Castle St., ☎ 091/567776) sells the best in modern household items and high-fashion, Irish-made clothing. **O'Máille's** (⊠ 16 High St., ☎ 091/562696) carries Aran sweaters, handwoven tweeds, and classically tailored clothing. Browse in **Treasure Chest** (⊠ William St., ☎ 091/567237) for china, crystal, gifts, and classic clothing.

JEWELRY

The **Claddagh Jewellers** (⊠ Eyre Sq., ☎ 091/562310) has a wide selection of traditional Claddagh rings and other jewelry.

MALLS

Slightly off the beaten path, **The Cornstore** (⊠ Middle St.) has some stylish shops that tend to be less crowded than their competitors on the main street. On the southwest side of Eyre Square and imaginatively designed to incorporate parts of the old town walls, the **Eyre Square Shopping Centre** (⊠ Eyre Sq.) offers a wide range of midprice clothing and household goods.

MUSIC

Specializing in Irish traditional music, **Mulligan** (⊠ 5 Middle St. Court, ☎ 091/564961) carries more than 6,000 CDs, records, and cassettes.

VINTAGE GOODS

Twice as Nice (⊠ 5 Quay St. ☎ 091/566332) sells a mix of new and vintage men's and women's clothing, linens, lace, and jewelry at reasonable prices.

The Aran Islands

③ *48 km/30 mi by boat from Galway City, about 24 km/15 mi by boat from Ros an Mhil (Rossaveal); flights from Connemara Airport.*

The Aran Islands—Inishmore, Inishmaan, and Inisheer—are remote western outposts of the ancient province of Connaught (though they are not the country's westernmost points; that honor belongs to the Blasket Islands [☞ Chapter 6]). These three natural wonders were once as barren and austere as the limestone pavements of the Burren, of which they are essentially a continuation. Today, the land is parceled into small fields surrounded by stone walls, the limestone having been lifted in great ramparts against the pounding ocean. The views from here are spectacular: Witness the uninterrupted expanse of the Atlantic on the western horizon; to the northeast, the Connemara coast and its Twelve Bens; and to the southeast, County Clare's Burren and the Cliffs of Moher.

The islands have been populated for thousands of years, and the Irish-speaking inhabitants have adhered to the traditions of their ancestors—hardy, plain-living fisher folk and farmers—while adapting to the changes brought by tourism: daily air service to Galway (subsidized by the government), motorized currachs, multichannel TVs, and all the usual modern home conveniences. Yet islanders retain a distinctness from mainlanders, preferring simple home decor, very plain food, and tightly knit communities. Crime is virtually unknown in these parts; at your B&B, you'll find no locks on the guest-room doors, and its front-door latch will be left open.

Many islanders have sampled life in Dublin or cities abroad but have returned to raise families, keeping the population stable at around 1,500. Through the years, the islands have also attracted writers and artists, including J. M. Synge (1871–1909), who learned Irish on Inishmaan and wrote about its people in his play *Riders to the Sea.* The film *Man of Aran,* made on Inishmore in 1932 by the American director Robert Flaherty, is a classic documentary recording the islanders' dramatic battles with sea and storm.

The best time to visit the islands is May and early June while the unusual, Burren-like flora is at its best and before the bulk of the more than 100,000 annual visitors arrive. (For details on getting to the Aran Islands, *see* Getting Around *in* The West A to Z, *below.*)

Inis Mór (Inishmore)

With a population of 900, Inishmore is the largest of the islands and the closest to the Connemara coast. It's also the most commercialized, its appeal slightly diminished by the existence of some road traffic. In the summer, ferries arriving at **Kilronan,** Inishmore's main village and port, are met by minibuses and pony and cart drivers, all eager to show visitors "the sights." More than 8 km/5 mi long and about 3 km/2 mi wide at most points, with an area of 7,640 acres, the island is just a little too large to explore comfortably on foot in a day. The best way to see it is really by bicycle; bring your own or hire one from one of the three vendors right near the quay: **Aran Bicycle Hire** (☎ 099/ 61132), **Costello's** (☎ 099/61241), **Burke and Mullin** (two outlets; ☎ 099/61402); all operate May through October. The **Aran Heritage Centre** explains the history and culture of the islanders who lived for many years in virtual isolation from the mainland. ☎ *099/61355.* ✉ *£2.* ⊙ *Apr.–Oct., daily 10–7.*

Leaving Kilronan, you'll see the tall, unmortared stone walls that enclose diminutive fields that are a telling human contribution to the islands. By building the walls, the farmers both cleared the land of rocks and at the same time created a buffer against Atlantic gales. Farmers then created soil, which did not exist on the island, by combining sand and rotted seaweed—the only available materials. As the road climbs the hill beyond Kilronan, panoramic views of the Connemara coast open in front of you. Footpaths lead across the fields to both stony and sandy beaches, most of them in small, deserted coves.

★   The main attraction on Inishmore is **Dún Aengus,** one of the finest prehistoric monuments in Europe, dating from about 2000 BC. Spectacularly set on the edge of a 300-ft cliff overlooking a sheer drop, the fort's defenses consist of three rows of concentric circles. Who were defending themselves against whom is a matter of conjecture. From the innermost rampart there's a great view of the island and the Connemara coast.

LODGING

The only hotel on the islands is on Inisheer (☞ *below*), but there's no shortage of B&Bs, mostly in simple family homes. The best way to book is through the **Galway City TIO** (☞ Galway, *above*). Each island has at least one wine-licensed restaurant serving plain home cooking. Most B&Bs will provide a packed lunch and an evening meal (called high tea) on request.

$ 🏨 **Kilmurvey House.** Situated in the island's second village about 6½ km/4 mi from the quay and the airport (accessible by minibus), this rambling, stone, 200-year-old farmhouse is the first choice of many visitors (about 60% of them American) to the island. Proprietor Teresa Joyce added five new rooms in early 1997 to the four large rooms in the old house and three previously added ones; she also added bathrooms to all the rooms that didn't previously have them. ✉ *Kilmurvey, Aran Islands, Co. Galway,* ☎ *099/61218,* 🖷 *099/61397. 12 rooms with bath. Dining room. MC, V. Closed Nov.–Apr.*

NIGHTLIFE

The place to go for traditional music is the **American Bar** (✉ Kilronan, ☎ 099/61130).

Inis Meáin (Inishmaan)

The middle island in both size and location, Inishmaan has a population of about 300 and can be comfortably explored on foot—in fact, you have no alternative. Conor Fort, a smaller version of Dun Aengus; the ruins of two early Christian churches; and a chamber tomb known as the Bed of Diarmuid and Grainne, dating from about 2000 BC, are the island's major antiquities. You can also take wonderful cliff walks above secluded coves. It's on Inishmaan that the traditional Aran lifestyle is most evident. Until the mid-1930s or so, Aran women dressed in thick, red-woolen skirts to keep out the Atlantic gales, while the men wore collarless jackets, baggy trousers made of homespun tweed with *pampooties* (hide shoes without heels, suitable for walking on rocks), and a wide, hand-plaited belt called a *crios* (pronounced "krish"). Most islanders still don hand-knitted Aran sweaters, though nowadays they accompany them with jeans and sneakers.

Inis Oirr (Inisheer)

The smallest and flattest of the islands, Inisheer may be explored on foot in an afternoon, though if the weather is fine, you may be tempted to linger on the long, sandy beach that lies between the quay and the airfield. In the summer, Inisheer's population of 300 is augmented by high school students from all over Ireland attending the Gaelteacht, or Irish-language school. Only one stretch of road, about 500 yards long, links the airfield and the village. The **Church of Kevin,** signposted to the southeast of the quay, is a small, early Christian church that gets buried in sand by the storms every winter. Every year the islanders dig it out of the sand for the celebration of St. Kevin's Day on June 14. A pleasant walk through the village takes you up to **O'Brien's Castle,** a ruined, 15th-century tower that sits on top of a rocky hill—the only hill on the island.

It's worth making a circuit of the island to get a sense of its utter tranquillity. A maze of footpaths runs between the high stone walls that divide the fields, which are so small that they can support only one cow each, or two to three sheep. Those that are not cultivated or grazed turn into natural wildflower meadows between June and August, overrun with harebells, scabious, red clover, oxeye daisies, saxifrage, and tall grasses. It seems almost a crime to walk here—but how can you resist taking a rest in the corner of a sweet-smelling meadow on a sunny afternoon, sheltered by high stone walls with no sound but the larks above and the wind as it sifts through the stones? "The back of the island," as Inisheer's uninhabited side facing the Atlantic is called, has no beaches, but people still swim off the rocks.

LODGING

$ 🏨 **Hotel Inisheer.** A pleasant, modern low-rise in the middle of the island's only village a few minutes' walk from the quay and the airstrip, this simple, whitewashed building with a slate roof and half-slated walls has bright, plainly furnished rooms. The five rooms added in 1990 are slightly larger than the other 10. The restaurant (open to nonguests) is the best bet on the island, although much of the food is imported frozen. ⌧ *Lurgan Village, Aran Islands, Co. Galway,* ☎ *099/75020,* FAX *099/75099. 15 rooms, 6 with bath. Restaurant, bar, bicycles. AE, DC, MC, V. Closed Oct.–Apr. 1.*

THROUGH CONNEMARA AND COUNTY MAYO

Bordered by the long expanse of Lough Corrib on the east and the deeply indented, jagged coast of the Atlantic on the west, rugged, desolate western County Galway is known as Connemara. Like the American West, it's an area of spectacular, almost myth-making geography—of glacial lakes; gorgeous, silent mountains; lonely roads; and hushed, uninhabited bog lands. The Twelve Bens, "the central glory of Connemara," as Brendan Lehane has called them, together with the Maamturk Mountains to their north, lord proudly over the area's sepia bog lands. More surprisingly, stands of Scotch pine, Norwegian spruce, Douglas fir, and Japanese Sitka grow in Connemara's valleys and up hillsides— the result of a concerted national project that has so far reforested nine percent of Ireland. In the midst of this wilderness, you'll find few people, for Connemara's population is sparse even by Irish standards. Especially in the off-season, you're far more likely to come across sheep strolling its roads than another car.

Two main routes—one inland, the other coastal—lead through Connemara. To take the inland route (our tour follows this route), leave Galway City on the well-signposted outer-ring road and follow signs for the N59—Moycullen, Oughterard, and Clifden. If you choose to go the coastal route, you'll travel due west from Galway City to Rossaveal on the R336 through Salthill, Barna, and Spiddle—all in the heart of the West's strong Gaeltacht, home to roughly 40,000 Irish speakers. Although this is one of the most impressive and unspoiled coastal roads in Ireland, it has been scarred by modern, concrete, one-story homes—a sort of faux-Spanish hacienda style favored by locals. (Most of the traditional thatched houses in the West are now used as holiday homes.) You can continue north on the R336 from Rossaveal to Maam Cross and then head for coastal points west, or pick up the R340 and putter along the coast.

Oughterard

③② *27 km/17 mi west of Galway City on N59.*

Small and pretty Oughterard (pronounced "*Ook*-ter-ard") is the main village on the western shores of **Lough Corrib** and one of Ireland's leading angling resorts. (The lough is signposted to the right in the village center, less than 1½ km/1 mi up the road.) From mid-June to early September, local boatmen offer trips on the lough, which has several islands. It is also possible to take a boat trip to Cong (☞ *below*), at the north shore of the lough. Midway between Oughterard and Cong, **Inchagoill Island** (the Island of the Stranger), a popular destination for a half-day trip, has several early Christian church remains. The cost of boat rides is subject to negotiation—expect to pay about £6 per person.

Lodging

$$$ 🏨 **Connemara Gateway.** This adventurously designed, modern low-rise with traditional, gray-slate roofs above whitewashed walls combines the best of old and new. With a nod to the traditional Irish cottage, the lobby and the bar are decorated with wooden and cast-iron artifacts, and chintz sofas. Guest rooms are decorated with modern furniture, floral wall panels, matching floral drapes, and fluffy, mohair coverlets. All have sitting areas beside the large teak-framed windows that look out over the gardens and the distant hills. There's a strong tour-bus trade, but it doesn't spoil its charm. The hotel is about 1 km/⅓ mi outside the village on the Galway side of the N59. ⊠ *Co. Galway,* ☎ *091/552328,* 🅵🅰🆇 *091/552332. 62 rooms with bath. Restaurant, bar, indoor pool, sauna, tennis court, fishing. AE, DC, MC, V. Closed Dec.–mid Feb.*

Nightlife

For good music try **Faherty's** (☎ 091/552194).

Outdoor Activities and Sports

Oughterard Golf Club (⊠ Co. Galway, ☎ 091/552131) has a parkland course suitable for novices and those who wish to improve their games.

En Route As you continue northwest from Oughterard on the N59, you'll soon pass a string of small lakes on your left; their shining blue waters reflecting the blue sky is a typical Connemara sight on a sunny day. Sixteen kilometers/10 miles northwest of Oughterard, the continuation of the coast road (R336) meets the N59 at **Maam Cross** in the shadow of Leckavrea Mountain. Once an important meeting place for the people of north and south Connemara, it's still the location of a large monthly cattle fair. Walkers will find wonderful views of Connemara by heading for any of the local peaks visible from the road. Beyond Maam Cross, some of the best scenery in Connemara awaits on the road to **Recess** (16 km/10 mi west of Maam Cross on the N59). At many points on this drive, a short walk away from either side of the main road will lead you to the shores of one of the area's many small loughs. Stop and linger if the sun is out—even intermittently, for the light filtering through the clouds gives such splendor to the distant, dark-gray mountains and creates patterns on the brown-green moorland below. In June and July, it's light out until 11 or so, and it is worth taking a late-evening stroll to see the sun's reluctance to set. In Recess, **Joyce's** (☎ 095/34604) carries a good selection of contemporary ceramics, handwoven shawls, books of Irish interest, original paintings, and small sculptures.

Cong

③③ *23 km/14 mi northeast of Maam Cross on R336.*

Resting on a narrow isthmus between Lough Corrib and Lough Mask on the County Mayo border, the pretty, Old World village of Cong—an optional detour from Maam Cross—is dotted with ivy-covered thatched cottages and dilapidated farmhouses. Cong is surrounded by many stone circles and burial mounds, but its most notable ruins are those of the **Augustine Abbey** (⊠ Abbey St., no phone), dating from the early 13th century, and still exhibiting some finely carved details. It can be seen overlooking a river near Ashford Castle (☞ Lodging, *below*). Cong's 15 minutes came in 1952, when John Ford filmed *The

Quiet Man, one of his most popular films, here. John Wayne plays a prizefighter who comes home to Ireland to court the fiery Maureen O'Hara. (Pauline Kael called the film "fearfully Irish and green and hearty.") The **Quiet Man Heritage Cottage** is an exact replica of the cottage used in the film, with reproductions of the furniture and costumes, a few original artifacts, and pictures of Barry Fitzgerald and Maureen O'Hara on location. ✉ *Cong, Co. Mayo.* ☎ *092/46089.* 🎫 *£2.50.* ⊙ *Mar.–Nov, daily 10–6.*

Lodging

$$$$ 🏨 **Ashford Castle.** Perched at the head of Lough Corrib, surrounded by neatly manicured lawns and gardens, this massive, flamboyantly turreted and crenellated castle was built in 1870 for the Guinness family in a mock Gothic "Baronial" style, incorporating an earlier 1228 structure built by the De Burgos family. Now American-owned, Ashford is one of Ireland's most luxurious castle hotels. Large oil paintings in gilt frames hang from the castle's carved stone walls above polished-wood paneling, illuminated by crystal chandeliers. "Deluxe" rooms have generous sitting areas, heavily carved antique furniture, and extra-large bathrooms. The suites are vast and faultless, furnished with Georgian antiques and blissfully comfortable. The bedrooms in the discreetly added new wing, though, are disappointingly like any other luxury hotel rooms. Extensive fitness facilities were added in 1995. ✉ *Co. Mayo,* ☎ *092/46003,* 🅵🅰🆇 *092/46260. 83 rooms with bath. 2 restaurants, 2 bars, sauna, steam room, 9-hole golf course, 2 tennis courts, health club, horseback riding, Ping-Pong, fishing, bicycles. AE, DC, MC, V.*

Cashel

③④ *8 km/5 mi south of Recess on R340.*

Cashel is a quiet, extremely sheltered angling center at the head of Bertraghboy Bay. General de Gaulle is among the many people who have sought seclusion here. A word of caution in this area: Stray sheep, bolting Connemara ponies, cyclists, and reckless local drivers are all regular hazards on the narrow mountain roads hereabouts.

Dining and Lodging

$$$$ ✕🏨 **Cashel House.** Quietly secluded at the head of Cashel Bay on 40
★ acres, with exotic flowering shrubs, woodlands, and Connemara ponies grazing out back, Kay and Dermot McEvilly's luxurious country house has more antiques and curios per square foot than any other hotel in Ireland. Intricately carved oak tables, Biedermeier bureaus, gilt mirrors, Georgian bookcases, ormolu clocks, and other knickknacks are scattered liberally around the lobby, lounge, library, and downstairs corridors. More antiques and curios turn up in the bedrooms, which have king-size beds (canopied in the 13 minisuites), pink-and-green drapes and spreads, and brass bedside lamps. For a view of the sea rather than the garden, ask for a front room. In the dining room, the table-d'hôte menu, with more choices than at many other country houses, is particularly strong on fresh local seafood: Plates of three smoked fish or local oysters are two of seven or eight appetizers; poached fresh brill with salmon caviar sauce and Connemara lobster are among the dozen entrées. ✉ *Co. Galway,* ☎ *095/31001,* 🅵🅰🆇 *095/31077. 32 rooms with bath. Restaurant, tennis court, horseback riding, beach, boating, fishing, bicycles. AE, DC, MC, V. Closed Jan. 10–Feb. 10.*

$$$ 🏨 **Zetland Country House.** Built for the earl of Zetland on a hill overlooking secluded Cashel Bay, John and Mona Prendergast's mid-Victorian hunting lodge is popular with anglers, hunters, and townsfolk

in search of a rural retreat. Basic bedrooms overlook the garden and are decorated in floral chintz. Twice as large as the other rooms and furnished with late-Victorian antiques, minisuites in the main house have sea views. Your best bet is one of the middle-grade "superior" rooms in the converted coach house, which also all have sea views, plus polished mahogany antiques, velvet armchairs, and fully tiled bathrooms with decorated washbasins. ⊠ *Co. Galway,* ☎ *095/31111,* FAX *095/31117. 19 rooms with bath. Restaurant, bar, tennis court, fishing, bicycles. AE, DC, MC, V. Closed Nov.–Apr. 1.*

Outdoor Activities and Sports

Cashel Equestrian Center (⊠ Cashel House, Co. Galway, ☎ 095/31001) offers scenic treks and the chance to try a Connemara pony on its home ground.

Ballynahinch

③⑤ *10 km/6 mi west of Cashel on R341.*

Along the shores of Ballynahinch Lake you'll enter more wooded country. Woodland in this part of Ireland indicates the proximity of a "big house" whose owner can afford to plant trees for pleasure and prevent them from being cut down for fuel.

Lodging

$$$ ⊞ **Ballynahinch Castle.** Built in the late-18th century on the Owenmore
★ River, Ballynahinch was once the home of Richard Martin (1754–1834), known as Humanity Dick, and the founder of the Royal Society for the Prevention of Cruelty to Animals. The large house sits on 40 walkable wooded acres; excellent fishing and shooting are at hand. Comfort without ostentation is the hallmark here. The tiled lobby with Persian rugs has two inviting leather chesterfields in front of an open fire. The biggest bedrooms, in the discreetly added new ground-floor wing, have four-poster beds, Georgian-style mahogany furniture, and floor-to-ceiling windows overlooking the river. Rooms in the old house are equally comfortable and quiet. The castle is signposted off the N59 between Recess and Clifden. ⊠ *Recess, Co. Galway,* ☎ *095/31006,* FAX *095/31085. 28 rooms with bath. Restaurant, bar, tennis court, croquet, fishing, bicycles. AE, DC, MC, V.*

Clifden

★ ③⑥ *23 km/14 mi west of Recess, 79 km/49 mi northwest of Galway City on the N59.*

In most places, Clifden, with roughly 1,100 residents, would be called a village, but out here it is looked on as something of a metropolis. It is, far and away, the prettiest town in Connemara, and its unrivaled "capital." Clifden's first attraction is its location—perched high above Clifden Bay on a forested plateau, its back to the spectacular Twelve Ben Mountains. The tapering spires of the town's two churches add to its Alpine feel. A good selection of small restaurants, lively bars with music most nights in the summer, some very pleasant accommodations, and excellent walks make the town a popular base. It's quiet out of season, but in July and August, crowds flock here, especially for August's world-famous **Connemara Pony Show.** Horse breeders come from around the world to check out Ireland's finest yearlings and stallions. A short (2-km/1¼-mi) walk along the quay road through the grounds of the ruined **Clifden Castle** is the best way to explore the seashore. It was built in 1815 by John D'Arcy, the town's founder, who laid out the town's wide main street on a long ridge with a parallel street below it. Take the aptly named **Sky Road** to really appreciate Clifden's breathtakingly scenic setting. Signposted at the west end of town, this high narrow circuit of about 5 km/3 mi heads west to Kingstown, skirting Clifden Bay's precipitous shores.

Dining and Lodging

$$ ✗ **O'Grady's Seafood.** A Clifden institution, this intimate, town-center restaurant serves fresh local produce, primarily seafood, more modishly than you might expect in the wilds of Connemara. Once a shop, the small main room is decorated in dark pinks and reds with wrought-iron dividers between the tables. Try the fresh crab and prawn bake gratiné to start, or marinated salmon with goat cheese in a sesame crust on raspberry coulis. Typical main courses might include a duo of monkfish and blackened scallops on a cilantro duxelle with two sauces, or crisp breast of duckling in its own juice with sweet caramelized onions. For dessert, the vanilla ice cream and sliced strawberries with Grand Marnier sabayon glazed under the grill is worth the indulgence. ⊠ *Market St., Co. Galway,* ☎ *095/21450. AE, DC, MC, V. Closed Nov.–Dec. 28, Jan. 10–Mar. 12, and Sun.*

$$$ ✗🖼 **Rock Glen Manor House.** Cross the bridge at the west end of
★ town and go ⅘ km/½ mi down the Roundstone road (the R341) to find John and Evangeline Roche's beautifully converted shooting lodge, built in 1815. On windy days, a tiny Connemara pony, Gregory, stands sentinel at the entrance gates and enjoys the breeze. Riding boots and tennis rackets in the hall make this feel more like a private home than a top-class hotel. A turf fire warms the large, sunny drawing room, with plump white armchairs, magazines, books, and board games. All the guest rooms are nicely furnished in the Georgian style, with fluffy mohair or chintz bedspreads and fully tiled bathrooms. In the Victorian-style restaurant, you might start with marinated herring with a honey and whole-grain mustard vinaigrette and move on to roasted rack of lamb with an herb crust and mushroom duxelles. The rhubarb crumble with ginger ice cream or crème brûlée grilled with banana make a tasty coda. ⊠ *Co. Galway,* ☎ *095/21035,* 🖷 *095/21737. 29 rooms with bath. Restaurant, bar, tennis court, horseback riding, Ping-Pong, fishing. AE, DC, MC, V. No lunch. Closed Nov.–mid-Mar.*

$–$$ ✗🖼 **Quay House.** A roaring turf fire in the sitting room greets visitors
★ to this three-story Georgian house, Clifden's oldest building (from 1820). It's a short walk from the busy town center, and an oasis of calm beside the harbor quay. All rooms but one have sea views, but the one without has a four-poster canopied bed to compensate. Proprietors Julia and Patrick Foyle have also added homey touches such as model boats and readable books. Dark-green walls hung with heavy, gilt-frame portraits set a tasteful tone in the highly regarded restaurant. Main courses include breast of chicken with goat cheese, pesto, and Parma ham or charcoal-grilled halibut with cardamom, basil, and orange vinaigrette. Desserts include "lethal chocolate pudding" and iced nougat mousse with fruit compote. ⊠ *Connemara, Co. Galway,* ☎ *095/21369,* 🖷 *095/41168. 7 rooms with bath. Restaurant, fishing. MC, V. Closed Nov. 8–mid-Mar.*

Nightlife

The best place in town for music is the **Abbeyglen Castle** (⊠ Sky Rd., ☎ 095/21201), which has sessions in the bar most nights from June to September, and occasional visits by big-name acts.

Outdoor Activities and Sports

BICYCLING

Explore Connemara by renting a bike from **John Mannion** (⊠ Railway View, Co. Galway, ☎ 095/21160).

GOLF

Situated on a dramatic stretch of Atlantic coastline, the par-72 course at the **Connemara Golf Club** (⊠ Ballyconneely, south of Clifden, Co. Galway, ☎ 095/23502) measures 7,174 yards.

HORSEBACK RIDING

Errislannan Manor Connemara Pony Stud and Riding Center (⊠ Connemara, Co. Galway, ☎ 095/21134) provides mountain treks, instruction, and courses for children.

Shopping

Millar's Connemara Tweeds (⊠ Main St., ☎ 095/21038) is a general crafts-and-art gallery with a good selection of traditional tweeds and handknits. The **Celtic Shop** (⊠ Main St., ☎ 095/21064) features good-quality general crafts. **Linda's Spinning Studio** (⊠ Derrylea, ☎ 095/21888) sells handwoven wool products and offers demonstrations of the craft.

En Route Continue toward Letterfrack through the **Inagh Valley,** which is flanked by two impressive mountain ranges with distinctive, conical-shape peaks, which rise almost directly to over 1,968 ft without any foothills.

Letterfrack

③⑦ *14 km/9 mi north of Clifden on the N59.*

The 5,000-acre **Connemara National Park** lies just to the southeast of the village of Letterfrack. Its **visitor center** covers the area's history and ecology, particularly the origins and growth of peat (and presents the depressing statistic that more than 80 percent of Ireland's peat, 5,000 years in the making, has been destroyed in the last 90 years). You can also get details on the many excellent walks and beaches in the area. ☎ 095/41054. ⌨ *Park free; visitor center £1.50.* ☉ *Park: accessible at all times; visitor center: May and Sept., daily 10–5:30; June, daily 10–6:30; July and Aug., daily 9:30–6:30.*

Dining and Lodging

$$$ ✕⊞ **Renvyle House.** A lake at its front door, the Atlantic Ocean at its back door, and the mountains of Connemara as a backdrop make for a triple-crown setting for this hotel 8 km/5 mi north of Letterfrack. Once the retreat of the man of letters Oliver St. John Gogarty, Renvyle's has a rustic, informal ambience, with exposed beams and brickwork and numerous open turf fires. All the comfortable guest rooms, elegantly decorated in a floral country-house style, have breathtaking views. The softly lit restaurant's table-d'hôte menu, based on the traditional country-house style, might offer wild mushrooms in a creamy sauce served in a savory tartlet to start, and local salmon poached in court boullion with cucumber butter sauce as a main course. Homemade ice creams and chocolate profiteroles tempt from the dessert menu. Live entertainment is usually on in the bar. The hotel is a great place to pursue outdoor activities: golf, fishing, and horseback riding are all at hand. ⊠ *Renvyle, Co. Galway,* ☎ *095/43511,* ℻ *095/43515. 56 rooms with bath. Restaurant, bar, outdoor heated pool, 9-hole golf course, 2 tennis courts, horseback riding, fishing, snooker. AE, DC, MC, V. Closed Jan. and Feb.*

$$$ ✕⊞ **Rosleague Manor.** Anne and Patrick Foyle's pink, creeper-clad, ★ two-story Georgian house sits on 30 lovely acres of wooded grounds overlooking Ballinakill Bay and the mountains of County Mayo and Connemara. Just inside, the clutter of walking and shooting sticks beneath the grandfather clock in the hall sets the tone, which is fairly informal. The solidly comfortable bedrooms are furnished with well-used Victorian and Georgian antiques, four-poster or large brass bedsteads, and drapes that match the William Morris wallpaper. The best rooms are at the front on the first floor, overlooking the bay. At dinner in the award-winning restaurant, you might start with a warm salad of roast quail with toasted pine nuts and walnut dressing. Baked monktail with crispy capers and balsamic vinegar is a typical entrée. Irish farmhouse cheeses and homemade ice cream are always on the dessert menu. ⊠ *Co. Galway,* ☎ *095/41101,* 𝐅𝐀𝐗 *095/41168. 16 rooms with bath. Restaurant, bar, sauna, tennis court, horseback riding. AE, MC, V. Closed Nov.–Apr. 1.*

Nightlife

For traditional music, try the **Bards' Den** (☎ 095/41042).

Outdoor Activities and Sports

Little Killary Adventure Center (⊠ Salruck, Renvyle, near Letterfrack, Co. Galway, ☎ 095/43411) provides sailing and windsurfing instruction on sheltered, coastal waters.

Shopping

Connemara Handcrafts (⊠ Co. Galway, ☎ 095/41058) carries an extensive selection of crafts and women's fashions made by the stellar Avoca Handweavers (☞ Chapter 3); there's also an above-average coffee shop.

Kylemore Valley

㊳ *6½ km/4 mi between Letterfrack and the intersection of the N59 and the R344.*

One of the more conventionally beautiful stretches of road in Connemara passes through Kylemore Valley, which lies between the Twelve Bens to the south and the naturally forested Dorruagh Mountains to the north. Kylemore (the name is derived from Coill Mór, Irish for "big wood") looks "as though some colossal giant had slashed it out with a couple of strokes from his mammoth sword," as John FitzMaurice Mills has

★ written. **Kylemore Abbey,** one of the most photographed castles in all of Ireland, lies about ¾ km/½ mi back from the Kylemore Valley road, visible across a reedy lake (one of three that lies along the road) with a backdrop of wooded hillside. The vast Gothic Revival, turreted, gray-stone castle was built as a private home between 1861 and 1868 by Mitchell Henry, a member of Parliament for County Galway, and his wife, Margaret, who had fallen in love with the spot on a carriage ride on their honeymoon. The Henrys spared no expense—the final bill for their house is said to have come to U.K.£1.5 million—and employed mostly local laborers, thereby abetting the famine relief effort (this area was among the worst hit in all of Ireland). In 1920, nuns from the Irish Abbey of the Nuns of St. Benedict, fleeing their abbey in Belgium during World War I, eventually sought refuge in Kylemore, which had been through a number of owners after the Henrys, and decades of decline. Still in residence today, the Benedictine nuns now run a girls' boarding school here. Three reception rooms and the main hall are open to the public, as are a crafts center and simple cafeteria. The grounds are freely accessible most of the year. A 6-acre walled Victorian garden, newly restored, is slated to be open daily in 1998. Ask at the crafts shop for directions to the **Gothic Chapel** (a five-minute walk from the abbey), a tiny replica of Norwich Cathedral built by the Henrys. (Norwich was built by the English Benedictines, in a felicitous anticipation of Kylemore's fate.) ☎ *095/41146.* 🎫 *Free.* 🕙 *Crafts shop Mar. 17–Nov. 1, daily 10–6; cafeteria Easter and May–Oct. 15, daily 9:30–6; grounds Feb.–Dec. 24, daily 9:30–6.*

Beyond Kylemore, the road travels for some miles alongside **Killary Harbour,** a narrow fjord (the only one in Ireland) that runs for 16 km/10 mi between County Mayo's Mweelrea Mountains to the north and County Galway's Dorruagh Mountains to the south. The harbor offers an extremely safe anchorage, 13 fathoms (78 ft) deep for almost its entire length and sheltered from storms by mountain walls. The rafts floating in Killary Harbour belong to fish-farming consortia who are artificially raising salmon and trout in cages beneath the water. This is a matter of some controversy all over the West, with some people fearing the long-term effect of pollution from certain fish-farming practices on wild salmon and trout, and others welcoming the employment opportunities.

Leenane

39 *18 km/12 mi northeast of Letterfrack on N59.*

Nestled idyllically at the foot of the Maamturk Mountains and overlooking the tranquil waters of Killary Harbour, Leenane is a tiny village noted for its role as the setting for the 1990 film *The Field,* which starred Richard Harris. Leenane's **Sheep and Wool Center** illustrates the traditional industry of North Connemara and West Mayo. More than 20 breeds of sheep graze around the house, and there are live demonstrations of carding, spinning, weaving, and the dyeing of wool with natural plant dyes. ☎ *095/42231.* ▭ *£2.* ☉ *Apr.–Oct., daily 9:30–7 (July and Aug., 9 AM–10 PM).*

Dining and Lodging

$$ ✕▥ **Delphi Lodge.** In the heart of what is arguably Mayo's most spec-
★ tacular mountains-and-lakes scenery, this attractive Georgian sporting lodge with a lovely lakeside setting is heavily stocked with fishing paraphernalia. Owners Peter and Jane Mantle are gracious hosts and valuable storehouses of information and stories. The bright, spacious bedrooms, some of which have lake views, have pine furniture, floral curtains, and wonderfully comfortable beds. Guests dine together; there is an excellent wine list and a self-service bar. ✉ *4 mi off the N59, northwest of Leenane, Co. Mayo,* ☎ *095/42211,* ℻ *095/42296. 12 rooms with bath. MC, V.*

En Route Westport is the next stop on our route, and you have two options for getting there. The first is to take the direct route on the N59. The second is to detour through the **Doolough Valley** between the Mweelrea Mountains (to the west) and the Sheeffry Hills (to the east) and on to Westport via Louisburgh (on the southern shore of Clew Bay). This latter route adds about 24 km/15 mi to the trip to Westport, but devotees of this part of the west claim that it'll take you through the region's most impressive, unspoiled stretch of scenery. If you opt for the longer route, turn left onto the R3356 1½ km/1 mi beyond Leenane. Just after this turn, you'll hear the powerful rush of the Aasleagh Falls. You can park over the bridge, stroll along the river's shore, and soak in the splendor of the surrounding mountains.

Either way you go, look out as you travel north for the great bulk of 2,500-ft **Croagh Patrick;** its size and conical shape make it one of the West's most distinctive landmarks. On clear days a small, white building is visible at its summit (it stands on a half-acre plateau), as is the wide path that ascends to it. The latter is the **Pilgrim's Path,** which about 25,000 people, many of them barefoot, follow each year to pray to St. Patrick in the oratory on its peak. St. Patrick spent the 40 days and nights of Lent here during the period he was converting Ireland to Christianity. The traditional date for the pilgrimage is the last Sunday in July;

in the past, the walk was made at night, with pilgrims carrying burning torches, but that practice has been discontinued. The climb can be made in about three hours (round-trip) on any fine day and is well worth it for the magnificent views of the islands of Clew Bay, the Sheeffry Hills to the south (with the Bens visible behind them), and the peaks of Mayo to the north. The climb starts at Murrisk, a village about 8 km/5 mi outside Westport on the R335 Louisburgh road.

Westport

★ ⓪ *32 km/20 mi north of Leenane on R335.*

By far the most attractive town in County Mayo, Westport is situated on an inlet of Clew Bay, a wide expanse of sea dotted with islands and framed by mountain ranges. The architect James Wyatt planned the town in the late 18th century when he was employed to finish nearby Westport House (☞ *below*). Westport's streets radiate from its central **Octagon,** where an old-fashioned farmers' market is held on Thursday mornings—look for work clothes, harnesses, tools, and children's toys for sale. Traditional shops—ironmongers, drapers, and the like—dot the streets that lead to the Octagon, while a riverside mall is lined with tall lime trees. The town is a popular fishing center and has several good beaches close by.

About 2 km/1¼ mi outside town (and clearly signposted from the Octagon) is Westport's **Quay.** (If you're driving north on the N59, you'll come to a left turn-off for the Quay before you arrive in Westport proper.) The Quay has some good bars and decent restaurants, but its central attraction is **Westport House,** a stately home built on the site of an earlier castle. The house was originally begun in 1730 to the designs of Richard Castle (☞ Leinster House *in* Chapter 2 and Powerscourt and Russborough Houses *in* Chapter 3), added to in 1778, and completed in 1788 by architect James Wyatt for the marquess of Sligo. The rectangular, three-story house is furnished with late-Georgian and Victorian pieces. Family portraits by Opie and Reynolds, old Irish silver, and a collection of old Waterford glass are all on display. The home is superbly situated beside a lake with a small formal garden; additional gardens are undergoing restoration. A word of caution: Westport isn't your usual staid country house. The old dungeons, which belonged to the earlier castle (believed to have been the home of the 16th-century warrior queen, Grace O'Malley) now house video games, and the grounds have given way to a small amusement park for children and a children's zoo. If these elements don't sound like a draw, arrive early when it's less likely to be busy. ☎ *098/25430.* ▣ *House only £6, family day ticket for all attractions £18.50.* ☉ *House only: May and Sept., daily 2–5; grounds and house: June, daily 2–6; July–Aug. 21, Mon.–Sat. 10:30–6, Sun. 2–6; Aug. 22–31, daily 2–6.*

Twelve kilometers/7 miles north of Westport on the N59 on the Beltra River, the pleasant village of **Newport** is popular from March to September with salmon fishermen.

Dining and Lodging

$$ ✕ **The Asgard.** This combination pub-restaurant fronts directly onto Westport's Quay. The pub serves better-than-average pub fare downstairs, with fresh fish from Clew Bay. Upstairs in the restaurant, you can enjoy predinner cocktails before the open fire in the anteroom. Large, nautical prints, white damask tablecloths, and red carpets and drapes decorate the dining room, which is cooled by a brass ceiling fan. Service is friendly and professional. Cream of nettle soup, roast stuffed duckling with orange sauce, and fillet of sole vermouth are typical menu

items. It's a reliable spot, popular with both locals and visitors. ⊠ *The Quay, Co. Mayo,* ☎ *098/25319. AE, DC, MC, V.*

$$ ✕ **Quay Cottage.** Fishing nets, glass floats, lobster pots, and greenery hang from the high-pitched, exposed-beam roof of this tiny, waterside cottage located at the entrance to Westport House. Both an informal wine bar and a shellfish restaurant, it attracts a youngish crowd in search of a good time and good food. Rush-seated chairs, polished-oak tables, and an open fire in the evenings add to the comfortable, none-too-formal atmosphere. Try the chowder special (a thick vegetable and mussel soup), garlic-butter crab claws, or a half-pound steak fillet, and be sure to sample the homemade brown bread. The restaurant is licensed to serve wine only. ⊠ *The Quay, Co. Mayo,* ☎ *098/26412. AE, MC, V. Closed Jan.–Feb. 1.*

$$$ ✕🖬 **Newport House.** This handsome, creeper-covered Georgian house beside the Newport River dominates the little town of Newport (12 km/7 mi north of Westport on the N59). Kieran and Thelma Thompson's grand and elegant private home has spacious public rooms furnished with gilt-framed family portraits, Regency mirrors and chairs, handwoven Donegal carpeting, and crystal chandeliers hanging from ornate stucco ceilings. In the dining room, oysters, smoked salmon, roast breast of duck, charcoal-grilled veal steak, and similar hearty country-house fare are served, along with homemade ice creams and sorbets for dessert. The sweeping staircase, lighted by a lantern and a glass dome, leads to an airy gallery and the bedrooms. Bright and less elaborate than the public rooms, these are decorated with pretty chintz drapes and a mix of Victorian antiques and merely old furniture. Most bedrooms have sitting areas and good views of the river and gardens; others have such compensations as the enormous Jacobean four-poster in Room 10. ⊠ *Co. Mayo,* ☎ *098/41222,* 𝖥𝖠𝖷 *098/41613. 19 rooms with bath. Restaurant, bar, fishing. AE, DC, MC, V. Closed Oct.–mid-Mar.*

$$ ✕🖬 **Olde Railway Hotel.** By far the best bet in Westport's town center, this Victorian railway hotel offers both character and comfort. Fishing trophies, Victorian plates, framed prints, and watercolors brighten up the lobby and lounge. A mix of Victorian and older pieces decorate the sunny bedrooms, which have double-glazed, Georgian sash windows. Two top picks: Room 209 has a heavy, Victorian bed and a river view; and Room 114, which has a Victorian chaise longue and a large Georgian wardrobe. Overlooking the landscaped gardens, the Conservatory Restaurant serves fresh local produce. Game in winter, such as Leenane woodcock or Connemara lamb, is typical fare. In summer, seafood such as Clare Island lobster and Clew Bay crab stars. The lively front bar serves good, inexpensive lunches and has live music in the evening in season and weekends. ⊠ *The Mall, Co. Mayo,* ☎ *098/25605,* 𝖥𝖠𝖷 *098/25090. 24 rooms with bath. Restaurant, 2 bars, fishing. AE, MC, V. Closed mid-Jan.–mid-Feb.*

$$ 🖬 **Hotel Westport.** A five-minute walk from the town center, this quiet, convenient glass-and-aluminum hotel overlooks the grounds of Westport House. The lobby, bar, and restaurant, decorated in an art-nouveau style, have heavy mahogany and stained-glass partitions. All bedrooms in the two-story bedroom wing are identical but pleasant, with Georgian-style mahogany bureaus and tables, off-white floral comforters, and fully tiled bathrooms. There's a large, modern swimming pool and leisure center. ⊠ *Co. Mayo,* ☎ *098/25122,* 𝖥𝖠𝖷 *098/26739. 128 rooms with bath. Restaurant, bar, indoor pool, hot tub, sauna, health club, bicycles. AE, DC, MC, V.*

Nightlife

A good spot to try for traditional music is the **Ardmore Pub** (⊠ The Quay, ☎ 09825994). In Westport's town center try **Hogan's** (⊠ The Octagon, no phone).

Outdoor Activities and Sports

BICYCLING

Enjoy the spectacular scenery of Clew Bay at a leisurely pace on a rented bike from **J. P. Breheny & Sons** (⊠ Castlebar St., Co. Mayo, ☎ 098/25020).

FISHING

Fishing tackle, bait, and licenses can be obtained at **Patrick Kelly** (⊠ Bridge St., Co. Mayo, ☎ 098/25982).

GOLF

Westport Golf Club (⊠ Carrowholly, Co. Mayo, ☎ 098/25113), beneath Croagh Patrick, overlooks Clew Bay; designed by Fred Hawtree in the early 1970s, it has twice been the venue for the Irish Amateur Championship.

HORSEBACK RIDING

Drummindoo Stud and Equitation Center (⊠ Castlebar Rd., Co. Mayo, ☎ 098/25616) will take you on the Clew Bay Trail, a three-day trek rising mainly on the superb beaches around Clew Bay and staying in farmhouses along the route. Alternatively, you can rent a horse by the hour.

Shopping

O'Reilly and Turpin (⊠ Mill St., no phone) sells knitwear, handwoven items, and pottery. **Carraig Donn** (⊠ Bridge St., ☎ 098/26287) has its own range of knitwear and a good selection of crystal, jewelry, and ceramics. **Satch Kiely** (⊠ Westport Quay, ☎ 098/25775) carries fine antique furniture and decorative pieces.

En Route If you're heading out to Achill Island, the N59 follows the shores of **Newport Bay** (the northern shore of Clew Bay) for 19 km/12 mi west from Newport to Mulrany, where the R319 branches off to the left for Achill. If you're driving inland directly from Westport northeast to Ballina (a total distance of 50 km/31 mi), the **Foxford Woollen Mills Visitor Center** makes a good stopping point. Besides looking at the crafts shop and enjoying the restaurant, you can stop at The **Foxford Experience**, which tells the story of the woollen mill (famous for its tweeds and blankets) from the time of the Famine—when it was founded by the Sisters of Charity to combat poverty—to the present day. ⊠ Foxford, Co. Mayo, ☎ 094/56756. ⊡ £3. ⊙ Sept.–June, Mon.–Sat. 10–6, Sun. 2–6 (July and Aug., Sun. 12–6); tour every 20 min.

Achill Island

★ **41** *16 km/10 mi west of Mulrany, 58 km/36 mi northwest of Westport.*

Heaven on earth in good weather, when its splendid scenery can be fully appreciated, Achill Island is a destination you'll probably want to head for only if you'll be able to *see it,* and to enjoy its cliff walks and sandy beaches. The largest island off the Irish coast (it's 147 square km/57 square mi, and only 20 ft away from the mainland), Achill is largely bog land and wild heather. A short causeway leads from the mainland to **Achill Sound,** the first village on the island. The main road runs through rhododendron plantations to **Keel,** which has a 3-km/2-mi beach with spectacular cathedral-like rock formations in the cliffs at its east end. There's a longer scenic route signposted ATLANTIC DRIVE. On Achill's north coast above **Doogort, Slievemore,** rising 2,204 ft, is the island's highest summit. Until just a few years ago, the people of Achill made a very poor living. Tourism has improved things, as has the establishment of cottage industries (mainly knitting) and shark fishing, which is popular from April to July.

Lodging

$ ⊞ **Ostan Gob A'Choire (Achill Sound Hotel).** In the first village you approach arriving from the mainland, this small, waterside, two-story town house has a brick-and-plate-glass bedroom extension. All bedrooms offer a sea view, but the nicer ones, with tweed curtains and reproductions of Georgian furniture, are in the old building. The smaller new rooms are already a little worn, but they are spotlessly clean and have pleasant views of the sound. *Ceilís* (Irish dancing and song) are staged in the Alice's Harbour Inn, as the bar is called, most weekends. ⊠ *Achill Sound, Co. Mayo,* ☎ *098/45245,* FAX *098/45621. 36 rooms with bath. Restaurant, bar, bicycles. MC, V. Closed Oct.–Mar.*

Outdoor Activities and Sports

Tour the cliffs of Achill on a bike from the **Achill Sound Hotel** (⊠ Co. Mayo, ☎ 098/45245). Bikes can also be rented from **O'Malley's Island Sports** (⊠ Keel P.O., Achill, Co. Mayo, ☎ 098/43125).

En Route   The road to Ballina runs for about 24 km/15 mi across desolate, almost uninhabited bog, some of which has had its turf cut away down to rock level by successive generations searching for fuel.

OFF THE BEATEN PATH   **CÉIDE FIELDS** – At the very north of County Mayo (signposted off the N59 about 27⅓ km/17 mi north of Crossmolina) on a bare stretch of hill overlooking the Atlantic Ocean, rows and patterns of stones have been preserved under a 5,000 year old bog, the remnants of dwellings, megalithic tombs, and stone-walled fields. A striking glass and steel, pyramid-shape **visitor center** uses well-designed displays and informative audiovisual presentations and tours to bring this strange landscape to life. The panoramic view from the promontory at the top of the pyramid is worth the stop. ⊠ *Ballycastle, Co. Mayo,* ☎ 096/43325. ☜ £2.50. ☉ Mid-Mar.–May and Oct., daily 10–5; June–Sept., daily 9:30–6:30; Nov., daily 10–4:30.

Ballina

42   *56 km/35 mi northeast of Mulrany, 40 km/25 mi northeast of Castlebar on the N59.*

The largest town in County Mayo (population 7,500), Ballina, a generally uninteresting town, is home to some light industry. Its chief attraction is fishing for salmon and trout on the River Moy and nearby Lough Conn.

Dining and Lodging

$$$ ✕⊞ **Enniscoe House.** A lovely, picture-perfect pink Georgian mansion 4½ km/3 mi south of Crossmolina and 20 km/13 mi west of Ballina, on the shores of Lough Conn, Enniscoe sits on 150 acres crisscrossed with pleasant walks and 3¼ km/2 mi of peaceful lakeshore. Owner Susan Kellett inherited the house, and she has been busy at once preserving it and enhancing the property. She's converted many of the property's farm buildings, which now house a number of independent organizations, including a Mayo genealogy center and the Cloonamoyne Fishery, which can provide angling services. Meanwhile, renovation has begun on the formal ornamental garden, while the fruits of the organic garden can be appreciated at mealtime. Colorful corridors, fishing motifs, pretty bedrooms, and quirky, slightly crooked stairways combine

to make this a wonderfully appealing spot. ⊠ *Castlehill, (near Cross-molina), Ballina, Co. Mayo,* ☎ *096/31112,* ℻ *096/31773. 6 rooms with bath. Restaurant, fishing. AE, MC, V. Closed mid-Oct.–Mar.*

$$$ 🏨 **Downhill Hotel.** Delightfully situated on 40 wooded acres beside a gushing tributary of the River Moy (just off the N59 Sligo road), this hotel is a popular spot with anglers and outdoor types. The late-Victorian main house feels a little gloomy downstairs, but it is comfortable. Rooms in the new wing tend to be smaller than those in the main house, but the former have good views of the river across the garden. Rooms in the main house are decorated with Georgian-style furniture and tastefully coordinated quilts and drapes. The recently revamped sporting facilities are the best in the area; there's music in the bar at weekends and midweek in July and August. ⊠ *Co. Mayo,* ☎ *096/21033,* ℻ *096/21338. 50 rooms with bath. Restaurant, 2 bars, indoor pool, hot tub, sauna, steam room, 3 tennis courts, aerobics, squash, fishing. AE, DC, MC, V.*

$$$ 🏨 **Mount Falcon Castle.** Owner-manager Constance Aldridge's rambling, Victorian-Gothic country house 5 km/3 mi outside Ballina is within easy reach of several beautiful, small beaches. Aldridge is renowned for putting guests at ease and encouraging them to mingle, and she makes children especially welcome. You can salmon fish on the River Moy right on the hotel's extensive grounds; horseback riding, sea fishing, and golf are nearby. Rooms are furnished comfortably with a mix of antiques and heirlooms, and they overlook the wooded grounds. In the dining room, the country-style home cooking, which takes advantage of local produce, has a fine reputation. The restaurant is licensed to serve wine only. ⊠ *Co. Mayo,* ☎ *096/70811,* ℻ *096/71517. 10 rooms with bath. Restaurant, tennis court, fishing. AE, DC, MC, V. Closed Feb.–mid-April.*

Outdoor Activities and Sports

BICYCLING

Head for the coast north of Ballina on a bike from **Gerry's Cycle Center** (⊠ 6 Lord Edward St., Co. Mayo, ☎ 096/70455).

FISHING

Fishing bait, tackle, and licenses can be obtained from **John Walkin** (⊠ Tone St., Co. Mayo, ☎ 096/22442).

GOLF

Enniscrone Golf Club (⊠ Enniscrone, Co. Sligo, ☎ 096/36297), 13 km/8 mi north of Ballina, is a 18-hole, par-72 course. West of Ballina (72 km/45 mi), the **Carne Golf Course** at Belmullet Golf Club (⊠ Belmullet, Co. Mayo, ☎ 097/82292) is a recent addition to the list of Ireland's renowned links courses (☞ Chapter 10).

Shopping

De Danaan Antiques (⊠ Teeling St., ☎ 096/21063) stocks old and antique country-pine furniture. Try **Maguire Martin Showrooms** (⊠ Tone St., ☎ 096/22598) for Victorian and Edwardian furniture, porcelain, paintings, and memorabilia. **Victorian Village Antiques** (⊠ Pearse St., ☎ 096/22127) carries Victorian furniture and bric-a-brac.

THE WEST A TO Z

Arriving and Departing

By Bus

Bus Éireann (☎ 01/836–6111 in Dublin, 021/508188 in Cork, and 061/313333 in Limerick) operates a variety of Expressway services into the region from Dublin, Cork City, and Limerick City to Ennis, Galway City, Westport, and Ballina, the principal depots in the region. Expect bus rides to last about one hour longer than the time by car.

By Car

The Dublin–Galway trip (219 km/136 mi) takes about three hours. From Cork City take the N20 through Mallow and the N21 to Limerick City, picking up the N18 Ennis–Galway road in Limerick. The drive from Cork to Galway (209 km/130 mi) takes about three hours. From Killarney the shortest and most pleasant route to Galway (193 km/120 mi; three hours) is the N22 to Tralee, then the N69 through Listowel to Tarbert and the ferry across the Shannon Estuary to Killimer in County Clare, joining the N68 in Kilrush, and then picking up the N18 in Ennis. The ferry leaves Tarbert every hour on the half hour and takes 20 minutes, avoiding a 104-km/65-mi detour through Limerick City. It costs £6 one-way, £10 round-trip. (Ferries return from Killimer every hour on the hour.)

By Plane

The West's most convenient international airport is **Shannon** (☎ 061/471444), 25 km/16 mi east of Ennis in the Southwest (☞ The Southwest A to Z *in* Chapter 6). **Galway Airport** (☎ 091/752874), near Galway City, is used mainly for internal flights, with steadily increasing U.K. traffic. **Horan International Airport** (☎ 094/67222), at Knock in County Mayo, is also used mainly for internal flights. A small airport for internal traffic only is also located at **Knockrowen,** Castlebar, in County Mayo (☎ 094/22853). Flying time from Dublin is 25–30 minutes to all airports. No scheduled flights run from the United States to Galway or Knock; use Shannon Airport (☞ The Southwest A to Z *in* Chapter 6).

Aer Lingus offers daily flights from London's Heathrow Airport to Galway and Knock via Dublin; the trip takes about two hours. **Ryanair** flies to Knock daily from London's Luton Airport; flying time is 80 minutes. **Loganair** flies to Knock from Birmingham, Manchester, and Glasgow.

BETWEEN THE AIRPORT AND THE CITIES

Galway: Galway Airport is 6½ km/4 mi from Galway City. No regular bus service is available from the airport to Galway, but most flight arrivals are taken to Galway Rail Station in the city center by an airline courtesy coach. Inquire when you book. A taxi from the airport to the city center costs about £7.

Knock: If you're flying from Dublin to Horan International Airport in Knock, you can pick up your rental car at the airport. Otherwise, inquire at the time of booking about transport to your final destination: No regular bus service is available from Horan International Airport.

By Train

Galway City, Westport, and Ballina are the main rail stations in the region. For County Clare, travel from Cork City, Killarney Town, or Dublin's Heuston Station to Limerick City (☎ 061/315555) and continue the journey by bus. Trains for Galway, Westport, and Ballina leave from Dublin's Heuston Station (☎ 01/836–6222). The journey time to Galway is three hours; to Ballina 3¾ hours; and to Westport 3½ hours. For train passenger inquiries, call 091/564222 in Galway, 096/71818 in Ballina, 098/25253 in Westport.

Getting Around

By Bus

In July and August, the provincial bus service is augmented by daily services to most resort towns. Outside these months, many coastal towns receive only one or two buses per week. Bus routes are often slow and circuitous, and service can be erratic. A copy of the Bus Éireann timetable (50p from any station) is essential. The main bus stations are located at **Ennis** (☎ 065/24177), **Galway City** (✉ Ceannt Station, ☎ 091/562000), **Westport** (✉ Railway station, ☎ 098/25711), and **Ballina** (☎ 096/71800).

By Car

A car is essential in the West, especially during September through June. Although the main cities of the area are reached easily from the rest of Ireland by rail or bus, transport within the region is sparse and badly coordinated. If a rental car is out of the question, your best option is to make Galway your base and take day tours (available mid-June–September) west to Connemara and south to the Burren, and a day or overnight trip to the Aran Islands. It *is* possible to explore the region by local and intercity bus services, but you will need plenty of time.

The West has good, wide main roads (National Primary Routes) and better-than-average local roads (National Secondary Routes), both known as "N" routes. If you stray off the beaten track on the smaller Regional ("R") or unnumbered routes, particularly in Connemara and County Mayo, you may encounter some hazardous mountain roads. Narrow, steep, and twisty, they are also frequented by untended sheep, cows, and ponies grazing "the long acre" (as the strip of grass beside the road is called) or simply straying in search of greener pastures. If you find a sheep in your path, just sound the horn, and it should scramble away. A good maxim for these roads is "You never know what's around the next corner." Bear this in mind, and adjust your speed accordingly. Hikers and cyclists constitute an additional hazard on narrow roads in the summer.

Within the Connemara Irish-speaking area, signs are in Irish only. The main signs to recognize are Gaillimh (Galway), Rós an Mhíl (Rossaveal), An Teach Doite (Maam Cross), and Sraith Salach (Recess). A good map, available through newsagents and TIOs, gives Irish and English names where needed.

By Ferry to the Aran Islands

Between June and September, **Aran Ferries** (✉ TIO, Victoria Pl., Eyre Sq., ☎ 091/568903 or 091/592447) has daily sailings from Galway Docks, a five-minute walk from Eyre Square, at 10:30 AM in June, July, and September, 9:30 and 1:30 in August. The crossing takes 90 minutes and costs £18 round-trip. The same company runs a boat from Rossaveal, 32 km/20 mi west of Galway City, that makes the crossing in 20 minutes and costs £12–£15 round-trip. The shuttle bus from Galway costs £3. For £20 round-trip on the same route you can have one night at a B&B on the islands.

Island Ferries (☎ 091/565414), which has a booking office on Victoria Place opposite the TIO in Galway City, has a one-hour crossing from Rossaveal for £12 round-trip, with up to five sailings a day in summer, weather permitting. Bicycles are transported free, and discounts are available for families, students, and groups of four or more. If you stay a night or two on the islands ask about accommodations when booking your ferry as there are some very competitive deals, including free nights in a hostel for backpackers.

If you are heading for **Inisheer,** the smallest island, the shortest crossing is from Doolin in County Clare (☞ The Burren and Beyond—West Clare to South Galway, *above.*).

Frequent **interisland ferries** are available in summer months, but tickets are not transferable, so ask the captain of your ferry about his interisland schedule if you plan to visit more than one island; otherwise, your trip can become expensive.

By Plane to the Aran Islands

Aer Arann (☎ 091/593034) offers four flights daily on weekdays, and two flights on weekends. During July and August flights leave every half hour. The flights call at all three of the Aran Islands and leave from Connemara Airport (☎ 091/593034) near Galway. The flight takes about six minutes and costs £35 round-trip. For £25 you can fly one-way and travel one-way by boat from Rossaveal. Ask about other special offers at the time of booking.

By Train

Rail transportation is not good within the West. The major destinations of Galway City and Westport/Ballina are on different branch lines. Connections can only be made between Galway and the other two cities by traveling inland for about an hour to Athlone (☞ Arriving and Departing by Train, *above,* and Chapter 4).

Contacts and Resources

B&B Reservation Agencies

For a small fee, **Bord Fáilte** will book accommodations anywhere in Ireland through their central reservations system. B&Bs can be booked at local TIOs (☞ Visitor Information, *below*) when they are open; however, even these reservations will go through the central reservations system. For more information, *see* Lodging *in* the Gold Guide.

Car Rentals

If you haven't already picked up a rental car at Shannon Airport (☞ The Southwest A to Z *in* Chapter 6), try the following:

Galway City and Vicinity: Avis (☎ 091/568886). **Budget** (☎ 091/566376). **Dan Dooley** (☎ 062/53103). **Hertz Rent A Car** (☎ 091/752502). **Murray's** (☎ 091/562222). **O'Mara's Rent-a-Car** (☎ 091/564663).

Horan International Airport, Knock: Diplomat Rent A Car (☎ 094/67252). **Murray's** (☎ 078/33029).

Emergencies

Police, fire, and **ambulance** (☎ 999 toll-free).

County Clare: Mid-Western Health Board (✉ Catherine St., Limerick, Co. Limerick, ☎ 061/316655). **Counties Galway and Mayo: Western Health Board** (✉ Merlin Park Regional Hospital, Galway City, Co. Galway, ☎ 091/751131).

Galway: Matt O'Flaherty (✉ 39 Eyre Sq., Co. Galway, ☎ 091/562927). **Westport: O'Donnell's** (✉ Bridge St., Co. Mayo, ☎ 098/25163).

Guided Tours

The only full- and half-day guided tours in the region start from Galway. Galway City's **TIO** (☞ Visitor Information, *below*) has details of walking tours of Galway, which are organized by request.

CIE offers two full-day tours, one covering Connemara and the other the Burren (each tour £9). Tours run from early June to late September only, with the widest choice available between mid-July and mid-August. Book in advance at Galway City's **Ceannt Railway Station** (☎ 091/562000) or the **Salthill TIO** (☎ 091/520500), which also serve as departure points.

Galway Tours runs a day tour through Connemara and County Mayo, and another to the Burren in July and August and on certain bank holiday weekends. Tickets can be booked at the TIO in Galway City (☞ Visitor Information, *below*).

Outdoor Activities and Sports

BICYCLING

All TIOs (☞ Visitor Information, *below*) in the West provide lists of suggested cycle tours. The Irish Tourist Board publishes a leaflet, "Cycling Ireland" (£2), that describes four circuits in the West.

BOARD AND DINGHY SAILING

One- and two-week courses in sailing and board sailing are available at the **Glénans Center,** based on an otherwise uninhabited island in Clew Bay near Westport. Contact the Center's head office (✉ 28 Merrion Sq., Dublin, ☎ 01/661−1481).

FISHING

Details of the numerous fisheries in the area are available from the local TIOs (☞ Visitor Information, *below*), or consult the Irish Tourist Board leaflet "Angling Ireland" (£2). Similar leaflets are available on coarse-angling (angling for freshwater fish) and sea-angling.

HIKING

For off-the-road walking, consult "Irish Walk Guides—The West," a pamphlet available at local TIOs (☞ Visitor Information, *below*), and take local advice on weather conditions.

Visitor Information

Bord Fáilte provides free information service, tourist literature, and an accommodations booking service at its TIOs.

MAIN OFFICES

The following offices are open all year, weekdays 9−6 and Saturday 9−1:

Ennis (✉ Clare Rd., Co. Clare, ☎ 065/28366). **Galway City** (✉ 1 Victoria Pl., Eyre Sq., Co. Galway, ☎ 091/563081, FAX 091/565201). **Westport** (✉ The Mall, Co. Mayo, ☎ 098/25711, FAX 098/26709).

SEASONAL OFFICES

These offices are generally open July and August only, weekdays 9−6 and Saturday 9−1:

Achill (✉ Co. Mayo, ☎ 098/45384). **Aran Islands (Inishmore)** (✉ Co. Galway, ☎ 099/61263). **Ballina** (✉ Co. Mayo, ☎ 096/70848). **Castlebar** (✉ Co. Mayo, ☎ 094/21207). **Clifden** (✉ Co. Galway, ☎ 095/21163). **Cliffs of Moher** (✉ Co. Clare, ☎ 065/81171). **Kilkee** (✉ Co. Clare, ☎ 065/56112). **Kilrush** (✉ Co. Clare, ☎ 065/51047). **Lisdoonvarna** (✉ Co. Clare, ☎ 065/51577). **Louisburgh** (✉ Co. Mayo, ☎ 098/66400). **Salthill** (✉ Salthill, Co. Galway, ☎ 091/520500). **Thoor Ballylee** (✉ Near Gort, Co. Clare, ☎ 091/31436).

8 The Northwest

Yeats Country, Donegal Bay, the Northern Peninsulas

On an island with no shortage of majestic scenery, the Northwest claims its fair share: Cool, clean waters from the roaring Atlantic Ocean slice the landscape into long peninsulas with breeze-swept, rocky crests. Clouds and rain sweep rapidly over proud mountains, soft glens, raw cliffs, sandy beaches, and tweed-color bogs—soon chased by sunlight and rainbows. Two brothers, William Butler and Jack Butler Yeats, immortalized this land in their work. Walk in their footsteps, and you'll be struck anew at the dance of nature and art.

Updated by
Jennifer Grimes

GLANCE AT A MAP OF IRELAND THAT HAS scenic roads marked in green, and chances are your eye will quickly be drawn to the far-flung peninsulas of the Northwest. At virtually every bend in the roads of counties Donegal, Leitrim, and Sligo, there's something to justify all those green stripes. But what that something is *now* may not be what it is an hour from now. The air, the light, and the colors of the countryside change like a kaleidoscope. Look once, and scattered, snow-white clouds are flying above tawny-brown slopes. Look again, and suddenly the sun has brilliantly illuminated some magnificent reds and purples in the undergrowth. The inconstant skies brighten and darken at will, bringing out a whole spectrum of subtle shades within the unkempt gorse and heather, the rocky slopes merging into somber peat and grassy meadows greener than any green you've ever seen.

The Northwest covers the most northerly part of Ireland's Atlantic coastline running from Sligo in the south along Donegal's remote, windswept peninsulas to Malin Head in the far north. These maritime landscapes are said to have given their colors to the most famous local product, handwoven tweed, which reflects the browns of the peaty heathland and the purples of the heather. Donegal, a sparsely populated rural county of small farms and fishing boats, shares its inland border with Northern Ireland; the border is partly formed by the River Foyle. Inland from Sligo is Leitrim, a county best known for its numerous lakes and loughs, some of which join up with the River Shannon, which forms the easterly border of this region (and is covered with greater depth in Chapter 4).

County Donegal was part of the near-indomitable ancient kingdom of Ulster, which was not conquered by the English until the 17th century. By the time the English were driven out in the 1920s, they had still not eradicated rural Donegal's Celtic inheritance. It thus shouldn't come as a surprise that County Donegal has Ireland's largest Gaeltacht (Irish-speaking area). Driving in this part of the country, you'll be either frustrated or amused whenever you come to a crossroads: Signposts show only the Irish place-names, often so unlike the English versions as to be completely unrecognizable. All is not lost, however—maps generally give both the Irish and the English names, and locals are usually more than happy to help out with directions (in English), sometimes with a yarn thrown in.

Tucked into the folds of the Northwest's hills, modest little market towns and unpretentious villages with muddy streets go about their business quietly. In the squelchy peat bogs, cutters working with long shovels pause to watch and wave as you drive past. Remember to drive slowly along the country lanes, for around any corner you may find a whitewashed thatched cottage with children playing outside its scarlet door, a shepherd leading his flock (or a wayward sheep or two looking philosophical about having strayed from their field), or a bicycle-riding farmer wobbling along in the middle of the road.

The Northwest is overwhelmingly rural and underpopulated, but it's not without a bit of hurly-burly, a smattering of culture. Letterkenny boasts the longest main street of any town in Ireland. The Northwest's boomtown, Sligo Town is in the throes of a major renaissance—on a typical weekday, its streets are as busy as those of Galway or Dublin, an amazing feat considering that the capital is an exponentially larger city. Sligo Town pulses not only in the present, but with the charge of history, for it was the childhood home of W.B. and Jack Yeats, the place that, more than any other, gave rise to their particular geniuses. Glenveagh National Park exemplifies the surprising alliance between nature and culture you'll find in the Northwest: Here, perched on the edge of a glorious lake in the midst of 24,000 acres of some of Ireland's most thrilling wilderness, sits a fairy-tale castle that reflects the life and times of its owner for 50 years: a leading American philanthropist and art collector whose Impressionist paintings now hang in one of the finest art museums in America.

Keep in mind, though, that the whole region—and County Donegal in particular—attracts plenty of visitors during July and August; this is a favorite vacation area for people who live in nearby Northern Ireland. To be frank, a few places are quite spoiled by popularity with tourists and careless development. The Rosses Peninsula on Donegal's west coast, still sometimes described as beautiful, is marred by too much building. Bundoran, on the coast between Sligo Town and Donegal Town, a cheap-and-cheerful, family beach resort full of so-called "Irish gift shops" and "amusement arcades," is another place to pass through rather than visit. On the whole, though, the Northwest is big enough, untamed enough, and grand enough to be able to absorb all of its summer (and weekend) tourists without too much harm.

Pleasures and Pastimes

The Brothers Yeats

Just mention Sligo to a Yeats lover and you'll get an immediate sign of recognition. Just as Dublin is, literarily, the city of James Joyce, Sligo and environs are bound to the life and work of W. B. Yeats (1865–1939)—and, no less, his brother Jack B. (1871–1957), one of Ireland's most important 20th-century painters, whose expressionistic landscapes and portraits are as emotionally fraught as his brother's poems are lyrical and plangent. Before you go, grab a volume of W. B.'s poems—as you gaze over Lough Gill, you really should have in hand "The Lake Isle of Innisfree"—or read Ray Foster's magisterial first volume of Yeats's life, which appeared in mid-1997, and in which Foster, professor of Irish history at Oxford, assessing W.B.'s accomplishments, notes that he was "both serially and simultaneously, a playwright, journalist, occultist, apprentice politician, revolutionary, stage-manager, diner-out, dedicated friend, confidant, and lover of some of the most interesting people of his day." Walking Sligo's streets today, or exploring the surrounding countryside, it's not hard to imagine yourself following in their steps—a feat made all the more interesting by how precisely, and with what feeling, the brothers Yeats captured the landscape in their poems and paintings. In 1923, W.B. was the first of four Irish writers to receive the Nobel Prize for Literature (George Bernard Shaw in 1925 and Seamus Heaney in 1995 followed him to Stockholm; in 1970 Samuel Beckett was in Tunisia when his Nobel Prize was awarded).

Dining

Although the Northwest has not been considered a great gastronomic center, in the last few years Sligo Town has established itself as a sort of last stop for food lovers, with a number of food-related shops worth visiting. On the dining front, here and there, newcomers are serving up well-above-average food in memorable settings, though overall, the majority of restaurants serve plain and simple fare, with generous helpings of potatoes (often prepared in at least two ways on the same plate). You're likely to find the finest food at the higher-quality country houses, where chefs elegantly prepare local meat, fish, and produce in a hybrid Irish-French haute cuisine. Another new trend: Several of the area's more successful restaurants have recently added accommodation, making them good overnight destinations. For price ranges *see* Chart 1(A) *in* On the Road with Fodor's.

Lodging

True, it's the farthest-flung corner of Ireland, but the Northwest has a steady stream of visitors—especially in July and August—when visitors seek out its joys. Residents of Northern Ireland are particularly apt to use the Northwest as a nearby weekend getaway. As a result, good bed-and-breakfasts and small hotels can be found throughout the region. In the Northwest's two major towns—Sligo Town and Donegal Town—as well as the small coastal resorts in between, traditional provincial hotels have been modernized (albeit not always elegantly), yet they retain some of the charm that comes with older buildings and personalized service. Away from these areas, your options are more restricted, and your best overnight choice, with some exceptions, is usually a modest guest house offering bed, breakfast, and an evening meal. Because of its large Gaeltacht population, you should consider staying in an Irish-speaking home; the local Tourist Information Office (TIO) can be helpful in making a booking with an Irish-speaking family. The Northwest is also home to a number of first-class country-house hotels where you can expect the gracious professionalism you'll find in comparable properties elsewhere in Ireland.

CATEGORY	COST*
$$$$	over £120
$$$	£90–£120
$$	£60–£90
$	under £60

All prices are for two people in a double room, including 12.5% local sales tax (VAT) and a service charge (often applied in larger hotels).

Nightlife

Like other regions in Ireland where there are few large towns, the pub is the center of nightlife. Always ask locally or at your hotel if there is a nearby pub with "sessions," informal performances of traditional folk music. Many hotels or large pubs, particularly at resort towns in season, put on some form of entertainment—a disco or live music—most nights of the week. Discos (often called "dances") are usually full of local and visiting teenagers and twentysomethings. These discos are far from sophisticated but are often a lot of fun (and a great place to meet people). When there isn't a disco, you will find some kind of live music, usually a local, traveling band that plays rock-and-roll standards and country-and-western music. These appeal to an older crowd, often the parents of the kids who danced the night away in the same place the night before.

Outdoor Activities and Sports

BICYCLING

Steep hills, winding and badly kept roads, occasionally strong winds, and the frequent possibility of cold weather and rain make the Northwest one of Ireland's most challenging areas for cyclists. On the plus side: plenty of low-cost accommodations, astonishing scenery, and empty roads make serious touring throughout all of the region or gentle meandering around a small area reasonable, depending on your inclination, time, and ability.

FISHING

The angling in Ireland's Northwest is of the highest class, attracting enthusiasts and connoisseurs from the world over. Yet there's so much space and so much water that it can feel as if you have the whole place to yourself. There are a dozen sea-fishing festivals during the season, open to visiting anglers. Anglers will find that the best area for brown trout is around Bundoran, including Lough Melvin. In western County Donegal, you'll have good opportunities for catching sea trout. Plenty of salmon and brown trout live in the rivers of southern County Donegal and northern County Sligo. More brown trout can be found in the loughs near Dunfanaghy in northern County Donegal, near Bundoran on the border of Donegal and Sligo counties, and in the border area of Sligo and Leitrim counties. Pike anglers and coarse anglers can cast their lines in the abundant County Leitrim lakes.

GOLF

The Northwest has a large number of 9- and 18-hole courses, most in seaside locations, and several of them are world-class. The Northwest's best 18-hole courses all welcome visitors; *see* Chapter 10 for the four best courses in the region. Expect to pay greens fees of around £15– £30 a day.

HIKING AND WALKING

Trails in the Northwest provide the experienced walker with challenging opportunities. It helps to be able to read a map, and on high ground you're wise not to take any chances with the weather, which can suddenly become wet and misty. The mountain districts (such as the Blue Stacks, near Donegal Town) offer rough walks with dramatic views. Long-distance footpaths may be found across County Donegal, in County Leitrim, and around Lough Gill in County Sligo. Good shorter trails are also accessible within Glenveagh National Park.

SURFING

There's great surfing along the Atlantic shores of Counties Donegal and Sligo. Head to Strandhill, Rossnowlagh, and Bundoran on the Sligo and south County Donegal coasts (if you need to rent equipment), or to Marble Strand and Rosapenna in north County Donegal (if you have all your own gear). These areas offer excellent conditions for world-class surfing.

Sweaters, Tweeds, and China

Most of the Aran sweaters you'll see throughout Ireland are made in County Donegal, the area most associated today with high-quality, hand-woven tweeds and hand-knit items. Made of plain, undyed wool and knit with distinctive crisscross patterns, Aran sweaters are durable, soft, often weatherproof, and can be astonishingly warm. Not so long ago, these pullovers were worn by every County Donegal fisherman, usually made to a design belonging exclusively to his own family. Today there's a greater variety in patterns, but most of the sweaters still have that unmistakable Aran look. High-quality, machine-made tweeds, especially tweed jackets, also have a long history in the area and are widely available. Locally made parian china is a thin, fine, and pale product of very high quality and workmanship. Elaborate flower motifs and a basket-weave design are two distinctive features of this china, which has been a specialty of Belleek, on the Donegal–Fermanagh border, for more than 100 years. In recent years, it has also developed in and around Ballyshannon.

Exploring the Northwest

Our coverage of the Northwest is organized into three autonomous tours, although they can easily be linked if you want to poke around the area over five or so days. The first tour begins in Sligo Town and covers its immediate environs—all the major sights within a roughly 24 km/15 mi radius—many of which have strong associations with Yeats. The second tour skirts the entirety of Donegal Bay, from Mullaghmore in the south to Glencolumbkille to the far north and west, before heading inland as far as Ardara. The last tour begins at the other end of Donegal, in Letterkenny, and covers the far northwest corner of County Donegal before swinging you back around to the Inishowen Peninsula, the tip-top of Ireland, delicately balanced between the Republic and Northern Ireland. If you decide to explore this chapter from back to front (this makes sense if you're arriving in the Northwest from Northern Ireland), begin with the last tour, in Letterkenny, skip the trip to the Inishowen peninsula, and pick up the middle tour from either Glebe House or Burtonport.

Numbers in the text correspond to numbers in the margin and on the Yeats Country and Around Donegal Bay, Sligo Town, and Northern Peninsulas

Great Itineraries

IF YOU HAVE 2 DAYS

Start your tour in **Sligo Town** ①–⑧, the bustling hub of County Sligo, dominated by the strange shape of Yeats's "bare Ben Bulben," a hill that rises up just north of the town. To get a taste for the works of Sligo's most famous poet, have a look at the memorabilia in the **Yeats Gallery Library Building** ③, where there are also some fine oils painted by his brother Jack. Take along a volume of Yeats's poetry (or at the least his poem "The Lake Isle of Innisfree") as you follow the sign-posted Yeats Trail around woody, gorgeously scenic **Lough Gill** ⑫, where you'll encounter the sites that inspired some of Yeats's finest poems. The road north passes Yeats's grave in a **Drumcliff** ⑱ churchyard, make a detour to **Lissadell House** ⑲, the aristocratic residence of the Gore-Booth family where Yeats was a frequent visitor, and then head on to **Creevykeel** ㉑, a ceremonial burial area dating from 2500 BC. Drive through **Ballyshannon** ㉓, where the River Erne empties into Donegal Bay, and continue on to ▦ **Donegal Town** ㉔, one of the larger villages of the Northwest and a good place to stay the night.

On the next day take the road to the thriving fishing port of **Killybegs** ㉕, beyond which point the views of Donegal Bay improve as the road twists and turns before descending into Kilcar, a village (like others hereabouts) known for its tweed-making. The road then crosses a stretch of barren moorland and reaches **Glencolumbkille** ㉖, a hamlet spread out around the rocky harbor of Glen Bay; it has associations with the early Christian missionary St. Columba. On the far side of the Glengesh Pass, the small village of **Ardara** ㉗ is the center of the region's tweed heritage and also a good spot to hear traditional music. Return from here southward to Donegal Town and either to Dublin (☞ Chapter 2) via Ballyshannon or to Galway (☞ Chapter 7) via Sligo.

IF YOU HAVE 5 DAYS

For your first two days, follow the *first* day of the 2-day itinerary above, but take *two* whole days to do it. You may want to push on at the end of your second day to ▦ **Ardara** ㉗ rather than ▦ **Donegal Town** ㉔, though both have a range of accommodations and some nightlife. On your third day, follow the coast road from Ardara up to Dungloe. Your rate of progress from here on will depend much on the weather and how leisurely you are, as the heathery headlands offer innumerable side excursions. North of Dungloe is a large Irish-speaking parish known as **The Rosses** ㊵, which has a wild Atlantic coast off which is the island of **Aranmore** ㊷, accessible form Burtonport. Working northward around this peninsula brings you to **Gweedore Headland** ㊴ and Bun Beag (Benbeg). From here another optional circuit can be made of the Gweedore Headland, with its bleak dramatic terrain, somewhat marred by modern bungalow development, which will bring you to Bloody Fore-

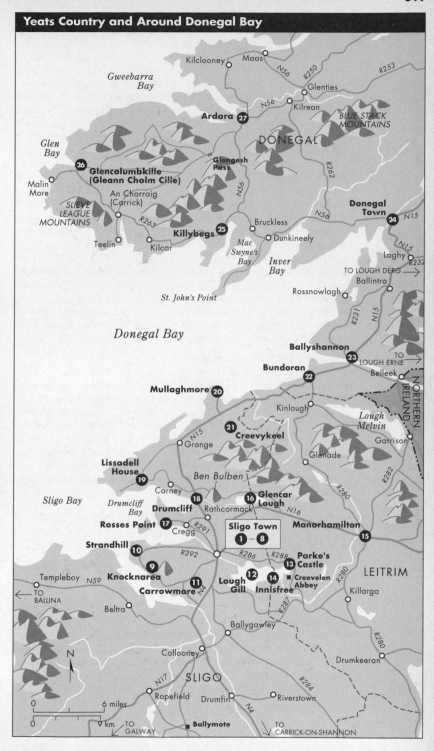

Yeats Country and Around Donegal Bay

land Head, named for the vivid reds that appear on the rock face during the long western sunsets. Meenlaragh, east along the same headland, is the departure point for **Tory Island** ㊳, a rocky, inaccessible place that has been inhabited since prehistoric times. Some of the Tory Island fishermen have developed a sideline producing naive art. **Dunfanaghy** ㊱ is a village built in the Plantation era on the shores of Sheephaven Bay, within easy reach of **Ards Forest Park** ㉟, which has trails leading to prehistoric sites. **Doe Castle** ㉞ occupies the southern end of Sheephaven Bay and stands at the foot of Muckish Mountain. **Carraig Airt** ㉜ (Carrigart), a small village with some enjoyable old-fashioned pubs, gives access to a signposted Atlantic Drive around the **Rosguill Peninsula** ㉝. From here either head south through Milford to **Ramelton** ㉙, a hilly little town on the edge of **Lough Swilly** ㉚, one of the loveliest of Donegal's big fjordlike inlets, to **Letterkenny** ㉘, a convenient base for exploring the rest of the county; or head north to **Rathmullan** ㉛, where a number of hotels are right on the shores of Swilly. If you enjoy modern and contemporary art, on your next day head for the **Glebe House and Gallery** ㊺, which exhibits work by major Impressionists, Picasso, Jack Yeats, and the art of the Tory Islanders. If the outdoors beckons, head west for **Glenveagh National Park** ㊸; if archaeology is your passion, then head east to **Grianan Ailigh** ㊻, which provides a spectacular panorama of Donegal, Derry, and the Inishowen peninsula. From Letterkenny head northeast across the border into Northern Ireland and the city of Derry (☞ Chapter 9) or south for Sligo Town and Galway (☞ Chapter 7).

When to Tour the Northwest

In July and August, the Northwest gets busy with families from Northern Ireland, Dublin, and the United Kingdom. Musicians play most nights at village pubs, and the weather may be warm enough for hardy folk to swim in the sea; accommodations may be hard to come by. Between November and February, in contrast, the area is empty of tourists, but with good reason: Gales of cold, lashing rain come in from the Atlantic, shrouding the wild, lonely scenery that is the Northwest's greatest asset. What's more, because so many of the area's hotels are seasonal, you'll have a limited choice. The best months to visit here are easily April, May, June, September, and October.

YEATS COUNTRY—SLIGO TOWN AND ENVIRONS

Just as James Joyce made Dublin his own through his novels and stories, Sligo is indelibly associated with the lyrical poems of William Butler Yeats (1865–1939), Ireland's first of four Nobel laureates. The poet intimately knew and eloquently celebrated in verse not only Sligo Town itself, but the surrounding countryside with its lakes, farms, woodland, and dramatic mountains that rise up not far from the center of town. Often on this route, you'll have glimpses of "bare Ben Bulben's head," as Yeats called flat-topped Ben Bulben Mountain, which looms over the western end of the Dartry range. The areas covered here are the most accessible parts of the Northwest, easily reached from Galway.

Sligo Town

★ ❶ *60 km/37 mi northeast of Ballina, 138 km/86 mi northeast of Galway, 217 km/135 mi northwest of Dublin.*

The only sizable town in the whole of the Northwest, Sligo (population 18,000) is the best place to begin a tour of Yeats Country. Currently in the throes of an economic boom—Europe's largest videotape factory is just outside of town, and it's the center of Ireland's plastics industry—Sligo retains all the charm of smaller, sleepier villages, yet by day it's as lively and crowded as Galway, its considerably larger neighbor to the southwest. Locals and visitors bustle past its historic buildings and along its narrow sidewalks and winding streets, and crowd its one-of-a-kind shops, eateries, and traditional pubs. More than any other town in the Northwest, Sligo has a buzz and energy that come as a surprise to anyone who hasn't visited recently.

Squeezed onto a patch of land between Sligo Bay and Lough Gill, Sligo is clustered on the south shore between two bridges that span the River Garavogue just east of where it opens into the bay. At press time (summer 1997), a pedestrian zone along the south shore of the river between the two bridges was under construction; when it's completed visitors will be able to enjoy vistas of the river right in the center of town. Sligo was often a battleground in its earlier days: it was attacked by Viking invaders in 807 and, later, by a succession of rival Irish and Anglo-Norman conquerors. In 1245, the town was fortified by the most successful of these victors, Maurice FitzGerald, earl of Kildare, although nothing is left of his medieval castle. Sligo's name in Irish, Sligeach, means "place of shells"; shells turn up at all kinds of historic sites in the area, the refuse of thousands of years ago, when its residents relied on seafood for their sustenance.

② At the **Yeats Memorial Building** the annual Yeats Summer School is conducted every August (☞ Seasonal Events *in* Nightlife and the Arts, *below*). The **Sligo Art Gallery** shows rotating exhibits of contemporary art. Across the street is Rohan Gillespie's modern **sculpture of the poet,** draped in a flowing coat overlaid with excerpts from his work. It was unveiled in 1989 by Michael Yeats, W. B.'s son, in commemoration of the 50th anniversary of his father's death. ✉ *Hyde Bridge,* ☎ *071/42693.* ✇ *Free.* ☉ *Mon.–Sat., 10–5:30.*

③ The **Yeats Gallery Library Building** houses one of Ireland's largest collections of works by Jack B. Yeats, who once said, "I never did a painting without putting a thought of Sligo in it" (Beckett once wrote that Yeats painted "desperately immediate images.") Among his works here are *The Island Funeral* (1923), *Sailor Home from the Sea* (1912), and *Leaving the Far Point* (1946). The collection also includes paintings by John Yeats (father of Jack and W. B.), who had a considerable reputation as portraitist. Other items at the **museum** that you can see on request are a collection of W. B.'s first editions and such intriguing memorabilia as the author's personal letters and the Irish tricolor flag that draped his coffin when he was buried at nearby ☞ **Drumcliff.** ✉ *Stephen St.,* ☎ *071/42212.* ✇ *Free.* ☉ *Library Tues.–Sat. 10–1 and 2–5, also Tues. and Thurs. 7–9; museum June–Sept., Tues.–Sat. 10–noon and 2–4:50, Oct.–mid-Dec. and mid-Mar.–May, Tues.–Sat. 2–4:50.*

④ The **Sligo Abbey,** the town's only existing relic of the Middle Ages, was built for the Dominicans by Maurice FitzGerald in 1253. After a fire in 1414, it was extensively rebuilt, only to be destroyed again by Cromwell's Puritans in 1641. Today the abbey consists of a ruined nave, aisle, transept, and tower. Some fine stonework remains, especially in the 15th-century cloisters. ✉ *Abbey St.* ✇ *Free.* ☉ *Usually open—if not, key with caretaker (name and address pinned to door).*

⑤ The **Courthouse** (✉ Teeling St.), built in 1878 in the Victorian Gothic style, has a flamboyant, turreted sandstone exterior; it is not open to casual visitors. After it was built, the structure became a symbol for

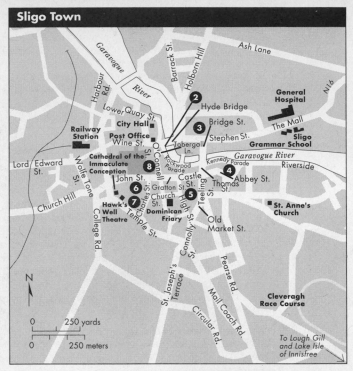

Sligo Town

English power. The Courthouse takes its inspiration from the much larger Law Courts in London. Just north of the courthouse on the east side of Teeling Street, look for the window designating the law firm of **Argue and Phibbs,** one of Sligo's most popular photo-ops. The **Dominican Friary,** still a functioning church, is west of the Courthouse on High Street; from High Street, take a left onto Church Street. At the end of Church Street, turn right onto Charles Street. You will notice along these streets that Sligo has numerous churches of all denominations. Presbyterians, Methodists, and even Plymouth Brethren are represented here, as well as Anglicans (Church of Ireland) and, of course, Roman Catholics. According to the Irish writer Sean O'Faolain, "The best Protestant stock in all Ireland is in Sligo." The Yeats family were part of that stock.

6 Designed in 1730 by Richard Castle, who designed Powerscourt and Russborough Houses in County Wicklow [☞ Chapter 3], little **St. John's Cathedral** (Church of Ireland) has a handsome square tower and fortifications; in the north transept you'll find a memorial to Susan Mary Yeats, mother of W.B. and Jack. Next door is the larger and newer **Cathedral of the Immaculate Conception** Roman Catholic church (with an entrance on Temple Street), consecrated in 1874. ⊠ *John St.* 🎨 *Free.* ☻ *No set hrs.*

7 County Sligo's **TIO** (⊠ Temple and Charles Sts.), useful for the whole of the Northwest, is around the corner from St. John's Cathedral, in the same building as the **Hawk's Well Theatre.**

8 Sligo's most famous pub is **Hargadon's** (⊠ 4 O'Connell St., ☎ 071/70933), a dark, old-style public house with cozy, private, wood-paneled snugs (cubicles) and a handsome golden-oak and green-painted facade. It's a good place for a bowl of soup or creamy pint of Guinness.

Dining and Lodging

$ ✕ **Bistro Bianconi.** The all-white decor—blond wood and white-tile floors—lives up to the name. But the minimalism ends there: the menu is a virtual display of fireworks, with a page-long selection of gourmet pizzas baked in the wood-burning oven, with toppings both traditional and innovative. Baked cannelloni and ravioli are other good Italian favorites. ⊠ *44 O'Connell St., Sligo,* ☎ *071/41744. AE, MC, V. No lunch.*

$$$$ ✕⊡ **Cromleach Lodge.** Christy and Moira Tighe run this highly regarded,
★ small, country hotel on a hillside overlooking Lough Arrow (off the N4 at Castlebaldwin, 27⅓ km/17 mi east of Sligo, 8 km/5 mi east of Ballymote). The modern building has a pleasant, country-style interior; bedrooms are spacious, decorated in relaxing pastel shades, and have views out over the lough. The restaurant, under Moira's direction, is particularly notable; all of the tables in the three small dining rooms offer panoramic views. A six-course table d'hôte menu makes use of fresh ingredients prepared with light sauces. Fillet of turbot with chablis and chive sauce and loin of lamb with rosemary juice are two typical entrées. Fresh fruits individually marinated in different flavored syrups, and homemade ice creams are staples on the dessert menu, while a selection of Irish farmhouse cheeses and homemade petits fours bring the meal to a close. ⊠ *Lough Arrow, Castlebaldwin, Co. Sligo,* ☎ *071/65155,* ℻ *071/65455. 10 rooms with bath. Restaurant, bar, fishing. Reservations required. AE, DC, MC, V. Closed Nov.–Jan.*

$$$$ ✕⊡ **Markree Castle.** From the front, this fortresslike 1640 castle looks slightly forbidding and cold, but seen from the garden in the back, it is spare and elegant. The ancestral home of Charles Cooper, who now owns and manages it with his wife Mary, Markree is Sligo's oldest inhabited castle. It sits on a 1,000-acre estate 11 km/7 mi south of Sligo Town just off the N4 Dublin road. The public rooms include the oak-paneled entry hall, with a large stained-glass window at the top of the grand staircase; a skylit gallery that doubles as one of the bars; and a formal dining room with ornate, Louis XIV plasterwork. Upstairs the layout is a bit warrenlike: bedrooms (somewhat haphazardly furnished) are spread over a number of floors and wings, though bathrooms have been modernized. Recommended dishes on the table d'hôte menus include fillet of smoked trout with horseradish cream sauce, medallions of venison with port and tarragon sauce, and a choice of sweets or a selection of Irish cheeses. On Sunday, a traditional lunch attracts a sizable, family-oriented crowd. ⊠ *Collooney, Co. Sligo,* ☎ *071/67800,* ℻ *071/67840. 30 rooms with bath. Restaurant, 2 bars, horseback riding. AE, DC, MC, V.*

$$$ ✕⊡ **Coopershill.** Seven generations of the O'Hara family have lived
★ in this three-story Georgian farmhouse since it was built in 1774. Beyond the elegant, symmetrical, stone facade, with its central Palladian window, the large public rooms are furnished with appealing period antiques and overstuffed furniture, while deer heads hang in the vast hallways. The spacious, beautifully furnished bedrooms have pretty floral wallpaper, and most have four-poster or canopy beds; there are no TVs. In the tranquil dining room overlooking the woods, Irish-style meals and a wide choice of wines are served by candlelight from a grand sideboard with family silver and crystal. The menu, which changes nightly, includes roast beef or lamb, fresh vegetables, and special soups. Guests can walk the 500 acres of grounds amid undisturbed wildlife. Coopershill is signposted from Drumfin crossroads, 17 km/11 mi southeast of Sligo on the N4 Dublin road. ⊠ *Riverstown, Co. Sligo,* ☎ *071/65108,* ℻ *071/65466. 6 rooms with bath. Dining room, tennis court, boating, fishing. AE, DC, MC, V. Closed Nov.–mid-Mar.*

$$$ ✕🍽 **Silver Swan Hotel.** Standing in the center of town on the Hyde Bridge, this comfortable, mid-range hotel and restaurant has a wonderful view of the Garavogue River rushing beneath the bridge. Although the '60s-style exterior is bland, the interior has been recently redecorated; bedrooms have been refurbished with dark-wood, modern decor. Wednesday nights feature live traditional Irish music, while Sunday morning there's jazz. Noise can be a problem, so ask for a room away from the louder public rooms below. ⊠ *Hyde Bridge, Sligo, Co. Sligo,* ☎ *071/43231,* 𝖥𝖠𝖷 *071/42232. 29 rooms with bath or shower. Restaurant, bar. AE, DC, MC, V.*

$$$ ✕🍽 **Sligo Park Hotel.** A mile out of town on the N4 (the main Dublin road), this is a modern, well-run property. Its predictable, reliable comforts appeal to business travelers, but it also makes a reasonable base for visitors to Yeats Country. The hotel offers dancing and piano entertainment on some evenings, and it has a first-rate fitness center. ⊠ *Pearse Rd., Sligo, Co. Sligo,* ☎ *071/60291,* 𝖥𝖠𝖷 *071/69556. 89 rooms with bath or shower. Restaurant, bar, indoor pool, 2 tennis courts, health club. AE, DC, MC, V.*

$$ ✕🍽 **Temple House.** Off the beaten track on more than 1,000 acres, this vast Georgian mansion and working organic farm has been in owners Sandy and Deb Perceval's family since 1665. Rooms are furnished with Georgian and Victorian furniture, with highly polished mahogany tables and sideboards and the original rugs. Guests can visit formal terraced gardens and a private lake with waterside footpaths. The huge bedrooms have authentic Victorian curtains, marble-top washstands, polished floorboards, dressing tables, and huge shuttered windows. Deb prepares the evening meal (book by 3 PM), using farm-fresh produce accompanied by fine wines. The traditional Irish breakfasts are generous. There are no TVs. Because of Sandy's allergies, guests are asked to avoid using perfumes, deodorants, and aerosols. ⊠ *Ballymote, Co. Sligo,* ☎ *071/83329,* 𝖥𝖠𝖷 *071/83329. 5 rooms with bath or shower. Dining room, boating, fishing. MC, V. Closed Dec.–Mar.*

Nightlife and the Arts

PUBS AND CLUBS

Open later than most pubs, **Toffs** (⊠ Kennedy Parade) has a sizable dance floor that teems with Sligo's younger set bopping to a mix of contemporary dance music and older favorites. A few miles south of town, a popular spot with the locals, the **Thatch pub** (⊠ Ballisodare, Co. Sligo, ☎ 071/67288) has traditional music "sessions" every weekend.

Sligo Town's **Sligo Park Hotel** (⊠ Pearse Rd., ☎ 071/60291) has bands, country-and-western shows, and discos during the whole week in high season.

THEATER

Sligo Town's **Hawk's Well Theatre** brings in amateur and professional companies from all over Ireland (and occasionally from Britain) to stage a wide variety of shows. Most of the summer season is devoted to the works of popular Irish playwrights. ⊠ Temple St., ☎ 071/61526. 🎫 £5–£10. ☉ Box office weekdays 10–6, Sat. 10–6; call for show times.

SEASONAL EVENTS

Begun in 1959, the **Yeats International Summer School** takes place during the first two weeks of August. Scholarly lectures, poetry readings, and various side events are open to the public. For details contact the Yeats Society (⊠ Yeats Memorial Building, Hyde Bridge, ☎ 071/42693, 𝖥𝖠𝖷 071/42780).

Dozens of high-profile and local performers take part in the **Sligo Arts Festival** (☎ 071/69802), held during late May and early June.

Outdoor Activities and Sports

BICYCLING

Explore Lough Gill, Rosses Point, and other areas of scenic beauty by renting a bicycle from **Gary's Cycles** (✉ Quay St., ☎ 071/45418).

GOLF

County Sligo Golf Club (✉ Rosses Point, Co. Sligo, ☎ 071/77186), also known as "Rosses Point," is one of Ireland's great championship links (☞ Chapter 10).

HORSEBACK RIDING

For hacking and trekking in the countryside around Sligo contact the **Sligo Equitation Centre** (✉ Carramore, Co. Sligo, ☎ 071/61353).

Shopping

Sligo Town has the Northwest's most thriving shopping scene, with a nice variety of food-related, crafts, and hand-knits shops, many with colorful storefronts. **The Cat & the Moon** (✉ 4 Castle St., ☎ 071/43686) specializes in an eclectic mix of Irish-made crafts ranging from jewelry and pottery to ironwork and scarves. The gourmet deli **Cosgrove and Son** (✉ 32 Market St., ☎ 071/42809) is a good place to stock up for a picnic or food for the road. **Cross Sections** (✉ 2 Grattan St., ☎ 071/42265) sells lovely tableware, glassware, and kitchenware. **Tír na nÓg** (✉ Grattan St., ☎ 071/62752), Irish for "land of the young," sells essential oils, organic foods, and other health-oriented items; a sister store across the street sells cards and posters. In addition to its own stylish sweaters, **Carraig Donn** (✉ 41 O'Connell St., ☎ 071/44158) offers a selection of pottery, linens, and children's kilts. The **Gourmet Parlour** (✉ Bridge St., ☎ 071/44617), across the Garavogue on the north side of town, sells breads, sweets, and homemade jams and chutneys.

Knocknarea

❾ *8 km/5 mi southwest of Sligo Town on the R292 Strandhill Rd.*

Knocknarea is the "cairn-heaped grassy hill," as Yeats called it, rising 1,083 ft to the southwest of Sligo Town on a promontory that juts into Sligo Bay. The mountain is also memorably depicted in W.B's brother Jack's painting *Knocknarea and the Flowing Tide.* A car park on the R292 gives pedestrian access (a 45-minute walk) to the summit, where there's a good view of the mountains of Counties Donegal and Sligo. At its summit, and visible from a huge distance sits a huge cairn—a heaped-stone monument made with 40,000 tons of rock. The cairn is traditionally believed to commemorate "passionate Maeve," as Yeats called her, a 1st-century AD Celtic queen of Connaught who is the heroine of many Irish legends. Archaeologists argue, though, that the cairn is more likely a 3,000-year-old tomb.

❿ Continuing west from Knocknarea on the R292, you'll come to **Strandhill,** a seaside resort that has a touch of charm. It has a good, sandy beach, stretches of which are favored by surfers (equipment can be rented at the beach).

A short drive southeast of Knocknarea (on the minor road back to Sligo **⓫** Town), **Carrowmore** is the largest group of megalithic tombs in all of the British Isles. The oldest of the 60 tombs, dolmens, and other ruins here predate those at Newgrange (☞ Chapter 3) by roughly 700 years; most are communal tombs dating from 4800 BC, though unfortunately, many have been badly damaged. A restored cottage houses a small exhibition about the tombs. ⊠ *Carrowmore, Co. Sligo,* ☎ *071/ 61534.* 🎫 *£1.50.* ۞ *May–Sept., daily 9:30–6:30.*

Dining

$–$$ ✕ **Strand Restaurant.** This casual spot serves appealing bar food from noon–5; dinner service begins at 6. Among the items on the restaurant's à la carte menu are rich paté marinated in red wine and scallops and crab claws served with herb butter and pasta. It's popular for its traditional Irish Sunday lunch, which might include a light grilled rainbow trout with parsley butter or a more substantial roast rib of beef with horseradish sauce. Light paneling, cozy booths, and a fireplace make the Strand's pub a comfortable place to relax on a breezy Sligo evening. ⊠ *Strandhill, Co. Sligo,* ☎ *071/68641. MC, V. Closed Mon.*

Lough Gill

★ ⑫ *1½ km/1 mi east of Sligo Town on R286.*

Beautiful, gentle Lough Gill lies just to the east of Sligo Town. If you're pressed for time, you can make a quick trip to it. (Take Pearse Road south out of town, go through one set of traffic lights, shortly after which you'll see a green sign for Lough Gill and Innisfree pointing to the left. Take this turn; you'll shortly see the Cleveragh Race Course on your left and then pass through a modern housing development before arriving at the crest of a hill offering a gorgeous vista of the lough and the Lake Isle of Innisfree [☞ *below*]. At the bottom of the hill, turn left, and you'll wind your way back to town.) Or you can make a more leisurely trip of it, making a 37 km/23 mi circuit of the lough; the tour that follows takes you on this longer drive. Leave Sligo Town via Stephen Street, which turns into the N16 (signposted to Manorhamilton and Enniskillen). Turn right almost at once onto the R286. Within minutes you will find some gorgeous views of the lake so adored by the young Yeats. In fact, Lough Gill in Irish means simply "Lake Beauty." The legend is that the bell from Sligo's Abbey lies at the bottom of the lake and those who are without sin can hear it pealing. No one has ever reported hearing it.

⑬ On the R288 on the eastern shore of Lough Gill, **Parke's Castle** is a sturdy, fortified house built in the 17th century by an English planter (a colonist settling on Irish lands confiscated from Catholic owners) who needed the strong fortifications to defend himself against a hostile populace. What made relations worse is that he obtained his building materials mainly by dismantling a historic fortress on the site, which had belonged to the clan leaders of the O'Rourkes of Breffni (once the name of the district). The entrance fee includes a short video show on the castle and local history. There's also a snack bar. ⊠ *Fivemile Bourne, Co. Leitrim,* ☎ *071/64149.* 🎫 *£2.* ۞ *June–Sept., daily 9:30–6:30; Apr., May, and Oct., daily 10–5.*

A short distance south of Parke's Castle, the handsome remains of **Creevelea Abbey** stand on the other side of the River Bonet and may be reached by a few minutes' walk along a footpath. In fact not an abbey but a friary, Creevelea was founded for the Franciscans in 1508 by a later generation of O'Rourkes. It was the last Franciscan community to be founded before the suppression of the monasteries by England's King Henry VIII. Like many such ruined abbeys, the place still has religious meaning for the local people, who treat it with reverence. One curiosity of this abbey is the especially large south transept; notice, too, its endearing little cloisters, with well-executed carvings on the pillars of St. Francis of Assisi. ⊠ *Signposted at Dromahair.* 🎫 *Free.* ۞ *Accessible all day.*

Lake Isle of Innisfree

⑭ *15 km/9 mi south of Sligo Town via Dromahair on N4 and R287.*

Though there is nothing particularly visually exceptional about Innisfree (pronounced Innish-Free), the "Lake Isle," is a must-see for Yeats fans; this is the site around which the poet wrote one of his most pastoral poems:

"I will arise and go now, and go to Innisfree,

And a small cabin build there, of clay and wattles made:

Nine bean-rows will I have there, a hive for the honey-bee,

And live alone in the bee-loud glade. . .

I hear lake water lapping with low sounds by the shore;

While I stand on the roadway, or on the pavements grey,

I hear it in the deep heart's core."

To reach Innisfree, drive through the little village of Dromahair to take the R287, the minor road that heads back along the south side of Lough Gill toward Sligo Town. Turn right at a small crossroads, after 4 or 5 km/2 or 3 mi, where signposts point to Innisfree. A little road leads another couple of miles down to the lakeside, where you can see the island just offshore. The small, tree-covered island is not the haven of peace that it must have been when Yeats wrote those words—excursions arrive by boat from Sligo Town, and visitors traveling by car turn up throughout the day.

Across the water on the southwestern end of Lough Gill, a little beyond the Innisfree turnoff, is a tranquil nature walk with particularly picturesque panoramic views of the lake and of Cottage Island from the top of **Dooney Rock;** this is where the poet daydreamed, contemplated the lake's islands, and imagined a fiddler on the rock who made "folk dance like a wave of the sea." A brochure from the wooden box in the parking lot details the particulars of the area's diverse flora, as well as a few interesting historical tidbits.

Manorhamilton

⑮ *25 km/15 mi west of Sligo Town.*

The small rural town of Manorhamilton was built in the 17th century for the Scottish planter Sir Frederick Hamilton, who had been given the local manor house by Charles I of England (hence the town's name). (To reach the town, come back along the R287 toward Dromahair, but instead of turning into that village, continue driving—the road number changes to R280—toward Manorhamilton.) The manor itself is now an ivy-covered ruin, and there's not much to see here. The surrounding scenery, however, is spectacular.

⑯ Take the N16, signposted to Sligo Town, for about 9½ km/6 mi until you reach the little turning that heads right to **Glencar Lough.** The turn is signposted "waterfall," and you'll discover several waterfalls here, with a parking lot and footpath leading to one of the highest. The lake is fed by the River Drumcliff and other streams at the foot of the Dartry Mountains: "Where the wandering water gushes/ From the hills above Glen-Car," as Yeats saw it.

Stay on Lough Glencar's right bank, and you'll reach a fork in the road: a left heads back to the N16 and Sligo Town, a right weaves across the country toward the N15 and the villages of Drumcliff and Carney.

You want to take the right, but even if you miss it, almost any other right turn off the N16 will lead you in the same direction.

Rosses Point

⑰ *8 km/5 mi northwest of Sligo Town on the R 281.*

Yeats and his brother, Jack, often stayed at Rosses Point during their summer vacations, and it is obvious why they returned. Glorious pink and gold summer sunsets wash over the seemingly endless stretch of sandy beach. **Coney Island** lies just off Rosses Point. Local lore has it that the captain of the ship *Arathusa* christened Brooklyn's Coney Island after this island, but there's probably more legend than truth to this, as it is widely agreed that New York's Coney Island was named after the *konijn,* Dutch for wild rabbits, that abounded there during the 17th century. Two popular sportsmen's havens, the County Sligo Golf Club, which has magnificent views of the sea and Ben Bulben, and the Sligo Yacht Club, are also here.

Drumcliff

⑱ *7 km/4 mi north of Sligo Town on the N15.*

W. B. Yeats lies buried with his wife, Georgie, in an unpretentious grave in the cemetery of Drumcliff's simple Protestant church, where his grandfather was rector for many years. Yeats actually died on the French Riviera in 1939, but it took almost a full decade for his body to be brought back here—to the place that more than any other might be called his soul-land. In the poem "Under Ben Bulben," he spelled out not only where he was to be buried but also what should be written on the tombstone: "Cast a cold eye / On life, on death. / Horseman, pass by!" It is easy to see why the majestic Ben Bulben (1,730 ft), with its sawn-off peak (not unlike Yosemite's Half-Dome) made such an impression on the poet: The mountain gazes calmly down upon the small church, as it does on all of the surrounding landscape—and at the same time stands as a sentinel facing the mighty Atlantic.

In addition to its significance as a Yeats site, Drumcliff is where St. Columba, a recluse and missionary who established Christian churches and religious communities in Northwest Ireland, is thought to have founded a monastic settlement around AD 575. The monastery flourished for many centuries, but all that is left of it now is the base of a **round tower** and a carved **high cross** (both just across the N15 from the church) dating from around AD 1000, with scenes from the Old and New Testaments, including Adam and Eve with the serpent and Cain slaying Abel.

Right next to the church, **The Old Stables Tea House and Craft Shop** (☏ 071/44956) is a good place to stop for a snack and to pick up some Yeats poetry and books about him; it's open March through October.

Lissadell House

⑲ *14½ km/9 mi northwest of Sligo Town, 3½ km/2 mi west of Drumcliff, signposted from the N15.*

Beside the Atlantic waters of Drumcliff Bay, on the peninsula that juts out between Donegal and Sligo bays, Lissadell is an austere but classic Georgian residence built by the distinguished Gore-Booth family in 1834; they still own it. Aficionados of all things Yeatsian will appreciate the house, for the family became good friends of Yeats, who recalled seeing the house often as a child from his grandmother's carriage. On a visit to the house in 1894, he met the two Gore-Booth daughters, Eva and Constance, and subsequently recalled their meeting in verse: "The light of evening, Lissadell,/Great windows open to the south,/Two girls in silk kimonos." Eva became a poet, while sister Constance Markievicz went on to lead a dramatic political life as a fiery Irish nationalist, taking a leading role in the 1916 Easter Uprising against the British. She survived the uprising, going on to become the first woman member of the Dáil (Irish Parliament).

"That old Georgian mansion," as Yeats called it, was designed by the London architect Francis Goodwin. Its two most notable features are a dramatic 33-ft-high gallery, with 24-ft-tall Doric columns, clerestory windows, and skylights; and the dining room, where Constance's husband, Count Markievicz, painted portraits of members of the family and household employees on the pilasters. A copy of Yeats's poem "In Memory of Eva Gore-Booth and Con Markievicz" is displayed on a sign beside the main gate at the entrance. The woods of the Lissadell estate have become a forestry and wildlife reserve—a fine place for birdwatchers, it serves as a home to Ireland's largest colony of the barnacle goose, along with several other species of wildfowl. ☎ 071/63150. ▧ £2.50. ⊙ June–mid-Sept., Mon.–Sat. 10:30–12:30 and 2–4:30.

AROUND DONEGAL BAY

As you drive north from Sligo Town to Donegal Town, the glens of the Dartry Mountains (home of Ben Bulben) gloriously roll by to the east, while coastal fields break open here and there to give startling views across the waters of Donegal Bay to the west. Off in the distance, the soaring Donegal hills beckon on the far horizon. This stretch is dotted with numerous prehistoric sites, and it has become the Northwest's most popular vacation area, though it is, alas, no French Riviera. You'll pass a few small and unremarkable seashore resorts, and, in some places, you may find that haphazard and fairly tasteless construction detracts from the scenery. In between these minor resort developments, you'll find wide-open spaces free of traffic and full of fresh air. The most interesting part of this tour lies on the north side of the bay—all that rocky indented coastline due west of Donegal Town. It's here where you enter the heart of away-from-it-all County Donegal.

Mullaghmore

㉑ *20 km/12½ mi northeast of Lissadell House, 37 km/20 mi north of Sligo Town.*

In the high season, the picturesque, usually sleepy fishing village of Mullaghmore becomes congested with tourists. Its main attractions: a 3¼-km-/2-mi-long sandy beach; the turreted, fairy-tale Classie Bawn, the late Lord Louis Mountbatten's home (he and his grandson were killed in a 1979 IRA bombing); and Ben Bulben, rising up off in the distance. A short drive along the headland offers unobstructed views beyond the rocky coastline out over Donegal Bay. When the weather's good, you can see all the way across to St. John's Point and Drumanoo Head in Donegal. **The Beach Hotel** (☎ 071/66103) serves terrific food, and if there's a chill in the air, it can be relied on to have a cozy fire awaiting; there's a wonderful view of the pier and the beach from the hotel's bar.

Creevykeel

㉑ *3 km/2 mi southeast of Mullaghmore, 16 km/10 mi north of Drumcliff on N15.*

Creevykeel is one of Ireland's best megalithic court-tombs. The site (sign-posted) lies off the road, just beyond the edge of the village of Clif-fony. You'll see a burial area and an enclosed open-air "court" where rituals were performed around 2500 BC. Bronze artifacts found here are now in the National Museum in Dublin (☞ Exploring Dublin *in* Chapter 2).

Bundoran

㉒ *12 km/7½ mi north of Creevykeel on N15.*

Just across the County Donegal line, Bundoran is one of Ireland's most popular seaside resorts, a favorite haunt of the Irish from both the North and the South. If souvenir shops and amusement arcades aren't your thing, north of the town center is a handsome beach at **Tullan Strand,** washed by good surfing waves. Between the main beach and Tullan, the Atlantic has sculpted cliff-side rock formations that the locals have christened with whimsical names such as the Fairy Bridges, the Wishing Chair, and the Puffing Hole (this last one blows wind and water from the waves pounding below).

Outdoor Activities and Sports

FISHING

Good fishing is 6½ km/4 mi away from Bundoran at **Lough Melvin.** Ask locally for **Pat Barrett's Tackle Shop** (⊠ Co. Donegal, no phone) for bait, tackle, and local information.

GOLF

Bundoran Golf Club (⊠ Co. Donegal, ☎ 072/41360) is an 18-hole course on the cliffs above Bundoran beach.

HORSEBACK RIDING

Stracomer Riding School (⊠ Co. Donegal, ☎ 072/41787) will take you on a hack along the coast.

Ballyshannon

㉓ *6½ km/4 mi north of Bundoran on N15.*

The former garrison town of Ballyshannon rises gently from the banks of the River Erne and has good views of Donegal Bay and the surrounding mountains. Its triangular central area has several bars and places to grab a snack. The biggest and most popular pub is the green-shuttered **Seán Óg's** (⊠ Market St., ☎ 072/51585), which serves light Irish meals all day and features traditional music in the evenings. The town was also the birthplace of the prolific Irish poet William Allingham. Each year in early August, the normally quiet village springs to life with a grand festival of folk and traditional music (☞ Nightlife and the Arts, *below*).

Exquisite chinaware and porcelain is made at the **Donegal Parian China Factory,** the Republic's largest manufacturer of parian china (so named because it resembles the clear, white marble from the Greek is-land of Paros). Both Donegal parian and the older, more well-known Belleek Pottery (6½ km/4 mi away, on the border between the Repub-lic and the North; ☞ Chapter 9) make delicate, cream-color pottery by traditional methods, to a large degree by hand. There's a free 15-minute tour, a 10-minute video, and a showroom, shop, and tearoom. ⊠ *On the N15 just south of Ballyshannon,* ☎ *072/51826.* ☉ *May–Sept., daily 9–6.* ☞ *Shopping, below.*

Just to the southeast of Ballyshannon, **Lough Erne** marks an ancient frontier, as the River Erne crossing here was for centuries the gateway into the Ulster region. Through the medieval period Ballyshannon was the southern stronghold of the O'Donnell clan, whose lands eventually became County Donegal. Today Lough Erne and its nearby sites are within the borders of the North; ☞ Around Counties Tyrone, Fermanagh, Armagh, and Down *in* Chapter 9 for full coverage.

Dining and Lodging

$$$ ✕⊡ **Sand House Hotel.** Behind the mock-manor-house exterior of this 19th-century former fishing lodge lies a large, modern hotel. Situated right on Donegal Bay (about 8 km/5 mi northwest of Ballyshannon and 16 km/10 mi south of Donegal Town), this makes a peaceful, well-positioned base for sightseeing the coastline (the hotel has access to 3 km/2 mi of beach). Renovated, well-kept bedrooms are beautifully decorated with antiques and overlook either the sea or the Donegal hills. The restaurant caters to the plain, hearty appetites of Irish vacationers looking for something a bit special. Fresh seafood, including Donegal Bay oysters and mussels, is the daily specialty. ⊠ *Rossnowlagh, Co. Donegal,* ☎ *072/51777,* ℻ *072/52100. 45 rooms with bath or shower. Restaurant, bar, tennis court, horseback riding, Ping-Pong, surfing, fishing. AE, DC, MC, V. Closed Nov.–Easter.*

Nightlife and the Arts

Held on the bank holiday weekend at the beginning of August, the **Ballyshannon Music Festival** (☎ 072/51088) is one of Ireland's largest and best folk-music events. Visitors can hear both well-known and unknown folk and traditional musicians, while impromptu "sessions" pop up at pubs. A party atmosphere prevails, attracting up to 12,000 visitors annually. In early June, during the **Ballyshannon Drama Festival,** the town hosts different drama companies for a program of mainly Irish plays.

Shopping

Donegal Irish Parian China Factory (☞ above) sells its wares at lower prices than you'll see in retail stores. The least expensive items (spoons or thimbles) cost around £5. A full tea set starts at about £250.

From Ballyshannon, the R230 runs along the south bank of the River Erne toward Belleek. You'll find **Celtic Weave China** (☎ 072/51844) right beside the Garda (Irish police) checkpoint, 1.6 km/1 mi before the border to Northern Ireland. This small, family business specializes in the basket-weave design and in elaborate floral decoration, and they can make a single piece of china to your own specifications. Extremely delicate-looking, hand-painted, china "flower baskets" are also available (though in fact this type of chinaware is not as fragile as it appears). Prices range from £6 to £1,500, but most pieces cost less than £100.

The goods of the best-known producer of Belleek chinaware, **Belleek Pottery** (☎ 01365/65501 in Northern Ireland), can be found in the shops of Donegal and Sligo. For more information on the factory, see Chapter 9.

OFF THE
BEATEN PATH

LOUGH DERG – From Whitsunday to the Feast of the Assumption (that is, from June to mid-August), tens of thousands determinedly beat a path to this lonely, out-of-the-way lake, ringed by heather-clad slopes. In the center of the lough, Station Island, known as St. Patrick's Purgatory, is one of Ireland's most popular pilgrimage sites, even though it is also the most rigorous and austere of such sites in the country. Pilgrims stay on the island for three days, taking no sleep and no food except black tea and dry toast. They walk barefoot around the island, on its flinty stones, to pray at a succession of shrines. The pilgrimage has been followed since time immemorial; during the Middle Ages, it attracted large numbers of devotees from foreign lands. To reach the shores of Lough Derg, turn off the main Sligo–Donegal road (N15) in the village of Laghy onto the minor Pettigo road (R232), which hauls itself over the Black Gap and descends sharply into the border village of Pettigo, about 21 km/13 mi from the N15. From here, take the Lough Derg access road for 8 km/5 mi. If you would like to know more about St. Patrick's Purgatory in order to become a pilgrim, write to Reverend Prior (✉ Lough Derg, Pettigo, Co. Donegal). Nonpilgrims may not visit the island from June–mid-August. Also, be sure not to confuse this Lough Derg with the Lough Derg covered in Chapter 4.

En Route   About a mile before you arrive at the next stop on the tour, Donegal Town, a sign on the right points to **Donegal Craft Village** (☞ Shopping *in* Donegal, *below*).

Donegal Town

㉔ *21 km/13 mi north of Ballyshannon on R232, 66 km/41 mi northeast of Sligo Town.*

With a population of about 3,000, Donegal is Northwest Ireland's largest small village—marking the entry into the back-of-the-beyond of the wilds of County Donegal. The town is centered around the triangular Diamond, where three roads converge (the N56 to the west, and the N15 to the south and the northeast) and the mouth of the River Eske pours gently into Donegal Bay. You should have your bearings in five minutes, and seeing the historical sights takes less than an hour; if you stick around any longer, it'll probably be to do some shopping—arguably Donegal's top attraction.

Donegal was previously known in Irish as Dun na nGall, "Fort of the Foreigners"; the foreigners in question were Vikings, who set up camp here in the 9th century to facilitate their pillaging and looting. They were driven out by the powerful O'Donnell clan (originally Cinel Conail), who made it the capital of Tyrconail, their extensive Ulster territories. Donegal was rebuilt in the early 17th century, during the Plantation period, when Protestant colonists were planted on Irish property confiscated from their Catholic owners. The triangular **Diamond,** like that of many other Irish villages, dates from this period. Once a marketplace, it has a 20-ft obelisk monument to the Four Masters (☞ *below*). On the north side of the Diamond, **McGroarty's Bar** (☎ 073/21049) is a good place to stop for a casual bite; lunch is served from 12–3 and dinner from 6–9, but snacks are served all day, including smoked salmon or dressed crab, and a variety of sandwiches. **Magee's** (☞ Shopping, *below*), also on the north side of the Diamond, is a general clothing store founded in 1866. Much of the stock that carries Magee's label is made in the store's own factory beside the River Eske, only a short walk from the shop. Magee's tweed jackets, said to be among the best in the world, are reasonably priced here. A 10-minute tour of the weaving factory, though a little rushed, shows how old-fashioned handwork is combined with the modern electronic looms. ✉ *The Diamond,* ☎ 073/21100. 🎫 *Factory tour free.* ⊙ *No set hrs; 1st tour starts about 11, last at about 3.*

Near the north corner of the Diamond, **Donegal Castle** was built by clan leader Hugh O'Donnell in the 1470s. More than a century later, this structure was the home of his descendant Hugh Roe O'Donnell, who faced the might of the invading English and was the last clan chief of Tyrconail. In 1602 he died on a trip to Spain to rally reinforcements from his allies. In 1610, its new English owner, Sir Basil Brooke, reconstructed the little castle, adding the fine Jacobean fortified mansion with towers and turrets that can still be seen today (he was responsible for the Diamond, as well). The small enclosed grounds are pleasant; inside, there are only a few rooms to see, including the garderobe (the loo) and a great hall with an exceptional vaulted wood-beam roof. Between the floor of the great hall and the ceiling there were once two additional floors, both used for sleeping quarters; you can see the fireplaces of one of these floors up on the walls. ⊠ *Tirchonaill St.,* ☎ *073/22405.* ⌷ *£2.* ⊙ *Easter–Oct., daily 9:30–5:45, Closed Nov.–Easter.*

The ruins of the **Franciscan abbey,** founded in 1474 by Hugh O'Donnell, are a five-minute walk south of town at a spectacular site perched above the Eske, where it begins to open up into Donegal Bay (take the N15, cutting off almost immediately for the parking area and pier behind the Hyland Central Hotel). The complex was burned to the ground in 1593, razed by the English in 1601, and ransacked again in 1607; the ruins include the choir, south transept, and two sides of the cloisters, between which lie hundreds of graves dating back to the 18th century. The abbey was probably where the *Annals of the Four Masters* was written from 1632 to 1636. The *Annals* chronicles the whole of Celtic history and mythology of Ireland from earliest times up to the year 1618. The **Four Masters** were four monks who believed (correctly, as it turned out) that Celtic culture was doomed after the English conquest, and they wanted to preserve as much of it as they could. At the National Library in Dublin, you can see facsimile pages of the monks' work (☞ Exploring Dublin *in* Chapter 2); the original is kept under lock and key. ⌷ *Free.* ⊙ *Freely accessible.*

Dining and Lodging

$ ✕ **The Blueberry Tea Room.** Across the street from Donegal Castle, this pleasant restaurant and café recently expanded downstairs from its second-floor perch. Proprietors Brian and Ruperta Gallagher serve breakfast, lunch, afternoon tea, and a light evening meal. Daily specials such as Irish lamb stew and vegetarian quiche (served from noon–5) augment the soups, sandwiches, and salads on the regular menu. Plain, fruit, and brown scones are baked daily. ⊠ *Castle St.,* ☎ *073/22933. AE, MC, V. Closed Sun. mid-Sept.–May.*

$$$$ ✕▦ **St. Ernan's House.** On its own wooded tidal island in Donegal Bay,
★ St. Ernan's is easily one of the most spectacularly set country houses in all of Ireland. The picture-book-perfect, two-story house was built by a nephew of the duke of Wellington in 1826. Today Brian and Carmel O'Dowd, the meticulous owner-managers, foster a relaxed, serene atmosphere. Bedrooms are simply but elegantly furnished with antiques and have spectacular views of the bay. Dinner orders are taken in the lovely drawing room, with its huge bay window, handsome yellow wallpaper, exquisite antiques, and sumptuous pink and green fabrics. Dinner in the intimate and elegant dining room is open to nonguests. The five-course menu changes nightly and relies on fresh local produce prepared in the Irish country-house style. Pigeon and quail sauté with oyster mushrooms is a typical starter; lamb in a rich red wine sauce or wild salmon with a fresh green herb sauce might follow. For dessert, try the homemade ice cream or the warm banana tartlet with butterscotch sauce. A stroll around the island is a perfect way to finish off the evening. The house is reached by a causeway a five-minute drive south of town. ⊠ *St. Ernan's Island, Co. Donegal,* ☎ *073/21065,* ℻ *073/22098. 12 rooms with bath. Dining room. MC, V. Closed Nov.–Easter.*

$$$ ✕▦ **Harvey's Point.** At the foot of the Blue Stack Mountains, nestled beside Lough Eske, this Swiss-owned hotel has spacious, well-equipped

bedrooms, all overlooking the lake. The split-level wood-paneled dining room, which also has lake views, has warm peach decor, Tiffany lamps, and locally made granite-top tables. The French cuisine leans toward a nouvelle presentation, with several lobster entrées on the menu; it might be served whole with a choice of two sauces, alongside rice and mussels, or garnished with tomatoes and red cabbage. Fisherman's Platter, a selection of five kinds of fish, is also served with two sauces, and sirloin steak is served with a demi-glaze sauce, topped with garlic butter. Homemade ice cream with profiteroles and chocolate sauce is a special dessert. ⊠ *Lough Eske, Co. Donegal,* ☎ *073/22208,* FAX *073/22352. 20 rooms with bath. Restaurant, bar, tennis court, boating, bicycles. AE, DC, MC, V.*

$$$ 🏨 **Hyland Central.** Right on Donegal's central square, this family-run hotel is affiliated with Best Western. The slightly shopworn public areas have a touch of Old World style. Although some of the bedrooms are spacious, their decor—simple built-ins and imitation black-leather and teak furniture—is nothing to write home about. On the plus side: Rooms in the back have huge picture windows with lovely views of Donegal Bay. The large dining room with its efficient staff serves good, filling food. The fitness center and good-size indoor pool are nice amenities. ⊠ *The Diamond, Co. Donegal,* ☎ *073/21027,* FAX *073/22295. 91 rooms with bath or shower. Dining room, indoor pool, steam room, health club. AE, MC, V.*

Nightlife and the Arts

During the summer people pack **McGroarty's Bar** (☞ *above*) for traditional music night each Thursday. **The Abbey Hotel** (⊠ The Diamond, ☎ 073/21014) has music every night in July and August, and a disco every Sunday night throughout the year.

Outdoor Activities and Sports

Rent a bike from **C. J. Doherty** (⊠ Main St., Co. Donegal, ☎ 094/31019).

Shopping

Long the principal marketplace for the region's wool products, Donegal Town has several smaller shops retailing local hand weaving and knits and lots of crafts stores. The main store in town, **Magee's** (⊠ The Diamond, ☎ 073/21100) carries their renowned private-label tweeds for both men and women (jackets, hats, scarves, suits, and more), as well as pottery, linen, and crystal. **Simple Simon's** (⊠ The Diamond, ☎ 073/22687), the local health-food store, has a nice selection of crafts, cards, essential oils, and other whole-earthy items. About 1½ km/1 mi south of town, right beside the main N15, the **Donegal Craft Village** is a complex of workshops where you can buy pottery, hand-woven goods, and ceramics from local young craftspeople and watch the items being made. A coffee shop sells snacks; shops are usually open 9 to 5.

En Route   The main road west is the N56, which runs slightly inland from a magnificent shoreline of rocky inlets with great sea views; it's worthwhile turning off the road from time to time to catch a better sight of the coast. About 6½ km/4 mi out of Donegal Town, the N56 skirts **Mountcharles,** a bleak hillside village that looks back across the bay.

Bruckless

19 km/12 mi west of Donegal Town on N56.

Don't be fooled by the round tower in the churchyard at Bruckless: It's a 19th-century belfry, not an authentic medieval structure. Soon after Bruckless, the N56 turns inland across the bogs toward Ardara, but this tour stays by the shore. The road now becomes the R263, which runs through attractive heathland and wooded hills down to Killybegs.

Dining and Lodging

$ ✕🏠 **Bruckless House.** A two-story, 18th-century farmhouse on the north side of Donegal Bay, 8 km/5 mi outside Killybegs, within an easy drive of Glencolumbkille, Ardara, and Donegal Town, this unusual bed-and-breakfast stands on 19 acres of woods, gardens, and a meadow where Irish draft horses and Connemara ponies roam. Public rooms have a fine view of Bruckless Bay; their Asian decor reflects years spent in Hong Kong by the owners, Clive and Joan Evans. The more conventional but comfortable bedrooms share a large bathroom upstairs. Wholesome dinners (which must be booked by noon) are prepared with fresh produce from the Evanses' garden, milk and cream from the resident cow, and seafood straight from the bay. ⊠ *Co. Donegal,* ☎ *073/ 37071,* 🅵🅰🆇 *073/37070. 4 rooms, 1 with bath. Dining room. MC, V. Closed Oct.–Mar.*

$ ✕🏠 **Castle Murray House Hotel.** Situated 1½ km/1 mi out on the 9½ km/6 mi-long St. John's Point Peninsula, this hotel has spectacular panoramic views of distant mountains, the sapphire-blue waters of Mac-Swyne's Bay, and the long, narrow unspoiled peninsula, punctuated at its tip by a lighthouse. The original house has been extended and modernized; rooms are basic but comfortable. Natives trek here for the restaurant ($$), where Thierry Delcros, the French-born owner-chef, prepares superb French cuisine. Selections might include phyllo-wrapped parcel of duck, or the specialty of the house, prawns and monkfish in garlic butter. The house is 21 km/13 mi west of Donegal Town. ⊠ *St. John's Point, Dunkineely, Co, Donegal,* ☎ *073/37022,* 🅵🅰🆇 *073/37330. 8 rooms with shower, 2 with bath. Restaurant, residents' bar. V, MC. Closed entirely mid-Jan.–mid-Feb. and Mon.–Tues. Oct.–mid-Jan. and mid-Feb.–Easter.*

Killybegs

㉕ *6½ km/4 mi west of Bruckless, 28 km/17 mi west of Donegal Town on R293.*

Trawlers from Spain and France are moored in the harbor at Killybegs, one of Ireland's busiest fishing ports. Though it's one of the most industrialized places along this coast, it's not without some charm, thanks to its waterfront location. Killybegs once served as a center for the manufacture of Donegal hand-tufted carpets, which can be found in the White House and the Vatican. The **Harbour Store** (⊠ Main St., ☎ 073/32122), right on the wharf, has plenty to make both fishermen and landlubbers happy, including boots and rain gear, competitively priced sweaters, and unusual bright yellow or orange fiberglass-covered gloves (made in Taiwan!).

Dining and Lodging

$$ ✕🏠 **Bay View Hotel.** Situated directly across from Killybegs's harbor, the Bay View is the town's most bustling spot. The lobby, redecorated in spring 1997, is spare and modish, nicely paneled in light wood. The modern, functional bedrooms are pleasantly decorated in pale colors. The Irish table d'hôte changes daily in the comfortable, efficient dining room. Bruckless mussels in a white wine and garlic sauce and braised young duckling served with market vegetables and an orange and cherry *coulis* (thick, pureed sauce) typify the fare. The hotel has extensive leisure facilities and is well placed for seeing the glorious north shore of Donegal Bay. Special rates include greens fees for golfers. ⊠ *Main St., Co. Donegal,* ☎ *073/31950,* 🅵🅰🆇 *073/31856. 42 rooms with*

bath. Restaurant, bar-brasserie, indoor pool, sauna, health club. AE, MC, V.

En Route   After Killybegs, the R263 narrows, climbs, and twists, giving even better views of Donegal Bay before descending again into pretty **Kilcar,** a traditional center of tweed making. The next village, signposted by its Irish name An Charraig (Carrick), clings to the foot of the **Slieve League Mountains,** whose dramatic, color-streaked ocean cliffs are, at 2,000 ft, the highest in Ireland and among the most spectacular. To see them, take the little road to the Irish-speaking village of Teelin, 1½ km/1 mile south from Carrick. Then take the narrow lane (signposted to Bunglass) that climbs steeply to the top of the cliffs. For an even more thrilling perspective, some hardy folk walk on the difficult coastal path from Teelin.

Glencolumbkille (Gleann Cholm Cille)

26   *8 km/5 mi west of Carrick, 27 km/16½ mi west of Killybegs on the R263.*

At the far end of a stretch of barren moorland, the tiny hamlet of Glencolumbkille (pronounced glen-colm-*keel*), clings dramatically to the rock-bound harbor of Glen Bay. Because it is at the heart of County Donegal's shrinking Gaeltacht, or Irish-speaking region, it has a strong, rural Irish flavor, as do its pubs and brightly painted row houses. Its name means St. Columba's Glen (or, alternatively, Columba's Glen Church); the legend goes that St. Columba, a Christian missionary (☞ Drumcliff *in* Yeats Country, *above*), lived here during the 6th century with a group of followers. Some 40 prehistoric cairns, scattered around the village, have become connected locally with the St. Columba myths. The **House of St. Columba,** on the cliff top rising north of the village, is a small oratory said to have been used by the saint himself. Inside, stone constructions are thought to have been his bed and chair. Every year on June 9, starting at midnight, local people make a 3-km/2-mi barefoot procession called An Turas (the journey) around 15 medieval crosses and ancient cairns, collectively called the Stations of the Cross. Near the beach in Glencolumbkille is the **Folk Village,** an imaginative museum of rural life. Three small cottages, with bare-earth floors, represent the very basic living conditions of the 1720s, 1820s, and 1920s. The complex includes a tea shop, which sells "an unusual kind of wine made from fuschias," and a crafts shop, selling local handmade products. ☏ 073/30017. ⊡ £2. ⊘ *Easter–May, Mon.–Sat. 10–6, Sun. noon–6; June–Oct., Mon.–Sat. 10–7, Sun. noon–7.*

Ardara

★ **27**   *28 km/17 mi northeast of Glencolumbkille. 40 km/25 mi northwest of Donegal Town.*

Fortuitously situated at the head of a lovely ocean inlet, the unpretentious, old-fashioned hamlet of Ardara (pronounced "ar-dar-*ah*") is built around the L-shape intersection of its two main streets. (If you come from Glencolumbkille, expect a scenic drive full of hairpin curves and steep hills as you cross over Glengesh Pass.) Ardara has been an important wool-trading center for centuries. Great cloth fairs used to be held on the first of every month, and although they have died out, cottage workers in the surrounding countryside still provide Ardara (and County Donegal) with high-quality, handwoven cloths and, especially, handknits. If you're looking for a chunky Aran sweater, "Ireland's capital of handwoven tweeds and knitwear," as Ardara bills itself, has no fewer than nine stores to choose from (☞ Shopping, *below*). The **Ardara Heritage Center** celebrates Donegal's history of producing tweed and knitwear. A weaver works at a traditional loom, while photographs and displays provide a historical overview; there's also an audiovisual show. ☎ *075/41704.* ⊠ *£2.* ⊙ *Daily 9:30–6.*

There are a number of good pubs where you can hear traditional music year-round (☞ Nightlife and the Arts, *below*). The long-established **Nesbitt Arms** (☎ 075/41103) is a good place for a reasonably priced drink and snack. If you're traveling in the high season, a word of caution: During the summer, it doesn't take a lot of visitors to overcrowd this small spot.

Dining and Lodging

$$ ✕⊞ **Woodhill House.** John and Nancy Yates's spacious home stands
★ on 4 acres of wooded grounds only ½ km/⅓ mi from Ardara. The cream-color exterior is Victorian, but parts of the interior date from the 17th century. High ceilings and marble fireplaces are in the fine public rooms; the hall has a lovely round table and stained-glass window. Bedrooms are less grand but large, with superb views of the Donegal highlands. Visitors and locals alike enjoy frequent Irish folk music sessions presented in the bar and dine in the fine, 40-seat restaurant. Fresh, local ingredients predominate on its Cordon Bleu à la carte menu, prepared in a French-Irish style. Entrées might include salmon with garlic and spinach sauce, accompanied by seasonal vegetables, or rack of lamb with herbs picked from the family garden. The elaborate desserts are all homemade. The Yates's own hens make the breakfast eggs as fresh as can be. ⊠ *Donegal Rd., Co. Donegal,* ☎ *075/41112,* ℻ *075/ 41516. 8 rooms with bath. Restaurant, bar, fishing. AE, DC, MC, V.*

$ ⊞ **The Green Gate.** If you're looking for an alternative to country houses and village hotels, Frenchman Paul Chatenoud's austere, remote cottage overlooking Ardara, the Atlantic, and some spectacular Donegal scenery may be for you. The four spare rooms, in a converted stone outbuilding with a thatched roof, have brand-new baths. Chatenoud, even more charming than his hideaway, is eager to point guests toward Donegal's best-kept secrets. It's worth visiting here for a peek at the comments in the guest book. ⊠ *Ardvally, Ardara, Co. Donegal,* ☎ *075/41546. 4 rooms with bath. No credit cards.*

$ ⊞ **Greenhaven House.** Only a few minutes from the village, Eileen and Ray Molloy's modern, one-story home has its own gardens and marvelous views of the nearby mountains and bay. You'll be warmed by a peat fire in the lounge and wake up to a hearty breakfast. The Molloys can advise you on shopping for handknits and other items. No evening meal is served. ⊠ *Portnoo Rd., Co. Donegal,* ☎ *075/41129,* ℻ *075/41129. 6 rooms with shower. V. Closed Dec.*

Nightlife and the Arts

For a small, old-fashioned village, Ardara offers a surprising number of pubs, many of them offering evenings of traditional music. **Peter Oliver's** (⊠ Main St., ☎ 075/41311), an atmospheric, recently done-up bar, provides music almost every night. One of the smallest pubs in the whole of the Republic, **Nancy's Pub** (⊠ Front St., ☎ 075/ 41187) has some rooms that make you wonder if you've wandered into the owners' sitting room; it finds space for a folk group several nights a week in the high season.

A **Weavers' Fair and Vintage Weekend** will be held on June 5–7, 1998, though it has as much to do with music, dance, and having fun as it does with selling homespun; for further details, call Bosco McGill (☎ 075/41262).

Outdoor Activities and Sports

Rent a bike from **Donal Byrne** (⊠ West End, Co. Donegal, ☎ 075/41156).

Shopping

Handwoven and locally made knitwear are on sale at no fewer than nine stores here; many commission goods directly from knitters, and prices are about as low as you'll find anywhere. Handsome, chunky Aran hand-knit sweaters (£60–£100), cardigans (similar prices), and scarves (£16) are all widely available. Stores also carry ready-to-wear tweeds; sports jackets for women run up to about £120; for men, up to about £150. Shops also stock a selection of traditional Irish products, such as glassware and linen, from other parts of the country. **Campbells Tweed Shop** (⊠ Front St., ☎ 075/41128), **E. Doherty (Ardara) Ltd.** (⊠ Front St., ☎ 075/41304), and **C. Bonner & Son** (⊠ Front St., ☎ 075/41303) are all recommended.

NORTHERN DONEGAL

Traveling on northern County Donegal's country roads, you'll feel that you have escaped at last from all the world's hurry and hassle. There's almost nothing up here but scenery: broad, island-studded loughs of deep, dark tranquillity; unkempt, windswept, sheep-grazed grasses on mountain slopes; ribbons of luminous greenery following sparkling streams; and the mellow hues of wide bog lands, all under shifting and changing cloudscapes. This tour, apart from Inishowen Peninsula, which is included as a separate excursion at the end, could take anywhere from one day to a week, depending on how low a gear you slip into after a few breaths of Donegal air. It begins in Letterkenny, the largest town in the county (population 6,500), but if you want to pick up the tour from Ardara, then follow the tour in reverse. If you choose to abbreviate the tour, try at least to catch the rewarding Fanad and Rosguill peninsulas and the drive around Sheephaven Bay.

Letterkenny

㉘ *55 km/34 mi northeast of Ardara, 51 km/32 mi northeast of Donegal Town, 35 km/22 mi west of Derry.*

Now one of the fastest-growing towns in all of Ireland, Letterkenny, like Donegal to the south, is at the gateway to the far Northwest; you're likely to come through here if you're driving west out of Northern Ireland. Letterkenny's claim to fame has been that it has the longest main street in the whole country, though none of its shops or pubs are particularly special, but lots of locals bustling around make it an interesting place to get a feel for what it's like to live in a modest-size Irish town today. The large, neo-Gothic Victorian St. Eunan's Cathedral towers over Letterkenny. The main County Donegal **TIO**, loaded with maps, literature, and advice, can be found 1½ km/1 mi south on the Derry road, N13. ☎ 074/21160. ☉ *Sept.–May, weekdays 9–5; June, Mon.–Sat. 9–6; July and Aug., Mon.–Sat. 9–8, Sun. 10–2.*

Dining and Lodging

$$ ✕🏨 **Mount Errigal Hotel.** One of County Donegal's smartest and most modern hotels, although not at all posh, this property appeals to both business and family-vacation visitors. Service here is friendly and professional. The clean and comfortable bedrooms are efficiently arranged, with characterless, pale-color furnishings. The Glengesh, the hotel's softly lit restaurant, decorated with Edwardian-style brass and glass fixtures, serves popular Irish cooking. The bar is popular with locals seeking a relaxed night out, and folk music, jazz, or dancing are

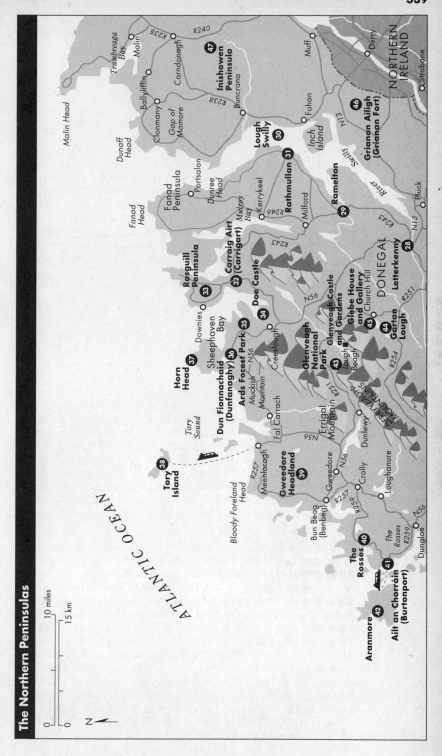

The Northern Peninsulas

ATLANTIC OCEAN

NORTHERN IRELAND

DONEGAL

DERRYVEAGH MOUNTAINS

Malin Head

Trawbreaga Bay

Malin

Ballyliffin

Clonmany

Carndonagh

R238

R240

Inishowen Peninsula **47**

Buncrana

Gap of Mamore

Dunaff Head

Muff

Fahan

Derry

Strabone

Grianan Ailigh (Grianan Fort) **46**

N13

Inch Island

Lough Swilly **30**

Rathmullan **31**

Ramelton **29**

Letterkenny **28**

Portsalon

Dunree Head

Fanad Peninsula

Fanad Head

Kerrykeel

Milford

R246

Midroy Bay

Carraig Airt (Carrigart) **32**

Doe Castle

Rosguill Peninsula **33**

34

Downies

Sheephaven Bay

Ards Forest Park **36**

35

Creeslough

Glenveagh Castle and Gardens

Glenveagh National Park **43**

Lough Beagh

Church Hill

Glebe House and Gallery **45**

Gartan Lough **44**

R251

R254

R255

R245

N56

Horn Head 37

Dun Fionnachaidh (Dunfanaghy)

Muckish Mountain

Fal Carrach

Errigal Mountain

R251

Dunlewy

Tory Sound

Tory Island **38**

Meenlaragh

R257

Gweedore Headland **39**

Gweedore

N56

Crolly

Loughanure

Bloody Foreland Head

Bun Beag (Benbeg)

R257

R259

The Rosses

Dunglae

N56

The Rosses 40

41

Ailt an Chorráin (Burtonport)

Aranmore **42**

10 miles

15 km

N

River Swilly

R245

N13

Pluck

R238

frequently scheduled on weekends. ⊠ *Ballyraine, Co. Donegal,* ☎ *074/ 22700,* ⅮⅩ *074/25085. 82 rooms with bath or shower. Restaurant, indoor pool, sauna, health club, nightclub. AE, DC, MC, V.*

Ramelton

㉙ *13 km/8 mi north of Letterkenny on R245.*

A handsome, small, former Plantation town, Ramelton (or Rathmelton, though the pronunciation is the same) climbs uphill from a river harbor close to Lough Swilly. The village was the birthplace of Francis Makemie (1658–1708), who preached here before emigrating and founding the American Presbyterian church, and it was once an important port that exported salmon, butter, grain, linen, and iodine (made from the local seaweed). The **Bridge Bar** (⊠ Milford Rd., ☎ 074/51119) has long been a favorite of locals and summertime visitors as a place to meet for a drink, enjoy a good, hearty meal (dinners are served upstairs, away from the bar), and take in the bands that regularly pack the place at night. Heading north to Rathmullan, take the waterside
㉚ road (the R247), which runs beside **Lough Swilly,** one of the loveliest of Donegal's big, fjordlike, ocean inlets.

Rathmullan (Rath Maoláin)

㉛ *11 km/7 mi north of Ramelton on R247.*

An ancient harbor village set among green fields, Rathmullan (its Irish name means "ring fort of Maoláin") looks across the broad expanse of Lough Swilly to the Inishowen hills on the eastern shore. In the last five years or so, holiday homes have sprung up near Lough Swilly's sandy shores, bringing with them vacationers who swell the town's ordinarily tiny population and make for a livelier summer scene. If you'd like to take an hour or two and familiarize yourself with the town's main sights, history, and flora and fauna, pick up *Rathmullan: A Walking Tour,* a lovely, handwritten, 28-page guide penned by resident Margaret Carton and published by the National Trust for Ireland. It's available at the County Donegal TIO (☞ Letterkenny, *above*), Letterkenny bookshops, Rathmullan House, or by contacting the author (⊠ Aughavannon, Rathmullan, Co. Donegal, ☎ 074/58244). There's nothing quite comparable for any other town in Ireland, so if this sounds like your cup of tea, don't pass it up.

Rathmullan's modest harbor was where English naval officers, posing as ordinary merchant seamen, captured Red Hugh O'Donnell in 1587. They invited him aboard to taste some of their "cargo of foreign wines," and the sociable clan leader fell for it. Once on board, he was shipped to imprisonment in Dublin Castle. After six years he escaped and returned to Donegal with added determination to defend his homeland—but to no avail. In 1607, Rathmullan's harbor was the scene of the Flight of the Earls, the great exodus of Ulster nobility that brought to an end the 13-year war with the English. The **Flight of the Earls Heritage Centre** commemorates this momentous event and the period that immediately followed, when the million-acre Ulster territories became part of the English domain. Two years later the Plantation era began: English and Scots colonists were "planted" here, and with them were sown the seeds of the Troubles that still dominate the affairs of Northern Ireland, across the border. ☎ 074/58229. ☞ £1.50. ☉ *Easter–Sept., Mon.–Sat. 10–6, Sun. noon–6:30.*

Dining and Lodging

$$$ ✕☐ **Fort Royal Hotel.** On 18 acres of verdant grounds beside Lough Swilly, Ann and Robin Fletcher's spacious, comfortable hotel, once an

aristocratic private home, is a decent alternative to the Rathmullan House (☞ *below*). It attracts a regular clientele, who enjoy its relaxed professionalism and marvelous location. Rooms are clean and meals are satisfactory. ⊠ *Co. Donegal,* ☎ *074/58100,* ℻ *074/58103. 15 rooms with bath or shower. Bar, 9-hole golf course, tennis court, squash, beach. AE, DC, MC, V. Closed Nov.–Mar.*

$$$ ✕▥ **Rathmullan House.** Behind the three-bay signature facade of this
★ two-story, cream-color mansion awaits one of Ireland's most appealing country houses—a rambling place that is elegant *and* relaxed, and well situated for visiting all of Donegal. Robin and Bob Wheeler are the friendly, gracious owner-managers. The public rooms, which include the bright yellow drawing room, library, and a coffee room, are decorated with fine antiques and oil paintings; all are elegant without being at all stuffy. Bedrooms vary from old-fashioned basic to grand, but all of them have antiques, well-appointed bathrooms, elegant wallpaper and fine fabrics. Rooms in the front overlook Lough Swilly, whose long, sandy, deserted beach lies steps from Rathmullan's front door, separated only by a ribbon of trees and the award-winning gardens. In a pavilion with a tented ceiling and floor-to-ceiling windows, the dining room has views of the gardens and the lake. The dinner menu changes nightly, and it takes advantage of locally available seafood and fresh produce. You might start with Donegal oak-smoked salmon sliced onto potato salad with a lemon dressing and move on to roast loin of lamb stuffed with bacon and herbs on a wild garlic sauce. Breakfast is itself a feast, with fresh fruit compotes, assorted freshly baked breads, fresh yogurt, and a variety of other hot and cold dishes. ⊠ *Co. Donegal,* ☎ *074/58188,* ℻ *074/58200. 21 rooms with bath or shower. Dining room, bar, indoor pool, sauna, steam room, tennis court, croquet, beach. AE, DC, MC, V. Closed Nov.–Easter.*

$$–$$$ ✕▥ **Water's Edge.** Dawn and Kevin Cairns recently added 11 bedrooms, nine with sea views, to their popular restaurant, set in a converted row of old cottages on the western shore of Lough Swilly. The cozy, romantic dining room has wooden beams, oak tables, deep-burgundy-red decor, and linen tablecloths and napkins. Influenced by the owners' travels, the menu is based primarily on fresh, local, seasonally available ingredients. Fish is the main event in summer (although it is available fresh every day of the year); steaks, chicken, duckling, and scallops predominate in the winter. Queen Sofia's Delight, a rich, meringue-based dessert made with seasonal fruit and fresh cream, is a specialty. ⊠ *The Ballyboe, Co. Donegal,* ☎ ℻ *074/58182. 11 rooms with bath. MC, V. Closed Nov.–mid-March.*

Outdoor Activities and Sports

Horses are available for excursions to the nearby Fanad Peninsula at **Rockhill Trekking Center** (⊠ Kerrykeel, Co. Donegal, ☎ 074/50012).

En Route Extending north from here is the barren and rock-strewn **Fanad Peninsula.** The signposted Fanad Scenic Drive takes you 27 km/17 mi up along the west shore of Lough Swilly to low-lying Fanad Head at its northern tip, then down again through the tiny resort village of Kerrykeel, with views of long, narrow Mulroy Bay twisting and turning to your right. If you want to cut the journey short, you can take the back road directly from Rathmullan to Kerrykeel for 9½ km/6 mi.

Carraig Airt (Carrigart)

㉜ *14 km/9 mi north of Ramelton on R245.*

A small village with a lot of charm and many old-fashioned pubs, Carraig Airt (Carrigart) is situated at the base of a slender isthmus. The
㉝ isthmus is the neck of the extremely beautiful **Rosguill Peninsula,** which

has a rocky heart and a fringe of sand dunes and beaches and is encircled by the signposted 15 km/9⅓mi **Atlantic Drive.** This area is not as far off the beaten track as you might think; you'll see several caravan sites and housekeeping cottages, popular with visitors from Northern Ireland. At the little resort of **Downings** (Na Dúnaibh), there's a long, sandy beach, good fishing, and a chance to buy linen directly from **McNutts of Donegal Ltd.** (☎ 074/55643) and tweeds from **John McNutt Homespun Tweeds Factory** (☎ 074/55158).

★ To the west of the Rosguill Peninsula, lovely **Sheephaven Bay** has shallow, meandering inlets and sandy shores. At the foot of Muckish Mountain and the southern end of Sheephaven Bay, protected on three
❸❹ sides by the sea and by a moat on its fourth side, stands **Doe Castle,** a tall, weather-beaten tower at the center of a complex structure enclosed within sturdy defenses. Described by attacking English forces in 1587 as "the strongest fortress in all the province," the impressive edifice dates from at least 1440, when it became the home of MacSweeney Doe, one of the "gallowglasses" (from the Irish *gall o glach*)—foreign mercenaries employed by the O'Donnell clan. Despite the castle's present poor condition, it was still occupied by his descendants until 1890. MacSweeney Doe's curiously carved tombstone is fixed to the southwest tower of the outer wall. ⊠ *Near Creeslough.* 🎫 *Free.* ☉ *Usually open; if locked, inquire at caretaker's cottage on approach path.*

Outdoor Activities and Sports

Horses for hacking or trekking on the Rosguill Peninsula can be rented at **Carrigart Riding Stables** (⊠ Co. Donegal, ☎ 074/55114).

Ards Forest Park

❸❺ *13 km/8 mi west of Carrigart on N56.*

Clinging to Sheephaven Bay's southwest shore, the 1,188-acre Ards Forest Park (reached by passing through adjacent Creeslough [pronounced *creesh*-la]) is the former wooded estate of a Capuchin friary; the friary itself is still occupied by the Capuchins. Four prehistoric, fortified sites and one dolmen lie within the grounds, which offer some of the most varied landscape of any of Ireland's national forest parks, including rivers, loughs, salt marshes, valleys, and, of course, the bay. If the weather is fine, the park's forest trails and picnic sites are great places to enjoy the scrubbed sea air. ☎ 074/53271. 🎫 *£2, free in winter.* ☉ *Daily 8 AM–9 PM.*

Dun Fionnachaid (Dunfanaghy)

❸❻ *8 km/5 mi northwest of Ards Forest Park.*

On the very edge of Sheephaven Bay, Dun Fionnachaid (Dunfanaghy) is a tidy, former Plantation village. If you're ready for a short break, both hotels noted below serve decent, unpretentious, local fare for about £8 for lunch. When the tide goes out, the vast sand flats of **Killyhoey Beach** are uncovered and the sea recedes into the far distance, but as it rises again, the sands are submerged in double-quick time. On the west side of Dunfanaghy, the signpost to **McSwyne's Gun** (McSwyne is the old spelling of MacSweeney) leads to a huge, natural blowhole that gives out a deafening bang when the tide rushes in during rough weather.

★ ❸❼ A little back road runs from Dunfanaghy up to **Horn Head,** the most spectacular of County Donegal's Atlantic headlands. From its sheer 600-ft cliffs, the views along the coast to the other headlands ranged one behind the other are spectacular. Bird-watchers take note: the cliffs are home to hundreds of seabirds, including puffin and guillemot.

Dining and Lodging

$$ ✕🖬 **Arnold's Hotel.** Situated right at the entrance to the village, this friendly hotel has been run by three generations of the Arnold family and is a favorite with Irish vacationers. Rooms are unassuming and relaxed; the best overlook the landscaped garden. Guests have the option of eating the generous, traditional Irish meals in the dining room or in the more casual Garden Bistro. The Arnolds offer special-interest classes for guests, such as painting and bird-watching. ⊠ *Main St., Co. Donegal,* ☎ *074/36208,* 𝔽𝔸𝕏 *074/36352. 31 rooms with bath and shower. Dining room, bar, tennis court, baby-sitting. AE, DC, MC, V. Closed Nov.–Mar.*

$ ✕🖬 **Carrig Rua Hotel.** On the shore of Sheephaven Bay, this unpretentious, two-story, former coaching inn (its name is Irish for "red rock") is friendly and modestly priced. It attracts many Irish family vacationers, especially those from the North. Children are made very welcome. The inviting rooms have new furniture and carpeting; some have bay views. Meals are plain and abundant in the traditional Irish style. ⊠ *Main St., Co. Donegal,* ☎ *074/36133,* 𝔽𝔸𝕏 *074/36277. 22 rooms with bath or shower. Restaurant, bar. AE, MC, V.*

En Route West of Dunfanaghy the terrain is rougher, wilder, and rockier; you're also likely to hear the Irish language being spoken. The N56 reaches round 11 km/7 mi to Fal Carrach (Falcarragh), the site of an Irish-language college. Another 13 km/8 mi around the rugged seashore, in good weather, you can catch a ferry from Meenlaragh (near Gortahork) to Tory Island.

Tory Island

❸❽ *14½ km/9 mi offshore.*

Harsh weather and difficult currents make Tory Island fairly inaccessible. (The boat trip lasts more than an hour on seas that are rough even on the best days; be prepared to get soaked, too.) Despite being rocky, ocean-battered, and barren (not even a single tree), the island has been inhabited since prehistoric times. Islanders speak their own dialect and refer to the mainland as "Ireland." Prehistoric and medieval relics are scattered about the landscape. Poised on the cliffs is the partly ruined, pink-granite **round tower** with its conical cap still intact. At Tory Island's eastern end, the prehistoric **Balor's Fort** was purportedly the residence of Balor, the terrifying, one-eyed, Celtic god of night and darkness. At the northeastern tip, the **Wishing Stone** has the power, it is said, to destroy enemies. Still talked about is the time (1884) when the stone's powers were invoked against the British gunboat *Wasp,* whose passengers (mainly policemen) had come to collect taxes—something the Islanders were unaccustomed to paying. The ship sank, and all but six of the crew were lost.

Most of the islanders live the simple life of fisher folk, though quite a few have unexpected sidelines as artists. In 1968, the well-known Irish painter Derek Hill met islander James Dixon, who felt that he could do a better job of painting than Hill. Many other Tory Island residents, thought they could, too, and today the Tory Island artists, depicting their own life and landscape in a naive style, are widely acclaimed and have exhibited elsewhere in Ireland (☞ Glebe House and Gallery *in* Gartan Lough, *below*) and abroad. **Dixon's Gallery** (☞ Tory Island Hotel, *below*) sells the work of the Tory Islanders; prices range from £50–£200.

Dining and Lodging

$ ✕⊡ **Tory (Ostan Thoraig).** After living and working in England for 10 years, native islander Pat Doohan returned with his wife Berney to build and run Tory Island's only accommodation. (He also watches over Dixon's Gallery [☞ *above*].) The comfortable guest rooms are large, sunny, and nicely decorated in a peach, blue, and green palette, with matching curtains and bedspreads; all have TVs and phones. A fireplace warms the bar, which is a popular local hangout and is the only place on the island that sells draft beer. Traditional music sessions and *ceili* dancing regularly liven things up. The restaurant overlooks the sea. ⊠ *Tory Island, Letterkenny, Co. Donegal,* ☎ *074/35920,* ℻ *074/35613. 14 rooms with bath. Restaurant, bar. Closed Dec.–Mar. MC, V.*

Gweedore Headland (Gaoth Dobhair)

39 *27 km/17 mi south of Meenlaragh on R257.*

When you return from Tory Island to Meenlaragh, you're on the edge of the Gweedore Headland, which can be circumnavigated on the coast road (R257). Gweedore is rocky, sparsely covered with heather and gorse, and low-lying until you reach its farthest point, **Bloody Foreland Head.** This dramatic name for once does not recall the slaughter of some historic battle, but describes instead the vivid red hues of the gaunt rock face when illuminated at sunset.

The Rosses (Na Rosa)

40 *13 km/8 mi south of Bloody Foreland Head on R259.*

The next distinctive headland south of Gweedore (on the road south after you pass through Bun Beag [Benbeg] and Croithli [Crolly]) is The Rosses (Na Rosa in Irish, meaning "the headlands")—even more beautiful than Gweedore. The bleak but dramatic terrain here, as at Gweedore, has not benefited from a liberal sprinkling of modern bungalows. The coast road (the R259) struggles over the inhospitable, stony landscape, crisscrossed with water channels and strewn with more than a hundred ponds. Yet quite a number of people manage to survive here, many of them Irish speakers (this is the heart of the Donegal Gaeltacht). The decline of population and living standards was reversed by Patrick Gallagher (1873–1964), who became known as Paddy the Cope. Son of a poor local family, he left school at 10, went to Scotland as a farmhand, and saved enough money to return home in the 1950s and buy a small holding of his own. Gallagher, affectionately remembered throughout the area, persuaded the citizens around The Rosses to set up cooperatives to bring in new farming methods and machinery, as well as cooperatively owned stores to keep prices down.

Ailt an Chorráin (Burtonport)

41 *16 km/10 mi southwest of Crolly on R259.*

This village of Ailt an Chorráin (Burtonport), which claims to land more salmon and lobster than any other fishing port in Ireland, is the departure point for a trip over to Aranmore, 6½ km/4 mi offshore. **Aranmore** means "big island," and it is indeed the largest and most populous of County Donegal's rocky offshore fragments. The ride out takes 25 minutes, but although it's fairly accessible, the island still feels remote and ungoverned. It has been inhabited for thousands of years (about a thousand people live on it today), and it offers good fishing as well as striking cliff scenery and views back onto The Rosses; there's a prehistoric fort on its south side. ⊠ *Ferry: £2.* ⊙ *7 crossings daily.*

Back on the mainland, if you follow the coast another 6½ km/4 mi southeast, the R259 rejoins N56 at **An Clochan Liath** (Dungloe), a pleasant little fishing town regarded as the capital of The Rosses, though there's little to do or see here.

En Route From Dungloe, start the journey back to Letterkenny. The N56 takes you 13 km/8 mi direct to Croithli (Crolly), a quicker journey than going back along the coast road. Stay on the N56 north until you're a couple of miles beyond Gaoth Dobhair (Gweedore) village, on the little River Clady, and take the R251 to skirt the south side of **Errigal Mountain** to the village of Dunlewy, 26 km/16 mi east of Dungloe. This whole drive passes through some of the best scenery in all of County Donegal. Serene Errigal looks especially grand from Dunlewy. On the edge of Dunlewy Lough, the **Lakeside Centre,** or Ionad Cois Locha, is an interesting spot to pause for a look at a reconstructed, 19th-century weaver's home where old-style weaving is demonstrated. There's also a café and crafts shop. ☎ 075/31699. ⌧ *Free.* ☉ *Apr. and May, Sat. 11–6, Sun. noon–7; June–Sept., Mon.–Sat. 11:30–6, Sun. 12:30–7.*

Glenveagh National Park

★ ㊸ *16 km/10 mi east of Dunlewy on R251, 27 km/16½ mi northwest of Letterkenny.*

Bordered by the Derryveagh Mountains (Derryveagh means "forest of oak and birch"), Glenveagh National Park encompasses 24,000 acres of wilderness—mountain, moorland, lakes, and woods—that has been called "the largest and most dramatic tract in the wildest part of Donegal." Within its borders, a thick carpet of russet-color heath and dense woodland rolls down the Derryveagh slopes into the broad open valley of the River Veagh (or Owenbeagh), which opens out into Glenveagh's spine: long and narrow, dark and clear **Lough Beagh.** (The park, in profile, looks like a backpacker marching off to the northwest.)

The Glenveagh lands have long been recognized as a remote and beautiful region. Between 1857 and 1859, John George Adair, a ruthless gentleman farmer, assembled the estate that now makes up the park. In 1861, he evicted the estate's hundreds of poor tenants without compensation and destroyed their cottages. Nine years later, Adair began to build **Glenveagh Castle** on the eastern shore of Lough Veagh, but he soon departed for Texas. He died in 1885 without returning to Ireland, but his widow, Cornelia, moved back to make Glenveagh her home. She created the four different **gardens** covering 27 acres and planted the luxuriant rhododendrons here and began the job of making this flamboyantly turreted and battlemented 19th-century folly livable.

The gardens and castle as they appear today are almost entirely an American invention—the product of the loving attentions of Glenveagh's last owner, U.S. millionaire Henry P. McIlhenny, who bought the estate in 1937 and, beginning in 1947, lived here for part of every year for almost 40 years (his other homes included a mansion on Philadelphia's Rittenhouse Square). McIlhenny's grandfather invented the gas meter, and he was a distant cousin of the creators of Tabasco sauce. An avid art collector and philanthropist (he was president of the Philadelphia Museum of Art, to which he bequeathed his outstanding 19th-century European art collection), McIlhenny decorated every inch of the house himself and entertained lavishly. (Greta Garbo slept in the Pink Bedroom on a visit.) McIlhenny was something of an eccentric: His staff of more than 40 were required to wear Austrian-inspired clothes—the women wore dirndls—he chose himself, inspired by his annual trips to Salzburg and other Austrian music festivals. The house has been maintained just as it was on his last occupancy in 1983; later that year, he made a gift of the house to the nation. (He had sold the government the surrounding land in 1975, which it opened to the public in 1984 as Ireland's third national park.) Beyond the castle, footpaths lead into more remote sections of the park, including the **Derrylahan Nature Trail,** a 1½-km/1-mi signposted trail where you may suddenly chance upon a shy red deer (the park is home to one of Ireland's two largest herds [the other is at Killarney]) or catch sight of a soaring falcon; guided walks are held May–October. The '70s-ish visitor center at the park's entrance has a permanent exhibition on the local way of life and on the influence of climate on the park's flora and fauna. Skip the sleep-inducing audiovisual and instead have a bite to eat in the cafeteria. ⊠ *Glenveagh National Park, Church Hill, Letterkenny, Co. Donegal,* ☎ *074/37088 or 074/37090.* ☞ *£2, guided tour of castle £2.* ☉ *Easter–Oct., daily 10:30–6:30 (until 7:30 in June–Aug.); closed Fri. in Oct.*

Gartan Lough

④④ *13 km/8 mi southeast of Glenveagh on R251, 17 km/10½ mi northwest of Letterkenny.*

Close to Church Hill village, Gartan Lough is technically within the national park and is administered partly by the park authorities. The lake and the surrounding mountainous country are astonishingly beautiful. St. Columba was supposedly born here in AD 521, and the legendary event is marked by a huge cross at the beginning of a footpath into the national park. Nearby are other dubious "relics" of the saint that are popularly believed to possess magical powers, such as the Natal Stone, where he is thought to have first opened his eyes, and the Stone of Loneliness, where he is said to have slept.

④⑤ On the northwest shore of Gartan Lough, just off the R251, sits **Glebe House and Gallery,** a fine Regency manor with 25 acres of gardens. For 30 years, Glebe House was the home of the distinguished landscape and portrait artist Derek Hill, who furnished the house in a mix of styles with art from around the world; in 1981 he gave the house and its contents, including his outstanding art collection, to the nation. Highlights include paintings by Renoir and Bonnard, lithographs by Kokoschka, ceramics and etchings by Picasso, and the paintings *Whippet Racing* and *The Ferry, Early Morning* by Jack B. Yeats, as well as Donegal folk art produced by the Tory Islanders (☞ *above*). The decoration and furnishings of the house, including original William Morris wallpaper, are worth a look as well. ⊠ *Church Hill,* ☎ *074/37071.* ☞ *£2.* ☉ *Easter and mid-May–Sept., Sat.–Thurs. 11–6:30.*

At the **Colmcille Heritage Centre** you can learn more about St. Columba and his times. Return to the R251 and turn right almost at once onto the R254 in Church Hill; straightaway you'll arrive at the exhibition and interpretation center, which features medieval manuscripts, stained glass, and displays tracing the decline of the Celtic religion and the rise of Irish Christianity. (From Church Hill, if you stay on the R251, you'll be back in Letterkenny after 16 km/10 mi.) ⊠ *Gartan, Church Hill,* ☎ *074/37306.* ☞ *£2.* ☉ *May, Sept., Oct., Mon.–Sat. 11–6:30, Sun. 1–6:30; June–Aug., Mon.–Sat. 10–6:30, Sun. noon–6:30.*

Grianan Ailigh (Grianan Fort)

★ ④⑥ *29 km/18 mi northeast of Letterkenny on N13.*

A circular stone Celtic fort, the Grianan Ailigh (Grianan Fort), definitely merits a visit, although it is, like the Inishowen peninsula (☞ *below*), northeast of Letterkenny, and thus closer to Northern Ireland

(☞ Chapter 9) than the majority of Donegal sites covered here. The fortress sits on top of an 810-ft hill; on a fine day, the immense panorama of the rolling Donegal and Derry landscape is breathtakingly glorious. To the north lies the Swilly estuary, flowing around Inch Island into Lough Swilly. On either side rise the hills of the Fanad and Inishowen peninsulas, though they're often partly veiled by mists. As for the fort, what you'll see is a circular stone enclosure with a diameter of about 76 ft that you can enter through a gate (it's open most of the year). Inside, earth ramparts and concentric defenses punctured by passages surround a sturdy central structure. No one knows when Grianan Fort was built, but it was probably an Iron Age fortress: Its position was accurately recorded in the 2nd century AD by the geographer Ptolemy of Alexandria. Later it became the seat of Ulster's O'Neill chieftains and remained so for many centuries, despite serious attempts by their enemies to destroy it, especially in the year 674 and again in 1101. The present-day fortress, however, owes a good deal to overzealous "restoration" in the 1870s by Dr. Walter Bernard, a Derry historian; before that, it was in ruins. To get here, take the main Derry road (the N13) from Letterkenny. Keep a lookout for signs to Buncrana, because the easy-to-miss sign for the fort is opposite. Instead of turning to Buncrana, take the narrow lane that climbs and turns for more than a mile to the top of the hill.

Inishowen Peninsula

㊼ *Peninsula circuit from Fahan to Muff via Malin Head and Inishowen Head: 161 km/100 mi.*

The most northerly point in all of Ireland, the huge Inishowen Peninsula is a grandly green, wild piece of land with a solid, mountainous interior. It is enclosed by Lough Swilly on one side, Lough Foyle on another, and the battering Atlantic to the north. Despite a string of small and untempting coast resorts, it remains unspoiled and less traveled than most other parts of the country. If you decide to make the 160-km/100-mi Inishowen circuit (known as the "Inishowen 100," for its length in miles) plus the 64-km/40-mi round-trip to reach it from Letterkenny, you'll need to allow at least one whole day, though it is possible to make an abbreviated visit in less time.

From Grianan Ailigh, go back to the N13 and cross straight over to take the Buncrana turning. You'll shortly meet the R238, the main route from Derry to Buncrana. Turn left here; the first town you'll come to is **Fahan** (pronounced "fawn"), which has monastic ruins that include the early Christian **St. Mura cross slab.** Just after the village, and opposite the North West Golf Club, signs on the right show the entrance to the IDA (Irish Industrial Authority) industrial estate. Turn in here, and you'll find the **National Knitting Centre,** which offers residential courses in traditional Irish hand knitting (☎ 077/62355 for details); the center also sells fine knit goods.

A popular, downscale beach resort favored by Derry denizens, **Buncrana** has a 14th-century O'Docherty tower that gradually became part of an 18th-century mansion. Shortly after you pass Buncrana, turn left at the fork in the road away from the R238 onto the coast road, which will take you past the 19th-century fort on Dunree Head, up and over the spectacular viewpoint of the **Gap of Mamore,** where the 1,250-ft **Croaghcarragh** rises up on one side, and the 1,361-ft **Mamor Hill** echoes it on the other. The road heads north toward **Dunaff Head,** where Lough Swilly opens into the ocean. Rejoin the R238 at Clonmany and take it through **Ballyliffin,** another small resort town with an O'Docherty tower on the beach, and a convenient place for a snack or meal. Ballyliffin's **The Strand Hotel** (☎ 077/76107) is a likable, family-run establishment where you can get well-prepared pub lunches; it also has 12 rooms ($), in the event you want to stay out here.

By the junction of the R238 and the R240, you'll see a church with a curious remnant of early Christianity against one wall, the decorated, 7th-century **Donagh Cross,** accompanied by a couple of pillar stones. The strange carvings on the stones clearly date from a pre-Christian period. Around the corner from the Donagh Cross, **Carndonagh,** the area's main market town, has several more medieval monastic remains; **Slieve Snaght,** Inishowen's highest peak at 2,019 ft, lies just southwest of town. As it runs up beside Trawbreaga Bay, the R238 turns into the R242 shortly before the picturesque village of Malin; it's another 16 km/10 mi up to **Malin Head,** the most northerly point in all of Ireland, and an important spot for birds migrating south in autumn. Although it does have good views, Malin Head is not as dramatic a spot as some of the other headlands.

From Malin Head, take the signposted route across the peninsula to **Moville,** a sleepy waterside resort on the Lough Foyle side. From here, it's 8 km/5 mi to **Inishowen Head,** the peninsula's rocky eastern tip. On the way to the head, at **Greencastle,** you'll see the fortifications of foreigners who tried to control the nine counties of Ulster: a 14th-century, Anglo-Norman fortress and an English fort built five centuries later to defend against French support for the Irish. The drive along the lough shore toward Derry (☞ Chapter 9), though attractive, is punctuated by small, uninteresting villages whose modernized pubs cater to visitors from Derry. If you want to turn away from Derry toward Letterkenny before reaching the border, take the R239 from Muff to **Bridge End,** home to one of the most attractive of Ireland's many new Catholic churches.

Dining and Lodging

$$–$$$	✕⊞ **Restaurant St. John's.** A cozy, old-fashioned, atmosphere pre-
★	vails at this restored, lakeside Georgian house, which has been known for 20 years for its restaurant. Recently owner Reg Ryan added five rooms. Pictures of old Derry hang in the turquoise-and-pink dining room, although white Donegal linen is used for tablecloths and napkins. Ryan, who does the cooking, is scrupulous about using only organic vegetables and local produce in the peak of its season. Homemade bread is baked daily to serve with the fresh garden soups and pâtés. The six-course table d'hôte menu changes monthly and offers appetizers such as seafood chowder or a terrine of salmon and monkfish wrapped in spinach. Fillets of brill with herbs and fennel sauce, or Donegal rack of lamb, served with sorrel and mint *jus,* are typical main courses. Desserts include homemade ice creams. ⊠ *Fahan, Co. Donegal,* ☎ *077/ 60289,* 𝕱𝕬𝕏 *077/60612. 5 rooms with bath. AE, DC, MC, V.*

Outdoor Activities and Sports

For hacking and trekking on the Inishowen Peninsula contact **Lenamore Stables** (⊠ Muff, Co. Donegal, ☎ 077/84022).

THE NORTHWEST A TO Z

Arriving and Departing

By Bus
Bus Éireann (☎ 071/60066 [locally] or 01/836–6111 [in Dublin]) can get you from Dublin to Sligo Town in four hours for £8 one-way, £11 round-trip. Three buses a day from Dublin are available. Another bus route, four times a day from Dublin (five on Fridays), gets to Let-

terkenny, in the heart of County Donegal, in 4¼ hours, via a short trip across the Northern Ireland border, for £10 one-way, £13 round-trip. Other Bus Éireann services connect Sligo Town to other towns all over Ireland.

By Car

Sligo, the largest town in the Northwest, is relatively accessible on the main routes. The N4 travels the 224 km/140 mi directly from Dublin to Sligo, but you need to allow at least four hours for this journey. The N15 continues from Sligo Town to Donegal Town and proceeds from Donegal Town to Derry City, just over the border in the province of Northern Ireland. The fastest approach for anyone driving up from the West and the Southwest is on the N17, connecting Sligo to Galway, though the landscape is undistinguished.

By Plane

The principal, international air-arrival point to the Northwest is the tiny airport at Charlestown, near Knock, whose official name is **Horan International Airport** (☎ 094/67247), 54½ km/34 mi south of Sligo Town. Locally it is known simply as Knock Airport; shortly before press time (summer 1997), Ross Perot announced plans for a major European distribution operation here. **Eglinton Airport** (☎ 01504/810784), at Derry, a few miles over the border, receives flights from the U.K. airports of Manchester and Glasgow and from Dublin. Eglinton is a particularly convenient airport for reaching northern County Donegal. A small, airfield is at **Carrickfinn** (☎ 075/48232) near Dungloe. **Sligo Airport** (☎ 071/68280 or 071/68318) at Strandhill, 8 km/5 mi west of Sligo Town is the other area airport.

Ryanair offers flights to Knock Airport from London and Irish airports. **Aer Lingus** has direct flights daily to Knock Airport, Eglinton Airport, and Sligo Airport from Dublin. **Macair** provides direct flights to Carrickfinn Airport near Dungloe from Birmingham and Edinburgh. **British Airways Express** flies to Carrickfinn from Glasgow, and also flies to Eglinton Airport from Manchester and Glasgow.

BETWEEN THE AIRPORTS AND YOUR DESTINATION

By Bus. If you aren't driving, Knock Airport becomes less attractive, as you'll have no easy public transportation link to your destination, except the once-a-day (in season) local bus to Charlestown (11 km/7 mi away). Nor can you rely on catching a bus at the smaller airports, except at Sligo Airport, where buses run from Sligo Town to meet all flights.

By Car. For car renters, Knock Airport has a convenient car-rental desk. You can also pick up rental cars at Sligo and Eglinton (Derry) airports.

By Taxi. Cabs sometimes stand waiting outside Knock Airport to meet incoming flights, but passengers arriving at the other airports may have to phone a local taxi company. Phone numbers of taxi companies are available from airport information desks and are also displayed beside pay phones inside the airport terminals.

By Train

Sligo Town is the northernmost direct rail link to Dublin. From Dublin three trains a day are available, and the journey takes 3 hours and 20 minutes. The fare is £12 one-way or day-return, £14 round-trip. The train stops at Ballymote (20 minutes from Sligo), Boyle (40 minutes), and Carrick-on-Shannon (50 minutes). However, if you want to get to Sligo Town by rail from other provincial towns, you'll be forced to make some inconvenient connections and take roundabout routes. The rest of the region has no railway services. Contact **Irish Rail** (☎ 01/836–6222).

Getting Around

By Bus

Bus Éireann services operate out of Sligo Town (☎ 071/60066) and Letterkenny (☎ 074/21309) to destinations all over the region, as well as to other parts of Ireland. From Sligo Town, you can reach almost any point in the region for less than £10. **McGeehans** (☎ 075/46150) is one of several local bus companies linking towns and villages in the Northwest.

By Car

Roads are uncongested, but in some places they are in a poor state of repair (French coach drivers refused to drive their buses in County Donegal a few summers back, as a gesture of protest about the state of the roads). In the Irish-speaking areas, signposts are written only in the Irish (Gaelic) language, which can be confusing. You need to prepare beforehand for this by checking the Irish names of places on your route.

Contacts and Resources

B&B Reservation Agencies

For a small fee, **Bord Fáilte** will book accommodations anywhere in Ireland through their central reservations system. B&Bs can be booked at local visitor information offices when they are open; however, even these reservations will go through the central reservations system. For more information, *see* Lodging *in* the Gold Guide.

Car Rentals

You can rent a car in Sligo Town from **Euro Mobil** (☎ 071/67291). **Murray's Europcar** (☎ 071/68400) rents cards from Sligo Airport. **Murray's Europcar** (☎ 078/33029) also has a branch at Knock Airport. A medium-size four-door costs around £50 per day with unlimited mileage (inclusive of insurance and taxes), or around £240 per week. If you're planning to tour mostly northern County Donegal, you may find it more convenient to rent a car in Derry from **Ford** (☎ 01504/360420). Conversely, if you're planning to drive a rental car across the border to Northern Ireland, inform the company in advance and check the insurance position.

Emergencies

Police, fire, and **ambulance** (☎ 999 toll-free).

HOSPITALS

Letterkenny General Hospital (✉ High Rd., Letterkenny, Co. Donegal, ☎ 074/22022). **Sligo General Hospital** (✉ Dromahair Rd., Sligo Town, Co. Sligo, ☎ 071/42161).

Guided Tours

Walking tours of Sligo Town depart twice daily, at 11 AM and 7 PM, in July and August from the TIO. They are free and last about 1 to 1½ hours. However, the guides are generally students, so a tip of 50p or £1 is welcome. For a friendly, relaxed, minibus tour of the area (in July and August) with a knowledgeable guide, call **John Houze** (☎ 071/42747) for his tour around Lough Gill (£5.50 for morning tour, £6.50 afternoon) and his tour north of Sligo Town to Drumcliff, Lissadell House, and Creevykeel (£6). **Bus Éireann** (☎ 071/60066 or 074/21309) has useful, budget-priced, one-day, guided coach tours of the Donegal Highlands and to Glenveagh National Park. These tours start from Bundoran, Sligo Town, Ballyshannon, and Donegal Town.

Nightlife and the Arts

Outside of Sligo Town, the Northwest features few serious arts activities and events, though there are a number of festivals and seasonal events (☞ Chapter 1). The local press, including *The Donegal Democrat, The Leitrim Observer,* and *Sligo Champion,* have useful events listings.

Outdoor Activities and Sports

BIRD-WATCHING

For more information, contact the **Irish Wildbird Conservancy** (✉ 8 Longford Pl., Monkstown, Co. Dublin, ☎ 01/280–4322).

FISHING

A **fishing license** is not needed for sea fishing or for coarse and pike angling. For game fishing (salmon and sea trout), the license costs £3 for one day, £10 for 21 days, or £25 for a full season. The full-season license is valid throughout the whole country; there's also a local annual license, valid only in the Northwest, for £12. Senior citizens are exempt from these costs. You can obtain licenses for County Donegal from the **Northern Regional Fishery Board** (✉ Ballyshannon, Co. Donegal, ☎ 072/51435). For licenses in Counties Sligo and Leitrim, contact the **North-Western Regional Fisheries Board** (✉ Ballina, Co. Mayo, ☎ 096/22623). Some tackle shops are also permitted to sell licenses.

If you want full **information** on fishing in the Northwest waters, suitable accommodations, details of boat rentals, etc., ask the Irish Tourist Board (☞ Visitor Information *in* the Gold Guide) for the annual *Anglers' Guide.*

Bait, tackle, and local information can be found at the following places:

County Donegal: John McGill (✉ Main St., Ardara); O'Doherty's (✉ Main St., Donegal Town); and Pat Barrett (✉ Finner Rd., Bundoran, ☎ 072/41504).

County Leitrim: The Creel or Geraghty's (✉ Main St., Carrick-on-Shannon) and Aodh Flynn (✉ Deerpark, Manorhamilton).

County Sligo: Barton Smith (✉ Hyde Bridge, Sligo Town).

GOLF

For a full list of golf courses in the region, contact the Irish Tourist Board (☞ Visitor Information *in* the Gold Guide) or local TIOs (☞ Visitor Information, *below*). For detailed information about the Northwest's championship courses, including Carn Golf Course, Donegal Golf Club, County Sligo Golf Club, and Enniscrone Golf Club, *see* Chapter 10.

HIKING

For information about Northwest walking routes, contact **Field Officer, Long Distance Walking Routes Committee** (✉ Cospoir, 11th floor, Hawkins House, Dublin 9, ☎ 01/873–4700).

HORSEBACK RIDING

For information on recognized establishments that offer full riding vacations including lodging, contact **The Association of Irish Riding Establishments** (✉ Mespil Hall, Kill, Co. Kildare, ☎ 045/77208 or 045/77299).

SURFING

Ask the **Irish Surfing Association** (✉ Tigh-na-Mara, Rossnowlagh, Co. Donegal, ☎ 073/21053) for specific information on surfing in the region.

Visitor Information

The TIO in **Sligo Town** (which is in the extreme south of the region) is the main visitor information center for the whole Northwest region. ⊠ *Áras Reddan, Temple St.,* ☎ *071/61201,* ℻ *071/60360.* ☉ *Sept.– May, weekdays 9–1 and 2–5; June, Mon.–Sat. 9–1 and 2–6; July and Aug., Mon.–Sat. 9–8, Sun. 10–2.*

If you are traveling in County Donegal in the North, try the TIO at **Letterkenny,** about 1½ km/1 mi out of town. ⊠ *Derry Rd.,* ☎ *074/ 21160,* ℻ *074/25180.* ☉ *Sept.–May, weekdays 9–1 and 2–5; June, Mon.–Sat. 9–1 and 2–6; July and Aug., Mon.–Sat. 9–8, Sun. 10–2.*

SEASONAL OFFICES

These offices are open only during the summer months (usually the first week in June to the second week in September):

Bundoran (⊠ Main St., Co. Donegal, ☎ 072/41350). **Donegal Town** (⊠ Quay St., Co. Donegal, ☎ 073/21148, ℻ 073/22762). **Dungloe** (⊠ Village Center, Co. Donegal, ☎ 075/21297).

9 Northern Ireland

Belfast, the Antrim Coast, Derry, Lough Erne, and the Mountains of Mourne

Peace—precarious peace—has returned to "the North," as the Irish almost universally call Northern Irland. What the future holds is anyone's guess, but the last four years have seen considerable progress toward an end to the longstanding conflict. Beyond the headline-making Troubles, the North's six counties have some of Ireland's most spectacular coastal landscape—including the aptly named Giant's Causeway—its tidiest towns, and two rapidly changing cities—Derry and Belfast—that offer many of the pleasures of other Irish locales: museums, theater, shopping, traditional pubs, and distinguished restaurants.

By Andrew
Sanger and
Ian Hill

Updated by
Ian Hill

IF THE CELTIC LEGEND IS TRUE, the giant Fionn MacCool built the Giant's Causeway off the coast of Northern Ireland to settle a score with his Scots cousin Fingal. Disguising himself as his infant son in swaddling clothes, he frightened Fingal off. After all, if this was the size of the son, how big must his father be? As in all legends there is a grain of truth, for the narrow and turbulent channel between Scotland and Ireland has never been much of a barrier to warriors—or farmers—moving in either direction, and this ancient Irish province of Ulster has always had close ties with its neighbor on the other side of the water.

But it isn't just the Scots influence that separates Ulster and its people from the rest of the island of Ireland. A natural barrier of low hills called drumlins, left behind by the last Ice Age 13,000 years ago, runs right across Ireland from east to west, isolating the old nine-county northern province of Ulster. In addition, a man-made barrier augments the natural one: Nearly 2,000 years ago the people of Ulster built the Black Pig's Dyke—a series of great ditches and earth barriers filling in the gaps between the drumlins—to mark the border between themselves and the other Irish regions to the south. To the southerners and would-be conquerors, Ulster was known as a tough, indomitable land, home of the Red Branch Knights, a warlike people. The "Red Hand" at the center of its flag tells a typically ferocious tale: Two great Celtic warriors raced from Scotland to Ireland's northern coast to settle a dispute between them for possession of Ulster. The first to touch the foreign land could call it his own. In the last moments, one of the rivals cut off his own hand and threw it onto the shore and so, by blood and sacrifice, won Ulster.

Present-day Northern Ireland, a province under the rule of the United Kingdom, includes six of the old Ulster's nine counties (the others—Donegal, Cavan, and Monaghan—lie in the Irish Republic) and retains its sense of separation, both in the vernacular of the man-made landscape and (some say) in the character of the people. The hardheaded and industrious Scots-Presbyterians, imported to make Ulster a bulwark against Ireland's Catholicism, have had a profound and ineradicable effect on the place. Not least of the Scottish legacies are the North's distinctive accents and its Ulster-Scots argot, most prevalent in the counties of Antrim and Down. The North appears to boast more factories, neater-looking farms, better roads, and—in its cities—more two-story, redbrick houses (which are typical in Great Britain) than does the Republic. And of course, you'll also see, in blue-collar Protestant districts, some of the more overt manifestations of the pro-British Loyalists' zeal: curbstones and lampposts painted in the British colors of red, white, and blue; entwined British and Red Hand Ulster flags fluttering from tall poles raised in pocket-handkerchief front yards; and countless signs and crests declaring proud devotion to Ulster and the Queen. (By contrast, in similar Irish Republican and Nationalist Catholic voting wards, you'll note the green, white, and gold of the Irish Republic's Tricolor flickering in the breeze.) For all that, the national frontier—"the Border"—which separates British Northern Ireland from the Irish Republic, is of little consequence to visitors, or even to residents, who may cross it freely at any time.

Ireland's ancient history begins in the North: Men and women first came to Ireland around 9,000 years ago, leaving their first traces—of their hide-covered huts, their kitchen middens rich in salmon bones and hazelnut and crab shells—on the banks of the River Bann, in the north of Ulster. Five thousand years later Bronze Age settlers built the great stone circles idiomatic to counties Down and Tyrone. The Iron Age brought the Celts who stayed to conquer and assimilate. Someone burnt a great structure at Navan in 94 BC. The Romans traded briefly, and were gone. The 5th century AD brought St. Patrick, son of a Roman official and once a slave in county Antrim, who re-landed in county Down, spreading, charismatically, the Christian faith. The marauding Vikings of the 9th and 10th centuries left little trace, but from the first Norman incursions in the 12th century onward, the English made greater and greater inroads into Ireland, endeavoring to subdue what they believed was a potential enemy and a collaborator with that great adversary of England's naval might, Catholic Spain. Ulster proved the hardest part to conquer, but in 1607 Ulster's Irish nobility were beaten and left their homeland in a great exodus known as the Flight of the Earls. Many went to France and Spain, abandoning their lands forever to confiscation by the English crown. In the 17th century the English distributed the territories among individuals called Planters—the name given to staunch Protestants from England and, even more often, from Scotland who came to Ireland to farm, work, and colonize. New Protestant towns were built, and Catholics became subjected to harshly repressive laws. Non-conformist Calvinist settlers fared better, but even they were subject to restrictions not placed on members of the Established (Anglican/Episcopalian) Church. Inevitably, tension between the various religious groups smoldered, often flaring into violence over the succeeding centuries.

1916 saw the Easter Uprising and then, in the parliamentary elections of 1918, an overwhelming nationalist vote across Ireland for Sinn Féin ("We Ourselves"), the party that believed in independence for all of Ireland; in the five northeastern counties of Ulster, however, just seven seats went to the Irish Nationalist Party (who were demanding Home Rule—local autonomy for an all-Ireland parliament within the United Kingdom), and Sinn Féin. Twenty-two constituencies voted for the Unionists (who wanted nothing less than to remain an integral part of the United Kingdom). At 2:10 AM on December 6, 1921, in the British prime minister's residence, 10 Downing Street, Michael Collins signed the Anglo-Irish Treaty, designating a six-county North to remain in British hands, in exchange for complete independence for Ireland's 26 counties as the Irish Free State. The North established its own parliament, housed in the imposing (now empty) Stormont building just east of Belfast. Thus the roots of the North's current sectarian conflict run deep into the soil of Ireland's history—a knotted complex, rich in a legends, invasions, enrichments, colonial exploitation, and alienation topped off with the Western world's late 20th-century's post-industrial malaise— apparent in incorrigibly high rates of unemployment.

Today visitors may be surprised by the high degree of religious observance in the North. Protestants divide about equally into Anglicans and a variety of more or less austere nonconformists, especially Presbyterians. From the 1780s to the 1920s, the Nationalist movement included many Presbyterians. However, the passage of time caused positions to become more entrenched rather than less. The various shades of Unionism today are closely identified with the "planted" Protestant population, while Nationalists and Republicans are inextricably associated with the "native" Irish community, which traces its genetic inheritance back to the Iron Age Celtic invaders and which is almost entirely Catholic.

In 1968, in the spirit of the student protesters in Paris and Washington, and after 40 years of living with an apparently permanent and sectarian Unionist majority, students in Belfast's Queen's University launched a civil rights movement, claiming equal rights in jobs, housing, and opportunity. The brutality with which these marches were suppressed in front of the world's press (for the Unionist Government took little note of the power of the television camera) led to world-wide revulsion, to riot and counter-riot. The Irish Republican Army (IRA), which had lain dormant for decades, hijacked what was left of the shattered civil rights movement, which once had a smattering of Protestant students among its ranks. Armed British troops who had been first welcomed by many in the Catholic ghettos as protectors from Protestant paramilitaries now found themselves welcomed by neither side. The Government in Stormont was prorogued. Britain imposed Direct Rule. No one was happy, and the decades of guerrilla conflict that ensued between the IRA, the UDA/UVF (Protestant/Loyalist paramilitaries), and the British Government continued in a mix of lulls and terrors—apart from the IRA's annual Christmas "truce"—until the summer of 1994 when the "Provos," as they are colloquially known, called an ongoing cease-fire.

Although it has been easy for Ulster's affluent middle classes to diminish the problems of recent decades by deeming them, deprecatingly, as the Troubles, the situation has been little less than full-scale guerrilla war for those from both traditions living in a handful of now internationally well-known enclaves: the run-down, inner-city, working-class neighborhoods of Belfast and Derry, and the rural southern border areas of counties Armagh, Down, Fermanagh, and Tyrone. In 1985 the London and Dublin governments signed the Anglo-Irish Agreement, which gives the Irish government a consultative voice in Northern Ireland's affairs, thus giving—in a roundabout way—the Nationalist/Republican vote a voice at the negotiating table. Moderate nationalists in the SDLP, the Social Democratic Labour Party, were delighted; republicans in Sinn Féin less so. Unionists of all shades were not amused. Traditionally, the great majority of workplaces and schools had been segregated by religion—Protestant versus Catholic. In 1990, a Fair Employment Commission was set up with the aim of bringing about integration in places of work. Similar legislation was enacted to offer the possibility of formal integration in schools. More and more people on both sides of the sectarian divide showed a sincere willingness to make compromises and live in peace with their neighbors.

The big unexpected breakthrough came in 1994 when—after some behind-the-scenes maneuvering by sympathetic American politicians—the IRA, on August 31st, called a cease-fire. Shortly afterwards Loyalist paramilitaries followed suit. Belfast reveled in its new peace: new hotels, shopping malls, and restaurants came off dusty drawing boards. People who had not seen the city's center for a quarter of a century gazed at its bright lights. But it was always an uneasy, nagging peace. Offstage, in the ghettos, paramilitaries on both sides continued to mete out the brutal assaults they deemed "punishment" beatings; after two years of talks, in February 1996, the IRA detonated bombs on the British mainland, sending a clear signal that the Peace Progress wasn't delivering alone what they wanted. For a while, while churchgoers of all religions prayed, the province held its breath, until, perhaps predictably, late in 1996 the IRA resumed its attacks on police and British army forces (but not civilian targets) in the North. At press time (summer 1997), the IRA resumed its 1994 cease-fire, although peace talks were stymied by disputes over disarmament.

Still, the North's turbulent history cannot mask the fact that it has some of Ireland's finest scenery—for example, on its County Antrim coast and in the tranquil green lake country of County Fermanagh. It also maintains close links with the United States and Canada, to which many of its people have emigrated over the last two centuries.

Pleasures and Pastimes

Dining
While it has nowhere near the number of innovative restaurants as Dublin (which is five times more populous), Belfast has witnessed an influx of international influences with new restaurants, bistros, wine bars, and—as in Dublin—European-style café-bars where you can get good food *and* linger over a drink.

By and large, though, hearty, unpretentious cooking predominates, with good-quality, fresh local fish or meat simply prepared. You're virtually guaranteed to find certain traditional dishes on menus here: The Ulster fry, an inexpensive café and pub dish, is something like an Irish breakfast—a sizzling portion of bacon, black pudding, mushrooms, sausages, tomatoes, and eggs, served with potato or soda bread; champ—creamy, buttery mashed potatoes with scallions; Guinness and beef pie; oysters from Strangford Lough; Ardglass herring; mussels from Dundrum; and smoked salmon from Glenarm.

Belfast has also discovered the convenience of neo-American fast food (McDonald's and Kentucky Fried Chicken) and ethnic restaurants (Chinese and Indian).

Without being formal, the Northern Irish tend to dress soberly. Men often wear a jacket and tie when dining out; but if you prefer to dress more casually, that is quite acceptable at most establishments, though jeans can be a bar to entry. By the standards of the Republic or the United States, or even the rest of the United Kingdom, restaurant prices are surprisingly moderate. A service charge of 10% may be indicated on the bill; it is customary to pay this, unless the service was bad. For price ranges, *see* Chart 1(B) *in* On the Road with Fodor's.

Festivals
Festivals, marches, and other excuses to gather fill the calendar in Ulster—certainly as much, and possibly more so, than in the South. Every village its own an annual celebration; such *fleadhs* (festivals) are especially common in June and July. If you're interested in the Troubles, you may want to see the often controversial Orangemen's (Unionist) March (July 12), and the Ancient Order of Hibernians (Nationalist) marches of August 15th, but be aware that in recent years some Orange marches have led to ugly confrontations as they've traversed nationalist/republican areas. The **Belfast Folk Festival** in September is a weekend of traditional Irish music and dance at downtown locations. The **Belfast Festival at Queen's,** which lasts three weeks each November, is the North's cultural high point of the year; its heady mix of drama, music, dance, and film are all centered on the Queen's University campus—the most pleasant area of town. *See* The Arts, *below, and* Festivals and Seasonal Events *in* Chapter 1 for more detailed information about these and other festivals.

Lodging
Since the advent of the 1994 cease-fire, major hotel chains both in the Republic and abroad have been investing in the North, but locals retain a loyalty to, and admiration for, the province's hotel dynasties (among them, the Hastings, Mooney, and Rana families) who maintained and expanded their operations during the years of the Troubles when hotels were a frequent target of IRA bombings. Low-cost guest houses (often family-run), offering bed and breakfast, are probably the best way to meet locals; most B&Bs provide an evening meal as well,

if needed. In Belfast's environs visitors can choose from the humblest terraced town houses or farm cottages to the grandest country houses. Dining rooms of country-house lodgings frequently reach the standard of top-quality restaurants. All accommodations in the province are inspected and categorized by the Northern Ireland Tourist Board, which publishes all names, addresses, and ratings in the handbook *Where to Stay* (£3.99). For additional lodging contact information, *see* Contacts and Resources *in* Northern Ireland A to Z, *below.*

CATEGORY	COST*
$$$$	over UK£135
$$$	UK£70–UK£135
$$	UK£40–UK£70
$	under UK£40

All prices are for two people in a double room, including 12.5% local sales tax (VAT) and a service charge (often applied in larger hotels).

Outdoor Activities and Sports

BICYCLING

Roads are good and fairly traffic-free, so cycling is popular. Once in the countryside you will often have the run of long, winding roads. There's no need to have a bike of your own—many towns offer places to rent them.

BIRD-WATCHING

The province has an unexpectedly wide range of habitats and bird species for such a tiny area. The best time to come is winter, but even in summer visitors can participate in first-class bird-watching, especially on the Antrim uplands, all down the Antrim coast, and on the offshore islands.

FISHING

With a 606-km/466-mi coastline, part on the Atlantic and part on the Irish Sea, as well as major lakes and an abundance of unpolluted rivers, the North is a great place for anglers. Set your rod for salmon on the Bann, Bush, and Foyle rivers and for brown trout in their tributaries. There are bigger lake trout in Loughs Neagh, Melvin, and Erne, while pike and other coarse (white) fish abound in the Erne. Good turbot and plaice are taken off the north coast where sea bass may be caught from the shore. For specific information on fishing, *see* Fishing *in* Contacts and Resources *in* Northern Ireland A to Z, *below.*

HIKING AND WALKING

Northern Ireland is magnificent walking country. Ask at tourist offices for details of their local walking and cycling trails, 14 of which spring off the **Ulster Way,** an 896-km/560-mi trek for the serious hiker that runs around the six counties and links up with marked trails on the other side of the border. The terrain never demands more than a pair of stout walking shoes, and of course, visitors do not have to walk the whole trail; some sections are easier than others. Many cities and towns have their own historic trails; for further information, *see* Hiking and Walking *in* Contacts and Resources *in* Northern Ireland A to Z, *below.*

HORSEBACK RIDING/PONY TREKKING

Sitting on the back of a horse or pony is a great way to travel into places that are out of bounds to motorists. Woodland, beaches, and rough country become accessible on guided rides, some suitable for complete beginners. Some 35 riding and trekking centers are around the province, and several of them offer accommodations (☞ Contacts and Resources *in* Northern Ireland A to Z, *below*).

Like the rest of the island, people in Ulster take their sport seriously, particularly Saturday's **soccer** and **rugby** and Sunday's **hurling** and **Gaelic football** events. Dates of local matches are listed in local newspapers. **Greyhound racing** has roots deep in the Celtic psyche. During the summer, you'll come across the very English sport of **cricket** matches being played throughout the province. There are two **horse racing** tracks—the one at Downpatrick is particularly atmospheric. One oddity is the ancient precursor of bowls, called **bullets,** which is still played in County Armagh. It involves throwing bowls (originally they were cannonballs, hence the name) along a narrow, winding country lane; the first to cover 3 km/2 mi is the winner. The All-Ireland Championship for this sport is held in early August in Armagh. Tourist offices carry details of local and province-wide events.

Shopping

The best of the North's traditional products, many made according to time-honored methods, include the exquisite linen and superior handmade woolen garments which you might associate only with the Republic of Ireland. Handmade lacework also remains a handicraft from the countrywomen of some Northern Ireland districts. Visitors should keep an eye out for hand-cut crystal from County Tyrone, and for the mellow, cream-colored parian china of Belleek. Traditional music CDs and the unadorned blackthorn walking stick are two good choices at the other end of the price scale.

Exploring Northern Ireland

Along the shores of the North's coasts and lakes, green, gentle slopes descend majestically into hazy, dark-blue water, against a background of more slopes, more water, and huge, cloud-scattered skies. The Antrim Coast is among the most scenic in all of Ireland; Dunluce Castle, the Giant's Causeway, and the small towns along the east coast offer the traveler a varied choice, and here the roads are excellent.

Belfast and Derry deserve a visit, if possible. Belfast is a naturally lively, friendly city with plenty of attractions; it is testimony to the spirit of the place that the long years of sectarian violence have not dimmed its vivacity. Derry too is looking to the future and has an appealing personality all its own. Much of the bad housing has been swept away; new developments are being built both in the suburbs and in the small city center, which is still enclosed by its medieval walls, making it one of Europe's best-preserved examples of a fortified town.

Enniskillen, in County Fermanagh, is bright and bustling; Lough Erne, surrounding it, has magnificent lake views, as well as one of Ireland's most impressive round towers, on Devenish Island. On the other side of Enniskillen stands Castle Coole, one of the most graceful mansions of the 18th-century, Anglo-Irish nobility.

Numbers in the text correspond to numbers in the margin and on the Northern Ireland and Belfast maps.

Great Itineraries

IF YOU HAVE 2 DAYS

The first day leave **Belfast** ①–⑪, the starting and ending point of your itinerary, and head north to the **Giant's Causeway** ⑰ and **Dunluce Castle** ⑱ via the **Glens of Antrim** ⑮, ending the day in ⚏ **Derry** ㉒. The next day head south to **Lough Erne** with visits to **Devenish Island** ㉖, the historic town of **Enniskillen** ㉗, and **Castle Coole** ㉘. Finish your second day back in ⚏ **Belfast.**

Malin Head

Tory Island

Fanad Head

Horn Head

Creeslough

Rathmullan

Milford

Ramelton

Malin

Culdaff

Carndonagh

Inishowen Head

Moville

Carrowkeel

Lough Foyle

Muff

Blackt
Aghadov

21 Limavady

B66

Letterkenny

Campsie

22 Derry

A2

Dungiven

B190

Glenties

Stranorlar

Castlefin

Lifford

Strabane

Sion Mills

Claudy

A6

B48

R. Foyle

B48

SPERRIN MOUNTAINS

DERRY

Tobermo

A6

BLUE STACK MOUNTAINS

Ballybofey

Donegal Town

Newtownstewart

A5

**Ulster-American Folk Park
and Ulster History Park 23**

Cookstown

A505

Pomeroy

Omagh

A29

A32

B46

TYRONE

Lower Lough Erne

A47

Kesh

B4

Dromore

Fintona

Dungannon

A4

24 Belleek

25 White Island

Castle Archdale
Country Park

A32

B82

Ballygawley

Clogher

A28

Augher

Aughnacloy

FERMANAGH

A46

Lough Melvin

Devenish Island

26

Ballinamallard

B80

Fivemiletown

27 Enniskillen

28 Castle Coole

Lisbellaw

A4

Florence Court

A32

Lisnaskea

Rosslea

Upper Lough Erne

Newtown Butler

R. Ern

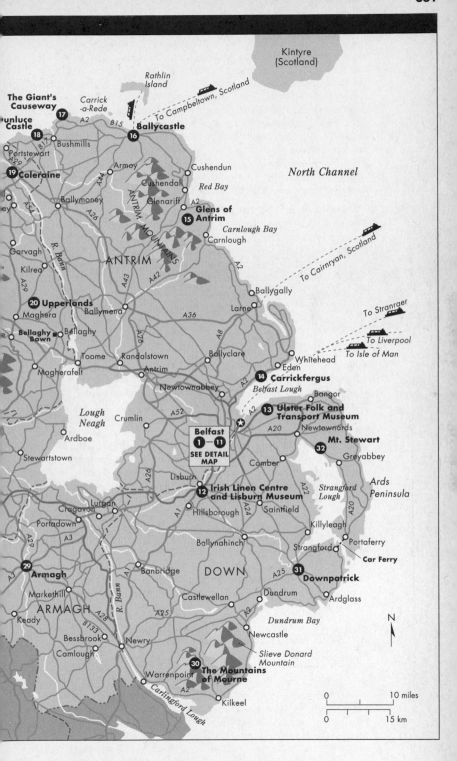

Kintyre
(Scotland)

Rathlin
Island

**The Giant's
Causeway**
Carrick
-a-Rede
17
A2
B15
unluce
Castle
18
Bushmills
To Campbeltown, Scotland
Ballycastle
16

Portstewart
19 **Coleraine**
A44
Armoy
Cushendun

North Channel

ey
A54
Ballymoney
A26
Cushendall
Glenariff
Red Bay
A2
**Glens of
Antrim**
15

Garvagh
R. Bann
ANTRIM
Carnlough Bay
Carnlough

Kilrea
A29
MOUNTAINS
A2

20 **Upperlands**
Ballymena
A43
A42
A36
A8
Ballygally
To Cairnryan, Scotland

Maghera
**Bellaghy
Bawn**
Bellaghy
A26
Larne
To Stranraer

Toome
Randalstown
Ballyclare
To Liverpool
To Isle of Man
Whitehead

Magherafelt
Antrim
Newtownabbey
A2
Eden
14 **Carrickfergus**
Belfast Lough
Bangor

*Lough
Neagh*
Crumlin
A52
**Ulster Folk and
Transport Museum**
13

Ardboe
★
A20
Newtownards
Mt. Stewart
32

Stewartstown
Belfast
1 — **11**
**SEE DETAIL
MAP**
Comber
Greyabbey

Lisburn
12 **Irish Linen Centre
and Lisburn Museum**
A22
*Strangford
Lough*
*Ards
Peninsula*

Cragavan
Lurgan
A26
A1
Hillsborough
A24
Saintfield
A20

Portadown
A3
Killyleagh
Portaferry

Banbridge
A1
R. Bann
Ballynahinch
Strangford
Car Ferry

29 **Armagh**
A28
DOWN
A25
31 **Downpatrick**

Markethill
ARMAGH
A25
Castlewellan
Dundrum
Ardglass

Keady
B133
A2
Dundrum Bay
N

Bessbrook
Newry
Newcastle
*Slieve Donard
Mountain*

Camlough
30
Warrenpoint
**The Mountains
of Mourne**
A2
Carlingford Lough
Kilkeel

0   10 miles

0   15 km

Leave **Belfast** ①–⑪ and head north to the **Glens of Antrim** ⑮ with a look at the characteristic towns of **Cushendall** and **Cushendun** before heading for the **Giant's Causeway** ⑰ and **Dunluce Castle** ⑱. Then follow the coast road via Downhill as far as 🎜 **Derry** ⑳, where you'll spend the night. The following day head south for **Belleek** ㉒ via the **Ulster-American Folk Park** and the **Ulster History Park** ㉓ and visit the islands of **White** ㉕ and **Devenish** ㉖. Spend the night in or around the historic town of 🎜 **Enniskillen** ㉗. The next day follow the road to **Armagh** ㉙, Ireland's ecclesiastical capital, its **Navan Centre,** and on to the **Mountains of Mourne** ㉚ via Bessbrook, Newry, and Kilkeel. Finish the day in 🎜 **Portaferry.** The last day make your way to Belfast along the shores of Strangford Lough to **Mount Stewart** ㉜ and the **Ulster Folk and Transport Museum** ⑬. Return to Belfast.

When to Tour Northern Ireland

The best time to tour the area is from May to September, when the weather is a little friendlier to travelers, especially in coastal and lake areas. Apart from holiday weekends there should be no trouble getting accommodation anywhere outside Belfast. If you go to Belfast, book in advance. Most of the city's cultural events—except early August's lively West Belfast Festival—take place in the autumn.

BELFAST

❶ *167 km/104 mi north of Dublin.*

Belfast was a great Victorian success story, an industrial boomtown whose prosperity was built on trade—especially linen and shipbuilding (the *Titanic* was built here). The key word here, of course, is *was*— linen is no longer a major industry, and shipbuilding has suffered severely. For the last two decades, news about Belfast was news about the Troubles. But the 1994 cease-fire began to change that; in the nearly three years since the cease-fire was first established, the North's capital city has benefitted from major hotel investment, gentrifying quaysides, a much heralded and brand-new performing arts center, and heartfelt efforts on the part of the tourist board to claim for the North their share of the visitors pouring into the Euro-buzzing Emerald Isle. On July 20, 1997, the cease-fire was officially reestablished, and few in Belfast have any doubts that there's no going back—that this embattled city is on its way to achieving a newfound identity. Like other places in the throes of a major historical transition, it's a fascinating place, with some of the warmest, wryest people in all of Ireland, a fair amount of new construction (although a disconcerting number of FOR RENT signs in and around its downtown commercial district), and most of all, a palpable will to move forward.

Some brief additional history: Before English and Scottish settlers arrived in the 1600s, Belfast was a tiny village called Béal Feirste (Sandbank Ford) belonging to Ulster's ancient O'Neill clan. With the advent of the Plantation period, Sir Arthur Chichester, from Devon in southwest England, received the city. His son was made Earl of Donegall; it was subsequently the second Marquis of Donegall's profligacy that led to the sale of his estates and hence the development of the city. Protestant French Huguenots fleeing persecution settled near here, bringing their valuable skills in linen work. In the 18th century, Belfast saw a phenomenal expansion—its population doubled in size every 10 years. Alas, a sectarian divide was always here: the Anglican gentry despised the Presbyterian artisans who, in turn, distrusted native Catholics. Belfast's growth continued at a dizzying speed. In 1849, Queen Victoria paid a visit (she is recalled in the names of buildings, streets, bars, monuments, and other places around the city), and in the same year, the university opened and took the name Queen's College. Nearly 40 years later, in 1888, Victoria granted Belfast its city charter. Today its population is 300,000—one-quarter of all Northern Ireland's citizens. In 1989, for the first time since the Great Famine, it saw its population swell slightly rather than decline.

Exploring Belfast

Belfast is a fairly compact city, its center is made up of roughly three contiguous areas that are easy to navigate on foot, though from the south end to the north it's about an hour's leisurely walk. At Belfast's southern end, the **Queen's University area** is easily the most appealing part of the city, with—first and foremost—the university, but also the Botanic Garden; entire streets of fine, intact 19th-century, two- and three-story buildings; and many good pubs, restaurants, and B&Bs. It's also the center of the city's nightlife. At this area's north end, between University Street and Shaftesbury Square, is the **Golden Mile**, with hotels, major civic and office buildings, and some restaurants, cafés and stores. The area doesn't quite glow the way the name suggests, but even if you don't end up staying here, you're likely to pass through it frequently. City Hall marks the northern boundary of the Golden Mile and the southern end of the (theoretically) pedestrian-only **central district**, which extends from Donegall Square north almost to St. Anne's Cathedral. Officially, only city buses and authorized delivery trucks are permitted to ply the streets here, but enforcement of this edict is inconsistent; still, it's overwhelmingly given over to pedestrians. This is the old heart of Belfast, and it's still a bustling, frenetic place—the equivalent of Dublin's Grafton and Henry streets in one—where both locals *and* visitors shop. Cafés, pubs, offices, and stores of all kinds—from department stores to the Gap and Waterstone's (there's even a Disney store), occupy the historic redbrick and white-Portland-stone buildings and modern in-fills that line its narrow streets. The buildings create a continuous street wall, giving the area a coherence that other parts of Belfast, where it seems like there's a parking lot on every block, don't quite share.

A Good Walk

Begin your stroll at the centrally located **Europa Hotel** ② and the **Grand Opera House** ③ next door. Even if you are just starting out, at least poke your head in the glorious **Crown Liquor Saloon** ④, right across the street from the Europa. Turn right from the Opera House onto Howard Street to reach Belfast's Donegall Square, dominated by its columned and domed **City Hall** ⑤. The gray building on Donegall Square's northwest corner is the **Linenhall Library.** Step around the corner of the library onto Donegall Place, Belfast's largely pedestrian-only, main shopping street. Stroll up to Royal Avenue, then turn right into Donegall Street to see **St. Anne's Cathedral** ⑥, and opposite it the main **Northern Ireland Tourist Board Information Centre** ⑦. Walk east down **High Street** into busy Victoria Street. From here, as you walk toward the leaning **Albert Memorial Clock Tower** ⑧, you'll see parts of Belfast's historic shipyards and two of the world's largest cranes. Return west to the city center by busy Chichester Street (the new Waterfront Hall [☞ Nightlife and the Arts, *below*] is on the river at the end of this street, one block east of Victoria Street). If you're ready for more walking, head south one block to May Street; you'll pass behind City Hall just before coming to Bedford Street, which turns into Dublin Road; together they constitute the eastern flank of the **Golden Mile.** Continue on to **Queen's University** ⑨, the **Botanic Gardens** ⑩, and the **Ulster Mu-**

seum ⑪, these last three in the **Stranmillis** area of the city. If you don't want to walk, head to Donegall Square East, where you can catch a black taxi or the Stranmillis or Malone buses.

TIMING

Belfast, a small, compact city, is suitable for walking tours. Owing to the Troubles, much of the city center is limited to pedestrians, and, therefore, traffic won't be a problem. The walking tour above could be completed in a couple of hours, but you'll want to leave yourself a little more time to browse at your leisure.

Sights to See

❽ **Albert Memorial Clock Tower.** Leaning a little to one side, not unlike Pisa's more notorious leaning landmark, the clock tower was named for Queen Victoria's husband, Prince Albert. The shipyard cranes beyond—Samson and Goliath—are two of the world's largest. The tower is not open to the public. ⊠ *Victoria Sq.*

★ ❿ **Botanic Gardens.** Laid out in 1827 on land that slopes down to the River Lagan, tucked between ☞ **Queen's University** and the ☞ **Ulster Museum,** these gardens are a glorious haven of grass, trees, flowers, curving walks, and wrought-iron benches. Begun in 1839 and completed in 1852, the **Palm House,** constructed of curved iron and glass, is the oldest such structure in the world—an early 19th-century technical marvel. The **Tropical Ravine House,** though not architecturally distinguished, has an outstanding collection of tropical flora. If you stay in the University area, this is easily the nicest place in Belfast for an early morning stroll or jog. ⊠ *Stranmillis Rd.,* ☎ *01232/324902.* ☞ *Free except during concerts.* ☉ *Gardens daily dawn–dusk; Palm House and Tropical Ravine House weekdays 10–5, weekends 2–5.*

★ ❺ **City Hall.** Built between 1898 and 1906, the massive, exuberant Renaissance-revival City Hall dominates Donegall Square. Before you go inside, take a stroll around Donegall Square, where you'll find statues of Queen Victoria; a monument commemorating the *Titanic* (built in Belfast); and a column honoring the U.S. Expeditionary Force, which landed in the city on January 26, 1942—the first contingent of the U.S. Army to land in Europe. When U.S. President Bill Clinton visited in November 1995, a huge reception was held on the green front lawn; it included a performance by hometown boy Van Morrison, whose "Days Like This" had become an unofficial anthem of the 1994–96 ceasefire. Head inside under the porte cochere at the front of the building. From the entrance hall, the base of what's called a **whispering gallery,** the view up to the heights of the 173-ft **Great Dome** is a feast for the eyes. With its complicated series of arches and openings, stained-glass windows, Italian marble inlays, decorative plasterwork, and paintings, this is Belfast's most exuberant public space—an homage to the might of the British empire. The guided tour gives access to the Council Chamber, Great Hall, and Reception Room, all upstairs. ⊠ *Donegall Sq.,* ☎ *01232/320202.* ☞ *Free.* ☉ *Mon.–Sat. 9–5; guided tours June–Sept., weekdays 10:30, 11:30, and 2:30; Oct.–May, weekdays 2:30.*

★ ❹ **Crown Liquor Saloon.** Directly opposite the Europa Hotel on Great Victoria Street and now owned by the National Trust (the U.K.'s official conservation organization), the Crown is one of Belfast's glories: A late-19th-century pub with richly carved woodwork around cozy snugs (cubicles), leather seats, colored tile work, and abundant mirrors. It's all been kept immaculate and is the perfect setting for a pint of Guinness and a plate of oysters. ⊠ *46 Great Victoria St.,* ☎ *01232/249476.* ☉ *Daily 11:30 AM–midnight.*

Albert Memorial
Clock Tower, **8**
Botanic Gardens, **10**
City Hall, **5**
Crown Liquor
Saloon, **4**
Europa Hotel, **2**
Grand Opera House, **3**
Northern Ireland
Tourist Board
Information Centre, **7**
Queen's University, **9**
St. Anne's
Cathedral, **6**
Ulster Museum, **11**

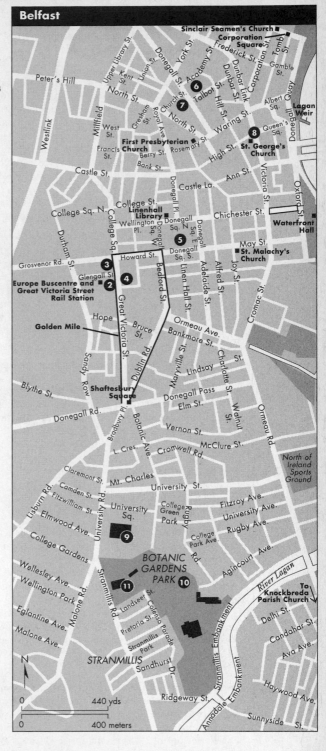

② Europa Hotel. A landmark in Belfast, the Europa is a monument to the resilience of the city in the face of the Troubles. The most bombed hotel in western Europe, it has been targeted by the IRA since the early '70s and refurbished countless times. Today it shows no signs of its explosive history. ⊠ *Great Victoria St. at Glengall St. (☞ Lodging, below).*

Golden Mile. The ☞ Europa and the ☞ Crown mark the northern end of this arrowhead-shape area extending from Howard Street on the north to Shaftesbury Square at the southern tip, bordered on the west by Great Victoria Street and on the east by Bedford Street/Dublin Road. The Crown (☞ *above*) is far from being the only impressive old pub on this stretch—most of Belfast's evening life takes place in bars and restaurants here. Alternatives include a number of nearby replicated Victorian bars with more locals and fewer visitors, such as **Robinson's,** next door to the Crown; **The Beaten Docket** on the other side of the Crown; **The Spinner's,** behind the Crown; and **Morrison's,** a haunt of media types on nearby Bedford Street.

★ **③ Grand Opera House.** Built in 1895, and an exuberant example of a Victorian theater, this redbrick and white stone structure has a richly decorated auditorium, where heavy gilt moldings, ornamental plasterwork, and frescoes depict Asian themes. It was the site of Van Morrison's 1984 album *Live at the Grand Opera House, Belfast.* By far the best way to see and enjoy the place is to attend a show; musicals, operas, and conventional theater all share billing. ⊠ *Great Victoria St.,* ☎ *01232/ 241919 (☞ Nightlife and the Arts, below).*

★ **High Street.** Off High Street, especially down to Ann Street (parallel to the south) run narrow lanes and alleyways called entries. Though mostly cleaned up and turned into chic shopping lanes, they still hang on to something of their former raffish character, including distinctive pubs with little-altered Victorian interiors. Among the most notable are: **The Morning Star** (⊠ Pottinger's Entry off High St.) with its large windows and fine curving bar; **White's Tavern** (⊠ Winecellar Entry off High St.), Belfast's oldest pub, founded in 1630, which, although considerably updated, still has a warm and comfortable ambience, with plush seats and a big, open fire; **Magennis's Whiskey Café** (⊠ 84 May St.), in splendid counterpoint to the Waterfront Hall's space-age ambience; and **McHugh's** (⊠ Queen's Sq.), in what is reckoned to be the city's oldest extant building, dating from 1710.

Linenhall Library. This gray building on Donegall Square's northwest corner is in fact a comfortable private library, founded in 1788. The library has an unparalleled collection of local material and ephemera relating to the Troubles; it is also a perfect hideaway for relaxing with a newspaper. On the walls are paintings and prints that show Belfast views and landmarks. Much of this artwork is for sale and makes excellent and original souvenirs or gifts. Library members can now peruse books while having a coffee and snack at the coffee shop inside the reading room. Membership costs U.K.£36 per year. ⊠ *17 Donegall Sq. N,* ☎ *01232/321707.* ☁ *Free.* ☉ *Mon.–Wed. and Fri. 9:30– 6, Thurs. 9:30–8:30, Sat. 9:30–4.*

⑦ Northern Ireland Tourist Board Information Centre. Located in an area now dominated by down market retail outlets, the main tourist office for the province may nonetheless be a pioneer in this neighborhood, as new zoning and planning efforts have targeted this area to become Belfast's version of Dublin's Temple Bar (☞ Chapter 2). As of press time (summer 1997), new construction is mostly just a promise, but as with Temple Bar, things may begin to change quickly. ⊠ *St. Anne's*

Court, 59 North St., ☎ 01232/246609, ℻ 01232/312424. ♡ Sept.–
June, Mon.–Sat. 9–5:15; July–Aug., Mon.–Sat. 9–7, Sun. 12–4.

NEED A
BREAK?

At the start of Royal Avenue, turn left into Bank Street to find **Kelly's Cellars** (✉ 30 Bank St., ☎ 01232/324835), a typical traditional bar with
character. Specialties include Ulster Fry and champ 'n' sausages. Two
centuries ago, Kelly's Cellars was the regular meeting place of a militant
Nationalist group, the Society of United Irishmen, whose leader, Wolfe
Tone (who was a Protestant), is remembered as the founder of Irish Republicanism.

⑨ Queen's University. Dominating University Road is Queen's University itself. The main university buildings, modeled on Oxford's Mag-
dalen College, were constructed in 1849 in a Tudor-revival style. The
long, handsome, redbrick and sandstone facade of the main building
has large leaded windows, with three square towers and crenellations
galore. **University Square,** really a terrace, is another treasure from the
same era. There is a new Seamus Heaney library. ✉ *Visitor Center,
Queen's University, University Rd., ☎ 01232/335253, ♡ May–Sept.,
Mon.–Sat. 10–4; Oct.–Apr., weekdays, 10–4.*

⑥ St. Anne's Cathedral. A somber heaviness and deep, rounded arches
are the hallmarks of the Irish neo-Romanesque style. Both elements
dominate at this large edifice, basilican in plan, begun at the turn of
this century. Lord Carson (1854–1935), who was largely responsible
for keeping the six counties inside the United Kingdom, is buried here
beneath a suitably austere gray slab. New landscaping around the
cathedral is one indication of the improving fortunes of this area. ✉
Donegall St., ☎ 01232/328332. ♡ Call for hrs.

Stranmillis. Once its own village, now the off-campus quarter, Stranmillis is one of Belfast's more appealing neighborhoods. Reached via
Stranmillis Road (on which the ☞ Ulster Museum sits), the neighborhood is home to home to "Little Paris," a stretch of shops and cafés
just up Stranmillis Road; tree-lined residential streets on which you'll
see scurrying academics; and a wide choice of ethnic eateries. The community reaches down to the riverside towpath along the Lagan. **Malone Road** joins the river farther south, close to the out-of-town **Giant's
Ring** (off Ballyleeson Road), a large, neolithic earthworks focused on
an impressive dolmen. To get this far, unless you're a vigorous walker
(it's possible to come all the way on the Lagan towpath), you'll be happier driving in a car or taking a bus: UlsterBus 13 passes close to the
site, and on the return journey it will take you back to Donegall
Square.

★ ⑪ Ulster Museum. Located in the southwest corner of the ☞ **Botanic Gardens,** the museum offers three floors devoted to the history and pre-
history of Ireland and, in particular, Northern Ireland, together with
a considerable collection of 19th- and 20th-century fine art. A skeleton of the now-extinct Irish giant deer is a highlight of the natural history section. Other major holdings are the trove of jewelry and gold
ornaments—as well as a cannon and other armaments—recovered
from the Spanish Armada vessel *Girona,* sunk off the Antrim coast in
1588. Perhaps the most imaginative, user-friendly sections are on the
first floor—one colorfully traces the rise of Belfast's crafts, trade, and
industry; the other tells the story of the Nationalist movement and explains the separation of the North from the rest of the country. Visitors have access to a small café on level three. ✉ *Stranmillis Rd., ☎
01232/383000. ☜ Free. ♡ Weekdays 10–5, Sat. 1–5, Sun. 2–5.*

OFF THE
BEATEN PATH

CHURCHES AROUND THE CITY – Belfast has so many churches you could go visit a different one nearly every day of the year and still not make it to all of them. The oldest house of worship is the Church of Ireland **Knockbreda Parish Church** (⊠ Church Rd. off A24 on the south side of city). This dark, sturdy, and atmospheric structure was built in 1737 by Richard Cassels, who designed many of Ireland's finest mansions. It quickly became *the* place to be buried—witness the vast, 18th-century tombs in the churchyard. Closer to the city center than Knockbreda, the **First Presbyterian Church** (⊠ Rosemary St.) dates from 1783 and has an interesting elliptical interior. It also hosts lunchtime concerts. **Church of Ireland St. George's** (⊠ High St.), built in 1816, has a tremendous Georgian portico and pretty box pews. Roman Catholic **St. Malachy's** (⊠ Alfred St.), built in 1844, features some fine stonework, including an astonishing fan-vaulted ceiling. By the riverfront is one of the most appealing churches, Presbyterian **Sinclair Seamen's Church** (Corporation Sq. off Donegall Quay). It was designed by Charles Lanyon, the architect of ☞ Queen's University, and has served the seafaring community since 1857. A maritime theme pervades the building; even the pulpit is shaped like a ship's prow.

Dining

With
contributions
from Vincent
Jamison

Cooking in Belfast is going through as profound a revolution as in Dublin. The choice of restaurants is more limited, but two or three of the best kitchens are a match for anything else in Ireland. The best chefs—Michael Deane, the Rankins, and Robbie Miller—have worked abroad and have brought back a sophisticated awareness of international cooking styles. Beyond the top-tier places, there are many spots where you'll find good-quality, fresh local fish or meat prepared in a simple style, but without much polish.

$$$–$$$$
★

✕ **Roscoff.** Celebrity TV chefs Paul and Jeanne Rankin, innovative cooks who travel widely, run this Golden Mile spot—consistently acclaimed as one of the best in the six counties and talked about a good deal throughout Ireland. The long, stylish room has a modern, minimalist decor, with chrome chairs and plain, buttermilk-color walls that show off local artwork. The Rankins (Paul is from Belfast, Jeanne from the Canadian Prairies) like to keep dishes interesting but simple. Marinated black olives and house bread greet diners. A typical starter is warm potato pancake with smoked salmon, crème fraîche, and chives. They also serve Asian-influenced dishes, such as pork with ginger, spicy fried cod with chili jam and a sesame vinaigrette, char-grilled Moroccan lamb with couscous, or roast monkfish with grilled tomatoes and black beans. The stellar desserts might include crème brûlée with fresh mango purée, or snap cigars filled with honey and pine nut ice cream served with sharp marinated plums. The Rankins do travel frequently, and the overall standards tend to suffer in their absence. ⊠ *Shaftesbury Sq. at end of Great Victoria St.,* ☎ *01232/331532. AE, DC, MC, V. Closed Sun. No lunch Fri.*

$$$

✕ **Deane's.** Chef Michael Deane became celebrated for his accomplished food in a tiny open kitchen in an equally tiny Victorian railroad station a few miles outside Belfast. Early in 1997, he sold out to move to a much larger two-story room—a brasserie downstairs and formal restaurant upstairs—in the center of Belfast, close to the City Hall. Deane's influences are eclectic, though he has worked in Bangkok, and Thai influences particularly shine in his subtle way with spices. Squab is a Deane specialty. He turns locally shot wild squab into a starter served in a light lasagna with celeriac leaves, spinach and foie gras, while for a main dish, he dry-marinates a squab with cinnamon sticks for two days, then serves it in an olive oil curried stock, with coriander seed and leaves, apple, ginger, and soy sauce, all on a bed of risotto. Although the restaurant is still in its infancy at press time (summer 1997), given Deane's record it's likely to become a standout. ⊠ *38–40 Howard St.,* ☎ *01232/56000. AE, MC, V. Closed Sun. and 2 wks in July.*

$$$ ✕ **Shanks.** Golf clubhouses don't usually spell welcome to peripatetic
★ gourmands, but Shanks is decidedly different. Robbie and Shirley Miller's cool temple to the contemporary, designed by London design guru Terence Conran, sits on a vast 3,000-acre estate. The bar is wood and zinc; David Hockney pieces hang on the walls. Like many of Ireland's best young chefs, Robbie Miller has done a stint under Roscoff's Paul Rankin, and he spares nothing to produce wonderful fish and game dishes. How demanding is he? A scuba diver handpicks large fresh scallops from the Copeland Islands in the Irish Sea, as they are more tender than scallops dredged by a trawler off the sea bottom. Typical starters include mille-feuille of lobster and eggplant, tempura of Dover sole with tagliatelle, and fine local prawns, served on a potato and basil frittata. Main courses include venison from deer shot on the estate and served in tender medallions with a sauce of red onion marmalade and wild mushrooms, or sliced breast of duck with polenta. For dessert, try the prune and Armagnac crème brûlée. Shanks is about 19 km/12 mi from Belfast, signposted off the Crawfordsburn Road (turn *right* off the Belfast–Bangor Road, or you can take a train from Belfast to Bangor and then a taxi). ⊠ *Blackwood Golf Centre, Crawfordsburn Rd., Bangor, Co. Down,* ☎ *01247/853313. Reservations essential. AE, MC, V. Closed 2 wks July. No lunch Sat.–Mon.*

$$ ✕ **Antica Roma.** Cecil B. DeMille's Rome cozies up with Little Italy in this restaurant's astonishing trompe l'oeil murals of the interior of a Roman villa, which justify anyone's first visit. The menu offers a surprisingly appealing Celtic interpretation of Italian cuisine. Seafood—especially clams, mussels, and squid, are particularly good. ⊠ *67 Botanic Ave.,* ☎ *01232/311121. AE, MC, V. Closed Sun. No lunch Sat.*

$$ ✕ **Café Society.** Though the little tables outside on the sidewalk in the summer may not give Café Society the Parisian air it may seek, upstairs the tables by the window offer the best view of bustling Belfast. The food is splendid too. Seared scallops with fennel and olives, or grilled buffalo mozzarella are among the distinctive starters. The mixed fish grill of grouper, red snapper, and salmon served with polenta is the delight amongst the entrées. ⊠ *3 Donegall Sq. W,* ☎ *01232/439525. MC, V. Closed Sun. No lunch.*

$$ ✕ **Manor House.** Much of Belfast's large Chinese community dines here late at night among lots of black lacquer on the staples of Cantonese cooking—dishes like beef in green pepper sauce and *char sui* (marinated and barbecued) pork. While you can't go wrong with these, this is a good place to abandon ordering by familiar numbers and take a risk with dishes such as duck's web or fish head soup, eel, and roasted pork belly. ⊠ *47 Donegall Pass,* ☎ *01232/238755. MC, V. No lunch weekends.*

$$ ✕ **Saints and Scholars.** Dirk Lakeman's University area restaurant complex offers four distinct sections, three of which make up Saints and Scholars (the fourth is Aubergines & Blue Jeans [☞ *below*]). The downstairs "library" has bookshelves on the walls, but the lively, noisy, and cheerful ambience could hardly be less studious. Upstairs, you'll find two calmer, more comfortable dining rooms (one with booths). Alsace onion flan is a particularly good starter; main dishes include a hearty cassoulet and wok-roasted monkfish. Many vegetarian dishes are available, both here and in Aubergines & Blue Jeans. The rich dessert crepes, supposedly made according to a recipe from

the Danish royal court, are truly fit for a king. ⊠ *3 University St.,* ☎ *01232/325137. Reservations essential upstairs. AE, DC, MC, V.*

$–$$$ ✕ **Chez Delbart.** Better known among locals by an alternative name—Frogities—this is the third and smallest of the trio of eateries founded by French exsubmariner M. Delbart, who promotes his heritage with the Eiffel Tower motif that adorns the exterior. Open in the evenings only, Frogities packs in a studenty clientele, particularly on weekends, who come back again and again for staples like the crepes and brochettes. ⊠ *10 Bradbury Place,* ☎ *01232/238020. AE, DC, MC, V. Closed Sun., Mon. No lunch.*

$–$$$ ✕ **La Belle Époque.** Relaxed and intimate, this well-established restaurant is charmingly French, with Art Nouveau decor reminiscent of Paris. The menu features smoked salmon stuffed with fish mousse in a horseradish sauce as an appetizer, and a main course of fillet of beef with seed mustard cream sauce. For dessert you can't go wrong with the freshly made fruit sorbets. The set-price lunch menu is an excellent value. ⊠ *103 Great Victoria St.,* ☎ *01232/323244. Reservations essential for dinner. AE, DC, MC, V. Closed Sun.*

$–$$$ ✕ **La Bohéme.** An accordion player who tinkers with Parisian tunes sets the tone at this sibling to La Belle Époque. The decor follows suit, looking as it does like a restaurant in a black-and-white French New Wave film of the fifties. The cuisine caps the French sensibility: chicken stuffed with prunes in red wine sauce and salmon with basil sauce are two typical entrées. ⊠ *103 Great Victoria St.,* ☎ *01232/240666. Reservations essential for dinner. AE, MC, V. Closed Sun. No lunch Sat.*

$–$$ ✕ **Nick's Warehouse.** Situated on a narrow cobbled street near the about-to-be-fashionable docks area, Nick Price's two establishments—wine bar downstairs, more sober atmosphere upstairs—are amongst Belfast's most relaxing watering holes. The busy street-level wine bar offers warm salads in a range of nut oils, plus tiny, tasty casseroles. Upstairs, favorites are duck with apple or halibut with langoustine and sweet peppers. The wine and imported beer lists are impressive. ⊠ *35 Hill St.,* ☎ *01232/439690. Reservations essential upstairs. AE, MC, V. Closed Sun. No dinner Mon.*

$–$$ ✕ **The Strand.** In the University area, this dark and intimate bistro with candlelighted tables attracts students and professors with its adventurous and unusual menu. Recommended dishes include Irish lamb noisettes and baked eggplant. For dessert try the cream-laden gâteaux. Several vegetarian entrées are available, such as a flan of broccoli and cashews. ⊠ *12 Stranmillis Rd.,* ☎ *01232/682266. AE, DC, MC, V.*

$ ✕ **Aubergines & Blue Jeans.** This downstairs café-bar, with its eclectic and modern decor, is part of the same building and management of Saints and Scholars (☞ *above*) and shares the same kitchen (though it has a separate entrance). The cuisine is simpler than its sister's, though, and it leans to hearty soups and hot, spicy baguettes. ⊠ *1 University St.,* ☎ *01232/233700. AE, DC, MC, V.*

Lodging

Airport and Environs

$$$ 🏨 **Aldergrove Airport Hotel.** This reliable, comfortable, modern four-story hotel at Belfast International Airport is 165 ft from the main terminal building and 27 km/17 mi from the center of Belfast. Rooms are generously equipped, with a double and a single bed, satellite TV, and full bathroom. The location is particularly good for anyone planning a brief visit to the province and not wishing to stay within the city. Nonsmoking rooms are available. ⊠ *Belfast International Airport, Belfast BT29 4AB,* ☎ *01849/422033,* 🖷 *01849/423500. 108 rooms with* *bath. Restaurant, bar, sauna, exercise room, meeting rooms. AE, DC, MC, V.*

$$$ 🏨 **Dunadry Inn and Country Club.** Set on 10 acres 10 minutes from Belfast International Airport, this spacious, whitewashed former mill is now a hotel of considerable charm. The renovation made use of large wooden components of the old mill's massive linen beetling (polishing) engines in the stairwell and a gallery over the bar. Its bedrooms are large (the best open onto the inner courtyard). The restaurant's cuisine is more competent than distinguished, but the excellent smoked eel from nearby Lough Neagh, brown trout from local streams, and poached salmon (when from the wild) are reliable. It is a popular spot for local weddings, so you may find yourself in the midst of a real Irish celebration. ⊠ *2 Islandreagh Dr., Dunadry, Co. Antrim,* ☎ *01849/ 432474,* 𝔽𝔸𝕏 *01849/433767. 67 rooms with bath. 2 restaurants, bar, indoor pool, hot tub, croquet, exercise room, meeting rooms. AE, MC, V.*

Golden Mile

$$$ 🏨 **Europa Hotel.** Another Hastings enterprise, this modern, high-rise, ★ city-center hotel has an explosive history, though you'd never know it. The polite, efficient management and staff are one of the reasons it has long attracted visiting journalists and business travelers. Though it doesn't offer much period charm, the overall ambience is comfortable. Bedrooms are blandly decorated, but they are warm, clean, functional, and offer all the modern conveniences. The Lobby Bar has traditional music on Friday evenings, and jazz on Saturday afternoons. ⊠ *Great Victoria St. at Glengall St., Belfast BT2 7AP,* ☎ *01232/ 327000,* 𝔽𝔸𝕏 *01232/327800. 184 rooms with bath. Restaurant, bar, café, laundry. AE, DC, MC, V.*

$$$ 🏨 **Holiday Inn Garden Court.** Centrally located between Great Victoria and Bedford streets in the city's Linen Conservation area, this modern seven-story hotel (until recently the Plaza) has a decor of muted grays and pretty, floral fabrics. Bedrooms and bathrooms are rather small and cramped, but all rooms have amenities including cable TV. The ground floor bar, the Spinners Inn, has a reputation for traditional music and *craic* (good conversation and fun); Amelia's Garden, the conservatory restaurant, is also a popular meeting place. ⊠ *15 Brunswick St., Belfast BT2 7GE,* ☎ *01232/333555,* 𝔽𝔸𝕏 *01232/232999. 83 rooms with bath. Restaurant, bar, room service, meeting rooms. AE, DC, MC, V.*

$$ 🏨 **Jurys Belfast Inn.** The first Jurys north of the border brings their flat-rate pricing formula (one price for up to three adults or two adults and two children) to the Golden Mile. Once you get past the forbidding warehouse-like exterior, a spacious tiled foyer and warm green and salmon hues await. Some rooms overlook College Square, the cricket lawn of the elegant dusky brick Royal Belfast Academical Institution, built in 1814 by Joan Soane. The Arches Restaurant offers well-prepared hotel fare. Tartan fabrics and dark wood decorate the Inn Pub, which serves a lunch-only hot buffet. ⊠ *Fisherwick Pl., Belfast BT2 7AP,* ☎ *01232/533500,* 𝔽𝔸𝕏 *01232/533511. 190 rooms with bath. Restaurant, bar, meeting rooms. AE, DC, MC, V.*

Outside the City Center

$$$$ 🏨 **Culloden Hotel.** Eight kilometers/5 miles from the city center on the A2, this 19th-century, former Scottish baronial mansion stands grandly amid 12 acres of parkland. It's the flagship in a fleet of hotels run by local hotelier Billy Hastings. Public areas have ornate woodwork, Louis XV chandeliers, decorative plasterwork, and stained glass. Guest rooms, both in the original section and in a newer wing, are decorated with silk-and-velvet fabrics and have fine views. The dining areas include the French Mitre Restaurant, with mahogany tables and a gar-

den view, and the Grill Bar, which serves both snacks and full meals. The hotel is in a peaceful part of town, close to the Ulster Folk and Transport Museum (☞ Side Trips, *below*). No-smoking rooms are available. ✉ *142 Bangor Rd., Holywood, Co. Down BT18 0EX,* ☎ *01232/ 425223,* FAX *01232/426777. 87 rooms with bath. Restaurant, grill, indoor heated pool, sauna, tennis court, croquet, squash, nightclub, laundry. AE, DC, MC, V.*

$ 🏠 **The Cottage.** Aptly named, this lovely little B&B in Mrs. Muldoon's immaculate, white home, 8 km/5 mi east of Belfast, has a charming, flower-filled garden in the back. It's as rural a setting as you're likely to find so close to the city center. The traditional country-house decor combines beautiful antiques and modern comforts in the bedrooms. ✉ *Mrs. E. Muldoon, 377 Comber Rd., Dundonald, Belfast BT16 0XB,* ☎ *01247/878189. 2 rooms with bath. No credit cards.*

University Area

$$$ 🏠 **Dukes Hotel.** Although this distinguished redbrick Victorian has only 21 rooms, it has such big-hotel amenities as a spacious lobby, extensive facilities, and a restaurant that leans toward healthful, local cuisine; the waterfall that runs down steps beside the stairs adds to the Dukes' unique character. The color scheme is smart gray, enlivened with plenty of greenery. The comfortable and well-laid-out rooms come with satellite TV; many have good views of the hills beyond the city. ✉ *65– 67 University St., Belfast BT7 1HL,* ☎ *01232/236666,* FAX *01232/ 237177. 21 rooms with bath. Restaurant, bar, sauna, exercise room, meeting rooms. AE, DC, MC, V.*

$$$ 🏠 **Wellington Park Hotel.** Formerly a private residence, this modernized establishment is among the best in this area of town. Many evening visitors enjoy the semi-singles bars, live music, and good food at this friendly hotel, run by the Mooney family. The quiet bedrooms are well designed, with built-in wooden furniture; some of them feature loft sleeping areas. 25 rooms were added in April 1997. ✉ *21 Malone Rd., Belfast BT9 6RU,* ☎ *01232/381111,* FAX *01232/665410. 75 rooms with bath or shower. Restaurant, bar, laundry service, meeting rooms. AE, DC, MC, V.*

$$ 🏠 **Ash-Rowan Guest House.** Award-winning former restaurateurs Sam
★   and Evelyn Hazlett own and run this outstanding B&B in a spacious Victorian home on a tranquil residential street. Every bedroom has been decorated in a tasteful, individual style, and each has a private bath and TV. Guests have access to a library. Breakfasts and dinners, prepared by the owners, are first-rate; the house is no-smoking. ✉ *Mrs. E. Hazlett, 12 Windsor Ave., Belfast BT9 6EE,* ☎ *01232/661758,* FAX *01232/663227. 4 rooms with bath. Dining room, library. MC, V. Closed Dec.*

$$ 🏠 **Madison's.** With the most stylish café-bar in the whole of the North, this is one of Belfast's liveliest spots, with a terrific location on tree-, café-, and shop-lined Botanic Avenue, just a few minutes' walk to the university. The hotel is run with gracious aplomb by the Mooney family (proprietors of the Dunadry Inn and Wellington Park Hotel [both ☞ *above*]). Its facade and public areas are done in a modish Barcelona-inspired take on Art Nouveau. The bedrooms, decorated in cool yellows and rich blues, are sparely furnished but comfortable. Guests have access to the extensive fitness facilities of Queen's University, including a terrific pool. ✉ *59 Botanic Ave., Belfast BT7 1JL,* ☎ *01232/ 330040,* FAX *01232/328007. 35 rooms with bath. Bar, restaurant, business services. AE, MC, V.*

$$ 🏠 **The Old Rectory.** Mary Callan's well-appointed house, built in 1896 as a rectory, is decorated in pastels and has good views of the countryside. Complimentary whiskey is served by the fire each evening. Rare

in Ulster B&Bs, a healthy alternative to the hearty Ulster Fry is served at breakfast. ✉ *Mary and Jerry Callan,* ✉ *148 Malone Rd., Belfast BT9 5LH,* ☎ *01232/667882. 4 rooms with bath. No credit cards.*

Nightlife and the Arts

Nightlife

Belfast has dozens of pubs packed with relics of the Victorian and Edwardian periods. Although pubs typically close around 11:30 PM, many city-center/Golden Mile nightclubs often stay open till 1:00 AM.

CITY CENTER/DOCKS

Pat's Bar (✉ 19–22 Prince's Dock St., ☎ 0232/744524) has regular first-rate sessions of traditional music. **Madden's Bar** (✉ 74 Smithfield St., ☎ 01232/244114) is another popular pub with traditional tunes. **The Kitchen Bar** (✉ 16 Victoria Sq. ☎ 01232/326473) is a real ale bar. Near the Kitchen Bar, **Bittles Bar** (✉ 70 Upper Church Ln., ☎ 01232/311088), on Victoria Square, has informal music sessions on weekends. **The Rotterdam** (✉ 54 Pilot St., ☎ 01232/746021) features folk, jazz, and blues performers. **Kelly's Cellars** (✉ 30–32 Bank St., ☎ 01232/324835), open since 1720, offers blues on Saturday nights.

GOLDEN MILE AREA

Robinsons Bars (✉ 38 Great Victoria St., ☎ 01232/247447), next to Crown Liquor Saloon, is a popular pub that appeals to a young crowd; it offers folk music in its Fibber Magee's bar Saturday, and rock in its Rock Bottom basement on Wednesday. **The Beaten Docket** (✉ 48 Great Victoria St., ☎ 01232/242986) is a noisier, modern pub that attracts an even younger crowd than Robinsons; it features up-to-the-minute music. **Limelight** (✉ 17 Ormeau Ave., ☎ 01232/325968) is a disco-nightclub with cabaret on Tuesday, Friday, and Saturday, and music on other nights. **Morrisons** (✉ 21 Bedford St., ☎ 01232/248458) has a music lounge upstairs where there's a mix of jazz, rock, and discussions for film buffs arranged by local directors in conjunction with the Northern Ireland Film Council; Saturdays, it's rock; Sundays, Irish music. At press time (spring 1997), the **Manhattan** (✉ 23 Bradbury Pl., ☎ 01232/233131), a.k.a. the M-Club, is Belfast's hottest club for dedicated clubbers.

UNIVERSITY AREA

The **Empire Music Hall** (✉ 42 Botanic Ave., ☎ 01232/328110), a deconsecrated church, is the city's leading music venue, with a varied music menu relieved by regular stand-up comedy nights (usually Tuesday) with much play on the Troubles. The **Botanic Inn** (✉ 23–27 Malone Rd., ☎ 01232/660460), known as the Bot to its student clientele, is a big, popular disco-pub. The **Eglantine Inn** (✉ 32–40 Malone Rd., ☎ 01232/381994), known as the Egg, faces the Bot across Malone Road. **Lavery's Gin Palace** (✉ 12 Bradbury Pl., ☎ 01232/327159) mixes old-fashioned beer drinking downstairs with dancing upstairs. The **Cutter's Wharf** (✉ 4 Lockview St., ☎ 01232/662501) down by the river south of the university, is at its best on summer evenings and at the Sunday jazz brunch.

The Arts

The Northern Ireland Arts Council (☎ 01232/381591) produces the monthly *Artslink* poster/brochure, which lists what's happening throughout Belfast and the North; it's widely available throughout the city.

ART GALLERIES

Ormeau Baths Gallery. The white airy spaces of this former municipal bathhouse now display the work of major contemporary international and Irish artists. ⊠ *18a Ormeau Ave.,* ☏ *01232/321402.* ☉ *Tues.–Sat. 10–5.*

Fenderesky Gallery. Iranian philosopher Jamshid Mirfenderesky's gallery is one of the few in Ireland whose stable of modern Irish artists are known throughout Europe. ⊠ *Crescent Arts Centre, 2 University Rd.,* ☏ *01232/235245.* ☉ *Tues.–Sat. 11:30–5:30.*

One Oxford Street. This spare, modern space facing the new Waterfront Hall features young, interesting, Northern Irish painters. ⊠ *1 Oxford St.,* ☏ *01232/310400.* ☉ *Weekdays 10–4.*

Bell Gallery. Nelson Bell's Victorian home in the leafy university suburbs is a mecca for many of Ireland's more traditional painters. ⊠ *13 Adelaide Park, Malone Rd.,* ☏ *01232/662998.* ☉ *Mon.–Sat. 9–6 and by appointment.*

FILM

Belfast has several city-center movie theaters that show the major new British and American box-office favorites. **Virgin Cinemas** (⊠ Dublin Rd., ☏ 01232/245700) has 10 screens. **Curzon Cinema** (⊠ Ormeau Rd., ☏ 01232/641373) has three screens. **Queen's Film Theatre,** Belfast's main art cinema, shows domestic and foreign movies on its two screens. ⊠ *University Sq. Mews, off Botanic Ave.,* ☏ *01232/244857.* ☉ *During university semesters only.*

MAJOR MULTI-PURPOSE VENUES

Grand Opera House. This beautifully restored Victorian playhouse has no company of its own but books shows from all over the British Isles and sometimes farther afield. It puts on a constant stream of West End musicals and plays of widely differing kinds, plus occasional operas and ballets. ⊠ *Great Victoria St.,* ☏ *01232/241919.* 🎫 *U.K.£4–U.K.£20.*

Waterfront Hall. Everyone in Belfast is singing the praises of this civic structure, which opened in January 1997. It looks like a hyper-modern version of Rome's Castel Sant'Angelo and houses both a major 2,235-seat concert hall (used for ballet, symphony, rock, and Irish music) and a 500-seat studio space (for modern dance, jazz, and experimental theater). The river-view Terrace Café restaurant and two bars make it convenient to eat or have a pint before or after your culture fix. ⊠ *Lanyon Pl.,* ☏ *01232/334400.*

MUSIC

King's Hall. Despite tricky acoustics, this is the major venue for pop and rock concerts. ⊠ *484 Lisburn Rd.,* ☏ *01232/665225.*

Ulster Hall. Home to the Ulster Orchestra, this has a splendid Victorian organ. Rock concerts are occasionally scheduled here. Led Zeppelin fans take note: The world stage debut of "Stairway to Heaven" took place here in March 1971. ⊠ *Linenhall St.,* ☏ *01232/323900.*

OPERA AND THEATER

Belfast Civic Arts Theatre. Near the University area, this venue specializes in comedies and lightweight productions. ⊠ *41 Botanic Ave.,* ☏ *01232/316900.*

Crescent Arts Centre. "The Crescent" to its habitués, this huge rambling black stone building off the campus end of Bradbury Place is a focus for experimental theater and dance, provocative art in its Fenderesky Gallery (☞ above), and experimental jazz. ⊠ *2–4 University Rd.,* ☏ *01232/242338.*

Lyric Theatre. In the south of Belfast, the Lyric stages thoughtful drama inspired by traditional and contemporary Irish culture. ⊠ *Ridgeway St.,* ☏ *01232/381081.* 🎫 *U.K.£6.50–U.K.£9.50; call to confirm prices.*

Old Museum Arts Centre (OMAC). A powerhouse of challenging, avant-garde theater and modern dance, OMAC also has a risk-taking art gallery. ✉ *7 College Sq. N,* ☎ *01232/235053.*

Opera Northern Ireland. Humperdinck's *Hansel and Gretel* is on the bill on the spring 1998 season (February 28–March 7); performances are at the Grand Opera House (☞ *above*). Britten's *A Midsummer Night's Dream*, Leoncavallo's *Pagliacci*, and Puccini's *Gianni Schicchi* will be performed in the fall (September 18–26). ☎ *01232/322338.*

Shopping

Belfast's main shopping streets include **Donegall Place, High Street, Royal Avenue,** and several of the smaller streets connecting with them. The whole area is mostly traffic-free (except for buses and delivery vehicles), so you'll find it pleasant to wander and window-shop. **Hoggs** (✉ 10 Donegall Sq. W, ☎ 01232/242232) stocks a good selection of linen, Tyrone crystal, Belleek china, and miniatures. **Castle Court** (✉ 10 Royal Ave., ☎ 01232/234591) is the city's largest, most varied upscale shopping mall. Opposite Castle Court, **Smyth's Irish Linens** (✉ 65 Royal Ave., ☎ 01232/242232) carries a large selection of handkerchiefs, tablecloths, napkins, and other linen goods, which make excellent souvenirs or presents. **Craftworks** (✉ Bedford House, 16–22 Bedford St., ☎ 01232/244465) stocks inexpensive crafts by local designers. The **Steensons** (✉ Bedford House, Bedford St., ☎ 01232/248268) sell superb, locally designed jewelry. If you've an interest in bric-a-brac, visit **St. George's Market,** a flea market you'll find on May Street every Tuesday and Friday morning. The long thoroughfare of **Donegall Pass,** running from Shaftesbury Square at the point of the Golden Mile, east to Ormeau Road, is a unique mix of biker shops and antiques arcades, and a good place to stroll.

Side Trips

The two sights below are closer to Belfast than the others covered in this chapter, so we've listed them here rather than as part of the full tour. However, none of the sites along the Ards Peninsula and the north coast is more than a few hours' drive from Belfast—perfect for day trips.

Irish Linen Centre and Lisburn Museum

In the 18th, 19th, and early 20th centuries, linen, a natural fabric woven from the fibers of the flax plant, was the basis of Ulster's most important industry—and thus of much of its folk history and song. A century ago, 240,000 acres were given over to flax, whose pretty blue flowers sparkle for just a week in early July, and 400 acres were designated as "bleach greens," where the woven fabric whitened in the summer sun. Eventually, American cotton and Egyptian flax killed off the mass-production linen trade, which had been centered on Lisburn, in mills powered by the River Lagan. What now survives of the of the linen industry does so by producing high-quality designer fabrics, plus old-fashioned expensive damask.

⑫ Today at the **Irish Linen Centre and Lisburn Museum** (12 km/8 mi southwest of Belfast), a series of rooms traces this history. Weaving is demonstrated on a turn-of-the-century hand loom. If you're looking for a more intensive investigation of the linen industry, tours of the **Linen Homelands** are offered. The 6-hour bus tour (with a break for lunch) visits three different sites: the Irish Linen Centre, a modern, operational linen spinning and weaving factory, plus the last working water-powered scutching mill (where flax fibers are broken down) in Ireland. In July you may catch the splendid sight of just a few fields of flax flowers bending in the light summer breeze. Tours are given May–September, Wednesdays 10–4 (the cost is U.K.£10, lunch extra), and begin at the Banbridge Gateway Tourist Information Centre (✉ 200 Newry Rd., Banbridge, ☎ 018206/23322). Reservations are essential for this more intensive tour. ✉ *Market Sq., Lisburn,* ☎ *01846/353246.* ✐ *U.K.£2.75.* ⊘ *Apr.–Sept., Mon.–Sat., 9:30–5:30, Sun. 2–5:30; Oct.– Mar. Mon.–Sat., 9:30–5.*

Ulster Folk and Transport Museum

⑬ Devoted to the province's social history, the **Ulster Folk and Transport Museum** is 16 km/10 mi northeast of Belfast, set in some 70 acres around Cultra Manor, encircled by a larger park and recreation area. It brings the North's past vividly to life with a score of reconstructed buildings brought here from around the region; these structures represent different facets of Northern life—a traditional weaver's dwelling, terraces of Victorian town houses, an 18th-century country church, a village flax mill, a farmhouse, and a rural school. You start your visit with the **Folk Gallery,** which explains the background of each building. Across the main road (by footbridge) is the **Transport Museum,** with exhibits showing every kind of transport, including a miniature railway on Saturdays during the summer. ✉ *Cultra, near Holywood,* ☎ *01232/ 428428.* ✐ *U.K.£3.30.* ⊘ *Apr.–June and Sept., weekdays 9:30–5, Sat. 10:30–6, Sun. noon–6; July–Aug., Mon.–Sat. 10:30–6, Sun. noon– 6; Oct.–Mar., weekdays 9:30–4, weekends 12:30–4:30.*

AROUND COUNTIES ANTRIM AND DERRY

Starting and finishing in Belfast, you can take a circular route through a portion of the North that allows you to pass through some fair-size towns, as well as drive in open country through splendid natural scenery. From medieval towns such as Carrickfergus, you'll travel past the natural wonder of the Giant's Causeway and the man-made brilliance of the castle at Dunluce before arriving in the old walled city of Derry.

Carrickfergus

⑭ *16 km/10 mi northeast of Belfast, 24 km/15 mi south of Larne.*

Carrickfergus, on the shore of Belfast Lough, grew up around its ancient castle. When the town was enclosed by ramparts at the start of the 17th century, it was the only English-speaking town in Northern Ireland. Not surprisingly, this was the loyal port where William of Orange chose to land on his way to fight the Catholic forces at the Battle of the Boyne in 1690. However, the English did have one or two small setbacks, including the improbable victory in 1778 of John Paul Jones, the American naval hero, over the British warship HMS *Drake.* (That, by the way, was America's first naval victory during the Revolutionary War.) After the sea battle, the inhabitants of Carrickfergus stood on the waterfront and cheered Jones because they supported the American Revolution.

Carrickfergus Castle, one of the first and one of the largest of Irish castles, is still in good shape. An impressive sight, perched on a rock ledge, it was built in 1180 by John de Courcy, provincial Ulster's first Anglo-Norman invader. The castle stood as a bastion of British rule right up until 1928, at which time it was still an English garrison.

Walk through the castle's 13th-century gatehouse into the Outer Ward; continue into the Inner Ward, the heart of the fortress, where the five-story Keep stands, a massive, sturdy building with walls almost 8 ft thick. Inside the Keep, you'll find the Cavalry Regimental Museum with historic weapons and an impressive, vaulted Great Hall. These days Carrickfergus Castle hosts entertaining medieval banquets (inquire at a local tourist office); if you're here at the beginning of August, you can enjoy the annual Lughnasa festival, a lively medieval costume entertainment. ☎ *01960/351273.* 🖼 *U.K.£3.* ☉ *Apr.–Sept., Mon.–Sat. 10–6; Oct.–Mar., Mon.–Sat. 10–4.*

The **Andrew Jackson Centre,** in a thatched cottage a mile northeast of Carrickfergus, tells the tale of U.S. President Jackson, whose parents emigrated from here in 1765. This cottage was not their home; it's a reconstruction of an 18th-century thatched cottage thought to resemble it. ⊠ *Boneybefore, Larne Rd.,* ☎ *01960/366455.* ☉ *Apr.–May, weekdays 10–4, weekends 2–4; June–Sept., weekdays 10–6, weekends 2–6.*

Structures that remain from Carrickfergus's past are **St. Nicholas's Church,** built by John de Courcy in 1205 and remodeled in 1614, and the handsomely restored North Gate in the town's medieval walls. Dobbins Inn on High Street has been a popular hotel for more than three centuries.

Dining and Lodging

$$$ ✕🖼 **Galgorm Manor.** The Gillies bar is decidedly Irish, the dining room cosmopolitan, the manor house itself photogenic, and the estate grounds—where guests may shoot, go riding, practice archery—cinematic. The River Maine, a good brown-trout river, flows within sight of many of the large rooms. Galgorm is off the A42 3 km/2 mi west of Ballymena, 32 km/20 mi inland of Larne, 40 km/25 mi north of Belfast. ⊠ *136 Fenaghy Rd., Ballymena BT42 1EA,* ☎ *01266/881001,* 𝔽𝔸𝕏 *01266/880080. 23 rooms with bath. Restaurant, bar, golf privileges, horseback riding, fishing, meeting rooms. AE, MC, V.*

En Route As you head away from Carrickfergus on the A2, you'll pass through the village of Eden, where **Castle Dobbs** was the home of Arthur Dobbs, the 18th-century British governor of North Carolina. Signposted on the left, 2½ km/1½ mi off the road, **Dalway's Bawn,** built in 1609, is the best surviving example of an early *bawn,* or fortified farmhouse occupied by a Protestant Planter.

Glens of Antrim

★ ⑮ *Nine glens in the 86 km/54 mi between Larne and Ballycastle.*

Soon after Larne, the coast of County Antrim becomes spectacular. Wave upon wave of high, green hills curves down into the hazy sea. Lower slopes are lush and intensively farmed, but rugged, too, while green moorland covers the rounded summits. Broad, rich glens, or valleys, cut through the hills toward the sea. A narrow, winding, two-lane road (the A2, known locally as the Antrim Coast Road) hugs the slim strip of land between the hills and the sea, bringing you to the magnificent Glens of Antrim, nine wooded river valleys running down from the escarpment of the Antrim Plateau to the eastern shore. Until the opening of this road in the 1830s, the glens were home to isolated farming communities—people who adhered to the romantic mystical Celtic legends and the everyday use of the Irish language. The Glens are worth several days of serious exploration. Even narrower B-roads curl west off the A2, up each of the beautiful glens where trails await walkers.

Carnlough

24 km/15 mi north of Larne, 22½ km/14 mi east of Ballymena, 43 km/27 mi from Ballycastle.

A little resort made of white limestone, Carnlough overlooks an endearing harbor within stone walls. The sandy beaches can be reached by crossing over the limestone bridge on main street, built especially for the Marquis of Londonderry. The small harbor, once a port of call for fishermen, now shelters pleasure yachts. Carnlough is surrounded by a group of hills that descend 1,000 ft into the sea. There is a small tourist office inside the post office.

Dining and Lodging

$$$–$$$$ ✕🏨 **Londonderry Arms Hotel.** This ivy-covered, traditional inn right on Carnlough Harbour, built as a coaching inn in 1848, has a lovely, seaside garden; gorgeous antique furnishings; regional paintings and maps; lots of fresh flowers; and Georgian-period decor. In 1921 Sir Winston Churchill inherited it; since 1947 it has been owned and run by the hospitable O'Neill family. A large addition in 1997 added 17 rooms. Both old and new rooms have lovely Georgian antiques and luxurious fabrics, and they are immaculately kept. The restaurant serves a substantial, traditional Irish meal that relies on fresh, local seafood, simply prepared; try the seafood gratiné or the lobster; homemade wheat bread is a perfect accompaniment. Traditional Irish music is performed during the summer months and every other Friday throughout the year. ✉ *20 Harbour Rd., Carnlough, Co. Antrim BT44 0EU,* ☎ *01574/885255,* 🖷 *01574/885263. 35 rooms with bath. Restaurant. AE, DC, MC, V.*

$$ 🏨 **Ballygally Castle.** At the Larne end of the North Antrim coast drive, 40 km/25 mi from Belfast, stands an impressive, turreted castle that faces Ballygally Bay. Built by a Scottish lord in 1625, the castle cheerfully invites visitors to enjoy a good night's sleep, a hearty breakfast, and its Dungeon Bar, whose substantial stone walls justify the name. Modern facilities integrate with old Scots Baronial design, though a recent extension jars with the original style. Bedrooms, some in the castle turrets—one complete with m' Lady's ghost—have been individually decorated with comfortable furnishings. In the dining room a decent table d'hôte evening meal is served (to music, on Saturdays), and a Sunday high tea is also available. ✉ *274 Coast Rd., Ballygally, Co. Antrim BT40 2RA,* ☎ *01574/583212,* 🖷 *01574/583681. 30 rooms with bath. Dining room, bar, fishing, baby-sitting. MC, V.*

En Route   Between Carnlough and Ballycastle the scenery becomes even more stunning. Glenariff, opening onto Red Bay at the village of Glenariff (also known as Waterfoot), is considered the loveliest of the glens. A good day trip is **Glenariff Forest Park,** the largest and most accessible of Antrim's glens. Inside are picnic facilities and dozens of good hikes, notably the 5½ km/3½-mi **Waterfall Trail** (follow the blue arrows), which offers outstanding views of Glenariff River and its waterfalls, and passes by small but swimmable loughs. Detailed maps are available at the visitor center, which has a small self-serve cafeteria. ✉ *98 Glenariff Rd.,* ☎ *012667/58232,* 🖷 *U.K.£1,* ☉ *Nov.–May, daily 8 AM–8 PM, June–Oct., daily 8 AM–10 PM.*

At Cushendall, you'll see a curious, fortified square tower of red stone—a 19th-century jailhouse—standing at a crossroads in the middle of the village. If you would like a break from the Antrim coast, stay on the A2 direct to Ballycastle. But if you would prefer to stay by the sea, turn left at the tower in the direction of **Cushendun,** a tiny jewel of a village. From this part of the coast you can see the Mull of Kintyre on the Scottish mainland. If you've got firm nerves, take the narrow and precipitous coastal road north past dramatically beautiful **Murlough Bay** to **Fair Head;** others will prefer to rejoin the A2 via the

B92, left, after a few miles and descend—passing on the left the ruins of the Franciscans' 16th-century **Bonamargy Friary**—into Ballycastle.

Ballycastle

🔟 *20 km/13 mi east of Bushmills, 16 km/10 mi east of Giant's Causeway.*

Ballycastle is the main resort town in the glens, at the northern end of the Glens of Antrim drive. People from the province flock here in the summer. The town is shaped like an hourglass—with its strand and dock on one end, its pubs and chippers on the other, and the ½ mi Quay Road in between. Beautifully aged shops and pubs line its Castle, Diamond, and Main streets.

From Ballycastle town you have a view of L-shape **Rathlin Island,** where in 1306 the Scottish king Robert the Bruce took shelter in a cave and, according to legend, was inspired to continue his armed struggle against the English by watching the patience of a spider spinning its web. It was on Rathlin in 1898 that Guglielmo Marconi set up the world's first cross-water radio link, from the island's lighthouse to Ballycastle. Rathlin provides a good sampling of the North's terrain, with cliffs and boulders on the island's west end, circular sandy beaches near the harbor, and velvet-green, rolling hills traversed by stone hedges in between. Bird-watching and hiking are the island's main activities. Unless the sea is extremely rough, a ferryboat makes regular journeys (twice daily in winter, more frequently in summer). Although the island is only 9½ km/6 mi away from shore, the trip can take 45 minutes; make sure that you'll be able to return the same day.

Every year since 1606, on the last Monday and Tuesday in August (the 24th and 25th in 1998), Ballycastle has hosted the **Oul' Lammas Fair,** a modern version of the ancient Celtic harvest festival of Lughnasa (Irish for "August"). Ireland's oldest fair, this is a very popular, two-day event at which sheep and wool are still sold alongside the wares of more modern shopping stalls. Treat yourself to the fair's traditional snacks, "dulse" (sun-dried edible seaweed) and "yellow man" (rock-hard yellow toffee).

Just off the coast, 8 km/5 mi west of Ballycastle, you can see the **Carrick-a-Rede** rope bridge, which spans a 60-ft gap between the mainland and Carrick-a-Rede Island. Carrick-a-Rede means "rock in the road" and refers to the island (the rock) that stands in the path of the salmon who follow the coast as they migrate to their home rivers to spawn. For the past 150 years salmon fishermen have set up the rope bridge in late April, taking it down again after the salmon season ends. Crossing over to the rocky outcrop, they cast nets in the frothy water and catch throngs of salmon as they rush by. The bridge is open to the public and offers some heart-stopping views of the crashing waves below. ⊠ *On the B15.* 🎫 *Free.* ☉ *Apr.–Sept., daily.*

The Giant's Causeway

★ 🔷 *19⅓ km/12 mi west of Ballycastle, 86 km/54 mi north of Belfast.*

The Giant's Causeway is Northern Ireland's premier tourist attraction—a singularly strange natural phenomenon consisting of a mass of 37,000 mostly hexagonal pillars of volcanic basalt, clustered like a giant honeycomb and extending hundreds of yards into the sea. Their creation dates back roughly 60 million years: Boiling lava, erupting from an underground fissure that stretched from Northern Ireland to the Scottish coast, crystallized as it burst into the sea, and formed according to the same natural principle that structures a honeycomb. "It's the original Lego building blocks," is how Philip Watson, the overseer of the site for the National Trust describes it. Less reliably, according to legend the columns were created when the legendary hero Fionn MacCool threw stepping-stones into the sea to make a causeway over to the Scottish island of Staffa.

To reach the causeway, you can either walk the 1½ km/1 mi trip down a long scenic hill or take a minibus from the visitor center. To the west of the causeway, **Port-na-Spania** is the spot where the 16th-century Spanish Armada galleass *Girona* went down on the rocks. The ship was carrying an astonishing cargo of gold and jewelry, some of which was recovered in 1967 and is now on display in the Ulster Museum in Belfast (☞ Belfast, *above*). Beyond that, **Chimney Point** is the name given to one of the causeway structures on which the Spanish fired, thinking that it was Dunluce Castle, which is 8 km/5 mi west.

Arriving by car at the Giant's Causeway, at first you'll reach a cliff-top parking lot beside the **visitor center,** which provides displays about the area and an audiovisual exhibition explaining the formation of the causeway coast. From the tearoom, enjoy panoramic sea views while you enjoy some tea, cakes, and scones. ⊠ *Causeway Head, near Bushmills,* ☎ *012657/31855.* ▦ *Visitor center: audiovisual exhibition U.K.£1, static exhibition U.K.50p, parking U.K.£2.* ☉ *Causeway: freely accessible; visitor center: May, June, Sept., Oct. daily 10–6; July and Aug. daily 10–7; Nov.–Apr. daily 10–5 (closes earlier according to demand).*

Bushmills

10 km/6 mi northeast of Coleraine, 14 km/8½ mi east of Portstewart.

The oldest licensed distillery in the world, Bushmills was first granted a charter by King James I in 1608, though historical records refer to a distillery here as early as 1276. Bushmills produces the most famous of Irish whiskeys, and what is widely regarded as the best. Enthusiasts who would like to see how it is made should call ahead to join one of the guided, 1-hour tours, which begin in the mashing and fermentation room, then proceed to the maturing and bottling warehouse. Tours are topped off with a complimentary shot of *uisce beatha*, the "water of life," in the visitor center–cum–gift shop. ⊠ *Bushmills Distillery, Bushmills,* ☎ *012657/31521.* ▦ *U.K.£2.50,* ☉ *Apr.–Oct., Mon.–Thurs. 10–4, Mon.–Sat. 10–4; Nov.–Mar., weekdays 10–4.*

Lodging

$$ ▦ **The Bushmills Inn.** Just off the diamond (as main squares are called in many Ulster towns) Roy Bolton and Richard Wilson have overseen a cozy transformation of an old coaching inn. Stripped pine, peat fires, and gas lights warm the public rooms. The livery stables now house the informal restaurant, serving fresh and hearty food, and the bar, always full of good spirits; out front are three tables so that you can dine and drink al fresco. The distillery is a stroll away, as is the salmon-filled River Bush. ⊠ *25 Main St., Bushmills BT57 8QA,* ☎ *012657/32339,* FAX *012657/32048. 11 rooms with bath. Restaurant, bar, meeting rooms. AE, MC, V.*

Dunluce Castle

★ ⑱ *8 km/5 mi west of Giant's Causeway.*

Halfway between Portrush and the Giant's Causeway, dramatically perched on a cliff at land's end, Dunluce Castle is one of the North's most evocative ruins. Originally a 13th-century Norman fortress, it was captured in the 16th century by the local MacDonnell clan chiefs—the so-called "Lords of the Isles"—who enlarged it, making it an important base for ruling northeastern Ulster. Maybe they expanded the castle a little too much, for in 1639 faulty construction caused the kitchens and the cooks to plummet into the sea during a storm. Nearby is the **Dunluce Centre,** an entertainment complex comprising rides, a live show about myths and legends, a viewing tower, shops, and a restaurant. ⊠ *Port Ballintree,* ☎ *01265/824444.* ⊑ *All attractions U.K.£4.* ⊘ *Mar.–Sept., weekdays noon–5, weekends 10–9; July and Aug., daily 10–9.*

Portrush and Portstewart are the two subsequent seaside towns. Portrush's main attraction is the **Royal Portrush Golf Club** (☞ Chapter 10), one of Ireland's premier, championship courses. **Portstewart Strand,** to the west of town, has some of Ireland's best surfing.

Dining

$$$ ✕ **Ramore Restaurant and Wine Bar.** On Portrush's picturesque harbor, where a haven of boats are tucked away from the resort's brasher amusements, this spot does double duty. The daily offerings at the wine bar ($) are posted on a blackboard. Upstairs, the draws are panoramic views and chef George McAlpin's Pacific Rim–inflected way with local Atlantic fish and shellfish. Start with the fan of tempura prawns served with diced peppers and Mexican tostadas. Main courses include char-grilled Thai chicken and monkfish with succulent scallops. Grand Marnier soufflé is an indulgent way to finish. ⊠ *The Harbor; restaurant:* ☎ *01265/824313; wine bar:* ☎ *01265/823444. MC, V in restaurant only. Restaurant: Closed Sun.–Mon. No lunch; wine bar: Closed Sun.*

Coleraine

⑲ *10 km/6 mi south of Portrush, 13 km/8 mi southwest of Dunluce Castle, 48 km/30 mi east of Derry.*

Dating from the 5th century BC, Coleraine became the seat of the University of Ulster in 1968. The River Bann, flowing through the town, here divides the county of Antrim from that of Derry. As well as being a fishing town, Coleraine boasts an important linen industry.

Some of Ireland's oldest remaining relics, dating from the very first inhabitants of this island (about 7000 BC), were found on Mountsandel just to the south of Coleraine. One of the many dolmens in this region is called Slaghtaverty after an evil dwarf who mesmerized women using his magical harp. He was buried alive and upside down by the great Fionn McCool (maker of the Giant's Causeway), so that the sounds of his harp would not escape from the ground.

Lodging

$$ ▥ **Greenhill House.** This charming, Georgian country house, about 13 km/8 mi south of Coleraine, is run by Elizabeth and James Hegarty and provides a peaceful retreat. Guests enjoy the pleasantly decorated bedrooms, the substantial breakfasts, and the excellent dinners of locally caught fish, Ulster beef, and homemade bread and cakes. ⊠ *24 Greenhill Rd., Aghadowey, Co. Londonderry BT51 4EU,* ☎ *01265/ 868241. 6 rooms with bath. Dining room. No credit cards. Closed Nov.– Feb.*

$ ▥ **Camus House.** Follow the road along the Bann valley south from Coleraine 6½ km/4 mi out of town, and you'll arrive at this appealing farmhouse, parts of which date from 1685. Today it's a relaxed and gracious guest house, elegantly furnished, with a snug sitting room with a stone fireplace. Proprietor and salmon fisher Josephine King provides a friendly atmosphere and a hearty breakfast. The pleasant bedrooms, decorated in pastel colors, have tasteful, modern furnishings, reading lamps, and large closets. ⊠ *27 Curragh Rd., Co. Londonderry BT51 3RY,* ☎ *01265/42982. 3 rooms share 1 bath. Breakfast room. No credit cards.*

Upperlands

20 *32 km/20 mi southwest of Coleraine, 56 km/35 mi northwest of Belfast.*

Upstream from Coleraine, the River Bann—rich in eels for roasting and smoking and in salmon for poaching—flows out of Lough Neagh. On its left bank are the towns and fortifications of the 17th-century planters, built by London's Livery Companies, whose descendants developed the linen industry. In the tiny town of Upperlands, visitors can tour **William Clark and Sons,** a working linen mill where age-old wooden machinery beetles (puts a shine on) threads for the linen linings of suits for England's Royals. There is also a small linen museum. ⊠ *Upperlands, Maghera,* ☎ *01648/42214.* 🖃 *U.K. £1.* ⊙ *Mon.–Thurs. 9–5, Fri. 9–noon.*

Dining and Lodging

$$$ ✕🏨 **Ardtara House.** A 19th-century Victorian home built by a de-
★ scendant of the founder of the town's first linen mill, Ardtara is the North's finest country house. In the mid-'90s, Maebeth Fenton—a New York–based public relations executive (her clients include the Northern Ireland Tourist Board) who grew up nearby—oversaw a luxurious renovation. The gorgeously furnished terra-cotta and pink drawing room, with original plaster moldings and a marble fireplace, looks out on the wide front lawn and tennis court. The eight large bedrooms are furnished with antiques; each has a fireplace, as do some of the elegantly appointed marble bathrooms. The hotel's restaurant is in the former snooker room, with dark paneled walls, a wallpapered hunting scene, and a huge skylight. Patrick McLarnon, the gifted young chef, prepares a daily menu that takes advantage of locally available produce. Starters might include potato and nettle soup or hot smoked salmon on a warm potato, olive, and bean salad. Peat-smoked rack of lamb with champ and rosemary gravy, or salmon with champagne sauce are stellar entrées. Plum and almond tart with angelica ice cream is one of the fine dessert offerings. You'll feel the calm and relaxed atmosphere Fenton, manager Mary Breslin, and the rest of the staff strive for the moment you walk in, and you won't want to leave it behind. ⊠ *8 Gorteade Rd., Upperlands, Co. Londonderry BT46 5SA,* ☎ *01648/ 44490,* 🖹 *01648/45080. 8 rooms with bath. Restaurant, tennis court, meeting room. AE, MC, V.*

OFF THE **BELLAGHY BAWN** – Fifteen kilometers (8 miles) southeast of Upperlands,
BEATEN PATH Bellaghy Bawn is a new, not wholly congealed hybrid museum. Half of it is devoted to the history and archaeology of the bawn itself, a representative Plantation-era stronghold, and the surrounding area, including nearby Lough Beg. The other half celebrates the life and work of Seamus Heaney, Ireland's fourth and most recent Nobel Literature laureate, who was born at nearby Mossbawn. It's Heaney's manuscripts, books, and other memorabilia that make this a must-visit for anyone interested in his work. ⊠ *Castle St., Bellaghy,* ☎ *01648/386812.* 🖃 *U.K. £2.* ⊙ *Oct.– April, Tues–Fri., 9–5, Sat. 12–4, Sun. 2–4; April–Sept., Tues–Sat. 10–6, Sun. 2–6.*

Limavady

㉑ *21 km/13 mi west of Coleraine, 34 km/21 mi northwest of Upperlands, 27 km/17 mi east of Derry.*

In 1851, at No. 51 on Limavady's Georgian main street, Jane Ross noted down the tune played by a traveling fiddler and called it "Londonderry Air," better known now as "Danny Boy." While staying at an inn on Ballyclose Street, William Thackeray (1811–63) wrote his rather lustful poem "Peg of Limavaddy" about a barmaid. Among the many Americans descended from Ulster emigrants was President James Monroe, whose relatives came from the Limavady area.

Dining and Lodging

$$$$ ✕🏨 **Radisson Roe Park Hotel & Golf Resort.** One of the North's most deluxe resorts, this sits on 155 acres of countryside on the banks of the River Roe. Bedrooms are decorated in cream and blue, with satellite TV and other amenities. Guests have a variety of dining options: The Courtyard Restaurant is formal and international; the Coach House, an American brasserie, is a relaxed place where golfers congregate; O'Cahan's Bar takes its name from a local chieftain besieged on a riverside promontory whose Irish wolfhound leapt an impossible chasm to bring relief—doubtless an inspiration to golfers flagging at the ninth. ⊠ *Roe Park, Limavady, Co. Londonderry BT49 9LB,* ☎ *015047/22222,* ℻ *015047/22313. 64 rooms with bath. 2 restaurants, 2 bars, indoor pool, beauty salon, sauna, steam room, golf, aerobics, fishing, horseback riding, baby-sitting, meeting rooms. AE, DC, MC, V.*

Derry

㉒ *109 km/68 mi north of Belfast, 53 km/33 mi north of Omagh.*

Derry's name is a shadow of its history. Those in favor of British rule call the city Londonderry, its old Plantation period name; the "London" part was tacked on in 1613 after the Flight of the Earls (☞ Rathmullan *in* Chapter 8), and the city and county were handed over to the Corporation of London, which represented London's merchants. They brought in a large population of English and Scottish Protestant settlers, built new towns for them, and reconstructed Derry within the city walls, which survive almost unchanged to this day. Both before then and after, Derry's sturdy ramparts have withstood many fierce attacks and have never been breached, which explains the city's coy sobriquet, "The Maiden City."

Whatever you choose to call it, Derry is one of Northern Ireland's most underrated towns. Despite the factories and low-income tenements along the banks of the River Foyle and a reputation marred by Troubles-related violence, the city has worked hard to move forward. Such efforts show in the quaint, bustling town center, encircled by 20-ft-tall, 17th-century walls. The city's winding streets slope down to the Foyle, radiating from the Diamond—Derry's historic center where St. Colomb founded his first monastery in 546. Fine Georgian and Victorian buildings, sit side by side with gaily painted Victorian-fronted shops, cafés, and pubs.

Derry, incidentally, has links to Boston that date as far back as the 17th and 18th centuries, when many Derry residents escaped their hardships at home by emigrating to that U.S. city and beyond. Aviation fans take note: Derry was where Amelia Earhart touched down, on May 21, 1932, after her historic solo flight across the Atlantic.

To really experience Derry's history, stroll along the parapet walkway atop the ramparts of the **city walls.** (You can do this on your own, or, in June–September, join one of the guided walks [£3], which depart from the town's **Visitor Information Office** [⊠ Ferry St., ☎ 01504/267284].) Pierced by eight gates (originally four) and as much as 30 ft thick, the gray stone ramparts are only 1½ km/1 mi all round; today most of the life of the town actually takes place outside the walls. At the entrance to the city, the ornate Victorian stone and sandstone **Guildhall** dates from 1890 and has impressive stained-glass windows. It is the site of musical recitals as well as some very heated political rallies. ⊠ *Guildhall Sq.,* ☎ *01504/377335.* 🎫 *Free.* ◷ *Mon.–Fri. 9–5; guided tours July–Aug. and by appointment.*

The **Tower Museum** is inside the reconstructed O'Doherty's Tower, originally built in 1615 by the O'Dohertys for their overlords, the O'Donnells, in lieu of tax payments. The vivid "Story of Derry" exhibition covers Derry's history, from its origins as a monastic settlement in an oak grove and including the beginnings of the Troubles. ⊠ *Union Hall Pl.,* ☎ *01504/372411.* 🎫 *U.K.£3.* ◷ *Sept.–June, Tues.–Sat. 10–5; July–Aug., Mon.–Sat. 10-5, Sun. 2–5.*

The Fifth Province is a high-tech celebration of the city's history from its earliest days, as well as its importance in creating the Irish diaspora. ⊠ *Calgach Centre,* ⊠ *4–22 Butcher St.,* ☎ *01504/373177.* 🎫 *U.K.£3.* ◷ *Sept.–June, Tues.–Sat. 10–5; July–Aug., Mon.–Sat. 10–5, Sun. 2–5.*

Butcher Gate, on the west side of Derry, opens onto the Catholic Bogside district. The graffito DOIRE CHOLMCILLE near this gateway is the old Irish name for Derry, meaning Columba's Oak. **Roaring Meg,** one of the original cannons from the 1688–89 siege, still looks out from Double Bastion, a fortified corner on the ramparts. Within the walls of Derry, Shipquay Street climbs steeply to the central square, the Diamond. Beyond the Diamond, if you walk on Bishop Street, you'll pass **St. Columb's Cathedral.** Built in 1633 in simple Planter's Gothic style, it is one of the first Protestant cathedrals built in the United Kingdom after the reformation. In addition to its intricate corbeled roof and austere spire, the church contains the oldest and largest bells in Ireland (dating from the 1620s). The church is a treasure house of Derry Protestant emblems, memorials, and relics from the 1688–89 siege. The **Chapter House Museum** has the oldest surviving map of Derry (from 1600). ⊠ *Off Bishop St.,* ☎ *01504/267313,* 🎫 *U.K.£1.* ◷ *Museum: Mar.–Oct. daily, 9–1 and 2–5; Nov.–Feb. daily 9–1 and 2–4.*

NEED A   **The Boston Tea Party** (⊠ 10 and 13–15 Craft Village, ☎ 01504/
BREAK?   269667), a small tea shop down an alley nearly opposite the Richmond Shopping Centre on Shipquay Street, is a nice spot for a snack or lunch break. Derry is packed with agreeable pubs, but **Badgers** (⊠ 16 Orchard St., ☎ 01504/360763) has the best range of simple wholesome food. Plus it's the watering hole for local media types, artists, writers, and musicians.

Dining and Lodging

$$$ ✗🏨 **Beech Hill.** Past a fairy-tale gatehouse and set among clumps of beech trees, streams, and a duck pond, Beech Hill is a grand 1792 country home very much attuned to the present. Chef James Nicholas, who trained with Paul Rankin at Roscoff (☞ Dining and Lodging *in* Belfast, *above*), draws many Northwest politicos from both sides of the border (with Eurocrats in tow) who appreciate his sophisticated menu. Confit of duck with pickled red cabbage and green peppercorn sauce, and lamb with a piquant mustard sauce typify the entrées. Cherry pie is a simple, delectable dessert. Some rooms have lovely Victorian antiques. The vast honeymoon suite, with a four-poster bed, overlooks the gardens. The house is 3¼ km/2 mi south of the city, left off the A6. ✉ *32 Ardmore Rd., Derry BT47 3QP,* ☎ *01504/49279,* FAX *01504/45366. 17 rooms with bath. Restaurant, bar, meeting rooms. AE, MC, V.*

$$$ ✕🖼 **The Trinity.** On the banks of the River Foyle, past the Guildhall and not far outside the city walls, The Trinity is Derry's only city-center hotel. The spacious bedrooms are decorated with rosewood and several hues of green; amenities include coffeemakers and satellite TV. The hotel is home to a number of watering holes: Nolan's Snug, the European-style café-bar, and the hotel's restaurant, which offers such specialties as blackened monkfish and seafood *boudin* (sausage). The roof garden makes a pleasant sanctuary. ✉ *22–24 Strand Rd., Derry BT48 7 AB,* ☎ *01504/271271,* FAX *01504/271277. 40 rooms with bath. Restaurant, 3 bar, meeting rooms. AE, MC, V.*

Nightlife and the Arts

It may be the North's *second* largest city, but to its residents, Derry is thought to be first in spirit.

ART GALLERIES

The **Orchard Gallery** (✉ Orchard St., ☎ 01504/269675) has gained a Europe-wide reputation in the fields of political and conceptual art. The **Context Gallery** (✉ 5–7 Artillery St., ☎ 01504/373538) is a close competitor.

PUBS AND CLUBS

Traditional Irish music can be found at **Peadar O'Donnell's** (✉ 63 Waterloo St., ☎ 01504/372318). The **Gweedore Bar** (✉ 16 Waterloo St., ☎ 01504/263513) is a favorite for hip-hop and house music. **Squire's Nightclub** (✉ 33 Shipquay St., ☎ 01504/266017) is the place for disco.

THEATER AND OPERA

Brian Friel, of *Philadelphia Here I Come* fame, premiered much of his work in the **Guildhall** (☞ *above*) through the **Field Day Theatre Company** (✉ Foyle Arts Centre, Lawrence Hill, ☎ 01504/360196). The **O'Casey Theater Company** (✉ 5–7 Artillery St., ☎ 01504/374253), managed by Sean O'Casey's daughter Shivaun, is one of several theater enterprises providing productions for the **Rialto Entertainment Center** (✉ 5 Market St., ☎ 01504/260516), the **Foyle Arts Centre**, and **The Playhouse** (✉ 5–7 Artillery St., ☎ 01504/268027). Touring operas play at **St. Columb's Theatre** (✉ Orchard St., ☎ 01504/262880).

Shopping

Shopping in the town is generally low-key and unpretentious, and some gems of Irish craftsmanship can be found here. Stroll up Shipquay Street to find small shops and an indoor shopping center. Stop at the **Donegal Shop** (✉ 8 Shipquay St., ☎ 01504/266928) for Irish linen, tweeds, and woolens. Off Shipquay Street, the **Derry Craft Village** offers a novel shopping experience: retail establishments, workshops, and residential apartments share an 18th-century setting, complete with crafts demonstrations, costumes and, of course, souvenirs galore. Where Shipquay reaches the Diamond, you'll find **Austin's** (☎ 01504/261817), a large store stocking Tyrone crystal, Belleek china, and other quality Northern Irish goods.

En Route From Derry, head across County Tyrone toward Enniskillen. Take the A5 south via Strabane to Omagh. **Strabane** does not offer much interest, apart from the well-preserved, 18th-century **Gray's Print Shop** (✉ 49 Main St., ☎ 01504/884094). John Dunlap (1746–1812), who apprenticed here as a printer before emigrating to Philadelphia, founded

America's first daily newspaper, *The Philadelphia Packet*, in 1771, and was also the man who printed and distributed the American Declaration of Independence. James Wilson, grandfather of President Woodrow Wilson, also emigrated from here. The original **Wilson family home** (☎ 01662/243292), a simple thatched cottage, still with much of the original 18th-century furniture, survives at Dergalt, 3 km/2 mi along the Plumbridge road. It can be visited by knocking at the farmhouse next door, still owned and worked by the Wilson family. For a delightfully rustic alternative route, drive along the minor road B48, which skirts the foot of the **Sperrin Mountains** and reaches all the way to Omagh.

Alternatively, you may want to head north from Derry to the **Inishowen Peninsula,** the northernmost point of Ireland (☞ Chapter 8).

AROUND COUNTIES TYRONE, FERMANAGH, ARMAGH, AND DOWN

During the worst of the Troubles, parts of these four counties that border the Republic were known as bandit country. But now visitors can enjoy a worry-free drive through the calm countryside and stop in at some very "Ulster" towns, distinct from the rest of Ireland. (You may see, few and far between, British army foot patrols and vehicle checkpoints.) The area includes the great house of Castle Coole; the ancient, ecclesiastical city of Armagh; and the wild Sperrin Mountains.

Ulster-American Folk Park and Ulster History Park

㉓ *27 km/17 mi south of Strabane, 5 km/3 mi north of Omagh.*

The **Ulster-American Folk Park,** which has been designed to re-create a Tyrone village of two centuries ago, includes a log-built American settlement of the same period, and re-creations of the docks and ships that the emigrants to America would have used. The centerpiece of the park is an old whitewashed cottage, now a museum, which is the ancestral home of Andrew Mellon (1855–1937), the U.S. millionaire banker and philanthropist. Another thatched cottage is a reconstruction of the boyhood home of Archbishop John Hughes, founder of New York's St. Patrick's Cathedral. Exhibitions trace the contribution of the Northern Irish people to American history. The park also features a crafts shop and café. ⊠ *Camphill, Co. Tyrone, on A5 between Strabane and Omagh,* ☎ *01662/243292.* ⊠ *U.K.£3.50.* ☉ *Easter–Sept., Mon.–Sat. 11–6:30, Sun. and holidays 11:30–7; Oct.–Good Fri., weekdays 10:30–5; last admission 1½ hrs before closing.*

On the B48, another 6 km/4 mi northeast of the Ulster-American Folk Park, the **Ulster History Park** documents Irish history from the first known settlers to the 12th-century arrival of the Normans. The open-air displays include lath and rawhide huts, primitive farms and stockades, a round tower, and an oratory. Hours are identical to those at the Ulster-American Folk Park (☞ *above*). ⊠ *Cullion, Lislap, Gortin,* ☎ *016626/48188.* ⊠ *U.K.£3.*

Omagh

43 km/27 mi northeast of Enniskillen.

Omagh, the county town of Tyrone, lies close to the Sperrin Mountains with the River Strule to the north. Playwright Brian Friel was born here. The town has two places of worship—a Church of Ireland church and a Catholic, double-spire church.

Belleek

 9½ km/6 mi southwest of Omagh.

The old town of Belleek sits on the northwestern edge of Lower Lough Erne and is home to the world-famous Belleek Pottery. On the riverbank stands the visitor center of **Belleek Pottery Ltd.,** producers of world-famous Belleek chinaware and porcelain. Here a factory, a showroom, a permanent exhibition, a Belleek pottery museum, and a café are all under one roof. On weekdays, a tour of the factory starts every half hour. You'll find hardly any noise coming from machinery in the workshops, however—everything at Belleek is handmade, using the exact process that was invented in 1857. The showroom is filled with beautiful gifts, but prices are high: A cup and saucer costs about U.K.£25–U.K.£30, and a bowl in a basket-weave style (very typical of Belleek) could cost you several hundred pounds. ✉ *Belleek, Co. Fermanagh,* ☏ *013656/58501.* ✆ *£2.* ☉ *Shop and showroom: Sept.–May, weekdays 9–6, Sat. 10–6; June–Aug., daily 9 AM–8 PM. Tours: Mon.–Thurs. 9:15–12:15 and 2:15–4:15, Fri. 9:15–3:15.*

En Route   North of Omagh the country is pretty and rustic, with small farm villages within sight of the bare Sperrin Mountains. Heading east from the town on the A505, you'll discover a pensive landscape of moist heath and bog. Left of the road, **Beaghmore** is a strange Bronze Age ceremonial site preserved for millennia beneath a blanket of peat: It has seven stone circles and 12 cairns. Farther along, the A505 reaches **Wellbrook Beetling Mill,** where locally made linen was first "beetled," that is, pounded with noisy water-driven hammers to give it a smooth finish. The mill is kept in working order by the National Trust. ✉ *Corkhill,* ☏ *016487/51735.* ✆ *U.K.£1.60.* ☉ *Apr., May, and Sept., weekends 2–6; Easter and June–Aug., daily Wed.–Mon., 2–6.*

About 6½ km/4 mi beyond Wellbrook is **Cookstown,** an odd Plantation village with a single, broad main street more than 1½ km/1 mi long. From here, head down on the back lanes to **Lough Neagh,** the largest lake in the British Isles (396 square km/153 square mi), noted for an abundance of eels. On its shore at **Ardboe** stands a remarkable 10th-century high cross. It is huge—more than 18 ft tall—and richly carved with biblical scenes.

Lough Erne

131 km/82 mi west of Belfast, 100 km/62 mi south of Derry.

On the journey beside Lough Erne, pause to catch your breath while eating up the lovely view of green hills extending down to the still lake water.

Castle Archdale Country Park, signposted down a narrow road about 6½ km/4 mi from the Kesh, has a lakeside marina, an open-air country museum, and a World War II exhibition featuring the Battle of the Atlantic. ☏ *013656/21588.* ✆ *Free.* ☉ *Call for hrs.*

Lake and River Cruising

Inland cruising on the Erne waterway—777 square km/300 square mi of lakes and rivers—is one of the North's major treats. Upper and Lower Lough Erne are enclosed by some of Ireland's finest scenery and are studded with more than 100 little islands. Out on the lakes and the River Erne, which links them, you'll have all the solitude you want, but you'll find company at lough-side hostelries. To hire a good, standard-size boat, contact **Erne Charter Boat Association** (✉ Belleek Charter Cruising, Erne Gateway Centre, Corry, Belleek, ☏ 013656/58027).

Expect to pay at least U.K.£300 to hire a four-berth cruiser for two or three nights.

White Island and Devenish Island

4 km/2 ½ mi and 16 km/10 mi north of Enniskillen.

From Castle Archdale a ferry (☎ 01365/21731) runs June–September, Tuesday–Sunday (U.K.£2.25), taking passengers to see the weird, ㉕ Celtic carved figures on **White Island.** After you drive 13 km/8 mi farther from Castle Archdale Park, where the B82 joins the A32, a small sign shows the way to catch the little boat (☎ 01365/323110) run-㉖ ning April–September, Tuesday–Sunday (U.K.£2.25) over to **Devenish Island.** The extensive but ruined 12th-century monastery on Devenish features Ireland's best example of a round tower—it is 82 ft tall—and a richly carved high cross.

Enniskillen

㉗ *43 km/27 mi southwest of Omagh, 77 km/48 mi west of Armagh.*

Enniskillen is the pleasant, smart-looking capital of County Fermanagh. The only place of any size in the county, its town center is strikingly situated on an island in the River Erne between Upper and Lower Lough Erne. The principal thoroughfares, Townhall and High streets, are crowded with old-style pubs and rows of redbrick Georgian flats, and the waterfront **Enniskillen Castle,** one of the best preserved monuments in the North. Built by the Maguire clan in 1670, this stronghold houses the local history collection of the **Fermanagh County Museum** and the polished paraphernalia of the **Royal Inniskilling Fusiliers Regimental Museum.** A **Heritage Centre** also stands within the curtilage of the castle. ✉ *Wellington Rd.,* ☎ *01365/325000.* 🎟 *U.K.£1.50.* ☉ *May–Sept., Tues–Fri., 10–5, Sat. and Mon. 2–5; July–Aug also Sun. 2–5; Oct–April, Mon. 2–5, Tues.–Fri. 10–5.*

The spires of the daunting 19th-century St. Michael's and St. MacArtin's cathedrals, both on Church Street, preside over the down. Farther west down Church Street are High Street's pubs and restaurants.

At the riverside in Enniskillen, the 16th-century **Water Gate** is handsomely turreted, a protection against enemies of the town.

Beyond the West Bridge in Enniskillen lies **Portora Royal School,** established in 1608 by King James I. Its grounds contain the ruins of Portora Castle. Among the writers who were educated there are Oscar Wilde—the pride of the school, until his trial for homosexuality, and Samuel Beckett.

Among the several relaxed and welcoming old pubs in Enniskillen's town center, the one with the most appeal is **Blake's of the Hollow** (✉ 6 Church St., ☎ 01365/322143) on the main street, a place hardly altered since it opened in 1887. Its name derives from the facts that the heart of the town lies in a slight dip or hollow, and the pub's landlord is named William Blake. Don't ask if he's related to the great poet of the same name—everybody does, and he isn't!

Castle Coole

★ ㉘ *3 km/1½ mi southeast of Enniskillen.*

In the 18th century and through most of the 19th, the Loughs of Erne and their environs were remote places—far from Ireland's bustling cities. But it was just this isolated green and watery countryside that attracted the Anglo-Irish gentry. They built grand houses—among them, one widely considered to be the finest: Castle Coole. The mansion stands in its own landscaped oak woods and parkland at the end of a long, tree-lined driveway. Although the Irish architect Richard Johnston did the original drawings in the 1790s, and is responsible for the foundation, the work is, for all intents and purposes, the work of James Wyatt, commissioned by the first Earl of Belmore. One of the best-known architects of his time, Wyatt, who was based in London, did much work in Ireland, but he only visited the country once, and he never visited here. Alexander Stewart was the resident builder-architect who oversaw much of the building's construction. The architect wasn't the only imported element; in fact, much of Castle Coole was brought over from England, including the main facade, which is clad in Portland stone shipped from Dorset to Ballyshannon and then hauled over land by horse and cart. And what a facade it is: In perfect symmetry, white colonnaded wings extend from either side of the mansion's three-story, nine-bay center block, with a pedimented central portico. It is perhaps the apotheosis in Ireland of the 18th-century's reverence for the Greeks, and it bears a touch of Palladian sensibility.

Inside, the house is remarkably well preserved. Most of the house's lavish plasterwork and original furnishings are still in place. (In a restoration completed in 1995–96, anything not in keeping with the original design was removed.) The saloon is one of the finest rooms in the house, with a vast expanse of oak flooring, gilded Regency furniture, and gray scagliola pilasters with Corinthian capitals. On its completion in September 1798, the construction had cost £70,000 and the furnishings another £22,000. The present earl of Belmore still lives on the estate and uses one wing of the house. ⊠ *Co. Fermanagh,* ☎ *01365/322690.* ⊡ *U.K.£2.80.* ☉ *Sept., weekends and Easter 1–6; May–Aug., Fri.–Wed., 1–6; Oct.–Apr., house closed.*

Horseback Riding/Pony Trekking
If you're over in the Enniskillen/Lough Erne area, the **Ulster Lakeland Equestrian Park** (⊠ Necarne Castle, Irvinestownick, ☎ 013656/21919) can teach you to ride or take you on a pony trek through the 200 rolling acres of this gothic-looking castle's rolling parkland. Rates begin at U.K.£6 for 45 minutes. There are rooms to stay in, a bar, and a restaurant.

Lodging
$$ 🏨 **Blessingbourne.** This faux Elizabethan, Victorian-era house, with mullioned windows, stables, and carriage museum, sits on a pretty circular lake. Meals can be eaten with the Lowry family, the proprietors. One of the bedrooms has a four-poster bed. A visit makes the diversion to Fivemiletown—so named as it is 5 Irish miles from anywhere—worthwhile. ⊠ *Fivemiletown, Co. Tyrone, BT75 0QS,* ☎ *013655/21221. 4 rooms. Restaurant (jacket and tie, reservations essential). No credit cards.*

$$ 🏨 **Jamestown House.** Tucked away in lush, tranquil countryside near
★ Lower Lough Erne and 11 km/7 mi from Enniskillen, this dignified country house dates from 1760 and is run by Arthur and Helen Stuart. The large, attractive bedrooms feature modern furnishings, and elegant drawing and dining rooms contain older, fine, polished-mahogany pieces. Staying here is just like visiting friends in the country. A river runs through the grounds—Mr. Stuart is keen on angling and advises visitors on the best spots to fish in the area. Breakfasts and the set dinners are generous and satisfying. ⊠ *Magheracross, Ballinamallard, Co. Fermanagh BT94 2JP,* ☎ *01365/388209. 3 rooms with bath or shower. Dining room. No credit cards.*

En Route Florence Court, about 11 km/7 mi south from Enniskillen on the A4
and the A32, is one of the most impressive of the North's grand Anglo-
Irish mansions; it was built in the 18th century for John Cole, father
of the first earl of Enniskillen. The house features abundant Rococo
plasterwork, 18th-century furnishings, and a fine porcelain collection.
You can stroll around the estate grounds and have a snack and coffee
at the tea shop. ☎ 01365/348249. 🖃 U.K.£2.80. ☉ *Mansion: Easter,
Apr., and Sept., weekends 1–6; May–Aug., Fri.–Wed. 1–6. Grounds:
May–Sept., 10–1 hr before dusk.*

Armagh

 64 km/40 mi west of Belfast, 77 km/48 mi east of Enniskillen.

The small but ancient ecclesiastical city of Armagh, despite the pleas-
ing Georgian terraces around the elegant Mall, east of the town center, can seem drab, having suffered as a trouble spot in the sectarian
conflict. Here St. Patrick founded a church, and the town has remained a religious center to the present day. In fact, *two* Armagh
cathedrals are dedicated to Ireland's patron saint. Despite the 1921 par-
tition of Ireland into two parts, the seat of the Catholic Archbishop of
All Ireland remains in Armagh, as does the seat of the Archbishop of
the Anglican Church of Ireland.

Armagh's main attraction is the **Astronomy Centre and Planetarium
and Observatory.** The observatory here has been in continuous use since
1791. The Planetarium contains fascinating exhibits, including models of spacecraft, video shows of the sky, and hands-on computer displays. The **Earthorium exhibition** displays the world from three
levels—its interior, surface, and atmosphere. The outdoor, 30-acre **AstroPark** features a model solar system. A **16-inch telescope** is open two
nights per month, September through April (call for specific dates). The
Planetarium's **Robinson Dome,** also known as "the 10-inch dome,"
for the 1875 Grub telescope it houses, is open in summer months. 🖃
College Hill, ☎ *Planetarium: 01861/523689; observatory: 01861/
524725.* 🖃 *AstroPark and Robinson Dome: free; hall of astronomy
and Earthorium: U.K.£1; special shows and other exhibitions:
U.K.£3.50.* ☉ *Planetariaum: Weekdays 10–4:45, weekends 1:15–
4:45; show weekdays at 3, weekends at 2 and 3. Robinson Dome: Apr.–
Sept., weekdays 9:30–4:30.*

Dedicated to St. Patrick, the pale limestone, Victorian-Gothic **Catholic
Cathedral,** with two pale spires, on a hill at the north end of Armagh
Town, is best seen from a small distance, allowing the viewer to take
in the full majesty of it.

Near the town center in Armagh, a squat, battlemented tower identi-
fies the **Protestant cathedral,** in simple, early 19th-century Perpendic-
ular-Gothic style. It stands on the site of much older churches and
contains several relics of Armagh's long history, including sculpted, pre-
Christian idols. This cathedral claims to be the burial place of Brian
Boru, the great High King—that is, king of all Ireland—who drove the
Vikings out of Ireland in the 11th century.

Past the 13th-century Franciscan friary ruins, in the stables of the former Archbishop's demesne, the **Palace Stables Heritage Centre** presents
a diorama of everyday life—upstairs and downstairs—in the 18th-cen-
tury days of the extremely wealthy Baron Rokeby, Church of Ireland
Archbishop Richard Robinson, who commissioned local architect
Francis Johnston—who designed much of Georgian Dublin—to create a new Armagh out of the slums into which it had degenerated. The
Archbishop gave the city a clean water supply and a sewer system, then

turned the city's racecourse into an elegant mall. He paved and lit the streets; financed improvements to the Bishop's Palace and the Protestant cathedral; and endowed the public library, the observatory, the Royal School, and the county infirmary. ⊠ *Palace Demesne, Friary Rd.,* ☎ *01861/529629.* ☎ *U.K.£2.80.* ☉ *Apr.–Sept., Mon.–Sat., 10–6, Sun. 1–6; Oct.–Mar., Mon.–Sat. 10–5, Sun. 2–5.*

Just outside Armagh, **Navan Fort** is Ulster's Camelot—the region's ancient capital. Excavations date evidence of activity going back to 700 BC. The fort has strong associations with figures of Irish history and legend. Thousands of years ago it is said to have been the site of the palace of Queen Macha; subsequent legends call it the barracks of the legendary Ulster warrior Cuchulain and his Red Branch Knights. Remains dating to 94 BC are particularly intriguing: A great conical structure, 120 ft in diameter, was formed from five concentric circles made of 275 wooden posts, with a 276th, about 12 yards high, situated in the center. In a ritual whose meaning is not known, it was filled with brushwood and set on fire. The Navan Centre rehearses the knight's tales—Ireland's *Iliad* and Ulster's *Camelot* combined. ⊠ *2 mi/3 km west of Armagh on the A28,* ☎ *01861/52550.* ☎ *Centre £3.95; fort free.* ☉ *Fort always open; Centre: Apr.–June, Sept., weekdays 10–6, Sat. 11–6, Sun. noon–6; July–Aug., Mon.–Sat. 10–7, Sun. 11-7; Oct.–Mar., weekdays 10–5, Sat. 11–5, Sun. noon–5.*

En Route   Leave Armagh to the southeast on the A28, driving toward Newry. Instead of going the entire way on the main road, after about 9½ km/6 mi, you'll have a more enjoyable drive if you take the B133, on the right. This will lead you through a rustic, drumlin landscape of vivid green pastures. The appearance of villages changes as you return toward the River Bann; houses and farms begin to resemble homes and farms in Britain rather than those in the Republic.

Lodging

$$$ ☷ **Drumsill Hotel.** On 15 acres of mature wooded grounds, this modern hotel is 1½ km/1 mi northwest of Armagh on the A29 road, signposted The Moy. The formal Gallery Restaurant has an adventurous menu, with a starter of Brie with rhubarb sauce wrapped in phyllo pastry, and main courses such as ostrich fillet with Dijon mustard and monkfish on a potato cake. Bedrooms are clean and functional. Bond's Wine Bar features live music weekends. ⊠ *35 Moy Rd., Armagh BT61 8DL,* ☎ *01861/522009,* ℻ *01861/525624. 10 rooms with bath. Restaurant, wine bar, meeting rooms. AE, MC, V.*

$$ ☷ **Dean's Hill.** Jill Armstrong's elegant guest house was built, as the name suggests, for the Cathedral's dean in 1760, and it has been in the Armstrong family for more than 100 years. The three bedrooms, with their period architectural features intact, each have their own bath. One has a four-poster bed, another a fireplace. A self-catering apartment in the courtyard sleeps four. Breakfasts include homemade jam and eggs plucked fresh from Armstrong's 80-acre working farm, which encompasses attractive wooded areas, a croquet lawn, and a tennis court. Despite the rural setting, Armagh's historic center is only a 10-minute walk away. ⊠ *College Hill, Armagh BT61 9DF,* ☎ *01861/524923. 3 rooms with bath, 1 apartment. Tennis court, croquet. No credit cards.*

Bessbrook

30 km/18 mi southeast of Armagh, 6 km/4 mi northwest of Newry.

Bessbrook is a "model village" built in 1846 by Quaker linen manufacturer John Grubb Richardson. It has a naive, dreamlike, toy-town quality, with its neat terraces and picture-book village stores. Richardson decreed that there would be no pubs at Bessbrook. Maybe that explains why there are no fewer than six in the neighboring village, Camlough.

Just south of Bessbrook is **Derrymore House,** a thatched cottage with a well-tended garden. Once the house of Isaac Corry, famous duelist and unpopular Chancellor of the Exchequer in the last all-Ireland Parliament, it was here, in 1880, that Corry and his cronies drafted the fateful Act of Union, which extinguished the Irish Parliament in Dublin, moving all political power to London. The house is now run by the National Trust. ⌧ *Derrymore Rd., Bessbrook,* ☎ *01693/830353.* ⌧ *U.K.£1.60.* ⊘ *May–Sept., Thurs.–Sat. 2–5:30*

The Mountains of Mourne

㉚ *16 km/10 mi south of Downpatrick, 51 km/32 mi south of Belfast.*

The Mountains of Mourne "sweep down to the sea" (in the words of a popular song) from 2,000-ft summits. East of the unprepossessing though historically important border town of Newry, this area was long considered ungovernable, its hardy inhabitants living from smuggling contraband into the numerous rocky coves on the seashore. Much of the Mourne range is still inaccessible except on foot. The countryside is gorgeous: high, windswept pasture and moorland—threaded with bright streams, bound by a tracery of drystone walls, dotted with sheep and whitewashed farmhouses snuggled in stands of sycamore. It's the perfect landscape for away-from-it-all walkers, cyclists, and serious climbers. (Climbers should inform their hotel or the Northern Ireland Centre for Outdoor Activities [Bryansford, Newcastle, ☎ 013967/22158] when and where they're heading before setting off.)

Newcastle, a bracing Victorian cold-water bathing station, is the main center for visitors to the hills. Looming above Newcastle is **Slieve Donard,** its panoramic, 2,805-ft summit grandly claiming views into England, Wales, and Scotland—"when it's clear enough," or, in other words, rarely, say the pessimists. **Castlewellan Forest Park** comprises 1,150 acres of forested hills running between the Mourne Mountains and Slieve Croob. With its lake, secluded arbors, and its **Arboretum,** the park makes an excellent introduction to the area. ⌧ *Main St., Castlewellan,* ☎ *013967/78664.* ⌧ *Car: U.K.£3; pedestrians: U.K.£1.50.* ⊘ *Daily dawn–dusk.*

Covering 1,200 acres and entered through picturesque Gothic gateways, **Tollymore Forest Park** extends up the valley of the River Shimna. There are many pretty stone bridges over the sparkling waters. ⌧ *Tullybrannigan Rd., Newcastle,* ☎ *013967/22428.* ⌧ *Car: U.K.£3; pedestrians: U.K.£1.50.* ⊘ *Daily dawn–dusk.*

Farther into the mountains, the road to the **Silent Valley** reservoir parklands leads to further glorious mountain views and excellent photo ops. Take the B27 from Kilkeel; after 6 km/4 mi, turn right. ☎ *01232/746581.* ⌧ *Car U.K.£3; pedestrians £1.50.* ⊘ *Apr.–Sept. 10–6:30; Oct.–Mar. 10–4.*

Outdoor Activities and Sports

The **Royal County Down** (⌧ Newcastle, ☎ 013967/23314) is considered by many golfers to be one of the finest courses in the world (☞ Chapter 10).

Lodging

$$$ 🏨 **Burrendale Hotel & Country Club.** Owner Sean Small's personality has made this low-slung, modern building, shaded by clumps of beech, into one of the most relaxing establishments on the North's east coast.

The staff is cheery; bedrooms are decorated in quiet tones. The Cottage Kitchen and Vine restaurants are competent (the former casual, the latter more formal) and particularly aim to please the many local customers, who like their plates overflowing. ✉ *51 Castlewellan Rd., Newcastle, Co. Down BT33 0JY,* ☎ *013967/22599,* FAX *013967/22328. 69 rooms with bath. 2 restaurants, 2 bars, indoor pool, hot tub, sauna, steam rooms, exercise rooms, meeting rooms. AE, MC, V.*

$$$ 🏨 **Slieve Donard Hotel.** A lavish, redbrick monument to Victoriana, this turreted, 100-year-old hotel stands like a palace on spacious, green lawns at one end of Newcastle's 6½-km/4-mi sandy beach. Guests will feel as if they are stepping back to the town's turn-of-the-century heyday as an elegant seaside resort, even though the rooms now have every modern comfort. Ask for a room overlooking the water. The relaxed Gatehouse pub/dining room serves adequate seafood dishes; folk music is presented every Saturday night. The Royal County Down Golf Club is next door. ✉ *Downs Rd., Newcastle, Co. Down BT33 0AH,* ☎ *013967/23681,* FAX *013967/24830. 120 rooms with bath. Dining room, pub, indoor pool, 2 tennis courts. AE, DC, MC, V.*

$$ 🏨 **Glassdrumman Lodge.** For those who wish to be pampered and even more immersed in the ancient Kingdom of Mourne, Graeme and Joan Hall's eclectically simple and stylish lodge is the place. Up a tiny road off the coast-clinging A2, the outside of the house is less than spectacular, but the estate grows its own crops, raises its own farm animals, churns its own butter, bakes its own bread, and lets its hens run free range. Inside, rooms are decorated in bright colors and have large windows that take advantage of the glorious views. The Halls think of everything: there is overnight laundry service and car washing, and they can arrange horseback riding and trekking. ✉ *Mill Rd., Annalong, Co. Down BT34 4RH,* ☎ *013967/68451,* FAX *013967/67041. 10 rooms with bath, 2 suites. Restaurant, business services, meeting rooms. AE, MC, V.*

Downpatrick

㉛ *35 km/22 mi south of Belfast, 50 km/31 mi east of Newry.*

Downpatrick used to be called plain and simple Down, but the town is proud of a claimed association with St. Patrick and changed its name in his honor. St. Patrick was a 5th-century Briton who, captured by the Irish, became a slave in the Down area; he escaped to France, where he learned about Christianity, and bravely returned to try to convert the local chiefs. Although it is not true that Patrick brought a new faith to Ireland (there was already a bishop of Ireland before Patrick got here), he must have been a better missionary than most because he did indeed win influential converts. The clan chief of the Down area gave him land at the village of Saul, near Downpatrick, to build a monastery.

Downpatrick's hilltop **cathedral,** built in 1790, preserves parts of some of the earlier churches and monasteries that have stood on the site since the 6th century. Even before that time, the cathedral site had long been an important fortified settlement. (Down takes its name from the Celtic word "dun," a fort.) In the churchyard, a somber slab has been inscribed "Patric"—it's supposedly the saint's tomb, which is a bit of a fraud since no one knows where Patrick is buried. It might be here, at Saul, or, some scholars argue, more likely at Armagh. A lot of such mystery and legend surrounds Patrick.

For some hard facts concerning the patron saint of Ireland, visit the **St. Patrick Heritage Centre** next to the cathedral; it's housed, together with the **Down Museum,** inside a former 18th-century jail. ✉ *The Mall,*

☎ 01396/615218. ⌨ *Free.* ☉ *Public and bank holidays plus mid-June–mid-Sept., weekdays 11–5, weekends 2–5; mid-Sept.–mid-June, Tues.–Fri. 11–5, weekends 2–5.*

OFF THE
BEATEN PATH

CASTLE WARD – From Downpatrick head northeast on the A25 to Strangford (13 km/8 mi) and the Ards Peninsula. Castle Ward, at Strangford, is an 18th-century mansion built in a bizarre mixture of styles—classical on one side, Gothic on the other. The 700-acre estate, ⅘ km/½ mi west of Strangford on the south shore of Strangford Lough, has a "Victorian pastimes center" for children, a wildfowl collection, a restaurant, an information office, and an old tower house that once guarded the shore. Holiday cottages are available for rentals as well. ☎ *01396/881204.* ⌨ *U.K.£2.60.* ☉ *House, shop, and restaurant: Easter, Sept., and Oct., weekends 1–6; May–Aug., Fri.–Wed. 1–6; estate daily dawn–dusk.*

Portaferry

30 km/18½ mi south of Newtownards, 13 km/8 mi east of Downpatrick.

You'll have to cross Strangford Lough on the 24-vehicle car ferry from Strangford to reach Portaferry (U.K.£4 per car and driver, 80p per additional passenger), another quiet fishing village with old fortifications to guard this once-strategic channel, which joins the lough to the sea. The ferry crossing takes 10 minutes or less, and boats leave every half hour throughout the day. Departures from Strangford are on the half hour and hour, and from Portaferry on the three-quarter hour and the quarter hour: weekdays 7:30 AM–10:30 PM, Saturday 8 AM–11 PM, and Sunday 9:30 AM–10:30 PM.

Exploris, Portaferry's unusual aquarium, has models of the underwater environment in Strangford Lough and examples of 70 species that call the lough their home. Some of these creatures may not be what you expect—seals and some large, long-lived species of fish still live in the lake. ⊠ *The Rope Walk,* ☎ *012477/28062.* ⌨ *U.K.£3.50.* ☉ *Apr.–Aug., Mon.–Sat. 10–6; Sun. 1–6; Sept.–Mar., Mon.–Sat. 10–5, Sun. 1–6.*

Dining and Lodging

$$$ ✕🏨 **Portaferry Hotel.** Standing on the quayside (or "strand") overlooking the narrow channel that connects Strangford Lough to the sea, this centuries-old, comfortable, whitewashed inn offers well-kept, simply furnished double rooms. The main action takes place in the popular bar and restaurant, home to huge breakfasts, country lunches, and old-fashioned evening meals. Live Strangford oysters, stuffed mussels, Dublin Bay prawns, scallops with bacon and garlic, and grilled turbot are briskly served to the Belfast and Dublin regulars who appreciate chef John Herlihy's fresh, frill-and-fad-free seafood. Watch the sun set across the water from the bar window, or better still, book one of the sought-after rooms at the front. ⊠ *10 The Strand, Co. Down BT22 1PE,* ☎ *012472/28231,* 🖷 *012477/28999. 14 double rooms with bath or shower. Restaurant, bar. AE, DC, MC, V.*

$$ ✕🏨 **Dufferin Arms Coaching Inn.** Next door to Killyleagh Castle, Kitty Stewart and Morris Crawford preside over this lively 1803 inn. The bedrooms have four-poster beds; there are also three two-bedroom apartments with kitchens. Rustic Irish cooking—entrées such as poached salmon and roast duck in cherry sauce—is served at the candlelit Kitchen Restaurant. One of the bars has snugs, another an open fire; diversions such as pub quizzes, traditional Irish storytelling, and Cajun and jazz music keep things lively. ⊠ *35 High St., Killyleagh, Co. Down*

BT30 9QF, ☎ 01396/828229, FAX 01396/828755. 7 bedrooms, 3 apartments. Restaurant, 3 bars, meeting room. AE, MC, V.

$$ ★ **Killyleagh Castle Towers.** Killyleagh, a pretty though somewhat run-down little port on the east shore of Strangford Lough, is home to this splendidly Baroque edifice. Hans Sloane (1660–1753), physician to George II and the man who founded the British Museum, was a village boy encouraged to educate himself in the castle's library. Travelers can rent three self-catering apartments—two in the 17th-century turrets and a larger one in a Victorian-style turret over the gateway. All apartments have cream walls, antique and modern furniture, and railed-off rooftop patios. Royalty watchers take note: Fergie, the ex-wife of Prince Andrew, has ancestral links here. ✉ *Lieut. Col. Rowan Hamilton, Killyleagh Castle, Killyleagh, Co. Down BT30 9QA, ☎ FAX 01396/828261. 3 apartments, each for 4 persons. Outdoor heated pool. No credit cards.*

Mount Stewart

32 *21 km/13 mi north from Portaferry.*

Mount Stewart is the grand, 19th-century family home of the marquesses of Londonderry. It was built in two stages, where an earlier house stood; George Dance designed the west facade (1804–5); William Vitruvius Morrison, the neoclassical main part of the building. The landscaped gardens are populated with surprising stone carvings of rare and extinct creatures. The house contains one of George Stubbs's most famous portraits, of the celebrated racehorse Hambletonian, after he had won one of the most celebrated races of the 18th century. The octagonal Temple of the Winds is a copy of a similar structure in Athens. ✉ *Newtownards,* ☎ *012477/88387.* *U.K.£3.50.* *May–Sept., Wed.–Mon. 1–6; Apr. and Oct., weekends and public holidays 1–6.*

Dining and Lodging

$$ **The Old Inn.** On the outside, the 1614 coaching inn that is reputedly Ireland's oldest looks the part: it's pure 17th-century Olde Worlde England, with a sculpted, thatched roof, half doors, and leaded windows. Inside there are roaring open fires in winter. Some of the bedrooms have four-poster beds and sitting rooms. The Churn Bistro's menu is solidly Irish, the staff jovial, and the locals are inquisitive. Crawfordsburn is 16 km/10 mi from Belfast. ✉ *15 Main St., Crawfordsburn, Co. Down, ☎ 01247/853255, FAX 01247/852775. 32 rooms with bath. Restaurant, 2 bars. AE, MC, V.*

NORTHERN IRELAND A TO Z

Arriving and Departing

By Bus

Northern Ireland's bus company, **Ulsterbus** (☎ 01232/333000), and the Republic's **Bus Éireann** (☎ 01/836–6111 in Dublin) both run direct services to and from Dublin. Buses arrive and depart from the Europa Buscentre; the ride takes three hours. Buses to Belfast also run from London and from Birmingham, making the Stranraer ferry (☎ 01776/702262) crossing.

By Car

Many roads from the Irish Republic into Northern Ireland were once closed for security reasons, but all are now reinstated, leaving drivers with a score of legitimate crossing points to choose from; "unapproved" routes across the border also exist but are not recommended.

Army checkpoints at all approved frontier posts are rare, and few customs formalities are observed. The fast N1/A1 road connects Belfast to Dublin (160 km/100 mi); sometimes you'll encounter delays at the border on this road as large trucks await customs clearance.

By Ferry

Norse Irish Ferries (✉ Victoria Terminal 2, West Bank Rd., ☎ 01232/779090) offers 11-hour, overnight car ferries that connect Belfast with the English west-coast port of Liverpool every other night. **P&O European Ferries** (☎ 0990/980980) has car ferries to Larne from Cairnryan, Scotland (2½ hours); infrequent trains take passengers on to Belfast. You can also cross on the **SeaCat** (☎ 0345/523523) or the **StenaLine's HSS** (☎ 0990/204204), both huge catamarans that carry cars and passengers from Stranraer directly into Belfast in just 1½ hours. The **Argyll and Antrim Steam Packet Company** (☎ 0345/523523) is a new 3-hour car-ferry service on the MV *Claymore* linking Campbeltown in Scotland with Ballycastle in county Antrim; it runs July 1– October 31. The **Isle of Man Steam Packet Company** (☎ 01232/313090) runs summer services to and from the Isle of Man–Belfast.

By Plane

Belfast International Airport at Aldergove (☎ 018494/422888) is the North's principal air arrival point, 30½ km/19 mi from Belfast. **Belfast City Airport** (☎ 01232/457745) is the second airport, 6½ km/4 mi from the city. It receives flights from U.K. provincial airports, from London Gatwick, and from Stanstead and Luton (both near London). **Aer Lingus** (☎ 01232/245151) flies once daily, Monday–Saturday, from New York's JFK directly to Belfast. Other scheduled services from the U.S. and Canada are routed through Dublin, Glasgow, London, or Manchester. Charter operators, including **American Trans Air** (☎ 01293/50237) run summer services directly into Belfast.

Frequent services to Belfast are scheduled throughout the day from London Heathrow, London Gatwick, Luton, and Stanstead (all four of which have fast coordinated subway or rail connections to central London) and from 17 other U.K. airports. Flights take about 1¼ hours from London. **British Airways** and **BA Express** (both ☎ 0345/222111) and **British Midland Airways** (☎ 0345/554554) operate the majority of flights into Belfast. Direct flights from Amsterdam on **Air UK** (☎ 0345/666777) and from Paris on **Jersey European Airways** (☎ 0345/676676) also arrive in Belfast.

City of Derry Airport (☎ 01504/810784) is 8 km/5 mi from Derry and receives flights from London Stanstead, Glasgow, Birmingham, and Manchester.

BETWEEN THE AIRPORTS AND THE CITIES

Belfast. Ulsterbus (☎ 01232/333000) operates a shuttle bus every half hour (one way U.K.£3.70, round-trip U.K.£6.40) between the International Airport and Belfast city center. From Belfast City Airport, you can travel into Belfast by train from Sydenham Halt to Central Station (✉ East Bridge St.) or catch a taxi from the airport to your hotel.

Derry. If you arrive at Eglinton Airport (8 km/5 mi from Derry), you may need to call a taxi (☎ 01504/811231 or 01504/263905) to get to your destination.

By Train

The Dublin–Belfast Express train—operated by both **Northern Ireland Railways** (☎ 01232/899411) and **Iarnród Éireann**—travels between the two cities in about two hours. Six trains (check timetables, as some trains are much slower) run daily in both directions (three on Sundays) from/to Belfast's misnamed Central Station (✉ East Bridge St., ☎ 01232/899411). However, a free shuttle bus service will drop you off at City Hall or Ulsterbus's city-center Europa Buscentre (✉ 01232/333000), or you can change trains for the de facto city-center Great Victoria Street Station (✉ Great Victoria St., ☎ 01232/230671), which is adjacent both to the Europa Buscentre and the Europa Hotel.

Getting Around

By Bus
Visitors can take advantage of frequent and inexpensive Ulsterbus links between all Northern Ireland towns. The main bus stations in Belfast are the Europa Buscentre (✉ Glengall St., ☎ 01232/333000), which is easiest to find using its Great Victoria Street entrance to the left of the Europa Hotel, and the Laganside Buscentre (✉ Donegall Quay, ☎ 01232/320111), around the corner from the Albert Clock and not far from Central Station.

If you want to tour the North by bus, a **Freedom of Northern Ireland Ticket** allows unlimited travel on bus or train (U.K.£9 per day, U.K.£28 per week). An **Irish Rover** ticket from Ulsterbus covers Ireland, north and south, and costs U.K.£36 for three days, U.K.£85 for eight. For specific fares and schedules, call **Ulsterbus** (☎ 01232/333000). Within Belfast, visitors have access to good city-bus service. All routes start from Donegall Square; you'll find a kiosk there where you can pick up a timetable. For **Citybus** inquiries, call ☎ 01232/246485.

By Car
In general, drivers will find that in the North the roads are in much better shape, signposting is clearer, and gasoline is cheaper than in the Irish Republic. Bad rush-hour delays can occur on the West Link joining the M1 (heading south or west) and the M2 (heading east or north). But on the whole, driving is quicker and easier in the North than in areas south of the border.

PARKING

Belfast has many parking garages, as well as street meter-ticket parking. Before parking on the street, check the posted regulations: during rush hours many spots become no-parking. Also always check, too, that you are not parking in a "control zone," where it is prohibited to leave a vehicle unattended. In the event there has been a recent bombing or other Troubles-related flare-up, city and town centers may introduce control zones; keep alert to these situations as you're traveling.

By Train
Northern Ireland Railways runs only four rail routes from Belfast's **Central Station** (✉ E. Bridge St., ☎ 01232/899411), which is not, in fact, that centrally located: northwest to **Derry** via Coleraine and the Causeway Coast; east to **Bangor** along the shore of Belfast Lough; northeast to **Larne** (for the P&O European ferry to Scotland [☞ *above*]); and south to **Dublin**. There are frequent connections to Central Station from the much more central Great Victoria Street Station (☞ Arriving and Departing, *above*) and from Botanic Station (✉ Botanic Ave., ☎ 01232/899411) in the university area. **Rail Runabout** tickets allow seven days' unlimited travel from April–October only (U.K.£30). **Freedom of Northern Ireland** tickets also apply to trains (☞ *above*). For more information contact **Northern Ireland Railways** (✉ 28 Wellington Pl., Belfast, ☎ 01232/899411).

Contacts and Resources

Banks and Money Exchange

The North uses British currency. Irish *punts*, or pounds, are not accepted. Rates change rapidly, but the British pound is generally worth slightly more than the Irish (☞ Money *in* the Gold Guide). You'll sometimes be given bank notes, drawn on Ulster banks, that are valid only in Northern Ireland; be sure not to get stuck with a lot of these when you leave, because they will be difficult to change at banks back home. Main banks are open weekdays 9:30–4:30, smaller branches weekdays 10:30–3:30. Changing money outside banking hours is possible at **Thomas Cook** branches. ✉ *Belfast Airport,* ☎ *01849/422536.* ☉ *Weekdays 7 AM–8 PM, weekends 7 AM–10 PM;* ✉ *11 Donegall Pl.,* ☎ *01232/554455;* ✉ *22 Lombard Pl., 01232/236044.* ☉ *Mon.–Wed., Fri.–Sat. 9–5:30; Thurs. 10–5:30.*

Car Rentals

Visitors can choose between several local rental companies, but car rental isn't cheap. A compact car costs U.K.£150 to U.K.£210 per week (including taxes, insurance, and unlimited mileage). If you're planning to take a rental car across the border into the Republic, inform the company and check its insurance procedures. Following are some of the main rental offices.

BELFAST

Avis (✉ Belfast International Airport, ☎ 01849/422333; ✉ Belfast City Airport, ☎ 01232/452017; ✉ Great Victoria St., ☎ 01232/240404). **Dan Dooley** (☎ 01849/452522). **Europcar** (✉ Belfast International Airport, ☎ 01849/423444). **Hertz** (✉ Belfast International Airport, ☎ 01849/422533). **Europcar** (✉ Belfast City Airport, ☎ 01232/450904). **Hertz** (✉ Belfast City Airport, ☎ 01232/732451).

DERRY

Ford (☎ 01504/810832); a U.K.£180 security deposit is required here.

Emergencies

Police, fire, and **ambulance** or **coast guard** (☎ 999 toll-free in all of Northern Ireland). **Belfast's main police station** (✉ 6–10 N. Queen St., ☎ 01232/650222).

HOSPITALS

Belfast: Belfast City Hospital (✉ Lisburn Rd., ☎ 01232/329241) is one of two main hospitals in the city with an emergency room. The **Royal Victoria Hospital** (✉ Grosvenor Rd., ☎ 01232/240503) is the other major hospital with an emergency room.

Derry: Altnagelvin Hospital (✉ Belfast Rd., ☎ 01504/45171) has an emergency room.

Guided Tours

Citybus (✉ Milewater Rd., ☎ 01232/246485) offers a Belfast city orientation tour that takes in the shipyards and heads out from the city center as far as Stormont (9½ km/6 mi east) and Belfast Castle on Cave Hill to the north. The cost is U.K.£6.50, including afternoon tea. The City tour leaves Castle Place June–September, Tuesday–Thursday at 2.

Ulsterbus (✉ Milewater Rd., ☎ 01232/333000) operates half day or full-day trips during June to September from Belfast to the Glens of Antrim, the Giant's Causeway, the Fermanagh lakes, Lough Neagh, the Mourne Mountains, and the Ards Peninsula.

LOWER LOUGH ERNE

Erne Tours (☎ 01365/322882) operates *Kestrel*, a 63-seat water bus; it sets off from Round O pier at Enniskillen during the summer for a two-hour trip on beautiful Lough Erne. On weekdays the boat makes a half-hour stop at Devenish Island (☞ *above*) From May to June there are Sunday trips at 3, and occasionally there are trips at other times of the year. Call for prices.

GIANT'S CAUSEWAY/BUSHMILLS

If you're seeing the province without a car, you could have difficulty reaching the Giant's Causeway. Apart from a tour to that destination from Belfast, Ulsterbus has also teamed up with the Old Bushmills Distillery to run the **Bushmills Bus,** an open-top tour bus running from Coleraine to the Giant's Causeway via the coast resorts; you also visit Bushmills to observe whiskey making. A bus leaves Coleraine daily at 9:20, 11:30, 2:10, 4, and 6. Call Ulsterbus (☎ 01232/333000 or 01265/43334) for prices.

Outdoor Activities and Sports

BICYCLING

Rentals cost around U.K.£7 a day, U.K.£30 a week; local TIOs can offer suggestions for good cycling routes (☞ Visitor Information, *below*). In Belfast rent from **McConvrey Cycles** (✉ 467 Ormeau Rd., ☎ 01232/491163). **ReCycle** (✉ 1 Albert Sq., ☎ 01232/313113) is another good place to rent in Belfast.

BIRD-WATCHING

Murphy's Wildlife Tours (✉ 12 Belvoir [pronounced "beaver"] Close, Belvoir Park, Belfast, ☎ 01232/693232) leads tours in all seasons, though if you're an advanced birder, you may want to concentrate on wintering wildfowl and waders that have migrated all the way from North America to the shores of Loughs Foyle, Neagh, and Strangford. For information, ideas, and details of field-study groups, contact Northern Ireland TIOs (☞ Visitor Information, *below*) and the **Royal Society for the Protection of Birds** (✉ Belvoir Park Forest, ☎ 01232/491547).

FISHING

Northern Ireland's system of pricing and administrating fishing licenses and permits can seem anachronistic, unnecessarily complex, and bewildering. No license is needed for sea fishing, but to catch freshwater fish, whether coarse or game, you need a rod license from the **Fisheries Conservancy Board** (✉ 1 Mahon Rd., Portadown, ☎ 01762/334666), another license from the **Foyle Fisheries Commission** (✉ 8 Victoria Rd., Derry, ☎ 01504/42100), depending on the area in which you're fishing, and you'll probably need a local permit. The good news is that all licenses and Department of Agriculture and Fisheries permits are available from the **Northern Ireland Visitor Information Centre** (☞ Visitor Information, *below*) as well as from a number of TIOs and tackle shops around the province.

In the main angling areas, the following are useful contacts: **Moyle Outdoor Angling** (✉ 17 Castle St., Ballycastle, ☎ 012657/69521), **Joseph Braddell** (✉ 11 North St., Belfast, ☎ 01232/320525), **Tommy McCutcheon** (✉ 114 Sandy Row, Belfast, ☎ 01232/249509), **Carlton Park Fishing Centre** (✉ Belleek, ☎ 0136565/8181), **Lakeland Tackle & Guns** (✉ Sligo Rd., Enniskillen, ☎ 01365/323774), **Albert Atkins** (✉ 67 Coleraine Rd., Garvagh, ☎ 012665/58555), **Hook, Line & Sinker** (✉ 43 South St., Newtownards, ☎ 01247/811671). **Joe Mullan** (✉ 74 Main St., Portrush, ☎ 01265/822209).

GOLF

All golf courses and clubs are listed in the Northern Ireland Tourist Board information guide No. 17, "Golf—Where to Play," available from main tourist offices. *See also* Northern Ireland *in* Chapter 10.

HIKING AND WALKING

More than 100 places to stay along the Ulster Way are listed in the Northern Ireland Tourist Board information guide, *Accommodation for Walkers on the Ulster Way.* The **Sports Council for Northern Ireland** (⊠ House of Sport, Upper Malone Rd., Belfast BT9 5LA, ☎ 01232/ 381222) can also give advice about the Ulster Way; it sells books covering each section of the route. Tougher walks in the hills are outlined in the informative handbook in the Irish Walks series, No. 4, *The North East,* by Richard Rogers, published by Gill & Macmillan (⊠ 15–17 Eden Quay, Dublin), which is available in local book and sporting goods stores in Northern Ireland; it gives precise details of 45 hill walks, complete with descriptions of the wildflowers you'll see along the way. For hikes in the Mountains of Mourne, you can obtain maps and details of suggested routes from the **Mourne Countryside Centre** (⊠ 91 Central Promenade, Newcastle, Co. Down, ☎ 013967/24059). **Celtic Journeys** (⊠ 111 Whitepark Rd., Ballycastle, ☎ 012657 69651) arranges wildlife and cultural walks.

Horseback Riding/Pony Trekking

About 3¼ km/2 mi south of center-city Belfast, the **Lagan Valley Equestrian Centre** runs pony treks and offers lessons—both group and private. ⊠ *170 Upper Malone Rd., Belfast,* ☎ *01232/614853.* 🖃 *Group lessons and trekking: U.K.£8 hourly; private lessons: U.K.£14.* ☉ *Weekdays 10–9, Sat. 10–3:30.*

Student Travel

For details on youth hostels in Belfast and elsewhere, contact **Y.H.A.N.I.** at the Belfast International Youth Hostel (⊠ 22 Donegall Rd., Belfast BT12 5JN, ☎ 01232/324733, ℻ 01232/439699). The Belfast hostel has 128 beds.

Visitor Information

The **Northern Ireland Tourist Board Information Centre** in Belfast is the main TIO for the whole of the North (☞ Exploring Belfast, *above*). ⊠ *59 North St.,* ☎ *01232/246609,* ℻ *01232/240960.* ☉ *Oct.–Easter, Mon.–Sat., 9–5:15; Easter–Sept., Mon.–Sat., 9–5:15, Sun. 12–4.*

Year-round local offices are also at these locations: **Armagh** (⊠ 40 English St., ☎ 01861/521800). **Ballycastle** (⊠ 7 Mary St., ☎ 012657/ 62024). **Bangor** (⊠ Quay St., ☎ 01247/270069). **Carrickfergus** (⊠ Heritage Plaza, ☎ 01960/366455). **Coleraine** (⊠ Railway Rd., 01265/ 44723). **Derry** (⊠ Ferry St., ☎ 01504/267284). **Downpatrick** (⊠ 74 Market St., ☎ 01396/612233). **Enniskillen** (⊠ Lakeland Visitor Centre, Shore Rd., ☎ 01365/323110). **Giant's Causeway** (⊠ Visitor Centre, ☎ 012657/31855). **Killymaddy** (⊠ Ballygally Rd., ☎ 01868/ 767259). **Larne** (⊠ Narrow Gauge Rd., ☎ 01574/260088). **Limavady** (⊠ Connell St., ☎ 015047/22226). **Lisburn** (⊠ Market Sq., ☎ 01846/ 660038). **Newcastle** (⊠ Central Promenade, ☎ 013967/22222). **Newtownards** (⊠ Regent St., ☎ 01247/826846). **Newry** (⊠ Town Hall, Bank Parade, ☎ 01693/68877). During June through August, many more towns and villages open TIOs.

Weather

Call **Weathercall** (☎ 0891/500427) or **Marine Call** (☎ 0891/505365) for a Northern Ireland weather forecast.

10 Irish Greens
Golfing in Ireland

If you come to Ireland to golf, you may hear the story about Mick O'Loughlin, a County Clare butcher who spent more time playing at the Lahinch Golf Club than behind his meat counter. "He can't be making much money," a visitor remarked, upon hearing where Mick could usually be found. Came the reply: "Maybe not. But he's sure making plenty of friends." In the last 10 years, Ireland has invested nearly $400 million in a gambit to become Europe's premier golf destination. While its you-know-who neighbor to the northeast still has more courses, Ireland's 330—and counting—are gorgeously scenic, designed by golf's greatest, and guarantee the welcoming warmth of Mick O'Loughlin and friends.

By Jonathan
Abrahams

Updated by
Dermot
Gilleece

ASK MOST GOLFERS WHERE TO FIND the golf vacation of a lifetime—a variety of breathtaking courses, beautiful settings, history seeping into every shot—and they'll probably point you in the direction of Scotland. Unless, of course, they've been to Ireland.

Indeed, Ireland's neighbor to the northeast gets more world attention when it comes to golf. It plays host to most of the British Open Championships and in many circles is considered the birthplace of the game. But Ireland doesn't lag far behind when it comes to golf history. Its oldest course dates back to 1881, and with more than 330 quality layouts, the Emerald Isle is second only to Scotland in the amount of golf it can offer per square mile. If you ask a local how Ireland's courses stack up against Scotland's, he'll fix you with a steely stare before defending his homeland on his life. Then he very well may buy you a pint of the local stout.

But you don't have to be a native to have such passion for the golf courses of Ireland (not to mention the stout). Golfers the world over who are "in the know" have long sung the praises of Irish golf. Tom Watson, winner of five British Opens, lists as his favorite not any Scottish course, but Ballybunion," as does the legendary writer Herbert Warren Wind, who, from an American standpoint, is credited with putting Irish golf on the map when he penned, "To put it simply, Ballybunion revealed itself to be nothing less than the finest seaside course I have ever seen." And although Ballybunion is generally considered the prize jewel of the Emerald Isle, it is reflective of the quality of courses found throughout the country.

So what makes Irish golf great? Architecture, perhaps the essence of a golfing experience, is one appropriate place to begin.

Connoisseurs of golf in America hold such courses as Cypress Point and Pebble Beach in the highest regard because their designers used the spectacular lay of the land to create a beautiful, challenging, but fair layout. In Ireland, however, there are many such courses. Of the estimated 150 top-quality links courses in the world, 39 of them are in Ireland. Most of the leading courses in Ireland were designed by celebrated British architects, such as Tom Morris, James Braid, Harry Colt, and Alister Mackenzie, who happened to have as their raw material a spectacular landscape: Ireland is one of those remarkable places where mountains and sea meet, so there is no need to manipulate the land. Nature—the scraggly coast of a links-land or rolling hills of heather—dominates the courses here, not the other way around.

There is also something to be said for the sense of history that comes with playing golf on a land that is, most assuredly, "Old World." Only 40 minutes from the airport in Shannon is the charming, 18-hole course at Adare, complete with a green nestled in the ruins of a 14th-century abbey. When you play Lahinch, one of the greats of the Southwest, you have the Cliffs of Moher as a majestic backdrop. Every step you take on an Irish golf course is a step back in history. Where in America can you find something comparable to the "Moon Hole" at Waterville, a par-3 built over a large hollow where Catholic priests used to hold services in secret, because praying was a capital offense at the time?

The land is spread out and often remote, not unlike the highlands of Scotland. There are great courses nestled in remote areas, away from any transportation hub, so the hordes of golf tour buses that traverse

Scotland are few and far between here. You can drive for miles on a seemingly endless, two-lane highway, enveloped by the sea of meadow and the smell of burning peat, then suddenly descend on such a hidden jewel as Waterville and have the course to yourself.

And you will be welcomed: There isn't a friendlier face than that of an Irish host, who treats a shared round of golf (or stout) as the forging of a lasting bond. A tour of the links usually winds up in the 19th hole, the local pub, which may easily stretch into dinner. Although pride runs deep here, there isn't any of the resentment or jealousy toward tourists that is sometimes found in Europe. They actually like Americans!

But the best part of Irish golf is what perhaps makes it most different from golf in America: simplicity. The game is remarkably unspoiled on the Emerald Isle, where you're far more likely to see goats grazing on a fairway than an electric cart roaming in the rough. Caddies are the staple here, and although they are famous for their slightly twisted advice ("It's a slightly straight putt." "You've got a strong crosswind against you."), they add a flavor lost to most of the world that hearkens back to the game's roots.

It's great stuff. But there are a few things you should know before you set out to conquer the courses of the Emerald Isle. Golf is a different game here, so be sure to address the following as you prepare:

The Weather Factor. Pack heavy. You see all different kinds of weather in Ireland, from high winds to rain and sleet to beautiful sunshine, and you may see it all in one round. There are no rain checks here. You play unless it's lightning, so pack your sweaters and rain gear, especially if you're planning your trip for the off-season months of the spring and fall.

The Sunday Bag Factor. If you don't have a golf bag that's light enough for you to carry for 18 holes, invest in one before your trip. Electric carts are generally available only at the leading venues in Ireland, so you usually have the option of a caddy, caddy car (pull cart), or carrying your own bag. Many courses have caddies but will not guarantee their availability since they're not employed by the course directly, so it's conceivable that you may be left with only one option: toting your bag yourself. To be safe, make sure you have a carry-all, or Sunday bag.

The Private Club Factor. Unlike America, most private golf clubs in Ireland are happy to let visitors play their course and use their facilities. It's important to remember, however, that the course is indeed there for the members first, and the majority of the club's concerns lie with them. Preferred days for visitors are listed below, but it's always a good idea to call in advance and make sure that the club will make time for you.

The Northern Ireland Factor. Some of the best and most beautiful courses are in Northern Ireland, where the leading venues are far less remote than in the Republic. Don't let media coverage from urban Belfast scare you away. Also, keep in mind that the region is under British rule, so all currency is in U.K. pounds, though the Irish pound, or punt, is always welcome.

And finally, a reality check. Ireland's best courses rank with the best of the world, but after that there's a bit of a drop-off. Of the 330-odd courses, only about 29 are worth crossing an ocean to play. Others are good, but nothing you can't find at home. Of that 29, all are happy to have visitors play, except Royal Belfast, in Northern Ireland. It's the oldest club in Ireland, and it's exclusive: If you belong to a club in America, they must write a letter of introduction to Royal Belfast to secure your playing privilege. The remaining 28 courses are listed below.

North of Dublin

County Louth Golf Club. Like many Irish courses, County Louth is better known as its hometown, Baltray, a village sandwiched by the Boyne Estuary to the west and the Irish Sea to the east. Long hitters will love the atypical layout, a par-73 that features five par-5's, but beware the well-protected, undulating greens. ⊠ *Baltray, Drogheda, Co. Louth,* ☏ *041/22329. 18 holes. Yardage: 6,783. Par 73. Fees: weekdays, £40; weekends, £45. Visitors: Mon. and Wed.–Fri. Practice area, caddies (reserve in advance), caddy carts, catering.*

The Island Golf Club. Talk about exclusive: Until 1960, the only way to get to this club was by boat. It was about as remote as you could be and still be only 24 km/15 mi from Dublin, but things have changed. The Island has opened its doors and revealed a fine links course that rolls in and around sandhills, with small, challenging greens. ⊠ *Corballis, Donabate, Co. Dublin,* ☏ *01/843–6205. 18 holes. Yardage: 6,625. Par 71. Fees: weekdays, £30; weekends, £35. Visitors: Mon., Tues., and Fri. Practice area, catering.*

★ **Portmarnock Golf Club.** Across an estuary from the easternmost point of Ireland, Portmarnock is perhaps the most famous of Ireland's "Big Four." (Ballybunion, Royal County Down, and Royal Portrush are the others.) Largely because of its proximity to Dublin, this links course has hosted numerous major championships, most recently the 1991 Walker Club. Known for its flat fairways and greens, it provides a fair test for any golfer who can keep it out of the heavy rough. ⊠ *Portmarnock, Co. Dublin,* ☏ *01/846–2968. 27 holes. Yardage: 7,051, 3,449. Par 72, 36. Fees: weekdays, £60; weekends, £75. Visitors: Mon., Tues., and Fri. Practice area, caddies (reserve in advance), caddy carts, catering.*

Royal Dublin Golf Club. Generally, links courses are in remote, even desolate areas (therein the charm), but this equally charming one is only 6 km/3½ mi from the center of Dublin, on Bull Island, a bird sanctuary. It's the second-oldest club in Ireland and is routed in the old tradition of seaside links: The front nine goes out in a line (wind helping), and the back nine comes back in a line (wind against). Don't expect to make a comeback on the way home if you've struggled going out. ⊠ *Dollymount, Clontarf, Dublin 3,* ☏ *01/833–6346. 18 holes. Yardage: 6,763. Par 72. Fees: weekdays, £45; weekends, £55. Visitors: Mon., Tues., Thurs., and Fri. Practice area, caddies, caddy carts, catering.*

St. Margaret's Golf and Country Club. Not all of the worthwhile golf in Ireland is played on links courses that are a century old. St. Margaret's is a parkland (inland) course that opened in 1992 and immediately received high praise from Ireland's golfing inner circle. If, after getting blown around on the seaside links, you long for a taste of Western golf, this is your haven. ⊠ *St. Margaret's, Co. Dublin,* ☏ *01/864–0400. 18 holes. Yardage: 6,965. Par 72. Fees: weekdays, £30; weekends and holidays, £35. Visitors: daily. Practice area, caddies, caddy carts, club rental, catering.*

South of Dublin and the Southeast

Gleann na Drioite (Druids Glen) Golf Club. Owner Hugo Flinn presented designers Pat Ruddy and Tom Craddock with the brief: "Build me the finest parkland course in Ireland, whatever the cost." After an outlay of more than $16 million their handiwork was opened to the public in September 1995. Only a few months later, it had been chosen as the venue for the 1996 Murphy's Irish Open, and it played host to the event again in 1997. Ruddy unashamedly admits to having copied some key elements of Augusta National—particularly the extensive use of water—in the layout. In the event, the course, situated about 40 km/25 mi south of Dublin in County Wicklow, is remarkably beautiful, particularly around the glen from which its name derives. It is essentially an American-style, target course incorporating some delightful changes in elevation, and its forbidding, par-three 17th has an island green, like the corresponding hole at TPC Sawgrass. ⊠ *Newtownmountkennedy, Co. Wicklow,* ☎ *01/287–3600. 18 holes. Yardage: 7,058. Par 72. Fees: £75 weekdays and weekends. Practice area, caddies, caddy carts, catering.*

★ **The K Club.** At just 27 km/17 mi west of Dublin, this 18-hole, Arnold Palmer–designed parkland course, one of the newest additions to the Irish golf scene, offers a round of golf in lush, wooded surroundings bordered by the River Liffey. From a challenge standpoint, the generous fairways and immaculate greens are offset by formidable length, which makes it one of the most demanding courses in the Dublin vicinity. Additional stress is presented by negotiating the numerous doglegs, water obstacles, and sand bunkers. Facilities on the premises are of the highest standard, allowing a wide choice of sporting and non-sporting activities. ⊠ *Kildare Country Club, Straffan, Co. Kildare,* ☎ *01/627–3333. 18 holes. Yardage: 7,171. Par 72. Fees: £110 (residents £60). Visitors: daily except 1:30–2:30, Sat. 9–1. Practice area, caddies, caddy carts, club rental, shoe rental, catering.*

Southwest

Adare Manor Golf Course. Situated in the ancestral estate of the Earl of Dunraven, this charming, parkland stretch was officially opened for play less than two years ago. Yet its immediate success was virtually guaranteed by the international profile of its designer, Robert Trent Jones. The grand old man of golf-course architects seemed far more comfortable with the wooded terrain than he was when designing the second links at Ballybunion. As a result, he delivered a course with the potential to play host to events of the highest caliber. The front nine is dominated by a man-made, 14-acre lake, the polyethylene base of which cost about $500,000. It is in play at the third, fifth, sixth, and seventh holes. By way of contrast, the dominant hazards on the homeward journey are the River Mague and the majestic trees. Both combine to make the par-five 18th one of the most testing finishing holes imaginable. ⊠ *Adare, Co. Limerick,* ☎ *061/395044. 18 holes. Yardage: 7,138. Par 72. Fees: £40, weekdays and weekends. Practice area, caddies, caddy carts, catering.*

★ **Ballybunion Golf Club.** Put simply, this is one of the finest courses in the world. The Old Course was a virtual unknown until Herbert Warren Wind sang its praises in 1968, and today Ballybunion is universally regarded as one of golf's holiest grounds. On the shore of the Atlantic next to the southern entrance of the Shannon, it has the huge dunes of Lahinch without the blind shots. No pushover, but every hole is a pleasurable experience. Watch out for "Mrs. Simpson," a double fairway bunker on the first hole, named after the wife of Tom Simpson, the architect who remodeled the course in 1937. The New Course opened in 1985, designed by Robert Trent Jones. ⊠ *Sandhill Rd., Ballybunion, Co. Kerry,* ☎ *068/27611. 36 holes. Yardage: 6,593 (Old), 6,216 (New). Par 71, 72. Fees: £45 (Old), £30 (New), £65 (both on same day). Visitors: weekdays. Practice area, caddies, caddy carts, catering.*

Cork Golf Club. If you know golf-course architecture, you know the name of Alister Mackenzie, who designed Cypress Point in California and Augusta National in Georgia. One of his few designs in Ireland is

Cork, better known as Little Island. There's water on this parkland course, but it's not the temperamental ocean; instead, Little Island is in Cork Harbour, a gentle bay of the Irish Sea. The course is little known but one of the Emerald Isle's best. ⊠ *Little Island, Co. Cork,* ☎ *021/ 353451. 18 holes. Yardage: 6,687. Par 72. Fees: weekdays, £30; weekends, £35. Visitors: Mon.–Wed. and Fri. Practice area, caddies, caddy carts, club rental, catering.*

Dooks Golf Club. On the second tier of courses in Ireland's Southwest, Dooks does not quite measure up to the world-class tracks. It is, nonetheless, a completely worthwhile day of golf if you're touring the area. Built in the old tradition of seaside links, it's shorter and a bit gentler, although the greens are small and tricky. It's an excellent way to take a breath. ⊠ *Dooks, Glenbeigh, Co. Kerry,* ☎ *066/68205. 18 holes. Yardage: 6,010. Par 70. Fees: £16. Visitors: weekdays. Caddy carts, catering.*

Killarney Golf and Fishing Club. Freshwater fishing is the sport here, for Killarney is an inland town, set among a stunning mixture of mountains, lakes, and forests. There are two golf courses, the Killeen Course, host of the 1992 Irish Open, and Mahony's Point, set along the shores of Lough Leane. Killeen is longer; Mahony's puts a premium on accuracy. Despite the abundance of seaside links, many well-traveled golfers name Killarney their favorite place to play in Ireland. ⊠ *Mahony's Point Demesne, Killarney, Co. Kerry,* ☎ *064/31034. 36 holes. Yardage: 7,056 (Killeen), 6,705 (Mahony's). Par 73, 72. Fees: £35. Visitors: Mon.–Sat. Practice area, caddies, caddy carts, catering.*

★ **Mount Juliet Golf Course.** The renowned, parkland, championship course, some 19 km/11 mi from Kilkenny Town, was designed by Jack Nicklaus and includes practice greens, a driving range, and, for those who feel a little rusty, a David Leadbetter golf academy. The heavily forested course has eight holes that play over water, including the three signature par-3s. The back nine presents a series of difficult bunker shots. A sporting day out comes to a welcome end in the Hunter's Yard or Rose Garden lodges, which cater to both the thirsty and the hungry. Greens fees are above average, and although visitors are always welcome, a weekday round is better than a weekend one, as tees can be crowded with members flocking to the course at week's end. ⊠ *Mount Juliet Estate, Thomastown, Co. Kilkenny,* ☎ *056/ 24455. Yardage 7,172. Par 72. Fees: weekdays, £65, weekends £70. Visitors: daily. Practice area, driving range, caddies, caddy carts, club rental, lessons, catering.*

Tralee Golf Club. Tralee is perhaps what all modern-golf-course architects *wish* they could do in the States: Find unspoiled, seaside linksland and route a course on it that's designed for the modern game. This is an Arnold Palmer–Ed Seay design that opened in 1984, and the setting is as classic as it gets, with plenty of cliffs, craters, dunes, and the gale-blowing ocean. Don't let the flat front nine lull you to sleep—the back nine can be a ferocious wake-up call. ⊠ *West Barrow, Ardfert, Co. Kerry,* ☎ *066/36379. 18 holes. Yardage: 6,738. Par 71. Fees: weekdays, £25; weekends, £30. Visitors: weekdays. Practice area, caddies, catering.*

Waterville Golf Links. Here's what you should know about Waterville before you play: The first hole of this course is aptly named "Last Easy." At 7,184 yards from the tips, Waterville is the longest course in Ireland or Britain, and it is generally regarded as their toughest test. Now the good news: The scenery is so majestic you may not care that your score is approaching the yardage. Six holes run along the cliffs by the sea, surrounding the other 12, which have a tranquil, if not soft, feel to them. ⊠ *Waterville, Co. Kerry,* ☎ *066/74102. 18 holes. Yardage:*

7,184. Par 72. Fees: £40. Visitors: weekdays. Practice area, caddies, caddy carts, buggies, catering.

West

Lahinch Golf Club. The original course at Lahinch was designed by Old Tom Morris, who, upon the unveiling in 1892, called it "as fine a natural course as it has ever been my good fortune to play over." That was when blind shots (when you can't see your target) were in vogue, and there are many here, where towering sandhills dominate every hole. Only a course with as much charm as this one could get away with that in today's modern game. ✉ *Lahinch, Co. Clare,* ☎ *065/81003. 18 holes. Yardage: 6,613. Par 72. Fees: £40. Visitors: daily. Practice area, caddies, caddy carts, catering.*

Connemara Golf Club. The local club for the small town of Clifden, Connemara is a links course where you can get carried away not only by the golf, but by the surrounding scenery as well. The Atlantic Ocean and Ballyconneely Bay are immediately to the west and the Twelve Bens Mountains are to the east. The course starts flat, then rises into the hills for the final, challenging six holes. ✉ *Ballyconneely, Clifden, Co. Galway,* ☎ *095/23502. 18 holes. Yardage: 7,174. Par 72. Fees: £25. Visitors: Mon.–Sat. Practice area, caddies, caddy carts, catering.*

Westport Golf Club. Twice the host of the Irish Amateur Championship, this inland course lies in the shadows of religious history. Rising 2,500 ft above Clew Bay, with its hundreds of islands, is Croagh Patrick, a mountain that legend connects with St. Patrick. The mountain is considered sacred, and it attracts multitudes of worshippers to its summit every year. All the prayers might pay off at the 15th, where your drive has to carry the ball over 200 yards of ocean. ✉ *Carrowholly, Co. Mayo,* ☎ *098/25113. 18 holes. Yardage: 6,667. Par 73. Fees: weekdays, £18; weekends, £22.50. Visitors: weekdays. Practice area, caddies, caddy carts, catering.*

Northwest

Carn Golf Links. This is a newer, Eddie Hackett–designed, links course that takes advantage of its location, far to the west on the shores of Blacksod Bay. From the elevated tees and greens you have a view of a string of Atlantic islands: Inishkea, Inishglora, and Achill. ✉ *Carn, Belmullet, Co. Mayo,* ☎ *097/82292. 18 holes. Yardage: 6,608. Par 72. Fees: £20. Visitors: daily. Practice area, caddies, caddy carts, catering.*

County Sligo Golf Club. A century old in 1997, the course at Sligo is one of the grand old venues of Ireland, having hosted most of the country's major championships. At 6,565 yards, this links course isn't particularly long; however, it still manages to have seven par-4s of 400 yards or more. Typical of Ireland's hidden jewels, Rosses Point clings to cliffs above the Atlantic. The third tee offers views of the ocean, the hills, and the unusual mountain Benbulben, which looks like a giant Irish arroyo. ✉ *Rosses Point, Co. Sligo,* ☎ *071/77186. 18 holes. Yardage: 6,565. Par 71. Fees: weekdays, £23; weekends, £27. Visitors: Mon., Tues., Thurs., and Fri. Practice area, caddies (summer only), caddy carts, club rental, catering.*

Donegal Golf Club. On the shores of Donegal Bay and approached through a forest, this windswept links is shadowed by the Blue Stack Mountains, with the Atlantic Ocean as a backdrop. The greens are large, but the rough is deep and penal, and there's a constant battle against erosion by the sea. Legendary golf writer Peter Dobreiner called it "hauntingly beautiful," perhaps recalling his experience on the par-3 fifth, fittingly called The Valley of Tears. ✉ *Murvagh, Laghey, Co. Donegal,* ☎ *073/34054. 18 holes. Yardage: 7,153. Par 73. Fees: weekdays, £17;*

weekends, £22.50. Visitors: daily. Practice area, caddies, caddy carts, catering.

Enniscrone Golf Club. Eddie Hackett designed this course on the shores of another bay, this time Killala. Hackett may be the Pete Dye of Ireland, due in part to the fact that he's blessed with wonderful land: Enniscrone's setting is a natural for good golf—a combination of flatlands, foothills, and, of course, the Atlantic. It's not overly long on the scorecard, but the persistent winds can add yards to almost every hole. It's among the small number of clubs in Ireland with electric carts, or, as they call them, buggies. ✉ *Enniscrone, Co. Sligo,* ☎ *96/36297. 18 holes. Yardage: 6,682. Par 72. Fees: weekdays, £18; weekends, £22. Visitors: weekdays, weekends by appointment. Practice area, caddies (weekends and holidays), caddy carts, buggies, club rental.*

Northern Ireland

Ballycastle Golf Club. Pleasure comes first here, with challenge as an afterthought: It's beautiful (five holes wind around the remains of a 13th-century friary), short (less than 6,000 yards) and conveniently located right next to Bushmills, the world's oldest distillery at nearly 400 years. ✉ *2 Cushendall Rd., Ballycastle BT54 6QP, Co. Antrim,* ☎ *012657/62536. 18 holes. Yardage: 5,882. Par 71. Fees: weekdays, U.K.£17; weekends, U.K.£22. Visitors: daily. Practice area, caddy cars, catering.*

Castlerock Golf Club. Where else in the world can you play a hole called "Leg o' Mutton"? Not in America, that's for sure. It's a 200-yard par-3 with railway tracks to the right and a burn to the left—just one of several unusual holes at this course, which claims, year-round, to have the best greens in Ireland. True or not, the finish is spectacular: from the elevated 17th tee, where you can see the shores of Scotland, to the majestic 18th, which plays uphill to a plateau green. ✉ *65 Circular Rd., Castlerock BT51 4TJ, Co. Londonderry* ☎ *01265/848314. 27 holes. Yardage: 6,499, 2,678. Par 73, 35. Fees: weekdays, U.K.£15, U.K.£7; weekends, U.K.£25, U.K.£10. Visitors: Mon.–Thurs. Practice area, caddies (reserve in advance), caddy cars, catering.*

Malone Golf Club. Fishermen may find the 22-acre lake at the center of this parkland layout distracting: It's filled with trout. The golf, however, is just as well stocked; large trees and well-manicured, undulating greens combine to provide one of the most challenging inland tests in Ireland. Bring your power game—there are only three par-5s, but they're all over 520 yards. ✉ *240 Upper Malone Rd., Dunmurry, Belfast, BT17 9LB,* ☎ *01232/612758. 27 holes. Yardage: 6,642, 3,138. Par 71, 36. Fees: weekdays (except Wednesday) U.K.£32 (men); £21 (women); Wednesdays and weekends, U.K.£37 (men), £29 (women). Visitors: Mon., Thurs., and Fri. Practice area, catering.*

Portstewart Golf Club. One hundred years old in 1994, Portstewart may scare you with its opening hole, generally regarded as the toughest starter in Ireland. Picture a 425-yard par-4 that descends from an elevated tee to a small green tucked between the dunes. The greens are known for uniformity and speed, and seven of the holes have recently been redesigned to toughen the course. Also, if you want a break from the grand scale of championship links, there's the Old Course 18 and the Riverside 9, 27 holes of downsized, executive-style golf. ✉ *117 Strand Rd., Portstewart BT55 7PT, Co. Londonderry,* ☎ *01265/832015. 45 holes. Yardage: 6,784 (Championship), 4,733 (Old Course), 2,662 (Riverside). Par 72, 64, 32. Fees: weekdays, U.K.£30 (Championship), U.K.£8 (Old Course), U.K.£10 (Riverside); weekends, U.K.£50 (Championship), U.K.£12 (Old Course), U.K.£15 (Riverside). Visitors: Mon., Tues., and Fri. Practice area, caddies, caddy cars, catering.*

★ **Royal County Down.** This is perhaps the most beautiful course in Ireland. Catch it on the right day at the right time and you may think you're on the moon; Royal County Down is a links course with a sea of craterlike bunkers and small dunes. Actually, for better players, every day is the right one. Harry Vardon labeled it the toughest course on the Emerald Isle, and, if you can't hit your driver long and straight, you might find it the toughest course in the world. It's a true masterpiece. ✉ *Golk Links Rd., Newcastle BT33 0AN, Co. Down,* ☎ *013967/22419. 36 holes. Yardage: 6,969 (Championship course), 4,087 (No. 2). Par 71, 65. Fees: weekdays, U.K.£50; weekends, U.K.£60. Visitors: Tues., Thurs., and Fri. Practice area, caddies, caddy cars, catering.*

★ **Royal Portrush.** The only club outside Scotland and England to have hosted a British Open, Portrush is perhaps the most understated of Ireland's "Big Four." The championship Dunluce course is named for the ruins of a nearby castle and is a sea of sandhills and curving fairways. The Valley course is a less-exposed, tamer track. Both are conspicuous for their lack of bunkers. The Dunluce course, in a poll of Irish golf legends, was voted the best course in Ireland. ✉ *Dunluce Rd., Portrush BT56 8JQ, Co. Antrim,* ☎ *01265/822311. 36 holes. Yardage: 6,530 (Dunluce), 6,054 (Valley). Par 72, 70. Fees: weekdays, U.K.£45 (Dunluce), U.K.£20 (Valley); weekends, U.K.£55 (Dunluce), U.K.£25 (Valley). Visitors: weekdays. Practice area, catering.*

11 Portraits of Ireland

IRELAND AT A GLANCE: A CHRONOLOGY

ca. 6000 BC   Mesolithic (middle Stone Age) hunter-gatherers migrate from Scotland to the northeastern Irish coast.

ca. 3500 BC   Neolithic (new Stone Age) settlers (origins uncertain) bring agriculture, pottery, and weaving. They also build massive megaliths—stone monuments with counterparts in England (Stonehenge), Brittany (Carnac), and elsewhere in Europe.

ca. 700 BC   Celtic tribes begin to arrive via Britain and France; they divide Ireland into "fifths" or provinces, including Ulster, Leinster, Connaught, Meath, and Munster.

ca. AD 100   Ireland becomes the center of Celtic culture and trade without being settled by the Romans.

432   Traditional date for the arrival of St. Patrick and Christianity; in fact, Irish conversion to Christianity began at least a century earlier.

ca. 500–800   Golden Age of Irish monasticism; as many as 3,000 study at Clonard (Meath). Irish missionaries carry the faith to barbarian Europe; art (exemplified by the *Book of Kells,* ca. 700) and Gaelic poetry flourish.

795   First Scandinavian Viking invasion; raids continue for the next 200 years. Viking towns founded include Dublin, Waterford, Wexford, Cork, and Limerick.

1014   Vikings decisively defeated at Clontarf by Irish troops under King Brian Boru of Munster. His murder cuts short hopes of a unified Ireland.

1066   Normans (French descendants of Viking invaders) conquer England and set their sights on Ireland as well.

1169   Dermot MacMurrough, exiled king of Munster, invites the Anglo-Norman adventurer Richard FitzGilbert de Clare ("Strongbow") to help him regain his throne, beginning a pattern of English opportunism and bad decisions by the Irish.

1172   Pope Alexander III confirms Henry II, king of England, as feudal lord of Ireland. Over the next two centuries, Anglo-Norman nobles establish estates, intermarry with the native population, and act in a manner similar to the neighboring Celtic chieftains. Actual control by the English crown is confined to a small area known as "the land of peace" or "the Pale" around Dublin.

1366   Statutes of Kilkenny attempt belatedly to enforce ethnic divisions by prohibiting the expression of Irish language and culture and intermarriage between the Irish and English, but Gaelic culture prevails, and the Pale continues to contract. Constant warfare among the great landowners keeps Ireland poor, divided, and isolated from the rest of Europe.

1477–1513   Garret Mor ("Gerald the Great") FitzGerald, eighth earl of Kildare, dominates Irish affairs as lord deputy (the representative of the English crown).

1494   Henry VII removes Kildare from office (he is soon reinstated), and initiates Statute of Drogheda (Poyning's Law), which is in force until 1782—Irish Parliament can only meet by consent of the king of England.

1534–40 Henry VIII's break with the Catholic Church leads to insurrection in Ireland, led by Garret Mor's grandson Lord Offaly ("Silken Thomas"). He is executed with five of his brothers.

1541 Parliament proclaims Henry VIII king of Ireland (his previous status was merely a feudal lord). Irish magnates reluctantly surrender their lands to him as their overlord. Hereafter, a constant English presence is required to keep the peace; no single Irish family replaces the FitzGeralds.

1558–1603 Reign of Queen Elizabeth I; her fear of Irish intrigue with Catholic enemies of England leads to expansion of English power, including the Munster "plantation" (colony) scheme and the division of Ireland into English-style counties.

1580–88 Edmund Spenser, an administrator for the Crown in Ireland, writes *The Faerie Queene*.

1591 Trinity College, Dublin, is founded.

1595–1603 Rebellion of Hugh O'Neill, earl of Tyrone (Ulster). Defeats England at Yellow Ford (1598), but assistance from Spain is inadequate; Tyrone surrenders at Mellifont six days after Queen Elizabeth's death.

1607 The Flight of the Earls, and the beginning of "the Troubles." The earl of Tyrone and his ally Tyrconnell flee to Rome; their lands in Ulster are confiscated and opened to Protestant settlers, mostly Scots.

1641 Charles I's policies provoke insurrection in Ulster and, soon after, civil war in England.

1649 August: British leader Oliver Cromwell, having defeated Charles and witnessed his execution, invades Ireland, determined to crush Catholic opposition. Massacres at Drogheda and Wexford.

1652 Act of Settlement—lands of Cromwell's opponents are confiscated, and owners are forced across the Shannon to Connaught. Never fully carried out, this policy nonetheless establishes Protestant ascendancy.

1678 In the wake of the Popish Plot to assassinate King Charles II, Catholics are barred from British parliaments.

1683 Dublin Philosophical Society founded, modeled on the Royal Society of London.

1689 Having attempted, among other things, to repeal the Act of Settlement, King James II (a Catholic) is deposed and flees to Ireland. His daughter Mary and her husband William of Orange assume the throne.

1690 James is defeated by William III at the Battle of the Boyne.

1704 First laws of the Penal Code are enacted, restricting Catholic landowning; later laws prohibited voting, education, and military service among the Catholics.

1775 American War of Independence begins, precipitating Irish unrest. Henry Grattan (1746–1820), a Protestant barrister, enters the Irish Parliament.

1778 Land clauses of Penal Code are repealed.

1782 Grattan's Parliament—Grattan asserts independence of Irish Parliament from Britain. Britain agrees, but independence is easier to declare than to sustain.

1798 Inspired by the French Revolution and dissatisfied with the slow progress of Parliament, Wolfe Tone's United Irishmen rebel but are defeated.

1800 The Irish Parliament votes itself out of existence and agrees to union with Britain, effective January 1, 1801.

1823 Daniel O'Connell (1775–1847), "the Liberator," founds the Catholic Association to campaign for Catholic Emancipation.

1828 O'Connell's election to Parliament (illegal, because he was a Catholic) leads to passage of Catholic Emancipation Act in 1829; later, he works for repeal of the Union.

1845–48 Failure of potato crop leads to famine; thousands die, others migrate.

1848 "Young Ireland," a radical party, leads an abortive rebellion.

1856 Birth of George Bernard Shaw, playwright (d. 1950).

1858 Fenian Brotherhood founded in New York by Irish immigrants with the aim of overthrowing British rule. A revolt in 1867 fails, but it compels Gladstone, the British prime minister, to disestablish the Anglican Church (1869) and reform landholding (1870) in Ireland. The government also increases its powers of repression.

1865 Birth of William Butler Yeats, the great Irish poet (d. 1939).

1871 Isaac Butts founds parliamentary Home Rule Party, soon dominated by Charles Stewart Parnell (1846–91, descendant of English Protestants), who tries to force the issue by obstructing parliamentary business.

1881 Gladstone's second Land Act opposed by Parnell, who leads a boycott (named for Captain Boycott, its first victim) of landlords.

1882 Phoenix Park murders—British officials murdered by Fenians. Prevention of Crime bill that follows suspends trial by jury and increases police powers. Acts of terrorism increase. Parnell disavows all connection with Fenians. Birth of James Joyce, novelist (d. 1941).

1886 Gladstone introduces his first Home Rule Bill, which is defeated. Ulster Protestants fear Catholic domination and revive Orange Order (named for William of Orange) to oppose Home Rule.

1890 Parnell is named corespondent in the divorce case of Kitty O'Shea; his career is ruined.

1893 Second Home Rule Bill passes Commons but is defeated by Lords. Subsequent policy is to "kill Home Rule with kindness" with land reform, but cultural nationalism revives with founding of Gaelic League to promote Irish language. Yeats, John Synge (1871–1909), and other writers find inspiration in Gaelic past.

1898 On the anniversary of Wolfe Tone's rebellion, Arthur Griffith (1872–1922) founds the Dublin newspaper the *United Irishman,* preaching *sinn féin* ("we ourselves")—secession from Britain; Sinn Fein party founded 1905. Socialist James Connolly (executed 1916) founds the *Workers' Republic.*

1904 William Butler Yeats and Lady Gregory found the Abbey Theatre in Dublin.

1912 Third Home Rule Bill passes Commons but is rejected by Lords. Under new rules, however, Lords' veto is null after two years. Meanwhile, Ulster Protestants plan defiance; the Ulster Volunteers recruit 100,000. Radical Republicans such as Connolly, Patrick

Pearse, and others of the Irish Republican Brotherhood (IRB) preach insurrection and recruit their own volunteers.

1914 Outbreak of war postpones implementation of Home Rule until peace returns. Parliamentarians agree, but radicals plan revolt.

1916 Easter Uprising—IRB stages insurrection in Dublin and declares independence; the uprising fails, but the execution of 15 leaders by the British turns public opinion in favor of the insurgents. Yeats writes "a terrible beauty is born."

1919 January: Irish Parliamentarians meet as the Dail Éireann (Irish Assembly) and declare independence. September: Dail suppressed; Sinn Féin made illegal.

1920–21 War breaks out between Britain and Ireland: the "Black and Tans" versus the Irish Republican Army (IRA). Government of Ireland Act declares separate parliaments for north and south and continued ties to Britain. Elections follow, but the Sinn Féin majority in the south again declare themselves the Dail Éireann under Eamon de Valera (1882–1975), rejecting British authority. December 1921: Anglo-Irish Treaty grants the south dominion status as the Irish Free State, allowing the north to remain under Britain.

1922 De Valera and his Republican followers reject the treaty; civil war results. The Irish Free State adopts a constitution; William T. Cosgrave becomes president. Michael Collins, chairman of the Irish Free State and Commander-in-Chief of the Army, is shot dead in his County Cork, not far from where he was born. In Paris, James Joyce's *Ulysses* is published.

1923 De Valera is arrested and the civil war ends, but Republican agitation and terrorism continues. William Butler Yeats is the first Irish writer to be awarded the Nobel Prize in Literature; he also takes a seat in the first Irish parliament.

1925 George Bernard Shaw wins the Nobel Prize in Literature.

1932 De Valera, who had founded the Fianna Fáil party in 1926, begins a 16-year term as Taioseach (Prime Minister).

1932–36 Tariff war with Britain.

1938 New constitution creates Republic of Ireland with no ties to Britain.

1947 The statue of Queen Victoria is removed from the courtyard in front of the Irish Parliament in Dublin.

1959 Eamon de Valera resigns as Taoiseach (Prime Minister) and is later elected President.

1963 John F. Kennedy, the first Irish-American President of the United States, visits Ireland.

1969 The annual Apprentice Boys' march in Londonderry, Northern Ireland, leads to rioting between Catholics and Protestants. British troops, called in to keep the peace, remain in Northern Ireland to this day. Samuel Beckett is awarded the Nobel Prize in Literature, but declines to travel to Oslo to receive it.

1972 Republic of Ireland admitted to European Economic Community. Troubles continue in the north: In Derry on January 30, British troops shoot 13 unarmed demonstrators on "Bloody Sunday." Stormont (the Northern Parliament) is suspended and direct rule from London is imposed. Acts of terrorism on both sides leads to draconian law enforcement by the British.

1979 Pope John Paul II visits Ireland and celebrates mass in Phoenix Park; more than a million people attend.

1985 Irish singer Bob Geldof, lead singer of the Boomtown Rats, raises $62 million for African famine relief in two Live Aid concerts.

1986 Anglo-Irish Agreement signed, giving the Republic of Ireland a stronger voice in northern affairs.

1988 Dublin celebrates its millennium.

1991 Mary Robinson becomes the first female President of the Republic of Ireland. Peace talks begin between the British and Irish governments and the main political parties of the North, excepting Sinn Féin.

1992 Ireland approves European Union. Sixty-two percent of the Irish vote in a referendum in favor of allowing pregnant women to seek an abortion abroad.

1994 The IRA, in response to advances made by the Irish, British, and U.S. governments, announces a complete cessation of activities. Protestant paramilitary groups follow suit one month later. Gerry Adams, the leader of Sinn Féin, speaks on British TV and radio.

1995 After 25 years, daylight troop patrols are discontinued in Belfast. Seamus Heaney receives the Nobel Prize in Literature, the fourth Irish writer in less than 75 years so honored.

1996 The IRA, frustrated by the slow progress of the peace talks, explode bombs on the British mainland, throwing the whole peace process into doubt. But violence has not returned to the province, and all parties say they are committed to peace.

1997 The Republic of Ireland legalizes divorce. Newly elected British Prime Minister Tony Blair apologizes for the British government's policies during Ireland's Great Famine, acknowledging that his predecessors' policies prolonged "a massive human tragedy." Ireland is rated the fastest-growing economy in the industrialized world. President Mary Robinson is named the High Commissioner for Human Rights for the United Nations. The IRA cease-fire is reestablished. Peace talks begin with the goal of bringing a permanent end to the conflict in Northern Ireland.

Antrim
Lynch
McDonnell
McNeill
O'Hara
O'Neill
Quinn

Armagh
Hanlon
McCann

Carlow
Kinsella
Nolan
O'Neill

Cavan
Boylan
Lynch
McCabe
McGovern
McGowan
McNally
O'Reilly
Sheridan

Clare
Aherne
Boland
Clancy
Daly
Lynch
McGrath
McInerney
McMahon
McNamara
Molon(e)y
O'Brien
O'Dea
O'Grady
O'Halloran
O'Loughlin

Cork
Barry
Callaghan
Cullinane
Donovan
Driscoll
Flynn
Hennessey
Hogan
Lynch
McCarthy
McSweeney
Murphy
Nugent
O'Casey
O'Cullane
(Collins)

O'Keefe
O'Leary
O'Mahony
O'Riordan
Roche
Scanlon
Sheridan

Derry
Cahan
Hegarty
Kelly
McLaughlin

Donegal
Boyle
Clery
Doherty
Friel
Gallagher
Gormley
McGrath
McLoughlin
McSweeney
Mooney
O'Donnell

Down
Lynch
McGuinness
O'Neil
White

Dublin
Hennessey
O'Casey
Plunkett

Fermanagh
Cassidy
Connolly
Corrigan
Flanagan
Maguire
McManus

Galway
Blake
Burke
Clery
Fah(e)y
French
Jennings
Joyce
Kelly
Kenny
Kirwan
Lynch
Madden
Moran
O'Flaherty
O'Halloran

Kerry
Connor
Fitzgerald
Galvin
McCarthy
Moriarty
O'Connell
O'Donoghue
O'Shea
O'Sullivan

Kildare
Cullen
Fitzgerald
O'Byrne
White

Kilkenny
Butler
Fitzpatrick
O'Carroll
Tobin

Laois
Dempsey
Doran
Dunn(e)
Kelly
Moore

Leitrim
Clancy
O'Rourke

Limerick
Fitzgerald
Fitzgibbon
McKeough
O'Brien
O'Cullane
(Collins)
O'Grady
Woulfe

Longford
O'Farrell
Quinn

Louth
O'Carroll
Plunkett

Mayo
Burke
Costello
Dugan
Gormley
Horan
Jennings
Jordan
Kelly
Madden
O'Malley

Meath
Coffey
Connolly
Cusack
Dillon
Hayes
Hennessey
Plunkett
Quinlan

Monaghan
Boylan
Connolly
Hanratty
McKenna
McMahon
McNally

Offaly
Coghlan
Dempsey
Fallon
(Maher)
Malone
Meagher
Molloy
O'Carroll
Sheridan

Roscommon
Fallon
Flanagan
Flynn
Hanley
McDermot
McKeogh
McManus
Molloy
Murphy

Sligo
Boland
Higgins
McDonagh
O'Dowd
O'Hara
Rafferty

Tipperary
Butler
Fogarty
Kennedy
Lynch
Meagher
(Maher)
O'Carroll
O'Dwyer
O'Meara
Purcell
Ryan

Tyrone
Cahan
Donnelly
Gormley
Hagan
Murphy
O'Neill
Quinn

Waterford
Keane
McGrath
O'Brien
Phelan
Power

Westmeath
Coffey
Dalton
Daly
Dillon
Sheridan

Wexford
Doran
Doyle
Hartley
Kavanagh
Keating
Kinsella
McKeogh
Redmond
Walsh

Wicklow
Cullen
Kelly
McKeogh
O'Byrne
O'Toole

THE MAGIC MOUNTAIN*

IT STARTED TO RAIN as soon as I drove out of Galway, and after a while it came pouring down, relentless and hard as though it was never going to end. I was going to Westport in County Mayo on the last Saturday in July. The following day pilgrims from all over Ireland traditionally climbed Croagh Patrick, the holy mountain outside the town overlooking Clew Bay. If this rain kept up, and if there was a wind, the climb would be even more difficult.

And then the rain lifted as I got closer to Westport as though I had entered a new climate or a new season. Suddenly, it was a summer's evening in a busy Irish town, with cars badly parked, slowly moving traffic and people wandering around, some on the way to early evening Mass. I had arranged to meet two friends; we discovered that all the hotels were booked, and we had to drive out of town to a bed and breakfast house.

When we went back into Westport the shoppers and the Mass-goers had gone home; the place was now full of young people and the evening was still warm. They stood outside the pubs, with pints of Guinness, talking and laughing, or they roamed the streets. The young men and women were well dressed and in good humour. In some of the pubs there was traditional music playing. Everywhere there was a sense of plenty, of security, of ease. You could make the mistake of thinking that it was prosperous here; you could mistake the atmosphere in a market town on a summer's night if you did not know that emigration had decimated Ireland in the previous five years, that in 1989 alone as many as fifty thousand young people had left the Republic of Ireland, which has a population of three and a half million. Whole villages had lost all their young people; there were countless stories of entire football teams leaving in one or two years, ending up in Boston or New York.

It had happened in Ireland before, not just after the Famine in the nineteenth century,

but again after independence. Four out of every five children born in the Republic of Ireland between 1931 and 1941 emigrated in the 1950s. I was born in 1955: two years before Ireland was admitted into the World Bank and the International Monetary Fund, three years before the government published its First Programme for Economic Expansion, which abandoned the failed protectionist policies and opened the country to foreign capital and investment. In the seven years after the Programme's publication industrial exports rose by one hundred and fifty per cent.

I came from that climate of hope; a world of free education, returned emigrants, television, reduced censorship. Even when unemployment began to rise again in the late 1970s, I did not think that people would emigrate, I thought they would believe enough in the future of the country to wait. But by the mid-1980s it had begun again, and it was hard, on nights like this in Westport, not to look around and know that things were less comfortable than they seemed, that many of these young people would leave too, that some were just home on holiday, that there was not much chance of things improving.

But you could misread the statistics too: you could watch unemployment rise above twenty per cent; you could be told that the entire revenue from personal income tax went to pay interest on the national debt; you could look at the emigration figures; but some people lived well in Ireland and maybe the young people we watched that night in Westport were not about to emigrate, but were going to stay to inherit what their parents and grandparents had consolidated. Since the end of the eighteenth century a new Catholic class had emerged in Ireland—people had opened shops, educated their children to enter the professions, slowly increased the size of their farms and gained control over the business life of the towns. This class remained extremely conservative and cautious. They were happier to put money in the bank than take any risks. This was, and is in general, the

---

This essay is excerpted from The Sign of the Cross: Travels in Catholic Europe, *published by Pantheon Books, New York.* Copyright © 1994 by Colm Tóibín. All rights reserved.

class from which the Catholic clergy come in Ireland.

It was easy for any external power to control the country once its population was suitably divided between the owners and the dispossessed. And gradually through emigration, and then legislation at the end of the nineteenth century which handed over land to tenant farmers, the threat from the dispossessed decreased and the country became stable but conservative, its population insecure and fearful, desperate to hold on to the small improvements in their lot.

Maybe what we witnessed as we sat on the ground outside Matt Molloy's public house in Westport that night, the music wafting out into the warm summer air, was a new confidence, a new generation wandering around on a Saturday night with no innate fear or insecurity. Or maybe as they grew older they would run their businesses and their lives with the same caution as their parents. For any outsider, it is difficult to judge a small community.

Later that night, we drove out to Murrisk at the foot of Croagh Patrick, and found a pub full of travellers, who sleep in caravans and move around the country, living off the dole and the sale of carpets and furniture. The tens of thousands of pilgrims (somewhere between twenty and sixty thousand) who would climb the reek the next day would each need a roughly-cut wooden staff for support, and there had been a fight outside the pub about who could sell where. The atmosphere in the pub was tense. Drinkers would get up and go outside to see what was going on and come back in to have animated and fierce discussions. Deals were done. A large and muscular traveller man grabbed one of our chairs when it was temporarily vacant. We did not protest.

I N THE MORNING there was a dull incessant drizzle which soon became soft rain. We sat having breakfast wondering if we should wait, if the weather would lift. Normally, the landlady told us, you could see Croagh Patrick in the distance from her kitchen window, but now you could see nothing. We drove into Westport and sat in a hotel lounge drinking coffee. I had spare shoes, but no real protection from the rain. My friends were in the same state.

Out at the foot of Croagh Patrick there were lines of cars parked and more making their way to the fields which were being used as car parks for the day. It seemed as though no one else had been worried about the rain. Some people had already been up the mountain and down again. As we bought our sticks for one pound I could see a line of people, like a small coloured stream winding up the mountain and disappearing into the mist.

This was where St Patrick, according to legend, had come and fasted for forty days and forty nights in the fifth century. But it was thought that the tradition of climbing the reek was a much older, pagan ritual which had been incorporated into the Christian calendar. There was also talk that the climbing of the reek had once been accompanied by great festivities, but this had been ended by the clergy, and now the day was dedicated to penance and penance only.

William Makepeace Thackeray was in Westport on the last Sunday in July in 1842 and he ventured out to Murrisk, having heard that 'the priests going up the mountain took care that there should be no sports nor dancing on that day.' He disliked the idea of the pilgrimage: 'it's too hard to think that in our day any priests of any religion should be found superintending such a hideous series of self-sacrifices as are, it appears, performed on this hill.'

We set off in a spirit of self-sacrifice. At first it was easy, like mild hill walking. Some people were barefoot, but most wore shoes. The mist was wet and the ground was uneven and soggy, the staffs becoming more and more necessary as we climbed. Soon, we separated; my two friends went ahead, joining the others who seemed to be vanishing into the sky. The climb became more difficult, and the rain came down harder. I was passed by a travelling woman in bare feet being helped along by her two sons. They did not speak to each other, appearing intent on the climb, a look of furious concentration on their faces. Then the man who had taken our chair in the bar the previous evening passed me, also in bare feet. I had thought that the travellers were only here to make money selling staffs and running stalls, but a good number of them climbed the reek that day, as though it were a crucial part of their fierce Catholicism.

Thackeray did not climb the reek, but received a report from a friend who told him that the ascent 'is a very steep and hard one . . . performed in the company of thousands of people who were making their way barefoot to the several "stations" upon the hill.' One hundred and forty-nine years later the stations are still there, and there are notices instructing pilgrims who arrive at the first station, for example, to walk 'seven times around the mound of stones saying seven Our Fathers, seven Hail Marys and one Creed'.

Beyond the first station there was no visibility. I could see only a few yards ahead as the mountain became steeper. A rescue team climbed past me carrying an empty stretcher; there must have been an accident higher up. A few people were coming down; one man smiled as he passed and said that it would not be long before I reached the top.

Suddenly, there was a shout from behind me. At first I thought that someone had fallen, but when I turned I found that the thick fog had lifted and we could see Clew Bay clearly—all the little islands, grey and silver in the dark water, with the soup of mist hovering over them and then gathering and closing in once more. Everyone had turned to look at it, like a small revelation. Now, we turned and trudged on, the terrain becoming more and more difficult. A few times the mist cleared again, and filtered sunlight shone on the sea so that it seemed like solid metal below us, and then gradually the clouds would block our view once more.

Nothing had prepared me for the last part of the climb. The rise was sheer and there was nothing to hold onto. At every step I sank into a bank of large slippery stones. I moved slowly on my hands and knees in the wind and the driving rain. I stood back to let the stretcher pass, as the injured man was carried down.

Everybody concentrated on each step, and on making sure not to fall and knock other people over. We clambered forward. It was impossible to see how close the summit was. At times progress seemed impossible; there was no foothold, and if you moved, you displaced rocks and stones, and there was still no foothold. Men and women walked down as best they could, pushing the staff into the ground ahead of them, letting it sink in between the stones,

then sliding gingerly down. If they caught your eye, they smiled in encouragement. People kept telling you that you would reach the summit soon.

When I got there I was exhausted and exhilarated. Mass was being said, and everybody, including all the young people, were paying attention. Later, huge numbers went to confession and communion. I felt so well, so happy to have made it that I was half-tempted to tell all my sins to the priest and then receive communion. But I sat back, instead, and watched. People had not climbed the reek simply to keep fit; now, as they reached the top, I could see that they were serious about this pilgrimage, as they all blessed themselves and joined in the prayers, including teenagers and men and women in their twenties. Age did not appear to affect the intensity of devotion.

WHY HAD CATHOLICISM survived like this in Ireland? Why did the Reformation never work? Why does the Catholic faith seem to thrive here among the young as it does not elsewhere? The previous week I had gone to Maynooth, the Catholic seminary and university close to Dublin, founded in 1795, and I had spoken to a lecturer in the Old Irish Department, Muireann Ní Bhrollcháin, about how Christianity had come to Ireland.

We know very little about pre-Christian Ireland, she said. The Celts did not build temples, but tended to honour their gods in open spaces. We know that they believed in another world, but there seems to have been no conflict between them and the first Christians, who came in 431 and 432. There were no martyrs in the early Irish church. The two worlds appear to have worked together. Saint Colmcille, for example, died in 597, and a long poem lamenting his death was apparently written by a pagan poet.

The Roman system did not catch on in Ireland until the mid-twelfth century, she explained, and this is significant. Instead, Christianity was spread by abbots and monks who ran autonomous monasteries. There was no central authority; there were no dioceses until the twelfth century. Thus the monks, instead of going and spreading the word or doing battle against pagan druids, spent time copying out manuscripts, or writing down stories from pagan times, incorporating Christianity with what came before, making gods and goddesses into saints. Some monks went to live in remote places; others founded richly-endowed monasteries where abbots and monks were like lords and tenants, and power was passed from father to son. Rules and regulations varied from one monastery to another.

Christianity, then, was never imposed on Ireland; Roman structures played no part in introducing the new religion. It grew slowly, and slowly the old set of beliefs faded. Christianity became the faith of the country over five or six centuries using the vernacular; it became a native religion. Having grown so organically, it was more difficult to change or dislodge.

Efforts were made to reform the Church in the ninth century, she said, but they had no effect. However, with the coming of the Vikings there were greater links between the east coast of Ireland and England, which was firmly under Roman control, and the possibility of restructuring the Irish Church increased once the Vikings in Dublin converted to Christianity. Between 1142 and the end of the century every monastery in Ireland was closed. The religious orders came in from Europe; they did not speak any Irish. It was the first and most significant invasion of Ireland, making the subsequent Norman and English invasions easier. It established structures in the society—parishes, dioceses, religious orders—which any invader would find useful. Ireland, which had been fully Christian, now became part of the Roman Church, but it did so much later than any other country in Europe.

I T WAS STILL RAINING on the summit of Croagh Patrick. I assumed that people had also come here on an appointed summer's day in the time before Christianity. And I imagined that the pre-Christian rituals may have been no battle between the rival religions, no year noted in chronicles when the big day on Croagh Patrick was turned over to the Christians. It is possible that both pagan and Christian rituals were carried on as part of the same thing, and then gradually the pagan disappeared.

I looked around. Another Mass had started and people were kneeling, while others queued for confession. The prayers were said with real seriousness, and when it came to the consecration people bowed their heads, ignoring the rain.

I set off down the mountain. By now the mist had cleared over the summit. Around the islands in the bay cloud was still melting and forming, and there were sudden darts of sunshine, as though the dawn were starting to break over the sea.

The first stretch on the way down was really hard. If anyone pushed against you, you would fall with nothing to hold on to. There had already been several injuries that day. You had to mind every step, use the staff for support and hope for the best. Once I was beyond the stones I knew I was past the worst. It was now the afternoon. The climb had taken about three and a half hours. There were still people coming up, but most were going down.

At the bottom of Croagh Patrick that day the Bishop of Clonfert, Dr Joseph Cassidy, stood dressed in his episcopal robes. He seemed part of what I had been thinking about—the Roman, the man in the official robes, civilised, from the diocese which did not exist until it was imposed from outside in the twelfth century. He was watching the pilgrims descend from their quasi-pagan encounter with rain and a holy mountain. He explained that he couldn't climb Croagh Patrick because of his bad heart. Instead, he waited there, greeting everyone warmly, being greeted in return. He smiled benignly at us all and spoke to anyone who approached him. He seemed pleased that the Church had so many pilgrims ready to climb Croagh Patrick, and happy to preside over the event.

— Colm Tóibín

Winner in 1995 of the American Academy of Arts and Letters' E. M. Forster Award, Colm Tóibín's books include three novels—*The South*, *The Heather Blazing*, and most recently, *The Story of the Night*—and five works of nonfiction including *Bad Blood*, his account of walking along the Irish border, and *The Trial of the Generals*, a collection of his journalism. Tóibín also edited the 1994 collection *New Writing from Ireland*.

BOOKS AND VIDEOS

Autobiography

Since it was published in September 1996, *Angela's Ashes,* Frank McCourt's enormously affecting memoir of growing up desperately poor in Limerick, has garnered every major American literary accolade, from the Pulitzer Prize to the National Book Critics Circle Award, and has become a fixture at the top of American bestseller lists. In *An Only Child* and *My Father's Son* (1969), Frank O'Connor, known primarily for his fiction and short stories, recounts his years as an Irish revolutionary and later as an intellectual in Dublin during the 1920s. Christy Brown's *My Left Foot* is the autobiographical account of a Dublin artist stricken with cerebral palsy (☞ Movies and Videos, *below*).

Guidebooks and Travel Literature

Exploring Ireland (2nd Ed.), also published by Fodor's, a full-color guide packed with photographs, is an excellent companion guide to this edition.

Peter Somerville-Large's *Dublin* is packed with anecdotes relating to the famed Irish city. *Georgian Dublin,* by Desmond Guinness, the founder of the Irish Georgian Society, explores the city's architecture, with photographs and plans of Dublin's most admirable buildings. The most up-to-date work on the Aran Islands is Tim Robinson's award-winning *The Stones of Aran: Pilgrimage.* Robinson has also written a long introduction to the Penguin edition of J. M. Synge's 1907 classic, *The Aran Islands.* Tomas Ó Crohán's *The Islandman* provides a good background on Dingle and the Blasket Islands.

In *Round Ireland in Low Gear* (1988), famed British travel writer Eric Newby writes breezily of his bicycle journey with his wife around the wet Emerald Isle. Fifty years older but no less fresh is H.V. Morton's *In Search of Ireland* (1938). Rebecca Solnit uses Ireland as a sounding board for her meditations on travel in *A Book of Migrations: Some Passages in Ireland* (1997).

History and Current Affairs

For two intriguing studies of Irish culture and history, consult Constantine FitzGibbon's *The Irish in Ireland* and Sean O'Faolain's *The Irish: A Character Study,* which traces the history of Ireland from Celtic times. J. C. Beckett's *The Making of Modern Ireland,* a concise introduction to Irish history, covers the years between 1603 and 1923. *Modern Ireland,* by R. F. Foster, spans the years between 1600 and 1972. Thomas Cahill's *How the Irish Saved Civilization* is a best-selling, lively look at how Irish scholars kept the written word and culture alive in the so-called Dark Ages. For an acclaimed history of Irish nationalism, try Robert Kee's *The Green Flag.* Peter De Rosa's *Rebels: The Irish Rising of 1916* is a popularly written, novelistic history of the defining event of modern Irish history. Irish country-house devotees should read *Aristocrats: Caroline, Emily, Louisa and Sarah Lennox, 1740–1832,* by Stella Tillyard; Louisa was the force behind Castletown House.

John Ardagh's *Ireland and the Irish: Portrait of a Changing Society* (1997) is the best current sociological and economic analysis of modern Ireland. *"We Wrecked the Place": Contemplating an End to the Northern Irish Troubles* (1996) by Belfast-based journalist Jonathan Stevenson is the best recent book on the subject. John Conroy's *Belfast Diary: War as a Way of Life* (1995) was reissued with a new afterword on the ceasefire. Neither Colm Tóibín's *Bad Blood: A Walk Along the Irish Border* nor Carlo Gebler's *The Glass Curtain: Inside an Ulster Community* are published in the U.S., but both are worth tracking down.

Rosemary Mahoney, a young Irish-American writer, moved to Ireland, where she wrote *Whoredom in Kimmage: Irish Women Coming of Age* (1993), a collective portrait of Irish women *and* men in the early 1990s.

Literary Biography and Criticism

Richard Ellman's *James Joyce* (1959) is recognized as the finest literary biography ever written, and is easily the best introduction to the man and his work. Ellman completed his second biographical masterpiece, *Oscar Wilde* (1988), shortly before his death, after more than 20 years of research. Ellman also wrote *Yeats: The Man and the Masks* (1978), although the first volume of Roy F. Foster's new biography, *W. B. Yeats: A Life—The Apprentice Mage 1865–1914, Vol. 1* (1997) has been welcomed as definitive, on the caliber of Ellman's Joyce and Wilde bios. Michael Holroyd's exhaustive, 4-volume biography of George Bernard Shaw (1988, 1988, 1991 and 1993) will tell you everything you want to know about the larger-than-life, Nobel Prize–winning dramatist, critic, and social reformer. Samuel Beckett himself asked James Knowlson to write his biography; the result, *Damned to Fame: The Life of Samuel Beckett,* was published in 1996 and is widely regarded as the definitive life of the writer. William Trevor's *A Writer's Ireland: Landscape in Literature* (1984) explores the influence of Ireland's changing landscape on its writers. *Inventing Ireland: The Literature of Modern Nation* (1995) by Declan Kiberd is a major literary history of modern Ireland.

Literature

Ulysses (1922) is the linguistically innovative masterpiece by James Joyce, one of the titans of 20th-century literature. Emulating the structure of *The Odyssey,* and using an unprecedented stream of consciousness technique, Joyce follows Leopold and Molly Bloom and Stephen Daedalus through the course of a single day—June 16, 1904—around Dublin. (Joyce set *Ulysses* on the day he and his future wife, Nora Barnacle, had their first date.) More accessible introductions to Joyce's writing include *A Portrait of the Artist as a Young Man* (1916) and *Dubliners* (1914), a collection of short stories (its most accomplished story, "The Dead," was made into a movie starring Angelica Huston in 1988). Joyce aficionados may want to tackle his final, gigantic work, *Finnegan's Wake* (1939), which takes the linguistic experimentation of *Ulysses* to an almost incomprehensible level. Arguably the greatest literary challenge of the 20th century, its pages include word plays and phonetic metaphors in over 100 languages. To prepare you for reading Joyce, you might seek out audio recordings in which he reads in his inimitable lilting tenor voice.

Samuel Beckett fills his story collection *More Pricks than Kicks* with Dublin characters; if you enjoy literary gamesmanship, you may also want to try Beckett's trilogy—*Molloy* (1951), *Malone Dies* (1951), and *The Unnamable* (1953).

If you're drawn to tales of unrequited love, turn to Elizabeth Bowen's stories and her novel *The Last September* (1929), set in Ireland during the Irish Civil War. Coming-of-age novels include *Under the Eye of the Clock,* a somewhat autobiographical work by Christopher Nolan, which takes as its subject a handicapped youth discovering the pleasures of language, and *Fools of Fortune* (1983), by William Trevor, which treats the loss of an ideal childhood, brought about by a changing political climate. Trevor's *The Silence in the Garden* (1988) is also worth looking for.

If you prefer reading more magical novels, take a look at James Stephens's *A Crock of Gold* (1912), a charming and wise fairy tale written for adults, and Flann O'Brien's *At Swim-Two-Birds* (1939), a surrealistic tale full of Irish folklore.

One of Ireland's foremost fiction writers working today, Edna O'Brien began her career with the comic novel, *The Country Girls* (1960), and has published seventeen books since, most recently *House of Splendid Isolation* (1994) and *Down By the River* (1997). Like many of her compatriots, she is a superb short-story writer. Her collection *A Fanatic Heart* (1985), is one of her best. Other superbly crafted story collections, full of acute observations of Ireland's social and political landscape, include Benedict Kiely's *The State of Ireland,* Mary Lavin's *Collected Stories,* Frank O'Connor's *Collected Stories* (1952), William Trevor's *Collected Stories* (1993), and John McGahern's *Collected Stories* (1993).

Thomas Flanagan's *The Year of the French* is a historical novel about the people of County Mayo, who revolted in 1798 with the help of French revolutionaries. *A Nest of Simple Folk,* by Sean O'Faolain, follows three generations of an Irish family between 1854 and 1916. Leon Uris's *Trinity* covers the years 1840–1916, as seen through the eyes of British, Irish Catholic, and Ulster Protestant families. In *No Country for Young Men,* Julia O'Faolain writes of two Irish families struggling to overcome the effects of the Irish Civil War. In John McGahern's prizewinning novel *Amongst Women,* modern-day Ireland attempts to reconcile itself to the upheavals of the early years of this century. For a more contemporary look at life in urban Ireland, try the phenomenally successful Roddy Doyle: His "Barrytown Trilogy"—*The Snapper, The Commitments,* and *The Van*—have all been made into films; *Paddy Clarke Ha Ha Ha,* another success, is sure to follow. Shortlisted for the Booker Prize, *Reading in the Dark* (1997) marks the novelistic debut of Seamus Deane, a poet, critic, and editor. It covers familiar territory—a family in 1920 Ireland riven by political strife—but does so with extraordinarily evocative language.

Movies and Videos

There has been a plethora of movies made in or about Ireland, and the number of Irish characters on screen is legion (the most numerous being priests, drunks, New York cops, and Old Mother Riley). *Juno and the Paycock* (known in the United States as *The Shame of Mary Boyle*) and *The Plough and the Stars* (1936), about the months leading up to the Easter Uprising, are early screen adaptations of Sean O'Casey's theatrical masterpieces. John Ford's superb *The Informer* (1935) is a full-blooded and highly stylized tale of an IRA leader's betrayal during the struggle for independence by a simpleminded hanger-on who wants to emigrate to the United States. Ford's boisterous comedy *The Quiet Man* (1952) is an Irish-village version of *The Taming of the Shrew,* with John Wayne playing a boxer who returns to his ancestor's village in the West of Ireland to claim local beauty Maureen O'Hara, and Barry Fitzgerald. David Lean's epic *Ryan's Daughter* (1970), is a four-hour pastoral melodrama of a village schoolmaster's wife falling for a British officer in the troubled Ireland of 1916; the film was a critical and commercial disaster for Lean, who didn't make another film for 14 years.

Daniel Day Lewis and Brenda Fricker give Oscar-winning performances in Jim Sheridan's *My Left Foot* (1989), a biography of Christy Brown, the Irish writer and painter crippled from birth by cerebral palsy. Alan Parker's *The Commitments* (1991), from Roddy Doyle's best-seller, humorously recounts the efforts of a group of young, working-class northside Dubliners trying to make it as a soul band. A made-for-TV version of another of Doyle's best-sellers, *The Snapper* (1994) is a touching, funny tale of a Dublin girl's struggles

to be a single mother in the face of an orthodox and often unforgiving society. *The Van* (1997) completes the "Barrytown Trilogy," as the books that were the basis of these three films are known. In *A Man of No Importance* (1994), Albert Finney plays a sexually repressed bus conductor whose passion for poetry leads him to stage Wilde's *Salomé.* John Sayles hooked up with acclaimed cinematographer Haskell Wexler to make *The Secret of Roan Inish* (1996), a magical realist fable about a Selkie—a creature from Celtic folkore who is a seal in the water and a woman on land—and the fisherman's family whose lives she changes.

Some of the best movies made in Ireland deal with the Troubles that have afflicted Northern Ireland. *Four Days in July* (1984), directed by Mike Leigh in classic *cinema verité* style, is a poignant and compelling portrayal of the sectarian divide in working-class Belfast. Based on actual events, Ken Loach's *Hidden Agenda* (1990) is a hard-hitting thriller about the murder of an American lawyer working for Amnesty International in the troubled North. As the plot unfolds, it becomes clear that the highest echelons of the British government and secret services are involved. Helen Mirren stars as the widow of an executed Protestant policeman in *Cal* (1984), based on Bernard MacLaverty's masterful novel about the Troubles. Daniel Day Lewis was nominated for an Academy Award for his portrayal of Gerry Conlon, the wrongfully imprisoned Irish youth, in Jim Sheridan's *In the Name of the Father* (1993). Neil Jordan's *Michael Collins* (1996) depicts the turbulent life of the heroic Commander-in-Chief of the Irish Republican Army from the Easter Uprising in 1916, when Collins was 25, until his assassination in West Cork six years later; it went on to become the highest-grossing film ever in Ireland. Helen Mirren again plays a widow in *Some Mother's Son* (1997), set during the 1981 Maze Prison Hunger Strike that claimed Bobby Sands.

Periodical

Billing itself as "A magazine for the Irish diaspora: An ongoing celebration of Ireland and the Irish around the world," *The World of Hibernia* (issued quarterly; US [$50], Canada [$60 U.S.], and rest of the world [$80 U.S.]: 340 Madison Ave., Suite 411, New York, NY 10164-2920; Ireland and Britain [£32]: 22 Crofton Rd., Dun

Laoghaire, Co. Dublin) has savvy, solid editorial coverage. Its production values are also high (on par with the finest art magazines), making it a magazine you're likely to keep on your coffee table months after the issue date.

Poetry

The poems of William Butler Yeats, Ireland's most celebrated poet, often describe the Irish landscape, including the Sligo and Coole countryside. A favorite poet among the Irish is Patrick Kavanagh, whose distinguished career was devoted to writing exceptionally about ordinary lives. Winner of the *Irish Times*–Aer Lingus Literary prize in 1993, Derek Mahon is the author of *Selected Poems* (1992) and many other books. Northern Ireland serves as the setting for many of Seamus Heaney's poems. *Selected Poems 1996–1987* (1990) and *The Spirit Level* (1996), his first collection published since he won the Nobel Prize in Literature in 1995, are both highly recommended introductions to his work. Though not as well known outside Ireland as Heaney, Paul Muldoon is another major Irish poet. His *Selected Poems: 1968–1986* (1987) and his most recent volume, *The Annals of Chile* (1994) are both good places to start. Eavan Boland is widely regarded as among the top tier of Irish poets, and the finest woman writing poetry in Ireland today. *An Origin Like Water: Collected Poems 1957–1987* (1996) and *Object Lessons: The Life of the Woman and the Poet in Our Time* (1995) are two of her recent books.

Theater

Ireland's playwrights are as distinguished as its novelists and short story writers. Samuel Beckett, who moved from Ireland to Paris and began writing in French, is the author of the comic modernist masterpiece *Waiting for Godot* (1952), among many other plays. Oscar Wilde's finest plays, *The Importance of Being Earnest* and *An Ideal Husband* (both 1895), were playing to packed audiences in London when he was charged by his lover's father as a sodomite setting in motion the trials that lead to his downfall. Among the many plays of George Bernard Shaw, who grew up in Dublin, are *Arms and the Man* (1894), *Major Barbara* (1905), *Pygmalion* (1913), and *Saint Joan* (1923).

The history of Irish theater includes a good number of controversial plays, such as J. M. Synge's *The Playboy of the Western World*, which was considered morally outrageous at the time of its opening in 1907 ("Playboy riots" took place in Dublin when the play was produced at the Abbey Theatre), but is appreciated today for its poetic language. Sean O'Casey wrote passionately about social injustice and working-class characters around the time of the Irish Civil War in such plays as *The Plough and the Stars* (1926) and *Juno and the Paycock* (1924). *The Quare Fellow* (1956), by Brendan Behan, challenged accepted mores in the 1950s and at the time could only be produced in London. Behan is also well known for his play *The Hostage* and for *Borstal Boy* (1958), his memoirs. Two more recently recognized playwrights are Hugh Leonard (*Da* and *A Life*) and Brian Friel (*Philadelphia, Here I Come!*, *The Faith Healer,* and *Dancing at Lughnasa*), whose work often illuminates Irish small-town life.

INDEX

NOTES

Fodor's Travel Publications

Available at bookstores everywhere, or call 1–800–533–6478, 24 hours a day.

Gold Guides

U.S.

Alaska	Florida	New Orleans	Seattle & Vancouver
Arizona	Hawai'i	New York City	The South
Boston	Las Vegas, Reno, Tahoe	Pacific North Coast	U.S. & British Virgin Islands
California		Philadelphia & the Pennsylvania Dutch Country	USA
Cape Cod, Martha's Vineyard, Nantucket	Los Angeles		Virginia & Maryland
	Maine, Vermont, New Hampshire	The Rockies	Walt Disney World, Universal Studios and Orlando
The Carolinas & Georgia	Maui & Lāna'i	San Diego	
Chicago	Miami & the Keys	San Francisco	Washington, D.C.
Colorado	New England	Santa Fe, Taos, Albuquerque	

Foreign

Australia	Europe	Montréal & Québec City	Scotland
Austria	Florence, Tuscany & Umbria	Moscow, St. Petersburg, Kiev	Singapore
The Bahamas			South Africa
Belize & Guatemala	France	The Netherlands, Belgium & Luxembourg	South America
Bermuda	Germany		Southeast Asia
Canada	Great Britain	New Zealand	Spain
Cancún, Cozumel, Yucatán Peninsula	Greece	Norway	Sweden
	Hong Kong		Switzerland
Caribbean	India	Nova Scotia, New Brunswick, Prince Edward Island	Thailand
China	Ireland		Toronto
Costa Rica	Israel	Paris	Turkey
Cuba	Italy	Portugal	Vienna & the Danube
The Czech Republic & Slovakia	Japan	Provence & the Riviera	
Eastern & Central Europe	London	Scandinavia	
	Madrid & Barcelona		
	Mexico		

Special-Interest Guides

Adventures to Imagine	Fodor's Gay Guide to the USA	Halliday's New Orleans Food Explorer	Rock & Roll Traveler USA
Alaska Ports of Call			
Ballpark Vacations	Fodor's How to Pack	Healthy Escapes	Sunday in San Francisco
Caribbean Ports of Call	Great American Learning Vacations	Kodak Guide to Shooting Great Travel Pictures	Walt Disney World for Adults
The Official Guide to America's National Parks	Great American Sports & Adventure Vacations	National Parks and Seashores of the East	Weekends in New York
Disney Like a Pro	Great American Vacations	National Parks of the West	Wendy Perrin's Secrets Every Smart Traveler Should Know
Europe Ports of Call	Great American Vacations for Travelers with Disabilities	Nights to Imagine	
Family Adventures		Rock & Roll Traveler Great Britain and Ireland	

Fodor's Special Series

Fodor's Best Bed & Breakfasts

America

California

The Mid-Atlantic

New England

The Pacific Northwest

The South

The Southwest

The Upper Great Lakes

Compass American Guides

Alaska

Arizona

Boston

Chicago

Colorado

Hawaii

Idaho

Hollywood

Las Vegas

Maine

Manhattan

Minnesota

Montana

New Mexico

New Orleans

Oregon

Pacific Northwest

San Francisco

Santa Fe

South Carolina

South Dakota

Southwest

Texas

Utah

Virginia

Washington

Wine Country

Wisconsin

Wyoming

Citypacks

Amsterdam

Atlanta

Berlin

Chicago

Florence

Hong Kong

London

Los Angeles

Montréal

New York City

Paris

Prague

Rome

San Francisco

Tokyo

Venice

Washington, D.C.

Exploring Guides

Australia

Boston & New England

Britain

California

Canada

Caribbean

China

Costa Rica

Egypt

Florence & Tuscany

Florida

France

Germany

Greek Islands

Hawaii

Ireland

Israel

Italy

Japan

London

Mexico

Moscow & St. Petersburg

New York City

Paris

Prague

Provence

Rome

San Francisco

Scotland

Singapore & Malaysia

South Africa

Spain

Thailand

Turkey

Venice

Flashmaps

Boston

New York

San Francisco

Washington, D.C.

Fodor's Gay Guides

Los Angeles & Southern California

New York City

Pacific Northwest

San Francisco and the Bay Area

South Florida

USA

Pocket Guides

Acapulco

Aruba

Atlanta

Barbados

Budapest

Jamaica

London

New York City

Paris

Prague

Puerto Rico

Rome

San Francisco

Washington, D.C.

Languages for Travelers *(Cassette & Phrasebook)*

French

German

Italian

Spanish

Mobil Travel Guides

America's Best Hotels & Restaurants

California and the West

Major Cities

Great Lakes

Mid-Atlantic

Northeast

Northwest and Great Plains

Southeast

Southwest and South Central

Rivages Guides

Bed and Breakfasts of Character and Charm in France

Hotels and Country Inns of Character and Charm in France

Hotels and Country Inns of Character and Charm in Italy

Hotels and Country Inns of Character and Charm in Paris

Hotels and Country Inns of Character and Charm in Portugal

Hotels and Country Inns of Character and Charm in Spain

Short Escapes

Britain

France

New England

Near New York City

Fodor's Sports

Golf Digest's Places to Play

Skiing USA

USA Today The Complete Four Sport Stadium Guide

WHEREVER YOU TRAVEL, *H*ELP IS NEVER FAR AWAY.

From planning your trip to providing travel assistance along the way, American Express® Travel Service Offices are always there to help you do more.

Ireland

American Express Travel Service
116 Grafton Street
Dublin
1/677-2874

http://www.americanexpress.com/travel